From
Milk
to
Meat

ADAM FIELD

ISBN 978-1-0980-6055-8 (paperback)
ISBN 978-1-0980-6056-5 (digital)

Christian Faith Publishing, Inc.
832 Park Avenue
Meadville, PA 16335
www.christianfaithpublishing.com

Printed in the United States of America

Foreword

If you were to cut my friend, Adam Field, he would bleed a love for Jesus and for souls. He has a passion not only to reach the lost but to train believers to have a broken heart for those who don't know Christ. It is not just a select a few who are to evangelize; it is every believer's duty and great honor to spread the message of salvation—a salvation in no one or nothing else other than in Jesus the Messiah. Adam refuses to look away from the despair he sees around him as the world careens toward the cliff of destruction. He has a desperation and urgency that is contagious. As you read this book, I pray that God will break your heart for the lost. I pray that God will bless you with an unshakable faith in His Word, in His presence, and in His calling to you and to me to be laborers in His harvest (Matthew 9:36–38; Luke 10:2). What a glorious time to be alive in these last days! Well done, Adam!

Patrick Dow BA MBA
CEO
Nicky Cruz Outreach/TRUCE

Adam is a tremendous young minister who reminds me a lot of me! He doesn't care what people think because he is absolutely devoted to Jesus and to reaching sinners. He unashamedly preaches repentance and a fear of God, not out of meanness or legalism but out of love. Like me, he is tired of playing church and of a Christian culture that is centered on self and personal blessing. It is as if the Western church is turning the music up loud enough to drown out the cries of the broken and the perishing. But we cannot go on like this. The days are evil, and the time is short. We must accelerate our efforts to pray, worship, obey, and proclaim the message of salvation in Jesus. We must speak of the cross and of His sacrifice and of His blood being shed for our sins.

For too long, the church has been spoon-fed a Gospel message that caters to self-interest and self-promotion. But we must hear the cry of the scripture that it is about Jesus and God's love and plan for reaching the world through us, His ministers of reconciliation (2 Corinthians 5:18–19). Like Ezekiel, Adam serves as a watchman on the wall who hears the Word of the Lord and faithfully warns us on God's behalf (Ezekiel 33). In this age of Christian celebrity and idolization of gifted speakers, are we content to decrease that He may increase? Can we be fulfilled by emptying ourselves and fulfilling the great commission?

We are bombarded by messages devoid of meat that implore us to quote certain passages lifted from the scripture that promise blessing and abundance but ignore the trials and struggles that are part of being true disciples. Adam's cry, like the apostle Paul, is to flee worldly teachings and to seek the great gain that comes from godliness and contentment in Him (1 Tim. 6). Our greatest glory—our ultimate purpose—and destiny are found in nothing else other than in loving Christ and glorifying Him in this lost and broken world. Everything else pales in significance to this eternal calling.

Dr. Nicky Cruz
Evangelist, author of *Run Baby Run*

Since my late teens, I have been writing devotionals. I have not stopped as those that have been following have seen. After hurricane Michael, the Lord led me to take the bushel of my writings for all to see into my relationship with God. Up until then, it was private between Christ and me. I started slowly publishing the unedited version of my writings on all our social media platforms. These devotionals are to challenge and provoke the reader to a nearer walk with Christ. None of it is God's Word; it's just opinions, challenges, and encouragements that hopefully enlighten many in my generation. After being raised in a Christian home, I've been through so many church trends; I went to Bible school, pastored, church planted, and currently am working as an evangelist in the United States. Many of these writings came out of seeing hypocrisy, being a hypocrite myself, and facing some of the hardest transitions a person can experience. Without writing out my heart to God, I would not have made it this far in my life. As David did in the Psalm, I wrote out my heart before the Lord. My generation and the younger generation need to read these nuggets of knowledge to preserve them from the hardships of this world, especially in the church.

In order for evangelism to take place, believers need to know whom they believe. The church must be discipled in the truth of the scripture and the direction our culture is going in. I learned more from my leaders about what not to do rather than what to do in times like these. The writings are direct, vulnerable and will be a resource to your everyday discipleship.

This book can be read as a daily devotional or all the way through. At the end of each devotional, take the time to meditate on the scripture that each one of these devotionals are based on. May our generation be open to the corrective words that are written for our betterment and never for condemnation. I hope they lift you nearer to the Lord and cause you to quote His Word more than any of my words. I want to leave a legacy for the next generation. Not all of today's preachers just tell their congregation what they want to hear; there is a remnant who love truth more than phony. The truth may not always be what we want to hear, but it's what we need to hear.

Adam Field,
Evangelist, president of Comission Inc.

1

"I have fed you with milk, and not with meat: for hitherto ye were not able to bear it, neither yet now are ye able" (1 Corinthians 3:2, KJV)

Living off of the milk is living for what we can get out of God but as we grow, we will move on to the meat, which means we will live for what God can get out of us. Initially we get saved for heaven's sake or one of the benefit's sake, but then after some time, we want to become more like Jesus. Jesus lived for the betterment of others; therefore, we are also called to live in such a way. We are conforming to the character of Christ every moment that we are living in Christ. We will never be perfect, but there will be a desire to be so. The Holy Spirit will lead us, grieve us, and keep us. Without the Holy Spirit, we have no power or desire for what is right. This may be a "me generation me" hour, but it is not too late for it to be a "generation Christ" hour. Why do we want to fit in so much? Why do we want to be conformed to the image of today's trends so badly? There is so much strife to fit in and find our identity in a false love. Love does not compromise truth. There is no love without truth. Truth is all we have. Truth may strip us of pride and carnality, but it wakes us up to our need for Jesus Christ. Truth is more than words and definitions, it's a person. Christ is truth. As we know Him in relationship, we will become like Him. The more we hang out with someone, the more their ways will be seen in us. We need to allow the chords of God's love to draw us near to Himself. God, draw us near. Grow us in your word so you can show up in our lives. We want all to know Jesus and remember Jesus's name once they are done talking with us.

"Howbeit when he, the Spirit of truth, is come, he will guide you into all truth: for he shall not speak of himself; but whatsoever he shall hear, that shall he speak: and he will shew you things to come" (John 16:13, KJV)

We need to be cautious of raising a personality above scripture. The only way a believer can be sustained is by scripture. When we raise a personality or experience above scripture, we become prey to deception and disappointment. Charismatic communicators, miracles, signs and wonders must be held accountable to the Bible. There is no other infallible word of God outside of the sixty-six books of the Bible. When the Church is built on the Bible then it will have a solid foundation. The Holy Spirit will never raise a personality above Christ. Once a person gains more attention than Christ then we can discern the spirit of antichrist is rising. The spirit of antichrist is spreading like wildfire. It spreads using a desire in people that want a personality more than Christ. The best preachers are those that make people rely on God's Word more than on themselves. We desperately need a biblical filter in this generation to discern the times. Most people only get an hour each week in the Word. No one can truly be discipled off of a forty-minute sermon a week. We need to stir one another in the Word and be disciplined to read it every day. Spiritual disciplines are essential to withstand the waves of life. The only way we can be concrete in our faith is if we choose to be disciplined in the word of God. Scripture memorization and studying the context of scripture is key to living spiritually full. If we don't get grounded in the Word then when the waves of life hit us, we'll get tossed back and forth. Let's quote scriptures more than preachers, let's quote scripture more than scholars, let's build on scripture and the Holy Spirit will do the rest. We need to be a Bible-based ministry. Our evangelistic teachings must be grounded in scripture. The more scripture leads our lives the less we will be tossed around by the waves of life. The Holy Spirit will only lead us to the truth of scripture. The Holy Spirit will lift Christ up and honor Christ through scripture. God in His sovereignty gave us the Bible we have today. We have seen the incredible influence of scripture on continents, countries, and cities for the good. Any nation that was influenced by scripture has prospered! "All scripture is given by inspiration of God, and is profitable for doctrine, for reproof, for correction, for instruction in righteousness: That the man of God may be perfect, thoroughly furnished unto all good works" (2 Timothy 3:16–17, KJV). Until we are content where we are, we will never be content where we are going with God. He is working contentment in us. Let's choose to be at peace with where God has us. God always takes His believers on a journey to work character and trust into His people. We won't always get it right but how we respond when we get it wrong really matters. Let's depend on God.

"So being affectionately desirous of you, we were willing to have imparted unto you, not the gospel of God only, but also our own souls, because ye were dear unto us. For ye remember, brethren, our labour and travail: for labouring night and day, because we would not be chargeable unto any of you, we preached unto you the gospel of God. Ye are witnesses, and God also, how holily and justly and unblameably we behaved ourselves among you that believe: As ye know how we exhorted and comforted and charged every one of you, as a father doth his children" (1 Thessalonians 2:8–11, KJV)

P reach like it is your last opportunity. This life certainly is not easy. Satan has lied to this generation and trapped so many in defeat. The lie that "because life is not going the way it was planned means God is upset with us"—needs to be exposed. Life is tough without Christ as much as it is with Christ. Life is hard for everyone. When it storms, it shows no mercy. Nature has been groaning since the fall. The consequences of the fall will always be evident until the return of Christ. The early church suffered martyrdom daily for their faith in Christ. The love of God is not defined by what we feel or see but by what the Bible says. Christ died to show us until we die, we will suffer. Life on earth will not be like heaven. There will be a new heaven and a new earth where there will be no sickness, pain or death. Until then we need to be aware lest the enemy heaps condemnation upon us because life is tough. Jesus prepared His followers for the worst. He told them of the troubles to come. He shocked them with his words when He said, "Eat my flesh and drink my blood," telling them that following Him included suffering. The early church was built and advanced by the martyrs. God loves us even when our life does not go as planned. He cares about us. It won't be this way forever. Don't take the easiest option when we are suffering. Believe that through the pain there is a fellowship with Christ that no other experience on earth could ever give. We may be in our valley of weeping and lamentation but take heart; God is working it all together for good. Look at the good God brought out of the crucifixion of Christ. Trust He will bring good out of our lives in affliction. Passion and fervency come from knowing that the enemy is lying and winning in so many minds on the earth. God, bring us back to you. Wake us up before it's too late. We speak awakening to this generation. God is the potter, we are the clay, have your way.

Note

4

*"Let not him that is deceived trust in vanity: for vanity
shall be his recompence" (Job 15:31, KJV)*

What God has for our lives is better than what we could ever get
for ourselves. Laying our will down is better than reaching the end
of our will and still not finding what we were chasing after. True
fulfillment is found in surrender. When we throw our hands up and
give up our plans, we don't realize that what we are getting from
God is going to be much better than what we could have imagined
in eternity. Our temporary pain is worth eternity's gain. What we
choose here will stand to us in eternity. Following God is better than
having God follow us. We were never designed to be god. We crum-
ble beneath the weight of trying to be gods leading our own lives.
When we are in our right position as sons and not fathers we are
protected by our Heavenly Father. "Call no man father," said Jesus.
Only our Father in heaven deserves that title. When we are under His
protection, leadership and counsel, then we are fulfilled. Removing
ourselves from His covering makes us open prey to the enemy to
pluck us away into depression. What God calls us to, may not fulfill
our fleshly desires but our souls will be full. When our souls are full,
our identity will not be in what we do but in who we are in Christ.
A peace that surpasses understanding will flood our mind, body and
soul. There is so much rest being right with God. When we are not
right with God, we will be tormented. We must be passionate about
what we talk about because eternity is a serious subject. Heaven and
hell are serious truths. The enemy has lied for a long time that God's

way is boring and restrictive, while his way is freeing and exciting. What he hides from his temptation is all the ramifications that follow long term willful sin. Sin is more than an action it's a state of mind. Are we relying on God? Are we seeking His will? Anything we seek more than His will, will become idolatry. Healings, miracles, visions can become idolatry if we are seeking anything more than Christ. The Holy Spirit will always put the attention back on Christ. When it's not on Christ and His will, then we will live disappointed feeling that God loves others more because He hears others prayers more than our own. His love is based on truth and not feeling or seeing.

Note

5

"I am crucified with Christ: nevertheless I live; yet not I, but Christ liveth in me: and the life which I now live in the flesh I live by the faith of the Son of God, who loved me, and gave himself for me" (Galatians 5:20, KJV)

Following Jesus is not only tough, hard and painful it's impossible in our own flesh. Our flesh can do nothing to follow God. The sooner we die to self-strength and come alive to Spirit-dependence, the less we will be living for self-gratification and we will become set on fire for Christ-glorification. This life can't be lived by flesh, only by faith can we see the power of Christ working through us what we could never do on our own. When we walk in the light, we will see very clearly what the Gospel is all about. Christ becomes the sole focus of our soul. What seems like reckless abandonment, giving over our will to the Lord Jesus Christ becomes the greatest decision ever made. We are not here to convert homosexuals to heterosexuals because no woman can do what only Christ can do. We are not here to preach a lifestyle only; we are here to preach the Lord's lifestyle through us. What He wants—we do. Where He goes—we go. Our souls are under the master and control of Jesus Christ. He is the King of kings. He is the supreme ruler of all. When He died, we died; and when He rose from the dead. The same Spirit that raised Him is in us, so that we too can rise in the power of His might. We are only alive when we reckon our own abilities dead so we become alive to the spirit of God. Christ is Lord. Christ is coming again. Next time it won't be through a Virgin, next time He is coming through the clouds. He is coming with fire in His eyes. He will be feared by all flesh. Every knee will bow and tongue will confess, "He is Lord" willingly or unwillingly. Free will be stripped from flesh. Judgement will begin and the pronouncement of His righteousness will be declared. Only those draped by faith in His blood will enter eternal life. Faith alone is our only access to heaven. Faith alone is our only means to redemption. It's time to raise up the preaching of the blood of Jesus. Life is in the blood. His Blood is our seal of the new Covenant. We stand only in the merits of the Blood. The Blood of Jesus is against Satan, Sin and death. We will preach this to the day we die!! May the Lamb that was slain receive the reward of His suffering.

Note

6

"And this is life eternal, that they might know thee the only true God, and Jesus Christ, whom thou hast sent" (John 17:3, KJV)

Why do we get so passionate with the message? We are passionate because we've seen countless young people make decisions without counting the cost. They buy into the lie that Jesus makes our lives easier. They don't realize that's our eternal promise but life here is not promised to be easy. Life takes so many twists and turns that we need to trust the Word in all situations. We will face many different seasons in life. The only consistency is the Word of God. Everything changes but God's Word. Scripture must be where our trust is rooted. Knowledge won't help us. Knowing Jesus will. A good seminary teaches their students that the cemetery is where we need to rest our flesh. Our flesh can get the best of us if not. The Word of God restrains our flesh. The Spirit of God mortifies the deeds of the flesh. If we live by the flesh, we will suffer great condemnation not from God but from ourselves. There is no stability outside of Christ. He truly has the whole world in His hands. Let's not sacrifice knowing God personally for only learning all about Him. Theology is good but when it becomes the focus over knowing Jesus intimately then we will fall into idolatry. We can make idols of doctrines and miss the person of Christ. Knowing Jesus is so important. He does not disappoint. We need to be prepared for the worst in life. We need to be prepared that life is going to be tough. We have the strongest fellowship with Jesus in suffering. It's in suffering that our self-strength dies. We have many that want to pray us out of suffering, but rather than praying out of it, be praying through it. God works all things for good if we love Him. If we don't love God and are not in it for His glory then life may not work out for good. *Romans 8:28* is conditional. Are we following God and seeking His purpose for our lives? If we are not, then that promise won't stand the test of time. God will get glory out of our lives but He wants to do it the gentlest way He can. It's our pride and stubbornness that makes the suffering even worse. The quicker we can get to surrender to His will the better it will be. God, use us to prepare this generation better than how we were prepared.

Note

7

"Jesus answered and said unto him, Verily, verily,
I say unto thee, Except a man be born again, he cannot
see the kingdom of God" (John 3:3, KJV)

If someone can be argued into salvation, then they can be argued out. Knowledge alone does not convert a sinner. All true evangelism is an outflow from the well of relationship with God. God is not interested in our public prayer life; He is interested in our private prayer life. We may "wow" the public with our prayers but does it "wow" God? Who are we trying to please? Can we fool God? If God does not have our heart, He does not have us. We need to break out of religion so God can break in on us. We need to come to a place of honesty with ourselves and God. Don't be scared. There is no shame or sin that Christ can't deal with. He can't work with us unless we are willing to let Him in on all of us. Confession in prayer is so important. If we don't confess unrepented sin, we will be harboring insecurities and grow callous in the leading of God in our lives. We can't lie to God. We can't put up religious smoke screens. He sees through our skin, rib cage, and all the way to the core of our heart. He knows what makes it beat, yet He still died for us. Knowing how desperately wicked our heart is, He still took our sin and wickedness upon Himself as He laid out on the cross. His blood made a way so that we can walk in transparency before God and find deep intimate fellowship with Him. As we walk in this type of relationship with God, His presence will spill out of us. We will overflow to everyone around us. We will become a wellspring and there will be no stopping the gushing of His river. This type of evangelism is powerful. We won't be arguing, we will be speaking power words and they will cause rivers in the desert of lost souls. We will have words of life for those that are dead in sin. God wants us to be Spirit-dependent. Not everyone will be saved to whom we talk to, but we will be a conduit for God to use. We don't have arguments, we have the only way, truth and life living in us. Christ does not need to be forced on anyone. His approach is never force; that's the devil's tactic. Our God knocks and waits for the invitation. God is self-existent. He does not need us. He is God with us or without us. However, even though He does not need us, He wants us. He desires a relationship with us. Let's know Him privately.

Note

_____

_____

_____

_____

_____

_____

_____

_____

_____

8

"And Samuel grew, and the Lord was with him, and did let none of his words fall to the ground" (1 Samuel 3:19, KJV)

"Jesus, have your way in me." This is a shout out to youth pastors that want truth over everything. They don't just entertain, they "enter-train." They are discipling the young people with faith, fun and friendships. They are willing to do what it takes to reach high schools and middle schools for Christ. They are willing to preach the whole counsel of God fearlessly. Discipleship and small groups are good but if they don't lead to soul-winning, then it's just another hang out educational time. We need to be intentionally winning souls for Jesus. Any discipleship that does not lead to evangelism is deficient and weak. We are here to be salt and light. Our students are salt and light in their schools. God is setting them on fire, for truth and His purpose, like He did Samuel. God called Samuel as a young boy by name. He knows our name. As we decide to seek God in the quiet place, we will start getting His heart for souls. Let's start local with our missions, then when we go global, we will have a weight to our words. Our audience will know if we mean it or not. If all we do is global missions, we will have very little impact on their souls because they will see through our words that we don't live this on the daily. It's going to take giving our all to reach the millennials. They can't handle the same old stuff. God is raising up a remnant that are awakened to His Word and life. Be found fanning into the flame and not fanning out the flame. It's easy to pour criticisms over this generation, but that could be done to every generation. It's easy for anyone in the peanut gallery to run commentary. Rather than being negative, outing the hope for this generation, let's have faith. Faith believing that God is sending an awakening. Faith, that God is going to have an incredible witness.

Note

_____

_____

_____

_____

_____

_____

_____

_____

9

*"Ye are our epistle written in our hearts, known and
read of all men" (2 Corinthians 3:2, KJV)*

"It's going to take you to reach your sphere of influence." God in an instant could have every human on their knees because of who He is. His choice of expression on the earth is you and I. We can wait around for Him to turn up but He is wanting us to turn up. We are waiting for a move of God while all along we are His move. We are His instruments He has chosen us. Our lives, our words, and our creativity will be used of God. We will die in the wilderness waiting for God to use us. God wants us to walk in the promised land now! Will we listen to the "Joshua and Caleb" who are telling us to believe? Believe that God has a purpose. We are waiting for the promised land, wandering in circles, chasing the tail. We are the promised land in Christ. The kingdom of heaven is within us. We are His hands and feet. We are His mouth piece. Stop putting it off to Aaron or someone else when God has called all of us to be a part of His body. We are His body collectively. Every one of us is significant. No preacher has access to the heart of those closest to you, like you do. It's going to take you to believe your calling because no one can believe it for you. Christ brought in the era of the "priesthood of all believers." We can't be relying on the pulpit or the skills of the few. That's like a human body relying on the face to walk. I've never seen anyone walk on their face. Let's assemble. Let's come together looking beyond our non-essential truths for salvation, so we can unite in Christ to be a light in the world. Let's let the world know what we agree on and not be known for what we disagree on. Jesus Christ is Lord, His Blood saves, His resurrection proves our assurance of eternal life for all that believe. Let's believe our significance; if we don't, we are tramping on Christ's blood. He died to redeem us. He rose to secure our fate. God so loves us. God is for us. The proof is in the death, burial and resurrection of Christ. Holy Spirit is anointing the message that elevates Christ and Him Crucified in this generation. Any watered-down message will not work for God today. Let's come back to scripture that saves souls right where we are at. This is our moment. We will be held accountable for eternity for what we do here. Are we in Christ for what we can get or are we in this for what He can get, glory?

Note

_____

_____

_____

_____

_____

_____

_____

_____

_____

10

"And then will I profess unto them, I never knew you: depart from me, ye that work iniquity" (Matthew 7:23, KJV)

Knowing Jesus is more important than knowing about Jesus. If Jesus is first in our lives, then we will obey Him. Ministry is obedience to His direction. Hearing His voice and knowing our purpose comes through scripture and prayer. Developing our relationship with God is essential for our soul's fulfillment. We can't control anyone around us but we can control ourselves. The Holy Spirit gives us self-control. When we are determined to know God, there are ways to develop it. Journaling, writing our hearts down on paper really helps. Writing to God helps get everything out that we could not verbally communicate. God is not looking for punctuation or a prolific writer; He is looking at the heart and seeing who is coming before Him with all that they are in Jesus's name. If God does not give us the discipline to write, we would never be able to stay committed. Writing is a release. If we don't write, then we won't rest well until we get everything off of our chest. We hope this inspires you. We hope to be writing to this very day. It's not for anyone else's sake but just God and you. God knows everything about you. Hide nothing from Him. There is nothing like being fully known and fully loved. God never forsakes. His love is unconditional. Start writing today and see how it works for you. You can be confident you will start getting more free time the more you write. Your intimacy with Christ will grow at a rapid speed. Live wide open before God, Christ made it possible so that we can.

11

*"And said unto them, It is written, My house shall
be called the house of prayer; but ye have made it
a den of thieves" (Matthew 21:13, KJV)*

We must never discredit prayer. Prayer is power. When we go to prayer, let's give our all. If ever prayer is needed, it's today. We can have all the education, wisdom and skill sets; without God we can even preach, but only God can bring the increase. We tend to pray when we are out of all other options. God knows when we are using Him as a means to our end. He sees our motives in our prayers. The prayer God hears is the one coming from the heart. He can see if we are engaged or if we are going through the motions. Formalities and ruts can disconnect us from a relationship with God. Prayer is the most important part of our day. It's the best gauge to determine how much we depend on God. Without including God in our decision making, Bible reading, sermons, or anything else are a sign that we are truly not under the Lordship of Jesus. God knows how to wake us up. He knows how to keep us going through this life. Affliction is our advantage as we look through the lens of our relationship with God. The harder or impossible the situation the more we will need God. Faith is not faith until we have nothing else to rely on but the Word of God. Prayer is not an excuse to not act. The book of Acts is well named. It's not the book of prayer meetings but the book of actions. When we are not about evangelism, our prayers will become inward focused. Praying for God to be glorified and Souls to be saved, moves the heart of God. Prayer is a great tool in evangelism. When we offer prayer to someone that is lost, they will hear our love and concern for them which breaks down their walls so we can preach the Gospel. People don't care about what we have to say until they know how much we care. When God reveals His love through us, we are able to speak the truth and it will be received. Not everyone will be converted but they will know us by our love for them and each other. Prayer is a great opener for any conversation, especially in evangelism. When we are walking in intimacy with God our audience will be able to tell something is different about us. When preaching is a lifestyle and not just a time of the week, our message will flow out of our mouths like a river of living water. Prayer is not repetition, it's a relationship.

Note

12

"Confess your faults one to another, and pray one for another,
that ye may be healed. The effectual fervent prayer of a
righteous man availeth much" (James 5:16, KJV)

Intercession is standing in proxy for another. Like Abraham did
when he bartered with God for mercy on Sodom. We need to pray
for mercy on our generation. The suicide rate is going up every day.
Most ministers need to sit down with the first responders in their
congregation and hear what is actually going on in their community.
After speaking with our first responders we will get a burden to pray
for them as well, a burden for our communities. Prayer has been
cheapened so much in our generation. The first meeting a "church
growth consultant" axes is the prayer meeting. Very few churches
have prayer meetings anymore. There are many believers that were
raised in the church and were never in a prayer meeting. When
prayer does not matter, then we are too self-reliant. If church growth
does not come by prayer and evangelism then we must question the
attendee's motive in being there. Getting crowds is easy if all we are
offering is self-reliance. Jesus did all He could to disperse the crowds,
to get with the one. Today we disperse the one to get to the crowds.
What defines God's blessing on our lives is how much we are drawn
to pray and how sound our doctrine is when we preach. God, bless
us with fellowship so that we may know you more in prayer. Let's put
prayer back to where it needs to be in our lives. Let's seek God with
all our hearts. Jesus bridged us directly to the throne of grace so that
we can obtain mercy in a time of need. In the book of Acts, we read

of a lot about prayer meetings. Why don't we have prayer meetings today? Do we need to wait until national calamities happen to pray? There may not be national calamities right now, but there certainly are individual calamities: suicide, drug addiction, domestic violence. Our first responders will help us see into the pain of the calamity. God raised us up to pray. Put a faith back in our church so that God listens. Prayer is a mystery, but nevertheless we still must pray. Prayer is a believer's weapon in Jesus's name. We can't fully understand how prayer and God's Sovereignty work but that did not stop the early church from praying. We need to live God-reliant, let's pray friends.

Note

13

"And lo a voice from heaven, saying, This is my beloved Son, in whom I am well pleased" (Matthew 3:17, KJV)

John the Baptist knew who Jesus was. He prophesied that Jesus was the Lamb of God, to be sacrificed for the sins of mankind. Jesus cast our sins as far as the east is from the west. Faith in Christ washes the sins of our past, present and future away. Faith brings us into salvation; unbelief takes us out. Our righteousness does not save us, it's the righteousness of Christ earned with blood that is ours. Our sin-debt is paid in full. We can have doubts but we need to be cautious of unbelief. Unbelief is a renouncement of the blood of Jesus. Under the law, obedience brought the Jews into right standing but under Christ, belief alone brings us into right standing. This is not a license to sin; this is not an excuse to live any sort of way that we want. Just like Jesus was accepted from the beginning, we are too. We don't do "for" God's acceptance or salvation, we do "from" God's acceptance and salvation. There is nothing we can add to the work of Christ that will bring us more acceptance in the sight of God. By doing that, we are calling for Barabbas rather than Christ. We are calling for works and wages to be given to us—which is death. Christ was the lamb of God. Our sins have been taken away by faith in Christ. We are compelled by His love and not duty to follow God in holiness and righteousness. Sons inherit, employees get wages. Christ's death and resurrection brought us into the family of God. We can call God our Father. We inherit eternal life and a relationship with God and nothing but unbelief can take it away from us. Let's believe to the day we die that no matter what our feelings tell us, no matter what our sight tells us, Faith in Christ is packed with the power to live different for the glory of God. We are accepted because Christ accepted us. He is our sacrificial lamb; that's why God allows the temple in Jerusalem to be in ruins for the last two thousand years to let all of mankind know there is only one sacrifice for sin and He paid it in full. God so loves us all that whosoever will believe in Him shall be saved. This is the greatest message that could be preached. The Gospel is truly good news with no "buts" attached.

Note

"Thou art all fair, my love; there is no spot in thee..." (Song of Solomon 4:7, KJV)

Christ makes the collective Church His bride. We are also collectively His body in the earth. He has chosen believers individually and collectively to be His expression on the earth. He could have chosen so many other ways to reveal who He is but He chose us. There is no spot in us or a flaw with us. Christ took all our sin and shame. We can either look at us the way we see ourselves or choose to believe the way God sees us. The Shulamite woman really struggled to believe King Solomon's love for her because of how unworthy she felt but she had to get over herself because he was the King and what he said is all that matters. As believers in Christ, we too need to surrender to what God says over us. Our biggest struggle is not living the Gospel, our greatest struggle is believing the Gospel. When our focus is on behavior more than belief, we will live in shame. The only way to have the right behavior is when we have the right belief. When we know we have no spots, that God accepts us in Christ, our behavior changes. Belief empowers us to behave but behaving will cripple our belief when it becomes our focus more than belief. We as the bride of Christ must believe that He washed all our sin away. What He says over us is of higher authority than anyone else. We love bad news as a society. Bad news sells, just look at the news headlines. Our news channel may as well be called "bad news" channel. We love to talk about bad news, we love to hear bad news, anything to distract ourselves from our badness. Christ came to bring good news and we could not handle it, so we nailed Him to a cross. It's time to believe the good news. God is for us and is never against us. If we are not willing to believe His grace, then we are the same as those that put Him on the cross. We can either believe the Blood is enough for our salvation or it's not. We can't mix faith and works for salvation, that's a lukewarm mentality. We are either saved by faith or not. It's time to believe the good news of the Gospel. Yes, it's that simple. We are His bride; we are His body on the earth. He has chosen us to be His hands and feet. Let's believe all God says over us.

Note

15

"But now hath God set the members every one of them in the body, as it hath pleased him" (1 Corinthians 12:18, KJV)

Every part of the body of Christ is important. Whether they are overseas or serving where they were born and raised. Where God has put us makes us important for His kingdom. Christianity is more than employment, it's family. We clock in and out as employees but we are family 24-7. Those that work for a ministry need to be cautious so that they don't get into a "clock in and clock out" mind-set. Every occupation is a mission and we are called to do everything as unto the Lord, not unto a check. It seems like people work harder for a paycheck than unto the Lord. This tells us that we put more value on provision than the provider. When we know that we are accepted and loved, it does not make us work less but makes us want to work harder for His glory with joy. Ministry is a "get" to. It's our "reasonable service." As we walk in relationship with God, we won't be living for the mission trip, we will be living on mission. If we want weight to our words, then we need to walk with God in a relationship. We are not just servants; we are sons and daughters first. There are lost sinners all around us every day. Let's be open to God's leading every day. Our audience will know if our faith is "from" God's love or "for" God's love. If it's "for" it, then we have nothing different to offer to anyone. Ministry is not a title we get from a church, it's a function that is evident in our life. Titles mean nothing to sinners. If we want to effectively reach the lost, then we ourselves must be walking in current relationship with God. All of our missions and ministries must be a byproduct of our relationship with Jesus. Christ died to reconcile us as sons and daughters more so than just servants. As we know God in relationship our ministry will flow out of us where we are. As you are reading this, you must believe that where God has you right now—He wants to shine through you. Be aware of those around you. You are not there by accident. This moment is not just a season to make money or raise support for missions in the future. Where you are at is your mission. Don't miss the souls that could be reached in this moment. We live for the next mission but miss out on the power of our moments. Don't listen to the liar who says we are not important.

Note

16

"That there should be no schism in the body; but that the members should have the same care one for another. And whether one member suffer, all the members suffer with it; or one member be honoured, all the members rejoice with it" (1 Corinthians 12:25–26, KJV)

Satan has used comparison and competition as an open door to the church for a long time now. When the human body competes with itself, it destroys itself. When every part of the body is content in the position God has placed it in, reaching the people they are called to be reaching, there would be unity. We have churches that don't talk and congregations that have the same Lord but don't know each other. There are slight variations on beliefs but most evangelicals agree on the same Gospel. When the local church is united, it becomes a force to be reckoned with. When every believer understands their value in the body, then the body would be a force to be reckoned with against darkness. Christ puts equal value on us all with His own blood. Before we are parts of His body, before we have functions for His kingdom, we are first and foremost His sons and daughters. God does not raise any human above another. We as humans love hierarchy, positions and titles but in the body, we are one. Some may seem more important because they are more visual. The hidden parts of our body are just as important as the visual parts, such as our organs. The Church is a body. When we unite, God commands His blessing. Rather than the eye trying to be what it's not when it is content being what it is then it functions at full capacity. Every believer is a part of the body of Christ; whether their part is ministerial, financial or prayerful every believer is important before God. When we are isolated or severed from the body of Christ, we are useless. We are only as useful as we are connected to the body. A hand by itself can do nothing. This is why forsaking the assembly was forbidden. We need one another. The body of Christ is interdependent just as our physical body is. Evangelists are a joint in the body of Christ connecting the local church with the intent of evangelism. Evangelizing is not promoting a church, it's promoting Christ. The church is not the solution for the sinner, it's the solution to the believer. The sinner needs Jesus more than anything else. By the shed blood of Jesus, we are flawless by faith. What God calls us is better than any title man can put in front of our name. Let's honor the Lamb by being content in His title given to us as sons and daughters.

Note

"For the life of the flesh is in the blood: and I have given it to you upon the altar to make an atonement for your souls: for it is the blood that maketh an atonement for the soul" (Leviticus 17:11, KJV)

There was nothing clean about the atonement of our sins. The gore and bloody sacrifice were very graphic on the day of atonement. Our worship is so clean today in comparison. Sin has terrible consequences; we can see it evidenced on the news every day. Sin had serious ramifications so God set up the sacrificial system to be bloody. When Christ died on the cross, there was nothing clean about it. He took our uncleanliness upon Himself and with the washing of His blood we have become His holy temple on the earth. We give God an address on this planet. There is no need to go to Jerusalem when the kingdom of heaven is within us now. Christ replaced the law sacrifices; He became the once-and-for-all lamb sacrifice for sin. Christ fulfilled the law and the prophets. Every prophetic word under the Old Covenant, Christ fulfilled. Now that we are His temple, we are His first choice to use to see others come to know Him. Like Moses, we love to talk back to God and tell Him what we can't do. We love to pray for others to do what God has called us to do. We rely on the TV, internet, prayer meeting, pastor, evangelist, etc., to do what He has called us to do. All our gifts are different but we are called to be a light. We are called to do the work of an evangelist. God can use our shadow, hanky, love, act of service, kindness, sermon, scripture quote, to see His name high and lifted up. Don't be too worried about our speaking gift or natural talents. God equips those whom He calls. Where God leads, God provides. There is no better way to minister, there is just the way God gave us individually. No one is supposed to do it the same. We just need to seek God for the way we are called to be a light. For some of us it is proclamation, for others it is Christ manifesting love through us, for some it's financially supporting ministries that are evangelistic. Our only footing to preach His name is faith in His death, burial and resurrection. We can't elevate ourselves above anyone because that type of pride comes before a fall. We are humans in need of a savior to the day we physically die. The serpent loves to lie to the saint "you should not need a savior by now," Jesus break these lies. We are what we are by the grace of God. Satan feeds our desire to compete and compare with each other, which incapacitates us in the body of Christ. Our importance is not in our position in the body of Christ but it's being in Christ. Christ's atonement was to reconcile us as sons and daughters. He did not atone for us to be servants or parts of the body alone. We are His family and our value is not determined by what we do or where we serve but by who we are as sons and daughters in Christ.

David said, *"It is good for me that I have been afflicted; that I might learn thy statutes" (Psalm 119:71, KJV)*. Affliction can be an advantage. It's in suffering where we have fellowship with God like no other experience can give us. *"That I may know him, and the power of his resurrection, and the fellowship of his sufferings, being made conformable unto his death (Phil 3:10, KJV)*. Three times Paul prayed to be delivered from his affliction and Jesus spoke back to Him, *"My grace is sufficient."* Affliction and sickness are not a disadvantage or God's punishment on us. Christ took all of sins' punishment on Himself at the cross. By His stripes we are healed spiritually and physically. There are mysteries and unknowns that we will have on this journey as believers. Everyone dies at some point, it's a matter of when our day is. No one lives forever here on earth. Lest God should tarry, we will all be six feet under one hundred years from now. Life is short. We all will face affliction but our perspective is through the lens of faith. Not just faith for healing but faith for God to turn our affliction into an advantage. He promises all things will work together for good for those who love God. God does not love anyone more because He heals them. Hezekiah got his healing but it did not work out good for him in the long term. The love of God toward us must never be defined by health or wealth. If we have a crack in our soul of God's love not being defined by the cross, then the enemy has a way into us. The love of God is only refined by the cross; not by our health and wealth. We need to fill the breach to our soul by not allowing any way for doubt to come in by not trusting the Cross. Christ's love for us is in the Cross. God's love for us is not based on anything other than what Christ already did for us. Satan has used the health and wealth message to shame suffering believers; also, charlatans have turned the message into a "cash cow." Any message that causes doubt in the cross of Christ as God's "so love" for us is anathema. We are loved more than we could ever know. Stephen and the early church embraced their martyrdom for the cause of Christ. They were unashamed of the price for following Christ. Suffering with Christ is better than suffering without Him. He can heal and deliver but it is a mystery if He does or does not. We must trust through it all that Christ will turn it for good. Rejoice in the prison cell, be at peace with the negative doctor reports, remember, God is sovereign! He is also good. Shall not the judge of all the earth do what is right?

18

"That I might know Him" (Phil 3:10, KJV)

Knowing Jesus in the power of His resurrection is the desire of the western church. The martyrs and persecuted church would tell us otherwise. There is a revelation in suffering that no other experience on earth can give to us. God is near to the broken-hearted. We like to read books on "ways to live furnace free" yet it is in the furnace that the revelation of Christ was made known to Nebuchadnezzar. It's in the lion's den that we learn that it was not the lion's den but God's den. It's in hardship that our faith becomes a reality. When we have no other options but for God to open up the path that is ahead of us is when we know Him the most. We can't define blessing by the western mind-set. To be blessed is to know God, period. Whether we know Him with wealth or without, nothing determines our blessing more than the death, burial and resurrection of Christ. We are blessed no matter the outward circumstances, whether that is martyrdom or deliverance, both are blessed outcomes for knowing Jesus through it all. We all want it easy but life is far from easy for both believers and unbelievers. It's better with Christ because He can heal, He can intervene, He gives us an eternal perspective. Without Christ our hardships become mountains but faith in God makes the mountains a mustard seed. God overcame sin, Satan, and death at the cross. We truly are more than conquerors. Don't let what we see or what we feel determine our faith. Don't listen to the false preachers that define blessing by anything more than the cross of Christ. Desiring more than what God has already given to us is such a slap in Christ's face. Friends, we need to call it what it is. There is nothing more that Christ could do for us to bring peace to our souls. Let's become believers through all circumstances. Believers are unmovable and unshakable. We are confident, we are conquerors, there is no scheme of hell that can make us doubt the goodness of God because His goodness is manifested in Christ. God is good, all the time. In all things we can be content, in all seasons, we can have peace, in all seasons, we can have a song. If He heals, amen, if He does not, amen, His will be done!

Note

_____

_____

_____

_____

_____

_____

_____

_____

_____

_____

19

"And he said to them all, 'If any man will come after me, let him deny himself, and take up his cross daily, and follow me'" (Luke 9:23, KJV)

Jesus teaches us how we can bear the cross the whole way to heaven. If we want to come after Jesus, we are to deny ourselves. Denial of self cannot be done by self. A lot of times we deny self; by self with the end goal which is for "our self." Denial of self is not denying stuff or things but it's denying self-strength. It's making Jesus Lord of our thought life. We try to deny ourselves but it's such an uphill battle. Jesus showed us what denial of self really looks like when He fell beneath the weight of the cross and Simon, the bystander, was called in to carry the cross the rest of the way. Jesus could have carried it all the way to Golgotha but He was teaching a lesson even in His dying moment. Simon represents the Holy Spirit. When we deny our self-strength, then the power of the Holy Spirit does in us what we could never do on our own. He enables the cross to be lifted in our lives and we are able to bear it by His power. Once we begin to live a Spirit-dependent life, then we are able to follow Jesus anywhere. Denial of self-strength is a daily decision. The only way to get the fruit of the Spirit is not by pruning the fruit of the flesh, we have to go to the root. The root is self-reliance. We are not the potter, we are not the vinedresser, we are not the one who can live this life following Jesus. We are the root, we are the clay; when we deny ourselves and let God be Lord, He brings life to our lives where there should be death. As we die to self-strength, we become alive to the Holy Spirit. God is interested in the root of sin while Satan has us all distracted by the fruit of sin. We are figuring out how to bear the cross, but we can't do it by ourselves. We must deny ourselves by honest communication to God that we can't do this. We can't carry this cross. We can't make it on our own. Without Christ we can do nothing. We can't have the fruit of the Spirit unless we have the root of the Spirit. As we abide in Christ, through Christ we can do all things. We no longer live but Christ lives in us. The life we live is by faith, which is revealed in honest relationship. As we walk transparently in Jesus's name, the Spirit will do the rest. Follow Christ, not self. Deny self-strength.

Note

20

"Again, the kingdom of heaven is like unto a merchant man, seeking goodly pearls: Who, when he had found one pearl of great price, went and sold all that he had, and bought it" (Matthew 13:45–46, KJV)

What is the pearl and the treasure in *Matthew 13*? Well we know Jesus is the redeemer and we are not. Jesus is not for sale. We can't buy Jesus. There is nothing we can sell or do to buy Jesus or earn Jesus because He is not for sale. The Pearl and the Treasure is you and I. Jesus laid aside His majesty to purchase us with His own blood. We are valuable and significant. Satan is doing all he can to devalue humanity to animals and to nothing. Preachers that tell their congregations they're nothing yet live like they are everything need to reevaluate their message. Christ redeemed everyone with His blood. We are blood bought sons and daughters. God shows no favorites. In Christ we are valuable and significant. We matter. God puts so much love on mankind. He does not discriminate like we do. Peter thought himself higher than the gentiles and he was Spirit filled. Paul had to confront this mind-set that one man is higher than another because of ethnicity or title. Paul counted all his earthly titles dung in comparing to the redemption of Christ. We are significant, we are loved, we are valued and when the enemy would try to add works to faith in Christ for our value, rebuke it in Jesus's name. We are pearls and treasures to God. He has given us 24-7 attention. He will by no means cast anyone away. God does not discriminate race, gender, or sinner. Christ made all sin a separator, whether it's self-righteous or self-gratification both get the same wage. Faith in Christ alone deems our value and salvation. There is nothing we can give to God that He needs. We could sell all and still it would not be enough without Christ. Let's fight for faith because there are many that would try to bewitch us to rob the simplicity of faith alone in Christ. He purchased us. He redeemed us. As we rest in our redemption, the Holy Spirit will transform our character and make us want to obey the leading of Christ. We are Christ followers and not man followers. Churches must be cautious when raising a man above the message. When a certain man is the only one that has the truth, then we are back in a papal mind-set. We are protestants for a reason. This is why the simple Gospel must be preached in the streets. God redeemed everyone.

Note

21

"Of how much sorer punishment, suppose ye, shall he be thought worthy, who hath trodden under foot the Son of God, and hath counted the blood of the covenant, wherewith he was sanctified, an unholy thing, and hath done despite unto the Spirit of grace?" (Hebrews 10:29, KJV)

"We are trampling on the blood of Jesus when we are working for salvation and not from salvation." The blood of Jesus gives us life and earned our right to come before God. The blood of Jesus washed our sins away. His blood was spilled on the cross so that ours would not have to be spilled for eternity. Life, healing and assurance is in the blood of Jesus. Without the shedding of His blood, there would be no forgiveness of sin. When we say we are just a member of the church, when we say we are just a volunteer, then we are lowering the justification that the blood was spilt for. We are "Just" because of Jesus. We are sons and daughters of God in Christ. That's a greater title than being an apostle, prophet, evangelist, pastor or teacher. Let's not say we are just anything and let's say the blood made us just. The just live by faith and not by titles or positions. When our justification comes by anything other than the blood of Jesus, then Christ died in vain. As we abide in Christ, which is not striving for salvation but resting from our salvation, then our works will be "want-to's" and not "have-to's." The just live by faith and not just think by faith. Our faith in Christ is power to behave like we believe. This life is by faith in the merits of the blood of Jesus. The blood of Jesus carries weight. It's a message packed with power. The blood of Jesus is against Satan,

Sin and death. The New Covenant was sealed in His blood. We have confidence and authority in Jesus's name. The Lamb that was slain will receive the reward of His suffering. His Blood was not spilt in vain.

Note

22

---

*"Trust in the Lord with all thine heart; and lean not unto
thine own understanding. In all thy ways acknowledge him,
and he shall direct thy paths" (Proverbs 3:5–6, KJV)*

"A great gauge to let us know if Jesus is Lord or not is by looking
back on our last major decision: did we include God in our decision-making process?" Jesus is Lord. As we give over our will in relationship and acknowledge Him in all our ways, then we can be confident that He will direct our steps. If God does not speak clearly, then
we can make the best decision we can and God will steer us as the
momentum picks up. We never have to be confused or wait longer
than normal. God is not the author of confusion. He will be with us
through all the ups and downs. Including God in all our steps and
decisions really shows ourselves that Jesus is Lord. Some just want
to be saved from hell but what about being saved from our will and
plans. Not only does Jesus have the best in heaven for us but He has
the best life for us too. The best life is the one with Jesus. It may look
tough and hard but it's the best. Life with Jesus is the most blessed
life. As we exchange our will for His will, we can trust that no matter
what is ahead, His grace will be sufficient. Knowing almighty God is
with us is such a huge comfort. At any moment He can intervene and
deliver. At any moment years of destruction can be put back together
in an instant. There is no sin that cannot be washed away by the
Blood of Jesus. Even if up until reading this, Jesus has not been a part
of your decision-making process, start today. Make Jesus Lord today.
It's not too late. There is no greater peace than turning over our will

to Jesus. God is in control. He is sovereign and we have no reason to fear. His perfect love casts out fear. We can be confident of the hand of God upon us when He is Lord.

Note

_____

_____

_____

_____

_____

_____

_____

_____

_____

23

"And he said unto me, My grace is sufficient for thee: for my strength is made perfect in weakness. Most gladly therefore will I rather glory in my infirmities, that the power of Christ may rest upon me. Therefore I take pleasure in infirmities, in reproaches, in necessities, in persecutions, in distresses for Christ's sake: for when I am weak, then am I strong" (2 Corinthians 12:9–10, KJV)

"Affliction is our advantage and not our adversary." When we are in a situation where we need Christ the most, there is such a grace. It's amazing. The peace that God gives is not even close to that of the world. There is no one or no place that can match the peace of God. There are so many counterfeit life styles and lures of the devil for peace but it's all a sham. Wealth and health do not give peace. Millions of people are living for the "break" but they don't know that what they are searching for will not fulfill them. Some of the most anxious people are wealthy and healthy. Peace is not found in a position, title, lotto card, etc. True peace is in Christ. He gives eternal peace and His peace is free with no price attached, just blessings. We have all tried the temporary peace of the world but it's never too late to find the peace of God. When we are in affliction, we rely on God the most, that's why affliction is an advantage. Our flesh hates pain and suffering but it's a way for us to depend on God the most. When we have everything we want, our flesh gets comfortable and we don't need faith because we have everything that we could want. That's why Jesus said it was harder for an independent rich man to enter heaven. Wealth and affliction do not have to determine our dependence on God. It just takes more discipline on our flesh to turn to God when everything is going great. May God keep us reliant in all seasons. If we are wealthy, may we choose to depend on God and if we are poor, we have no option but to depend on God. God, keep us leaning on you through it all. Teach us to not see affliction as an adversary. We need to have a right perspective through it all. God is good all the time, in all seasons because our definition of His goodness is not in what we experience but in *John 3:16.*

Note

_____

_____

_____

_____

_____

_____

_____

_____

24

"I beseech you therefore, brethren, by the mercies of God, that ye present your bodies a living sacrifice, holy, acceptable unto God, which is your reasonable service. And be not conformed to this world: but be ye transformed by the renewing of your mind, that ye may prove what is that good, and acceptable, and perfect, will of God" (Romans 12:1–2, KJV)

The best way for us to live is in total surrender to God. When we give over our desires, dreams and expectations to God, we find peace. God has a better and a more exciting life than any one of us could conjure up for ourselves. There is no way any of us should sell out our call for a bowl of soup like Esau did. None of us should sell out our call for pieces of silver like Judas did. There is no purpose outside of the purpose that God has for our lives. Our biggest enemy is ourselves. We are our own worst enemy. That's why Jesus wants to be Lord. He does not "need" to be the Lord. He is Lord. He is self-existent and needs nothing. God chose us. God desires us not out of need but out of love. It's not a blind love; God is calling us to surrender. He proved His love for us when Christ went to the cross. We can be confident as we open ourselves to His will. He will give us the grace and peace to see it through. The enemy has sown into our culture that God is not good. Just a crack of doubt in our souls in the goodness of God can lead to a crash. We must fight to believe the goodness of God, not because of what we see, but because of what Christ did for us. This life is so exciting. We just never know what God is going to do next or how He is going to provide next. He will take care of us. We will see His provision as we live by faith, nothing compares to the wonders of our God. God will never abandon us. I gave Jesus my whole life many years ago. In my imperfections, sins, confusion, sickness, unforgiveness, not one time did He abandon me. Not one time did He turn His back on me. He has not failed me yet. I'm far from perfect, I'm not someone who *used* to be like you, but someone who is *just* like you. I need Jesus as much as anyone on the street. I've never needed Jesus more in my life than right now. God keeps on providing. His grace is sufficient. His grace forgives, enables and empowers. Without His grace, none of us could have made it. We can never cast judgment because it was grace that saved us and grace that keeps us. May the lamb that was slain receive the reward of His suffering.

Note

_____

_____

_____

_____

_____

_____

_____

_____

_____

25

"And Jesus came and spake unto them, saying, All power is given unto me in heaven and in earth. Go ye therefore, and teach all nations, baptizing them in the name of the Father, and of the Son, and of the Holy Ghost: Teaching them to observe all things whatsoever I have commanded you: and, lo, I am with you always, even unto the end of the world. Amen" (Matthew 28:18–20, KJV)

"A disciple without spiritual discipline is not a disciple of Christ but a disciple of their flesh." Our flesh will try to get the best of us but we need to decide for our faith to get the best of us. As we surrender to God and live in a state of repentance, the power of the Holy Spirit will empower us to be disciplined. Stepping out in faith by setting an alarm, buying index cards, buying a pen and a journal are all essential tools to help us be spiritually disciplined. As we step out, we will form good habits in our lives. Habits are formed over time and discipline. When we put God's word in our souls and cast our sins, fears and anxiety on God, then we are able to live differently. It's what we were created for. "Whatever a man sows, he will reap." If we sow into the Word, prayer and evangelism, we will reap fulfillment. We were created for a purpose. God is not looking for braindead believers. He loves our minds and our creativity. He gave authority to Adam to name the animals. He wants a relationship where we don't only consume but we where we produce. The consumer mentality is not what Jesus is desiring from us. He gives, so we can give. As He is, so are we in the world. He that is in us is greater than us. Even though we are not naturally disciplined as we make decisions of faith, with our time and passion, the Holy Spirit will enable us to commit. We don't have to be led by our flesh and emotions. Our feelings must not be lord of our time or lives. Our flesh will destroy us. We are self-harming creatures if we are left to our passions. We are to come under the Lordship of Jesus and beat our self-strength into submission to Christ. Let's fight to believe that God can overcome our flesh. As we believe, our behavior will follow suit. Faith in Christ will always lead to action. This is not a gnostic teaching that only affects our thinking. Our faith works. We work *from* our salvation and not *for* our salvation. Christ compels us from the inside as we walk in relationship with Him. As we let Him be Lord of our lives, which is giving over to His will and including Him in our decision-making process, then we will see disciplines formed in our lives.

Note

"Ye ask, and receive not, because ye ask amiss, that ye may consume it upon your lusts" (James 4:3, KJV)

God rarely answers prayers when He knows we already have what it takes to do what we are asking Him to do for us. God is not going to do for us what we can do for ourselves. God is not going to do what we can do; He is going to do what we cannot do. God won't teleport our food to our stomach but He will bless it, when we pray before we eat. If we want to be free from fear then we need to stop feeding fear in our lives and pray for the spirit of fear to be broken off of us. If we want to be free from depression, then we need to pray but also change up our music, media intake and movies. Are we feeding our fears? Are we feeding our depression? I've never heard of Jesus making someone thin, who was obese. That miracle has not happened yet. He has healed the sick but when it comes to discipline, exercise and diet, that's up to us. God will do what we cannot do. As we live in a state of surrender to God, which includes surrendering our movies, music and anything of the world that would feed sin, fear or depression, then we will see answered prayer. God cares about our mind and lives. He enjoys seeing our creativity. He wanted Adam to name the animals, which was a big responsibility since there were millions of animals. God never wants us to lose self-control. As believers in Christ, we receive self-control and a sound mind in the Holy Spirit. God reinforces our mind with His Word and Spirit. We can follow through on what is right because we are choosing to walk not after the flesh but the Spirit. When we walk after the Spirit, we will not fulfill the lust of the flesh. When we walk this life out in our self-strength, we will fulfill the lust of the flesh. We have seen that happen numerous times as believers. The only way to live free from sin is to live Spirit-dependent which is more than a state of mind but a relationship with Christ. As we are in relationship, communication and dependence on Christ, then we will see power in our lives to do what we could never do in our flesh. We are never on our own as believers. God is with us. Christ made a way with His blood to receive us sinners into His family but not to leave us the way we are; because the way we are is destructive. Christ hears our cry for salvation out. When it comes to our prayers for things that we are responsible for, God will not always answer.

Note

27

"Draw nigh to God, and he will draw nigh to you. Cleanse your hands, ye sinners; and purify your hearts, ye double minded" (James 4:8, KJV)

Prayer is relationship and not a replacement of our effort. Prayer is not a means for God to work so that we don't have to. God has not chosen prayer as His means to evangelize. God has not chosen prayer as His means to souls being saved. Prayer is a partnership where God and the believer walk in a relationship. Out of that relationship comes the leading of God on our lives to do what we could never do, like evangelize effectively. God chose preaching as His primary means to see souls saved. Just like we pray before we eat, and then we partake, it's the same with what obedience looks like for the believer. We pray, then obey. Obedience may be tough, but it's easier with prayer because God enables us to do what we could never do on our own. Prayer is a lot more practical than we may have thought. Prayer is simply a relationship. Including God in our decision making, bringing Him into our every day, seeking the Word of God for counsel, releasing stress, sin, and frustration to God, all show that we were designed for this relationship with God. Only God listens and never interrupts. Only God listens and has the power to take the pain of our soul away so that we can have peace. Once we pray, He will give us the motivation to do His will. Prayer is power. Prayer in Jesus's name will always lead to action. God calls us to a purpose and action. It's not only to tithe for someone else to do our purpose for us. God calls all of us. That model is not working. God has called each one of us to rise in our own unique call. There is only one man that gets the attention, and that is Jesus; this is about His glory, His mission, and His will to be done. The papal mind-set is easy for us to cave into. We need to stop lifting people above God. Christ leveled the ground, the five-fold ministries are functions; they are not titles. Our titles are sons and daughters, brothers and sisters. Christ is the greatest equalizer for humanity. He leveled the ground. Christ is our mediator. We can know God for ourselves. We have direct access. We have the Bible, the Holy Spirit, and a relationship with Jesus and the church, what more do we need, to do what God has called us to do? Let's choose to grow as believers. Let's not look for the easy way out. Let's ask, seek, knock and "do" in Jesus's name.

Note

28

"Then Peter opened his mouth, and said, Of a truth I perceive that God is no respecter of persons" (Acts 10:34, KJV)

"If we draw near to God, He will draw near to us." We can know as much of God as we want. We don't have to read of the characters of the Bible and wish that we knew God as they did. We can know God as much, even more than any of the Old Testament characters. Every Old Testament character did not have faith in the shed blood of Jesus. They were veiled from the presence of God. Thanks to Christ's death, the Veil was torn from top to bottom to show those at the top that they are just as equal as those at the bottom. Christ's resurrection proves our resurrection that we truly never die. We live forever. Our flesh will die, but our souls will live forever. One day we will be in our glorified bodies, and we will be whole, both in soul and body. Right now, our flesh needs to be submitted to our faith. Our feelings cannot get the best of us. We must keep our flesh in check. We can take every thought captive and make it obey Christ. We can know God. He is no respecter of people. He has no favorites. Whosoever will believe in Christ has equal access to God almighty. We can know God as our Father. We can cast our cares on Him; we can know His Word, we can seek His face. We need to be intentional about our time with God so that He gets uninterrupted time with us. Let's be cautious that we are not giving God the scraps of our time but the best of our time, like the first moment when we wake up or go to bed. We can know Him throughout the day, but don't forget quality time with God and His Word. Just like we set up appointments with officials or those who are important, God deserves this same respect. It is our reasonable service. Laying our time down to focus on God, laying our lives down as a living sacrifice, so we are to live as He is the center of our world rather than someone or something else. Only God is God. No one can replace Him in our soul. If we let someone or something else into our soul, we will be unfulfilled. Intentionality is important. Having a structure is healthy. If our bodies had no bones, we would be like jelly. We need both structure and life. We need both prayer time and prayer life. Let's remember the importance of our relationship with God. It's what Christ accomplished, reconciliation.

Note

29

"Even so faith, if it hath not works, is dead,
being alone" (James 2:17, KJV)

Our relationship with God takes faith. Faith produces the effort. As good as Christian books and devotionals are, none of it compares to Scripture. When the scripture is our least read book, then we are open prey to deception. The Bible alone is where our faith comes from. Faith comes by hearing the Word of God. Any other opinion cannot replace the scripture. Sermons, references, and aids are good, but they are all fallible. The only infallible Word, the only anointed Word is the Bible. God won't get the Bible into our mind unless we soak in the Word of God; unless we memorize the Word, we pray the Word, we study the Word, and we preach the Word. The authority of scripture is our only "go-to" for life and godliness. "Oh, that we would be baptized in the fire of the Holy Spirit." That the Word of God would be our life source and not anything of our flesh. The Holy Spirit fire is not passion, but it's purification. The Holy Spirit sets fire to our laziness and makes us eagerly desire the Word of God. The fruit of the Holy Spirit will always accompany the Gifts of the Spirit. The only way to try the Holy Spirit is with scripture. The Holy Scripture is our soul's fuel. Our evangelism is not "outreach" it is the proclamation of the Gospel. The gospel will always be a message. The Gospel is about knowing Christ; it's about glorifying Christ. "Oh, that we would be set on fire for His glory; that we would live every day like it's our last." We have nothing else to live for because we were created for God's pleasure and not our own. When we take steps to seek God and intentionally seek God, He will meet us every time. His omnipresence is true, but those that seek Him will experience His manifested presence: Christ with us, Christ in us, the hope of glory. Just like it takes working out to be physically healthy, it takes spiritually working out to go deeper in our faith. As we work out our own salvation, then God will use us to see others get saved. As we know God for us, then He makes Himself known through us to others around us. Our words become action-packed. They will hear from us, not the boldness of our flesh but the boldness of the Spirit. They will know that we are not another "teacher" but that it is God who works in us.

Note

30

"All scripture is given by inspiration of God, and is profitable for doctrine, for reproof, for correction, for instruction in righteousness: That the man of God may be perfect, thoroughly furnished unto all good works" (2 Timothy 3:16–17, KJV)

If the Bible is the least-read book in our daily reading, we can be sure that we are prey for deception. Biographies, commentaries, sermons, etc., are just resources. Our core text is the Bible. Sermons must be held accountable by scripture. Understanding the context and having two to three verses to verify our point is essential. Anything can be taken out of context. Just like we never look up a novel and read whatever we flick open to, neither should the Bible be read so flippantly. We need to be intentional when reading scripture. No one needs to hear our stories, jokes, opinions, or pet topics; we are to rightly divide the Word of God and not elevate our personality above Christ. The mandate on a preacher for truth is very serious. We won't always get it right, but we should want to. Even though our words are fallible, this does not mean that we have a license for fallibility and malpractice. No, we should study to show ourselves approved. Our message is serious. There is nothing light about this life. The Gospel is not a cheap, betterment program. This is not about our goosebumps or our knowledge base; this is knowing the truth, and the truth setting us free. As we nourish our faith with God's Word, we will become unshakable. Some of us need to have a "Bible-only" diet for a season: leaning not on opinions or our own understanding but the Word of God. If we grow the church any other way other than by the preaching of the Word, then those congregants are temporary. Community is empty; worship is empty, entertainment is empty, the only thing that feeds the soul like bread feeds our flesh is the Word of God. When the teaching of the Word is the draw to our assembly, then we have a true community, true worship, and true entertainment. People will come and go; fads will come and go, but God's Word stays the same. Take a break from music, take a break from movies, take a break from entertainment and seek God in His Word. Samuel did. As a young man, he heard the voice of God. God still speaks purpose, direction, and conviction. He will never speak new doctrine because the Bible is the only infallible Word of God for doctrine and instruction. Let's go right to the source. It'll save you a lot of money at the Christian book shop. Read your Bible and pray.

Note

31

"And I saw heaven opened, and behold a white horse; and he that sat upon him was called Faithful and True, and in righteousness he doth judge and make war. His eyes were as a flame of fire, and on his head were many crowns; and he had a name written, that no man knew, but he himself. And he was clothed with a vesture dipped in blood: and his name is called The Word of God. And the armies which were in heaven followed him upon white horses, clothed in fine linen, white and clean. And out of his mouth goeth a sharp sword, that with it he should smite the nations: and he shall rule them with a rod of iron: and he treadeth the winepress of the fierceness and wrath of Almighty God. And he hath on his vesture and on his thigh a name written, King Of Kings, And Lord Of Lords" (Revelation 19:11–16, KJV)

When Christ comes back, it will not be through a virgin. He will be coming with all power and authority. He will be riding a horse with a heavenly military. Christ is the only one that is coming through the clouds. There is no other alien presence that is going to be coming through the clouds. There are no other aliens or flying saucers. Christ is coming. He is coming, prepared for war. Vengeance will be in His heart toward the antichrist, sinners, and Satan. He will not be mocked. Jesus Christ will be hailed as king by every human. Every false religion from Islam to Hinduism will be defeated, and their followers will be brought to their knees for judgment. Only Jesus Christ is the way, the truth, and the life. We have the only way to the Father. There is no other way. Every human without Christ is damned to hell unless they repent and leave their religion, works, and culture behind. We are now citizens of heaven. Our culture is a Jesus culture. We are either in Christ or not. All our cultures, ways, customs will pass away, and all things will become new. The Bible is the only X-files we will ever read. The words of the Bible are from heaven. The Bible is God-breathed. The UFO we need to be looking for is Jesus coming on a horse. We have so much to look forward to. Believers in Christ are not perfect, but we know Christ is perfect. We are those that have realized a need for Jesus but have not graduated from a need for Jesus. The second we think we have graduated from a need for Jesus because of our knowledge, works and maturity is the second we have bitten the apple of the anti-Christ. The spirit of anti-Christ has risen. Churches have axed the prayer meeting. There is no dependence on God. We have silver and gold but we have no power from God. We are building the church by personality, human strategy and fleshly ideas. We are not hearing from God. We are following the trends rather than following Christ. When trends decide worship and sermons, Jesus is not Lord. Music and entertainment have taken over the house of God. The most basic understanding of God is all that people want. "Just give us enough truth to get us into heaven," "please don't wake us up," "sing us lullabies, don't challenge our faith."

32

"Whose end is destruction, whose God is their belly, and whose glory is in their shame, who mind earthly things" (Phil 3:19, KJV)

In Christ we receive the habituation of God. We become the temple of God. The Holy Spirit indwells the moment we place faith in Christ. Once we repent and make Jesus Lord, the Holy Spirit lives in us. Friends, this is not a natural life as a believer, it's a supernatural life. This is not a gnostic religion that deals with our thinking. God changes our thought life so He can change our lives. He is calling us out from the life of sin, pain and turmoil. He calls us to a life of peace. We have so much reason in Christ to live free. We have the Bible, the power of the Holy Spirit, and the church. We have everything we could ever need to be free. The Bible says, *"Dearly beloved, I beseech you as strangers and pilgrims, abstain from fleshly lusts, which war against the soul" (1 Peter 2:11, NIV)*.

We are called to live a life of Spirit-dependence and not self-reliance. As we depend on Him who is in us, He will overcome our self-strength so Christ will be glorified in our behavior. We are aliens in Christ. We receive power from heaven to be different. This is a supernatural life. This is not a natural life. We are called to walk in power and might from God. The more we believe who we are in Christ, the more different we will live. Living the Gospel is much easier than believing the Gospel. If we would only believe the benefits of the cross that we gain, imagine how different we would live. Believing is our only way to right behavior. Believing the goodness of God, believing the love of God, believing the kindness of God, this all leads us to right behavior. We generally put behavior ahead of belief. This will condemn us because we will never be good enough. We can never be "God" enough. We need a savior; we need a God. Everyone has a god today, it's either their "belly" or their self-gratification. They worship by eating their pain away or by entertainment, taking a five-star cruise to hell. God, may Christ always be Lord of our lives. Burn up all the compromise and mediocrity. Make us more like you Jesus. We can't but He that is in us can. So, Holy Spirit, have your way in us so Christ can be seen in our lives. As we walk in the light before God, all power that we need to glorify God is accessible.

Note

33

*"For the preaching of the cross is to them that perish
foolishness; but unto us which are saved it is the
power of God" (1 Corinthians 1:18, KJV)*

The preaching of the cross is powerful. The Gospel is power. It's more than just power to see the lame walk. It's more than amplification. It's more than goosebumps. The preaching of the Cross is power unto salvation. The Bible spells out our salvation and our purpose. God wants us saved. The world has treated the preaching of the cross as foolishness. All some people want to hear about is destiny and purpose, as if talking about it will cause it to happen. If we are not preaching about the cross, then talking about purpose is like a lifeguard teaching someone drowning how to do a breaststroke. Every sermon on TV lately is all about our purpose, our peace, our pleasure, our wealth. Have we conjured up a "lapdog" God, like He's a genie in a bottle? The preaching of the cross reminds us that, yes, we are saved but Christ will get glory from our lives. Most people believe in a god that they get the most out of. Their god is a resource through life. They sing songs to him and "amen" a sermon but once the church service is over, they are on with their lives. "Oh, that our preachers would preach fervently the cross of Christ again." We have turned sermons into teachings, showing off our knowledge and wisdom. It's hard to stay awake. Most are going to church for the music. The sermon is a part of the church that everyone has to endure. Music is more valued today than the Word. Artists are bouncing around the stage performing but have no power in their personal life. Once their circus act is up, they live no different than the world. My friends, it's time to realize that artists are not what we really need. What we really need is the preaching of the Gospel. The shallow faith of our artists today would shock our parents' generation. Very little prayer, very little depth in the word, they are leading in clothing and hair-cuts, more than in the Word of God. Their outward appearances, the tattoos, ear piercings, and torn jeans, have become their identity. We need mercy on this generation more than ever before. "Oh, that God would bring back a depth in His Word." Some of our generation is so scripturally illiterate, that some are chasing signs and wonders, not realizing that those who chased Jesus for wonders and got them, were the same ones shouting for Barabbas to go free.

Note

34

"For it had been better for them not to have known the way of righteousness, than, after they have known it, to turn from the holy commandment delivered unto them" (2 Peter 2:21, KJV)

The Bible is from God. It is the infallible Word of God. The evidence of its authority is all over the western society. From the Government to the Economy, we have the influence of scripture everywhere. Everyone has a moral compass that they rely on; whether it is from Hollywood, videos, games, religion, or culture, we all get our moral compass from somewhere. The Bible has been tried and tested for thousands of years. The Bible influences the whole person; it's not just a spiritual book, it's practical and its principles have prospered society. The West would have to be steeped in arrogance to not give credit to the Bible that we are as free and blessed as we are today. Any nation that has been influenced by any other religion or moral compass is nowhere near Christian countries. To know we have the Truth is such an amazing assurance. The Bible is the only God-inspired book. We have the way, truth and life in Christ. If it was not for biblical truth, we would still be pagans, doing foolish pagan practices. When we decide to follow biblical truths for our life, society and community, we will find prosperity. Wherever Christianity influenced the constitution and culture of a country or community, we find prosperity. God's way is always the best, even though it may be the most difficult way. God's way will always be the most rewarding. Let's not be ashamed of the Bible in a generation where we could be mocked for what we believe. There is too much evidence all around us that the Bible is true. The Word of God will bear witness inside us when we hear it preached. It will feel like a cleansing and nourishing to our soul. The Word of God is food for our soul. As we decide to memorize it and apply it to all of our lives, we will see the most amazing fruit. We have a real enemy and persecutor. So, in Jesus's name, we need to submit to God, resist the devil and he will flee. When we take stands for a truth like this, we can be sure there will be a backlash.

Note

35

"Enter ye in at the strait gate: for wide is the gate, and broad is the way, that leadeth to destruction, and many there be which go in thereat: Because strait is the gate, and narrow is the way, which leadeth unto life, and few there be that find it" (Matthew 7:13–14, KJV)

The Gospel is an offense. The Word of God cuts between bone and marrow. Jesus came to bring a spiritual sword which circumcises the heart. It's time to go all in or all out. We can't be lukewarm anymore. There is no power in a lukewarm message. All it does is lull us to sleep so that we are of no threat to the devil. It's when we begin to raise up the name of Jesus and the truth of His Word that the Devil is enraged. There is such a hunger for truth today. When the truth is preached with no compromise, it clears out the cobwebs of the soul. It's so refreshing. Truth will call us all to repentance. If anyone says they don't repent anymore this means they don't sin anymore, and if they say they are without sin then they have deceived themselves and the truth is not in them. We live repentant because we live in a state of dependence on God. As unbelievers, we repent once to be saved but after that we repent to stay in a right relationship with God. God wants us to walk in the light, which is transparency. No matter what sin is being done, it can be cleansed. When we confess it and believe, then we are clean. Jesus will wash us clean with His Word. His cleansing is not an excuse to continue in sin. He gives us the grace to turn from sin and empowers us to live. Let's rest in His grace, which not only receives us as we are but does not leave us the way we are. Christ cleanses us spiritually and physically as we walk in the light. God desires real fellowship. The blood of Jesus made it possible for us to live open and transparent. Rather than God saying, "Shame on you for sinning," He says, "Shame off you" because He dealt with sin at the cross once and forever. Let's put our trust in Christ. Let's trust Him to make us "white hot" for His Word!! We may be a minority on earth but we are a majority in heaven.

Note

36

*"Nay, in all these things we are more than conquerors
through him that loved us" (Romans 8:37, KJV)*

The Cross and an empty tomb symbolize to us that the power of sin, Satan and death was taken away. We are not hoping to win the race to eternity. We won the race to eternity; not because we won but because He won. We have nothing to ever fear. Our enemies are fighting the King of Kings. God is our protector. People today are tired of political correctness. We desperately need biblical correctness. Let's live unashamed of the Word of God. If we are going to be ashamed of Christ, then He will be ashamed of us. We have nothing to be ashamed of. We know the Christ, the risen Savior who makes us conquer. When we have belief that the battle is won, we can enter the rest. Christ accomplished more than we could ever imagine for us.

37

For we are his workmanship, created in Christ Jesus
unto good works, which God hath before ordained that
we should walk in them" (Ephesians 2:10, KJV)

God wants to honor Christ through us. We are His workmanship. We can't do this on our own. The best we can do on our own is sin. When we put faith in Christ, we become a disciple. A discipleship without the teaching of the Lordship of Jesus is like someone drowning but the lifeguard is teaching them the breaststroke. We must understand what it means to be saved. We can't do this on our own. If we are in this relationship only to "get," then we are going to have a shallow relationship with God. We should not be in this relationship with God for what we can get but for His glory. Christ gave us all we could ever need or want at the cross. God cares about us and will take care of us. As we yield to His power and will, then we will have peace. It's when we are trying to muster up the peace on our own or become so focused on our own need for peace, that we end up in turmoil. The peace Christ gives us is the peace that we are never on our own. We are His workmanship. It is God that works in us. We can't be anything for God by might or strength but only by His Holy Spirit. Discipline comes out of our relationship with God. Good works come of our relationship with God. We are called to walk in them. Our discipline will never save us, our works will never save but our faith in Christ produces works and discipline. Let's eagerly desire to grow. We will always need Christ; even the desire for more of God comes from Him. Our only part is faith and surrender. As we yield to God and step out in faith, then we see His work in us. Let's pray that Christ will be glorified through our lives.

38

"So shall my word be that goeth forth out of my mouth: it shall not return unto me void, but it shall accomplish that which I please, and it shall prosper in the thing whereto I sent it" (Isaiah 55:11, KJV)

"Scripture memorization." If it was not for the Word of God, we can't imagine how depraved our society would be. We are to hide His Word in our hearts. Some find it easier to memorize entire chapters and books; that's not the only option. Simply memorize the scriptures that mean most to you—the verses that are charged with doctrine are the best. The Holy Spirit uses verses that we have memorized as arrows in His quiver. The Holy Spirit will use the Word of God to evangelize through us, as well as our testimony. Memorizing the Word of God nourishes our soul. It also is a weapon against darkness when we start sharing the Word of God. *John 3:16* is the most common to memorize but verses 17 and 18 would be great to memorize too. In the dark seasons that we go through, its the Word of God that gets us through. God's Word is a lamp to our feet. His Word has lights up the way before us. His Word edifies our faith when we fear that we have none. There is no way that we could make it on our own. The KJV is the easiest Bible to memorize because it is outside of our common vernacular. Bible translations closer to our everyday language are harder to retain. The poetic language of the KJV is so impactful when quoting it over and over. For those that battle depression, anxiety, fear…you need to memorize the Word of God. The scripture keeps our emotions in check and keeps us in a healthy mind-set. God's Word will never return void.

39

"Jesus answered and said unto him, Verily, verily,
I say unto thee, Except a man be born again, he cannot
see the kingdom of God" (John 3:3, KJV)

Jesus said to Nicodemus "you must be born again." The born-again experience is a regenerating experience. Under the law there was "have-to's" in order to please God. In Christ, He gives us the desire to "want to" and "get to" obey Him. We that believe in Christ receive the Holy Spirit who does through us what we could never do on our own. The enemy loves to put anxiety on us and make us feel like "we have to" scripture memorize but we can't entertain those thoughts. God accepts us not because of our works but because of Christ's work on the cross. We don't do "for" salvation but "from" salvation. As we believe in His grace and love, then the desire comes into us to want to be spiritually disciplined. Christ died for relationship with us. As we walk in relationship with Christ, open about our shortcomings and sin, then we see the power of Christ working through us. We can't do this on our own. We are totally defeated when we try to attain God's acceptance. All we will do is fall flat on our face over and over again, until we stop listening to the lies of the enemy. Lies that we have to earn God's love for us. Christ earned the love of God for us. He cares about us. We can be born again. There is hope for us all in Christ. A new mind, a new heart and redeemed soul. We get it all in Christ.

40

*"I am crucified with Christ: nevertheless, I live; yet not I,
but Christ liveth in me: and the life which I now live in the
flesh I live by the faith of the Son of God, who loved me,
and gave himself for me" (Galatians 2:20, KJV)*

The born-again message is so powerful. Jesus came to take upon Himself all of our sins so that He would cleanse and make us a habitation for the Holy Spirit. God does not live in bricks or mortar or gold chalices, He lives in us. The excellency of the power is in us and it is of God. We don't have it in of ourselves. As we realize more and more how much we need Jesus and His power, the more God will shine through our lives in culture and character. As we face trials and hardships, our flesh gets weakened, so that the power of Christ can work through us. We must not despise brokenness. We must not despise learning to depend on Christ. It is never easy for our self-strength to be beaten into submission but submission to Christ is life and freedom. When we take every thought captive and bring it to the obedience of Christ, then we are living a God-reliant life. Let's walk in relationship with God. Let's bring God in on our daily life and our schedule. As we are under the Lordship of Christ, there is so much safety and peace that we can access. God will change up the "have-to's" to "want-to's." God will work through us, both to will and to do of His good pleasure. "You must be born again." Christ in us is the hope of glory. He that is in us is greater than our own self-strength so that we can do what God has called us to do.

41

"And they overcame him by the blood of the Lamb, and
by the word of their testimony; and they loved not their
lives unto the death" (Revelation12:11, KJV)

When testimonies become only emphasis, then we will have a lot of "testifonies." We have a better story than our story, we have History. Christ and what He accomplished is the only story that saves a soul. Testimonies verify the preaching of the Gospel. We overcome first by the blood of the lamb and then by the word of our testimony. The Gospel is the greatest message on earth. If we don't feel comfortable with our testimony, then we always have something to talk about for the glory of Christ. We never have to feel insecure because of our testimonies. We have a greater security and message which is Christ. Christ and Him crucified is the greatest message that could ever be preached. When souls are saved, Satan is plundered. We have to fight through a lot of negativity from hell to do what God has called us to do. We hear opinions, our own reasoning, logic and the devil telling us what we can't do. Paul found the greatest "can do" mentality and that is through Christ who strengthened him. Listening to every voice but God's is very dangerous. We crave to please people but it must be balanced with the fact that we already are pleased in the sight of God. Faith in Christ causes God to be pleased with us. He took our sin, shame, and fear at the cross. God can do so much through us if we just believe. We will fight to believe when we know that God has called us. When we give up on faith, then our feelings will get the best of us. Only God wants to give us "a hand up." We can wait around for people but we will be disappointed. People are impossible to please. It's bottomless when we people please. When we are assured of God's love for us, then we can work from God's acceptance and not for it. As we know God and follow Him, we will have peace. Pleasing people will only lead to our own displeasure. We are what we are by the grace of God. Let's preach Christ! Let's preach His Word and when He leads us, we can share our personal testimonies of what Christ did in our lives. The greatest message that can never be exaggerated from scripture is Christ and Him crucified.

Note

42

"For I am not ashamed of the gospel of Christ: for it is the power of God unto salvation to every one that believeth; to the Jew first, and also to the Greek. For therein is the righteousness of God revealed from faith to faith: as it is written, The just shall live by faith" (Romans 1:16–17, KJV)

Our testimonies don't save anybody, only Jesus Saves. The Gospel is not a betterment program, it's a salvation message. Jesus wants to save sinners more than change sinners. The change follows after the salvation. We worship change, we honor change, we desire change but it's Jesus that saves and only Jesus that changes. When change becomes the emphasis over salvation, then we are missing the mark in our message. A lifeguard does not rescue someone that is drowning by teaching them how to swim, but by doing all that they can to get the drowning to live. The church of Jesus is to preach the Gospel as serious as a lifeguard rescues someone that is drowning. Those that preach the Gospel will give an account of their message. We are not to lead anyone astray or we should look for a millstone and cast ourselves into the sea. Jesus won't put up with preachers that mishandle the word of God. We are to rightly divide the word of God. We are fallible and will get it wrong, but we need to approach our message with soberness. The Gospel is a message and always will be. The first strategy of the devil is to axe the Gospel from being preached. That's why we have outreaches going on today all over the country with no emphasis of the Gospel being preached. There is no passion for winning souls. We give our community free food, bounce houses, entertainment, live music and some positive stories, but the most important message is cut out. It's such a shame. The Gospel is the greatest message, yet it's the least preached. We have emphasized discipleship so much in the church, that we have many who have been in the church for years and couldn't tell a soul what the Gospel is. There are many in the church that have never heard the Gospel. Discipling the unsaved is like teaching someone who is drowning how to breaststroke. It's impossible. Discipleship can resemble Saul's armor in so many ways. David did not need Saul's armor; he had all he needed in his slingshot and five smooth stones. As we know God intimately, we have the Bible, prayer and the Holy Spirit to be all that we need to be. We can't save anyone but we can preach Christ who saves. God has chosen the foolishness of preaching to be his means for people to get saved. Let's be unashamed of the Gospel.

Note

43

"For God so loved the world, that he gave his only begotten Son, that whosoever believeth in him should not perish, but have everlasting life" (John 3:16, KJV)

What we are saved from is more important than what we are changed from. We are saved from way more than bad manners, sins, poverty, sickness, etc. Christ saved us from hell. The fires of hell, the lake of fire, and the bottomless pit was all designed by God for Satan and his demons. It was not built for humans; but we get the same consequence as the devil because we want to live his life over God's way. We all serve someone. We either serve God or we serve the devil but we can't serve both. We are either under the Lordship of Jesus or the lordship of Satan. There is no middle ground. We are either all in with God or we are not at all. Few are those that walk in this revelation. One of the best ways to measure if we are under the Lordship of Jesus is by asking ourselves, "Was God a part of our last major decision? Is God a part of our decision-making process?" When Jesus is Lord, we will include Him in all our ways. When we acknowledge Him in all our ways then we can be confident that He will direct our path. We need to bring our ways to God. If our dreams, our plans, our desires are not sinful, God may let us continue, or He will shut them down and lead us down a better path. God's way always ends better than our way. Our way may look better, but the end will be destruction. Lifeguards take their job seriously, first responders take their responsibility seriously, and it's about time we take our mission seriously too. There is so much unbelief in this generation. We don't like hearing hard words. Salt hurts but heals; sugar is sweet but hurts. Salt heals wounds, but it stings at first. Friends, if our message is not salty and does not wake up our audience, then our message is weak. In the Western world, it's going to take urgency and fervency to jolt this sleeping generation. Life is too easy. Everything is handed to us. We have it much easier physically, yet spiritually we have it much harder. God, wake up this generation in any way you can. Make us preachers that treat every opportunity like it's our last time to preach or like someone is listening the last time to hear the Gospel.

Note

44

"Take therefore no thought for the morrow: for the morrow shall take thought for the things of itself. Sufficient unto the day is the evil thereof" (Matthew 6:34, KJV)

We put so much stock in tomorrow as a generation. We miss out on hundreds of opportunities a week to share the Gospel because we are so busy. Busyness is not good. It can become white noise drowning out the voice of God to lead our lives. Sitting quietly before God and listening to His Word is an important habit to form. We can drown out the voice of God with the worship music playing, with our prayers, and with our busyness, that we don't take time to listen in silence. We hate silence but silence is where we hear the heartbeat of God. It's in the still small voice that He speaks the loudest. Salvation is more than change, its being saved; which is being saved from hell. When we have a revelation of hell, a shift happens in our gratefulness and purpose. We need a Holy shift to happen in this generation. Shift happens when we are waiting on God. As we intentionally desire to sit, He will give us the direction to serve. He will reveal to us the deeper doctrinal truths rather than just all the self-gratifying truths our flesh wants to hear. If we were to poll the evangelical church today on how many believe in hell, we would be shocked. Most live every day like there is no hell because they treat sinners carelessly. We keep Christ to ourselves "because all that matters is that we are saved and have our fire insurance." If salvation is just fire insurance, then we better fasten our seatbelts. Jesus is not just a ticket to heaven. He calls for friendship and relationship. After salvation comes, all the benefits, which are reconciliation, sanctification, change, healing, and more, we can't forget the benefits but we can't put the benefits above the giver. No gift must be priced higher than the giver. That's a slap in the face of the giver. Let's honor the salvation Christ wrought for us. Let's believe the depth of His saving grace!

Note

_____

_____

_____

_____

_____

_____

_____

_____

_____

45

"Preach the word; be instant in season, out of season; reprove, rebuke, exhort with all long suffering and doctrine" (2 Timothy 4:2, KJV)

Here is a warning of focusing on the testimony more than the gospel. When the testimony is emphasized more than the Gospel, there will be "testifonies." I've met young people that felt so insecure because they had no testimony, that they went out and made one. The only air time someone's testimony gets is when it's suspenseful. There are testimonies that have made individuals millions of dollars because they wrote a book about themselves. We have to be cautious when our testimonies become so much about money-making, that we are embellishing our story for the "wow" factor. We are prone to exaggerate and lie. As believers, we are not perfect. We are as sin-sick as anyone else. We just acknowledge a savior and He keeps us living righteously but when we are not dependent on Him, we will sink like Peter did after stepping out of the boat. Our only hope is living dependent on Jesus. We can never get it wrong when preaching the Gospel from scripture. We don't need to have a graphic testimony to be useful to God. Our testimonies will not save anyone. They are useful but God does not need it to use us. He needs nothing to use us. Our God does not need. He is self-existent. God has chosen to use us and our words as we preach the Gospel to see people saved. We are His vehicle of expression on the earth. Let's build our ministries on the gospel and not on our personalities. We are on dangerous ground when our ministries are more revolving around our testimonies and personalities than the preaching of the Gospel. We need to have a Jesus message because what the lost need is Jesus more than our stories. Let's get to the point where instead of waffling on about ourselves, we are preaching about the gospel. The greatest preachers preach Christ and Him crucified. At the end of the sermon, the whole focus is on Christ. They forget the preacher and all they can do is follow Jesus more.

Note

46

"But be ye doers of the word, and not hearers only,
deceiving your own selves" (James 1:22, KJV)

There is so much concern and talk about the day we live in. The problem with concern and talk is, that is all that it is, concern and talk. We are called to action. Our concern must lead to conviction because conviction will lead to action. The book of Acts is not the book of concern but the book of action. The Holy Spirit will always call us to action. If all the Spirit does for us is give us experiences and emotions, then that is not the Holy Spirit. Jesus said the Holy Spirit will convict of sin, righteousness and judgment. The Holy Spirit will lead us to action. He will call us to pray and preach; it will be motivated from a state of peace. We don't act out of anger or anxiety but we act out of a state of dependency on the Holy Spirit. Jesus gives perfect peace. His peace does not empty our brains and bring us to a state of meditation only. His peace leads us to action. It's not enough to talk about it and be concerned, let's go to prayer about it. If there is nothing we can do, then we can pray. We have undervalued prayer so much today. Prayer is power. God can do more through one man's prayer, than all the effort of our youth. We are limited beings. God can use prayer to change the government, to change the weather, to change a whole generation. We are called to prayer. It's time to intercede. Rather than the news leading us to talk, let's let it lead us to prayer. Talk is cheap but prayer is powerful. God is calling us to action. It might be prayer but it won't always be prayer only, it might be doing something about the issue too. God gives us wisdom beyond our years as we pray and read His Word. Let's never limit what God can do through us. We need to wake up from our slumber. This is not a day to sleep. We need to be toiling because the harvest is over seven billion souls. We need to believe for souls. We need to believe that on our watch we can see one more great awakening. Let's not give into the signs of the day. God, one more time have mercy. We want to see the greatest awakening the world has ever seen. We believe our biggest soul winning hour the earth has ever seen is right before us. It's time to shake doubt off! The darker it gets the brighter we will shine. The more impossible it gets; the more Jesus will get glory.

Note

47

"And he said unto them, Go ye into all the world, and preach the gospel to every creature. He that believeth and is baptized shall be saved; but he that believeth not shall be damned" (Mark 16:15–16, KJV)

The Great Commission is the mission statement of most organized Christianity. The evangelical church needs to awaken to the age we are living in. Our models draw crowds but do they make disciples? Are we raising the pulpit above the pew, have we forgotten where we came from as Protestant Believers? Are the clergy the only ministers? Are we the only ones with the insight to interpret the Word of God? Is the organized evangelical church returning to a "papal"[1] mind-set of raising a man above another? It's the level ground at the cross of Christ. When it comes to the ministry, there is no difference between sacred and secular for believers. All that we do is unto the Lord. We all have the Bible, and the Holy Spirit, and we need the church for accountability. There will be a global awakening but God won't let it be one man or one denomination. It won't just happen under the roof of a church; it will happen in every believer's sphere of influence. The unlikely will testify of the most fruit in the kingdom. The tables will be turned. Gifting, charisma, wealth, and influence won't be what God is looking for. He will take the broken, dependent "whosoever," and anoint them to preach, confounding the world of what God can do through a yielded vessel. To all the churches that are soul winning, raising disciples and sending missionaries, keep on keeping

---

[1] "Papal" means going to a mediator more than Christ.

on. To those that have gotten stuck in a rut and only sing lullabies on Sunday mornings just to wait out until the return of Christ, it's time to wake up. It's time to sound the alarm or you will be left behind on this awakening. Many will be left in the peanut gallery throwing cynical opinions rooted in jealousy. This is a call to whoever has an ear to hear. Our greatest days are ahead as a church. It's time to shake fear off and be all God has called us to be in prayer. When we pray, God will lead us in a selfless life, considering others more than ourselves. When we celebrate the victories of another, we can be confident that God has revealed His love to us. Jealousy, competitiveness and cynicism are doors opened to the enemy. Through this, he is getting a foothold in the church. Let's believe again, like never before. There are too many without the Gospel and we are God's choice for today.

Note

48

"Now then we are ambassadors for Christ, as though God did beseech you by us: we pray you in Christ's stead, be ye reconciled to God" (2 Corinthians 5:20, KJV)

Praying is not a mantra but a relationship with God. In the beginning, we see God wanting a relationship with mankind. He delighted in man as He would walk in the cool of the day, listening to Adam naming the animals. Even though the relationship with man was broken in Eden because of man's sin, God still wanted us to know Him. He did not abandon us, no not even once. We forsook Him all the way through history, rejecting His grace and mercy, yet He has never given up on us. In our generation He has a remnant; those that want to press past religion, mantras, robotics, organization, and want to know God relationally. Very few believers ever decide to go deeper in prayer. We get busy studying, evangelizing, preaching and doing awesome work for God, but if we miss knowing Jesus relationally, we will be void of life. God is interested in our lives and our purpose. He has chosen to use us as believers in Jesus Christ, to be His ambassadors to the lost. We are His hands and feet. God rarely bypasses the Church to win the lost to Christ. The church, which is more than a structure is what God has chosen to be His expression on the earth. Every believer makes up the church of Jesus. God has no favorites. We can know God no matter who we may be. The least in our sight are the closest in His sight. Those we would overlook are the ones who God anoints. We have elevated charisma over character, emotionalism over doctrine, and busyness over prayer. A shift is happening in Churches all across this country. One of the greatest awakenings is right before us. Those that decide to pray, seek, ask, and knock will be a part of this great move. We are not called to go through the motions, waiting for the return of Christ. Every enemy enjoys watching their opposers shrink back behind the walls. Evangelistic ministries are what will take believers all across this country out from behind the walls to take back what the enemy has stolen from Christ. The gates of hell will not prevail a church that goes out from behind their own gates. We are going to see our streets taken back for Jesus Christ. We must have faith. God is a rewarder of those that will diligently seek Him. Let's get out of our ruts and decide to go deeper in prayer.

Note

_____

_____

_____

_____

_____

_____

_____

_____

_____

49

"But Peter, standing up with the eleven, lifted up his voice, and said unto them, Ye men of Judaea, and all ye that dwell at Jerusalem, be this known unto you, and hearken to my words" (Acts 2:14, KJV)

The book of Acts is well named. It could also be named the book of works or the book of purpose. We are not called to be "human beings," we are called to be "human doings." If we were called to be just a "being," then we would never get out of bed in the morning. We were not called to just "be." We were called to do. If our heart stopped beating, we would be dead. We have to get up, work out Salvation ("out," not "for"), and fulfill our purpose. If we don't work out our salvation, we will grow lazy, expecting everything, but getting nothing. God won't give us what is in our reach to get. We need to study the Bible, memorize the Word, attend church, intentionally evangelize. If we lose intentionality, we will crash. Any human that lives on "auto pilot" will crash. We must take responsibility for what we can do. Anything outside of what we can do, we are to trust God to do His will. The church has been using too many excuses for laziness. Whether it's having prayer meetings only or community groups only, we have been distracted from doing by the enemy. The Holy Spirit calls us to action. He quickened the early church to do missions. It's why Christianity spread at such a rapid rate. They were not wanting a God that would do everything for them, but they wanted to do everything they could for God's glory. Today we want a God that stays out of our lives. We want heaven without following Christ to get there. We want to follow our flesh, we want to follow our desires, we want to follow anything and anyone but Christ. We will call a friend or a counselor before going to God in prayer. Once a crisis occurs, God is not our first, second or third choice to talk to. We are talking to everyone but God. Only God can truly get us through life, yet we push Him out. No matter what season you are in, it's not too late to seek God. Read His Word and memorize His promises. We need intentionality, for without it we will do circles in a wilderness. Let's be doers. Let's dream big. Let's follow His leading in our lives. God has an action for us, God has work for us, God has a purpose for us. Ask Him, acknowledge Him, lean on Him, He will not fail or be silent…He will direct our paths.

Note

50

"The Spirit of the Lord is upon me, because he hath anointed me to preach the gospel to the poor; he hath sent me to heal the brokenhearted, to preach deliverance to the captives, and recovering of sight to the blind, to set at liberty them that are bruised" (Luke 4:18, KJV)

When the Spirit of the Lord is upon us, we will go preach the Gospel. A deceiving spirit is pulling the charismatic church away from seeking first the kingdom of God to seeking signs and wonders. We want an emotional experience more than obeying the great commission. God does not just celebrate when we have spiritual self-gratifying experiences; He celebrates when one sinner repents. We are chasing the crowds and fanfare; but are we chasing God privately? We love numbers and masses but Jesus had time for that one individual every time. Mass crusades have their place but believers must not rely on an evangelist or a church service to reach their family. We need to rely on God individually, more than just corporately. Our daily life matters to God as much as our two-hour Sunday service. Our private prayer life interests God more than our public prayer life. When we come back to a personal relationship with Christ, we will be surprised at the impact we will have for the kingdom of God. Let's seek first His kingdom. Let's obey Jesus and fulfill the great commission. Jesus wants His church back. When He builds His church, the gates of hell will not prevail. As long as we are building His church with no prayer, no dependence on God, no acknowledgment of "except the Lord build the house the laborers labor in vain," then the gates of hell will look like it's prevailing. God wants every church thriving.

God wants every believer thriving. Come what may, Christ will be glorified. We have seen the fire kindled by works of the evangelist. We should be excited for all that God is going to do through the evangelist. Pray for the revitalization of the evangelist.

Note

51

"But avoid foolish questions, and genealogies, and
contentions, and strivings about the law; for they are
unprofitable and vain" (Titus 3:9, KJV)

Very few young people have cash to spend on just anything. We don't pay for something for the sake of it. We intentionally count the cost and make sure that we are getting our money's worth. We can't squander what we don't have. When we are living paycheck to paycheck. We need to run a tight budget. When times get tight, we watch our quarters. We are living in a spiritually serious time. The mandate of the Great Commission needs to come to the forefront. While the church is debating non-essential doctrine for salvation, eschatology and what our evangelistic event is going to look like, souls all around us are on their way to hell. We have soothe-sayers—telling everyone to chill, relax and just be. The problem is that we will have eternity for that. We need to urgently seek God for a revelation of why we are here. Sitting around offices, preparing sermons all week, and figuring out doctrine that only faith can answer is not going to advance the kingdom. We are all called to do the work of an evangelist. It's time for the congregation to be raised up. Warming pews and writing checks is not a calling. It may be a season, but at some point, one must grow. We grow in faith and we grow in calling. The church is an incubator to grow. If you are not growing, go where you will grow. We are called to grow. Friends, let's not just grow in knowledge, but in service. Find an outlet to serve as a greeter, small group leader, the rescue mission, lead Bible studies on the job, and more. Let's utilize every sphere of influence to reach the lost. It's water off a duck's back to preach to those we know want to hear what we have to say; it's a real challenge to evangelize to those that could care less if they are going to hell. We have leaders and not lords as believers in Christ. There is only one Lord. Our mission is to equip the whole church to be a witness. We all are on a mission field. Our families, friends, and communities are mission fields. It's going to take intentionality. It's time to wake up and realize our potential. We should tithe and give to ministers so that they raise you up to be all God has called you to be. Leaders are equippers. Churches are equipping communities, desiring everyone to walk out their full potential in Christ.

Note

52

*"All we like sheep have gone astray; we have turned
every one to his own way; and the Lord hath laid on
him the iniquity of us all" (Isaiah 53:6, KJV)*

We may not fully be able to explain why we do what we do. We do crazy things as humans. We leave each other down. We leave ourselves down. We are sheep without a shepherd on our own. There is no shepherd for us like Jesus. If we look to man as our shepherd, we will realize they are just "hirelings." There is only one Good Shepherd who fulfills His function night and day, yet never complains. He does not distinguish between race, gender or sinfulness. He receives all as we are and before anyone says a word, He knows our thoughts. The good shepherd is not interested in tithe or service, He is not interested in social status or wealth, He sees the soul and loves us the same. The Good Shepherd never slanders accents whether from the north side or the south side. The good shepherd receives all as we are but loves enough to not leaves us as we are. The primary difference between goats and sheep is that sheep need a shepherd and goats do not. There are many goats that don't need prayer, they don't need God, they are not desperate for His leading because they can do it on their own. We have entire populations of Christians that are goats herded by hirelings. The hirelings watch sheep for a wage but once they clock out, they could care less for the sheep. Hirelings celebrate only over crowds of sheep but care less for the lost alone sheep that needs to be rescued. They go from one large herd to the next, with no desire to shepherd. This is why there is only one good shepherd.

Don't be shocked by another human's choice no matter what title is in front of their name. Be shocked by our own need for Christ and pray for mercy on all the others around us. Mercy is all a human has to boast in. Without grace, where would we be? Imagine if our insides were put on display for all to see. The Bible is true. Our hearts are deceitful and desperately wicked. Look to Jesus Christ, He is Lord, He is the Good Shepherd. The Lord is my Shepherd, with Him I have no lack. All these years have I followed Him and He has not failed me yet. Even when I failed, great is His faithfulness. Church, we are about Jesus. Jesus wants His church back. We are preachers that want to get the attention on Jesus as quickly as we can!

Note

_____

_____

_____

_____

_____

_____

_____

_____

_____

53

"Yea, though I walk through the valley of the shadow of death, I will fear no evil: for thou art with me; thy rod and thy staff they comfort me" (Psalm 23:4, KJV)

It's through the valleys of the shadow of death that we learn to fear no evil. We learn that Christ has made us more than conquerors even when we feel written off. When people write us off, God writes us in. God is near to the broken. Don't stop believing. It's not over, it's just beginning. The cries of the people have been heard. The greatest day to honor Jesus Christ is right before us. His name will no longer be mocked but revered. Anyone that uses His name in vain should fear and repent. Jesus Christ is Lord. There is no other false god that has been mocked as much as the only true God has been mocked by Hollywood or the world. They will be short lived. When He returns, vengeance will be in His heart. For all those that have lived affluent lives off of His blood will be shocked at the ramifications. God has given so many slack, desiring to wake them up. The reverence of Jesus Christ will be returned to the Church. All the nonsense of gold dust, weird experiences, loud emotionalism will be quenched, and Christ will be glorified. The Holy Spirit is being quenched when He is used for emotionalism more than the conviction of sin, righteousness, and judgment. There is no excuse for biblical ignorance today. We have never had so many Bibles in print yet have so much deception. Charlatans have schools of worship and all sorts of ministry schools, but we need biblical schools today. Techniques, methods, business, skills are all secondary to the truth of scripture. All we do must be verified by scripture or convicted by scripture. There will never be a day we live without scripture. The Spirit will use scripture to convict us and lead us on in His Word. None of us are exempt from sin or deception. We daily need Christ and His Word. As we live in a state of repentance, which is an acknowledgment of a need for Christ, we will see so much power flowing through us to do what we could never do on our own. It's time to be biblically literate and biblically correct. Biblical correctness is essential if we want to see Christ honored in Spirit and truth.

Note

---

54

*"But lay up for yourselves treasures in heaven, where
neither moth nor rust doth corrupt, and where thieves do
not break through nor steal" (Matthew 6:20, KJV)*

The hearts of so many are hurting. Countless people are weeping themselves to sleep. If we could see the pain, tragedy and anguish of millions of souls right now across the world, we would not be able to bear it. Our minds are not able to bear the worlds issues. We have an influx of bad news everywhere we go. The Gospel is "good news," yet when we hear it preached by some we wonder where is the good news in all that. We like to say "the gospel is good but…" The "but" is where most tune out. It's either good or it's not. Can the gospel be good news? Can it be true that God loves us with no "buts" attached? Yes, it's true. Christ loves us unconditionally and equally. His blood is enough to reach the darkest corner of our soul. There is nothing God can't forgive and cleanse. The key is repentance. Repenting before God keeps an open heaven between us and God. We must keep our relationship with God current. The outflow of our relationship with God is that we will be more like Jesus. As we communicate and let God in all of us, the Holy Spirit makes us more like Jesus. The Gospel is good news to all that believe; but to those that will not, it's the worst news ever. It's a fearful thing to stand before God in our sin. Unless we are believers in Christ, we will answer for our decisions for all eternity. The believer's judgement will not be a matter of heaven or hell but a matter of rewards. Faith in Christ leads to repentance and dependency on His salvation, which was won for us at the cross.

Satan will use guilt, fear and manipulation to crack open the door to doubt in the goodness of God. Once we doubt the goodness of God and His great love for us, then we will walk into the snare of condemnation. The only way to keep that door shut is to believe the word of God. The scripture is our sword to cut through unbelief. The Word of God cleanses our soul. As we allow the goodness of God into our mind and soul, then we gain a whole new outlook. What we will have will be contagious. Everyone will be jealous because of the peace that we will have. People will ask why we have joy, how do we keep going, where are we getting confidence from; we will point to scripture. The Bible truly nourishes our souls unlike anything else in the world. Only God can cope with life's hardships. Rest in His Word.

Note

_____

_____

_____

_____

_____

_____

_____

_____

55

"A man that hath friends must shew himself friendly: and there is a friend that sticketh closer than a brother" (Proverbs 18:24, KJV)

Friendship is a gift to us all. Working with pastors, evangelists, worship leaders and administrators is a joy. Knowing we pray for one another. Knowing we respond to each other's messages and phone calls. Knowing we can dream with one another in a safe place. These are the authentic friendships. We must choose accountability. Friendship must be built on reciprocation. Friendships are earned and not given. As believers, we are to text back, call back, email back better than the world's friendships. We value people by our strong communication gift. When we don't reach out or respond promptly, then we give off the vibe that friendship does not matter. We need to raise the standard of communication. How we communicate will determine our ministry and friendship. Just as much as communication is essential between man and God, so is the communication between one another important. Satan has used miscommunication and a lack of communication to divide and destroy. We really have no excuse for bad communication. We have so many platforms to communicate today. Friendship takes work. It can't be a one-way street. We can't live expecting to get, when we are not giving. All friendships are toxic when everyone is in it for what they can get rather than what they can give. How are our friendships? Are we living to get or living to give? God lives to give. He loves us so much that He gave. Make the decision to work on our friendships. Be committed to returning texts and phone calls. Reach not for something, but to listen and encourage. Let's value our friendships and realize the importance of communication. Value people as Christ values us.

Note

_____

_____

_____

_____

_____

_____

_____

_____

_____

56

"They are new every morning: great is thy faithfulness" (Lamentations 3:23, KJV)

We are called to give our all. It's all or nothing. We are either all in or all out. There is either cold or hot. Goat or sheep. Wheat or tare. Believer or unbeliever. We can't walk by faith and feelings. Every morning we need to rely on mercy from God. His mercy is new every morning. There is no middle ground. We either believe that Christ is enough or we don't. We are not on a roller coaster called life, that's how the world lives. Faith in God's Word keeps us in check. His Word holds our perspective accountable. No matter what is in front of us, we either do it unto the Lord or not. There is so much in life to side track us from our call. It's up to us to choose unto this day whom we will serve. Only God can change a goat to a sheep. We are all naturally cold, goats, tares, doubters…we are lovers of darkness more than lovers of light. That's why being born again is so incredible. We can be regenerated. Old things pass away and all things become new. We are called to rely on faith and the Spirit of God; to be what He wants us to be. When we approach the lost, we can't come off like we are saviors. We will set them up for disappointment. The quicker we can get our witness to Christ, the better. Christ saves. Christ transforms. It's all about Jesus Christ. We can all evangelize and share no matter our testimony because Christians have Jesus to talk about. Our savior is all we brag on; His death, burial and resurrection are our message. As we are depending on Jesus and rely on His new mercy, the outcome will be evangelism. We love to boast about our hobbies, restaurants, vacations, etc., because they were such great experiences. It's the same mentality when it comes to Christ. Those that are forgiven much, love much. Let's fight Luke warmness and mediocrity. Faith is a fight in our flesh. We must choose to believe or we will have no power in our lives. Believe that we are clean. Believe we have a purpose. Believe that where we are is where God wants us to be. Give no place to the enemy. Close all cracked doors that would make us doubt the goodness of God. No matter the crowd, location, or people, we give our all. All that we do is unto the Lord. May we always stay white hot, honoring Christ over all.

Note

57

"Who shall change our vile body, that it may be fashioned like unto his glorious body, according to the working whereby he is able even to subdue all things unto himself" (Philippians 3:21, KJV)

The Scribes and Pharisees listened to Jesus to find fault. They never listened to learn. We are fault finders and thrive off of gossip and bad news. We can be prone to self-destruct when we give ourselves over to negativity. They brought three charges against Jesus: He loved sinners, He healed on the Sabbath day, He claimed to be the Son of God. Jesus had to put up with bad press but His accusers got His charges right. Jesus loves sinners. We all are sinners and we will never be without sin while we are in these bodies of sin. Finger pointing and fault finding is only going to heap up judgment on ourselves. When we kick someone when they are down, we can expect judgement. Jesus loves sinners. Whether they are believers or not, He loves people. We might try to differentiate between believers and unbelievers but both are the same in their flesh. It's not until we get our glorified bodies that we will be without a sin nature. We are making ourselves a target when we become stone-throwers on any level. This is a healthy reminder. We need to hear this every so often to keep ourselves in check so that we don't get puffed up by knowledge. Love covers a multitude of sins. When our default is not mercy but judgment, there is something wrong with our understanding of Jesus. To be more like Jesus is to love more, it's to put our love for people ahead of traditions, it's to believe that we are sons of God in Christ. Faith alone brings us in as family. Some people's fruit take longer to grow than others. Just because the fruit is not where we would like it to be, dare anyone judge the fruit as bad? Only God can see the soul. Like Samuel, we all will be rebuked for looking at the outward appearance because only God sees the heart. Our level of cynicism is going to tell us how much of the forbidden fruit we are eating because we think that we are now like god, casting judgment. Anyone that dares to take God's throne over will get the same judgment as Satan. Who God calls clean by faith let no man call unclean. Casting judgement is worse than any sin committed. It's playing God. That's what Satan did in heaven. It's what he tempted man with to make him fall. It's what the Scribes and Pharisees were doing with Jesus.

It's amazing to see the favor of God. When one door shuts, He opens an even better one. God only makes things better in time, as we wait on Him. It will take time, so don't grow impatient in the waiting. Tune out every other voice so the only voice that is clearly speaking is His. When we follow God, the opinions will fly but at the end of the day we will answer to God and not to the people's opinions. Don't put anyone ahead of God in our lives. Selling our soul for someone else's happiness is not worth it. Decide to be grateful where God has you. It may not be where you want to be but His way always has the best outcomes. God bless the United States of America. "I pledge allegiance to the flag of the United States of America, and to the republic for which it stands, one nation under God..."

58

"And the lord said unto the servant, Go out into the highways and hedges, and compel them to come in, that my house may be filled" (Luke 14:23, KJV)

We are called to the streets. From downtowns to community parks, we have seen the Gospel make an eternal difference for many. We are just sowers, we can't always discern the soil that the seed lands in. Only God sees whether the soil is ready or not. The soil for every soul is difficult for us to discern. The external appearance of a person does not determine the state of the soul. All we are called to do is scatter the seed of the Gospel. How it takes root is a mystery. The Spirit of God and the soul take the seed of the Gospel but only God knows the outcome. The wrestle between the Spirit and the will of a person is real. The process of someone's salvation is a mystery. We are called to scatter as much seed of the Gospel as we can. We can't discriminate or profile because only God knows who will respond. Unlike a farmer, the evangelist does not scatter seed for fruit sake. We scatter the seed of the Gospel to obey the Great Commission. Evangelism is obedience and must never be done only for fruit. When evangelism is done for fruit-sake, we will be disappointed. The fruit is of the Spirit and not of our flesh. More will reject than accept. We can expect rejection; after all none of us are better than Jesus or the apostles. If they were rejected, yet loved not their lives unto death, how much more should we obey? As of right now, none of us in the West are going to die for the Gospel, but the future is getting darker. We might get our feelings hurt; we might get moved on by the authorities. We have freedom of speech here in the West yet we keep the message confined to the Church. Church services are supposed to be for believers to get built up to do the mission in their everyday life. We have turned church into an outreach center rather than a discipleship center. That model has worked but evangelism should be about going to where the need is at, more than telling everyone to come to church. We need to be going to where the souls are at. Every believer can be a light everywhere. That's a more influential evangelization than relying on an evangelist to do your calling. An evangelist is to equip you to do what they do. An evangelist is to ignite the church for evangelism both in information and demonstration.

Note

59

*"But when Peter was come to Antioch, I withstood him to
the face, because he was to be blamed. For before that certain
came from James, he did eat with the Gentiles: but when they
were come, he withdrew and separated himself, fearing them
which were of the circumcision. And the other Jews dissembled
likewise with him; insomuch that Barnabas also was carried
away with their dissimulation" (Galatians 2:11–13, KJV)*

The Worldly Proverb "Curiosity killed the cat" may sound true,
but o sot true for the believer? Jesus calls us to ask, seek and knock. If
we are stuck in a routine and take life as it comes, without intentionally seeking God, we need to wake up. We will miss out on all that
God wants us to do. By faith, the saints of old accomplished so much
for the kingdom of God. It was not by logic or even by power of God
alone but by faith. Their faith in God accomplished miracles. We are
such a faithless generation. We have silver and gold but we have no
power to preach the Gospel. We rely too much on media, preachers and evangelistic resources. God wants us to believe. It's time to
believe again. It's time to wake up while we are here on earth and
have a pulse to believe for God to do through us what we could never
do on our own. Run from pastors that hoard and never raise up.
Flee the model of church that raise the pulpit above the pew. Jump
the ship that points to a personality more than Christ. When only a
certain person has all of discernment, we are in a cult. The Bible is
in all of our hands. We can hold the pulpit accountable; we can hold
our churches accountable. Anyone that gives without making sure

how their gift is going to be used is not using faith but foolishness. If we would start giving with intentionality then truth-speakers would be raised up more than tickling ear-speakers. Most large ministries today are riddled with politics. Denominations need to have their swamp drained. We are seeing nepotism taking over the house of God. Eli and his sons will only go so far but won't last in God's sight. God is not mocked. Our mission is to stay curious. What is God is up to next? How will He come through for us now? We will live unashamed of the Gospel of Christ. The age-old proverb that says, "He who pays the piper, calls the tune" sheds light on what happens when the preacher depends on the audience's generosity more than the scripture. We are currently not bought out by any big ministry or church. We are here to honor Christ and believe for an end-time global revival. May you always see our humanity so Christ will always be glorified. We are not people who used to be like you we are people just like you. We will be utilizing every platform to honor Christ.

Note

_____

_____

_____

_____

_____

_____

_____

_____

_____

60

*"That I may know him, and the power of his resurrection,
and the fellowship of his sufferings, being made
conformable unto his death" (Philippians 3:10, KJV)*

Can we be loved for who we are? Is there a love that will accept us as we are? Is everyone's love based on our resources and wealth? Are all friendships dependent on what we can do for each other? When we talk to someone, do we only see influence and dollar signs? Are all of our friends a resource to us, or do we truly love them as family? Believers in Christ are family and we will spend eternity with each other. Christ is the only one that loves us as we are, with no conditions attached. If we are looking for love, we will never find it until we experience the love of Christ. The only one with whom we can relax and be ourselves with is God. Every human will disappoint. Christ never disappoints. There is no other love like Christ's. If people don't like us and want to constantly change us, then we need to move on because we are who we are by the grace of God. Our personality makes us unique and won't fully change. Trying to change for others' approval what God does not want to change, won't change. God created us with our own facial structure, fingerprints and DNA. God loves us for who we are and the way we are. He does not leave us the way we are if the way we are is harming us or will hurt us. Jesus loves our differences as individuals. Our personality is what God loves about us. We are fearfully and wonderfully made. While we were in the womb, He knit us together. We can be confident that God loves us. Christ died to save us, so we can walk in relationship with God. We can be loved the way we are. God loves us not for what He can get out of us but because He loves us unconditionally. God does not value a person because of their influence, wealth or bloodline. His desire is for all to be saved. The more we walk with God, the more we will love as He loves. When we dodge the poor, broken and hurting, we are shallow in our walk with God. If all our friends are suit wearing, wealthy, influential people, then we are nothing like Jesus. We can understand the new covenant doctrine but if we don't have the character of Christ, we are as ignorant as new believers. We are shallow spiritually when we know doctrine but don't have love like Christ. Depth is not found in our knowledge; it's found in our knowing of Jesus.

Note

61

*"The fool hath said in his heart, There is no God. They
are corrupt, they have done abominable works, there
is none that doeth good" (Psalm 14:1, KJV)*

Time waits for no one. There is no way to turn back time. There is no way to pause time. How many millions of people have sailed the sea before us? How many millions walked the path we walk on? Atheism is a cancer on our society. Darwinism is a disease. Religion is an offense to God. We have so many that feel insignificant and so many that have taken their lives. We have others that compare themselves to mammals and when life gets tough, they take their lives. There are other humans that have failed their religious duties and can't live with themselves because they have sinned against their god and they take their life. Here is why knowing the Bible is so important. Satan has infiltrated our educational system and religious systems to steal, kill and destroy. Fools believe there is no god. Fools believe "chance" put us here. Fools believe in any other way to salvation except through Jesus Christ. Abundant eternal life is in Christ alone. If we don't know our personal Savior, who knows every detail about us, we will feel so insignificant and devalued. God cares for us. God formed us in the womb. God knows the number of every strand of hair. God was with us from our conception to the age we are today. God wants to walk with each one of us personally. We are not another mammal. We are sinners that could never attain the righteousness of God, so we need a savior. Christ died, was buried, and rose from the dead so we can have life. Life is found in Christ. Life is found in our

God. There is no other religion that gives life, values life and cares for life as much as Christianity. We are the only ones that are right here on this planet for life and salvation; life and salvation is found only in Christ. This is an absolute truth that has been tried and tested for two thousand years. Our time will be up here soon. Take time with Jesus. Take time with His Word. Know God intimately. The more we invest into God's Word, the more our state of mind will be peaceful. The peace Christ gives is unlike any counterfeit peace that the world offers. Faith in Jesus Christ gives us peace. He is our creator; we were created in His image and He became our savior. Turn from any counterfeit peace that would tempt us so Christ alone is our peace.

Note

62

"For all have sinned, and come short of the
glory of God" (Romans 3:23, KJV)

Hypocrisy needs to be defined in this generation. Hypocrites are those that preach one thing but live the opposite. Hypocrites put pressure on others to do what they are not doing themselves. Hypocrites teach "do as I say but not as I do." They are professors and preachers but they are not doers. They know what is right but don't do what is right. They teach on evangelism but don't evangelize. They sing worship of Jesus on Sunday and sing worship of the world on Monday. They honor Jesus with their lips on Sunday yet honor everything else during the week. The greatest definition of a hypocrite is "someone that is not willing to acknowledge they are one." We are all hypocrites in the church and as believers. There is no believer that is Christ. A believer is not perfect but someone who acknowledges their need for Christ. You are a hypocrite. I am a hypocrite. There is not a person that has graduated a need for Christ while in these bodies of flesh. This is not a license to sin, but the process to victory is transparency before God. Tearing down all the veils of religion and false pretense is a daily battle for each of us. We are prone to live in the shadows but God is calling us into the light. Jesus took our shame and guilt so that we can approach the throne of God with boldness. We can have confidence before God. Jesus took our sin penalties so we can be in the light with God and have no shame. Any shame we feel is from Satan. God convicts but does not shame. Satan, the world and ourselves are the greatest "shamers." Jesus took our condemnation for us. This takes the emphasis off of religion and shows us the depth of the relationship that God wants to have with us. God knows us yet loves us the same. God is willing to come into the shadows where our dark secrets are and pull us out into the light. He clothes us with a robe of righteousness and welcomes us as family. This is the power of the blood of Jesus. Just as Adam was clothed by God in his fall, we are clothed too. Embracing our hypocrisy is not a license to continue in sin but frees us to live in honesty. As we walk in the light, the Holy Spirit will manifest the character of Christ through us. He will wrestle our flesh and subdue it.

Note

63

"He must increase, but I must decrease" (John 3:30, KJV)

The toxicity of insecurity needs to be exposed. Every human has insecurity. We are all looking for security in wealth, position, community or something. We desire recognition. We want to be noticed. We judge people that look for security and recognition but we all suffer with it. We enjoy diagnosing someone and their problems but rarely look for solutions. We discuss what's wrong with people more than what is right with people. It's time to walk away from those that don't want solutions but just more problems. There is only one place for us to be secure and that is in Christ. I have seen insecurity go unchecked, opening the door to jealousies and divisions. Satan uses insecurity as a way to divide and destroy. We must keep insecurity in check lest we turn the resources around us into threats. What God sent to be a helper we have turned them into a threat all because we are insecure. We cast spears because we are jealous, we throw stones like we are better than anyone else. Saul ended up falling on his own sword. The judgmental Jews dropped their stones because Jesus exposed their own sin. He that is without sin cast the first stone. The Scribes, Pharisees, and Sadducees need to be studied in today's church age. I fear many have been given over to a religious spirit. Jesus wants His church back. We are supposed to be conforming to His image, not the celebrity pastors' image. We are supposed to be finding our security in Christ, not how big our churches are. Insecurity is one of the most toxic attributes of the flesh. It drives families, churches, and friends to turn on each other. Insecurity will make someone that drives a Ferrari jealous of someone that drives a Corolla. Insecurity is toxic. Choose the security that Christ offers. Filter everyone's opinions through scripture. Don't cave into those who are in the peanut gallery. God decommissioned and defrocked the peanut gallery at the cross. Jesus could not stand the religious spirit. The more we know Jesus, the more allergic we will become to religion. Walk away from religion and walk into a relationship with Jesus. He will never abuse us, take advantage of us, or use us as stepping stones. He will never use us to secure funds for his own lust. Jesus is better.

Note

64

*"Cast not away therefore your confidence, which hath great
recompence of reward" (Hebrews 10:35, KJV)*

We can be in the valley of the shadow of death but still have confidence. We never have to cast away our confidence. Confidence is not arrogance or pride. Confidence is trust. Trusting God's Word and His sovereignty is what will get us through every valley. Arrogance leads to our falling; pride leads us to a fall but confidence leads us to trust. As believers, we can be the most confident and bold. We should never under any circumstances cast away our confidence. Casting away confidence is removing our faith in Christ and His Word. The Holy Spirit will manifest confidence through us in our weakest times. When the Spirit came upon the Old Testament characters, they accomplished great exploits and expressed illogical confidence. Believers in Jesus Christ get the same Spirit, except He does not come upon us, He resides within us. We are the residence of the Holy Spirit. We have a constant presence of confidence in us. Quenching the Spirit is not believing that He, which is in us is greater than He that is in the world. Our flesh may be weak, our circumstances may look dire, the opinions around us may say we are not going to make it but whose report do we value the most? God's Word leads us into a higher reality; a reality of God with us, the reality of God's sovereignty, a reality of our God is true and every other is a liar. Our confidence is in the Lord. Our confidence is in His Word. We become unshakable as we grow in the confidence that the Word of God gives. Let's believe again, let's be confident again, let's trust the Spirit and the truth so we can worship with confidence, approaching the throne of God with boldness. His bloodshed makes us bold before our great God. Be strong and courageous. We have a sure footing to walk on. It's not over, it's just beginning. Don't lose heart but fight past feelings and sight to trust in the goodness of God. He is not playing a game with us. He will work this for good. Read the Old Testament, God always worked it out. Not one was abandoned by God, no not even one. There is a circumstance somewhere in scripture that can relate to what we are going through. Look it up, read it, and be surprised that God always worked it out. God will turn this for good.

Note

65

*"But thanks be to God, which giveth us the victory through
our Lord Jesus Christ" (1 Corinthians 15:57, KJV)*

There is no stopping what God wants to do. When anyone stands
in the way of God, they are asking for trouble. There is no way of
anyone trying to thwart the will of God. Satan will try, sinners will
try but God will always win. In fact, He already won. Going against
the current of His will is so hard. He will not let us go that easily.
As far as we try to run from His will, He knows exactly how to get
us back on track. There is nothing we could do that would surprise
Him. It's best to just give in and let His current take us where He
wants us. If we could disengage our anxiety and enter the rest, we
would do ourselves a favor. Stress brings on so many health conditions. Finding ways to relieve stress is so important. Prayers, scripture
memorization, worship and evangelism are the most stress-relieving
practices we could do. We were designed for God. Healthy community is also important. God knew Adam's need for a companion. Just
like we need Jesus as our savior, we also need community. We need
tangible community. As good as media and technology may be, it
cannot replace the church. A hand shake, a side hug, a greeting is so
important for our need for community. Jesus set the church up to
be His hands and feet. When one part of the body hurts, we all hurt
(that's if we are connected to the body). If we are not connected to
the body, then the body won't know if we are hurting. Jesus and His
church are essential. There is no separation between the two. We can
know Jesus without the church but we can't know the church without

Jesus. Going to church without Jesus is like going into a den of lions. The church is a sin-sick community who acknowledge their need for Jesus. They are just as much human as any other community. Jesus makes the church alive. Jesus unites the church. Jesus is what we have in common. The church will never be Jesus and will never save a soul. We talk about Jesus. It's all about Jesus. When we miss Jesus, then we have a religion running like a for-profit business. If Jesus is the focus of the Church, then it's leaders would be a lot like Jesus in character and love. When a church is built on a personality, then it is borderline cult. Church is all about Jesus, He will be glorified.

Note

66

"And Saul said unto Samuel, I have sinned: for I have transgressed
the commandment of the Lord, and thy words: because I feared
the people, and obeyed their voice" (1 Samuel 15:24, KJV)

How well do we celebrate others? Do we take joy in others successes? How does it make us feel when someone outperforms us? Do we reach for a spear or do we get inspired? Our nature loves to throw spears. We are professional spear-throwers. Our nature scorns others naturally. We don't even have to try. This type of culture is so destructive. Rather than giving a hand up, we are casting those that have needs down by only giving what perpetuates them down rather than the solution. Jesus was about others. Believers are to be about others. Jesus was never threatened by anyone. We are to fan into flame, not pour out contempt because we are jealous. Our society is riddled with envy. If we are short on giving encouragement, then we are short on Jesus. If we can't celebrate over others then our flesh is more lord than Jesus is Lord. God wants us to be conformed to the image of Jesus. He wants to work the heart and character of Christ in us, yet many of us mirror Saul more than Jesus. We see anyone that takes our attention as a threat rather than a resource. "Others" must be ahead of ourselves. The more we want to mature in the faith, the more others will have our attention. If our discipleship makes us more about ourselves than others, then we are not being discipled. The model of Church today is going to run its course. It's time for the congregation to be discipled rather than the congregation paying for the one man behind the pulpit to be discipled. We are to disciple the church; they are not to be discipling us alone. Ministers are equippers of others and not equippers only of themselves. When a minister is insecure, he sees the outperformers as a threat rather than a resource. The difference between a legend and a legacy is a legend is about one person but a legacy is about others. Let's choose legacy over legend. God forbid we ever throw a spear; Jesus took our spear in His side at the cross. Dare anyone throw a spear. God has ways of turning spears in midair to come right back at us. If we can't celebrate others successes, then we are babies in the faith. If our encouragement tank is empty, then our faith is on empty. The more secure we are, the more we can encourage others. Drop the spears, let's fan into flame the gifts in us and around us.

Note

67

*"To the weak became I as weak, that I might gain the
weak: I am made all things to all men, that I might by
all means save some" (1 Corinthians 9:22, KJV)*

We do our best to show our best. We are professional actors. We
can learn how to perform. We know how to adapt to our audience
and setting. We have become all things to all people, but in the midst
of it, God is knocking on the outside, desiring to be let in. God wants
us as we are. When it comes to our relationship with God, there are
no eggshells. In Christ, God is our Father. When we lock away hurt
and live in shame because of it, God knocks at that door. God wants
all of us. There is no hurt, pain or sin that the blood of Jesus can't
heal and cleanse. Only God knows us fully yet loves us the same. We
can't pretend with God. Every human is a hypocrite, tare, goat, and
sinner. This is why we repent and live a life of trust in Christ—letting
God have all of us, matters for us to have it to the end. We want to be
known. It's in our nature to be noticed. There is no overcoming that
when it's essential for us to develop, a child that is neglected will not
blossom. God takes notice of us like no other. God does not see us as
resources, servants, workers, or just a part of His plan. Our Father sees
us as sons and daughters. Employees get wages, we that are in Christ
get an inheritance. The only salary we deserve outside of Christ is
death. Satan's lie would be to either accuse us or graduate us from a
need for Christ, telling us that we can do it on our own. Whichever
way his prey is most vulnerable, one of those two will be his strategy. Some fall because of his accusations, but others fall because of

his puffing up. Faith is a fight. The just live by faith. Let's not think of ourselves higher or lesser than we ought. Let's believe what God says about us. Christ's death, burial, and resurrection bring us into a relationship with God, where He is our Father. We can rest in His presence. Christ gives us rest. He knows us all the way yet wants to be with us. We will never graduate from needing Jesus. Jesus Christ will bring tears to our eyes when we survey the wonders of the cross. The content of our message as believers should always be Christ and Him crucified. "Oh, that the Lamb who was slain would receive the reward of His suffering from each one of our lives."

Note

68

"And as it is appointed unto men once to die, but after this the judgment" (Hebrews 9:27, KJV)

It may seem like forever, but there is an end in sight. We are all given a time, but when it's up, it's forever. There are heights that we will reach, but we will always be reminded that the only experience which satisfies the soul is being planted in Christ. No matter how high we get, what is more, important is how deep our roots go with Christ. Height without deep roots is very dangerous. This is why abiding is a state of mind. If we don't learn to take all thoughts captive and make them obey Jesus, then our thoughts will get the best of our faith. Only God should get the best of our faith. When our faith is in our thoughts, then our faith will be tossed by every wind of life. As we grow in height, let's also grow in depth. May we value our roots more than we value our height. We can get cut down to a stump by life, but as long as our roots are in Christ, there is still hope for life. Abiding is the state our minds need to be during the day and night. As we enter the rest of the dependency on God, no matter what happens above the soil, it will not determine our health. It's what happens below the soil that sustains us through all of life's trials. There are ways we can deepen our roots: repentance, prayer, scripture reading, scripture memorization. Always remember, it's not how we start that matters; it's how we finish. If we don't nurture the soil and grow our roots, then we will be blown away by life. Let's ground ourselves in the scripture allowing the Word to get the best of our faith. As we develop our private intimacy with Christ, our public life will be safeguarded by the grace of God. It won't always be this way. This is not an eternal moment. His return is imminent and our time on earth is like a vapor in light of eternity. God, deepen our roots. No matter what we feel, keep our faith in scripture. Teach us only to see what matters. Abiding is our only way to growth. Abiding believes that God is growing His will through the seed of our faith in Christ. Even though we don't know the day or the hour of His return, or our departure, we have nothing to worry about as long as we are abiding in His sovereign hand leading our lives. Abide in Christ. Plant our souls in His Word. Root our faith in the truth.

Note

69

"And I fell at his feet to worship him. And he said unto me, See thou do it not: I am thy fellowservant, and of thy brethren that have the testimony of Jesus: worship God: for the testimony of Jesus is the spirit of prophecy" (Revelation 19:10, KJV)

Angels are lesser beings than our Lord Jesus. Calling on Angels when we could be calling on Jesus, does not make sense. There are so many distractions in our generation. One of them is angels. Our society is fascinated with them. Why would anyone want an angel when they have Jesus? Why would anyone want the strength of an angel when we have the Holy Spirit? Satan does his utmost to get us distracted from Jesus and His Word. We chase signs, wonders, movements of God, crazy experiences like truth is not enough. Freedom is found in truth. Experiences are great but cheapen faith. It's more blessed to have not experienced yet believe. We need to come back to simple faith in God's Word, or else we will get distracted with gold dust, visions, prophesies. Things get weird quickly when we open ourselves up to the spirits without truth. The Holy Spirit works in sync with His Word. He does not contradict His Word. Any spirit that contradicts His Word is not the Holy Spirit. Any experience or expression that is not biblically explained is not the Holy Spirit. We need to be about souls. He who wins souls is wise. If our discipleship is not equipping the disciples for evangelism, then we are wasting valuable time. Bible studies and classroom settings are okay, but that is not how Christ taught. We have too many teachers today. We need some doers leading the way. It's one thing to have a "teaching" gift, but it's better to have a "doing" gift. We learn best doing rather than warming a pew. Jesus did life with His disciples. Discipleship is not an hour on a Sunday; it's our life. When people ask, "what is your follow up?" We simply ask, "what is your evangelism?" Much of today's discipleship is Saul's Armor. It's like teaching someone drowning how to do specialty swim techniques; it just does not make sense. How we make disciples has more to do with what we do than it does what we say. Our education system of learning only in the classroom is not how Christ taught, and we wonder why our discipleship is ineffective. So many get saved believing but leave church doubting. They go to a seminary believing but graduate doubting. Knowledge puffs up, but knowing Jesus sustains us to the end. We need to be cautious of anything that would try to distract us from Jesus.

Ireland, isle of my birth. Ireland was once known for its saints and scholars. Today it's known for its jokers and drunkards. The serpents that Patrick chased out, the Irish welcomed in with open arms. Patrick was a British young man that was taken by bandits to Ireland as a slave around 400 AD. He was able to escape and stowed away on a ship to France. It was in France that he heard the call of God to go back to Ireland to preach the Gospel. He used the shamrock to explain the Trinity and converted the chieftains and kings to Christ until the whole nation became Christian. Patrick was not an Irish man, yet had one of the biggest impacts on Irish History. Patrick is an example of an evangelist. If only he knew of how he is remembered today, with drunkenness and sinfulness, he would weep. Ireland must repent. The church is riddled with politics, money-hungry, egotistical leaders. Abuse has been covered over; their god is their belly. The people are not flocking to churches because they see through the suit-wearing charlatans. Patrick is one that must be studied as he accomplished more than most preachers ever did. He won souls to Christ, sought the face of Christ and honored the Trinity. I'm proud of this heritage, but the corruption of socialism, communism, homosexuality, and the support of Palestine is sickening. "Oh, that the Irish would come back to the Bible and flee dead religion like the Roman Catholic Church. Oh, that the Irish would have a Patrick to resist the serpent and watch him flee in Jesus's name." Ireland, I devoted my all to your streets while I was there. May we see a return on thousands of seeds of the Gospel that were planted. Let's run from a Europe that has bought our independence and flee the Roman Catholic Church that raped our ancestors. A reformation is needed today more than ever. A "Patrick" is needed today more than ever before. God bless Ireland and send a mighty revival, exposing the Ananias and Sapphira, so the name of Jesus is revered again. We can take encouragement from Patrick's witness that the Gospel is powerful. The preaching of the Gospel changes nations. The Gospel affects every aspect of life. It's not gnostic teaching that only changes minds but lives too! Tiocfaidh ár lá.

Note

70

*"For God hath not given us the spirit of fear; but of power,
and of love, and of a sound mind" (2 Timothy 1:7, KJV)*

The spirit of fear can take faith out of the best of us if we give up
the fight to believe. Spiritual oppression is real. Every time God does
something great, brace for the ramifications. The buffeting of Satan
looks different for everyone. Our enemy's strategies of attacks have
no etiquette and are always when we least expect it. Our adversity
waits to find a breach in the wall to attack. Ministry brings on the
worst attacks in every way imaginable. Living ignorant of spiritual
oppression is asking for a major onslaught. It's good to be aware, so
there are no surprises. The temptation is to give up on following God
because of the pain of the attacks. It can be so lonely stepping out
to follow God. Each one of us most likely has a long list of spiritual
attacks and batter demonic oppression. Not once will God fail you.
Pray that Jesus will use you to slap the smile off of Satan's face. The
blood of Jesus is against Satan. Whenever the hoard of hell comes
against you, call on the name of Jesus Christ. Don't call on angels or
any other distractions; the name of Jesus is good enough. Jesus and
the Holy Spirit are greater than any angel or any spiritual force that
could pull you out of the pits. When we say the name of Jesus Christ
from the heart, it incapacitates evil. Jesus Christ is Lord. Spiritual
warfare is a mystery, but it's real. Anyone that makes the right decision will face the hardest of times, but the outcome will always be
the best. Even though we will be buffeted, the grace of God won't let
go of us. He will preserve it to the end. We can be assured it won't

be this way forever. Satan will try to deceive us by making now seem like forever, but it will end. Seasons come and go. Christ is the same yesterday, today and forever. We fight off the oppression with faith in God's Word. When we know the promises of God and His Word, it exposes the evil one. He is a toothless lion with just a roar. Satan has no hope; that is why he is after ours. Satan has no future; that's why he wants ours. Satan is damned. We are more than conquerors over him in Jesus's name. When we submit to God, we can resist the devil, and he must flee. We don't have to give in to a spirit of fear! Choose to surrender to the Spirit of power, love and a sound mind.

"The fruit of the righteous is a tree of life; and he that winneth souls is wise" (Proverbs 11:30, KJV).

He who wins souls is wise. There is only so much that we can do, but the saving of souls is up to God. We are not called to pray in the lost; we are called to preach in the lost. We have relied on God so much that we want to escape responsibility for souls around us today. God has chosen to use us and our steps of faith to make Himself known. It's time not only to pray but preach. God will not usurp His source of revealing His truth, which is scripture. We are His expression on the earth. God does not want to hide us behind the cross; He wants us out preaching the cross. Everyone is looking for a way out from obeying the great commission. They will use prayer, theology, and all other excuses not to fulfill the great commission. As if we can earn our way for God to use us. When we need others' approval to evangelize, we are in trouble. There is no process to get someone ready to share Jesus. God is not interested in doctorates or skill sets; all He is looking for is faith. When we replace faith with discipleship, education and man's approval, we are hindering the Holy Spirit. The only reason it's being taught is that much of our leaders are insecure and afraid that someone might outshine them. The problem is that their candlestick is about to be blown out. Control will be stripped from any controlling personality. Every one of us that tries to control

God, and what He desires to do will be confounded. Some of them will be carried out because the Spirit will not always strive with them. There is a moment when the Spirit of God will hold them accountable because they have no board or eldership around them. The Holy Spirit will hold back no punches. It would be better for them to pick out a millstone before He intervenes. No one will stand in the way of what God is going to do. You have been found out. There is none holier than another. Jesus, come and be our everything. We surrender so Jesus can have His way. Use all our efforts but show off what only you can do as we step out in faith. At this point, we did what we could; now it's up to God for the increase. When we complain about budgets for evangelism, when we complain about efforts and time because only a few were saved, we are proving our lack of belief in the infallibility of scripture. We teach the scripture, but if we don't believe that when one sinner repents all of heaven rejoices, then we don't have a scriptural perspective. God values the one, yet we value the crowd more. It's time to realize that scripture renews our minds; it does not just accumulate in our minds. Jesus came so that old ways of thinking would pass away and all things become new. We need to start rejoicing over what God rejoices in. If God saw the cross as worth it for one, how much more should we see our time, treasure and talent spent for one. If all we accomplish our whole lives are one soul introduced to Jesus, then that is accomplishing a lot. Friends, we do evangelism because it is obedience to God, not because of the outcomes. The fruit is of the Spirit and not of the flesh. If the fruit is of the flesh, then the fruit is temporary. Christ saves, yet all we can do is "nearly persuade." Our persuasion won't keep anyone saved. Christ saves but also saves to the uttermost. We can be confident that what God begins, He always finishes. All of the sowers, the mystery of the seed and soil bearing fruit will always be a mystery to us. Only God knows the state of the soul. We can see the state of the soil, but only God sees the state of the soul, whether it's ready or not. Let's not profile or discriminate on who is ready for the seed of Christ because we will always be confounded. God wants us to live believing. Let's believe for a mighty revival in the open air. We should be equally excited to be ministering to groups and "one-on-ones."

Note

_____

_____

_____

_____

_____

_____

_____

_____

_____

71

"For to be carnally minded is death; but to be spiritually minded is life and peace. Because the carnal mind is enmity against God: for it is not subject to the law of God, neither indeed can be. So then they that are in the flesh cannot please God. But ye are not in the flesh, but in the Spirit, if so be that the Spirit of God dwell in you. Now if any man have not the Spirit of Christ, he is none of his. And if Christ be in you, the body is dead because of sin; but the Spirit is life because of righteousness" (Romans 8:6–10, KJV)

Evangelism is spiritual. We are not merely apologists convincing the world through logic that our God is true. When we lift the name of Jesus, God supernaturally draws the lost to Himself. It is up to us to lift His Name and it's up to Him to do the rest. He won't do our part, and we can't do His. God chose this partnership between the Church and His Spirit. When we go, He will meet us as we step out. If we never step out, we will never see Him work. Discipleship is not biblical discipleship if the purpose is not to evangelize. Most of the Church's Bible studies are well abbreviated to LOL. If we are not equipping the church to evangelize, then why are we still here? The whole purpose of remaining on earth after we get saved is to be a light in the darkness. Believers are the church; Jesus never intended a structure to be a church. We spend all our money on buildings, furniture, bills, staff, and overseas missions yet neglect to evangelize to our own communities. These structures that we call churches have become country clubs, community centers, entertainment centers, concerts, rather than equipping centers where disciples are raised up and sent out each week to be a witness. The music is like lulla-bies, and the sermon is like a feel-good motivation message where an unbeliever would be able to say amen at the end of it. The statement of faith is rarely preached, and the pillars of the church don't resem-ble the Great Commission. In fact, in some cases, they could call it the Great Omission. Everything we do overseas will be powerless if we are not doing it here. We emphasize a one-week mission trip over an everyday mission life. For some, Jesus is a time of the week that they obey Him, but the rest of the time, they follow their own dreams. When Jesus is not a part of our decision-making process, when we don't pray or acknowledge God in all our ways, then who is Lord of our lives? Either He is Lord or we are Lord; we can only have one Lord. When Jesus is Lord, we will obey Him. That's what Lordship means. It means He calls the shots for our lives. It's impres-sive what flesh can do without God. What is worse than blatant sin or building the church independently from God? They both get the same judgment.

Note

72

"Go to now, ye that say, Today or tomorrow we will go into such a city, and continue there a year, and buy and sell, and get gain: Whereas ye know not what shall be on the morrow. For what is your life? It is even a vapour, that appeareth for a little time, and then vanisheth away" (James 4:13–14, KJV)

If today was our last day on this planet, how would we preach? As a generation, we live from one high to the next. We expect tomorrow. We expect next week but an hour from now is not promised. As humans, our finite minds cannot bear eternity. God is so big and alien to our tiny minds. We spend all of our years trying to explain what will always be a mystery to us. Faith will be essential no matter what sign or evidence we can prove. Once we think we have figured out God, we have become a god. Jesus purposely taught parables. The Bible is full of deeper meanings, typologies, and prophecies, so that we would rely on the Spirit to interpret. When we get saved, it's more than a logical persuasion, it's a born-again experience. The Spirit of God comes and lives in us. We are transformed. The supernatural presence in us affirms our faith and bears witness with our spirit that Jesus is God. In Christ, we become co heirs with Him. Even greater things than He did, we can do. We are not on our own. When logic and knowledge is all that we depend on to persuade sinners to Christ, our audiences' conversion would be by logic, just as they were persuaded in by logic, they too can be persuaded out by logic. The preaching of the Gospel is spiritual. This is why the Gospel has so much power. The gospel is power. Real power. We can never neglect the spiritual component to our faith. Our faith is packed with real power to honor Christ in boldness and truth. The warfare that takes place on those that preach the Gospel is real. Unlike the military, there is very little resources, help and back up naturally for the evangelist. If anyone knew what we face, then no one would ever step out. Evangelists need prayer covering. Without partnership in prayer and finances, we would not continue with what we are called to do. God chose to build an interdependent church to see His name lifted up. There is so much more that we can do together. Souls will be saved; the Gospel will be preached. The battle will be great spiritually and in every other way. Spiritual warfare is real. In Jesus's name we will continue. Against all odds He made us make it this far. May the Gospel always be preached like it's our last opportunity for His glory.

Note

73

"Bear ye one another's burdens, and so fulfil the law of Christ" (Galatians 6:2, KJV)

Be so grateful for friends that always reach out to pray and encourage. We live in a culture where we treat people like resources more so than friends. We only reach out when we want something. It got so bad a few years ago all I'd say when someone would call is "what do you want?" Real friends call just to check in on how we are doing. Set aside time to call friends just to pray with them and encourage them. Friendship is more than stepping stones to get to where we want to go. When our friends just want to get resources out of us all the time, then we need to draw the conclusion that they are not friends. Our friendships must be more than what we can do for each other. When was the last time you called someone to see how they are doing? People are valuable not for what they do but for who they are. If we have no one around us that we can go deep within friendship, then we are not living. We are called to go deep with one another in friendship. We need real community. Without someone asking us the tough questions or having a good laugh, we are lonely. We need Jesus for salvation but we need the church for community. Jesus wants us to be more than friends, but family. The word *brother* has been cheapened today. We call everyone our Brother. The words friendship and brother need to be defined today. Friendship is more than a "like" or a "follow" on social media. It's reaching out in prayer, it's making a call to check in, it's asking how are you doing? If you find yourself making all the effort in a friendship and there is no reciprocation, make a new friend. Reciprocation is what a friendship is built on. God has real friendship for His church. He does not look at us as resources but as sons and daughters. Today's organized church values the wealthy, talented, and influential more than the average person. In fact, some duck and dive the poor. They will delegate it out to the members of the congregation but they themselves run from the broken. The people Christ went to some of our leaders today would not be caught dead around. It would be healthy for this generation to read the book of James. Friends that run from us in time of need were never friends; they were just leeches. God thank you for the church.

Note

74

"And fear not them which kill the body, but are not able to kill the soul: but rather fear him which is able to destroy both soul and body in hell" (Matthew 10:28, KJV)

There is no way that we can please everyone. We can try but people are never fully pleased. The sooner we wake up from pleasing people, the better life will be. Living up to people's expectations that change with the weather is worse than the law of Moses. At least the law of Moses was written down, people's expectations change with their emotions. If we can't be comfortable being who God has made us then we need to move on and believe we are who we are by the grace of God. God created each one of us unique and there are certain unalterable traits that will never change: our DNA, our person and our soul. In Christ we will live forever. The grace that is upon us is unique yet equal at the same time. As much as God loves each one of us equally, He also loves each one of us uniquely. As we read the scripture, which is totally infallible, we still read the personalities of the authors coming out in the text. God loves our voices, thoughts and personality. As we grow in believing God loves us because we are in Christ, we become confident. We are valuable and significant in Christ. God is pleased with us and is totally at peace with us by faith in Christ. Christ redeemed us and purchased us. We are the pearl of great price; we are the treasure in the field. He sold all He had to purchase us. Jesus is not for sale and there is nothing we have that He needs. He wanted us. He desired us. He first loved us. While we were yet enemies of Him, while we were yet sinners, Christ died for us.

For God so loved the world. For God so loved the lost sheep, the lost coin and the prodigal son that when we believe in Christ, He finds us. When we decide to believe, we are found. When we are found, God celebrates over us for all eternity. Believe that we please Him. We are His beloved sons and daughters in Christ in whom He is well pleased. We have acceptance in Christ. This is so important for our spiritual growth to believe. People will make us double minded because they are unpleasable. Unless we are trusting in Christ, we will never be satisfied. God gives us a reason to stand tall for His glory. We are His and He is ours. We have nothing to be ashamed of. Let's live shaming the devil and shameless before man in Christ!

Note

_____

_____
_____
_____
_____
_____
_____
_____
_____

75

"But I have prayed for thee, that thy faith fail not: and when thou art converted, strengthen thy brethren" (Luke 22:32, KJV)

Setting up and tearing down "street church" services for years was the best season of our lives. Sometimes three times a week. We have had so much training for what is to come next. Cities all across the US will be reached with the Gospel of Jesus Christ. As we are in this season of sowing and setting the stage, soon the curtains will be open wide for all that God is going to do. Souls will be saved; churches will grow and Christ will be glorified in spirit and in truth. We will never forget the countless souls we reached with the Gospel. Evangelism is the most exciting part of our spiritual development as believers. The Gospel is the greatest message on earth. We are calling on intercessors to join us today as we wait on God. Prayer is the initial seed we scatter before we ever say a word. The most important part of evangelism and our gospel presentation is prayer. Prayer is the gauge whereby we know our level of dependency on God. When we pray, we need God. May we discipline our prayer life so we don't pray only at crunch time but we are praying without ceasing. We have many that cease to pray until crisis strikes. As if God is on standby, so when we need Him, we dial 777, 7 being the number of perfection, to get His attention. Jesus wants a relationship with us. He is not our protector only. He desires to be our Father. Praying in the good times is building a storehouse of bread for the hard times. We will face famine times on the earth. We will face all seasons. Let's pray as hard as we would in famine times during all seasons of our lives. God can stabilize us like no other. Where some would lose their faith, God can fuel our faith as we learn to walk with Him moment by moment. The opening prayer is the most important part of the sermon. Preachers are not teachers for this reason. We are littered with teachers today. We need preachers more than ever. Preachers, pray. We know that without God we can't do anything. Our charisma, passion, storytelling is white noise without the anointing of God on our lives. We are not here to inform; we are here to preach. Teachers give information, preachers demand a decision. Our end goal is to get a response out of someone to obey Christ in salvation or to a call on their lives.

Note

76

"Ye are my witnesses, saith the Lord, and my servant
whom I have chosen: that ye may know and believe me, and
understand that I am he: before me there was no God formed,
neither shall there be after me" (Isaiah 43:10, KJV)

He who wins souls is wise. Evangelism is our primary purpose while we are here. When we die, it's final. There is no evangelism in heaven. The short time we are here we are to pray and preach that people would be saved. Believers in Christ will not perish but will have everlasting life. Jesus was the one that preached hell more than heaven. When ignorant Christians mock those that preach hell, fire and brimstone, they are mocking their own savior. Jesus preached more on hell than heaven. The eternal consequence to sin needs to be to emphasized. Very few consider eternity anymore. They live as if there is no afterlife. The teaching on hell will reinforce the conviction for life and we won't see as much suicide if we taught it. When a person has a revelation of hell, they will see souls differently. We have a more important job than a lifeguard, but just as if a lifeguard does not save the drowning but instead paddles out to the drowning and teaches "how to do the breaststroke," that lifeguard would be fired, or worse, sued and potentially prosecuted for not saving a life. Every preacher will be held accountable to the message they preach. Some today could try on a couple of millstones for size. There is no excuse for ignorance in this generation. Fools chase gold dust, fools chase angel wings, fools seek manifestations more than souls being saved. If we want to be wise let's do what Jesus did, after all we have the

Holy Spirit in us. We have the Holy Spirit yet resist His conviction to preach motivational sermons that tickle the ear. Preach the whole counsel. Don't worry about the tither that gets offended, fear God who not only has the power to take your life but also cast you into hell. Jesus Christ is either your Lord or He is not. This is love. Truth is love. Love without truth is perversion. We have all fallen short. We all have sinned. We are not above anyone else, which is not an excuse to do whatever sin we want. Those that know better will be held to account. This type of preaching levels the ground. There is no hierarchy. No one can pull rank but Christ. When it comes to our relationship with God, it is level ground. Jesus made it possible that we all can know God equally. Ignorance saves nobody.

Note

77

"Ye also, as lively stones, are built up a spiritual house, an holy priesthood, to offer up spiritual sacrifices, acceptable to God by Jesus Christ" (1 Peter 2:5, KJV)

The Gospel is the only message worth preaching every week. Growing up in the church, we went through a lot of different cycles of teachings; from fear mongering eschatology, to lunatic Pentecostal (where the spirit they wanted took away their self-control), to boot camp Christianity, to new covenant teaching. By the time we were on the other side of one fad another sweeps its way in. As if the Gospel is not good enough. Like we can have a new revelation. Like our small church has all the answers while the rest of the Christians don't have a clue. There was also a strong discrimination toward accents and where someone was from. There was very little to no accountability at the top, unless they were thousands of miles away in the US. There were so much cover ups and politics, it would make communist China look great. We wonder why our congregations are at the bars and tuned out of what is being preached. We preach Christ in suits and with passion yet have no power in our lives to have the character of Christ. We have the gifts of the Spirit but the fruit of the Spirit is missing. We will build the church on any donation we can get even if it takes the elderly to do so. As a society, the culture of the Jewish and Papal priesthood is flooding the church. Rather than us teaching the priesthood of all believers in Christ, we are dumbing down our congregation so they never grow past the pew. We will only give enough truth to keep people coming back for more. Anyone that grows past the pew and actually embraces biblical discipleship are called rebels and practice witchcraft. The pulpit is used to shame, manipulate and control its audience. The congregation is being worn out by pastors that live off their backs. They talk about how hard their job is yet would struggle to spell the word "work." Ministers need to sit more with their first responders, doctors and surgeons and see what a work week looks like. Ministers are not paid to play golf and make disciples of their own kids. It's time to wake up. Our organized church needs the swamp drained before we can see revival.

Note

78

"I can do all things through Christ which strengtheneth me" (Philippians 4:13, KJV)

Preaching to people that want to hear what we have to say is not what our calling as preachers is to be about. We have grown so accustomed to the pulpit like it's our only designated place to preach. As soon as the mic is off, what happens? It's easy to love our own, even the pagans do that. Loving those that we know will give back to us is not the love of God manifests in us. That's common love. It's loving the broken and unlovable; that's where we will see the love of God manifest. We are called to love the unlovable. There is nothing natural about the will of God. God does not only make it hard, He makes it impossible. God makes it so difficult that the obstacle is impassable. We can't do it. It takes some of us longer to get to this point than others. Hopefully we learn it here and are not so stubborn that we carry that independence into eternity. God uses sinners. It is independence of Him that He chooses to not work with. There is always hope for a sinner but for an unbeliever there is no hope. When we strive to be all that God has called us to be on our own, even preaching becomes difficult. When we spend hours preparing for a sermon and days recuperating, then we have forgotten who builds the church. Jesus will build His church with or without us, we are all replaceable. He waits until we get out of the way and at times, He will take us out of the way. It's a mystery as to how long God will strive with us. There is a point where He removes the candlestick and "Ichabod" will be proclaimed. History shows us what happens when an anointing is removed. Total chaos floods in. There is no clarity. Run from this as quickly as you can. The writing is on the wall. When ministry is a burden all the time, then what are you doing it for? Preaching each week to people that want to hear what you have to say is rudimental. Our mission while we are here is for the streets. We are to go and are going after the lost in the open air.

Note

79

"For we walk by faith, not by sight" (2 Corinthians 5:7, KJV)

Following God is adventurous. When we turn over our lives to Him, He takes the reign. It's certainly a faith walk. Every step is painful for our flesh but obedience will always be worth it. The way He leads can look the most difficult and at times we just want to be in heaven but God has a way of turning it all for good. There will be nights of anguish, nights of anxiety, and nights of anger. We can wonder "why" we are facing such turmoil when all we want to do is follow God. We don't teach enough on hardship in the western church. We have bitten into the fruit of Satan that prosperity, size and wealth is our blessing. God defines blessing far differently than we do; we want the blessed life to be material and physical. What does it mean to be blessed? I've learned in good times and hard times to believe that I'm blessed. I'm blessed in health and I'm blessed in sickness. Belief in Jesus is being blessed. There is no fulfillment that God could add to our lives outside of giving us His Son. We can become spoilt brats in the west, as if Salvation in Christ is not a good enough gift for us. Whatever gives us a sense of peace and blessing outside of Christ is an idol. We are mini-idol factories and produce idols every day. That is why Paul learned to die daily. He had to learn to die to himself, so do we. God can turn us over to our own definition of blessed but don't take it as a blessing because when we reach where we always wanted to be, we will realize we are still unfulfilled. Our minds will always race to the next thing. We will spin our wheels but go nowhere. Rather than letting another person, budget, or fad rob your blessing, find blessing in Christ. No one can lead us in peace like God can. The focus must never be on money, family or health. May Christ be our focus through it all. Every other focus will lead us to a crash. No one can satisfy the soul like Christ will. We can have it all yet still not find what we were looking for. There is only one that never abandoned me, used me, or expects the impossible from me and that is Christ. Christ met my impossibilities. Christ never once forsook me. Christ never uses me. We are His family. My hope is that when anyone hears me preach, that Christ will get as much glory as possible.

Note

80

"For ye are bought with a price: therefore glorify God in your body, and in your spirit, which are God's" (1 Corinthians 6:20, KJV)

Freedom always comes at a price. Nothing is free. Freedom is not a license to do whatever we please. Freedom is not a life without boundaries. Freedom must be defined to this generation, a generation that have had everything handed to them. We have freedom in the West because of brave men and women that laid down their lives to fight tyranny. Salvation is free because Christ laid down His life. Christ dealt with all sin. There are no degrees of sin. Sin is sin. We have all broken the laws of God; breaking one is breaking them all in the sight of God. If we think we can earn freedom by fighting in our own righteousness, then we will miss heaven. So many are weighing up their good with their bad and if their good outweighs their bad then they feel good enough for heaven. The second we feel good enough is the second we are unqualified for heaven. When we feel we have earned to take communion because of our work, we have become obsolete for heaven. Our behavior, music, obedience, etc., must never be for salvation. By working for salvation, we have made Christ of no effect. Our righteousness is wicked rebellion in the sight of God. There is only one way to the Father; if we go any other way we will be treated as thieves. Our salvation is based on faith and faith alone. Cursed is the one that teaches another gospel. The apostle Paul took the gospel so serious that he told the church of Galatia that they were bewitched. If discipleship ever graduates us from a need for faith in Christ, then we have strayed from the truth.

We are not under any law for righteousness in the sight of God. Faith in Christ and faith alone is our only hope of holiness. The Holy Spirit will always honor His word and He will not leave the believer in anything that will harm them. The Holy Spirit brings liberty and freedom from the bondages of sin in our lives. We will see the power of God at work in our lives. This is the Good News. It's not about what we can do, it's about what He did. Sons and daughters don't earn their inheritance, they inherit it. We have a great inheritance waiting for us. When we believe in Christ, we live forever. When we don't believe in Christ, we will burn forever. Ignorance won't get anyone to heaven. This is why we preach.

Note

_____

_____

_____

_____

_____

_____

_____

_____

_____

81

"And all things are of God, who hath reconciled us to himself by Jesus Christ, and hath given to us the ministry of reconciliation" (2 Corinthians 5:18, KJV)

The Gospel is so good; how can we not share it? The Gospel is a "get to" message and not a "have to" message. It's such good news. Christ reconciled us. We were all separated and afar off because of sin, but Christ saved us. Christ washed us. We are clean by His Word. Who God calls clean, let no man call unclean. God took down all the walls that man built up. He tore all veils that man was separated by. He comes to us all and knocks on our hearts. His Spirit is convicting every soul. Some respond, but most reject. Most turn a deaf ear to God. God nailed down our salvation. We are saved by faith in Christ. What an assurance we truly can have. If only we would believe more. It's harder to believe the Gospel than it is to live the Gospel. We can all through grit and discipline and live an outwardly modest life. What the Gospel does is make a person born again. This change we see happens in the interior and affects our exterior. God does not want us just to dress modest, live moral, and be a model citizen; He wants a relationship with us. Religion can make good citizens out of us, but Christ wants us to be a citizen of heaven. Earthly, carnal, socialized gospel messages are spreading like wildfire in the western church. Christ has become nothing more than a human betterment crutch. We are a humanistic society where we come to God for our own benefit. As long as God benefits us and does what we need Him to do, we serve Him. It's when life doesn't go as planned, and we get to the top of all we want in life but still are empty, that's when Christ is nearest to us. We are born again when we die to our old selves. When we realize that God is the treasure in these earthen vessels, then any power we have is because Christ is in us. Our only way forward is dependence on God. The Gospel truly is the best news ever. The author of Hebrews calls it a better covenant. We have a better way. There is no competition with Christ and His goodness. This is what an evangelist preaches, the Gospel. It's not a "have to" for us; it's a "get to."

Note

82

"And I saw a great white throne, and him that sat on it, from whose face the earth and the heaven fled away; and there was found no place for them. And I saw the dead, small and great, stand before God; and the books were opened: and another book was opened, which is the book of life: and the dead were judged out of those things which were written in the books, according to their works. And the sea gave up the dead which were in it; and death and hell delivered up the dead which were in them: and they were judged every man according to their works. And death and hell were cast into the lake of fire. This is the second death. And whosoever was not found written in the book of life was cast into the lake of fire" (Revelation 20:11–15, KJV)

W e will be with Jesus whether He comes through the clouds or we pass into eternity to be with Him. We can be assured of our salvation in Christ. On the day of judgment, the unbeliever will be judged to hell and the believer will be judged for their works. A believer is assured of heaven but our works will be rewarded too. God is interested in the "why" behind our work than our quantity of work. There are rewards for those that allow the grace and conviction of God to have its way. Many of our works will be burned up because we were spiritual gluttons. God saw the politics, lies, underhanded deals, cheating, and bullying techniques to get some of our church leaders where they are today. They have respect here but what about heaven? God is interested in who we are when the camera is off; the miracles that took place while no one was watching. God is interested in the times with Him when no one knew it. God is interested in our evangelism with the cashier more so than our large evangelistic crusade. The way Jesus judges us is not the way pastors select their conference speakers. God does not look at quantity, resumes, or books written; God sees the heart. We put value on what was done in public, God puts value on what was done in private. Rewards will be given out for faithfulness to Him. The "first" here will be last in heaven. The famous here could be unknown in heaven. Don't be envious of the wicked, it may look like their prospering but their wealth is taking them to hell. Don't be envious of the Christian that seems to be at the top; in heaven they most likely will be at the bottom. The only one worth imitating is Jesus. We have none of the twelve apostles around us today. There will only be twelve apostle thrones in heaven. Every church leader has the same access to God as their congregants. Rather than the people raising a man, the man needs to be raising the people. That's the model Jesus gave to us. Who are we making disciples of? What matters more is how we are making disciples. There is an even more important question, why are we making disciples? The "why" matters most to God. God cares about motives a lot more than actions. We care a lot more about actions than motives today.

83

"Lest Satan should get an advantage of us: for we are not ignorant of his devices" (2 Corinthians 2:11, KJV)

There is a fight for our souls. We have an enemy. It's a mystery to us how Satan attacks and has his way at times. We will never fully figure it out. The Bible encourages us to not be ignorant of the wiles of the devil. *"Put on the whole armour of God, that ye may be able to stand against the wiles of the devil" (Ephesians 6:11, KJV).*

Cracking the door to him is the worst decision we could ever make. His mission is to steal, kill and destroy. Our message is serious because souls' matter. God went to huge lengths to save us. Mediocrity must go. We either need to be all in or all out. It's time to slam the door shut in Satan's face, in Jesus's name. Satan wants our soul. Well it's not for sale, we have been redeemed. What he offers is independence from God. He gives us religion, works, busyness, wealth; anything to divert us from Jesus. None of us are exempt. If you have a pulse, then this word is for you. There is a sinister demonic influence on our educational system. Our society teaches us that we are mere mammals, that we only matter as much as the ant we step on which has no funeral, that from the womb we come and to the tomb we go. When a human believes they will nourish worms when we die, what keeps the fight in us to keep going? Life is hard. If our society is true, then we need to all take the easy way out. Here is the truth, only one God values a soul to the point of shedding His own blood to save us and that is Jesus. No one saves the soul like Jesus. No one puts as much value on wretched sinners like

Jesus did. Humans are made in the image of God. Satan wants that image destroyed. Satan is destroying society by leading people into aids, addictions and suicide. Satan wants our soul. In Jesus's name, slap the smile off Satan's face by trusting that we are significant. We matter. Anyone that says otherwise is a liar. God's Word tells us we are fearfully and wonderfully made. We are eternal. Life here is not it. Life begins when our bodies die. To be absent from the body is to be in eternity. Where will you spend eternity? We have so many buying and selling houses, planning vacations, living for the next toy, but how is your soul? Where is your soul going when you die? Our souls are eternal. There is no authority to give assurance of eternal life outside of scripture. Don't look for assurance anywhere else.

Note

84

"Beloved, think it not strange concerning the fiery trial which is to try you, as though some strange thing happened unto you: But rejoice, inasmuch as ye are partakers of Christ's sufferings; that, when his glory shall be revealed, ye may be glad also with exceeding joy. If ye be reproached for the name of Christ, happy are ye; for the spirit of glory and of God resteth upon you: on their part he is evil spoken of, but on your part he is glorified" (1 Peter 4:12–14, KJV)

I have seen miracles. I have seen signs. I have seen provision. I have seen healings. Nothing compares to seeing Jesus in His Word. Just as food is fuel for our bodies, so is the Word of God fuel to our soul. Seeing Jesus in the furnace is the clearest revelation we will ever get. Our flesh needs the furnace so our faith rises to the top. Without ever going through a furnace our faith is not refined. I've gone in and out of many furnaces. The fire still has not burned my faith away but increased my faith, as I've seen Jesus in the furnaces of my life. Satan made the furnace ten times hotter over the last couple of years but still Jesus did not abandon me. How much hotter will it get? I don't know what our future on earth holds, but I know who holds my future. Preaching from the furnace and doing life in the furnace is impossible for flesh but possible for faith. Our furnaces can look different but trust that Jesus is with us. The three Hebrews, Shedrach, Meshach, and Abednego, had the Son of God with them. None of us are like them. In fact, we all have bowed to Nebuchadnezzar's image. We have all sinned. We all deserve the furnace we are in and the eternal furnace that awaits those who don't believe. Knowing Jesus gives us assurance in the earthly furnace of hardships that it won't be this way forever. Those that believe in Jesus will not perish but have everlasting life. Following after Jesus is not a furnace-free life but is a furnace-free eternity. Knowing Jesus, seeing Jesus in scripture, walking with Jesus cannot be compared to; He gives us assurance and confidence like no other. Jesus Christ is my Lord. Though I bowed to the image, while I yet sinned, Christ died for me. Christ took upon Himself our sin, our furnace and our shame so we can know God for all eternity. While on earth, there will be furnaces. We have enemies here: Satan, our flesh and others flesh. As we read His Word, it fuels our faith. As we memorize His Word and hide it in our hearts, we will have faith for what is ahead. God did not bring us this far for no purpose. The furnace season will end. Our revelation of Christ will only be stronger. There is no furnace hot enough to take our faith as we yield to Christ. Make a bed in the furnace, preach in the furnace, worship in the furnace, let all see Jesus through all of our life experiences.

Note

_____

_____
_____
_____
_____
_____
_____
_____
_____

85

"And above all things have fervent charity among yourselves: for charity shall cover the multitude of sins" (1 Peter 4:8, KJV)

Love covers a multitude of sins. When Christ died, all sin was dealt with. When we repent to get saved, all our sins are forgiven. Every individual sin is taken away. It's the merit of the blood of Jesus. His death speaks of forgiveness. What we deserved Jesus took for us. As believers we confess our sins to the Lord, not for salvation sake but for our relationship sake. We can be assured of salvation not because of our perfection but because of His. We can be assured of eternal life because He lives. Christ lives not only because the Bible tells us but I've been born again and millions of others too. We have seen Christ work in our lives. We have seen His miracles. We have experienced old things pass away and all things become new. Knowing Jesus is more than knowledge, it's experiential. We can encounter the resurrected Christ. Once we encounter Christ through repentance, we are born again; our lives will never be the same for the better because no one walked away from Jesus worse off. Ye must be born again. All the "have-to's" of religion pass away and the "want-to's" of Christ come in us. The love of God not only covers us but takes away our sin. In the sight of God, we are righteous but in own sight faith is all we have to hold on to. Our flesh is far from righteous. Until these bodies of flesh die and we gain our glorified bodies, we will battle to the day we die. Don't give up fighting our flesh with faith. We are to fight the fight of faith. Our flesh would love to cave in our faith. Fight for faith. Believe against all we can see. Trust even when our truth condemns us. Satan does not need to lie to condemn us. Satan preaches truth when he condemns. We give him ammunition on a daily basis to attack us. All we need is Christ for assurance. Christ is our assurance. Christ is our hope. Christ is our savior. Jesus Christ saves souls. Mine saved. We can encounter the person of Jesus. We can know that He is real because He lives in us. His grace is upon us. Not once has He failed us. Call on the name of Jesus and be saved; He loves, He covers, He forgives. Look to His nail-scarred hands. See the piercing in His feet. God so loves us. Anyone that questions the love of God is a fool. How can we question the love of God after surveying the cross?

Note

86

"Peace I leave with you, my peace I give unto you: not as the world giveth, give I unto you. Let not your heart be troubled, neither let it be afraid" (John 14:27, KJV)

All to Jesus believers we must surrender. All to Him we freely give over our will. It's our reasonable service to lay our lives down as a living sacrifice. The raising of hands is a symbol of surrender. Surrender all and we will have Christ's peace. As long as we are holding on, white knuckling through life, we will never have peace. Open our fists and be in a posture of surrender. Whatever we surrender is nothing in comparison to what we receive. When we surrender, it's like surrendering nothing and receiving everything. What God has for us is better than whatever the world would offer. Our enemy will want us to hold on and live in anxiety. Anxiety is evidence of our lack of surrender. Anxiety never accomplished anything but destruction. Fear and stress bring on all forms of sickness. Only the believer in Christ can be anxious for nothing. Peace is a state of mind for the believer. Loosen the fist, open our palms and surrender so we can receive the power of the Holy Spirit. Discipleship without surrender is educating our mind but not empowering our minds. It's time to surrender so the mind of Christ will have its way. Let His mind be in us. Surrender to God. Stop trying to figure out what will always be a mystery. Be okay with the mystery. Trust, God will reward those that diligently seek Him, we may not see but we believe. This is the most blessed believer. The believer that has not seen, yet believes. The strongest believer is the one that takes God at His Word. Experiences, revelations, and words of knowledge are great, but faith is not seeing, it is surrendering. When we surrender, faith can have its perfect way. Surrender is faith that God has something better than what we already have. Surrender is not defined by talent, time or treasure, it's a state of mind. Trust God. If peace can be earned by what we do then we would have it every night. Peace is inherited by what we believe. Surrender starts in our mind and then is evidenced in what we do. As long as we are trying to earn peace, we will never attain it. Peace is inherited in Christ. We can't get peace until we surrender. God is not interested in what we have, He is interested in who we are. We can't earn peace; we inherit it in Christ. Surrender!

Note

_____

_____
_____
_____
_____
_____
_____
_____
_____

87

"But the Lord said unto Samuel, Look not on his countenance, or on the height of his stature; because I have refused him: for the Lord seeth not as man seeth; for man looketh on the outward appearance, but the Lord looketh on the heart" (1 Samuel 16:7, KJV)

Internal sickness is worse than external sickness. Just because the outside is healthy that does not mean the inside is. We ignore what we can't explain. When a hand is broken, we know how to fix it. When the mind is broken, we don't know what to do. The church does not know what to do with internal sickness. Very few have discernment. We can diagnose the physical because our naked eye sees, but what about the mental or spiritual health. If ever there was a generation needing discernment, it's this one. Common sense is not common anymore. The Western world desperately needs discernment. We have charlatans all around but because we can't see the heart like God does. Millions of dollars are being wasted on lavish lifestyles. Discernment is both a gift of the Spirit and is learned by reading scripture. The Holy Spirit will always reinforce scripture so we can discern what we are up against. We may look good on the outside but we could be cut to pieces inside. We may be physically free but, on the inside, we are locked up in depression. The attack is far more sinister in the West than it is in the persecuted church. The persecuted church divides the real from the fake real fast. In the West the wheat and tares live side by side. The tares look so like the wheat that it's hard to tell the difference. Satan has done a great job refining the counterfeit. We are primed for the angel of light to step on the scene.

We have foolish Christians already elevating angels and getting them tattooed on their skin. They are waiting for some strange manifestation to come out of Toronto again.[2] This is known as the "Toronto Blessing." Like the first one did not do enough damage. The Spirit of God gives a sound mind and self-control. Any spirit that behaves contradictory to the Word is not the Spirit of Christ. We need to seek the gift of discernment, or even the elect will be deceived. We need to use common sense, or at least make sense common again. We are getting close to the day where as a society we will not be able to endure sound doctrine. We can barely endure it today. Preachers on TV are apologizing for the Word of God. We have nothing to be ashamed of. We need discernment. We need wisdom. We can have it in Christ.

Note

_____

_____

_____

_____

_____

_____

_____

_____

_____

[2.] "Toronto Blessing." *Contemporary American Religion*, Encyclopedia.com, 21 Feb. 2020, www.encyclopedia.com/philosophy-and-religion/christianity/christianity-general/toronto-blessing.

88

"Wherefore I say unto thee, Her sins, which are many, are forgiven; for she loved much: but to whom little is forgiven, the same loveth little" (Luke 7:47, KJV)

The more we have been forgiven the more forgiveness flows from our lives. The nearer to Christ we get the more of our wretchedness gets exposed. The brighter the light of the Word gets in our lives, the more we see in ourselves. Anyone that graduates from a need for Christ because of their own self-righteousness makes Christ of no effect in their lives. If we say we are without sin, then we are liars and have strayed from the truth. The more mature we get, the deeper our worship of Jesus will be. As we are discipled, God's salvation will become even greater. When we grow in the grace of God, it keeps our fire for Christ stoked. It's when we can do it on our own that we lose the fire of God. Some of our discipleship teaches, informs and equips us to rely on our own understanding rather than being discipled in surrender. Our teachings must lead to surrender where our audience walk away with "not what they can do" but "with what they cannot do." The believer's life is not possible in their own strength. We can only do what God graces us to do, to follow after Him. Disciples will always rely on Christ no matter how mature they get. The most mature spiritually will have the most childlike faith. As we mature, our faith will become simpler. Most of our discipleship today makes growing in Christ possible rather than impossible. The more possible we can do it the less faith we need. A day without faith empowers our adversity. Let's disciple the way Jesus did. After three years with

His disciples, they still could not follow Jesus on their own. They needed God to do what God was calling them to. Jesus knew their weakness. He knew they would not be able to follow Him until they were endued with power. We can't forgive like Christ can. We can't live like Christ can. We can't save like Christ can. We can do all things through Christ that strengthens us. Christ strengthens us and not Himself in us. We are able to do what He did when we surrender. As we surrender via prayer, and communicate honestly with Him our state of inability, He makes us able. We no longer live but Christ lives in us as we surrender. We are not justified by what we do but by what He did. He Justifies, He strengthens, He keeps.

Note

89

"And I say also unto thee, That thou art Peter, and upon this rock I will build my church; and the gates of hell shall not prevail against it" (Matthew 16:18, KJV)

"Stay behind the walls" Satan. It's time to silence Satan's "amen" every Sunday morning. As long as we only do church behind the walls, we are of no threat to him. He loves the walls we have built. He loves that all of our miracles are recorded under roofs and behind walls. As long as our faith is confined to a time of week and in a structure, he will leave us alone. It's time to go beyond the walls and declare war on the power of darkness. We have been in the coup for too long. It's time to get out. The walls are coming down in this generation. The pulpit is where God has placed us every day and not just a podium we look to. Church is an organism and not just an organization. Jesus gave no blueprints for a structure but gave us the indwelling of His Spirit so that wherever we are, He is there 24-7. In Jesus's name Satan's smile is going to get smacked off his face. We are going after the lost and those in his death grip. Jesus has empowered us to go into all the world and preach the Gospel. We can, because God can. We go because He goes, so let's decide to go. What are we waiting for? The same spirit that raised Christ is in us. We can't be educated to obey God; we simply step out in faith and believe God is with us. God catches us every time we step out. We need to mobilize to take Jesus to the streets. Every believer is a threat to the devil. Not only are we threats individually but together we are stronger. God sends blessings when the church unites to win souls to Christ. Our intent is to win souls to Jesus and not any one church. Churches can't save souls. We are here to win people to Jesus. Only Jesus saves. This is why churches can come together to win our streets, communities and parks back. Satan welcomes outreaches but detests evangelization. It's time to realize as the evangelical church what our mission is. So many ministries have the great commission up on their walls and as their mission statement but there is no gospel being proclaimed by their ministry. Billions of dollars are spent on ministering to the mind and the body. What about the souls of men? It's when we begin to preach the Gospel that Satan's world falls apart. Evangelists exist to take the church beyond the walls proclaiming the Gospel, Jesus saves.

Note

90

"Neither give place to the devil" (Ephesians 4:27, KJV)

Satan and demons can use animals and people as hosts. There can be thousands of demons in one person. Witches, fortune tellers, and the demonic world are real. It's why Hollywood bring out new horror movies every week. Horror movies used to only be released during Halloween but now Satan's will toward us is being watched in all seasons. Satan's will is to steal, kill, murder, and destroy. In the West we take our demonically possessed off our streets and put them in prisons or hospitals. In Jesus's day the demonic hosts wandered the streets. There were no institutions for them. A while ago a psychiatric doctor got saved because He saw the power of Jesus's name in a Hospital while on duty. He said that he heard the voice of demons coming out one of his patient's mouth. It was enough to convince him of the spirit realm. He started attending church and gave his heart to Christ. There is power and authority in the Name of Jesus. We need to start saying the name of Jesus with reverence and authority. When we summon the name of Jesus and His authority, every demon flees. As believers, we are hosts for the Holy Spirit. A believer in Christ is possessed by the Spirit of God. Christ in us is our assurance against the enemy. When we preach the Gospel, it's more than truth, it's power unto salvation. The Gospel is more than a lecture, it's power. This is why the Gospel is the answer to sin, poverty, and oppression. The Gospel does not just educate the mind, it saves the soul. The Gospel breaks the power of the will of Satan over our lives so the will of God can have its way in our lives. God's will for us is life and life to abundance. In this world we will have trouble because of sin but when we pass to eternity, it's abundance forever. Let's believe the power of the Gospel again as a church age. In Jesus's name we call on the Holy Spirit to manifest His power through us so the enemy of souls will be resisted and put on the run. It's time for the believer to slap the smile of Satan's face in Jesus's name. It's time to rise in the power of Christ's might. Don't doubt but be confident of the will of God toward us. When doubt sets in of the goodness of God, just look to the Cross. Life gets tough for us all but through it all we have the name of Jesus for peace, comfort, and authority. We are empowered by the Holy Spirit to do everything God has called us to do. Just be willing and watch God do what only He can. Humans are not natural beings we are supernatural when empowered.

Note

_____

_____

_____

_____

_____

_____

_____

_____

_____

91

"Whereas ye know not what shall be on the morrow. For what is your life? It is even a vapour, that appeareth for a little time, and then vanisheth away" (James 4:14, KJV)

Days turn into weeks and months turn to years, we wither like the grass. Today will end. There is no stopping time. All the money in the world cannot buy time. If only we could speed up time and slow it down to suit us. We were never created to go faster than three miles an hour. Automobiles, mobile phones, internet has sped up our lives. We can accomplish so much in a minute. We can be anywhere in the world in twenty-four hours. When the night draws in and all we hear is our pulse, do we hear God? God wants our attention. We have so much fighting for it but when we give it to God, we can have peace. Worry does not accomplish anything. God gives us a new language that is heavenly. Rather than filtering every thought through our earthly perspective, when we filter our thoughts through the Spirit, we are edified. God builds our faith. Even though time is fleeting, God is the same. He knew us from the womb. We are not on our own. Jesus Christ is God and He is with us. Pause, slow the pace of our thoughts, breathe, say the name of Jesus. Speak the name of Jesus. He is the same yesterday, today, and forever. We change, we age, but God is the same. Return to the quiet place, find peace in His Word. Remember Jesus as the toils of life will pull us away into busyness. If we don't, one day it will be too late. Break free from the rut, don't tell anyone, unplug, and sit with Jesus. He can do more in us as we sit at His feet and listen than all of the strength of our youth.

God wants us to withdraw to worship, read, and listen. He will fill us with His language, which is of faith, hope, and love. The fears, anxiety and pain will be washed away in His presence as His Word renews our minds. We are never alone. His hand is outstretched to any that would be drowning in fear. Relinquish worry and war in faith. Fight aggressively to believe, believe to the day we pass into eternity. Our faith makes a difference on others. Many will look on and marvel how we made it this far but there is only one that can take credit, Jesus. We change but He remains the same. We falter but He is faithful. We may not have much time but we do have eternity. Time is of the essence. Give God time and God will give us peace. Come Lord Jesus.

Note

92

"For the love of Christ constraineth us; because we thus judge, that if one died for all, then were all dead" (2 Corinthians 5:14, KJV)

The price paid to be saved was so great. When we have a glimpse of what Christ went through at the cross, He is worth giving up everything for. Whatever it is that He asks of us does not come close to what He has given to us. Walking away from the world's lures becomes easier when we get a revelation of Christ and Him crucified. Letting go may seem like a huge burden but once we release, we will find ourselves held the whole time. We are more held than we could let go. What we thought would make us freefall, now is our source to soaring. Faith in Christ goes against our logic and reason but has the most amazing outcome. Faith in Christ never disappoints. The more we see Christ, the easier it is to bend our knee. The world abuses us, takes advantage of us, and when we are in need, the world is nowhere to be found. There is only one that can find us. We are only found when we are found in faith. Without faith there is no pleasure for our soul and it is impossible to please God. Christ paid the price with His death and sealed the reward for our faith with His resurrection. When we have an eternal perspective, we will see the importance of all to know Christ. The world distracts us with busyness, bills, and worldly pleasures. It's healthy and true to take life one day at a time. We make plans and live in the future but everyone faces a "suddenly." We are only a pulse away from dying. As real as all of the distractions are, so is the fact that today could be our last. We spend all our time securing an insecure future. There is only one assurance in this world and that is the face that He lives. Christ is alive. How do I know? He lives in me. His Word is true and millions are still worshipping His name every week. Jesus is the most famous and well-known person in history. Jesus Christ is Lord. We need to get used to being on our knees. Whether it's willingly or not, every knee will bow, every tongue will confess Jesus is Lord. He paid the price. He came as a savior. He is coming as King of Kings. The greater the revelation we get of Christ, the more we will evangelize the lost. If we don't know Christ, then we won't have anything to talk about with the lost. Our evangelization is the measure of our revelation of Christ. Revelation of Christ leads to evangelization.

Note

93

*"For do I now persuade men, or God? or do
I seek to please men? for if I yet pleased men, I should not
be the servant of Christ" (Galatians 1:10, KJV)*

Keeping up with appearances is such a waste of time. The facade never leads to peace. A culture of phonies is the most destructive. As humans, we hide behind our stuff, talents, and reputation. If everyone knew our thought life and our internet history, what would they think of us? Jesus knows us, yet loves us the same. Religion imposes dress codes, standards, and exterior religiosity. The tree of the knowledge of good and evil could be called the tree of religion. Adam and Eve immediately hid themselves from God, clothed themselves and lived in blame. They did not want to take personal responsibility. Any Christian that judges another is usurping God's throne and taking God's position. When we peel back to our hearts, we will realize quickly that none of us are righteous. If we are gossipers, judges, maligners, scorners, mockers, scoffers, then we need to come out from behind the bush. Jesus introduced us to relationship. Much of Christianity today could be compared with the sects of Judaism like the Pharisees that resisted Jesus. One of the gauges to see if we resemble Jesus is by asking ourselves "how many sinners are our friends?" If we only mix with "Ned Flanders"[3] Christianity, then we are nothing like Jesus. Our religion today produces great citizens but horrible followers of Christ. Run from religion. Religion will take you to the

---

[3] Character from *The Simpsons*

same place as some of our "criminals" in the prison system. God does not judge the action; He judges the intent. We are all condemned and have fallen short. Christ and Christ alone is our savior. If we mix our salvation with what we do, with what He did, then we nullify what He did, and will face hell. Run from religion. Run from dress codes, rules, and behavior modification because religion sends everyone to the same place as "criminals." From God's perspective, religion will make a spiritual criminal out of us. Let's run into a relationship with Jesus, where we can be honest and open with Him. We can't be that way with anyone but Jesus. We were made for a relationship with Jesus. If we miss knowing Jesus in relationship then we will miss heaven. Let's conform to the character and teaching of Jesus and not a pastoralism or denomination. Are we becoming more like Jesus?

Note

_____

_____

_____

_____

_____

_____

_____

_____

_____

94

"Yea, so have I strived to preach the gospel, not where
Christ was named, lest I should build upon another
man's foundation" (Romans 15:20, KJV)

Titles don't entitle respect anymore. We are in a generation that desire authenticity more than anything else. The discernment of this generation for what is real is increasing by the day. So many are tired of entertainment, the show, and the comedian. The act worked for a long time but today it won't. The pulpits are full of comedians, controllers, and money hungry businessmen. The church is wondering why we are on the decline but if we were to look at our everyday life, do we resemble Jesus. Everyone wants their feet washed today yet their "Lord" was looking to wash others feet. When was the last time leaders "washed feet"? The pompous leadership of today are no different than the papal regime[4] we came out of. Rather than our ancestors having one pope now, every church has their own pope. Rather than one Vatican, every church has become a Vatican. We rarely hear preached about the priesthood of all believers, in case someone in the church will "fall out of rank." Dear church leader, stop trying to cram as many "found sheep" as we can in the pew. Church plants are becoming the "new thing." We have hirelings thriving off of building on another man's foundation. If we want respect, then we are to live like Jesus and not just talk like Jesus. If our theology excuses us from being conformed to the character of Christ, then we are heretical;

---

4. The Roman Catholic Leadership

demanding titles, controlling people's lives, and taking advantage of the elderly is detestable. The congregation may look the other way but God won't. We are going to be surprised when we get to heaven. Those that hoarded control, held others back, manipulated to grow their reputation will face judgment. We have so many hirelings running our ministries today. They don't have the people's interest. They love the sound of their own voice. Rather than the church being known as the church, it's known for the pastor, "that's pastors so-and-so's church." The church is not a family-run business. It's a 510c3 (nonprofit) and in the eyes of the government it should be run like one. Are we like Jesus in character and nature? If not, our Christianity is a religion. Do we want to imitate a preacher more than Christ? If we look to a man more than to Christ, we will be so disappointed!

Note

_____

_____

_____

_____

_____

_____

_____

_____

_____

95

"Now when the sun was setting, all they that had any sick with divers diseases brought them unto him; and he laid his hands on every one of them, and healed them" (Luke 4:40, KJV)

No one walked away from Jesus worse off in their health. God wants us to prosper in every way. In heaven there will be no more employment, sickness, worry or bills. When we have faith in Christ, we can taste the heavenly benefits here. God does not will poverty, sickness and persecution. God's will is blessing, eternal life and good gifts. What good father would want to hurt their kids? Yet we are earthly fathers. Jesus took our sins upon Himself; all good and perfect gifts come from above. We can have assurance God is good. Anyone that teaches that the Gospel is bad news is a heretic. The Gospel is such good news, that living it is not the issue, it's believing it that is the problem. We have no excuse for doubting, complaining or being negative. We can have a positive attitude in all things because we are more than conquerors. We may be impoverished here but that's a good thing because we can be confident that we are going to heaven. We need to research how we lay up treasure in heaven, if we are smart. Most of this generation is busy securing temporary assurances. Unlike the world, we can be joyful with much and with little. We can celebrate in sickness and in health, because this is not our home. When we have a revelation of Christ, nothing can get us down but our own unbelief. When following Christ is a drudgery and all we do is complain, then we may need to relook at our salvation. If all we do is be miserable where we think God has put us, then quit and do something else. If serving God is not an honor or a "get-to," for most it's a "have-to," then we will get the same reward as every other sinner. The sooner we die to ourselves, the more of His attitude, culture and favor will come into our lives. Prison doors will open as we sing praise to our God. We can have a right attitude if we would grow up spiritually. We have so many adult spiritual babies today. It's time to grow up. Stop allowing feelings to get the best of our faith. Get up with a smile and serve God because it's a privilege. If it's not, then quit and get an honest job. Serving God is the most conquering life we could ever live. We are victorious. Shine bright, smile, decide to be joyful, get over ourselves and believe in what is to come. Jesus changes our minds!

Note

96

"And the Lord God said, It is not good that the man should be alone; I will make him an help meet for him" (Genesis 2:18, KJV)

We can't make it through this life on our own. We were not designed to. God leaves a void in all of us that only real community can give us. That's why we assemble as often as we can. Connecting with others is a huge need in all of us. This is why Jesus and His Church go hand in hand. If we are not in a fellowship or a church community, then we are going to fill the void with another form of community. Sports and colleagues at secular employment are good, but not the best type of community. A Christ-centered fellowship is the best kind. It not only fills our void for friendship and accountability ut also nourishes our soul. Community takes intentionality. Don't wait for a phone call or a text. If every believer would intentionally initiate, we would have such a healthy community. Communication is essential to God but is also important to us. As believers, let's give a phone call, let's reach out in text, let's look to shake a hand at church. Don't always wait around on the receiving end because Jesus taught us that it is more blessed to give than to receive. The more we reach out, the more connected we are. Respond by the end of every day. The same value that is on us is on everyone else. We are called to show value to all as we have been valued in Christ. Let's intentionally seek God. Let's intentionally be in a community. Everything good takes intentionality. If we are not, then the enemy will isolate us and pour out depression on us. Stay in a community. It takes intentionality. Set aside time to be in a Christ-Centered community. Who we choose to surround ourselves with will determine who we will be in the future. Fight isolation. Use all the tools we have been given, whether that is social media or a phone call. We need to stay connected. We have very little reason to be isolated or alone. God is always with us but a listening ear or someone to pray with is vital too. It is not good for us to be alone. Just reach out. Be intentional. Don't expect community, intend community. Let's stop consuming and start producing. Christ was not given only for us, but we are called to share Christ. We are to do unto others as we have been treated by God almighty. He reached out to us and never stopped. He responds to us every time and never delays. His Word is a 24-7 communication to our soul!

Note

_____

_____

_____

_____

_____

_____

_____

_____

_____

97

"Beloved, when I gave all diligence to write unto you of the common salvation, it was needful for me to write unto you, and exhort you that ye should earnestly contend for the faith which was once delivered unto the saints" (Jude 1:3, KJV)

We are called to contend for the faith. Faith is not the ignorance of truth. Faith is in truth. Faith is just a word if it's not backed up with truth. Faith and truth may seem like a paradox but they go hand in hand. When we are contending for the faith, we are deepening our own revelation of the truth. Faith without action is laziness and is not faith at all. Faith in truth teaches us to take a step and trust God to firm up the ground under our feet. Faith will make us uncomfortable. Faith is not the easy option. Faith is obeying God against all feelings. Faith is trusting that God's way is better. Faith trusts that God has a great outcome no matter what it initially looks like. Faith mutes the opinions and silences the "peanut gallery" so that all we hear is God's leading. Faith that does not lead to obedience to God is not scriptural faith. Faith demands action. Faith is not the absence of actions; it is the motivator of action. Belief is all we have as a human race to keep going. Without faith we could care less. Faith makes us care. Faith reminds us that we are not God. Without faith we cannot please God. God rewards faith, which means God rewards works. We were not saved from good works; we were saved unto good works. We have created a faith today that makes God out to be a resource rather than our source. Jesus is not a resource. God is not a resource. God does not revolve around us. We are not the center of the universe. We serve God; He does not need to serve us. He may choose to serve us but we can't take His grace in vain and treat His service with contempt. God is to be revered. God is to be worshipped. God is to be obeyed. He knows our fragility and that's why He honors faith. By faith we can get through this life. By faith we can obey Him. By faith we can follow Him. By faith we have a purpose to make His name known. It's by faith and not just by God. We have to decide, to believe or not. Break out of all the molds that the world would put on us, break out of the armor Saul tried to put on us, be all God has called us to be. Follow God no matter what. Put faith to work. Fight to have faith. Defend faith. Faith leads to a fearless life that is built on a soul's cry to depend on Jesus Christ, to make Him known to the end. Contend for the faith—follow God.

Note

_____
_____
_____
_____
_____
_____
_____
_____
_____
_____

98

"For I know the thoughts that I think toward you, saith the Lord, thoughts of peace, and not of evil, to give you an expected end" (Jeremiah 29:11, KJV)

God's thoughts toward us are good. Religion portrays God as cold and distant. The religious love a God that is impersonal. The God of the Bible teaches us that God is good. There is no other God but the God defined to us is in the Bible. Every other god is false and their followers must be converted in order to be saved. When we believe, scripture evangelism becomes an urgency. Christians that have no burden to share their faith do not have the heart of God. We can sing songs, study theology, listen to sermons but if we are not concerned for souls, we have missed the heart of God. How can we say "amen" to evangelism yet not evangelize? Every Christian agrees with the great commission but very few take it seriously. There are far more lost in this generation than we know. We can know the Word, know the times and even say that we know God, but if we don't act, then we must call into question what we know. Knowing God always leads to a purpose and action. Friends, there is no intercessor in the five-fold ministry. We can spend hours in prayer but does that lead to hours of evangelism? An evangelist should not only evangelize but is to equip the church for evangelism. When was the last time you shared your faith with the lost? How can we say we love Jesus but not follow Him? How can we sing songs to Him but not obey Him? Friends, we are all the Chief of failures. We are weak and fearful as anyone else. We sin like every other human sins. We are still human as believers.

There is nothing different about me. We still get convicted as believers. Oh Jesus, we want to follow you, we want to obey you, we want whatever you want for our lives. Friends, this life is about surrender. When we realize our reasonable service and where we are at in life, we can't help but throw our hands up in the air and surrender. Our God is good. Our God is worthy of our lives after all that He did for us at the cross. As we surrender to His goodness, His power quickens us to do His will. Jesus come and have your way in us. We must be so thankful that we are not in a false religion or cult like the Jehovah Witnesses' or Mormons. It's time to surrender. Billions are going to hell while much of the church members are playing with their hobbies and planning their vacations. God's will be done, amen!

99

*"And he gave some, apostles; and some, prophets; and some,
evangelists; and some, pastors and teachers; For the perfecting
of the saints, for the work of the ministry, for the edifying
of the body of Christ" (Ephesians 4:11–12, KJV)*

How are we equipping? An evangelist's goal is to see every believer
be the best witness or evangelist they can be. We are all called to be
a witness and we all have a testimony but not everyone is an evangelist. Igniting a passion in the church to share Christ requires anointing from the Holy Spirit. As good as someone can teach, it takes an
evangelist to equip the church to evangelize. This is why we have the
office of an evangelist. We are inundated with teachers today that
teach "do as I say, but not as I do." That form of leadership worked
for the previous generation but this generation will have none of it.
It's why most of them are walking away from Christianity because
they hear from so many teachers but see very few doers. Inspiring a
generation with passion is easy but inspiring them with action takes
anointing. Scripture memorization, daily relationship with Christ
and intentional evangelism cannot be done in a pulpit alone. This
is a lifestyle. If we are ministers yet are too busy to pray and spend
quality time with Christ then we should look for an honest job.
Ministers are not event organizers or businessmen; they are people
who have been with Christ. They are followers of Christ. They hear
from Christ and obey. We need far fewer teachers and far more doers
in the church today. Everyone wants a pulpit but they won't get it
until they start preaching where they are at. God wants our private

life more than our public life. We crave the public life of position, power and influence, but a man of God values His private life with Christ more. We are shallow if we don't walk with God. We can have great ideas, build big ministries, accomplish a lot; it will never cease to amaze me what we can do for God without God. We are still eating the serpent's fruit to this day—"the fruit of independence from God." Ministers are not entertainers, sitters, teachers, or preachers; we are sons and daughters of God. Everything we do is an outflow of our relationship with Jesus. There will be many disappointed with what I'm writing, but it's the truth. If we don't know God where we are, don't think we will know God where we want to be. Don't wait around to know God in the future. Tomorrow is not promised. Be a light in season and out of season by knowing Jesus in season and out of season.

He has risen. Believers know He has risen. Who else has given us life? Who else has brought us this far? We can preach Him with every fiber in us because I know He lives. Some have even seen Him. His hand has led me since I was six years old. Every step of my journey He has been there. I will only get more undignified than this. I would not be doing what I do if He was still in the grave. Two thousand years later, He is still changing lives. He is still healing lives. He is still saving souls. Jesus Christ is the same and has not changed. For all eternity He is Lord of all. Each one of us as believers have a testimony. Our story matters. Not only is the death of Christ important but the Word of our testimony is proof that Christ lives. Buddha, Muhammad and every other religious leader is dead. Our Lord Jesus is alive. I'm never the same when I'm with Jesus. He has wiped the tears of my soul away, calmed the storms that raged in me, warmed my cold heart. He has given me life like no one or no thing could. May I preach Him with even more passion, may I serve Him with even more tenacity. I want the world to know my Savior lives. I want the world to be converted to the Lord Jesus Christ. He went to the cross as a lamb but He is coming back as a Lion. Confess with your mouth and believe in your heart that Jesus Christ is Lord. Repent, today is the day of salvation. Trust Christ, He never fails.

Note

100

"And he said unto me, My grace is sufficient for thee: for my strength is made perfect in weakness. Most gladly therefore will I rather glory in my infirmities, that the power of Christ may rest upon me" (2 Corinthians 12:9, KJV)

It may seem like God disappoints us, but if we stay believing, with time, our unanswered prayers will make sense. He won't leave us down. There will be temporal disappointments as a believer. There will be set backs. Things won't go the we want it to go just because we are believers. Life doesn't get easier because you're a believer. In this world we will have trouble. We get bad reports, our cars break down, our structures fail us, we even let ourselves down. If someone comes to Jesus for a better life, then they have been lied to from the beginning. For most of the early church, their lives got worse when they became believers. They lost their employment, status, freedom and some even faced martyrdom. The western gospel is very similar to the gospel that Judas wanted to believe. Judas was is in it for the better life. Judas was in it to get his dreams answered. Judas wanted it easy. Judas wanted prosperity but had no value for eternity. Religion offered his desires to him but left him empty. Religion offers silver but, in the end, there is no hope outside of Jesus. The best that an organized religion can offer is silver, benefits, education and a happier life here on earth. Jesus gives to us what nothing else can, peace. How much peace a believer has is a great gauge to tell how discipled we are. Peace is found in the presence of Jesus. Peace is found in a relationship with Jesus. In this world we will get let down but God does not leave us down. This life will be tough. It will get complicated but God is with us. It's a bigger miracle to have faith in the storm than for the storm to cease. It's a greater testimony to sing in prison than to sing free. Let's go deeper in our discipleship. God, deepen our faith. God take us further in discipleship so we can experience the peace of Christ. Don't wait for the chains to break to sing. Don't wait for the miracle to praise. Faith is expressed to God when we have no reason to rejoice in our feelings. Let's let faith get the best of our feelings. This is how we can be a witness to the lost. They are looking on and seeing Christ with us in the furnace. That speaks more to the lost than having it all together and trying to shine for Christ. Vulnerability makes us relatable and gets the attention on Christ. We have heaven to look forward to!

Note

101

*"And whosoever doth not bear his cross, and come after
me, cannot be my disciple" (Luke 14:27, KJV)*

Jesus discipled His twelve apostles for three years and look how they responded on their own. One would think that after three years with Jesus no one could fall away. Yet they did. Our discipleship is not based on how well we disciple but on how well we get people to depend on Jesus. Only Jesus can keep a believer to the end. If people are not saved by Jesus, then they won't be kept to the end by Jesus. Discipleship is impossible for anyone to accomplish without Christ. Our forms of discipleship can be worse than the law of Moses. The worst slogan that came out of our previous generation is "What Would Jesus Do." Bracelets were made and millions of dollars spent on the "WWJD" acronym. The problem is, if we could do what Jesus did, then we would never have needed Jesus to save us in the first place. Trying to be like Jesus in our own strength is impossible. We can't do anything without God. Religion emphasizes what we can do but Christ emphasizes what He can do in us. The Christian life without surrender will condemn anyone. We can't do what God wants us to do in our own flesh. We can try but we will fail. Peter had to hear the rooster crow before he would learn that he can't do what he wants to do in his own sin-loving flesh. We are prone to wander, prone to fail. When we try in pride, we deny God doing what only He can do. This life is lived by surrender. As we yield, God brings the increase. Let's get out of the way and watch how well He can live life through us. If we want life, then we need to die to ourselves. As we die to ourselves, He becomes alive in us, doing through us what we could never have done on our own. It's not over. Today is a new day, today is a new beginning. We have the right to forgiveness and to start over in Christ. Surrender our weak selves and gain God's strength. We can't, but He can. It's time to throw up our hands and surrender. Surrendering to God is the best state of mind we could have. God does not take away if He does not have something better in mind. Believe to the day that we die because it won't be this way forever. Jesus was the best disciple-maker yet look how his disciples turned out when He died. Jesus knew they would fail, so He sent the Helper. We have the comforter. We have power to live today. The Holy Spirit was given to us! Surrender!

Note

_____

_____

_____

_____

_____

_____

_____

_____

102

"That at the name of Jesus every knee should bow, of things in heaven, and things in earth, and things under the earth; And that every tongue should confess that Jesus Christ is Lord, to the glory of God the Father" (Philippians 2:10–11, KJV)

The Lord Jesus Christ will be hailed King of Kings and Lord of Lords on the earth. Every knee, everywhere will declare Him Lord, willingly or not. Those that are ashamed of His name, He will be shamed on the day of judgment. How can believers be ashamed of their Lord for the sake of money. So many ministries have sold out their Lord for the sake of funding. An awakening is coming. It is not an awakening of socialism or community development, it's an awakening of the preaching of Jesus Christ and Him crucified. A ministry that does not preach Christ with a Gospel presentation is not a ministry of Christ but a scheme of hell. A revival is coming, but it's not a revival of demonic manifestations that are not evidenced in scripture. It is a revival of the Gospel being preached in the open air. Jesus is coming with judgement and authority to take out revenge on His enemies. He won't be coming back on a donkey but on a horse, ready for battle. Those that sold out the Gospel for temporary pleasure and self-seeking motives will be shamed. The goats and the sheep will be separated. Christ's day will come. All sinful flesh, satanic control and demonic hordes will be vanquished forever. Practice the posture of being on our knees. Remind ourselves of our state before God almighty. Willingly and joyfully go on your knees in submission to Jesus, as a symbol to our flesh and all those around us who is Lord of our lives. Our Lord has all authority in heaven and on earth. Jesus Christ is God. His Name is to be revered, His death is to be remembered, His resurrection is our assurance and His commission is to be obeyed. I have encountered Jesus more times than I could count. I have seen His Hand do what only God could do. I have met the resurrected Christ. My life has never been the same since. We preach from an encounter and not just from theory or a book. We overcome not only by the blood of the lamb but by the word of our testimony. The believers' born-again experience shields us from any argument of the world. Does it move you to know that souls are going to hell? Do you feel called to action, knowing you have the answer to eternal life? Don't give to outreaches, give to the evangelization of souls. Let's GO!

Note

103

"For God sent not his Son into the world to condemn the world; but that the world through him might be saved" (John 3:17, KJV)

Lifeguards save lives; they are not swim instructors primarily. Most lifeguards don't get paid to do swim instructions while they are on duty. The last thing someone needs to hear when they are drowning is a new swim technique; all they need is to be saved. There are swim instructors that can teach how to swim but that is not the job description for the lifeguard. Jesus came to save souls. We emphasize discipleship over salvation in this generation. We downplay salvation and emphasize discipleship. Discipleship for a sinner is ridiculous. It's like a lifeguard training someone drowning on how to do a new breaststroke swim technique. Discipleship will be followed by salvation, but if it's not in that order then we are not fulfilling our call. There is only one "lifeguard" that can save the soul and that is Jesus. An evangelist is not a savior, neither is any of the other four offices of ministry.[5] We are all sinners and never can be saviors. The minister that assumes a savior complex is functioning in an antichrist spirit. Our mission is to let people know who are drowning, to reach out to Jesus who alone can save the soul. Jesus wants to save. His intent was to save. He is passionate about salvation. As good as our discipleship may be, we will never be able to save the soul. Our generation has attempted to make model Christians but we can't save a soul.

---

5. *"And he gave some, apostles; and some, prophets; and some, evangelists; and some, pastors and teachers." (Ephesians 4:11, KJV)*

Religion masks the need for salvation. Religion makes "saviors" out of sinful gluttons. We all need to be saved and never graduate from needing to be saved by Jesus. We will always need Jesus. He was our savior; He is our savior and He will be our savior. When Jesus saves, discipleship will look different for everyone. Much of our discipleship today is like Saul's armor. We see people get saved by faith and then we throw works, burdens and conditions upon them. Salvation produces works but discipleship produces condemnation for those that were never saved. Discipleship without being saved can condemn worse than the law of Moses. The reason why we don't see awakening is because we are trying to awaken a group of people that potentially have never been saved. Salvation never graduates us from a need for Christ. We are saved and we are being saved. Call on Jesus.

Note

104

"Not forsaking the assembling of ourselves together, as the manner of some is; but exhorting one another: and so much the more, as ye see the day approaching" (Hebrews 10:25, KJV)

Running from the assembly is running from God. We were not to do life on our own. Accountability is essential for our wellbeing. Community is essential to continue in the faith. Isolation is Satan's play against us to destroy us. We are stronger together. It's time to wage war on isolation. We have amazing tools to stay in community. Take advantage of every means we have to stay in community. Jesus lived in community. He only spent short spells of His ministry alone with His Father. A healthy balance is essential. Adam was not made to be alone. As much as we need Jesus, we need the body of Christ. Jesus and His Church come hand in hand. We can't have one without the other. We can't love one and hate the other. God hates hate. Hatred is Satan's fuel to sidetrack God's people. Hate makes haters. Hatred must be shunned. Love destroys hate and empowers us to overcome hate. This is why the love of God is powerful. We overcome hate when we are overcome by the love of God. When we believe that we are loved, then we will love. Our level of love is a revelation of how much we believe we are loved. We hate because we think we are hated. We do to others what we feel was done to us. Yet, look what Jesus did for us. When we encounter Jesus, we get a replacement of our love for His love. Pray for a revelation of love. Survey the cross. See the depth, width and breadth of God's love for us. Love covers sin. Love seeks truth. Love contends for truth. True love does not compromise but is fuel for truth, life and confidence. Community must be built on Christ. When community is built on Christ, we are able to unite. When we unite, God commands blessing. When we are in one accord, the Spirit does what only He can. Let's put away division and seek what unites. Let's run to the assembly. Let's run to church. Let's stay in community!

Note

_____

_____
_____
_____
_____
_____
_____
_____
_____
_____

105

*"So then because thou art lukewarm, and neither cold nor hot,
I will spue thee out of my mouth" (Revelation 3:16, KJV)*

Mediocrity and compromise leads to comfort. When we are comfortable, we are no longer walking in faith. If we are not challenged and competing to know God, we will quickly become lukewarm. Eagerly desire challenge, eagerly desire growth, eagerly desire to be discipled. Stagnancy leads to bacteria. We were not made to stand still. We were made for movement. There are times to stand still but that's not a lifestyle. We are to take the enemies ground by force in Jesus's name. We are to seek gifts to make us more of a threat to the enemy. Cowards get the same reward as any sin we could list. Bravery is much more than doing what we can do, it's allowing God do what we cannot do. The Western Christianity is breeding cowards. Martyrdom is a lost word. Preaching the gospel is seen as outdated. As if the proclamation of the Gospel does not work, so we have to put together weak social strategies to change the world. Trying to compete with the government and other social projects is such a waste of resources when we have a message that can make all things become new. When we make the Gospel a demonstration or a work (effort) other than a message, then that is evidence that we don't believe its power. When we are all about music, concerts and motivational words more than being equipped to preach the Gospel, we have neglected biblical discipleship. If the preacher is the only one that is being raised up, more than the congregation, then there is a fundamental issue. As a Protestant believer, we hold to the priesthood of all believers. No one stays a "sheep" but God with time makes everyone shepherds in their families, workplaces and communities. A butcher crams his sheep in the pen for fear he would lose profit. If there was ever a day where the church is lacking equipping, it's this generation. Discipleship does not only mean making better citizens out of our congregants but making better believers. We are called to make disciples. We assemble to get emboldened to do ministry. If we have a pulse, then we have a purpose. There is no one higher than another in the sight of God. His calling is irrevocable. When He calls, no one can hinder His work. His call makes a way for the "called." Where He leads, He provides.

Note

106

*"That if thou shalt confess with thy mouth the Lord Jesus,
and shalt believe in thine heart that God hath raised him
from the dead, thou shalt be saved. For with the heart man
believeth unto righteousness; and with the mouth confession
is made unto salvation" (Romans 10:9–10, KJV)*

Confession with the mouth and belief in the heart that Jesus is Lord leads to salvation. Our closing prayer in response to the Gospel is a confession but only God sees the belief in the heart. I've seen thousands confess with their mouth but the belief in the heart is what makes a Christian a disciple. I am very aware of my brokenness but the one thing I know for sure is that I believe in my heart that Jesus is my Lord. Just because Jesus is my Lord does not mean I get it right all the time. I have to wrestle just like we all wrestle. Preachers are not saviors. Preachers need salvation as much as their audience do. We never move on from needing Jesus as our savior. It's a dangerous place to have a savior complex. It's easy to fall into this mind-set; as if we can save anyone. We are not doctors who take care of the sick in a hospital. We are the sick taking care of the sick by reminding ourselves of the only doctor that can save. The church is a hospital and it's full of the sick. That's why so much happens in the church and it seems like the church is failing society. The church should be made up of honest sinners that are fully aware of their need for a savior. Somehow our discipleship graduates its disciples from sheep to goats today. Our discipleship makes sheep so self-sufficient on knowledge that they forget that they need a shepherd like everyone else. Who has bewitched us? Goats have no need of a shepherd. One of the signs that our discipleship is raising goats is the lack of prayer meetings in the church. Prayer is the measure as to how much we rely on God. Sheep need a shepherd, goats don't. If we need God, we are praying to God. If we don't need God, we are leaning on our own understanding. It's time to remind ourselves what Jesus called His house. It was not just a house of music, or a house of Bible teaching but a house of prayer. When discipleship is producing goats and not sheep, it's time to reevaluate our scriptural literacy. We never graduate from needing Jesus, no matter what title we hold. When we rely on anything other than faith in Christ for anointing or salvation, then we are set up to fail. We will constantly fail and end up frustrated when we have become goats. Let's remain sheep.

Note

107

"But whereunto shall I liken this generation? It is like unto children sitting in the markets, and calling unto their fellows, And saying, We have piped unto you, and ye have not danced; we have mourned unto you, and ye have not lamented. For John came neither eating nor drinking, and they say, He hath a devil. The Son of man came eating and drinking, and they say, Behold a man gluttonous, and a winebibber, a friend of publicans and sinners. But wisdom is justified of her children" (Matthew 11:16–19, KJV)

Jesus never got upset with blatant sinners but He did with the blatant religious. Religion is a cancer on society. What holds back people from experiencing God is religion. Religion has sent more people to hell than any "sin" we could list. In fact, religion is the root of all sin, which is independence from God. Religion stones sinners, whereas Jesus welcomes sinners. The religious detest sinners, yet live no different in private. The religious talk about their self-denial yet indulge on "self" at the "buffet." The religious try to correct everyone and prescribe help to everyone, yet in their own lives they are falling apart. Religion puts up a front that God won't work with. Sin can be convicted and dealt with but religion leads to blaspheming of the Holy Spirit. The story of Ananias and Sapphira is a sobering illustration of how religion kills. Read the Gospels. If you are judging sinners and loving the religious, you are not mirroring your savior. We are supposed to be conforming to the character of Christ and not the apostles. Peter reached for a sword and that's exactly how the religious use the word of God. The Word of God should be used to reconcile and not cut sinners to pieces. The only people that should be offended when we preach are the religious ones. We live in a society steeped in religion. You will never hear me be hard on a sinner. When it comes to the religious though, they need to hear the truth. Their religion is giving them a false assurance. Their works are not good enough for God. Their sacraments are filthy rags in the sight of God. Their holiness before God is sinfulness. There is none Holy but God. Faith alone in Christ makes us holy. All Jesus rewarded and encouraged was belief. If faith alone is not enough, then Christ's sacrifice was not enough. It's time for the Gospel to be preached in the church. Most of the Church have been bewitched by tithe teaching, works driven, and church going Christians. There is nothing we can do to earn salvation. Our discipleship does not lead to our salvation. Discipleship follows salvation. We are saved by faith. We live by faith. We die with faith. Faith is not only needed at the beginning of our lives but should be needed more at the end of our lives.

Note

108

"Preach the word; be instant in season, out of season; reprove, rebuke, exhort with all long suffering and doctrine" (2 Timothy 4:2, KJV)

When people are connected to local missions, their faith becomes a lot more sustainable. There are so many that fell through the cracks of our previous church structure. When we only do missions once a year to an overseas country, the students of today see through that charade. When we connect students to local missions, then they are prepared for global missions. Most indigenous ministries will not benefit spiritually from a team that is not serving locally. Our church age loves to go overseas, but will not go across the street. Jesus never said, "Go and build buildings." Missions that are not proclaiming the Gospel are not the missions that Jesus was talking about. Using humanitarian aid and other ploys to bring the Gospel is very deceitful. The Gospel won't be advanced through any type of deceit. We are all prone to use human wisdom to advance the Gospel. Obedience to the great commission, which is to preach the Gospel to every creature is the best way to see the Gospel advance. Young people must be inspired to share their faith. If they are told "do as I say, but not as I do" that youth group will never make it. This generation wants authenticity. If we are not displaying dependency on God, no one will listen to us. It's time to get scripture literate and follow Jesus. The current system of our so-called "discipleship" is not what Jesus had in mind. Bible studies are great, but if the "why" is not communicated to them, then it's just an accumulation of knowledge. Our ministries must never forget the "why" behind us being here. When we are not winning souls, we are nullifying salvation. We are saying that salvation is not as important as knowledge of the length of the temple. We have so many distracted by knowledge but never fulfill the great commission. It's time to wake up to our "why." Having a burden for those that are thousands of miles away yet not sharing locally is foolishness. Our mission's departments have missed it here in the US for years now. They don't have a burden for their neighbors or city, but they do for those overseas. Christ put a value on all humans. He was always concerned about those right in front of Him. He was delayed by those that were in His periphery. When our evangelism is only when we are behind a mic, something is wrong.

Note

109

"Now concerning virgins I have no commandment of the Lord: yet I give my judgment, as one that hath obtained mercy of the Lord to be faithful" (1 Corinthians 7:25, KJV)

We get so distracted as a society. We are the most distracted generation of Christians, yet this generation is the most needy generation ever to hear the Gospel. The days of relying on the "few" is over. It's time for the few to rely on the majority to reach this generation. God has shifted the attention from the pulpit to the pew. God has heard the cry of the congregant. For too long, we have relied on the clergy to do ministry, but that's not what God intended. The clergy was set up to make disciples and see them raised up. The average believer must walk in their call. The ordinary believer must take responsibility for their walk with God. Crying out for a preacher or a man of God to do what each believer was called to do will not be heard. God is shifting the anointing from a personality-driven ministry to His "people-driven ministry." Church, we are called to equip our congregation. The best leader is the one that is working their way out of a job so others can carry on the legacy. Rather than leaders being threatened by their gifted congregants, they should be fanning them into flame. Our current system dumbs down the congregation and allows them to have enough truth to keep them coming back for more. The leaders at the top surround themselves with people that could never outperform them. It breeds the spirit of Saul rather than raising up disciples. We can't be intimidated or insecure in ministry. Every believer should be passionate about seeing every other believer thrive. Jealousy, covetousness, and competition are against the spirit of Christ. It is the antichrist. The spirit of antichrist is everywhere today. When a personality is raised higher than the person of Christ, we are in trouble. It's time for all believers to be raised up in their call. Go to a church where you are equipped to minister. Church has been set up for consumers in the West, but that model has failed our generation. Believers can only consume for so long until they start to desire to minister. There are believers who, for years, have been spiritually consuming. They may be adults, but they are spiritual babies because they have not been discipled to disciple. Our system keeps the congregation in the "pen" and feeds only milk lest the sheep grow and produce. Go where you will grow.

Note

110

"I the Lord search the heart, I try the reins, even to give every man according to his ways, and according to the fruit of his doings" (Jeremiah 17:10, KJV)

Asking "why" before we do anything is a healthy strategy to make sure God is in it. How do we know if God is in it? Is what we are doing about others? Is what we want to do going to reach others? When we are "others" centered, then we are "Christ" centered. The nearer to Christ we are, the nearer to the sinner we will be found. Christ left us here to reach sinners. The monastic mind-set is a scheme from hell to keep us from being a light in the world. When all the Christian kids are pulled out of public schools, we shouldn't be surprised by how dark the schools will get. When believers are not going to the streets to preach the Gospel, we shouldn't be surprised by the six o'clock news. We have been called to preach the Gospel, but if we don't, then Satan will take ground. He has taken ground in many of our neighborhoods and city streets. Pulling back to our structures and waiting out until the return of Christ is a coward belief system. Cowards will get the same consequence as every sin we could list according to Revelation 21:8. Cowards only preach behind pulpits and share with those that want to hear what they have to say. Cowards teach the church service on Sunday to be all that a believer is called to. We are called out of a coward's lifestyle. It's time to awaken from just warming a pew and being lulled to sleep by our lullabies on Sunday mornings. The church has become a huge bedroom, and the congregation is saying, "please don't wake us up." The alarm is sounding. Billions of people are unreached today yet we are keeping our assurance of eternity to ourselves. We have lost ground in our streets, politics, businesses, and communities. The church is awakening. There is going to be such a move of God that the chief of cowards will be preaching like a lion. When the Holy Spirit moves, we will be burdened to preach the Gospel; people will hear and be converted. This is what revival will look like. We need awakening. It's going to take challenging sermons to awaken us. We have been told all that we want to hear and are still not satisfied. What we want to hear does not quench our need for purpose. It's sermons that make us uncomfortable and provoke us to obedience is what will satisfy us the most. When our "why" is for others, God will turn up! Let's go.

Note

111

*"Either what woman having ten pieces of silver, if she
lose one piece, doth not light a candle, and sweep the house,
and seek diligently till she find it?" (Luke 15:8, KJV)*

We have seen tremendous results from prisons to youth conferences to street preaching to rescue missions and church revivals. God has anointed an evangelist to ignite a passion in the church for souls. No matter what setting we are in, each of us gets saved for a great purpose. If evangelism is not a part of the discipleship at your church, then they are in direct rebellion to Jesus's final mandate. On the day of Pentecost, everyone was empowered to preach the Gospel in a relevant way so all could know Jesus. Thousands were added to the Church through that one big street revival. The Holy Spirit was given so every believer can be useful to preach the Gospel. If we can do ministry without Him, then we should tremble out of fear. We are saved to go to heaven, but we are also saved to depend on Him until the day we die. How do we gauge if we are dependent on Him? Are we in personal prayer? Does your church have a prayer meeting? A prayerless church is a powerless church. The book of Acts is full of prayer meetings. They knew where to get the boldness to preach the Gospel. If you have no burden for souls, if you are a coward when it comes to sharing Jesus, if you do not intentionally want to see the Great Commission fulfilled, there is something off in your relationship with God. Paul told Timothy to do the work of an evangelist. Timothy was timid, but Paul told him he had no excuse because the Spirit we all received is a Spirit of power, love, and a sound mind.

Let's pray that the Holy Spirit fills us with power so that we can speak the Gospel with passion. The best tongue the Holy Spirit wants to fill us with is the tongue that preaches the Gospel. The gifts are to show unbelievers that Christ lives and not to entertain the believer. The Holy Spirit is not your entertainer, and the church is not your circus, although some of our leaders today are clowns. Once we take steps of faith toward obeying the Commission, we will see the power of God working through our ministries. Any church growth strategy that does not include discipling the church in evangelism needs to be cut off. We need to stop building the church with might and human power; it's time to rely on the Spirit of God. Take the makeup off, and let's get about God's will!

Note

112

*"Verily I say unto you, All sins shall be forgiven unto the sons
of men, and blasphemies wherewith soever they shall blaspheme:
But he that shall blaspheme against the Holy Ghost hath never
forgiveness, but is in danger of eternal damnation. Because
they said, He hath an unclean spirit" (Mark 3:28–30, KJV)*

All sin can be forgiven except blaspheming the Holy Spirit. There
is no sin that we repent of that can separate us from God. We like to
define sin by all of its fruit, but the root of sin is independence from
God. Jesus had very little time for the Pharisees. Like the Calvinists
today, they felt they were the only elected ones. Jesus drew sinners
near. The type of sinner that no one would have thought would have
been elected to Salvation. Jesus repeatedly said, "Your faith made
you whole." He marveled at the faith of the centurion. He said of
him, "there was no greater faith in all of Israel," which disturbed
His followers and the Jews. Jesus rewarded faith and always rebuked
unbelief. Read the Gospels. Anyone that believes in limited atonement should be ashamed of themselves. Christ shed His blood for
every sinner. He desires all to be saved. He wants all men to be drawn
unto Him. We believe in unlimited atonement and resistible grace.
The Spirit of God is wrestling with every person's will so that they
would be saved. Any theology that cheapens evangelism and free will
is demonic. What is a human that we should cheapen the great commission to just relying on the sovereign will of God? Jesus told His
followers to "go and preach the Gospel." Religion loves to sit around
a coffee table and value books more than souls. Religion loves to

distract itself with anything other than evangelizing sinners. Religion confines its followers to a box with a steeple on it. Jesus was out in the streets while the religious leaders were behind walls, coming up with techniques to keep the sheep in the pen for as long as they could. Religion breeds hate and judgment, and it ruins society. A greater cancer on society than any sin we could list is religion. Jesus was an offense to the religious, yet was embraced by prostitutes and loved by sinners. Go to a church where sinners are welcomed and the religious feel uncomfortable. We are here to evangelize the religious because their assurance is built on sand. All our works are filthy rags. There is nothing we can do to save ourselves. Faith is an internal decision to trust Christ and His finished work on the cross. There is no one out of arm's reach of our God. All are elect, but few believe! Let's preach, so they will hear and believe in Jesus.

Note

113

*"And hope maketh not ashamed; because the love of
God is shed abroad in our hearts by the Holy Ghost
which is given unto us" (Romans 5:5, KJV)*

When our whole life source is in Christ, we can't help but get passionate for Christ. When all we have is Christ, to get through each day, we can't help but get passionate for Christ. When Christ is our all, and we have nothing else to drive us, then we can't help but be white-hot for Him. In order to get on fire for God, we need to allow the fire of God to burn off all our dross, so all we have is Christ to trust in. Christ will compel us to be fervent when He is all we have. It's when we have multiple "Christ's" in our lives to get us through life that the passion flickers. Only Jesus quenches the thirst of our soul. When we mix Jesus with all our other crutches, we become lukewarm. Passion is not anointing because passion can be manipulated. We need an anointing that breaks depression and puts darkness on the run. When we are forgotten, and all that is remembered from our sermons is Christ, then we are on a healthy track. The best preachers get the attention on Jesus as quickly as they can. When our church growth comes from anywhere but Christ, something is wrong. When our sermon series comes from anywhere but scripture, then something is wrong. The church is sacred. It's not a business. Jesus wants His church back from some that feel they can build it better than Him. Jesus will build His Church with or without us. He clearly laid out how to make disciples. Let's read His Word for church growth and disciple-making, it will save us a ton of money and time. Let's not do what works; let's do what He says. Taking matters into our own hands may seem like a temporary way to success, but it never works out in the end. We have testimony after testimony to teach us that our ways don't work out in the end. Jesus is our life source. There is no life outside of Him. Once we taste life in Him, nothing else will ever satisfy. Earthly pleasures will only leave us depressed in comparison to a life in Christ. Christ never leaves us. Christ never disappoints. When we read of the crucifixion of Christ, it will motivate us to surrender our all. As we give over to God, He gives in return to us peace, life, and hope. We let go of our stress to gain His peace. Surrender all, let Christ have His way.

Note

114

"That the trial of your faith, being much more precious than of gold that perisheth, though it be tried with fire, might be found unto praise and honour and glory at the appearing of Jesus Christ" (1 Peter 1:7, KJV)

Throughout scripture, we see that God likes journeys, processes and seasons. Even in the creation of the earth, what God could have done instantaneously, He took His time. God is not in a rush for anything. It took thousands of years from the fall to get to the incarnation. It's been over two thousand years since Christ walked on earth. We must never give up when the journey is long and rough. It will be worth it by the time we reach our destination. We read of many in history that gave up on the journey or grew impatient with the journey and took matters into their own hands. Nothing ever worked out when they tried to speed up God's process. The scripture teaches us what not to do in life, as well as teaches us what we should do. We may know the right thing to do but keep choosing the wrong thing. If we could do the right thing all the time, then we would never need a savior. Jesus is our savior, not only to get us to heaven but also to live through us so we can have the power to do the right thing. What God calls us to do may look like the shadow of death, but remember it's just a shadow. The hardships of this life will be nothing in comparison to the eternity ahead. Don't rush. Be patient. Anxiety opens the door to the wrong decisions. Be anxious for nothing. Set your mind on the Lord and He will give you peace. Slow down. Breathe. When we sit still, then we will see the salvation of the Lord. When we are anxious, we will fall every time. Our anxiety measures our level of faith in Christ. Prayer, scripture reading and repentance are keys to living a believing life. Living repentant is living honestly with our ongoing need for a savior. When we say we have no sin and have no need of repentance, we have been lied to. Jesus called the churches in revelation to repentance. Only the arrogant would say that we don't need to repent after we believe. Repentance is an empowering word. Jesus has forgiven and will forgive every time. The Holy Spirit works through repentance to make our character more like Christ. As we are on this journey, remember that it's never too late to repent. Remember that it's not over. Death is just a shadow. Those that believe in Christ do not die but step into eternal life with Christ. We have so much to look forward to. This is not "It."

Note

115

*"And I, if I be lifted up from the earth, will draw
all men unto me" (John 12:32, KJV)*

The atonement of Christ is unlimited and it's for whosoever will believe in Christ. Every human is elect to salvation but few believe it. Following the passion of Christ, an evangelist wants all to believe by preaching the Gospel to everyone. Faith comes by hearing the Word of God. Faith does not come by God alone, but He designed the preaching of the Gospel as the means to people responding with faith and being saved. We cannot excuse evangelism by a theology that keeps us from doing the call of God, which is the Great Commission. No matter how much sin, tattoos, abortions, or brokenness, anyone can be forgiven and all can be saved. God loves sinners. We see this by reading the kindness that Jesus showed sinners. The only time Jesus got upset was with the religious. Jesus loved sinners. Who we all thought were the elect, were the very ones that wanted Jesus to die on the cross. Peter had to be told by Jesus to not call the unclean what God has called clean. Whom Peter thought were not the elect were elected because Christ's atoning blood was for every sinner everywhere. We evangelize with no discrimination, we evangelize everyone as if they are elect, their decision is on them, not us. The mystery of salvation will always be a mystery but we are not to judge the outward appearance. Who we thought would never get saved, got saved. Who we thought were not paying attention or would never listen are the ones that respond the most. Evangelists must never profile or show favoritism. We are called to treat every sinner as God treats us.

We are no better than anyone else. We bleed red and we die physically. No matter how sanctified we think we are, we will never be perfect. If we could be perfect, then we would never die. If we could be perfect, then we would never need Jesus. Jesus was our savior; Jesus is our savior and Jesus will be our savior. We have not been saved to be saviors as evangelists. There is no evangelist that can atone for sin. Only Jesus saves. He has chosen preaching as His means to see people converted. Jesus's blood was shed for everyone. We believe in unlimited atonement for whosoever will believe. Jesus has saved the most unlikely throughout history. God always confounds the proud; let's pray that He will do it again.

Note

116

"And he commanded us to preach unto the people, and to testify that it is he which was ordained of God to be the Judge of quick and dead" (Acts 10:42, KJV)

Evangelism will always include a message. God wants His Church to be ambassadors to see people of all walks of life converted and saved. The Gospel is not only a demonstration but a definition. The truth of the Gospel is more than an action, it's good news. The emphasis of Christianity is Christ. It's not "church-ianity" or "ministry-ianity," it's Christ-ianity. We are all fallible beings pointing to our infallible savior. Jesus Christ Saves souls, but we don't. The message we preach is Christ and Him crucified. Each believer is called with a purpose to make Jesus known, whether that is as an evangelist or a witness. We are all called to be salt and light. We are not here to wait out until we get to heaven. We are here to work out our salvation. Evangelism needs to be intentional because our flesh will never evangelize. This is why the Bible lists out the names of the apostles and men of God that were used for His kingdom. Each one of us matter to God. Our personalities, skills and purposes matter to God. Where He has put us is our mission field. Let's not rely on an evangelist, rely on Christ in you. Only you have the greatest influence on those around you. Christ will shine through anyone that surrenders their will to God. The Holy Spirit will empower us to preach Christ. When the Holy Spirit fills us, we will be a witness unto Christ everywhere we go. If the spirit that fills us does not make us evangelize or make us a witness unto Christ, then it is not the Holy Spirit that filled us. We need to try the spirits. As we yield to the Holy Spirit, He will break our hearts for what breaks His. It takes steps of faith for faith to be faith. Without faith no one can please God. Faith is not knowledge, it's an action that goes against our self-strength so that all we can do is rely on God. Believers "do," believers are not "Gnostics."[6] We don't sit back and vegetate, we use all we have to glorify God; and when we are without, we still will glorify God with faith. Let's preach the Gospel! It's the greatest love that we can show another human! The Gospel is more important than any humanitarian needs that a person may have. We can meet needs but we must never lose the conviction to preach the Gospel. Jesus saves. Our faith works. Our faith is the only faith that works. Knowing Christ is knowing the way, truth and life. Without Christ, there is no access to the Father. Narrow is the way to eternal life and few will find it. By faith, the saints of old accomplished the will of God. It was not just by God or the Holy Spirit, but by faith. Faith is God's economy to see the kingdom of God advance.

---

6. Gnostics focus on mental ascent than obedience.

117

"That at that time ye were without Christ, being aliens from the commonwealth of Israel, and strangers from the covenants of promise, having no hope, and without God in the world" (Ephesians 2:12, KJV)

Outside of Jesus Christ I would be hopelessly lost. There is not a day that goes by that I don't need Him or rely on Him. His word has been a lamp unto my feet and His purpose fulfills my heart. I knew His call on my life from a young age. All I ever wanted to do was lead people to my savior. I've seen Muslims convert, Roman Catholics leave their religion, Homosexuals become straight, gang members become model tax-paying citizens. When Jesus saves a soul, that life will not remain the same for the better. The truth of scripture enlightens and gives understanding. It's as if everything in the world makes sense when we have Jesus. A relationship with Jesus eases the soul, lifts the weights of life and completes the purpose we are looking for. Before I am any title of the world or of ministry, I am an adopted son in my Father's household. Knowing that God is my Father, anchors my soul. I bring all my sin, brokenness and fears to my Father. Jesus makes this relationship possible. I am not affiliated with a religion or theology. My allegiance is to Jesus Christ and His Word, the Bible. An evangelist exists to ignite a passion for souls in the church. First and foremost, we are to emphasize a relationship with Jesus. Evangelism without a personal, ongoing relationship with Jesus is just an argument. Evangelism is not a debate. The Gospel is not open for discussion. The Cross is power unto salvation. When the

Gospel is preached from a relationship with Jesus, it will be packed with power so we can be an effective witness. The call that God has on my life as an evangelist is to see souls converted. We believe the Gospel can change lives for the better. We are unashamed of the Gospel. Whether that's on a platform or one on one, we take the Gospel seriously. Will you support our endeavor to ignite a passion for souls in the Church? Evangelists not only want to preach behind the pulpit of churches but we want to take the church with us to the streets. An evangelist does not teach on evangelism alone, that's just a teacher. An evangelist evangelizes. The title is a function. First, we are in the family of God, but God has a calling for each of us. Mine happens to be an evangelist.

Note

118

"He that loveth not knoweth not God; for
God is love" (1 John 4:8, KJV)

When we love people, all the walls come down. When people feel love, there is no guile. When people feel fully accepted and comfortable around us, we can go deep in our friendship. There is such a need for authenticity today. We can be so plastic as a society. We are pressured to save face. One of the greatest qualities we could ever have is being real. Real with our pain, real with our brokenness, and real with our sin. God will only work with those that are willing to be themselves before Him. God does not want robotics; He desires a relationship. The cross is the extent of God's passion for relationship. When we feel loved as we are, then we gain motivation to change. When we are living to fit a mold and are being insincere, we will never change. We can't be this way with everyone but we must be this way before God. God knows all of us anyway. We are only hurting ourselves by holding back from Him. As we pour out our pain and anguish before God, He heals us. Holding back the tears only hurts us. It's okay to cry. It's okay to be real. God will only use us when we are walking in openness before Him. Let's love as we have been loved. Let's comfort as we have been comforted. Let's accept as we have been accepted. Trust God, He won't leave us as we are, but always takes us as we are. God will always turn our situations for good. There is nothing we have done, or do, that would surprise God. Deliverance is not found in positive thinking but it's found in honest communication to God. Christ made this type of relationship possible. It's the love of God that compels us and it's love that compels healthy relationships. God first loved us. He not only defined love but demonstrated love. As we embrace the love of God for ourselves, then we can show the love of God for others. We love as we have been loved. While we were yet sinners, Christ died for us. God so loves sinners that He dealt with all our sin at the cross. Now He can call sinners, sons, if we believe in Christ. The Gospel is the only answer to our society, relationships, and friendships. The Gospel is the least preached message from our pulpits today. We must never forget the power of the Gospel. Satan hates it but we are going to preach it.

Note

_____

_____
_____
_____
_____
_____
_____
_____
_____
_____

119

*"For we are his workmanship, created in Christ Jesus
unto good works, which God hath before ordained that
we should walk in them" (Ephesians 2:10, KJV)*

God prepares His people when He is about to show His glory. So many have been baptized in anguish over the last few years. Despair nearly took them out. The afflictions were so back-to-back that no one knew if we were going to make it. Some of us, because of the affliction and wrestle, have a lifelong limp either emotionally or physically from the intensity of the season. The weakness, shame, and regrets can crash in so heavy that you can't breathe. It's at this point, when we are trusting God for every pulse and thanking Him for every breath, that we are ready for what He has planned next for us. No military will send someone to war without boot camp and training. This mind-set is the same for everything in life. God's boot camp is not designed to be passed. It's designed to get us to fail. Once we embrace our failure and make weakness our friend, then we can stand in the strength of almighty God and do the impossible. It's in the affliction that all the stuff that would hold us back from our call surfaces. Jealousy, insecurity, sin, bitterness, self-pity, selfishness: these are all traits of the flesh. When we die to ourselves then we become alive to Christ. God replaces our self-strength with His strength. What was once impossible, God makes possible. Whatever it is that reminds us of our need for Christ, don't be quick to pray it away. Take pleasure in it. Let the physical or emotional limp be a reminder of our humanity. We tend to pray out what God gave as a weapon against the enemy. The deceiver loves to get our focus on ourselves because it's how he disarms us as a threat to him. When our focus is on Jesus then we are a weapon. When we are walking in Christ's strength, we are treading on our enemy's necks. When we are submitted to God, Satan can be resisted and he must flee. It's time for the resistance to rise. We have been in affliction but we have learned that it is an advantage and not a disqualification. The more we depend on Christ, the more qualified we become. Silence Satan in Jesus's name. Stand in the name of Jesus. Press on with the strength of Christ. We are not on our own. Christ will see us through. His glory will shine on the earth again. His remnants have been interceding. God, have mercy.

Note

120

"Ye shall know them by their fruits. Do men gather grapes of thorns, or figs of thistles?" (Matthew 7:16, KJV)

Discipling is not only teaching; it is also a demonstration. Jesus demonstrated His teaching to His disciples. Anyone can teach today. Teachers are simply buying sermons online. Western churches have become so scripted, mechanical and ordered, that God is not needed. Worship teams sing to tracks like they prepped for karaoke. It's become so timed and professional, that we can grow a church without God. Our generation is chasing fads, whatever the biggest and best do, most imitate today. The average congregant is tired of imitations. People are burned on mechanics. We were designed for authentic relationship. The American pace of life is so busy, that church is not prioritized. An hour of church a week is not going to disciple anyone. Rather than Sunday being a morning to be discipled, we have turned it into an outreach to grow numerically; but where is the growth in the Word of God? God is not interested in a "photo-op." Sunday is for the edification of the church. Every other day is for evangelism of our friends and family. Today Sunday is the only day that ministry happens for most believers. That's a great model for whoever gets propped up behind a pulpit. However, it's not how Christ intended it to be. Monday through Saturday, while we are working, raising kids or are in school should be the days for ministry and evangelism. Sunday is to rest and be built up to live on mission. The assembly is not our mission. It's supposed to be where we get the pep talk so that we can live on mission. God deserves for us to be evangelizing

Monday through Saturday, as well as inviting someone to church to be evangelized to on Sunday. If Sunday Church is the only expression of Christ that the lost could have, and the believer is not an expression of Christ, then the one man in the pulpit should be busy night and day doing what every believer is called to be doing, evangelizing. Church in the West is a very expensive club that not only expect money but time too. Rather than the church being equipped, the ministers are the only ones being equipped today. Rather than ministers serving, some expect to be served. They delegate so much out, that their volunteers work harder for nothing and God is used by these ministries as a bait-and-switch to work the volunteers while the leaders are out boating, golfing and fine dining on the ministry credit card.

Note

121

"If ye then, being evil, know how to give good gifts unto your children, how much more shall your Father which is in heaven give good things to them that ask him? Therefore all things whatsoever ye would that men should do to you, do ye even so to them: for this is the law and the prophets. Enter ye in at the strait gate: for wide is the gate, and broad is the way, that leadeth to destruction, and many there be which go in thereat" (Matthew 7:11–13, KJV)

If an earthly father, who is a sinner, knows how to give good gifts to his kids, how much does our Father in heaven? Jesus taught us that God is our Father. Jesus took upon Himself our sin so that we can be a family again. Our Father loves us way more than any earthly dad. Every earthly dad will fail at some point. We are broken as a race. Christ alone can bring us in on a family where there is unconditional love. The Family of God loves with no strings attached. The family of God does not gossip, they don't laugh when you are down, they don't take advantage of one another. The family of God will be together for eternity, where there will be love, peace and harmony. Heaven will be full of family. Christ saved us into His family. We have been counted as sons and daughters of God. We have been accepted and welcomed to the table of God. He delights to do good; He delights to protect us; He delights to provide for us. We see all of this in the death of Christ. Love is best defined by how God so loved us so much that He would send His Son to adopt us that believe. The love of our Father, who is in heaven is a love that we all have been looking for in earthly relationships. No one can be what only God can be to us. Not once has He forsaken us. Not once does He forget us. We are His family. Satan hates our identity in Christ. Satan hates our fate. Satan is after our faith. Let's fan into flame our faith in the goodness of God. Jesus Christ is Lord, God and Savior. His wounds, His blood, and His death is why we have life. God is good. Just look to the cross and all of our doubts will be washed away. He will meet us where we are. He takes us as we are, in our sin and depression. He is not ashamed of us. Christ took our shame upon Himself. Call on His name; Jesus, and eternal peace will flood your soul. Not for a minute was a believer ever forsaken. We never will be either. We are loved more than we know. We are cared for, more than we know. His thoughts toward us are to bless us. Parents would do anything for their child, and no parent is perfect. The Lord said to us, "I would do anything for you!" What more could He do after sending Jesus to do what He did? Our God is good. Trust Jesus, He is faithful.

Note

122

*"Except the Lord build the house, they labour in vain
that build it: except the Lord keep the city, the watchman
waketh but in vain" (Psalm 127:1, KJV)*

Evangelism without prayer is an argument. It's like a car without gas. We can't do what God can. Only Jesus can make new creatures. We can get responses, but only God can make someone born again. The Gospel saves lives but also changes lives for the better. Jesus never leaves us the same. Jesus never said, "Just get saved." He wants us to sin no more. Jesus takes away the pleasure of sin in our lives and makes holiness our hearts' cry. This does not mean that we will be sinless, but it does mean that we will "sin less" in Christ. Sin will grieve the Spirit inside the believer. It's how we will know that we are saved because sin will not be pleasurable anymore. If it is, then we need to repent and allow the Spirit of God to convict us. The New Covenant is not just a legal agreement of our sins being forgiven but also it is the power to live as He lived. The Gospel is not a license to sin but it's a relationship that empowers us to grieve when we sin. We don't have a license to sin and if we do sin, then we are not walking in a heartfelt relationship with God. Jesus will always take us as we are but He won't leave us as we are. Everyone who was sick or caught in sin always walked away better and holier. He does not want to see any of us perish. We are forgiven in Christ. We also are made new in Christ. We are not free to sin but we are free to repent and trust Christ to change us to be more like Him. We will always be a work in progress. We are under construction until the day our bodies die;

then construction will be complete with new glorified bodies. We are called to a relationship with Christ. Our evangelism is an outflow of our relationship with Christ. Prayer is relationship. Relationship speaks of a heart connection and that is what God wants with us. There will be a difference that everyone will see when we are walking in relationship with God. People will feel His presence from us. It's not us, it's Him being active in us because we are walking in a relationship with Him. Knowing Jesus intimately is powerful. Sitting still, reading His Word including Jesus in all our decisions, surrendering to Him all of our fears, shame, guilt and is what intimacy looks like. Satan is resisted when Jesus is known intimately.

Note

123

"And if it seem evil unto you to serve the Lord, choose you this day whom ye will serve; whether the gods which your fathers served that were on the other side of the flood, or the gods of the Amorites, in whose land ye dwell: but as for me and my house, we will serve the Lord" (Joshua 24:15, KJV)

Salvation is a decision. When people made their decision for Christ in the Gospels, they stepped forward and were baptized. Baptism was symbolic of a new direction. It was a conversion. Making disciples of people that were never saved is like telling someone lame to walk. We have so many people that are making "disciples" but their discipleship has become more rigorous than the law of Moses. The disciple-maker is not a god, nor is the disciple-maker a mediator. Jesus did not make disciples in sanctuaries or classrooms. Our model today has reinvented the priesthood and elevated the "anointed" above faith in Christ. There is no man of God. There is a man, and there is a God. There is no medium; there is no certificate that makes anyone have more access to God than another. When we look to people more than to the Bible, we fall into another religion. Religion always elevates the pulpit. Religion always elevates one person above another person. Religion breeds discrimination. Religion expects titles to be given to their minions. The audacity of this generation's leaders to expect titles in front of their names, yet when it comes to Jesus, they call Him by His first name. Today's model of Church feeds their congregants milk lest they grow and take their money with them to become what God calls them to be. Religion loves to control. Religion rarely equips and is shy to raise anyone up lest someone outperforms its system. Religion celebrates laziness and criticizes evangelism. Religion looks to every easy way out from obeying God. Like Saul, religion taxes and breeds nepotism. Religion forms monarchies. Religion is a cancer on our nation and is sending more people to hell than any one particular sin. Jesus had no time for religion, yet we can't get enough of it. Religion is a deceptive sin that looks like an angel of light yet it's full of darkness. The honor must go to Jesus. Jesus is who we are to imitate. Jesus is who we should be quoting. The religious quote everyone and everything but the Bible. The religious heap up teachers but never read the word for themselves. It's time to get off the milk and onto the meat. It's time for disciples to grow up. Our words are fleshless bones if we are not in relationship with Jesus.

Note

124

*"But the Comforter, which is the Holy Ghost, whom
the Father will send in my name, he shall teach you
all things, and bring all things to your remembrance,
whatsoever I have said unto you" (John 14:26, KJV)*

No one comforts like the Holy Spirit. When the Holy Spirit is yielded to, His love pours through the church to all those around. When we yield to the Holy Spirit, community is established and pure love is manifested. Love is found in the church. Community is found in the church. There is no greater love felt than when the Holy Spirit manifests love in a community of believers; it's unconditional love, pure love, sacrificial love, a love that lays itself down for another. Love from our nature is only a shadow compared to the love Christ gives us. We have felt love but when we are caught up in the love of God nothing else compares. The love of God quenches our need for love. His love is like no other. His love has no strings attached. His love takes us as we are, yet it is packed with power to love us out of what is unhealthy for us. The love of God compels an evangelist. The love of God compels sinners to Christ. The love of God melts the hardest heart like wax. Love has won, and love will win. Love one another. Christ is the example of love. He first loved us. Let Him tell you He loves you. Loving others without believing first that we are loved will make a hypocrite out of us. We have so many that want to give love to everyone, which looks religious, but that is all it is, religious if they don't first receive the love of God. We can only give what we have been given. We first have been loved. If we want to love like Christ, we must first believe that we are loved. Only someone that believes they are loved can love like Christ loves. We are not the source of love for anyone. We will disappoint. We can only give what we have been given. Only Christ's love is the source, we are only resources. He has chosen us to be His hands and feet. Let's embrace one another. Let's look at everyone as Christ looks at us, as a family. We are family. Believers are family. We are more than members, congregants, and friends, we are family. Family fights for one another. Family loves one another. If you have never experienced family, then you can in the church of Jesus Christ. The Church is more of our family than our biological family if they are not in Christ. We are brothers and sisters in Christ. Christ ties us all together and makes us one. Pray the fervent love of God to be manifested today.

Note

125

"And we know that all things work together for good
to them that love God, to them who are the called
according to his purpose" (Romans 8:28, KJV)

Processing our life experiences can be very disheartening. Having an outlet and hoping it helps others along the journey is so important. There is no wasted time or experiences. Jesus makes good of it all. Every season has its benefits; we just need to focus on the benefit so we can make it through. God brings purpose to our past. When our expectations are dashed and dreams have become nightmares, it's then that we can feel the nearness of God. God is near to the broken hearted. He is near to those that find themselves in gray situations. It's not black or white. God can bring clarity to confusion if we surrender to Him. Saying "I surrender" is a process. It's not a one-time confession but it's a lifelong profession of surrender. When we are at the end of our strength, then we graduate religion and enter into a relationship with Jesus. Regret only hurts those that regret. It's a wasted emotion. It's time to believe that God can turn all things for good. Humans love to heap shame, guilt, and condemnation on themselves and others. It's why bad news sells so much in our world. The Gospel is good news. We even try to focus on the bad news of the good news when it comes to the Gospel. There is no question that Jesus preached good news for the sinner, good news for the confused and broken. The only people that found Jesus message as bad news are the religious. The religious thrive off of bad news. Jesus came to proclaim the good news. The good news is that Jesus reconciled us back into a relationship with our Father. Nothing can separate us from Him. There is no sin outside of the reach of God's grace. It's the religious that need to fear hell and not just the repentant sinner. The religious spirit must die in us or we too will face judgment. As we process our life experiences with Jesus, all our guilt and shame are washed away. We are clean by His Word. God can work all our experiences together for good. Don't be disappointed. Don't regret. The dream may have turned into a nightmare but the dream is not over. We know the end of all the stories of God's people in scripture. Their circumstances always turned for good. Stomp fear out in Jesus's name. Live shameless. Lift your head. You are not who you were and you are not who you are going to be. God is good and does good.

Preach like Jesus is about to break through the sky. Preach like we just got left out of hospice for an hour. Preach like there is no tomorrow. Preach the Word without guile. Preach only to glorify God and not for any other reason. This is Comission. The Holy Spirit has put a fervency in this ministry to simply preach the Gospel. We are not just teachers; we are evangelists that believe evangelism is the heart of God for the church while we are here. Evangelism is not only obedience to His Word; it's our purpose in Him leaving us here after we are saved. We resist legalists; we challenge the religious, and we love sinners. Loving sinners is the love Christ produces in us. Religion segregates, separates, flees, judges, and discriminates. Whom Jesus calls clean, let no man call unclean. We have been made clean by His Word. Christ made way for sinners to be saved. Christ is near to the broken sinner. That means He is near to me. I am not someone who used to be like the people I preach to; I'm someone just like them. Preachers are beggars telling other beggars where we found bread. Evangelists are not saviors. They are broken messengers telling the world who is healing them on a daily basis. If ever the church needed evangelists, it's today. We are not just guest speakers; we are gust preachers. We are not itinerant speakers; we are not motivational speakers; we burn for souls to be saved. We burn for souls whether the mic is on or off. We burn for souls everywhere we go. Evangelism is a lifestyle. An evangelist is simply someone who loves Jesus, and out of their love for Jesus, He shares His desires with us. Jesus lived for others. If we love Jesus, we will love others. That's what His love does in us; it multiplies. When we are selfish with Jesus, and He is our only focus, we will naturally become selfless to reach others. To be Christ-centered will lead us to be others-centered. We are not a church that gets weekly support.

Note

126

"She said, No man, Lord. And Jesus said unto her, Neither do I condemn thee: go, and sin no more" (John 8:11, KJV)

The Gospel is not good news to sin, it's good news not to sin. The Gospel is not a license to do whatever we want; yet the Gospel does not mean we are sinless or conditionally righteous either. The Gospel will make us grieve over sin and not have joy in it. The Gospel takes us as we are but then teaches us to "go and sin no more." The wrestle is real between sin and the Spirit in our bodies. We won't always get it right. Repentance is not an easy escape; it's a genuine remorse for grieving the Spirit of God. When we understand that Jesus loves us no matter what, our relationship with Him will convict us of wrong in our lives. His Word and His Spirit in us will challenge every decision that is contrary to Christ. The nearer we get to Christ, the more sin we will see in our hearts. The closer we are to Christ, the more sin kicks against the Spirit in us. Repentance is our assurance of making it to the end. The further from Christ that we are, the more self-righteous we become. The further from Christ we get, the less the light shines on our nature. When we make a decision to draw near to the Lord, we need to not be surprised what will surface from our hearts. Our own hearts will condemn us. We are our own worst enemies. Overcoming our own self-strength is only accomplished by total surrender to the Lord and being quick to repent. God, keep us repentant. God, keep us grieving over sin. Thank Jesus that He not only takes us as we are but that He makes us new creations. Old things pass away. Are our old things passing away or are they alive and well?

Old things pass away as Christ becomes the focus more than the things that need to be changed. When change is the focus, we will never change. When Christ is our focus, change happens organically. Our only boast will be in what the Lord has done because we will be so aware that by ourselves, we are the Chief of sinners. Paul was not ashamed of reminding himself who he was and who he is. He was not sinless and neither are we. We will always need Christ. We will always be calling on Him. There will never be a day where we made it through by ourselves. The believer's life is a life of dependency on God. Anyone that says we can make it on our own is in for a rude awakening. Jesus, I need you.

Note

127

*"For ye were sometimes darkness, but now are ye light in the
Lord: walk as children of light" (Ephesians 5:8, KJV)*

We are emotional beings. We have five senses. God gave them to us. The presence of God is not theory. We can feel the weight of God's presence. We can feel His peace. We sense His conviction. God is not afar off. He is nearer to us than we know; in fact, He is in us, and we can encounter Him. Blessed are those that have not had an encounter yet believe. Blessed are those that have never felt Him yet believe. God's Word must be enough even though He does manifest His presence. If we draw near to Him, He will draw near to us. We need Him to draw near in our generation. When we get desperate for His presence, He never fails to show up. God's Word is our plumb line. Our emotions can get the best of us. The Word of God keeps our emotions in check. As we grow in His Word, we can discern His presence in a greater way. An evangelist wants people to encounter God's presence. People are not won to Christ by an argument but by the anointing of God's Spirit. We need power summoned through prayer for God to use us in a mighty way. He lives. May all know that He lives in us just as He lives through us. Once we are born again and we have seen old things pass away, then all things become new. We are assured that He lives. The Spirit bears witness within us. Jesus Christ can be experienced. The born-again life is real. This is not a theory. This is not a theology. This is a supernatural power. The is an experience that cannot be denied. The Word of God is enough. We don't need to seek His presence. When we seek His Word, His presence will become a reality. God will never contradict His Word. Let's burn for Christ. Let's get fervent in our prayers. Let's worship relentlessly. God wants all or nothing. As we give God our senses, He gives us discernment and power to express the fruit of His Spirit. He never leaves us nor does He forsake us. Let's not be ashamed of our passion for Jesus. Let's get more undignified than this. Set us on fire God. Use us to light up the darkness. We don't want to contain it. God all this is for you. Show up in a supernatural way everywhere we go.

Note

128

"And whatsoever ye shall ask in my name, that will I do, that the Father may be glorified in the Son. If ye shall ask any thing in my name, I will do it" (John 14:13–14, KJV)

There is power in the names of Jesus. When we say "Jesus" from the heart, demons tremble. All authority in heaven and on earth is in the name of Jesus. Praying in Jesus's name gives us access to Him. When we stand on our own name, we stand in our own shame. The authority for salvation, miracles, and healing is in Jesus's name. There is no other name that can give us access to the throne of God. There is no other name that is packed with as much power. Satan has cheapened the name by making it a filler word like any other cuss words. What he has actually done is highlighted the deity of Jesus. No one uses other false gods' names in vain. There is so much evidence that the name of Jesus is sacred and that His name is powerful. As believers, we have power in the name of Jesus to put the devil on the run. Never pray without saying "in Jesus's name." Prayers are unheard if they are not "in Jesus's name." Only Jesus gives us access to the throne of God. None could stand on their own. Only the perfect have access to the holiness of God. Jesus makes us perfect because He took our imperfection on the cross. Praying in Jesus's name testifies to God and to ourselves that we are unworthy to come to God on our own authority. A church that does not pray is a church that tells God that they don't need Him. A believer that prays without using Jesus's name is a believer that has been lied to by being told that we can have access to God without Jesus. We never graduate as disciples from needing to call on the name of Jesus. When we leave our first love, we get distracted and forget what salvation was all about, a relationship with Jesus. Many today have left their first love. We are fascinated by singing songs, we live in "communes" Sunday mornings, we consume, but God is calling us to contribute. How do we contribute? God does not need money. God wants willing believers that are passionate to make Jesus known. We contribute when we fulfill the great commission. The only way to fulfill the great commission is to preach Jesus, in Jesus's name. It's time to preach Jesus. His message must be heard. Jesus never said, "Go and show me to the world." We are imperfect people until we die as believers. We are not to elevate ourselves lest we stumble our followers.

Note

129

*"Thy word is a lamp unto my feet, and a light
unto my path" (Psalm 119:105, KJV)*

With God we don't know what is next. The journey He takes us on, no one could plan it. It's wise to plan but the Lord orders our steps. We live so pressured from day to day that we take no thought for the moments given to us. Sometimes God slows us down to a grinding halt where He is our only focus. We are never alone on our journey. There will be mountain tops and low valleys. We will face every season. Life favors no one. Just when we think we are on top of it, we are reminded again of our humanity. It's when bad reports come in and we feel totally surrounded by our enemies, the only way left to look for hope is up. Our horizon can fuel our evil foreboding. We just assume the worst. Our mind spirals into the worst-case scenario when we get wind of a bad report. We are to set our minds on things above as believers. "To set our minds" means to make a conscious decision. No matter what our horizon may look like, look up. God will never fail us no matter the season. He did not bring us this far to let us fail now. God completes the work He began. He still heals, the wind and the waves still obey Him, He still turns all things for good to those that love Him. God is faithful to His Word. He is our only anchor when we are thousands of miles out at sea on our journey. We are all on a journey individually. Our relationship with the Lord is always personal. There are no mediators. The only one we will have to give account for is ourselves. We can't get anyone to heaven. Only Jesus can get us to heaven. We came into the world as our own person and we will leave as our own person. Wherever we find ourselves on our journey, call on His name. Honor Him in the good times and honor Him in the bad times. It's all about Jesus. The quicker we repent, the quicker we get our minds in Him, the quicker we vent to Jesus, then the more whole we will become. God wants to bring us through every journey as a whole. God wants us whole. This does not mean being perfect but it does mean being unmovable in our faith. God is good. His plans toward us are good. He does not want any to perish. God is love. God is just. We won't understand every season and there will be natural doubts through life as to why we face what we face, but God knows.

Note

130

"This is a faithful saying, and worthy of all acceptation,
that Christ Jesus came into the world to save sinners;
of whom I am chief" (1 Timothy 1:15, KJV)

We do everyone a favor by getting the attention on Christ in us as quickly as we can. There is no denying that He uses us but we are called to be intentional about giving glory to Jesus Christ. God allowed the names of His sons and daughters to be used in the Bible. He was not insecure about their representation of Him, whether it was good or bad, because He will get glory one way or another. The end of all human existence is not the glory of flesh but the glory of God. God is God. He does what He pleases. His calling is irrevocable. We may write someone off but all along God is writing them in. God always confounds the proud. Pride is assuming that we have God figured out. Pride is living independent from God. We can try to hide behind false humility, we can put up spiritual smoke screens but it's of no avail. We have been, and we currently are, but we won't always be the Chief of sinners. There will be a day when our soul will enter our eternal, sinless bodies, and forever we will honor our Lord perfectly; but while we are here, the Spirit and the bride say, "Come, Lord Jesus." Are we anticipating heaven? Are we investing in heaven? Having a nest egg here won't do anything for us in heaven. We could leave our kids everything but if we don't give them Jesus, we will be separated from them for eternity. Anyone that knows us should not know us as religious but by our flaws they will know we need Jesus as much as anyone else. Jesus is unashamed of us. Let's be unashamed of Him. The shame we deserved; He took upon Himself. We are not the Chief of religiosity; we are called to be the Chief of believers. Believers believe against all odds, obstacles, and obstructions. Believers won't always have their five senses condoning them, for most of us our five senses condemn us. This is why we build our belief on scripture and not on our feelers. Our senses will deceive us. This is why we worship Jesus; this is why we get the attention on Jesus. For He alone saves. God will use us but don't look to us, look to Him that works in us. We are not the assurance anyone is looking for, Christ in us is the hope of glory. Our maturity in the faith does not lead to further independence from God but a deeper dependence on Him. God, we need you.

Note

131

"For the which cause I also suffer these things: nevertheless I am not ashamed: for I know whom I have believed, and am persuaded that he is able to keep that which I have committed unto him against that day" (2 Timothy 1:12, KJV)

Still not ashamed. The devil is still a liar. Not much has changed. Jesus stays constant through it all. To be ashamed of Him leads Him to be ashamed of us. Our fervency dwindles and our passion matures but one truth remains the same, Jesus Christ is Lord. We don't have to have changes in life that shift our faith. We can be grounded in the Lord in knowing that we are great sinners but Jesus is a greater savior. I know He lives. The world will debate with logic, reason, and science but I know He lives because He lives in me. There is no doubt in my soul of our Savior's grace. He conquered death to break in on us so we would never be the same forever. We have the heart of God. We have a new heart and a new mind, but our bodies have yet to be made new. Where He is, so are we. Let's get more "undignified" than this. Let's get even more white hot as we mature. Forget the opinions of the world and set fire to our souls with the power of the Gospel. Nothing sets our face like flint but Jesus. When we have encountered Him, there is no turning back. His love is unmatched. His grace is unbeatable and His presence is spiritual. The spirituality is "factuality" for the believer. We march to a different drum. The rhythm of heaven calls us forward. He is the sinew on our dry bones. He is the pulse of our life. May we make Jesus Christ known to the day we pass or He returns. If it was up to us, the lies of the devil and the logic of the world would spiral us down into depression; but God...God is faithful to complete what He began. Don't lose heart. Don't grow weary. Fan into flame. Choose to be passionate, choose to be fervent, choose faith over feeling and our faith will rule our feelings. Don't be led by our feelings but be led by His faith. His Word is a sure foundation. Our words are weaker than water. Paul was not ashamed because he had a revelation of Christ. He was not standing in his own confidence but the confidence that was given to him. We have no confidence of our own. The best we have on our own is confusion and timidity; but God...God gives grace and His grace gives boldness. When we know we are loved boldly, we love boldly.

Note

132

*"Two are better than one; because they have a good reward
for their labour. For if they fall, the one will lift up his fellow:
but woe to him that is alone when he falleth; for he hath
not another to help him up. Again, if two lie together, then
they have heat: but how can one be warm alone? And if one
prevail against him, two shall withstand him; and a threefold
cord is not quickly broken" (Ecclesiastes 4:9–12, KJV)*

Fellowship and community is what we were designed for. We can't do life on our own. God won't replace the church in our lives. The Church loves like no other community could on this planet. The Church is a community of grace and truth. We can do more together. Every animal predator has the same strategy of attack: isolate its prey and then pounce. Don't cave into isolation. Fight past isolation. There are hands outstretched to help. They won't gossip, they don't laugh at your stumbling, they believe in one another, they live to see others raised up, they don't build on others foundation, they live for the betterment of others, they rejoice in being last, they live to decrease so others increase, they are faithful to the end. This may not have been our experience all the time but it's how Jesus is toward us and He lives in us. The more mature we become, the more like Him we will be. Discipleship today produces students but does it produce the characteristics of Christ in us? We can win arguments but are the lost feeling Christ from our words on their skin? The more mature we get, the more of Christ's love will be manifested. Our suit and knowledge are a form of maturity but Christ shining through us is the evidence of maturity. The greatest compliment is not how well we look but how well He looks in us. The fruit of the Spirit must be intentionally sought after. As we radiate His grace and love, all will know we have been with Jesus. Being with Jesus is more than being with a book or singing a song, it's a heartfelt relationship that lets Him in on all of us so we are taken over by love. It's rare to find this kind of community, but when you do, fight for it. Stay in community. We can't make it alone. It's God's will for us to be in community. Fellowship is not showing up after the first song of worship and leaving as the pastor says amen. It's more than a Sunday morning. Fellowship must happen daily. We have so many resources to stay in fellowship with phones, social media, coffee shops, etc. We are just a text away from tangible help; but even better, we are a prayer away from heavenly help. "God, draw us deeper. Mature our faith so that it's not just puffed up knowledge but it's Christ being puffed up in us." Amen.

Note

_____

_____

_____

_____

_____

_____

_____

_____

133

*"Cast me not away from thy presence; and take not
thy holy spirit from me" (Psalm 51:11, KJV)*

"Cast me not away from your presence, take not your Holy Spirit from me." Ananias and Saphira, Herrod Agrippa, Demas, and the Church of Ephesus are sure reminders that we are not to take the grace of God in vain. When God takes away our candlestick, we are left with no light. When even the elect departs, and the falling away happens, where will we be found? Have we grown so calloused that we are not moved emotionally by our lukewarm state? Have we grown desensitized to our own sin? Where is the remorse of sin? Do we love sin more than the holiness of God? When God says enough, and we get turned over to Satan, how will we respond? How do we go that far? God will not always strive with us. The day has come where our fig leaves must come off. The reverence for the Lord is being kindled once again. When God manifests His holiness, he will first run out the money changers, convict of sin and establish His holiness. Jesus did not come to bring liberty to sin but to bring freedom from sin. Jesus takes us as we are, forgives us of all our sins but also empowers us to overcome sin progressively. Sin does not have dominion over us. Christ does. He is Lord. This does not mean we are Christ and will be perfect, but our perfection is in Christ. Jesus called the Churches to repentance. Everyone is called to repentance and is warned multiple times before judgment. No one is destined for hell. He desires none to perish. His foreknowledge knows the end from the beginning, so He knows who will remain faithful through repentance. We don't have that foreknowledge for ourselves or anyone else. Those that repent are stating their need for Jesus. Those that are stiff-necked assume perfection in their flesh and have chosen a wage over an inheritance. Believers don't get "wages." Jesus paid the wage for us, which was death. He cleared our debt and gave us everlasting life. It won't be this way forever. We inherited an abundant eternal life, but while we are here, we will have trouble. This is not a "have it your way gospel," this is a "have it His way Gospel." Most get saved today by a ploy for what they can get out of God but all they get over time is a disappointment. They love this world and desert the call of God on their lives.

Note

_____

_____

_____

_____

_____

_____

_____

_____

_____

134

"I am the vine, ye are the branches: He that abideth in me, and I in him, the same bringeth forth much fruit: for without me ye can do nothing" (John 15:5, KJV)

Only God can do what we cannot do. We can't change ourselves and we can't change others to meet God's standard. We are either received as we are or we are not received at all. When we are not received as we are, we strive to become what we could never be. Living to please people is like attempting to jump and reach space. We can't fulfill one another. We can't be what is expected of us from anyone. The only way we can have peace is in Christ. The refining of Christ in us means we are letting go of what we think of ourselves and we are holding on to what He says of us. When we assume that we can be fulfilled by anyone other than Christ, we will be disappointed. Satan wants our soul. He will tempt us like Jesus was. Jesus was tempted in the area of provision, God's faithfulness, and to worship him other than God. We have the same temptations today coming at us. The enemy will make us believe that God won't provide, that God won't be faithful to His promise, and that worshipping God is to no avail. Jesus responded to his enemy with the Word of God. God will provide in His timing. God's faithfulness does not need to be tested. Worshipping God is what we were made to do. Beware of the lies of our enemies. They sow into us doubt, oppression, and shame. They love to accuse and manipulate. When the spirit of Satan is at work, it's a condemning voice to get you to do anything but the will of God. Resist the devil in Jesus's name. Stand on God's Word. Cast away the demon in Jesus's name. Don't sit and take it over and over again, stand up in Jesus's name. We are not called to cower; cowering is not humility. Being humble does not mean to live like a coward. We are to be bold, to be confident, and to have authority in Jesus's name. The Holy Spirit will baptize us with all these traits so that we don't need to live under the hammer of the accuser. Jesus took our accusers' words and blotted it all out with His blood. Salvation comes through faith in God's Word and not in the words of others. Other people's words mean nothing compared to God's Word. Don't quote men, don't quote preachers, don't quote songs, but instead quote the Word of God, for God's sake. No matter what intelligent catch phrase or buzz word going around, none of it compares to God's Word! Bible = Power.

Note

135

"Even the youths shall faint and be weary, and the young
men shall utterly fall: But they that wait upon the Lord
shall renew their strength; they shall mount up with wings
as eagles; they shall run, and not be weary; and they shall
walk, and not faint" (Isaiah 40:30–31, KJV)

Every day as believers, we fall on our knees physically or spiritually. Everyone's knee bends. We run hard but the second we run in our own might; we are reminded that we are but flesh. We can get bewitched by society, religion, and even our own minds deceive us. We can't make it through a day without repentance, which is an acknowledgment that we still need Jesus. We don't know how many steps peter made before he began to sink, but the sooner he began to sink the louder his cry for Jesus became. Some can go weeks, months and even years by themselves but I can't go a day without Jesus. The thorn in our flesh is real. Our humanity is very evident. The more unmasked we become before Jesus, the greater we see our need for Him. When we are far from Jesus, we seem to be able to live independently from Him; but the nearer we get to His light, the greater the need for Him we gain. As His light shines on all of us, we see that we are flesh. In our flesh there is no good thing. We can smokescreen using religion and makeup but God knows all. God knows all yet loves us the same. As we kneel physically or more importantly surrender spiritually before Him, we find rest. The posture of surrender is where peace floods our soul. Shame, guilt and defeat is washed away from our soul as we kneel in repentance before our God. Pray that we grow in a mind-set of dependency on our God that is not only daily, but hourly or even better every second. We can grow so familiar with time. Familiarity is such a curse. It takes intentionality in our relationship with God to not allow familiarity to set in. Once it does, contempt takes over. Decide for God to take over. Let His power take over. Open the flood gates and let His power flood our soul. Daily choose His will over yours. Jesus prayed His Father's will to be done on earth as it is in heaven. He prayed that way, He taught His disciples to pray that way, and we should pray this way as well. God wants us to ask, seek, and knock but God delights in our surrender before Him. It's our reasonable service to live sacrificially before God that He would have His way in us. Our only peace is in Him. Our only abundant life is in Him. Abundance is not materialism, healing or wealth. Abundance is in Christ.

Note

136

"This is a true saying, if a man desire the office of a bishop, he desireth a good work" (1 Timothy 3:1, KJV)

Anyone that quenches spiritual ambition other than God is on thin ice. When we try to out the passion for God in others, we are being inspired demonically. Peter tried to talk Jesus out of his purpose and Jesus rebuked Satan. We can assume we know best but God will always surprise us. When we scoff at another person's ambition to glorify God, we may seem logical but we are behaving like antichrist. The antichrist spirit wants to quench the believers' faith. Cult leaders love to destroy any spiritual ambition in their congregation so that they have no threats to their position. When the Holy Spirit filled the early church, they were filled with Godly ambition to preach the Gospel everywhere. Ambition in the church must be cultivated and harnessed. Cults quench ambition. Cults cap their congregations' growth. Cult leaders are more interested in raising themselves up rather than raising up their congregation. Personality cults are what a lot of our non-denominational churches have become today. These churches are known for their pastor more than known for their ministries. Beware of dream quenchers. Beware of the cynical spirits that believe in no one else's idea but their own. These types of cult leaders don't partner. They aim to herd as many as they can into a building, to fleece them of every resource they have in the name of God. They use God as a means to get their audiences time, treasure and talent. They are the only ones that gain financially and keep all their staff on minimum wage. God will not be used as a cash cow for charlatans much longer. The church should be full of believers that not only believe for their salvation but for their growth too. God wants us all to grow. Jesus put out of "business" the middle man at the cross. He made the way for all to know Him and for all to do great exploits in His name. Flee from churches that are known for their pastor more than their ministries. Flee from churches that raise a pulpit above the pew. Flee churches where pastors are more respected than the Bible. Flee pastors that demand titles but don't function in their job description. We need to get intelligent as a church. What we feed—grows, what we starve—dies; let's feed faith and not fame.

Note

137

"But I say unto you, That whosoever looketh on a woman to lust after her hath committed adultery with her already in his heart" (Matthew 5:28, KJV)

In the sight of God, the thought of sin and the action of sin receive the same judgment. All have sinned. Every human has broken every law of God. Railing against one particular sin while we are struggling with gluttony or we are covetous is hypocrisy. While we are judging, our own lack of self-control and inability to wait on God is condemning us. One person's sin is not worse than another's in the sight of God. God does not judge as we do. God can work with someone caught in the act of sin, but he can't with someone living in the thought of unrepentant sin. Religiosity is more damning than secularization. For decades, religion kept sin in the closet or hidden in the basements of our hearts. Our society is not getting worse, it's just getting more shameless. God can't work with shame; but the more shameless our generation gets, the more we will experience the physical consequences of our sin which leads us to repentance. Don't fear secularization or the liberalism of our society, it's only preparing the way for a move of God. Once people reach the end of all their sinful lusts, hopelessness sets in and they become primed for the Gospel. Religion dulls the conscience and sears it. Religion stitches up the veil that God tore. Jesus had very little time for the religious. He spent most of His time with sinners. Does the church today mirror the life of Jesus in character and passion? Jesus cared more for people than He did building projects. Jesus cared more for people than He did singing songs. Jesus cared more for people than He did preaching sermons. Why is it not encouraged to be more like Jesus today? We want to be like preachers, teachers, and pastors but what about aspiring to be like Jesus? Friends, there is nothing good in any of us. The only trait worth emulating is the character of Christ. The more of Christ one sees in us the greater our impact will be. The religious are cloaked in suits and ties. At the end of the day, they are as human as anyone else. On this side of eternity, we will never be perfect. This is why getting the attention on Jesus as preachers is the best thing we could do for our congregation. When we attempt to share glory with God, we will be let down by ourselves.

Note

138

"Jesus answered and said unto him, Verily, verily,
I say unto thee, Except a man be born again, he cannot
see the kingdom of God" (John 3:3, KJV)

The Gospel is enough to change a person from the inside out. We are hurting a person by only meeting the exterior needs. When we give Jesus, we are giving dignity and value. Rather than giving someone a hand out, the Gospel gives a hand up. Silver and gold cannot change the heart of a person. The church today is flushed with cash but we need to be flushed with the Spirit of God. If the church was stripped of its financial dependency, we would see God at work in the church again. Depending on music, aesthetics, and marketing is not what grows the church spiritually. This does not mean that we should have obstacles for people to be at church but the power is in the Gospel to add to the church. The Gospel is power. Education, self-help, and resources make no dent on the heart of a person. It's like leading a horse to water but "only the horse has the will to drink." Changing the culture and the will of a person cannot be done from the outside; it's a work of God on the inside. The born-again experience is the least preached doctrine and the least believed truth in the Western Church today. We give out everything but what really matters. "Outreaches" have become the coward's bed to sleep in; they sleep in humanism, they plan through the lens of human-ism, they seek to show Jesus as if they are Jesus. Jesus never said "Go and show me," instead He said "Go and preach." It's the message that has power; not the food we give out, not the show we put on, not the music we sing, not the testimonies we share. The power is in the preaching of the cross. Cowards only preach to people that they know want to hear what they have to say. Cowards tell their congregation to do as they say but not as they do. Cowards love the pulpit more than people. Cowards hide in green rooms. Cowards hide in their offices. Cowards never roll their sleeves up to do the work of an evangelist. When soul winning is not our vision, then our vision is not from God. When the majority of our prayer life is not for laborers in the harvest, then we are praying amiss. We don't need orators today. We don't need clever speeches. We need power. The power is in the Gospel. God is setting a fire in the church cleansing, purifying and awakening us. We are coming back to "why" we are still here.

Note

139

"And this is his commandment, That we should believe on the name of his Son Jesus Christ, and love one another, as he gave us commandment" (1 John 3:23, KJV)

Choose a community of faith. A community of faith is not only a community that believes in God but they believe that God can do anything through each one of us as we yield to Him. It's a community not built on sarcasm and comparison. There are so many that believe in God but when it comes to believing what God can do through others, they are full of unbelief and limitations. When our community is full of limitations and ceilings, we need to flee that community. Our community today can look like two crabs in a bucket. If we only worked together, we would "get out of the buck," but we are too busy pulling each other down. Hypocrites believe God for themselves but don't believe in the same God that lives in others. Even Satan believes in god. When our community leader is insecure of one that outperforms him, they ostracize and call him a maverick. This type of culture is full of laziness and sloppiness. This type of leaders should look for millstones. Leaders that hold back the call of God on those that look up to them should be ashamed of themselves. Our culture of leadership celebrates laziness and sneers at success. They may profess faith in god but their god, the devil is no different than them. Jesus's style of leadership put others ahead of Himself. Today's style leaders only raise themselves up. They vote republican but do church like a monarchy. Is our community full of growth, life, and opportunity or is that growth, life and opportunity only for the "monarch"? Nepotism is a cancer on the church today. Many of our churches are run by families and the rich. Positions are given based on how much money one has or gives. The "monarchs" are obese and cling onto their positions like Saul did his. We have a ton of Ananias and Sapphira's leading today's ministries. They have sold out their conviction for silver and gold. They are willing to do whatever it takes to secure their "thrones." Just as the Jews craved a king versus a judge, today Christians crave a pastor over a personal relationship with God. We give titles to leaders yet call Jesus by His first name. Our leaders expect titles yet they talk about Jesus by His first name. They say "give of time, talent or treasure" with no accountability. They call accountability, rebellion. Truth is not rebellion, it's freedom.

Note

140

"For the wages of sin is death; but the gift of God is eternal life through Jesus Christ our Lord" (Romans 6:23, KJV)

Employees get wages; sons and daughters get an inheritance. We don't "do" to earn, we "do" because we want to. We don't do what we have to; we do what we want to. Believers in Christ will want to do what God has called them to. The law and religion give us "have-to's," but Jesus gives us "want-to's." When we are born again, we receive a new heart and a new mind. This means that we get new desires. Don't let Satan tempt you with "have-to's." Surrender to Christ, and He will give you the "want-to's" to obey Him. Christ's way is not up to us, it's up to Him to work in us both to will and to do of His good pleasure. Faith in Christ makes us supernatural beings. What was once impossible for us is now made possible because He is in us. The only wage we can earn in ourselves is death. We have inherited the power to live differently. The "just" don't just believe the "just" live. We have a new life working in us as we surrender to our inheritance. We have inherited a new bloodline, a new pedigree, a new citizenship, and a new spirit. It's time for us to stand in authority as sons and daughters of God. Christ made this available to whosoever will believe by paying our wage at the cross. Before we can know our purpose, we must first understand who we are. Our purpose does not define us; Christ does. In Him, we live. This is not a "have-to" religion; this is a "get-to" relationship with God. Let's arise from the false definitions of the world and awaken to our inheritance in Christ. Don't let Satan deceive us as mere sinners, slaves, and workers. We are free sons and daughters in Jesus's name. As we surrender to who God says we are, we will want to obey everything His Word tells us to do. Our faith will appeal to everyone that comes in contact with us. They will want our joy, peace, and boldness. Before we say a word, people will want what we have. We have what is greater than anything that could ever compare. There is none like Jesus. Our souls were made for Him. Our thirst for life is quenched in Him. As we let Him live, we simply observe what only He could do in us. Years of brokenness is healed in an instant. What would take years to fix is healed in a moment. Our God works in the immediate. He loves to bring on a "suddenly."

Note

141

"And he said unto me, My grace is sufficient for thee: for my strength is made perfect in weakness. Most gladly therefore will I rather glory in my infirmities, that the power of Christ may rest upon me" (2 Corinthians 12:9, KJV)

God's grace is always sufficient. Many of us compare with the martyrs of old and think to ourselves that there is no way we would make it through what they did. There are some looking at our lives right now and wondering how we are making it. We all have grace on us for what we are facing. We can make it through anything because we are in His grace. The grace of God puts metal in us. It's by grace that we can face each day. We can shout grace to every mountain in our lives. This is the age of grace. Grace is our only assurance of salvation in life. Grace empowers us to do what we could never do on our own. We could never earn the power of God. As we mature as believers, we will grow in a deeper need for grace. The further along in life we get, the more desperate for grace we are. Grace was not cheap; it cost God His Only Begotten Son for us. Grace can be taken in vain if we use grace as grease or as an excuse to do what we want to. God's grace is not for us to do what we want to do but it is there to do what He wants. Grace is a comforting word for all believers. There is always forgiveness for the repentant. Repentance is not an empty apology but a heartfelt cry before God to do what is right. God's grace does not leave us in our brokenness but heals us. His grace is always available, all the way to death's door. It's never too late to call on God and trust His grace. It's by grace that we are saved and not of our works. None can boast because all have sinned. If it were not for the grace of God, we would all be cut off. Rest in His grace, let Him carry us through whatever it is that we are facing. Everyone will wonder why we have peace in the hardest of times, and our declaration will be "the grace of God is sufficient." Jesus won't fail us and He will never leave us. We are never forsaken in Christ. His grace is always sufficient. Let's be open with God. Let's depend on God. Let's pray to be "white hot" for His glory sake. Grace sets us on fire for the Lord. Grace fuels our desire to obey and to lift Christ up in all situations. Grace takes the strife out of our relationship with God. We can rest, relax, breathe, and watch God do what only He can do. Worry changes nothing. His grace changes everything together for good.

Note

142

"Ye are the salt of the earth: but if the salt have lost his savour, wherewith shall it be salted? it is thenceforth good for nothing, but to be cast out, and to be trodden under foot of men" (Matthew 5:13, KJV)

Don't live lukewarm. Live ice cold or white hot. God wants all or nothing. God wants all our heart, mind, and soul. We are either all in or all out. Living lukewarm is so miserable. Many live this way and never really live. Religion breeds Luke warmness. Religion teaches, "Warm the pew and don't grow beyond it." Religion quenches the desire to lead, for fear of rebellion. Religion esteem resumes and caps spiritual growth to just below where the leadership is at. We can only take people as far as we have gone ourselves. Religion judges, religion packages the Holy Spirit and tells God how He is going to build His church. Religion is an organization that teaches a form of godliness but lacks power. It's like planting a seed in a mechanical structure. It won't grow. Mechanics cannot give life. Jesus did not give us a blueprint to a religion. He did not give us an order of service or a set list of songs to sing. When the Spirit of God is heeded and the Word of God is esteemed more than the leadership, then we will see the church built. Paul exposed Peter's fallibility in Galatians to teach us that every human is fallible. We may have faith but we are always fallible. Only God's Word is infallible. Religion covers up and makes the outside look good. When we are born again, the Spirit of God makes all things become new in us. His life is lived through us. We will always be aware of our humanity to the day we die. There is no escaping our humanity while we are in these bodies. As we walk in open communication with God about our thoughts and sins, the power of God breaks the dominion of sin off us. He can make us new. We will never graduate from a need for Christ, no matter what religious title we hold. The closer to the top one gets, the more we see. Jesus wants us to grow to be at the top. Desire to be a leader. Don't settle. We are all chiefs. Chiefs of sinners. Let's decide to grow in Christ. When Christ is our focus, all the limitations of religion are shattered. Jesus called average, ordinary men to follow Him. His candidates would have failed every church or ministry interview for every position. God calls whom He wills, let Him set you on fire for His glory. Everyone dies but not everyone lives!

Note

143

*"Study to shew thyself approved unto God, a workman
that needeth not to be ashamed, rightly dividing the
word of truth" (2 Timothy 2:15, KJV)*

Hours upon hours are spent in the Word and in prayer before a sermon is birthed. It's the secret behind the boldness. Learning to withdraw is a discipline in itself. We have so many people buying sermons
online, spending time reading books but what we need today is simply scripture exposited. Anyone can read a script. We are overladen
with resources today, but we need to come back to the source. Prayer
and scripture are what is needed to equip one to be a preacher. If we
don't withdraw like Jesus did from the crowd, we will not hear from
our Father. God is jealous for us. He defrocked all mediators between
Him and us when Christ died on the cross. The veil being torn tells
us that we all have access to the source. We have more understanding
than any ancient prophet. We have more understanding than Moses.
All the concealed truths of the Old Testaments have been revealed by
the New Testament. We can know God with a better understanding
because we have a better covenant than that of the law of Moses. The
believer in Christ has access to the throne of God yet we would rather
lean on another man's opinion than go to the source ourselves. There
are seasons when we need to close everyone's book but the Bible.
Having a diet of only scripture is the best spiritual diet we could
ever have. Choose His Word, Choose His presence, listen to Him.
Biographies are helpful, studying revivals encourage us, but God's
Word is the raw material for faith and revival. Jesus taught us that

the only thing worth looking back on is His death, burial and resurrection. Behold, He is doing a new thing. Biographies and history books can create counterfeit expectations and reliance on imitations. We are entering an era when God will call us to Himself and when we leave that time of intimacy with Him, we will walk in the power of God. We will not be a "carbon copy." God will organically do through us what only He can do. Come back to the raw materials of Christianity. Put away all the fads, styles, and personalities. God has more for us than anyone or anything else. When the church decides to seek His will above their own, then the power will start to flow. As long as we are full of agendas and guile, we will see little progress.

Note

_____

_____

_____

_____

_____

_____

_____

_____

144

"And God shall wipe away all tears from their eyes; and there shall be no more death, neither sorrow, nor crying, neither shall there be any more pain: for the former things are passed away" (Revelation 21:4, KJV)

The Gospel is assurance of eternal prosperity, health and wealth. Jesus was famous for His healings and casting out demons. As long as He did what people wanted Him to do, they were happy with Him. Many had expectations on Jesus to rally a Jewish army to conquer the Romans and expand the borders of Israel. They thought the Messiah would reinforce their significance as a race and make everyone convert to Judaism. They read what they wanted to read out of the scriptures. The Jews were offended at Jesus because He was offering salvation to "whosoever will," and taught that salvation was by faith alone. It was no longer by bloodline, rituals or animal sacrifice. He even prophesied the destruction of the temple. When Jesus started talking about troubles, persecution and the cross, many turned away. All they could see was here and now. They could not understand the eternal kingdom that awaits. Judas was so desperate for temporal prosperity, that he sold out eternity for a few pieces of silver. Satan lures us with materialism, fame, prosperity and health. Anything to distract us from what really matters. We are easy to distract. We have heretical ministries today craving the same thing the Jews wanted, temporal prosperity. Rather than desiring to glorify God, they desire for their pleasures to be fulfilled. In this world we will have trouble. It's appointed for us all to die and then we face judgement. Are we living for the glory of God or our own pleasure? If we get saved by being lured into a health and wealth message, we will end up bitter and disappointed. The prosperity Gospel is not a sure foundation while we are here. For eternity we will be healthy and wealthy but while we are here, if we seek to glorify God, we will face trouble. Life is not easy for believers and unbelievers. However, it's easier for believers because we have the assurance of eternal life. We can be in the darkest of situations and have joy. Everlasting life is what made the martyrs of old face such horrid deaths. Our freedoms today cost their blood. Our eternal life cost the blood of Christ. Are we living for the glory of God? The only way to gauge that is by our obedience to the Great Commission. If we don't have a passion to see the lost saved, then we don't have the heart of God.

Note

_____

_____

_____

_____

_____

_____

_____

_____

_____

145

"There is neither Jew nor Greek, there is neither bond nor free, there is neither male nor female: for ye are all one in Christ Jesus" (Galatians 3:28, KJV)

Christ did away with discrimination between Jews and gentiles, men and women, rich and poor, nationalities and races. In Christ we are one. God tore down all the walls of religion. The people He chose, rejected Him, so He made a way for the "whosoever's." Salvation is for all that would believe in Christ. Jesus sat with Samaritans, touched lepers, ate with sinners, walked with tax collectors and healed on the Sabbath day. In the eyes of the chosen, Jesus was a rebel. The Church is His bride and everyone in His bride are one in Christ. No one person has any more access to God than another. Nothing other than faith in Christ can save the soul. There is no bloodline, pedigree, gender or race that can inherit the favor of God. Christ earned it only for those that will believe. Churches that accumulate one demographic or one race or one nationality is anti-Christ. It is antichrist to love conditionally. As we have been loved, we are called to love. As we have been received, we are called to receive. Discipleship is not head knowledge, it's knowing Christ and letting His life be conformed in us. If Christ does not break down discrimination in us, then we are not His disciples. How can we claim Christianity and not strive to be like Christ? Today, some churches would escort Jesus out if He attended. Some scorn the very people that Christ loves yet claim to be Christian. Christianity is a culture and not a theory. Christ affects the whole person and not just the intellect. His character is what we should desire; not the culture of a people group but a Jesus culture. Peter brought discrimination into the church and had to be confronted by Paul. We need "Pauls" today. We are falling back into "Peter's"[7] mind-set, elevating a people group above another. We are not to elevate a race above Christ. We are not to elevate a culture above Christ. There is no discrimination in the sight of God for salvation. All God is looking for is faith. Faith to believe our value in Christ and to count all of our other values as dung in His sight. All other cultures are dung compared to Christ.[8] Christ receives us all as we are but does not leave us the way we are. He conforms us to His image. As we surrender to Him, His culture is formed in us.

Note

_____

_____

_____

_____

_____

_____

_____

_____

_____

[7.] Galatians chapter 2

[8.] This is what Paul valued in Phil 3:8. *"Yea doubtless, and I count all things but loss for the excellency of the knowledge of Christ Jesus my Lord: for whom I have suffered the loss of all things, and do count them but dung, that I may win Christ." (KJV)*

146

"And Jesus said unto him, Verily I say unto thee, Today shalt thou be with me in paradise" (Luke 23:34, KJV)

When someone tells you that they want to die and they have a rope in their backpack, how would you respond? We may think we always have the right thing to say but actions speak a thousand words. Jesus sees the heart. Not once did He lead someone in a robotic sinner's prayer. With the repentant thief on the cross, He said, "Today you will be with me in paradise." There will be many that will make it in that we would never suspect. There will be many turned away too. Evangelism is easy when people feel Christ's love for them through us. When people feel genuine love, they will genuinely respond. Evangelism without heart is a debate. The Gospel is not open for debate. Jesus did not have to debate with anyone. All He wants is our soul. He is not looking for perfection. If we could have earned it, He would not have laid His life down. Bringing our pain into the light is our first step toward victory. Jesus never judges or casts us away. There is nothing He can't heal, fix or forgive. The only way to condemn ourselves is to hide our souls from Him. Satan has set up religions to hide our souls far from God. He has distracted the masses with methods, rituals and works. Religion separates the soul from God. Christ wants us to renounce religion and give Him our soul. Religion is worse than sin. Sin tears down the walls of religion and exposes the need for a savior. Religion callouses the heart. Sin rips the heart to shreds and shows us our deep need for a savior. Rejoice that religion is crumbling down in our society. The sooner it's torn down to the foundation, the better; then God can start saving sinners. God loves sinners and has very little time for the religious. Jesus prophesied the destruction of the temple and it happened soon after His resurrection. Buildings are not God's habitation, Believers are. He that is in us is greater than religion. God lives in us, giving us purpose and value. Don't throw your life away to the devil. Believe in Jesus, give Him your soul or someone else will take it. Satan steals, kills, and destroys. Life is in Jesus. He embraces us as we are but loves us enough to not leave us the way we are. We are His habitation on earth. Let Him love through us.

Note

_____

_____

_____

_____

_____

_____

_____

_____

147

"There shall no man be able to stand before you: for the Lord your God shall lay the fear of you and the dread of you upon all the land that ye shall tread upon, as he hath said unto you" (Deuteronomy 11:25, KJV)

Let no one tell you "no" when God says "yes." There is no other calling that would ever fulfill outside of the call of God. Each of us are on our own journey. Scripture teaches us that there will be mountaintops and valleys low. We never have to feel forsaken no matter what we are going through. As we read scripture, we see God brings good out of every situation. No matter what deviation, mistake, or intentional sin, if we surrender right now to the Lordship of Jesus, He will always get us back on track. Whether He uses a big fish, famine, persecution, burning bush, donkey or writing on the wall, God will speak to us. If we would filter our decisions through scripture, prayer and godly counsel, we would save ourselves a lot of time in confusion. God does not want us to be in a wilderness doing circles but our unbelief keeps us there. Push mute to the opinions all around you, follow the pillar of fire by night and the pillar of smoke by day. His leading is not confusing. He is not the author of confusion. What good father makes His will confusing and difficult to know? God only spoke once through a still small voice yet we have built a doctrine off of it in our church age, not realizing the majority of times God calls there is no question on the "still small voice." If God called us to something, we would not be indecisive about it. With God's calling comes the confidence to complete it. We have the indwelling of the Holy Spirit. He will complete the work

He started in us. All we have to do is say yes. Yes, to His will. Yes, to His call. When we say yes, every qualification, skill, and wisdom necessary is given to us to complete His will. The less abilities we have to complete His call, the better for Him. God loves to show off His glory through the least likely. Look at the disciples of Christ. We can tell from His pick that He does not interview as we would for a leadership position. Where are the leaders that hear from God? Have we grown so calloused to the voice of God that we can't hear Him when He calls our name? I fear that much of our church today is full of Eli's, whose ministries are producing Ichabods.[9] Eli was the high priest of Israel and he would not hear the conviction of God. He would not repent. His stubbornness led to his sons dying, the ark of the covenant being captured, and his daughter-in-law called her baby Ichabod, which means, "The glory of God has departed." We need a reformation. The swamp must be drained before a Samuel Generation can be raised up. It took a whole generation to die before God could take His people into the promised land.

[9.] *"And she named the child Ichabod, saying, The glory is departed from Israel: because the ark of God was taken, and because of her father in law and her husband."* (1 Samuel 4:21, KJV)

148

*"And as it is appointed unto men once to die, but after
this the judgment" (Hebrews 9:27, KJV)*

Everyone dies, but not everyone lives. It is appointed for us once to die and then the judgment. Are we laying up treasure in heaven? If we were, would we be about our Father's business a lot more? If eternity was in our hearts every day, how would we be talking to those around us? If His imminent return was believed, would we be living like we are today? We are more led by our senses today than truth. If we saw someone in physical need, some would feel compassion, but where is the compassion for their spiritual need? We would give to alleviate poverty but what about the souls around us going to hell? Does it not bother us that people without Christ are going to hell? Does someone's physically state matter more than their eternal state? Anyone can write a check to alleviate poverty, but we are more than check-writers. We, too, have a voice; we also have a message. This broken earth will always have poverty, but this earth won't always have the hope of Christ. Ministries in the West have lost their value of the soul. They have bitten the apple of humanism. They can dig wells, educate and make the community self-sustainable, but what about souls? These ministries have a savior complex because they think that by making the community better, the communities' lives will get better. We can see here in the West, that making them like us only comes with its own set of problems. The Gospel is what changes lives. When our discipleship makes people less God-reliant and more self-reliant, then we are not biblically discipling. Dignity is given when Christ is given. He values the soul; He gives them the motivation to alleviate their own poverty. The Born-Again message does not need socialization to help the process. What makes the West successful is the influence of Protestantism, which teaches the priesthood of all believers. Roman Catholicism teaches us to rely on man, Protestantism taught us to rely on Christ in us. We don't need a government, mediator, pastor, or priest to be saved. Believers have the source of all life living in us. When this message is preached and is the primary ingredient of a community, then abundant life is found! Christian majority countries thrive! Travel the world and see for yourself! Let's come back to the raw material.

Note

149

*"For whatsoever things were written aforetime were written
for our learning, that we through patience and comfort of
the scriptures might have hope" (Romans 15:4, KJV)*

Don't wait for the feeling. Decide. Feelings should follow our decisions. We can't let our feelings decide our decisions. Animals live off of their senses. We are not animals. We did not evolve from mammals. We are made in the image of God. We have souls, and no other creature does. We live forever. People that follow their feelings get lured into the devil's snare. Faith can trump feelings and cause us to rise from the valley of life. God puts us together and breathes life into us. We have been called to a decision. Follow Jesus or follow our feelings. Everyone is following someone. Few decide to follow Jesus. They have been fooled to believe that what they have is more valuable than what He has. So many have sold out their call for the temporal ease. Check your feelings, check your emotions, only God's Word should be what we anchor to. If we are out of line, decide to get in line. Once the decision is made, we realize that what we are getting with Jesus is better than any pleasure in the world. We can face the most horrid of circumstances yet have overwhelming peace. Follow Christ; let no one be Lord, but Jesus. No one defines you as Jesus can. No one will love you as Jesus does. No one can lead you as Jesus can. Jesus is better than everyone; He is way better than what we think is best. Leave the valley of decisions, follow Christ. Include Him in your decision making. If you don't, He is not your Lord. There will be many that will say "Lord, Lord," but Jesus knows the truth. Do your feelings always get the best of you? Do your emotions rule your faith? Repent, make Him Lord, and His fruit will grow in you. It won't be immediate, and we will never be perfect, but that is not an excuse to settle. Don't let the devil knock the fight out of you. It's time to fight to believe against all the odds. This is what belief is. It's time to believe beyond what we can see. It's time to grow up. Babies follow feelings. We follow Christ. We "live" by faith and not just "think" by faith. Renounce the gnostic doctrine that we only "think" by faith. Faith is a "following Jesus" kind of faith and not a mental ascent faith. Faith works. Submit, resist, and let's smack Satan's smile off his face in Jesus's name. We have decided! Have you?

Note

150

"And this is life eternal, that they might know thee the only true God, and Jesus Christ, whom thou hast sent" (John 17:3, KJV)

There are times to sit, there are times to serve. God can do more in our sitting than He can in our serving. More can be done through one person's prayer than all of the strength of our youth. If we don't cultivate prayer now, there might be a day when "sitting" is not optional. There are many that cannot "serve" as they would want to. Their health or circumstances have disabled them. It's so important for them to know that they still matter. Our value is not in what we do or preach but in our relationship with Jesus. Jesus paid the price so that we can know Him personally. We were designed for life and eternal life to know God.[10] As we grow in prayer, hours become seconds. He calls us away to Himself. Prayer is experiential. Once we engage in Jesus's name, we are right before the throne of grace, and we are encouraged to go boldly. Prayer has caused the universe to stand still; prayer shut the lions' mouths; prayer fed the five thousand people. After three years of discipling the apostles, they still did not value prayer. They could not pray for an hour without falling asleep. We spend a lot of our time evaluating our discipleship programs, good thing Jesus did not live off of our evaluations, would we have approved of the way Jesus did His ministry? We are so concerned about creating disciples that we have forgotten to whom those disci-

---

10. *"And this is life eternal, that they might know thee the only true God, and Jesus Christ, whom thou hast sent." (John 17:3, KJV)*

ples belong. In Acts, the apostles dedicated themselves to prayer and the Word of God. When prayer is cheapened, people will perish. As we get caught up in prayer, we will see results. When we make our prayers about others, we will not pray amiss. Intercession is when we begin to pray for others. Paul requested prayer; Jesus prayed, so why don't you? Jesus set aside an hour to pray. Do you set aside time to pray? The "prayer life only" teaching is an excuse. That mind-set only gives God a scrap of your time. Jesus had both; so should you. When was the last time you spent an hour in prayer? That will tell you how dependent you are on God. It's amazing how much church we can do without God. Jesus never said, "my house will be a house of songs, preaching, and entertainment," He said, "It will be a house of prayer." What is God's house? Believers are! We house Christ in us. What you should be desiring is a relationship with Jesus; without it, you will remain empty.

Note

_____

_____

_____

_____

_____

_____

_____

_____

151

"For the preaching of the cross is to them that perish
foolishness; but unto us which are saved it is the
power of God" (1 Corinthians 1:19, KJV)

Ministry should model the character and vision of Jesus, but today very few resemble Him. They talk about Him, they use His Word, but they are so far from His heart, it's frightening. Evangelism is not on their agenda. If they were asked when the last time was, they intentionally evangelized, they would squirm. They are more interested in being "Jesus" than preaching Jesus. Some frown at the preaching of the Gospel. They have held to a heretical slogan, "preach the gospel and use words when necessary." They feel like their life is the gospel. Their help is the gospel. Their money is the gospel. Their aid is the gospel. They neglect that the Gospel is a message. Their founders thrived because of their passion for the Gospel to be preached. This generation is more interested in being the messiah to the poor than preaching the messiah to the poor. If our ministry is lacking the preaching of the Gospel, then it's just a weak humanistic club. Humanists believe the end of all human existence is the prosperity of man. Their gospel is human-centered. If ministries were for the glory of God, they would be spending a lot more of their budget preaching the Gospel than on conferences for people that just want to be pampered. The pampering and laziness of the western church is shameful. They are squandering money on wasted projects, websites, buildings, staff, so little gets done. One wonders how they sleep at night. Have they seared their conscience? The world works harder than these ministries today. The world values a paycheck more than the ministries value their Lord's heart. Ministries and government agencies have a lot in common. One works unto the "lord" and takes advantage of the weak, and the other takes advantage of the taxpayer. It's time for donors to become shrewder with their giving. Taxes must be paid but why are we giving to ministries that are ashamed of the Gospel? Ministry leaders have felt untouchable and have used scripture to beat the people down from holding them accountable. Reformation is coming. The day of judgment for religion is at hand. The religious budgets will be dried up, the "tares" will be exposed, and the "Ananias and Sapphiras" will be carried out. Hophni and Phineas have been warned. There will be more to come.

Note

_____

_____

_____

_____

_____

_____

_____

_____

152

"Be still, and know that I am God: I will be exalted among the heathen, I will be exalted in the earth" (Psalm 46:10, KJV)

Stop, stay still, pause, stand firm, wait, don't rush. Timing is important to God. What God could have done in an instant, He did in six days and rested on the seventh. Did God need to rest? Does God need anything? After all, He is God and self-existent. He rested to teach us the importance of rest. We are constantly on the go. The best way to slow us down sometimes is for God to send something our way to get us out of the rut and to wake us up to who He is. God does not have any needs. He has desires, but He is completely self-existent. We are in need of rest. When life happens to us, then we realize our need for God quickly. This is not laziness; this is commanded rest. God can do more in our rest than He can in our work. We toil, we pine, we covet, we desire, but in the end, it all doesn't even matter. Poverty perpetuates these motives to live but when we get it all, what is it all anyway? Mere titles, fame, wealth, friends. We came into the world dependent, and we will leave the world dependent. What we live dependent on will determine our eternity. What do you do when God gives a revelation of hell? How does one live each day knowing thousands die per minute without hearing the Gospel? Jesus taught us that the way is narrow, and few find it. The beckoning for people to be saved is arising in the church today. When the Bible is read, we won't enjoy the same pleasures anymore. When the Bible is read, we will crave prayer and souls to be saved. The reason many don't read the Bible is that they don't want their lives to change. "Tell me

I'm going to heaven, but don't tell me to change my dreams." Jesus changes lives but not always for our definition of good. Our definition of good, blessed and abundance is very similar to the disciples of Jesus's definition prior to the Cross. When they saw Him being taken away beaten and bloodied, they went back to their old lives. They were disappointed. Jesus did not turn out to be the messiah they hoped. Their reading of the messiah was self-seeking, self-gratifying and self-indulgent. They wanted a savior that gave them everything they wanted and more. Jesus did not come to give what we want but what we need. We should desire what we need more than what we want. The one thing that is needed is to know Him.

Note

_____

_____

_____

_____

_____

_____

_____

_____

153

"Iron sharpeneth iron; so a man sharpeneth the countenance of his friend" (Proverbs 27:17, KJV)

We need mercy from God. The needs are overwhelming. The brokenness is everywhere. Our streets are filled with demons. Suicide is affecting every home. Sickness, depression, and all other forms of spiritual wickedness is covering the nation. Once we start engaging with our community, we will hear the cries of the people for healing and hope. Our first responders would be the first to let us know what is going on. They have a better understanding than most of our ministry leaders of what is going on. Once we start engaging with the pain of our generation, we will begin to have prayer meetings again. Our cliquish mentality, our discriminatory feelings, and political affiliations have no foothold in believers. As ministers, we must be engaged with our community. What are we if we are not? How would Jesus be doing our job description every day? How would He be doing it? Does it even matter to you what He desires, what He wants, what His purpose for you is? Jesus would be doing what a lot of our first responders do every day. I don't know how anyone can justify not living like Jesus, preaching like Jesus, and yet claiming to be a Jesus follower. Would Jesus look at people the way you do? Would He talk about people the way you do? Does it even matter to you that you are not doing what He has called you to do? Or have the roles been reversed, and you are His lord rather than Him being your Lord? We resent the Lordship of Jesus. This is why we have so many cults that emphasize Mary or make Jesus out to be a prophet, but He is Lord. We need His mercy. The same Jesus that spoke to the seven churches is speaking to the churches of today. If we are not about winning souls to Jesus, then we are not about His will. We need to get out of our comfort and buildings and cliques. It's time to engage with our community. It may not be appealing to the flesh, but it's the will of God; and if you don't desire His will are you even saved? How can you have Jesus but not care as Jesus did for the lost to be saved? These are hard questions, but how would you know if you were never asked the challenging questions? We don't get better by staring at each other; we get better when we sharpen each other. To sharpen, you need friction. God have mercy, wake us up.

Note

154

"And to make all men see what is the fellowship of the mystery, which from the beginning of the world hath been hid in God, who created all things by Jesus Christ" (Ephesians 3:9, KJV)

We will never know the full extent of our faith until we get to heaven. So many have come and gone; they wandered through their journey, but what did they accomplish? Whatever we do in faith will be laid up in heaven for us. Faith is God's economy on earth. Faith is His choice channel for miracles and power to flow through. Jesus healed based on people's faith. Jesus marveled at people's faith. Faith gets the attention of God. When we believe, our faith moves Jesus. If we want God's attention, we are called to believe. Faith is audacious; faith is scandalous; faith levels the ground for all people to gain the attention of God. God is not interested in our legacies, knowledge, or works; He is moved by our faith. Faith in the Word of God alone is the most moving faith in the sight of God. Encouraging spiritual experiences is not what we need to be chasing; those that have not experienced yet believe are even more blessed. The Word of God is our anchor and fuel for our faith. Renounce all other sources for our faith, such as experiences, so that our souls' anchor is only the Word of God. Having a spiritual diet of only the Word of God is the purest soul food we could digest. What we believe for will store up as treasure in heaven. Let's choose to live by faith and not by experiences, works, purposes, etc., seeking God for our purpose is what we are encouraged to do today. Why not seek God for who He is? If we would drop our agendas before God and surrender to Him, we would save ourselves a lot of time chasing a secondary purpose. Our primary purpose is to know God; to know God is to know His Word. Out of that focus, our purposes will be in our periphery. Don't be purpose-driven. Be faith-driven. Believe God, know God, seek God and everything else will work itself out. Seeking our purpose has become idolatry today. Any purpose we find our identity in, other than in Christ is idolatry. That purpose is less than the position we already hold as sons and daughters in Christ. Like the prodigal son and the elder brother, they both could not see the value of being in the family. We have many "elder brothers" today in the family and they are not happy. They are seeking identities outside of Christ, but they will never be fulfilled.

Note

_____

_____

_____

_____

_____

_____

_____

_____

155

"Submit yourselves therefore to God. Resist the devil, and he will flee from you" (James 4:7, KJV)

Satan is taking ground by the day but the resistance is rising. A church fully submitted to God. We will take our faith seriously. We are not perfect but we know Christ's perfection covers us. We don't look to man for affirmation. We follow only God's voice. We march to the beat of His drum. We don't fear what people think. We say what needs to be said. We are violent in prayer; prayer is our weapon. We are taking back what was stolen from the church in Jesus's name. Our journey has trained our hands for war and fingers for battle. We are in a spiritual war not with flesh and blood but with spiritual wickedness. We wield His Word as our sword. His Name is our defense. We are serious about Christ and His glory. We are not here to cruise through life to get to heaven. We are intentionally desiring to glorify God. We are not ecumenical, we are not wishy-washy, we are rooted in the Word and fundamental in the teaching of the supremacy of Christ. The Holy Spirit is in us, dare anyone resist Him. We are fully yielding and rising in His might for the name of Jesus sake. His blood was not spilled in vain. By grace we will live for Him and with grace, we will die for Him. We will not take the mark, we will not renounce Christ, we will not stop preaching Jesus. We are going into the darkness to dispel the wickedness. We won't take no for an answer. In Jesus's name all Satanic hoards will flee. The army is rising. Our shields are interlocking and unity is commanding the blessing. God, in Jesus's name advance your will, mission and kingdom in our generation. Use us as you see fit. Set a fire in us and fan it until it's white hot. We despise complacency; mediocrity is our enemy and we detest lukewarmness. We want to be all in, like never before. We live today like it's our last day. Your imminent return is what we are expecting. Give us your armor-clad. Be our rear guard as we go. We won't go unless God goes with us. We don't have what it takes but God does. If God is for us, we pity those that stand in His way. When Christ comes back, it won't be by a virgin as a baby. He is coming with vengeance in His eyes, every knee will bow before Him willingly or unwillingly and declare Him Lord. Vengeance is the Lords. In Jesus's name let this be, I surrender.

Note

156

"All the ways of a man are clean in his own eyes; but the Lord weigheth the spirits" (Proverbs 16:2, KJV)

All lives matter. Jesus does not see the outward appearance; He sees the heart. Our hearts are all the same. He knows us all the way, yet loves us the same. Don't let what people see about you define you. If you live your life based on the opinions of people, you would never get out of bed. People will always gossip, people won't always believe in you, people will not always help you, people thrive off of bad news about you more than good-news. It takes faith every day to believe what God says about you. The freest people are those that listen only to God's voice. The religious voice condemns, the voice of others mocks, the voice of our friend's doubts, but God's voice cuts through all unbelief and establishes confidence. The world marveled at the disciple's boldness. They must have battled with so many insecurities from friends and family for following Jesus. They probably were told a bunch of "I told you so's" when Jesus was taken away. People cannot be trusted with your soul. God can be trusted, just look at the cross if you doubt. God does not gossip. God is not insecure about whom He calls. God's ways are not our ways. God gives Good News and wants to tell us Good News. The Gospel means Good News. The toughest part of the Gospel is believing it. Be challenged to believe the Good News for you. Your life may not be turning out as planned but your eternity will, if you trust God. Satan's ploy is to make this life out as if it's all we have. Atheism and evolution teach that nonsense. This is not our home. We did not evolve. We are created in

His image. We are fearfully and wonderfully made. We matter as a race. God knows us more than anyone. He knows every detail. No one can get closer to us than God can. Only God has been with us through every high and every low. Jesus is the safest person we can talk to about the deepest wounds, the darkest sins and all that we are. Leading people to Jesus by preaching the Gospel is the greatest honor. Letting people know that they were/are never alone, that God does not distinguish between people, that He loves unconditionally is such an honor. The reason evangelism does not happen as much as it could is because believers don't believe as much as they should.

Note

157

*"Therefore if any man be in Christ, he is a new
creature: old things are passed away; behold, all things
are become new" (2 Corinthians 5:17, KJV)*

God loves you as much today as He ever will. The love of God does not grow as we grow "holier." We can't get any holier from the day we first trusted in Christ. The love of God cannot be earned, it's given. "For God so loved that He gave." God gave His love to us unconditionally. To doubt His love is to mock Christ's death. To question God's passion for you is to scoff at His scars and blood. Unbelief is unforgivable. God is not looking for perfection. He is not looking for obedience. How can sinners do anything to earn His love for we have all sinned? Sin is not what we have done but it's who we are from birth. We are born in sin. This is why we must be born again. God's love is not comparable to any human love. Our love is emotional and contractual. His contract of love was sealed with His own Son's blood. Jesus sealed the eternal love of God toward us forever. The love of God takes us as we are. God loves us not for what we have or what we can do but for who we are. We are not just tools, resources, or servants; we are cherished sons and daughters because of our new birth. To be born again is to be brought into God's family; we become co-heirs with Christ for eternity. God is passionate for you. God chose you. Believe that He loves you. Believe that He loves others. If there is anything to hate, hate unbelief. He went to great lengths so that we could believe that He loves us. His love does not grow, He loves us as much today as He will tomorrow. No matter what our sin is, no matter what our lifestyle is, God loves you and will take you as you are but love you enough to not leave you as you are. God will straighten what needs to be straight, He will bring health, right desires and discipline to our lives. It's Christ in us that produces this life. We can't do it on our own but as we believe in the love of Jesus and when we confess Him as Lord, He changes everything about us for the better. No one walked away from Jesus worse off. No one came to Jesus sick and walked away sicker. Jesus betters our lives, betters our perspective, and betters our reason to live. God's way leads to eternal prosperity, health and blessing. Every Country influenced by the Bible is blessed because the love of God radiates from His church.

Note

_____

_____

_____

_____

_____

_____

_____

_____

158

"He hath made every thing beautiful in his time: also he hath set the world in their heart, so that no man can find out the work that God maketh from the beginning to the end" (Ecclesiastes 3:11, KJV)

How do we get the heart of God? How do we desire His desires over our own? Prayer. Not mantras, but honest communication. Hold nothing back from God. Be blatantly honest. Be bold before His throne. Walk in the light before Him. This type of prayer defines repentance. Repentance is letting God in on all of us. Once God has our thought life, He shares His passions with us. Ministry is done from our relationship with God and not for a relationship with Him. Religion organizes a relationship that's supposed to be an organism. God will not be formalized or understood by us. We will need faith until we die. Jesus made this relationship possible. Let no one bewitch you into thinking that we can earn a relationship with God by what we do. What we do spills out of who we know. Jesus wants to give us living water. It's water that quenches our soul's thirst. No religion or relationship can make us who we were designed to be but Jesus. Eternity has been set in all our hearts.[11] Only Jesus can fill that void. We know His heart by knowing Him in relationship. Write your prayers out, speak them out, think them out, get them all out before God. Let Him in. Jesus made intimacy with God possible for whosoever will. He is no respecter of people. Don't ask for our desires to be met, ask for His desires. Most of us have had our fleshly desires

---

[11.] *Ecclesiastes 3:11*

and it got us in a mess. Only God's way is the best; it may be the hardest but it's the most rewarding. Jesus is the way. Knowing Him in truth leads to us knowing His life for us. He is the way, truth and life. We can't get to the Father without Him. He made this relationship possible. Know Him, seek Him, hear from Him, get His agenda. Don't push yours. Hezekiah did that, he got what he wanted but look at the consequences. We don't want what we want. Ask anyone that has had it. Don't live perpetually in want. Be fulfilled in Christ. Let Him be our source of contentment; after all, what could God give us outside of His only Son that could add to the joy we have in Christ? Is Christ's sacrifice enough for you or have you grown familiar with His blood? Do you trample on His blood every day, living like Christ is not enough, pining for our own desires to be met?

Note

159

"Is any among you afflicted? let him pray. Is any merry? let him sing psalms. Is any sick among you? let him call for the elders of the church; and let them pray over him, anointing him with oil in the name of the Lord: And the prayer of faith shall save the sick, and the Lord shall raise him up; and if he have committed sins, they shall be forgiven him" (James 5:13–15, KJV)

Offering to pray with someone is the easiest way to open the door to evangelize. Once someone knows you genuinely care about them by praying for them, their walls come down. When people know you care for them, they will care to listen to what you have to say. Simply offer to pray. Pray for the sick. Pray for their broken. Jesus healed many that never made Him Lord. Miracles are signs to the unbelievers; they are not for the believers' entertainment. All the gifts of the Holy Spirit are not for the believers' entertainment or indulgence. The gifts and the power are to make us an effective witness of Christ to the lost. The Holy Spirit was not given for our own euphoria but so we can exalt Jesus in power and demonstration. The authentic gifts of the Spirit will be manifested in the believers that have the "fruit" of the Spirit. The gifts of the Spirit can be mimicked by sorcery. The fruit of the Spirit cannot be. We can test the spirits by the "fruit" of the Spirit in the believer that walks in the "gifts" of the Spirit. The fruit of the Spirit will have a longer impression on someone's life than any show of miracles. The Holy Spirit gives self-control and a sound mind. Flee assemblies where the gifts of the Spirit are emphasized more than the fruits. The Holy Spirit is not the ringmaster for your circus. He is to be revered. He is a consuming fire. He is in us to convict us of sin, righteousness and the judgement. This is what we need to be listening for. The content of the message is more important than the goosebumps we feel. Don't be led by what you feel or see. If you are, you are open prey to deception. The antichrist will appear as an angel of light but he really is a wolf in sheep's clothing. Wolves see sheep as food. We have a lot of wolves using sheep today for their own gain. They don't care for the sheep; they care for the delicacies of the food in the green room. The people are mere sheep. "Somehow, they believe that they are higher than the sheep." As if they have graduated from being a sheep in the sight of God. Only Jesus is the good shepherd. Every believer is just a sheep compared to Him. Let's live for the benefit of others and watch the Power of the Holy Spirit be fanned to flame.

Note

160

*"Let no man despise thy youth; but be thou an example
of the believers, in word, in conversation, in charity, in
spirit, in faith, in purity" (1 Timothy 4:12, KJV)*

It's not over. It's not too late. We are not too young. We are not too
old. We have not sinned too much. We have not gone too far. We
are not too poor. We are not too sick. "Too" is a smack in the face
of faith. "Too" limits what God wants to do. Christ came to tear the
limitations in two, that we or society have placed upon us. He tore
up the writings against us. What we thought disadvantaged us, He
can turn it into an advantage. With God, impossibilities for us are
possible for Him. Dream and believe, don't let facts nullify what God
can do in us. Christ takes all our inadequacies and makes us adequate
for His will. Fight past people's thoughts about us, fight past our own
opinions about ourselves, fight to believe what God says. Scripture
teaches us that Christ picks us up in our brokenness and multiplies
life through us to glorify His name. We believe that He takes us as we
are and produces through us; He will confound those that have written us off. He puts our pieces together perfectly without one blemish.
No matter how disadvantaged we may feel, don't let it determine
faith; in fact, let it fuel faith. Scripture was given to teach us that faith
is greater than fact. Don't grow weary; the pain was not in vain. He
turns all things together for good. Remember His death, remember
His resurrection; if God can bring life out of death, He can bring a
lot out of our little, He can bring beauty out of our ashes. Offer to
Him what we have. Don't be ashamed. Christ took our shame. Come

like a child with faith, offer what we have, let Him take it, and watch what He can do. Lay down heavy burdens, lay down comparisons, lay down doubts, and believe that God will make Christ's death and resurrection count in us. Don't hold onto the "too," hold on to faith in "Christ in us." We know Christ lives because He lives in us. Who else could have brought us this far? Who else keeps us going from day to day? It's Christ in us turning all our "thought disadvantages" into "real advantages" for His glory. God will get glory out of us one way or another. God will be who He says He is. Fight to believe and watch what He can do. Don't be led by sight, be led by what He said, "I am with you always, even unto the end of the age" Jesus.[12]

Note

_____

_____

_____

_____

_____

_____

_____

_____

_____

_____

_____

---

12. *"And Jesus came and spake unto them, saying, All power is given unto me in heaven and in earth. Go ye therefore, and teach all nations, baptizing them in the name of the Father, and of the Son, and of the Holy Ghost: Teaching them to observe all things whatsoever I have commanded you: and, lo, I am with you always, even unto the end of the world. Amen." (Matthew 28:18–20, KJV)*

161

"Draw nigh to God, and he will draw nigh to you. Cleanse your hands, ye sinners; and purify your hearts, ye double minded" (James 4:8, KJV)

When we are alone, withdrawn from the busyness of life, it's in this place that we find our true identity. It's in times of isolation and stillness where we find out who we are. If we do what we do only in front of people, then what we are doing will have little weight. It's in the lulls that we find our desperate need for God. We live in a generation that lives for highs, experiences and entertainment. In the down times they pine for the next buzz. God wants us to value the wilderness. See the significance of the stillness. Some will be in it for longer spells than others. We see this in scripture. In the mundane, God is working His masterpiece. He has reasons for everything; some of which we will only know in hindsight. Find value, recuperation and identity in the lonely times of life because power is drawn from being with Jesus. Nothing will compare to the time spent with Jesus. No experience is higher than the revelation He gives from scripture. What we do does not give us significance but who we are in Christ does. What we thought was loneliness, isolation and "the wilderness" is actually God getting our attention. Read the Bible, pray, worship. Before God release us, He desires to renew us. Engage with God in all seasons. Out of this place comes His heart for people, out of this place anointing is kindled, this is where we find value. Jesus does not change even though we do. As we age, our need for God gets stronger. Our primary calling is to worship Jesus; all other gifts and purposes will only disappoint. Jesus never disappoints. As we cultivate our love for Jesus, ministry will be an outflow, not the source. With Jesus we can work any job and have joy. When our significance is in Christ, what we do will not define us. Don't seek purpose more than Jesus. Knowing Jesus is our purpose. Being purpose driven is being idol driven. Love Jesus, seek Jesus, and all the purposes He has for us will open. We won't have to elbow our way to where we need to be, we will be invited. Know Jesus, be at peace in Him. Let believing in Him be our identity. Rest in Him and watch Him work, or work for Him and watch Him wait. God will wait until we learn to wait on Him. God will work when we learn to wait.

Note

162

"For where two or three are gathered together in my name, there am I in the midst of them" (Matthew 18:20, KJV)

We can only go so far on our own. Interdependence as believers is what it means to be a part of the body of Christ, which is the church. Our body has many parts, seen and unseen. Naturally, the internal are more important than the external to live. We elevate the external parts of the body of Christ today but Christ honors all parts equally. He sees the body as without blemish. His church is altogether lovely. No matter where you have been positioned in the church or in the body of Christ, God does not value one part above another. The church is not a business, the church is not a hierarchy, the church is not a corporation in the sight of God. God does not see mediators, titles, positions or pulpits. He sees sons and daughters that need Him for their every decision. The church is not a building or an organization. The church is an organism. Believers collectively are the church. God does not live in our buildings. When parts of the human body compete with itself, we get diseases. When one part is working but another is not, then our bodies get sick. When one body part hurts, the whole body feels it. Is this the type of church community you're in? Are you in a church or a corporation? If the body of Christ came together united, we would see the "suddenly" we all desire. It starts with the leadership. Jesus exemplified leadership as He washed His disciple's feet. Great leaders want to "wash feet"; toxic leaders want their own "feet washed." True leaders understand that they exist for the people's success and not their own. Leaders exist for the people;

the people do not exist for the leader. There should be a body of Christ "appreciation month." The church is not about one part of the body, it's about each part being about Christ the head. In the sight of God, every member is equal, loved and cherished. Unity comes when issues are diagnosed and healed. Unity does not come by overlooking what needs to be dealt with. Diagnose the sickness and treat the wound. The diagnosis is tough, but once it's treated, it grows back stronger. We have gone undiagnosed for a long time. The body can only make it so long on its own. The diagnosis is never a condemnation, it's conviction to make us stronger.

Note

163

"Sanctify them through thy truth: thy word
is truth" (John 17:17, KJV)

Truth is offensive but not for the sinner. Biblical truth offends religiosity. The truth that Jesus preached drew sinners but the religious detested it. The truth that Jesus came to bring was a sword toward the religious and salvation for the sinner. If we want truth that offends sinners, condemns sinners, and judges sinners, don't read the teaching of Jesus. Religion does not make someone free; it gives more laws than God gave. The freedom and liberty that Christ won was for sinners. Today's Christianity has more traditions, discipleship rules, and standards than the law of Moses in some cases. It has become a ministry of condemnation breeding hypocrites. Actors and actresses can make it through the ranks of ministry today. Skill sets, education, and qualifications do not entitle the call of God. They can resource the call but they are not the source. The call of God is not a career. Our callings are encounters with God, where He interjects in our trajectory to get us in His direction. Everyone wants to hear the "hard truths." The "hard truth" is while we were yet sinners, Christ died for us. The tough truth is Jesus attracted sinners and repulsed the religious. Our Christianity today looks so different than our Christ. Our forms of religion, forms of ministry, and forms of church have attempted to organize an organism, which only leads to death. Reflections have no power. Our generation does not want a reflection; it wants the radiation of Christ. Once we encounter the resurrected Christ, we will go and sin no more. We will have Him living in us rather than attempting to be Him. The "What would Jesus do?" bracelet may as well say, "What would the law tell us do?" Sinners can't do what Jesus did, if we could, He would never have had to die. Jesus died because we could not save ourselves. When He reigns in us, we will desire His culture and His ways. The change Christ brings interior but leads to the exterior. All that religion can do is change the exterior, but Jesus came to deal with the source of our sin and that is within us internally. Jesus empowers repentance; however, religion despises repentance because its system is built on a "graduation" from a need for God. Jesus did not come to tempt us like Satan did, to make us "like god." Jesus calls us to a life of repentance, a life of dependency. Discipleship is dependency on God.

Note

164

"And whosoever liveth and believeth in me shall never die. Believest thou this?" (John 11:26, KJV)

Getting to the top is not what it makes itself out to be. We can get everything but still have nothing. So many are living for everything. They never get enough, so they pine for anything. They are never full. This lifestyle is causing many to crash. Living for everything will leave us with nothing in the end. Things won't satisfy. Things disappoint. Things corrode, rust, and age. Why live for everything when those that have gone before us could not bring anything with them? Nothing leaves with us. All our fame stays here, all our wealth stays here, none of it carries over to what's next. We focus on what's the next thing but what about the next life? What about the afterlife? Our generation is numb to eternity. The least read words of Jesus are "What happens to those that live for everything, die with nothing and spend eternity the way they deserve?" Jesus spent more time talking about eternity than He did talking about our purpose. We spend more time living for our purpose and neglecting what life here is all about. So many sell out their eternity for their dreams to be met here. They would rather have it easy here, but in the end, it does not work out eternally. Earthly dreams, earthly purposes, earthly fulfillment costs eternity. Godly dreams, godly purposes and godly fulfillment is all that is worth living for. It may not get nobility here. Look what treatment Jesus got. There is no gain without pain. Everything good takes sacrifice. "Sacrificing" for Christ is like giving up a bicycle but gaining the ability to fly. Time here is like a grain of sand, compared to eternity. Do we want life here, or do we want everlasting life? Most want both but few get both. For most of us to have one means we have to sell out the other. Don't live for everything, live for everlasting life. Christ gave His life so that we can have Him live in us; with whom we never die. We live forever. Death for the believer is an open door to heaven. Death is only death for the unbeliever. Believers don't die, we pass into eternity. To be absent from the body is to be present with the Lord. For the short time we are here, let's preach the Gospel. Souls are all that we can bring with us to heaven or hell.

Note

---

165

*"Yea doubtless, and I count all things but loss for the excellency
of the knowledge of Christ Jesus my Lord: for whom
I have suffered the loss of all things, and do count them but
dung, that I may win Christ" (Philippians 3:8, KJV)*

God defines us. No one else should. When we define ourselves based on our own understanding, it will be measured by our status, wealth and education. When all of these slip out of our grip, what do we reach for to find our identity? What defines us? We are all seeking to build a definition of ourselves. God has a better definition than our resumé, no matter how good it is. The world values credentials, doctorates, and accomplishments but none of it gets a standing ovation in heaven. All God is looking for is repentance. Without faith, it is impossible to please God. God is not interested in our accomplishments; He is interested in how we are honoring His Son. If we lift up our accomplishments, our gender, our lifestyle, our obedience above Christ, we are going to be disappointed. Glorifying Christ with all our heart and bending our knees to declare Him Lord is where life is found. Every other way leads to disappointment, devastation and death. When our focus is lifted from ourselves, from our situation and from what others think, then we will have peace. To be a believer is to lay down OUR rights, desires and dreams to gain Christ's rights, desires and dreams. We are not our own, we belong to Him. We all belong to someone or somebody. Only Jesus knocks, everyone else intrudes. While we are here, we have the option to choose. Once our pulse stops, the choice is gone forever. "Choose you this day whom you will serve."[13] You have to serve someone and you can't have two masters. God does not change. He remains the same. Anchoring to Him will promise to us that we can weather any storm. No one else is designed to be the anchor for our soul. Others may appear that way, but no one is a sure foundation like Christ. If we are feeling like we are sinking, if the cracks are on the walls, it's not too late. The outstretched[14] arm of Jesus is outstretched to whosoever will. Anyone that comes to Him, He will by no means cast away. God wants us. He cares for us. When all we get is the backs of people, know that today we have the face of Christ looking at us. His eyes are upon us. We matter. Don't heed the opinions of people, heed the Word of God. His word defines us. It is written *Christ will never leave us nor forsake us."[15]*

---

13. *"And if it seem evil unto you to serve the Lord, choose you this day whom ye will serve; whether the gods which your fathers served that were on the other side of the flood, or the gods of the Amorites, in whose land ye dwell: but as for me and my house, we will serve the Lord." (Joshua 24:15, KJV)*

14. *"With a strong hand, and with a stretched out arm: for his mercy endureth for ever." (Psalm 136:12, KJV)*

15. *"And the Lord said unto Moses, Behold, thou shalt sleep with thy fathers; and this people will rise up, and go a whoring after the gods of the strangers of the land, whither they go to be among them, and will forsake me, and break my covenant which I have made with them." (Deuteronomy 31:16, KJV)*

166

"And ye shall know the truth, and the truth shall make you free" (John 8:32, KJV)

Our senses must not lead us. God designed us with our five senses. They should not be denied. We are emotional beings. Our feelings and emotions must be held accountable to scripture; otherwise our feelings and emotions will lead us astray. Balancing our emotions with truth takes time. The closer the gap between our emotions and scripture, the more well-rounded we will be. Emotionalism is when our emotions are held to a higher esteem than scripture. The biblical Holy Spirit will give us self-control and a sound mind. Any spirit that does not is not the Spirit of Christ. Any manifestation that cannot be verified with scripture is emotionalism and is a step toward falling away. Emotionalism, signs, wonders, etc., cannot keep a person. The same people that saw Jesus in action was the same crowd wanting Him crucified. Jesus emphasized the authority of scripture. If the scripture is not enough for our faith to be edified, then we are on the brink of deception. There is no other authority outside of scripture for us to live by. Our emotions can start cults. Our emotions can lead us astray. Truth is what sets us free, not emotionalism. Flee wanting to feel the presence of God and run into His presence by faith. Run into His courts with praise. Goosebumps are not the gauge of the presence of God. The gauge for God's presence is faith in His Word. He never leaves us. If you don't feel His presence and you don't get goosebumps during church anymore, welcome to maturity. Maturity is graduating from "milky emotionalism" to a "meaty" faith walk in His Word. Anointing has little to do with passion, fervency, or emotionalism. Anointing is when the truth of scripture is preached rightly. God anoints His Word. The preacher is replaceable. God's word is true to the end. This does not negate the presence of God. We can feel His presence. We can experience His Word. We can get revelation from scripture. The Holy Spirit does fill us. We can walk in the power of God and do what we could never do on our own. Jesus promised us the comforter. No one comforts us like the Spirit. Nothing can get a handle on our emotions like the word of God. Emotions are subject to Scripture. Scripture alone, "Sola scripture."

Note

167

"Therefore hearken not ye to your prophets, nor to your diviners, nor to your dreamers, nor to your enchanters, nor to your sorcerers, which speak unto you, saying, Ye shall not serve the king of Babylon" (Jeremiah 27:9, KJV)

The prophetic words being given by some are mostly pathetic. A prophet is not a fortune teller, tarot card reader, or a mediator. If God wants to talk to someone, the Bible is the source. Anything He says through someone else will not be new to you, it will be a confirmation and a rightly divided word from scripture. The fads that are sweeping through the church are mostly weightless. There is no power in their words. We all want to hear "a Word" for us, but the Scripture is our only source for that. Humans are manipulators, wanting to swindle something, whether for influence or wealth. Scripture is all we can hear that won't return void. No one has "a Word," they have the Bible as everyone else does. "The Word from heaven" is scripture and not someone's interpretation. The pulpit is not there to be used as a form of control and manipulation. I remember when I first started feeling the effects of psoriatic arthritis in my feet. It was excruciating. Everyone could see it. The pastor did not approve of a decision that I made for my life, so he had "a Word" for the church "from the Lord," which was taken from King Asa in Chronicles, who was cursed with a foot condition for rebellion against God. Everyone could see for over a week that I was struggling with my feet. As I sat through that message, I knew I was not dealing with a man of God but a man of manipulation. Friends, if we are not grounded in the

Word, we will be prey to those that use the Word for their own gain. I rejoice in the Gospel that is going forward; it's the discipleship I'm concerned about. Discipleship was never to cost just 10 percent of your income. A lot of it is like Saul's armor today. A relationship with Jesus, the Bible, and fellowship that raises the Word of God above the pulpit is discipleship. So-called prophets need to read Jesus's words to the seven churches and get honest with their assumption of themselves. When Jesus gave a prophetic Word to the seven churches, it was full of conviction. "God, have mercy on the gluttons that exercise in little to no self-control but demand a spiritual title." We all will give an account before God. The day of repentance is at hand. This is our opportunity to repent. Repentance is a lifestyle.

Note

_____

_____

_____

_____

_____

_____

_____

_____

_____

168

*"That I may know him, and the power of his resurrection,
and the fellowship of his sufferings, being made
conformable unto his death" (Philippians 3:10, KJV)*

Prayer is not a ritual. Prayer is vital. When we call on God in Jesus's name, immediately we are before Him in His presence. We are seated with Him. If we are not in prayer, we may not be a house of God. We are God's house by faith in Christ. By Christ's death we are made righteous to be the dwelling place of God. His house is not a structure made with bricks. Believers are the temple of God. How prayer is answered is a mystery. If Jesus prayed, we should be praying. The early church prayed for hours. The day for nonchalance is over. The urgency is right before us. We can't go through a day without seeing the despair of our society. Prayer is no longer a choice. Prayer gauges our dependence on God. When we are praying, we are basically walking in relationship with Jesus. We are letting Him in on our thought life and allowing Him to renew our mind. When we include God in our decision making, pain, hurt and anguish, we are doing ourselves a favor. We were not designed to carry the weight of the world. Telling someone other than God, helps; but telling God, opens the opportunity for impossibility to become possible. The effective fervent prayer is what avails much. Fervency in prayer is what is needed today. Our routined, robotic, ritualistic prayers need to be trashed. It's time to put religion aside and get desperate like the persistent widow. It's time to travail again in prayer. Prayer is not a wish. Prayer is a relationship with Jesus. Anyone that sought out

Jesus, got a healing, answer or a result of some magnitude. We have not because we ask not. It's time to ask, seek and knock. Put away the weak Calvinistic approach to prayer. Lay down our intellect and cry out to God. Any teaching that quashes prayer should be revoked. As if we are greater than the early church and have graduated from the need to pray. Our savior taught us to pray. Follow His lead rather than some weak prayerless teacher. Put formalities aside, go in the name of Jesus, and pour out your anguish to God. *Weep, wail, wrestle but be real before God.* Holding back is only hurting us. Christ reconciled us in relationship so that we can know God. When we draw near, He draws near to us. Pray fervently.

Note

169

"O foolish Galatians, who hath bewitched you, that ye should not obey the truth, before whose eyes Jesus Christ hath been evidently set forth, crucified among you?" (Galatians 3:1, KJV)

True fervency for God can't be manufactured. We can't save people; we can only evangelize. We can't disciple without God. We never graduate from a need for God. This is why repentance is a lifestyle and not a one-time confession. If we are truly being discipled, then we would need God more today than we did yesterday. Satan's temptation in the garden was to get Adam to be like god. Satan did not want Adam to need God and Adam was lured by that idea. Some of the gospel presentations today sound a lot like Satan's "gospel." "Jesus" is the "fruit" and we Satan's minions are preaching "come to Jesus and you will be healthy and wealthy," basically they are saying "you won't need God, you can be 'god.'" Jesus did not come to make us gods where we become Christ. We don't get saved and then graduate from a need for God. We grow in a dependency on Him. Some of today's discipleship is "Ten steps to be a Christian without God." Discipleship is much easier than we have made it. The reason it's so weak in a lot of churches today is because discipleship is taught that it's up to us to live this life after we get saved. We get saved by faith but we live by works, which is wrong. The Bible is clear, we live by faith. We are not just saved by faith but we grow in faith. The older we get, the more fragile life gets. If we attempt to grow in holiness, we will be on a roller coaster journey; as long as we are in these bodies, we will wrestle with sin. If we grow in faith, then our relationship with God becomes consistent. We don't need to have highs and lows in our relationship with God. He is the only unchanging one. God stays the same. He is truly our most intimate relationship. There is no one that knows us like Him. Just like we can't save people, we can't disciple people if God is not our life source. Discipleship is dependency on God. After three years of discipleship, the disciples still failed. Was that Jesus's fault? Was He a bad disciple maker? No, they just did not get the "Spirit dependence." They did not understand until Pentecost that this life is not to be lived by our own might. Discipleship is not only an education; it's depending on God to be faithful to complete the work that He started. "Spirit dependence" makes us truly fervent.

Note

170

"The Spirit of the Lord is upon me, because he hath anointed me to preach the gospel to the poor; he hath sent me to heal the brokenhearted, to preach deliverance to the captives, and recovering of sight to the blind, to set at liberty them that are bruised, To preach the acceptable year of the Lord" (Luke 4:18–19, KJV)

Jesus of Nazareth was the Messiah that the Jews were waiting on. Some are still waiting for the Christ, but the evidence of Jesus being the Messiah is all over. How could a man, born in a small town in Israel, be so famous? His fame did not come by military power nor political persuasion, His fame came by His Resurrection. His own disciples, if it were not for His resurrection would have went on with their lives. The Bible is clear: His closest abandoned Him. They missed what they were waiting for their whole lives. Many still miss it to this day. Jesus Christ of Scripture is the Messiah, Savior and the soon coming King. We are in the age of grace but that age is coming to an end. While we are in this age of grace, the Spirit of God is convicting the world of sin, righteousness and judgement. Our hearts can get so hard, that we escort Salvation right out of our lives. Many agree that Jesus was a prophet and a good man, but that does not save the soul. Jesus was God in flesh, He is Lord of all. Jesus read out His mission in Luke chapter 4, and the same Spirit that was upon Him is upon the church to do the same mission. The Spirit of God anoints the Gospel to be preached to the poor. Church outreaches that do not preach the Gospel, deceive those that they want to reach that salvation is in the services they off rather than in the person of Christ. Jesus preached everywhere He went. He educated about His Kingdom and preached that His Kingdom is at hand. Jesus will reign on earth for thousands of years. During that reign, we will have plenty of time to vacation, sight see and enjoy creation. While we are in this age of grace, we need to surrender to the Holy Spirit's mission. Preaching is His choice expression on the earth. A willing vessel, a living sacrifice, a yielded believer is whom He chooses to use. He is the treasure in our earthen vessels. In our flesh, we can only do what Moses did prior to His encounter with God. Moses's own good intentions only accomplished the murder of a slave driver and he could only set free one Hebrew slave. We can't do the will of God on our own. It was never for us to do. His will is accomplished by the power of the Holy Spirit. We have built many golden calves today and have called it places of worship. Jesus is not our cash cow. He wants to be our Lord; when He is, what we do will be by His might, His strength and for His glory.

Note

171

"Come unto me, all ye that labour and are heavy laden, and I will give you rest. Take my yoke upon you, and learn of me; for I am meek and lowly in heart: and ye shall find rest unto your souls. For my yoke is easy, and my burden is light" (Matthew 11:28–30, KJV)

Are you weary and heavy laden? Jesus said to come to Him with no shame if you are heavy laden. Go to God in the realest emotional state we are in. Don't go as someone we think that He wants us to be, go as we are. Jesus did not work well with people that hid behind religion, hid behind their emotions or were full of pretense. There is nothing we could talk to Him about that would embarrass Him or surprise Him. God knows everything, yet loves us. He is not sarcastic. God will not shame anyone. While we are all doubters, sinners, and worriers, God wants us in the light before Him so we can have real fellowship with Him. God listens like no one else. When God speaks from scripture, it sets us free like no one else could. God is free; He requires no charge. Christ paid the bill for us. What Christ accomplished in reconciling us to the Father is more favor beyond that of any other creature has received. God loves us. The proof is in the cross. Don't let the enemy make you lose sight of the cross. He will try to question "does God really love you, look at what you are going through." Remember Christ's death and resurrection. God demonstrated His love toward us. The cleansing blood of Jesus gives us access to God. We can pour out our soul to the lord and find rest. With God, life becomes easier and the weights become lighter. We are not on our own, for the creator of everything is with us. Christ's sacrifice was for us to be assured that we can go to God as we are. As we walk in transparency before God, with our worry, fear and panic, God has the power to break these attacks off us. Religion stitches up what God tore from top to bottom. Don't put up a veil between you and God. It was torn once and forever. We can go to God with all formalities aside. Anyone that calls on the name of Jesus will have the attention of God. He will by no means cast anyone away. Jesus said, "Come to me." What are we going to do in times of weariness? Only Jesus can carry us through. Let's be careful what we turn to first. Jesus must be our first go-to; then a godly counselor and then a trusted friend. Don't store up how you feel. Break the damn in Jesus's name. Jesus works. Call on His name. It's from this relationship that evangelism happens. Others will want what we have, Jesus is contagious in us.

Note

_____
_____
_____
_____
_____
_____
_____
_____

172

"It is good for me that I have been afflicted; that I might learn thy statutes" (Psalm 119:71, KJV)

When we are in anguish and our soul is in turmoil because of what we see, there is only one thing to do, worship Jesus. Worshiping Jesus by song and by declaring His promises causes the chains of life to break open, our palpitations begin to level, our minds are brought to peace. A lot can happen in twenty-four hours. Cultivating a life of worship in the good times gives us a reservoir of assurance in the hard times. Let's sow now so that we can reap later. Dedicate time to worship, dedicate time to pray, memorize the Word of God. Don't let the ease of life blunt the sword of truth. Stay in the Word of God. No matter what season we are in, choose to worship God. The chains of life can be physical, mental and spiritual; only worshiping Jesus will set us free. Sing, read the promises of God out loud, and write out your prayers before God; these are practices that aid us to work out our salvation. Once we take the initial step, God will sustain our discipline. God won't robotically do it for us. He gives us self-control so that we can make the right decision, for it is God who works in us to do and to will of His good pleasure. Worshiping Jesus refocuses our perspective of the mountains that we are facing to the grains of sand. God is bigger than all of life's circumstances. The more we heed of His conviction, the more prepared we will be for what is to come. Sow in whatever season we are in and reap the blessing. Sow in the Word, Sow in the Spirit, Sow in the Gospel. Believers never sow in vain. God always brings a harvest. We serve the God of the harvest.

Don't let the mind race. Take captive every thought and bring it to the obedience of Christ. Christ is looking at what we are facing from a heavenly perspective. We have access to this perspective by faith. Worship Jesus. Right now, take time to worship Jesus. Sing praises to Him, read His promises, write your prayers, and His Word out. These disciplines will be a step toward breaking out of the anxiety and fear that come crippling in. Jesus has the power to get us through to the other side. Don't grow weary. Choose to grow in faith. God's way is attached to blessing and peace. It may look like the most difficult way, but it's the most rewarding in the end. God is a rewarder.

Read Matthew chapter 23. Sinners loved Jesus but He repulsed the religious. The four Gospels testify to Jesus's love of sinners. Thieves would seek Him out; He would receive them as they were, but His love would change them to the point that they would want to make things right with those they stole from. Jesus made sinners curious of His love and His holiness. He loved but never participated in their lewd lifestyle. Jesus changed their culture, but they had no impact on His. This is the same for believers today. When Christ is in us, Satan's temptations are crushed. Believers are influencers and culture-changers. When the church is known for their love of sinners, they are known as Jesus was. Jesus was seeker friendly. Religion is seeker hostile. Jesus never came up with dress codes, hair styles and formalities for Him to be approached. Religion that claims to be Christian but acts nothing like Christ should be ashamed of themselves. Church is a hospital for the sin-sick and not a club for the model citizens. Jesus changes people not by pointing out the obvious but by saving the person as they are. When we come before Him, Jesus could care less about our image, clothing, color or pedigree. Jesus loves sinners. That means He loves all of us. Jesus is not partial. He shows no special privileges or expresses partiality. Jesus had a "come as you are policy." Knowing Jesus means that we, for the first time, know total acceptance. He shed His blood so we could be accepted as we are. When we come before Him repentant and sincere, He takes us as we are; but loves us enough to not leave us as we are. He conforms us to His character. We are not sinless but we sinless. Jesus affects the whole person when we are born again, mind, body, and spirit. Believing is not a mental ascent, it's power for Christ to live through us. We have been called to influence. We have been called to evangelize. We are not here to be monastics; we are here to influence the world toward Jesus. A relationship with Him changes everything for His glory. No one walked away from Jesus sick. He came to heal the broken hearted. Jesus left us here to be His hands and feet. He did not come to give us a new to-do list. He came to give us life. That life is not defined by stuff but by Christ in us.

Note

173

"Jesus said unto him, Thou shalt love the Lord thy God with all thy heart, and with all thy soul, and with all thy mind" (Matthew 22:37, KJV)

God wants 100 percent, not 10 percent. Doing only 10 percent of what we're capable of doing is so destructive. It's like a jet engine being used to power an electric toothbrush. Few ever tap into the 90 percent of what God can do through their lives. Due to a lack of vision, belief and comfort, we never leave the wilderness. We make the belly of the whale a home. What was only supposed to be a couple of nights has turned into years. Unbelief will put every limitation imaginable upon us. We live with a "can't do" mentality, wasting away in slothfulness. This lukewarm lifestyle is what caused a whole generation to live and die in the wilderness. Excommunicate people that only tell us what God can't do in us. The church is a culture of faith, where dreams are born and not crushed, where impossibilities become possibilities, where limitations become unlimited. A culture of faith bursts with creativity and godly ambition. Choose a community of faith where everyone believes in Christ but also puts no limits on what He can do in one another. Be around people that inspire in the Lord, flee gluttonous realists that cave into evil foreboding and squalor in sarcasm as their only means of laughter. As long as we have a pulse, Christ is not done with us. It's never too late to do what God has called us to do. Don't listen to critical manipulators that feed off of keeping us down so it makes them feel better about their own sin. God is in the business of expansion, multiplication and abundance.

Listen for God and follow Him. Mute the voices that don't have our interest at heart; God does, surrender and let Him lead us to mountains high or valleys low. Yesterday's manna is worms today. Our generation could care less about "the olden days"; we want God today. We are tired of the charlatans bringing yesterday's manna. *"Behold I will do a new thing,"*[16] *"His Mercies are new every morning,"*[17] *"in Christ we are a new creation, behold, all things will become new."*[18] God does not look at age. We emphasize the youth today as if their millennial wisdom could fend off a Nazi invasion. God does not cap age to be called! Whatever our limitations are, in the sight of God are qualifications for Him to use us. Rely on our weaknesses for God to show off His strength. Fan into flame and live white hot.

Note

16. *Isaiah 43:19*
17. *Lamentations 3:22–23*
18. *Corinthians 5:17*

174

*"And he cometh unto the disciples, and findeth them
asleep, and saith unto Peter, What, could ye not watch
with me one hour?" (Matthew 26:40, KJV)*

When Jesus did not live up to the expectations of the apostles, they forsook Him. They would not even pray with Him for an hour. Judas got so disappointed that his bitterness drove him to sell out Jesus. They felt that they gave three years of their life to Jesus for nothing. Like many today, their expectations of Jesus were for health, wealth and fame. Jesus did not follow through on their expectations so they gave up on Him. He warned them *"in this world we would have trouble."*[19] His eternal kingdom was clearly taught but they heard what they wanted to hear. Somehow humanity has made a religion of Jesus but live nothing like Him today. Religion spends more money on its buildings and staff than on the mission they claim to be about. Some of the religious leaders live better than the for-profit business owners in their communities. They claim non-profit status but the percentages of the donations that they spend on buildings and staff is shocking. Their statements of faith are rarely taught and their claim to evangelize rarely materializes. The great commission is an unpracticed slogan. Once trouble hits, many of today's Christians will scatter because their faith is built on a one hour a week emotional experience. The gospel they are hearing is no different than the expectations the apostles had on Jesus. Just like the apostles scattered

---

19. *John 16:33*

when Jesus was taken away, many will scatter from Jesus once following Him does not go the way they thought. Following Jesus is not about our will, our betterment, or our agenda, it's about the glory of God. Jesus is used like a pharmaceutical drug but when He does not seem to work, we move on to the next high to cope through life. Jesus never said that life would be easy. He never said to follow Him and live a problem free. We have heaped up for ourselves false teachers today that tell us everything we want to hear so that they can secure their income and their lavish lifestyle. We should be preaching the truth, whether it fills a room or empties a room. It's the truth that sets us free. We are not Lord of Jesus. We are fragile people that are here today and gone tomorrow. When our gratefulness is sourced in the cross, we will never have a reason for disappointment. What more could God give us after giving His only begotten Son?

Note

_____

_____

_____

_____

_____

_____

_____

_____

_____

175

"And thou shalt love the Lord thy God with all thy heart, and with all thy soul, and with all thy mind, and with all thy strength: this is the first commandment. And the second is like, namely this, Thou shalt love thy neighbour as thyself. There is none other commandment greater than these" (Mark 12:30–31, KJV)

Read the Bible like you are going to be preaching every Sunday. We know our level of intimacy with God by how much effort we study His Word for others verses our own relationship with Jesus. Preachers and teachers can fall into the trap of only reading the Word with their congregation in mind but miss out on what God is speaking to them. When we only approach worship and the Word of God for others sake, we are missing God's sake. Before we can get an effective ministry to others, we must make sure our relationship with God is effective. Otherwise we can be like the Shulamite woman in Song of Solomon[20] taking care of her brother's vineyard but neglecting her own. Churches can fall into a "works" mentality where prayer and worship become secondary to "works." Jesus wants us to do the one thing that is needed, which is to sit at His feet not for any other reason but to worship Him for who He is. Discipleship is not always serving but requires sitting. Critics will always have an opinion but Jesus will say back to them "what about you." Like Peter, we can be so concerned about how others are following Jesus, that we are not following Him ourselves. We are called to work out our own salva-

---

[20.] *Song of Solomon 1:6*

tion. We can't save anyone. Our cleverest speech cannot save a soul. We have so many script-readers in the church that can communicate well but they have no heart, no passion and no anointing. Jesus wants us to follow Him and not fads, trends, and soundbites of the latest book we have read. What about the scripture being your spiritual diet for a season? Read the Word as if you were preparing a sermon or teaching every word but it's for your own intimacy with Christ. Value your personal relationship with Christ and the congregation will get a lot more out of what you have to say. Don't value anyone more than Christ. Don't seek God for anyone else's sake but for Christ's sake! Watch the difference when you choose to live for the glory of God rather than the pleasure of man. Once a believer catches a hold of this intimacy with Christ, Satan will say to the charlatans, "Jesus, I know, _____ I know, but who are you?" Satan does not see anyone that does not know Christ personally as a threat. Satan could care less for our songs, sermons and service when it's done in our might and strength.

Note

_____

_____

_____

_____

_____

_____

_____

_____

176

*"Whether therefore ye eat, or drink, or whatsoever ye do, do
all to the glory of God" (1 Corinthians 10:31, KJV)*

Seek God for who He is and not for what He has. When we use
God or people for our own gain all the time, we will find ourselves
empty. Using God for our own gain and our own agenda won't get us
very far. Using people for our own gain and agenda also won't get us
far. Selfishness never satisfies. When we live only for our own security, gain and ambitions, we will wake up one day disappointed. We
will have no legacy. Living for others is the fruit of living for Christ.
Worship Jesus like there is no other benefit attached other than salvation. Don't use Jesus in the hard times only. He sees our motivation
behind our worship and prayers. God judges the heart. He knows
those that worship Him for who He is and those that are using Him
for what He has. For most today, salvation is not enough for them.
The cross is not enough for them. They only worship until life goes
the way they want and once it does, they stop worshiping. Jesus is
just a help or a resource in low times; but when they get a break, they
forget God and chase their dreams. God cannot be fooled. People
can be fooled, and congregants can be fooled, but God sees all. It's
best to be as blatant as one can be before God. Examine motives,
don't just pray. The more real we are with God the more He works
in us. Jesus would rather have honesty than empty words. Repent of
selfishness before God. Let Him in on the ambitions of the heart. He
is not surprised by any of our thoughts or desires. He knows all of
us. While we were sinners Christ loved us to death. He rose from the

dead so we can walk in open relationship with Him. Keep nothing in the closet with God. Hide nothing from Him. He works with repentance but not with dishonesty. Don't let fear of what He thinks hold you back, He already knows everything. Repentance opens the way for the Spirit of God to work change in us. To live for others, to pray His will be done, to surrender to His Lordship is not natural for our flesh to do. We naturally are brats, pining for our own agenda, using God to get all we can out of Him, and if He disappoints us, we move onto the next thing or god. Our hearts will never be full. God is not our cash cow. He is not our genie in the lamp. God won't always give us what we want but He gave us what we need.

Note

177

"Paul, an apostle, (not of men, neither by man, but by Jesus Christ, and God the Father, who raised him from the dead;) And all the brethren which are with me, unto the churches of Galatia: Grace be to you and peace from God the Father, and from our Lord Jesus Christ, Who gave himself for our sins, that he might deliver us from this present evil world, according to the will of God and our Father" (Galatians 1:1–4, KJV)

What sin separates us from God? We like to categorize sin. In the sight of God sin is sin. Jesus leveled the ground with sin. The thought of sin condemns us as much as the action of sin in the sight of God. The temptation from Satan was to get man to think that he could be god. "Eat the fruit and be independent from god." The gospel in the west has a similar message. Jesus is the "fruit." If we eat of him, we won't need him again, "We will be healthy and wealthy, Jesus will make us problem-free." That's not the Gospel. We need Jesus to the day we die. Earning God's salvation is mocking the blood of Jesus. Thinking that what we do gets us saved is like banging in the nails into Jesus's hands and feet. Religion teaches independence from God by teaching reliance on their rituals, traditions and discipleship. If discipleship makes us independent from God that is not discipleship. We will never graduate from a need for God. We can "do" all we want but none of it earns salvation. We don't do what we do *for* God's salvation, we do what we do *from* God's salvation. Someone has bewitched you if you were saved by faith but now you think you're kept by your works. Jesus not only saves us by faith but keeps us by faith too. All our works are filthy rags in the sight of God. Whatever we do independent from God is no different than any sin we look down upon on. There will be many turned away on the day of Judgment. Their years of ministry will be burned up along with them in hell. There is no "look what I did." The attention will be on Jesus and his accomplishments for salvation. All we did was place Jesus on the cross because of sinfulness. Independence from God will get us the same reward as any sin committed. Those who are famous here will be potentially nobodies in heaven. He does not give out rewards as we would. The first will be last. Striving for success here could end you up in eternal loss. If Christ is not enough for your soul, you will never have peace. Nothing and no one will give peace like Jesus. Does Jesus know you? Do you have a transparent relationship with Him? What gives you purpose outside of knowing Jesus? Don't be bewitched by religion. Satan's "apple" has an imitation Jesus on it today. Jesus never promised happiness here, He warned us that in this world we will have trouble.

Note

178

*"Judge not, that ye be not judged. For with what judgment
ye judge, ye shall be judged: and with what measure ye mete,
it shall be measured to you again. And why beholdest thou
the mote that is in thy brother's eye, but considerest not the
beam that is in thine own eye?" (Matthew 7:1–3, KJV)*

Jesus said, *"Judge not, lest you be judged."* Assuming the position as
judge in any courthouse will get you escorted right out. No one can
just walk into a court house without the qualifications of a judge
and cast judgement. No human can judge anyone to hell. Only God
has the right to judge eternity. If we assume the throne of God, we
are in rebellion and could face the very judgement we would pro-
nounce on those that sin differently than us. Eternal judgment is
God's right alone. Any religion or religious person is arrogant to
assume that position. Jesus defrocked the religious leaders of the day.
Their stone-throwing days were over when Christ went to the cross.
He decommissioned the priesthood and prophesied the destruction
of the temple. He leveled the ground for all humanity to be saved
by faith. Only He that is without sin can judge. That means every
human has no right to judge another's eternity. There is no greater
sin than assuming to be God and judging those that He died for. The
religious are bound to all forms of closet sin. Those that judge the
hardest are normally those that are depraved the most. Evangelism
is not done from judgment but it's done from love. It's the kindness
of God that leads us to repentance. It's with chords of love that He
draws us to Himself. The religious wanted Jesus to call fire down

upon sinners and militarize His people so they can have their king-dom here on earth, but Jesus loved sinners and rebuked the religious. We don't evangelize because we are better than anyone; we evangelize because if we can be saved, anyone can be. He that is forgiven much loves much. The religious that get saved need to know the severity of their sin. Their religion put Jesus on the cross. Religion is a darker force than any one sin we could list. Religion starts wars, abuses chil-dren, squanders money has a form of godliness but denies the power of God. Flee religion. We need to be pleading with the religious like we would with someone in a burning house when they don't know that it's on fire. Paul begged, "Be ye reconciled." God wants sinners and not phonies. Go to God as you are. Don't stitch up the veil that God tore in two. If we say we are without sin we have deceived our-selves. Many are deceived by religion.

Note

179

*"Being confident of this very thing, that he which hath
begun a good work in you will perform it until the
day of Jesus Christ" (Philippians 1:6, KJV)*

How we finish matters more than how we start. That is why "now"
is more important than what's next. Our nature naturally grows
familiar with "now" and craves what's next. God wants our "now."
Without God, our "now" never matters. Once we take God out of
life, nothing matters. When our conscience removes any reverence
for the afterlife, what we do today does not matter. God keeps our
mind grounded. If He was to take His grace from the earth, total
chaos would break out everywhere. God is all that matters. Knowing
Him gives us value for everything that matters in our lives. Nothing
earthly can be God to us. Jesus Christ is God. He alone can put the
value on us that we are craving for. He is the love that we all crave. He
is the acceptance that we all long for. Knowing Christ in relationship
makes all circumstances turn for good. We can be in any situation
and see good. He gives us a "good" perspective that makes us strike
up a song even in the prison cell. The greatest freedom we can get
begins in the mind. We can be free no matter where we are or what
we are going through. Once we tap into this love relationship with
Jesus, nothing else matters other than knowing Him. Everything else
grows strangely dim when we are with Him. He makes our darkest
days like a honeymoon when He is the center of our lives. Welcome
hardship, greet pain, kiss our enemies because we are free. Once He
has our thought life, then we are engaged in a "powerful" life. Let

God define us, for He is the finisher. We can't complete the work He started. He began it so we could not complete it on our own. What He starts, He completes. The lie today is that we are saved by faith but then we are kept by works. Works won't keep us. God does. We are kept by His grace. The same grace that saved us, keeps us. Striving to be kept by God for our future only perpetuates familiarity in our lives for the thing that matters now. As we surrender to Him in prayer, God does what we could never do. God is the completer. When we assume to finish His work in us by ourselves, we end up in a worse situation than we did before we got saved. The more we let God lead our lives, the more we see that He is a better leader. Trust God with your life here and watch what He does. God makes us consistent; there are no peaks or valleys with Him.

Note

180

"Casting all your care upon him; for he careth for you" (1 Peter 5:7, KJV)

Knowing Jesus fills the void of the soul that religion or anything else could never fill. If we miss Jesus, then we have missed out on life. The abundance of life is best defined by knowing Jesus. The western definition of abundance is materialism and health, but that's not what Jesus always has in mind for us while we are here. Eternally we will have abundance as we want it. There will be no sickness, bills or hardships in heaven. While we are here, we will have trouble. No one is exempt from storms or sickness while we are here. Our definition of being blessed is to be healthy and wealthy yet independent from God. The real blessing of God will not make us independent from God but would keep us dependent on Him. When we pray to be blessed, God may not bless us as we want but will bless us as we need. To be blessed is to be eternally assured in Christ. When we anchor our definition of blessing to scripture, it will keep us anchored through the storms of life. We are blessed even when the world thinks we look cursed. This teaching got the Martyrs of old through to heaven with joy in their soul. We can have consistent faith. Consistent faith comes when we are not led my sight but by faith. Consistency can be reached when we decide to live by faith. Living by doctors' reports, bank accounts, or employers will mean that we will live a life of ups and downs. We can take our thoughts captive in Christ and reach contentment. There is no religion or state of being that can give the type of peace that Christ can provide. No one and nothing can compete with Him. We go to church not because church saves our soul but because the Church is supposed to keep our focus on Christ. Any church that lifts Christ above its music and preachers is the church that one would want to be attending. They are hard to find. Unfortunately, some of our western leaders demand titles but call Jesus by His first name. Christ is the only one that will never disappoint. When we know Jesus, we can't help but talk about Him. That's what evangelism is. If evangelism is not secondary to knowing Jesus, then it's just an argument. Every title and everything must be second or last to Jesus. If we are not content being alone with Jesus, then there is something wrong.

Note

181

"And a certain ruler asked him, saying, Good Master, what shall I do to inherit eternal life? And Jesus said unto him, Why callest thou me good? none is good, save one, that is, God. Thou knowest the commandments, Do not commit adultery, Do not kill, Do not steal, Do not bear false witness, Honour thy father and thy mother. And he said, All these have I kept from my youth up. Now when Jesus heard these things, he said unto him, Yet lackest thou one thing: sell all that thou hast, and distribute unto the poor, and thou shalt have treasure in heaven: and come, follow me. And when he heard this, he was very sorrowful: for he was very rich. And when Jesus saw that he was very sorrowful, he said, How hardly shall they that have riches enter into the kingdom of God! For it is easier for a camel to go through a needle's eye, than for a rich man to enter into the kingdom of God. And they that heard it said, Who then can be saved? And he said, The things which are impossible with men are possible with God. Then Peter said, Lo, we have left all, and followed thee. And he said unto them, Verily I say unto you, There is no man that hath left house, or parents, or brethren, or wife, or children, for the kingdom of God's sake, Who shall not receive manifold more in this present time, and in the world to come life everlasting" (Luke 18:18–30, KJV)

Jesus alone saves. Jesus eloquently taught the rich young ruler that there is none "good" but God. All our works, titles, pomp, wealth is "dung"[21] in comparison with who God is. God has no competitor. Satan is no

---

21. *"Yea doubtless, and I count all things but loss for the excellency of the knowledge of Christ Jesus my Lord: for whom I have suffered the loss of all things, and do count them but dung, that I may win Christ."* (Philippians 3:8, KJV)

match for God. Satan is just a fallen angel. Our God is the uncreated One. God is complete and self-existent. Our God has no lack or need. He is not driven by need but by want. His love for us is a choice and not a forced love. God chose to love us even while we were at enmity with Him.[22] Only God is good. Only God is love. The love of God is the love we are looking for. We search for it in all the wrong places and sometimes even in the "right" places but no one loves like Jesus. As much love as we can experience from our community or church, it will always disappoint compared to the love of God. His goodness cannot be competed with. The goodness of God is gifted to us. For some this can be offensive but for others this is good news. We don't have a relationship with God because of something we did or because we earned it. In fact, earning salvation is just as bad as the most blatant act of sin we could commit in the sight of God. Our definition of good is not God's definition of good. Read the law of Moses. For thousands of years we read of Israel's failed attempts to be good for God. That's why God gave the sacrificial system because He knew no one could be good enough for Him. Christ replaced the sacrificial system. Christ replaced works with faith as the means to salvation. We are saved by faith. Our best works are filthy rags compared to His holiness and perfection. The church does not save, Jesus does. No one can replace Jesus for Salvation. The reason we see so many failures in the church is because the church is a hospital for the sin-sick that need Jesus in their lives. When Church is full of "good" people, then it's full of closet sinners. Christ's church is the most accepting community we could ever have when Jesus is the focus. When any doctrine, dress code or behavior is focused on more than Jesus, then we are out of sync. The Holy Spirit would not outshine Jesus. The Holy Spirit will always honor Jesus above experiences, signs and wonders. If a spirit does this, it's not the Holy Spirit. Lift Jesus Christ up above everything.

---

[22] *"Because the carnal mind is enmity against God: for it is not subject to the law of God, neither indeed can be." (Romans 8:7, KJV)*

182

"Wherefore also we pray always for you, that our God would count you worthy of this calling, and fulfil all the good pleasure of his goodness, and the work of faith with power" (2 Thessalonians 1:11, KJV)

Let no one tell you what you can't do if God has called you to it! Every calling comes with challenges. When God calls, it will always require faith. If it does not take faith to do what God has called you to do, then one must question if you even heard it from God. Our Western Christianity has little need for faith in ministry. Actors and actresses can make it through the ranks of ministry. We are so organized that we hire based on qualifications verses the call of God. Carnal business-minded "Christians" have infiltrated ministry. They make the budget look good at the expense of the anointing and faith. Faith and anointing cannot be hired, bought or inherited. You may not want to be reminded of this, but it's healthy to remember that God always has a process to get us to our purpose. When the process takes longer than expected, we can grow weary. Don't grow weary. You did not fight so much to give up now. The more resistance, the more negative opinions, and the longer the process, the greater the work of faith will be in us. Our faith will never return void, whether in this life or in the next. It's a fearful thing to assume the position of God and determine someone else's calling. What man would stand in the way of what God wants to do? It may take ten plagues but God knows how to get through to the "naysayer." No one in scripture was qualified or fully ready for what God called them to do; all that God requires is faith. Only Satan would try to discourage you from following God. There are voices and opinions you need to say "get behind me" to. There will always be opinions when you get out of the norm. There will always be "prophets" telling you all of the obstacles ahead. They will put on quite a presentation. Christ died so you don't have to answer to them. We have no mediators. No one can share the throne of God in our life. Though none go with you, follow Christ. Alone with Christ makes you a stronger force than having everyone around you without Him. The first here will be last where He is. Our faith here will be treasure in heaven. Your journey is not in vain. Don't sell out now. Fan your flame and get more undignified than this. The scorners will be put to shame. This season has trained you to fight, so fight for faith.

Note

183

"For we walk by faith, not by sight" (2 Corinthians 5:7, KJV)

Consistent faith is when we decide to walk by faith and not by sight. The Bible is clear that by faith we can make it through any obstacle. Faith is a conscious decision to trust God's Word over everything else. This does not mean that we deny our doubts or live by fakery. This is not a fake walk. Faith may seem fake but faith is different than fake. Faith empowers the Word of God in us, to do through us, what we could never do on our own. Fake is relying on our own wisdom and strength. Being fake will only get us so far. Believing will get us to the end. Our minds rely on logic, facts and what we see. If we live our way, then we will spiral down when life happens. Believers are not led by anything other than faith in God. As we mature in faith, we will not be moved by our circumstances or emotions but be led by God's promises. God has a greater purpose for us here than we could ever know. Some of us won't know all that God did through us until we get to heaven. Some of us may feel like it's taken us more faith to get through life than others. Comparison removes our eyes from faith. The more faith we have needed from day to day the more of God we needed from day to day. Faith is what God rewards. When we diligently seek Him, when we are consistently believing Him, God will reward us. To be diligent means to be consistent and disciplined to have a fight to believe what God said is true. Choose this day whom you will believe. Believing the report of the Lord always gives us the best eternal outlook. Believing the promises of God always leads our minds to the healthiest perspective. If we want a crystal-clear outlook, we need to believe God. Jesus takes us out of the mire and brings clarity to our minds. Confusion sets in when faith is ignored. Faith in Scripture answers every question we could have for our origin, purpose, or destiny. There is no alternative. Our finite minds will never understand this life. Once we believe Scripture as our sole authority for life and purpose now, we can have a sure foundation. Doubt not only hurts the doubter but all those around them. A community of doubt is a brood of vipers. We need to be in a community of faith. Choose wisely who we put around us. Do we walk away with faith from our community?

Note

184

"But when he saw the multitudes, he was moved with compassion on them, because they fainted, and were scattered abroad, as sheep having no shepherd" (Matthew 9:36, KJV)

When we live wide open before God and bring our outcry to Him, it moves Him to compassion.

God is moved with compassion when He hears the state of our brokenness. God wants what no one else would want from us, He wants us. He wants us for who we are. Christ made the way to the throne for us to go boldly before God. Go to God wide open. Connect our thoughts to His heart. Walk in openness before almighty God like we can't with anyone else. Only God can carry us, no other being was designed to bare our anguish. There is no earthly person that was designed to bare our cares like God can. Preachers are in need of their message as much as their audience; sometimes they need the message more because of the onslaught that a preacher faces from Satan. Preachers get buffeted[23] by Satan daily. Pray for truth speakers. If Satan can strike the preacher, the people will scatter. Preachers are not mediators. Preachers are humans who need Christ as much as anyone else. We all need to be held. Let's call on God for our generation. On our watch, millions are lost and going to hell. We are here to be a witness of Christ so that all people will have a chance to

---

[23.] *"For this thing I besought the Lord thrice, that it might depart from me." (2 Corinthians 12:8, KJV)*

hear the Gospel. God desires all to be saved. The same compassion He has for us, He can give us for others. When we are going to the throne of God and experiencing His grace, we will want everyone to know this experience. There is no greater experience than knowing God intimately. Knowing Him is our peace. It's from this foundation that ministry is built. Our effectiveness will be based on our intimacy with Christ and not on our accomplishments without Him. If we miss knowing Him, we could miss heaven. Having a heart connection to God is why Christ died. He did not die to make us servants. He died to makes us family. Know God our Father and everything else will fall into place. Take time to nurture this relationship with Him. He is our anchor through the storm; everyone and everything changes but Him. God stays the same. He is a sure foundation. To preach reconciliation, we must be reconciled. The Gospel won't be advanced by actors or actresses. Take our relationship seriously with Jesus and He will handle the rest. Jesus exemplified this relationship with His Father.

Note

185

"Let this mind be in you, which was also in Christ Jesus: Who, being in the form of God, thought it not robbery to be equal with God: But made himself of no reputation, and took upon him the form of a servant, and was made in the likeness of men: And being found in fashion as a man, he humbled himself, and became obedient unto death, even the death of the cross" (Philippians 2:5–8, KJV)

We can circumstantially be free, yet be bound mentally. The Western Church comes under the most sinister attacks. Our mental health is so important. It needs to be discussed. Religion does not know what to do with mental health because it requires discernment and that is something no religious person has. The persecuted church needs prayer too, yet we can make sense of their need because we can see it. When it's internal, it's much harder for us to show grace. We have millions of Christians in the West that circumstantially are free, but mentally they are bound. Our minds are the worst prisons. Being mentally chained to depression, doubt, guilt and shame will destroy any person over time. We have many in our pews that look free but are mentally bound. Pharmaceuticals are not always the answer. Counseling will not always work. These chains are only broken by prayer and fasting. The effective fervent prayer avails much. We have many around us daily that are being tormented and keep it to themselves. Their own minds condemn them. There is no logical reason why they feel the way they do. No one understands them because they look physically free, but they are in a torture chamber in their minds. We desperately need discernment in the West. Mental health must be addressed with grace and tenderness. It has affected every home and every family. Shame keeps us isolated; isolation is the devil's strategy. Trying to get free on our own seems to only bind us more. It's like quicksand, the more we move to get out, the more we sink. Bringing these weights into the light before God will help us guide our way to His rest. God can pull us out but we have to let Him. We won't be able to break free until we bring our mental chains to God in prayer. When we watch a family member face this, all it can do is fill us with compassion if we have discernment. Judging only damages our own health. May God have mercy on our mentally ill. May God grant us power so that when we preach, it will drive out the darkness and break the mental chains. The love of God is set toward the mentally ill. Internal sickness or mental-health victims would much rather a cast or sling so that they can be understood. When we see it, we understand it and give more grace. We are never alone. Pray for discernment. We need power in Jesus.

Note

186

"But ye shall receive power, after that the Holy Ghost is come upon you: and ye shall be witnesses unto me both in Jerusalem, and in all Judaea, and in Samaria, and unto the uttermost part of the earth" (Acts 1:8, KJV)

If we say we have the Holy Spirit but have no power to witness for Christ, then what spirit do we have? If we want the Holy Spirit just for our own experience, then we are after the wrong spirit. The Holy Spirit is not our entertainer. He is not the ring master for our circus. The Holy Spirit is a person who grieves. He is not an "it." There are so many misconceptions of the Holy Spirit today. He is to be revered but He has not been sent to take the attention from Christ. He was sent to empower us to be a witness. We are naturally weak, shy, timid and quiet. Religion beats out vision and ambition from its participants. Its system caps its followers to being seat warmers and tithe givers only. It caps the Holy Spirit and it caps believers as well. Religion nearly always works those that are genuinely called of God mavericks and lists out all that they cannot do. Some of the best worship leaders were told by the religious that they could not sing. Some of the most impactful preachers were told that they could not preach. The religious thought they were burying the "called of God" but really, they were planting them. God does not bury, He plants. God uses the pompous religious to raise up His called by allowing His "called" to never rely on religious bigotry. God blows the limitations of man off so all will know that He is God and we are not. We must be slow to tell a fellow believer what they can't do.

The words of doubt will come back on us. When we attempt to limit faith, God will surprise us every time. When the Holy Spirit comes into a believer, anything is possible; any calling, any gifting, any purpose is made possible. As we surrender to the Holy Spirit, Christ will get glory out of us. The more people say we "can't," the more the Holy Spirit does through us. Don't listen to people's voices, listen to God's voice. Tune into God and mute everyone else. Give ourselves to the Holy Spirit and for the glory of Christ; watch what God does with our life. The Holy Spirit will shame our enemies and shut their mouths. Speak life over people. Let the Fruit of the Holy Spirit be poured through us to everyone around us. Don't seek the gifts of the Spirit more than the Fruit of the Spirit. Honor Christ, preach Christ and always use words.

Note

187

"But of that day and hour knoweth no man, no, not the angels of heaven, but my Father only" (Matthew 24:36, KJV)

Life here as we know it is about to change. It will not be this way forever. We look through the lens of tomorrow but it's not promised. As sure as the rain falls, so will our lives end here. We all fall in life. We have all fallen. We are fallen. There is no one that has made it through this life without feeling the effects of the fall. All of our calamities we brought upon ourselves because of sin. We can't blame anyone else because even the best of us would not have done any better than Adam. The fall of man happened thousands of years ago and we still see the effects. We are always looking for someone else to blame. Personal responsibility removes the blaming mind-set and steps us in the right direction of repentance. Blame won't work before God. He knows us inside and out. Every hair is numbered. In our fallen state, we all reach for something to pacify our emptiness. Whatever it is that we are reaching for every day outside of Christ will not deliver us from our fallen state. When we fall, there is only one that can lift us up. Christ did not come to kick us further down but He came to raise us up from our fallen state to a family state with God. We know more with Christ in us than Adam did in the garden. The Bible gives us revelation that none of our ancestors ever had. We are no longer fallen. We are family. We no longer are mere sinners who are cut off from God. He reached out to us with His only Son and all we could do is brutalize Him. He was not caught by surprise. It was His plan to save us. God is never caught by surprise. Our eternal, uncreated God loves us. Even in our fallen state, He wants us. This is a mystery to all of us who believe His Word. If God was not a mystery, we would never need Him. There are many mysteries about our God but when faith is applied to scripture, the mysteries turn to revelation. We don't have to live in the unknown. We can be confident that our God is with us no matter what our state is. Life changes but God stays the same. When God is our focus and is not just in our periphery, we can have stability through it all. Don't reach out to anyone more than Christ. Christ is faced toward us with love and grace. He won't change toward us until we breathe our last. Our faith determines our eternity.

Note

188

"For what shall it profit a man, if he shall gain the whole world, and lose his own soul?" (Mark 8:36, KJV)

The American dream has become a nightmare for many. Materialism, keeping up with appearances, zip codes, salaries, titles, etc.; these are all motives for significance. Significance is what we all crave. We were designed to be loved and feel worth. How we determine our worth should alarm us. Whatever we give worth to, we will give worship to. Learning our "stuff" does not give our soul the significance it needs. It is vital to live joyful. Happiness is gauged by happenstance. Our happiness must not be our pursuit because it will always be dependent on what happens. Joy is not a pursuit; joy is a choice. Significance is a choice. Worth is a choice. None of these emotions are given or earned they are chosen. If we don't choose it, we will search for it in all the wrong places. Even the "right" places won't give us the significance our souls desire. Jesus is our joy; Jesus is our significance. Look at the worth that Christ put on us at the cross. When we choose Jesus and decide to follow Him, we gain everything our souls desperately crave. When a society removes Jesus, what started out as a dream turns into a nightmare of debt, depression, anxiety, low self-esteem. God is the One that makes dreams come alive. His ways have no vain imaginations attached. We can choose to believe that "it won't be this way forever." God does not disappoint because His promises are completed when we pass into the next life. Don't let stuff determine significance. Don't build identity on the zip code or on the size of our house. Bigger is not always better. Don't sellout Jesus for a nightmare. Satan lures us by appealing with us to be god. A human crumbles at the top because they realize that there is no fulfillment outside of Christ. We can't handle being a god. Once we get to the peak, we realize no height is high enough for our flesh. There is nothing that satisfies. When you were poor, you were lured into thinking that wealth and achievement will satisfy, but once we get it, we are so let down, disappointed. Our souls were not designed to be filled with junk; we were designed to be filled with Jesus. Having everything but not Jesus is having nothing at all. Jesus is our everything. It takes a long journey to realize this; some longer than others, and some unfortunately never realize it.

Note

189

"Come now, and let us reason together, saith the Lord: though your sins be as scarlet, they shall be as white as snow; though they be red like crimson, they shall be as wool" (Isaiah 1:18, KJV)

God welcomes us to reason with Him. God welcomes doubters that sincerely seek truth. Sincerity is not salvation, but when we sincerely seek God, we will get answers. Nicodemus did not have the courage to meet Jesus in public, so he requested a private meeting at night. He was seeking truth. Jesus welcomed him and must have gotten through to him because Joseph of Arimathea and Nicodemus requested the body of Jesus after He died.[24] Jesus never ran from doubters but welcomed them, knowing their thoughts and motives before they said a word. Jesus knows our thoughts. That's why our prayers must begin in our thoughts and not just with our mouths. God discerns our words and sees deep into our motives. When we say "God wants our heart," we are saying "God wants our motives and thoughts." We focus so much on our words and behavior, but it's evident in scripture that God is not looking for righteousness; He is looking for sincerity. When truth reveals that we are sincerely sinful, we then are in a state of genuine repentance. This repentant relationship gains us the ability to discern. We will be able to hear past the words of others and hear deep into their motives. "Church" people can be the least discerning. The pastors that some church people listen to are stealing from

---

24. *"And after this Joseph of Arimathaea, being a disciple of Jesus, but secretly for fear of the Jews, besought Pilate that he might take away the body of Jesus: and Pilate gave him leave. He came therefore, and took the body of Jesus." (John 19:38, KJV)*

their time, treasure and talent for their own elevation. The lack of authenticity in our churches has made church out to be just a concert with a motivational speech that sounds a lot like a "self-help," "positive thinking" speech. Our discernment is not sharpened by music or motivating speeches. Discernment is developed through the hearing and studying of scripture. Discernment is different from judgement. Judgment is only for God. Discernment is for the believer. We gain discernment by using the scripture as a "plumb" line for life and doctrine. When a church elevates the personality behind the pulpit above scripture, then people will congregate for the personality more than for the scripture. This mind-set is preparing the way for the antichrist, "even the elect will be deceived." The Scripture must always be held to a higher esteem than any personality. Let's nurture discernment. Bring the Bible to Church. We gather for the scripture and not for the teacher. Truth sets free, not the teacher.

Note

190

"Hereby know we that we dwell in him, and he in us, because he hath given us of his Spirit. And we have seen and do testify that the Father sent the Son to be the Saviour of the world. Whosoever shall confess that Jesus is the Son of God, God dwelleth in him, and he in God. And we have known and believed the love that God hath to us. God is love; and he that dwelleth in love dwelleth in God, and God in him. Herein is our love made perfect, that we may have boldness in the day of judgment: because as he is, so are we in this world. There is no fear in love; but perfect love casteth out fear: because fear hath torment. He that feareth is not made perfect in love. We love him, because he first loved us" (1 John 4:13–19, KJV)

Christ did not only define the love of God but He demonstrated His love by going to the cross. Each one of us can testify of His love that is still being demonstrated to this day. The cross has not lost its relevance. All across the earth, people are still encountering Christ and being saved. His Word is still relevant. Each one of us are living epistles, showing the Lord's current work on the earth. We might be the only "Bible" that someone will ever read. Our lives should look very similar to the characters in scripture. The scripture is full of failing humans but testifies of a faithful God. Our failures speak more of the grace of God than our successes. This is why most of our testimonies point to how lost we are and how faithful God is. The evidence that Christ lives is the Church. There are millions of believers that still testify of Christ all over the world. Our testimonies need to be shared and not just our successes. People relate better when we talk about our failures because we have all failed and fallen short of the glory of God. God knew this, so He gave us the Bible to show us that no matter how far we may have gone in sin, He is faithful. The religious emphasize their righteousness; believers in Christ emphasize His righteousness. When we judge who is righteous, we think of a "good" living person and when we judge an unrighteous person we think of a sinner, but Jesus declares the repentant sinner righteous, and an unrepentant "good" person as unrighteous. Jesus came to teach that righteousness is for those that trust Him for righteousness and not trust their works. The religious hate repentance and want to talk about it as little as possible. They want their discipleship to graduate sinners from repentance by works of self-righteousness. They are deceived to think they graduate from a need of a savior after they "get saved." This mind-set leads to all forms of closet sin and is normally evident in the waistline of the religious. Religiosity cultivates gluttonous consumers that look nothing like Christ. They conform to the image of self rather than be conformed to the image of Christ. They are professional stone throwers. They see fault with everyone but themselves.

191

"The name of the Lord is a strong tower: the righteous runneth into it, and is safe" (Proverbs 18:10, KJV)

How are we coping through life? When it comes to issues of life, one person's mountain is another person's pebble. We can be quick to play down another person's problem because we are not in their shoes. Spectators can only be counselors, but they cannot be saviors. Counselors can help us with our perspective, but they cannot compete with the Wonderful Counselor.[25] Jesus is the greatest coping mechanism. He listens but also has the power to save. He does not gossip, charge, or give ill advice. His Word gives us direction like no other could. We can cope through life with Jesus and His Word. Make Him the coping mechanism for life and His Word for our peace. Whatever situation we are in, remember the darkest valley only has shadows of death. Believers don't die. We live forever. This life is not it. Eternity awaits. Knowing Jesus and believing His Word is our only assurance through life. Everything else is fleeting. When we pray, our faith gets the attention of God in Jesus's name. Heaven is our home. As long as we are here, we will never feel entirely at home. These bodies are aging and time is ticking. Don't get too comfortable here. Some spend all their time securing themselves for the short time they are here. Our minds trick us into thinking that this life is all we have. Jesus did not come so we could have heaven here.

---

[25] *"For unto us a child is born, unto us a son is given: and the government shall be upon his shoulder: and his name shall be called Wonderful, Counsellor, The mighty God, The everlasting Father, The Prince of Peace." (Isaiah 9:6, KJV)*

Our time here as believers is for one purpose and that is to be His ambassadors. We are only given one shot at life here. It goes by so quick. Don't sell out because you are in a valley. There is nowhere else to go. There is no one else to turn to. Once we encounter Christ, there is no other rest that can compare. When we cast our cares on Christ, don't reel them back in. Leave them with Him and reel in His promises. Don't make the problem bigger than God. Our minds will deceive us. His promises will remind us that God is bigger than every problem. All our problems and trouble here, compared to eternity in heaven are only a pebble and not a mountain like our minds have made them out to be. The Bible keeps our minds in check and shows us how to cope through all the valleys of life. For some, their whole life is a valley. No matter how dark it is, cope with Christ and believe that heaven is our home.

Note

192

*"Then saith he to Thomas, Reach hither thy finger, and behold
my hands; and reach hither thy hand, and thrust it into my
side: and be not faithless, but believing" (John 20:27, KJV)*

Thomas would never have gotten the revelation he did if he simply accepted the testimony of the other apostles. Thomas represents most of us. There is no one that should be convinced by another person alone. That's a cult. Cults hate to be questioned and control everything they can. They hate social media and any truth source outside of themselves. Cults teach that they are the source of truth. They focus on one doctrine or experience and name themselves after it. Satan has severed the church over so many "nonessential truths" for salvation. We have built up walls around worship styles, fads, age and culture. It has been so easy for Satan to divide us. When a church sees another as a threat because of a trivial expression, we know who is behind it. Churches that only gather one race, yet live in a multicultural community is a cult. God levels the ground between us all. Leaders that demand titles yet call their Lord by His first name are cultish. Churches that have thrones and lift up their leaders above Christ are cults. Most "church people" vote republican yet allow their leaders to lead the church like a monarchy. Jesus alone is King. His desired relationship with us is personal. The priesthood was defrocked by Jesus. No church has a priest. Anyone that assumes to be a priest is anti-Christ. There is only one Holy Father and He is in heaven. Most of the epistles in the New Testament dealt with apologetics and contending for the faith. We desperately need this style preaching. Some of the preaching today is more for first-graders. We need to contend for truth and not remain passive by just "praying" about it. Jesus did not say "Go and pray"; He said, "Go and teach." Preaching should be fervent and urgent. Yet by the way some people talk, one would wonder if they even believe what they are saying. The "career" ministry mentality has opened the floodgates for Satan's wolves to infiltrate the church. Their shrewd business-minded strategies have turned Jesus into a cash cow. They could care less about contending for the truth as long as the place is packed. We have the scripture; we have no excuse for deception. Jesus removed mediators between us and Him. Know Him, read the Bible, flee cults.

Note

193

"But by the grace of God I am what I am: and his grace which was bestowed upon me was not in vain; but I laboured more abundantly than they all: yet not I, but the grace of God which was with me" (1 Corinthians 15:10, KJV)

We all want significance. It's natural to want to be known, to have a voice, to make our lives count. It's normal to want to be respected and valued. Evolution cheapens us to mammals, atheism cheapens us to coincidences, religion cheapens us to predestined sinners. Jesus showed us love even while we were yet sinners. Jesus did not come to condemn. For the first time, humanity experienced tangible, unconditional, passionate, and emotional love. God came among us. He loved those that religion has cast out. He valued what evolution deemed "burdens on society." He showed "nobodies" that they were not coincidences but were the love of His life. Jesus loved us to death. There is no greater love that a human can experience outside of the love of God. His love compels us. When we experience His fierce love toward us, that He would beat sin and the grave for us, how can we but respond with an attitude of total worship? Everyone can know significance, everyone can be heard, for everyone can be saved. No matter how far we have gone in sin or unbelief, sometimes those that have gone the furthest will see Him the clearest. Jesus loves us. Why do we care so much that others don't? When God loves us, values us, cares so much for us; why do we care so much when others don't? Friends, let's find our worth in Christ. Don't live off of the mere opinions of others. "Others" are not as important as God. Let's not fear "others." Only Fear God, who loves us relentlessly. If anyone attaches any "but" to the love of God toward us, they are blasphemous and enemies of the cross. Their gospel of works and conditions are anathema and have left their first love. Don't just preach the love of God to your neighbors when you hypocritically won't believe His love for yourself. Don't preach to sinners what you don't believe for yourself. If you don't believe it for yourself, how will your foolish self-convince anyone else? Jesus loves you. Jesus loves me. How does it make you feel to say "Jesus loves me"? It rolls off our tongue to say, "Jesus loves you" that's what religion wants us to say to everyone. Today I'm telling you, Jesus loves me, even me. You may not, others may not, but I know for sure Jesus does. If Jesus does, to hell with the opinions of others! Amen.

Note

194

"Then he answered and spake unto me, saying, This is the word of the Lord unto Zerubbabel, saying, Not by might, nor by power, but by my spirit, saith the Lord of hosts" (Zachariah 4:6, KJV)

Why are we going to the whole world when we are not "going" to our own worlds? When missions are a trip or a destination but it's not a lifestyle, then how do we expect to make an impact worldwide. Missions is not something we do, it's who we are. We have idolized missions as if we or our services are "Christ" to those we feel called to. When we are walking in a personal relationship with Christ, we will live on mission. Our mission won't be racially profiled or class profiled. As we are walking in a personal relationship with Christ, He will lead us as He was led in the Gospels. How many times did Christ set out to reach someone but along the way was distracted by the leading of the Spirit? Following Christ cannot be organized or listed out in bullet points. Following Christ will look more like an amazon jungle verses a manicured golf resort. It's not as clear as we would want it. When God leads, it's more like a lamp to our feet, than a lamp to our future. Our eternal future is secured but our life here can change in twenty-four hours. As we walk in relationship with Christ, He begins to lead us like no one else could. Many years from now, we will wake up one morning and wonder how did we get here. As we surrender our lives to God, He takes us on the greatest adventure of our lives. Most likely we won't know our "tomorrows" but we can be confident that God holds our tomorrow. It's when we take matters into our own hands and try to make sense of faith which can't be done, that we get discouraged and confused. Jesus wants a relationship with us that is more than just workers. We fall so naturally into routines and "busyness." When we grow familiar with our relationship with Jesus, we fall beneath the weight of a checklists. We can create more checklists than the law of Moses. Christianity that strays from scripture can lead to greater legalism than the law. Our works won't save is, our missions won't save us; as long as we are here, we will need Jesus in every detail. We plan, dream and do everything without including Christ and expect a great return. God put us here for relationship. Since the fall of man God has wanted reconciliation with us. Evangelism is not an event. It is an outflow of our relationship with Christ. Pray to reach "our" world.

Note

_____

_____

_____

_____

_____

_____

_____

_____

195

"Beware of false prophets, which come to you in sheep's clothing, but inwardly they are ravening wolves" (Matthew 7:15, KJV)

Don't give if the ministry is ashamed of the gospel. We have so many ashamed of the gospel today. They are dropping the name of Christ from their mission statement. Their vision looks no different than a humanitarian charity. They shun the proclamation of the Gospel. They are more interested in surveys of what donors want than preaching scripture or doing what God wants. They are more moved by human need than God's wants. They proclaim a gospel that puffs their works up above Christ. They feel like their ministry is equal to the work of Christ. By not preaching Christ, they are honoring their works above His. If we are ashamed of Him, He will be ashamed of us. When the preaching of the cross is seen as foolishness and outdated, we can be sure that we are nearer to the end than ever before. Concerts, entertainment and charity has outshone the preaching of the gospel in this generation. The Gospel is no longer a message but it's an action. Heretics preach the gospel but never use words. As if their works and righteousness is enough for someone to be saved. This generation cares for the glory of mankind more than the glory of God. Don't give to ministries that could care less about the glory of God but pocket the money for themselves and their families. You complain about Christianity and the church, but why are you funding it? Why don't you start putting money where your mouth is and support a ministry that is sold out to the preaching of the Gospel? As believers, we are a body and we are interdependent.

Will you support a ministry that says what needs to be said? Will you support a ministry that wants to see the gospel great again in the USA? Will you support a ministry that is willing to contend for the truth? Will you support a ministry that will preach truth whether it fills a room or empties the room? No one should be getting rich off of your generosity. Give financially to ministries that preach fervently and relentlessly the Gospel of Jesus Christ.

Note

196

"Cast thy burden upon the Lord, and he shall sustain thee: he shall never suffer the righteous to be moved" (Psalm 55:22, KJV)

Suppressing doubts, fears and anxiety is exactly what religion wants us to do. "Show no weakness." "Don't be vulnerable." "Live fake so you stay out of the way of gossips." "Isolate from everyone because no one really cares." Satan lies through any outlet possible; the worst is religion. We can't understand it but when Peter tried to talk Jesus out of the Cross, Jesus rebuked Satan. Sometimes those closest to us can be used in the worst way. Religion gives Satan a very effective weapon to keep us condemned, and that is self-reliance. It takes our eyes off the only One that can get us through life and puts it on our works, circumstances, and anything our minds' eye will entertain to distract us from Christ. Religion is so crafty. This is why billions are caught up in dead religions. Jesus wants us as we are, even with doubts, fears and sins. When He went to the cross, He made a way where we can come boldly before God. Religion gives us a set of steps, verses, promises, and rituals, but God sees past our words into our motives. All God wants is the bare us. No guile. No religion. Just a relationship that is fully in the light. God welcomes doubters, sinners and anyone who is willing to believe that Christ made the way to Him. God won't leave us in what hurts us, He changes us for His glory. Relationship with God is where the power is kindled. As we interact with Him, He empowers us to overcome. Without relationship, all we are left with is a dead religion, based on dead works, that keep us bound in condemnation. Religion will never set us free. Fakery will never set us free. Only truth sets us free. This is why we need to walk in the light as He is in the light. Live transparently with God. Paul gave Timothy some medical advice for his stomach issues. Any religion that overrides medical advice need to stay out of our journey with Christ. God can use any means to heal us. Only narrow-minded cult leaders would try to limit God's healing to just miracles. God does miracles but He also uses natural means and sometimes He calls us Home. False religions that look down on the sick should be ashamed of themselves. It's better to be sick in a relationship with Jesus than to be healthy without Him. Live wide open.

Note

197

*"A man's heart deviseth his way: but the Lord
directeth his steps" (Proverbs 16:9, KJV)*

There are no coincidences for the believer. We live in a generation that relies on coincidence. A life relying on coincidences is an anxiety filled life. The mystery of why certain things happen, drives us into a state of panic and upset. On this side of eternity, there is no way of knowing the mystery of "why"? What we must trust through it all is that God is good. There are times where the goodness of God is clouded with sickness, mental illness, death, sorrow and rejection. As long as we are here, there will be mysteries. Only fools would try to wrap their minds around faith in the goodness of God. Our minds are futile. We are like grass; we grow today and wither tomorrow. Our sure foundation is scripture. The cross is the definition of the goodness of God toward us. A popular question is: "If God is good, then 'why' this?" A better question is "If God was not good, then why the cross?" There are so many perspectives to "why" but the best is scripture. When we have a biblical perspective, our faith becomes metal. Life throws at us a lot of reason to doubt, but the cross throws at us a lot more reason to believe. Jesus Christ did not die in vain. His death sealed the goodness of God toward us. His resurrection sealed the eternal love of God toward us. Jesus gives us the best outlook on life. "Jesus, I love you. Be known through me. Be famous. Be Lord. Be God. Be all that the world hears from me." This is the prayer of the believer that knows Jesus. There are no coincidences. He is Lord of our every breath. We may not understand His methods but there are "methods to His 'seemed' madness."[26] God knows when we don't. We'll know one day. Life won't diminish our faith, because our faith is rooted in scripture. Believers live by faith. We don't live by sight. We choose to believe even when all we see is darkness. Our light is in Him. Nothing is a coincidence. Don't stop believing. Watch God turn this for good, look how He turned the crucifixion for good. He can turn this for good. Jesus loves us. Jesus cares. Even in the darkest storm His Word is our brightest light. It won't be this way forever. Forever will be abundant, but in this life, we will have trouble. There are no coincidences. Jesus is Lord. Trust.

Note

---

26. Based on an old saying "Method in madness."

"Let your conversation be without covetousness; and be content with such things as ye have: for he hath said, I will never leave thee, nor forsake thee. Let your conversation be without covetousness; and be content with such things as ye have: for he hath said, I will never leave thee, nor forsake thee" (Hebrews 13:5–6, KJV)

Are you tired of walking around with your tail between your legs? Giving yourself to the pleasures of the world will only leave you abused. The world's head may have been turned from you. They may not approve of you but who are "they" anyway. Why have you given the world so much authority to determine your value? The only person you are responsible for is yourself. If we don't believe His Word for ourselves, we will have no impact on others around us. Judas wanted to be "Christ" to the world more than trusting Christ for himself. A prostitute had more revelation than the apostle. She was willing to give what she had to worship Jesus knowing only Jesus could fulfill her deepest need of love. She knew that what Christ had, no other man could give her. Jesus always had time for the one. There are more records of Jesus being one on one, than Him being with a crowd. Jesus cared for the one. No matter who you are or what you have done, believe that you have the attention of Jesus. It was the desperate and broken people that had His attention more than anyone else. You are a perfect candidate that He went out of His way for. No one else may have gone out of their way for you but Christ did. He went out of His way for the one. You are the one. You are the apple of His eye. Just because you are overlooked by people, does not mean that you are overlooked by God. His eye is not only on the sparrow. Don't listen to the condemnation that you are "too…," whatever. God's eyes are on you. It's time to come out from the religious closet. The religious money changing days are nearly over. Their walls are coming down. Religion wants crowds but could care less for relationship. Those that don't have the character that Christ had, don't need to be listened to. If we are to be conformed to His image, then why do we value a crowd more than the one? God is interested in you. When you talk to Him, you have His full attention. God is a "one-on-one" God. Jesus proved His passion for relationship throughout the gospels. Judas the apostle missed out on what was most important. His ministry, fame or charity did not do it for him. He missed out on what religion destroys, relationship. You are the head and not the tail. Be who God wants you to be before His throne, yourself. He will do the rest.

Note

199

*"That ye may be the children of your Father which is in heaven:
for he maketh his sun to rise on the evil and on the good, and
sendeth rain on the just and on the unjust" (Matthew 5:45, KJV)*

Christianity is the world's largest religion. It was not always this way. There are more professing Christians on the planet than ever before. Doubting Christ today is foolish. How could Jesus have become so famous after dying on a cross? Even His followers abandoned Him. It's obvious that He rose from the dead. Every other religion fails their society and their followers. Look how Christianity has influenced the West. Even though many Christians don't follow Christ, He still does good to those that despitefully use Him. Why would anyone look to the failing religions and governments of the world when Christ has been tried and true for hundreds of years? No other race or religion can compare to those that trust in Jesus Christ as Lord. There is no other way to the Father but through Jesus. There is no person, no race, no pedigree that can get the attention of God. Faith alone in Christ gets the attention of God. He leveled the ground between gender, race and nationality. Only Jesus Christ is the way, truth and life. When we elevate one people group above another, we need to be rebuked like Paul did Peter.[27] There is no discrimination in the heart of Jesus. "Whosoever will" can be saved; this is what Jesus taught. Peter reached for a sword to defend Jesus but Jesus does not need

---

[27.] *"But when Peter was come to Antioch, I withstood him to the face, because he was to be blamed." (Galatians 2:11, KJV)*

our weapons or defense. Even after Pentecost, Peter needed to be sat down and be corrected. We all need accountability. Don't follow any church that claims Peter as their founder. We look to Christ as our founder; not a pope, priest or pastor. We don't need help with interpreting scripture; we have the Bible and the Holy Spirit. The more we believe in Jesus and apply His Word to our lives; the more favor and blessing will be poured out on us and everyone else. Those that are from other parts of the world or believe in false god should assimilate, convert or live quietly. The evidence of Jesus being Lord is right before our eyes and there is no other that can compare. Evangelists should pray for the conversion of every one that has not come to faith in Christ. Profession is not enough. Jesus said, "You must be born again." The church must rise in the boldness of the proofs of Christ. The church must not be influenced by failed practices but wholly trust in Scripture as our source for life and truth. Jesus does not need our help; He wants our faith. Let's remain unashamed.

Note

_____

_____

_____

_____

_____

_____

_____

_____

_____

200

"For God hath not given us the spirit of fear; but of power, and of love, and of a sound mind" (2 Timothy 1:7, KJV)

Our minds can run out of control in dark times. We can play out scenarios and cave into fear. Our minds can be very sensitive to unexpected changes. When our minds are flooded and our thoughts accumulate, we can get crippled with fear. What keeps our minds balanced is the truth of scripture. Scripture harnesses our thoughts and makes them accountable to the Word of God. This is why abiding in His Word is so important. Scripture is fuel for our faith, faith anchors our thoughts. Faith takes captive fear and brings it to the obedience of Christ's Word. When we build our thought life on God's Word, we become strong. The emphasis is always the Word of God. As good as our soundbites or our exposition may be, it's the truth of scripture that brings freedom. The freedom that God brings to the mind is really a willing submission to His Word. When we yield to His Word, we find freedom. Our minds can spiral as our thoughts roam freely. God wants our thought life; once He has our thought life, then we can have a prayer life. We gain a new mind in Christ. We gain the mind of Christ. We choose to think through His mind. A believer can have their thoughts processed through a biblical filter. As we are studying the Word, memorizing the Word, He gives us a new filter/mind. So, in the dead of night, we have the light of His Word filtering our fears through His truth. We all have filters, whether they are cultural or personal, some filters are more reserved than others. God is the greatest filter. When we hold every thought accountable to God's Word, then we can take every thought that is contrary to the Word captive and bring it through prayer to Christ who destroys the spirit of fear. This is why the believer needs a renewing of the mind. Christ renews our minds daily as we are reading His Word. It is written that we don't live by food alone but by the truth of scripture. Let the mind of Christ reign in us. We will be fearless when we give over to the truth of scripture. Oh, what a freedom we have when our Faith is fueled by His Word.

Note

201

"To the one we are the savour of death unto death; and to the other the savour of life unto life. And who is sufficient for these things?" (2 Corinthians 2:16, KJV)

The mind of Christ gives us a God-perspective of what we are facing. Believers need a renewing of our minds. There is an ongoing battle in our minds between fact and faith. We can either filter our sight through our mind or through the mind of Christ. We are to "put on the mind of Christ" as believers. This is a conscious daily decision to choose a "God point of view." When our past haunts us and our present torments us, remember Christ. There is nothing worth looking back on or looking forward to more than Christ. Our past and present must not determine our point of view. To have a "God point of view," we must choose to put on the mind of Christ. His perspective makes our mountains become mustard seeds. There is no such thing as a big faith or a small faith. With a mustard seed of faith, we can have a God perspective of our mountains. We are to focus; our periphery is what feeds our mind doubts. When our minds' eye is focused on Christ, we will have God's point of view throughout our life. Don't compare ourselves with others, don't mix facts with faith. We either believe or we don't. There is no way that a believer can live by sight and faith. Scripture gives us a single focus as we study it. Most don't have time for scripture and they hope the guy behind the pulpit has "a word" for them. Our model today has millions set up for deception. No preacher has an infallible word. We can nourish our own faith by reading scripture for ourselves.

What we hear should be a confirmation and not a new revelation. If we never get weaned off depending on the pulpit to dependence on scripture, we will be open prey to deception. If the preacher does not elevate scripture above their oratory skill, then we are in trouble. Our generation will pack out for an orator but they won't study scripture for themselves. Humanity craves mediators more than going to God for themselves. That's why we quote everyone but scripture. This craving will leave us unsatisfied. Christ made a way for all to know God for ourselves. If we want a "God point of view," we need to put on the mind of Christ. His mind is laid out by scripture. It's up to us to take doubts captive and bring them to obedience of Christ. This is a daily decision. Continue in faith.

Note

202

*"Judge not, that ye be not judged. For with what judgment
ye judge, ye shall be judged: and with what measure ye mete,
it shall be measured to you again. And why beholdest thou
the mote that is in thy brother's eye, but considerest not the
beam that is in thine own eye?" (Matthew 7:1–3, KJV)*

Don't you dare judge anyone's eternity. Who do any of us think that we are to look down upon one another for any reason? There is no room for "snootiness" in the believer. When we gossip, malign or mock another person because we feel better than them, we are set up to fall. The Bible is clear that we have all sinned. We all have reason to be ashamed. We all have secrets in our closet. If our thoughts from our whole life were put on display, we would all be ashamed of ourselves. The people we judge to hell are no different than any of us. What we feed grows; what we starve dies. When our flesh is left without correction or instruction, we will be surprised at what our flesh is capable of doing. When we understand how much we have been forgiven, it's easier to forgive others. No matter what sin or self-righteous life style we live, both sides put Christ to the cross. Don't you dare judge, lest we be judged. How can we throw a stone at anyone when we ourselves are under our own boulders? We can discern, but we must not judge. Judgement is not our place; it's God's. Don't assume to be God. That never worked out for anyone. Discernment is not judgement; it's spiritual insight. We need discernment so that when we are conversing, we can hear past the words and into the motives of what is being communicated. God will show us the heart of the tatted criminal who was abused, rejected and hated his whole childhood. God will give us discernment so that we can preach truth in the most compassionate way. When we preach, we need the right emotion and the right approach to each of our audiences. This is why we need discernment. Discernment will fill us with compassion and not judgment. When we discern, we can see the person as God sees them. Rather than relying on a strategy and condemnation, we need to rely on God. Methodology will not work with evangelism; it only leads to arguments. Arguments don't convert anyone. Judgement does not convert anyone. Jesus never had to argue with sinners; Jesus never judged sinners; only the religious felt the weight of His anger. Not once did Jesus take a whip to sinners, but he sure did to the religious. We know that we have the heart of Jesus when sinners feel comfortable around us but the religious are repulsed. Read the Gospels.

Note

203

"It is the spirit that quickeneth; the flesh profiteth nothing: the words that I speak unto you, they are spirit, and they are life" (John 6:63, KJV)

The ignoramus religious think their methodology of evangelism will argue people into salvation. Jesus came to fulfill the methodologies of the Law. What Jesus fulfilled we have been reinventing since Pentecost. Christianity is not a religion, lifestyle or culture; it's a relationship with God first. Christ did not come with a new set of rules so that we can be justified by works. Jesus taught that faith in Him is what God determined as righteousness. The law taught that obedience was righteousness; but none could fully obey this law, therefore we kept falling short. Jesus obeyed all the way to the cross so that we can be saved by faith alone. When the pompous religious boasted in their works and a sinful tax collector hit his chest trusting God to be merciful, Jesus told His followers that the repentant sinner was justified. The way God deems justification is by faith in Christ. Faith in Christ is evidenced by repentance and a need for His mercy. Justification cannot be earned. The repentant sinner was honest and had no religious garb to hide behind. It's harder for the religious to be saved than it is for the sinner. Jesus offended the religious by exposing their hearts, thoughts, agendas, motives and character. Run from the ignoramus religious that talk themselves up above Christ and demand titles in front of their names but demean their Lord by calling Him by His first name when they refer to Him in their sermons. Repentant sinners are the community we want to surround ourselves with rather than with self-righteous gossips. When we are walking in relationship with Jesus, evangelism will be discerning and tailored to our audience; it will be a "want to" and not a dead religious "have to." Don't be "bewitched" by human methods and all other charades to be a Christian or to evangelize. They have sold out an authentic relationship for a dead "Methodist" religion. Jesus died to reconcile us into an eternal relationship with Him. If we miss knowing Him and depending on Him, we will get the same judgment as all the blatant sins we rail against. Jesus taught very clearly who He came to save and it was not the "found," it was the lost. Those that were "found" were more lost than those whom they would have defined as "lost" at the time of Jesus.

Note

_____

_____

_____

_____

_____

_____

_____

_____

_____

204

*"For there is nothing covered, that shall not be revealed;
neither hid, that shall not be known" (Luke 12:2, KJV)*

There are more people coming out of the "closet" in our generation than ever before. Some are shocked, others are mortified. The religious for decades have loved to keep all these lifestyles secrets and tucked away behind closed doors. Coming out of the closet is fuel for God to do something great. When we come out to be who we are in its fullest sense, then we are ripe for God to turn up in our lives. Religion suppresses who we really are, clothes us, and makes us hide behind our works as a smoke screen. Jesus died so that we could come to Him as we are. Going to God as someone else or with pretense will not get us anywhere in our relationship with Him. There is no human that can fully know us and fully love us. Only God can do that. We search for that kind of love in all types of relationships, hobbies and careers but never seem to find "peace." We never seem to find the right person or people that can be to us what only God can be to us. Religion builds walls, establishes formalities and distances who we really are from God. God loves us for who we are. While we were yet sinners, He loved us. His love is toward all of us. There is no sin that His blood can't cleanse or wash away. Sin is more than a list of certain behaviors. We are not sinners for what we do, we are born in sin. In ourselves, we are sinners for who we are and not just for what we do. Christ did not come to just make us all behave a certain way. He came to save us, reconcile us and draw us into a relationship that our soul has been longing for since Eden. Jesus is the answer to the intimacy we are all looking for. What He gives us, quenches every thirst for relationship, identity and love. Jesus is the bedrock of Christianity. Religion focuses on fruits, behaviors and lifestyle, but Jesus dealt with the root, sin. He took on Himself everything religion despises. When we receive Him, we become whole. He replaces the old heart that kept disappointing us with a new heart that satisfies our wants. Jesus makes the crooked path straight. He takes us as we are but never leaves us as we are. He preserves us from aids, disease and makes us the healthiest reproducers we could ever be. No one walked away from Jesus physically sicker. Go to Jesus as you are and leave as He is, whole.

Note

_____

_____

_____

_____

_____

_____

_____

_____

_____

205

"Through mighty signs and wonders, by the power of the Spirit of God; so that from Jerusalem, and round about unto Illyricum, I have fully preached the gospel of Christ" (Romans 15:19, KJV)

The Holy Spirit in us is a river and not a reservoir. He is there to flow through us the character, culture and holiness of Christ. The Holy Spirit does not work with our consumerism. He is not in us so that we can Lord over Him or use Him for self-gratification. When the Holy Spirit is flowing through us, we will be witnesses of Christ to the lost. Signs and wonders follow the preaching of the gospel, not precede it. Signs, wonders, and the Holy Spirit have been idolized in some circles. Anything sought after more than glorifying Christ is idolatry. Seeking anything but to glorify Christ blocks the Holy Spirit from flowing through us. Gathering to call on the Holy Spirit for any other reason but to evangelize is idolatry. The revivals of the past that elevate preachers and miracles are abhorrent in the sight of God. An authentic move of God won't gratify the flesh but will glorify Jesus Christ. Honoring the Holy Spirit above Christ will not be anointed and the spirit behind it is a strange spirit. Few are discerning the spirits today. They care more about an experience than truth. Manifestations must not "wow" us more than Scripture or we will be open prey for deception. If God does not give self-control and a sound mind, then the Spirit of Christ is not at work in the midst. The sixty-six books of the Bible are our infallible Scripture for instruction and correction. The Spirit of Christ is the Spirit of truth and He never contradicts Himself. Uncontrollable laughter is unbiblical; uncontrollable falling back wards for believers is unbiblical. There is no evidence that the Holy Spirit does that in Scripture. We should be known as a Jesus church and not elevating any doctrine or experience above Christ. Any church that does is potentially a cult. Are we burdened for sinners to be saved? That's the only manifestation of the Holy Spirit that we should be excited about. The preaching of the Gospel is the most important gauge to determine how mature we are in the faith. No one must excuse the preaching of the Gospel only to the evangelist. We are all called to do the work of an evangelist. If there is no desire to witness for Christ or share the Gospel, there might be no Holy Spirit in you.

Note

_____

_____

_____

_____

_____

_____

_____

_____

_____

206

"My people are destroyed for lack of knowledge: because thou hast rejected knowledge, I will also reject thee, that thou shalt be no priest to me: seeing thou hast forgotten the law of thy God, I will also forget thy children" (Hosea 4:6, KJV)

When common sense is not common anymore, where do we get our sense from? What is the basis of our sense? When we are left without instruction, we are susceptible to any base action. Jesus Christ gives us "heavens' sense." It may not be common, but He's a better sense than anything the world offers. When we are walking in relationship with Jesus, we become creative, wise and discerning. As we fuel our faith with scripture and know Jesus in relationship, our limitations become our qualifications. Surrounding ourselves with Jesus-lovers is the greatest community. A community where everyone has each other's back. A community that is encouraging, edifying and enriching. This is the Church. No community can compare to the Church. Common sense within the church is the most productive sense that we could ever get as believers. Let's be common sense believers. Our senses are not what lead us. We are led by Christ. We do not want to follow our hearts or our desires; most of us did in the past, and it left us empty. Fulfillment is in Christ. May we be set alight with a conviction like no other generation. The Church may be sleeping; some have incorrectly deemed her dead, but she is awakening. We are on the brink of dawn. The greatest days of the church are right before us. Truth will prevail. Christ is coming back for a bride that is white hot in evangelism, worship, scripture and prayer.

A generation of truth-seekers that want common sense preaching is rising today. We don't want wishy-washy messages. We are tired of all the political correctness. We want biblical correctness. The pulpit is not for politicians. For too long, the church has been riddled with politics. People see past the smiles and know "Eli's" generation is ending. "Samuel's" generation is rising. The storehouse is ready for the genuine to rise up with a "biblical sense" message to replace the weak "common sense" message of today. We have been mandated to contend for the truth. The "Peters" of our generation must be confronted to their face as to why they are so gospel light in their content. Why have they attempted to conform the church to their culture rather than conforming to the image of Christ? Conform to the image of Christ; quote Jesus more than everyone else.

Note

207

"The fear of the Lord is the beginning of wisdom: and the knowledge of the holy is understanding" (Proverbs 9:10, KJV)

The fear of the Lord is the beginning of wisdom. Jesus will be taken seriously. We have many that would make Jesus out to be our peer but He is Lord. We will always be created beings. None of us were there in the beginning. Growing familiar in our relationship with Jesus never worked out for anyone. He is the last person that we should grow familiar with. When our prayer life is a cheap repetitive sentence, when our Bible reading is done out of duty, when our church going is just what we do, we are not taking Jesus seriously. The fear of the Lord is not living scared of God. It's not putting on religious fig leaves. God wants to be taken seriously. When we pray, we are bringing our thoughts, agendas and motives to God. When we do ministry, it's because He told us to do it and not just a good idea. Our relationship with Jesus is not a mental ascent, but it leads to an action of obedience. Ministry is obedience and if it's not, don't do it. Satan is not threatened by our might or strength. Even the angels would not rebuke him; the Archangel Michael said, "The lord rebuke you."[28] Obeying Jesus will offend natural thinkers. We can know it's of God by how much faith it takes us to do what God has called us to. We can expect nay sayers and every attack possible. God uses it all to refine our faith and work a fight in us where only

---

[28]. *"Yet Michael the archangel, when contending with the devil he disputed about the body of Moses, durst not bring against him a railing accusation, but said, The Lord rebuke thee." (Jude 1:9, KJV)*

He is focused on. We will be held responsible for our faithfulness to our call. Fearing God means not seeking to be the fan of man. When we are submitted to God, Satan can be resisted and he will flee in Jesus's name. Sara scoffed the will of God when she heard that she would give birth. Don't scorn or mock the will of God. It's playing with fire. Michal scorned David's joy of the Ark being returned to Israel. Rebellion against the will of God leads to anxiety and is equal to witch craft. If we want wisdom, fear God over everyone. Take God seriously today; tomorrow is not promised. There is nothing that is more important than our relationship with God. When Jesus is not first in our lives, our whole life will be out of order. We will never find fulfillment in any job, location or materialistic possession. The call of God must not be resisted. Read of those that resisted the call of God. Pharaoh would beg all of us to be teachable, don't harden your heart.

Note

208

"Yea, a man may say, Thou hast faith, and I have works:
shew me thy faith without thy works, and I will shew
thee my faith by my works" (James 2:18, KJV)

Loving God is not evidenced only in song or prayer but in action. Believers are called to feed faith to others. If Peter loved Jesus, He would have been equipping others. This is why Jesus told him: "If you love me, you would feed my sheep."[29] God loved us by giving. Love is not an emotion; love is an action. The emotions follow the actions but actions rarely follow emotions. Faith nearly always works contradictory to feelings. When God speaks, our feelings will generally kick against faith. The actions God calls us to do are not easy; in fact, if it's not impossible, God may not have called us to the action. Peter could not do what Jesus called him to do, even if he wanted to. Like us, he had to be endued with power. God's kingdom can only grow so much in our strength. Anything we build without God is like a sandcastle to the enemy. This is why we see the enemy taking ground. We have all these seminars, conferences, marketing experts, etc., that teach how to build the kingdom of God without evangelism, prayer and sound doctrine. Aesthetics, music style, and trendy clothes may pack a room, but what about packing the hearts in the room with faith? Jesus spent most of his ministry in the open air,

---

29. *"He saith unto him the third time, Simon, son of Jonas, lovest thou me? Peter was grieved because he said unto him the third time, Lovest thou me? And he said unto him, Lord, thou knowest all things; thou knowest that I love thee. Jesus saith unto him, Feed my sheep." (John 21:17, KJV)*

with the sick, preaching to sinners! Does it bother us that we are not conforming to His likeness and mission? We have charlatan evangelists in the pulpits across America. They are using evangelism to pack their rooms but the Gospel they preach tickles ears. Pastors should be discipling their congregants and not poaching from other churches. If an evangelist is the leader, the church will be a mile wide but an inch deep. Sunday mornings are for the church, it's not an evangelistic outreach. Peter was mandated to feed his sheep. Believers must be fed to grow and not kept as a dollar amount in the pew. Churches equip to send out, not equip to keep in; that's a cult. They should not be intimidated losing tithe or numbers to the mission field. Disciples start as sheep but grow to become shepherds. We don't stay sheep; we morph to become shepherds as we grow. We believe in the priesthood of all believers. We are saved to be multipliers and not consumers. Producing is way more satisfying than consuming. Feed the sheep, don't just feed yourself. Faith in His Word is our fuel to action.

Note

209

"Whereas ye know not what shall be on the morrow. For what is your life? It is even a vapour, that appeareth for a little time, and then vanisheth away" (James 4:14, KJV)

The way it is now, won't be forever. We live in an ever-changing world. Millions have gone before us. Our time here is like a vapor. Seasons in our lives can feel so long. Don't rush the season. Process the purpose of the season because God is intentional with every believer. God does not waste time. Every character that He called, went through all types of seasons. Some longer than others. Some were only a matter of hours, like Samuel, but others took forty or more years to start their next season, like Moses. Don't rush the season. Moses did and all he accomplished was killing an Egyptian slave driver. There is no telling how long each season lasts for each of us. We are all on our own tailored journey. Scripture sheds so much light on the fruit of waiting on God. No one waited on God and was disappointed in the end. Why God waits is a mystery; why God took six days to create the earth; and even why God rested is a mystery. Our God is a God of process. Our generation could care less for the process; we want everything immediately. Hardly nothing of quality happens immediately for us. Does that mean that God does not function in the immediate? God does what God wants. That's what makes Him God. We can trust that God turns all things for good to those that love Him. For those that don't, eternal life does not fare well. Loving God and wanting His will, even when our flesh can't stand it is mega faith in His sight. If we want this to turn for good, we need to check our love for God. Life can feed our blame and bitterness toward God. It will try to corrode our trust in the love of God. This is why we anchor to scripture and relationship with Him. Even if we don't feel the love of God or see His love in what we are going through, we can believe His love is there. The crucifixion of Christ is enough evidence for us all to believe that God is love. This is why Jesus wanted us to remember what He accomplished. He knew the trouble we would face from life: Satan and the flesh. Don't buy into the western gospel, which says that we will have heaven here. We will wrestle within and without until the day we die. All things will work together for good. This promise can be trusted because God has a purpose to our calling in this season. Don't rush, wait.

Note

210

"Be sober, be vigilant; because your adversary the devil, as a roaring lion, walketh about, seeking whom he may devour" (1 Peter 5:8, KJV)

Satan has unleashed spiritual wickedness all across the earth. He is seeking whom he may enter. Drugs, alcohol and substances which make us lose control, open the door for his possession. He can't force his way in but we can leave the door open for him. It's up to us to steward our decisions. We are all one decision away from our lives changing forever. We live in the valley of decision-making until we die. We must choose this day whom we will serve. Whatever we feed—grows, whatever we starve—dies. Whatever we sow—we reap. To be a disciple of Christ, means filtering our decisions through Him in prayer. Do we include God in our decision making? If we don't, then who is Lord of our lives. We can only serve one of two masters. There are so many people wide open to be possessed by Satan. They open themselves up to everything and anything. We desperately need to repent and only open our hearts to Jesus. Making Jesus Lord is the safest decision we could ever make. Having His leading in our lives makes us wiser than those without Him. Having reverence for life is so important. We have such a party mind-set as a generation. It's time to take life seriously. We need to put away the foolishness. It's time to pray, read our Bibles, and repent of sin. We have been lured to sleep. The enemy has distracted us with entertainment. The Church is the only force on earth to withhold the darkness. When the church is caught up, and the grace of God is removed from the earth, there will be violence, bloodshed and all forms of wickedness. We are reaching the peak of grace. Everything is pointing to the return of Christ. The prophecies are unfolding by the day. We are one day away from life changing forever. As believers, we need to shut the door to sin, compromise, and passivity. We are so passive as a generation. We have been dumbed down by the pulpits. Where are the men of conviction, passion and anointing? Where are the men that lift their voices and are fervent for the things of God? We burn for sports, hobbies, and everything else but Christ. God set a fire in us for holiness, scripture and prayer. Repentance must be preached. The haughty have no weight in their words. The repentant before Christ are the only threats to the enemy here. Repent.

Note

211

*"Knowing that whatsoever good thing any man
doeth, the same shall he receive of the Lord, whether
he be bond or free" (Ephesians 6:8, KJV)*

God can place such a burden for souls that in the opening prayer of a sermon, the call can be given to follow Christ. Our sermons can't persuade anyone to be saved. Being Spirit led in the presentation of the Gospel, calls for immediate response to His prompting. Our opening prayer is the most important part of the sermon. We can discern the opening prayer if the preacher is reliant on themselves or on God. Sinners have more discernment than the Christians of America. The people that pay tithe will be held accountable for feeding the preacher who tickles their ears. We can complain about the pulpits, but it's the congregations that are funding it. If people started giving to what God has called them to and not to what they want, we would see a very different Church. Churches are doing what seems to be right; congregants are doing what seems to be right; but what about doing what God tells you to do? Why are so many people afraid of bringing God in on their decision-making? God is good. Anything God asks is always in our best interest. We don't fully trust that God is good, so we end up keeping God out of what's important to us. We want what we want, at all cost but we will pay for it in the end. The greatest life we could live is the life that God has for us and not the life we want for ourselves. Maturity as believers has got nothing to do with our knowledge, journals, scripture memorization, or ministry experience. Maturity is following the leading of Christ; doing what Christ has told us to do. A child put the apostles to shame by showing more spiritual maturity when he came in faith to provide his loaves and fish for Jesus to multiply. When we can't learn, when we can't be instructed, when we rely on yesterday's manna, all we will have is worms for today, just like yesterday's manna is the wilderness.[30] Yesterday's awakening must not be relied on today. God calls us to relationship where His mercy is new every morning. When we plateau spiritually, we will become lukewarm. A lukewarm life gets spat of Jesus's mouth. There are many that are about to get spat out of the body of Christ. Their charlatan, prayer-less, money hungry days are coming to an end. Judgement is going to start in the church. Only the sincere in their relationship with God will make it.

Note

---

30. *"Notwithstanding they hearkened not unto Moses; but some of them left of it until the morning, and it bred worms, and stank: and Moses was wroth with them." (Exodus 16:20, KJV)*

212

"If a man say, I love God, and hateth his brother, he is a liar:
for he that loveth not his brother whom he hath seen, how can
he love God whom he hath not seen?" (1 John 4:20, KJV)

The military care for their wounded on the front lines. They don't leave their own for dead. They do all they can to rescue, deliver or take care of their injured soldier. Religion is totally the opposite; they abandon their fallen and trust God to either heal them or take them home. Some even mock their fallen or throw a cheap shot at them while they're down. Religion is so cold and hateful. It starts wars and breeds judgment. How does it make you feel when someone in ministry falls? Do you pray for them or sarcastically mock them? The seat of the scoffers is a fearful place to sit. That pride will lead to our own demise. There has been so much child abuse and financial abuse covered up. Where there is religion, these two abuses are prevalent. Religion is so dark and manipulative. The bait is shame and the switch is judgment. Religion takes our time, talent and treasure, and then leaves us with nothing. Religion tortures faith until the faith is starved to death. Religion is faithless. It has big budgets, buildings and business. Jesus had none of it, yet so many have made Him a cash cow and look nothing like Him in character, culture or compassion. Judas felt the full brunt of trying to make a living off Jesus. If ever Christ needs to be preached, it's today. The bodyguards, armored vehicles, and adoration of those behind the pulpit is so different than the way Jesus lives. They crave titles; they crave to be heard; their clothing alone gives them away. Religion uses fear to keep everything buried for the "testimony" of the Gospel. The end justifies the means for the religious. It takes from the vulnerable. If Jesus is our Lord shouldn't we be looking like Him in character and culture. We quote all sorts of preachers, but what about Jesus? When was the last time we got excited from His Sermons? Does it matter to us that we have so many churches but very few of them care to reflect Christ? They will reflect successful preachers and singers, but what about Jesus? Have we all drank the Kool-Aid of passivity. Prayer is not passivity. The book of Acts is appropriately named because it's the book of actions. The Holy Spirit worked through the Church. Let's contend, for Christ's sake.

Note

_____

_____

_____

_____

_____

_____

_____

_____

_____

213

"And surely your blood of your lives will I require; at the hand of every beast will I require it, and at the hand of man; at the hand of every man's brother will I require the life of man. Whoso sheddeth man's blood, by man shall his blood be shed: for in the image of God made he man" (Genesis 9:5–6, KJV)

Humanity has dominion over the earth. We are superior beings on planet earth. Our bodies are designed. Only a fool would think that coincidence or evolution put us here. Our design is too detailed to come from nothing. God created us. God had no beginning; He is the uncreated One. He was not caught by surprise when man fell or when we fall. God knows all of us, yet loves us the same. In our total depravity, God chose relationship with us. He desired us over and over again. His plan from the beginning was to reconcile us to Himself. Christ saved us from sin, Satan and ourselves. Salvation is not only a response to the Gospel, but it's a journey of following Him to the day He calls us home. Not everyone makes it to the end of the journey. How we finish matters more than when/how we start. God wants to finish the work He began in us. There has been an increase in falling away and departures from the faith in the West. Where are the no-nonsense preachers for our generation? We have been left with smooth-talkers from the pulpits that have no power to live what they preach when the mic is turned off. It's time to break the bushels of the world, religion and hell. Let His light shine in us. Show no shame. Get more undignified than this. In Christ, we have authority and benefits. Let's not forget what we gain in Christ. Let's not forget

His benefits given to us. Let's not live as slaves, when we are free sons of God in Christ. Let no one diminish the benefits of the cross in us. Be who we are called to be and be it boldly. Don't fall into the snare of false humility and pity; that's the cowards form of leadership. We are what we are by the grace of God. We find our security in Christ and not in man. God is for us; we pity those that stand in His way. Embrace those that stand in our way because they are fueling God to lead us further than the limitations that they put on us for His glory. God always chooses the least likely so that no one shares His glory. The uncreated One will not share His glory with limited created beings like us. Jesus Christ will be glorified and get the full reward of His sufferings. He did not get crucified in vain. His day of reckoning will come. Jesus is to be revered. He is in us.

Note

214

*"Wherefore come out from among them, and be ye separate,
saith the Lord, and touch not the unclean thing; and
I will receive you" (2 Corinthians 6:17, KJV)*

Living in hiding will keep us bound. We are ingrained to come before God as we would come before an employer for an interview. This is why the believer needs a renewing of mind, renewing of culture and renewing of attitude. When the biblical Gospel draws sinners, they hear, "Come as you are!" Is our Gospel biblical? Do we preach good news? Jesus came to bring good news, but critics today call it light, cheap and weak on sin. Preaching sinners can only be justified by faith in Christ repulses those that have heeded the temptation of Satan. Satan not only tempts with sin, but with religion too. Satan hates faith. Self-righteousness is his lure to deception; he wants us focused on works for salvation. Have you read Jesus's sermons to the sinner? What would you have said of Jesus's style of evangelism? Those that reject the Gospel as good news for the sinner should look for a millstone. Their Gospel of "faith" and discipleship for salvation must be challenged. Discipleship is not for salvation. Salvation leads to discipleship. If discipleship is for "salvation," then you have made Christ of no effect and should expect the fires of hell. "Anathema"[31] to the gospel of works. Our self-righteousness secures our eternal destination in hell. Every sinner gets saved the same way. Faith in Christ.

[31.] *"If any man love not the Lord Jesus Christ, let him be Anathema Maranatha." (1 Corinthians 16:22, KJV)*

Christ alone is the way to the Father. Any other man-made way, discipleship or work, makes us thieves in the sight of God because we did not enter by the door. Faith in Christ is evidenced by a genuine need for Christ, which is called repentance. Anyone who preaches that we don't need a repentant attitude has been bewitched by the tempter. We will need Christ to the day we die. The Holy Spirit is grieved by the "gospel" that graduates us from a need for Christ. The Holy Spirit will convict us of sin. When a believer sins if He is in us, we will feel His grief. Do we grieve over sin? Does sin even bother us? Does trying to be righteous without Christ repulse us? The Holy Spirit will convict the believer as the believer confesses their need for Him. We can't change ourselves. Trying to change ourselves is like trying to keep the law of Moses. We can't. If we could, we would not have needed Christ to save us. Just as much as we can't save ourselves, we can't sanctify ourselves.

Note

_____

_____

_____

_____

_____

_____

_____

_____

215

"By this shall all men know that ye are my disciples, if
ye have love one to another" (John 13:35, KJV)

How can we say we love Jesus but hate His Church? How can we worship Jesus in song but curse our brother? Loving Jesus yet hating His Church is where many have ended up in their walk with God. The church was never supposed to be our savior. The church is like a Hospital but everyone in it is a patient. No one in the church is immune. Church attracts sinners. Jesus did, so will His Church. When we are let down by the church leaders, we should not be surprised. Jesus's last written words in Revelation speak of issues with His Church. The Church will always be a work in progress but it will never perfect. We will never find a perfect church or a perfect leader. On the leader's best day, we still fall short of the glory of God. We must beware of raising anyone above Christ or His Word. Cults love to honor man above God. Cults love to emphasize man's interpretation, over scripture interpreting itself. The church was never supposed to be a building. The church was always flesh and blood. Jesus never gave blue prints to buildings. We as believers are His Church. We are His ambassadors. We are not "mini-Christs." We need Him as much as anyone else. Our life will teach what depending on Him really means. We live contrite, repentant and dependent on God. The church of Jesus lives. It's not bricks or mortar. Events, missions, and buildings seem to be more important than making disciples today. Teach what Christ taught. Love like Christ loved. When a sinner knows how much they have been forgiven, it enables them to forgive others. When we understand that our sins put Jesus on the cross, we are enabled to forgive others of our offense against them. It's when we don't understand our own need for forgiveness that we hold on to bitterness. Self-righteousness is the filthiest of sins that we could commit in the sight of God. He calls our righteousness filthy rags in Isaiah 64:6.[32] It makes us independent of God. We emphasize the moral law to show our sin nature but we are not only sinners by what we do, we are sinners by who we are. We were born in sin. We were born with an independent nature from God. The Church is a Hospital where only Jesus is the Doctor because we are all dying. There is no spiritual doctor but Jesus. Every person is sin-sick. Love the Church as Christ loves you. Be gracious; do not forsake the assembly. Honor Christ by loving others.

Note

[32] *"But we are all as an unclean thing, and all our righteousnesses are as filthy rags; and we all do fade as a leaf; and our iniquities, like the wind, have taken us away." (Isaiah 64:6, KJV)*

216

"But now thus saith the Lord that created thee, O Jacob, and he that formed thee, O Israel, Fear not: for I have redeemed thee, I have called thee by thy name; thou art mine" (Isaiah 43:1, KJV)

God knows you by name. In a world where wealth, fame and pedigree determine significance, billions believe the lie that they don't matter as much. When titles, gifting and influence feed discrimination, that foundation will not stand the storm of life. Jesus walked past those that the religious catered to and called to Him those the religious would have judged. He called by name those, that the religious would have cursed by name. The religious discriminated between rich and poor. Jesus drew the discriminated. When we only associate with those that are richer than us, those who look like us, those who behave like us, then we are no different than the religious that called for the crucifixion of Christ. How many preachers are seen in our urban communities? How many preachers invite the poor to lunch? If preachers don't resemble Christ in character, they will have no weight to their words. Their words will fall on deaf ears. It's convenient to do missions one week out of the year but what about living on mission? How can we say we know Jesus but know nothing of the life He lived? Mega-church pastors and best-selling Christian authors are not the example of success, Jesus is. Haircuts, trendy clothes, and fancy suits are not the image we should be aiming for. What about conforming to the character of Christ? We have very little biblical churches but thousands of personality cults. When a pastor or teacher pushes anything more than reading the Bible for ourselves or knowing Jesus for ourselves, they are in rebellion to God's mandate on them. Leaders foolishly think that the people exist for their gain. Jesus put the people ahead of Himself, but today leaders put themselves ahead of their congregations. Rather than congregations getting discipled, they are paying so the pastor hoards all the discipleship for himself and his staff. Seminaries have replaced the mandate on the local church. Professors can't teach what a local pastor can. Jesus never sent people to text books or class rooms. He demonstrated; we have so many dead head teachers that have a form of godliness but our lives teach better than any text book we could give anyone. Why isn't the Bible enough? You can have as much of Christ as anyone else!

Note

217

"And grieve not the holy Spirit of God, whereby ye are sealed unto the day of redemption" (Ephesians 4:30, KJV)

Grieve over sin before it's too late. Sin kills. Look what sin did to Jesus. He never sinned, yet He bore our sin. Jesus was the final lamb slain for remission of sin. Animal sacrifice was God's way of showing Israel the consequence of sin. Sin is the root of death. Christ dealt with sin once and for all. Faith in Christ makes us sinless in the sight of God. God receives us as we are by faith. Under the old covenant, the blood sacrifice for atonement had to be continual because the sinners sinned. Christ took our title of sinner upon Himself so that He can call us sons. From sinners to sons. This does not mean we are sinless from our perspective. Every believer can testify of the wrestle between the flesh and Spirit. This battle won't be won until these bodies are redeemed. This does not license sin. The Spirit of God can put to death the sinful desires, but He calls for a relationship with Him. When we are living in communion with Him, He enables the life of Christ in us. We will not be Christ, and our flesh will remind us daily of our inferiority to Him. Our need for Christ daily is not shameful; it's normal. Sin will be grieved over and not be enjoyed by believers. The Holy Spirit will grieve us if we are dependent on Him. We are warned against taking the grace of God in vain, trampling on the blood of Christ, or willfully sinning. Satan wants to knock the fight out of us. The fight is not with sin; it's believing that Christ in us is our hope of glory. Pray, "do not take the grief of sin away from me. Make me grieve over what grieves You." This is an honest cry. Holiness, purity, and righteousness are what our Spirit man is parched for. As we believe in the atonement of Christ, the Holy Spirit empowers us. Truth does not set us free; "knowing the truth" sets us free, knowing that Christ is our only way to make it to the end. We can know about truth, but it's knowing the truth, where the power is. Jesus is the truth. Life is not found in what we know; it's found in who we know. This is why a relationship with Christ is vital; we can bring our sin to Him shamelessly and trust Him to do in us what only He can do. God won't leave us in what hurts us. His power is available to rescue no matter how deep you are in. Believe that it's not over.

Note

218

"For by grace are ye saved through faith; and that not of yourselves: it is the gift of God" (Ephesians 2:8, KJV)

Discipleship and Evangelism must never be done for salvation or merit. Any work for salvation is a dead work. Any effort done for God without God is rebellion. God does not need our efforts. God does not need help. God is not limited to our strength or wisdom. All we can do is mess it up on our own. Look what man has done without God. We can do a lot but we can't save the soul. The soul has been undervalued by our current Christianity. The mind and the body are our focus as a culture. What about the soul? The mind and the body are not as important as the soul. The crowd wants their minds and bodies bettered, but what about their soul? The soul is the way to our mind and body being made whole. Jesus came to save the soul. There were many that got their minds right and their bodies healed but lost their souls. We have ministries built on healing of the mind and body, but true ministry would be about the soul. Let's stay in our lane. Ministry is to focus on Christ and His mission. Leave politics to politicians. Leave business to businessmen; but if we are sons of God, let's be about the mission of God. For Christ's sake, we are not Muslims. We are not a political force, we are not a social justice pusher, we are Christ pushers. We have never been so ignorant as a generation of the mission that Jesus gave to us in The Great Commission. We could care less for the glory of God; our ministries want finances so badly, that they realized the glory of man brings in more resources than the glory of God. Wealth and influence do not evidence "blessing." Biblical accuracy defines what it means to be "blessed." We don't need any more Vaticans; we have one of those demonic strongholds already. We need biblical truth. The reformation never ended. The contending for truth will affect every facet of our current ministries. A voice is shouting in the wilderness. "Longshanks" will not be king for long more. A freedom is rising from the underbelly of ministry. Hope is coming. Truth will prevail. The remnant is still alive and well in the West. We may not be many but we will not take the knee. Truth preachers will be popular again. Music has taken over the house of God. Singing and music is not the only way to worship Christ. Worship is primarily obedience to Christ's Word. Faith alone saves.

Note

219

*"Therefore if any man be in Christ, he is a new
creature: old things are passed away; behold, all things
are become new" (2 Corinthians 5:17, KJV)*

Salvation transforms the whole person. The born-again experience doesn't need any crutches to produce change in a person's life. Discipleship was never to be a means to salvation; discipleship follows salvation. Discipling the unsaved is impossible; a "discipleship only" ministry is a ministry of condemnation. Discipleship can condemn worse than the Law of Moses when someone is not saved. We can't disciple anyone if they are not saved. Many ministries spend billions on discipleship, but what about increasing the budget for the only means for people to be saved which is by the proclamation of the Gospel? How will anyone hear if no one is preaching the Gospel? We have taken for granted the most important Commission given by Christ Himself in Mark 16, to preach the Gospel. A true disciple will want discipleship. We don't need to make it difficult, but we can't compromise it or cater to lure people to be discipled. Discipling is teaching all that Christ taught. How much of our discipleship is done the way Christ did it? Why are our strategies so different than the way Jesus did it? We disciple from books and pulpits but Jesus demonstrated it with His life and preaching in the open air. The only time recorded that He discipled the way we do, which is from a pulpit, He was nearly thrown off of a cliff.[33] Biblical discipleship looks very different than our Sunday schools, seminaries and conferences. We want awakening but we don't want biblical accuracy; we want to do it our way. We want to do it without Him and without His Word. As if our foolish selves can do anything better than Him. Evangelist's that just "guest speak" or "pulpit preach" are not evangelists. There is no ministry in scripture of a revivalist. The word revival is not even a biblical word. Evangelists disciple and equip by doing it, by demonstrating it, as well as teaching. When we do our evangelistic outreaches with the local church, we are discipling the congregants and volunteers like Jesus did.

Note

[33.] *"And rose up, and thrust him out of the city, and led him unto the brow of the hill whereon their city was built, that they might cast him down headlong." (Luke 4:29, KJV)*

220

"And my speech and my preaching was not with enticing words of man's wisdom, but in demonstration of the Spirit and of power" (1 Corinthians 2:4, KJV)

Lives restored, friendships reconciled, souls saved. This is what the Gospel did and does. No message compares. When religion would say "Shame on you," Jesus says "Shame off you." Jesus was shamed so we could be shameless. Jesus bore our shame on the cross. We can live unashamed. The grace of God always takes us as we are. Jesus says, "Neither do I condemn you." He did not come to condemn but to save. His salvation has no downside for the believer. The Gospel is good news. After He receives us as we are, He empowers us to "go and sin no more." This does not mean we will never sin again, but when we do, He says the same thing to us after we repent. Jesus empowers us to overcome. Our perfect and sinless state is by faith. We will need Christ and repentance to the day we die. Jesus never condoned sin. He was condemned because of our sin. The Spirit of God in us is Holy. He makes us Holier in lifestyle if we let Him, but there will always be a reminder in our flesh that we need Jesus Christ. We will never be comfortable with the thorn in our flesh. As we walk genuinely with Him, our cry will be "come, Lord Jesus." We will never be able to rely on self for holiness. We can't get any holier in the sight of God than when we first put faith in Christ. As we abide in Christ, then the Spirit produces the fruit. It's when we replace the Spirit and the "vine dresser," we form religion. We can have a form of religion but deny the power. We need to abide in faith in Christ.

Abiding is what Martha could not understand about her sister and it frustrated her. As believers we need to run frustration, anxiety and comparison out. As we surrender to Christ, He will do what only He can do and that is make us everything He wants us to be. No one ever leaves Jesus the same way. When we repent, God cleanses us and what would take years for a counselor to fix, Jesus the wonderful counselor does it in an instant. Jesus immediately restores us back into a relationship with Him. He is faithful to forgive and cleanse. This is not just for the sinner; this is for the believer. Believers can fall into gluttony in every way and try to excuse it. Jesus never licensed sin; He gives power over it. Repentance keeps us abiding. Repent.

Note

221

"Lest Satan should get an advantage of us: for we are not ignorant of his devices" (2 Corinthians 2:11, KJV)

Theology in the West makes many ignorant of the strategies of Satan. We make light of Satan and the demonic forces. That's one of hell's strategies to become fictional. Even though it's a mystery, we see through scripture that Satan tempts, the demons destroy and we are not to give place to them in our lives. They seek whom they can devour. They want to steal, kill and destroy. We need spiritual armor more than ever. We need to utilize the spiritual weapons that we have been given. These are not cute verses that we memorized as kids. The fight is real. Jesus is praying that our faith will not fail. Faith in the Word of God shuts the door to darkness. It is written "knowing truth sets us free." Jesus is to be known. When we only know about the truth, the enemy will scoff at us. We are called to know truth.[34] It's not what we know that matters, it's who we know. The name of Jesus is our main weapon but it can't be used as a charm. Learn from the seven sons of Sceva.[35] Jesus calls us to know Him, not just about Him or just to use Him, but to actually KNOW Him. We are good at discipling about Jesus but are we teaching to "know Jesus." Knowing Jesus means having a relationship with Him. Satan knows those that know Jesus by name. We are only threats to darkness when we walk in relationship with Jesus. This is why religion is powerless. It teaches a

---

[34]. *"And ye shall know the truth, and the truth shall make you free." (John 8:32, KJV)*
[35]. *Acts 19:11–20*

form of godliness but denies the power that is found in a relationship with the God. Christ died the death of the cross to reconcile us into a relationship that God tried to bridge all the way through the Old Testament. Reconciliation is the opposite to religion. Religion ritualizes what God wants, which is relationship. We need be praying in the name of Jesus. We need to stand in the authority of Christ when hell rages against us. It may seem like hell is prevailing all around us but we have authority in Jesus's name. When we submit to God and resist the devil, he will flee. We are to submit our sin, weakness and doubt to God. Jesus takes us as we are but does not leave us the way we are; as prey to the devil. Without Jesus, we as humans are "low hanging fruit." Those that are not under the Lordship of Christ will have every horror conceivable done to them in this life and for sure in the next. Call on Jesus and be saved.

Note

222

"And this is the condemnation, that light is come into the world, and men loved darkness rather than light, because their deeds were evil" (John 3:19, KJV)

We learn best the hard way. Thank God Jesus went the hard way so that we don't need to. He made the way so we can walk through the wind and on the waves. We have so many talking about issues and teach on solutions but Jesus called us to actions. Talk is cheap if we are not willing to do something about it. We learn best when we live what we talk. As we live what we preach, we will realize that we don't have what it takes. The need is too big; the issues can't be tackled by us. As we depend on God, what would be typically impossible for us, with God is possible. We learn the "hard" way because it's hard for our flesh but simple for the Spirit of God. We have nothing to be ashamed of when it comes to our lack; in-fact our lack is our boast. The book of Acts was not the acts of the apostles or early church but the acts of the Holy Spirit. God is no respecter of who He decides to advance His will. He delights to use what the world would deem foolish to confound the wise. Let's not grow weary in doing good because as we do what seems impossible to the flesh, God will prove His glory in it and He will get the full glory. An evangelist desires to glory in Christ above everything. As we live dependent on Him, He makes the yoke easy and the burden light. In Him, there is rest. In us there is strife. When our eyes are fixed on Him, we become fearless. We don't need to have what it takes, Christ does. This is the key to making it to the end. *We are a mess, but Christ came to bless our mess.* What we thought would be hindrances, Christ turns it as His means to use us. There is no one that His blood can't redeem. The same forgiveness we preach is accessible for us too. We are to remind ourselves of these truths every day. The USA needs evangelists. We have plenty of churches and pastors but evangelists are lacking. An evangelist is not a humanitarian or an outreach pastor. An evangelist equips the church to proclaim the Gospel and preaches the Gospel in such a way, that decisions are made to follow Christ. How do we fund evangelists? We need evangelists who want to convert sinners and add to the church. Evangelism is the only biblical church growth strategy! Will you support the office of an evangelist?

Note

223

*"For the word of God is quick, and powerful, and sharper than
any twoedged sword, piercing even to the dividing asunder of
soul and spirit, and of the joints and marrow, and is a discerner
of the thoughts and intents of the heart" (Hebrews 4:12, KJV)*

"Just tell me like it is." This is the cry of our generation. We can't
handle wasting time; we just want the bottom line. It's amazing to
see the power of God's Word. We have seen incredible conversions.
Never write off a generation. Those that we would write off, often
times God is writing in. His ways are not our ways on purpose to
teach us that we should always rely on Him. Just when we think we
have figured God out, He takes us deeper. If we are not baffled at
God, then He is not God. We are Trinitarian believers because if God
could be explained, then He would not be God. We serve a God that
our finite brains will never be able to comprehend. Let's stay in faith
and not in logic. Faith is the answer to creation, purpose and peace.
Without faith in God, we have a hole that cannot be whole until we
come to the end of ourselves. God loves us and, in His love, He will
do whatever it takes to wake us up to who He is. Sometimes the only
way to wake us up is to shock us. We need to be shocked today. If our
words don't shock, life will. Life wakes us up from our complacency.
Let's embrace uncomfortable truths. Let's seek challenging sermons.
Don't settle for the tripe that does not challenge us to read the Bible
for ourselves. Any entity that wants 10 percent of our income needs
to be preaching the Gospel and evangelizing to their communities.
We would never pay a coach to not challenge us to be better. Why

would we pay a pastor if he does not challenge us in the Word? If all He does is feed our mental need for information, then we need to move on. It's time for preachers to equip and raise up. Keeping the sheep in the pen for too long will only lead to rebellion. "Sheep"[36] don't stay "sheep"[37] but are all raised up to be shepherds[38] in their own way. Shame on the shepherd that keeps his flock as sheep. The pastor is to be giving his secret sauce and raising up his congregants to be better than him as a minister. Every pastor should be paid for how many pastors he can reproduce. It's embarrassing when we are known for our crowd more so than the individuals we have raised up. Instead of raising people up, they are spearing those that might outshine them, so that they can keep as many sheep in the pen as they can. That is not the heart of Jesus.

Note

[36.] Believers in Christ
[37.] Just believers
[38.] Leaders

224

"For I know that in me (that is, in my flesh), dwelleth no good thing: for to will is present with me; but how to perform that which is good I find not" (Romans 7:18, KJV)

"I don't like myself. I know who I am." The good you see in me is of Him (God); it's what He did. The reason I love Jesus is that He still loves me. I understand that some don't, but He does. Preaching Christ and Him Crucified is not a "have to," it's all I want to do until I die, no matter the setting. It's His goodness that you see in me; if you knew me, you would not want to know me. You see me, but I hope you see Him. You hear me, but I want you to listen to Him. As you read this, I want you to hear the core of what motivates me to get up every day, Jesus. The more discipled we become, then the more dependent on Him we get. The nearer to Him we get, then the more we learn to lean on Him. The closer to the light we get, then the more we see of ourselves and the extent of grace He has poured out on us. The more we walk with Jesus, then the more we see His love for us; it's unlike any love we could ever receive on earth. Religion gives us a form of godliness, but Jesus provides us with a relationship that sustains us daily. There is never a day that we can come before the Father in our own righteousness. We get saved by faith, but some falsely believe that we are kept by works. We are kept by faith. Faith becomes more of a reality as we age. Religion is sinister because it puts the emphasis on our works rather than Christ's work. To truly be a disciple of Christ means we, like Peter, live a life of need for Christ. Our dependence on Christ will be evidenced in our prayer life, decision-making and worship of Jesus Christ. We will be serious about giving honor to whom honor is due. We will have no temptation to share the glory of God. Our whole thought process will be FOR the glory of God. We will be careful to get the attention off of us and on to Christ. There is no way of hiding us because He has chosen us to have His treasure in our earthen vessels. When people see us, let's be unashamed of the Gospel. We know who we really are. Who could stand before the holiness of God? The only way to have a clean heart and clean hands are by Jesus making us clean by His Word. Let's live for the glory of God. We are what we are by the grace of God. I'm sorry you may not like me, but I can't change me, but Jesus can. Look up to Jesus.

Note

225

"And brought them out, and said, Sirs, what must I do to be saved? And they said, Believe on the Lord Jesus Christ, and thou shalt be saved, and thy house" (Acts 16:30–31, KJV)

"What must I do to be saved?" This is a common question that comes up. Everyone is wondering what do I do? Inside of us, we want to do something to get saved. This is why we have so many religions. Religion teaches what we must do to be saved. It's full of check lists, rituals and works. This is why the religious wanted Jesus dead. They were offended that God would want no work of our own to be saved. We want to be self-sufficient. We want it our way. We try to make sense of faith; we try to understand God, but faith can't be made sense of and if God could be understood, He would not be God. The Bible is the inerrant word of God. God is One yet is a Trinity. Salvation comes through faith in Christ. Heaven is accessible to all that believe in Christ. Belief in Christ makes us a habitation for the Spirit of God who works the life of God through us as we live in relationship with the Father. Belief is more powerful than duty. No believer does the will of God out of duty but are compelled to follow their savior wherever He leads. It's His treasure in our earthen vessels that we boast of. Christ saves to the uttermost for those who believe. Belief in Christ is defined as confession of sin to Him, repentance of those sins and a declaration of dependence on Him. When we mean it, belief in Christ makes us never the same again for the better. Christ's way makes life better not because His way is easier, or prosperous but because He is with us. God being with us is the most abounding and prosperous truth that we could ever experience. Knowing Jesus in power, knowing Jesus in suffering or knowing Jesus in death does not change up the richness of simply knowing Jesus. Knowing Jesus is what salvation accomplishes. It's not just a ticket to heaven; it's a relationship of fulfillment. Knowing Jesus causes us to have joy in shackles as much as we have joy in freedom. It's the message that compels us. It's not the need or pity that drives us; it's knowing Jesus which makes us want everyone to know Him. As we are intimate with God, He leads us to those that want to be saved. He leads us to those that are crying out "what must I do to be saved?" Evangelism is an outflow of knowing Jesus.

"And rend your heart, and not your garments, and turn unto the Lord your God: for he is gracious and merciful, slow to anger, and of great kindness, and repenteth him of the evil" (Joel 2:13, KJV). Outside we look happy. Outside we look blessed. Outside we look wealthy. However, inside we are parched. Inside we are shredded. Our inside is insecure, needy and empty. All our insides are the same. We bleed red; our organs, bones and minds are aging. We can search religion, business, vacation, food, luxury, but in the end it all feeds our depression. The end of time here is death for us all. It is appointed for us all to die. Death does not discriminate. The angel of death can come as a thief in the night. Friend, don't take life for granted because we don't know how long we have. Before we start comparing ourselves of where we are at in life, before we set out another day seeking fulfillment, just know that you don't have to live in disappointment. Religion disappoints and those that claim to be God's ambassadors will fail us, but they were never there to elevate themselves in any way. They and all of us are human. We are all the same. Some sin differently than another but we all come before God the same way. Faith in Christ is our only way to the Father. Trying everything but Christ to get fulfillment will only make us idol worshippers in His sight. There is no idol, there is no life, there is no peace outside of Christ. In our futility we search but to no eternal avail. Jesus Christ can take our "need" away and we will never "need" again. He fulfills. We can let Him in on what no counselor, friend or clergy could do for us. Christ made a way where all can come before Him as they are but never leave as they were. He keeps us coming back for more and more of His Word. Daily He gives us manna; His mercy is sufficient to this very day. We want Him more and more as we trust Him with our lives. Jesus is Lord. Jesus can be our closest friend. Jesus is our all in all. To Jesus Christ be glory. Our whole soul, life and mind we are to give to Him daily. Making Him Lord brings peace like nothing else. He is cost-free for us because He paid the cost with His own Blood. Serving Him is never a duty. Jesus compels us to do what we do for His glory. Abundance of life is in Him. Selling out Jesus for our will, agenda and dreams is not worth it in the end. Pharaoh would tell us this if could. His story always repeats itself. What will it take for you to know Jesus? Will it be too late, as it was for Pharaoh?

Note

_____

_____

_____

_____

_____

_____

_____

_____

"Not forsaking the assembling of ourselves together, as the manner of some is; but exhorting one another: and so much the more, as ye see the day approaching" (Hebrews 10:25, KJV)

No one should ever have a reason to forsake the assembly. Church attendance is a must for every believer. Internet church, live stream church, tv screen church is not church. Singing songs and listening to sermons is not the main purpose of church, fellowship is. A hand shake, side hug or meet-and-greet is not fellowship. We need to get to know each other. Pray with each other. Build one another up. This is why serving in the church gets you the best fellowship; because you get to know your serve team. Media church is not church. God wants us to do life together. There is no accountability with a TV screen. We are a generation that is parched for fellowship. Rather than the church being a solution, they are catering to it. TV screen church just makes the lead teacher bigger than what he is. If he can't raise up teachers for his campuses, then he is not making disciples. Those that attend are not being discipled by these internet churches. Jesus did not disciple like that. He commanded us to disciple like He did, teaching what He taught. Go to a church where the leaders know you by name. Get involved and expect to be let down. Don't get involved for the leader's sake, get involved for Christ sake. If you have to deal with a Saul leader, don't touch the hem of his garment. God put them there, God can take them from there. We are to contend for the truth. We are to follow Christ but we can't say we love Christ yet despise His church. The forgiveness Christ showed us, we are commanded to show others. If we don't forgive, Christ won't forgive us. This does not mean that we have to turn a blind eye, but there is a time to be a lion and there is a time to be a lamb. As we are surrendered to Christ, He will lead us in the way that we need to go about dealing with the wolves. Choosing peace is the best default but there are times where God will lead us to take a stand as a prophet. We need real prophets and not the smooth-talking "pathetic" we have today. Much of the prophetic ministry today is pathetic because they tickle the ears of their audience. They say everything people would want them to say for a dollar. We need men of God in the pulpits that will preach the Truth, whether it fills the room or empties the room. Fear God only; to hell with the fear of man.

Note

227

*"Looking unto Jesus the author and finisher of our
faith; who for the joy that was set before him endured the
cross, despising the shame, and is set down at the right
hand of the throne of God" (Hebrews 12:2, KJV)*

Jesus Christ is who we are called to look up to, imitate and esteem. His character is what we are conformed to when we are in Him. Do we resemble Him in character? Believers need to be reading the Gospels to get an understanding of our Lord. It's amazing how our church age talks very little about the character of Christ. Read how He loved on sinners and repulsed the religious; do the religious want to crucify us? Do sinners love us? We are to draw sinners; but most churches cater only to the religious. The religious may give more money, but Jesus loved sinners and trusted His Father for provision. We cater church to those that give the most. We tailor the sermon to those that sustain the pulpit financially. Jesus did the opposite. The Lord of our faith would not wear the garb of the religious. If He was to walk in today into most of our churches with His followers, they would be escorted out. Church needs to look more and more like Jesus in character. Everything that the Christian culture has taught us needs to be brought into alignment with Christ. The Roman Catholic Papacy is nothing like our Christ. It's pomp and wealth are detestable in the sight of God. If that's the Christianity you have seen, read the Gospels. Jesus never abused anyone or took anyone's tithe; Jesus never used a weapon or bullied anyone to follow Him. He has had so many misrepresent Him throughout the last two thousand years. We have no excuse today. We are literate and have the scripture in our language, yet we still lift up every mega-church pastor we can to imitate. If any of the men we look up to don't push us to Christ, then we are in a cult. No one should ever dare elevate themselves above Christ. Our sound bites, cleverness of speech, and our interpretations should never be elevated above Christ. God will remind us and everyone else that we are but flesh. He will not share His glory with another. Most of what we see on TBN is so contrary to Christ. The "Jesus plus prosperity" teaching is Satanic at the core. Their Jesus is not biblical. Satan has turned their Jesus into the apple in Eden. Eat of their gospel and you will never need God again. Jesus's words to the seven churches could not ring truer today. God have mercy.

Note

228

"That if thou shalt confess with thy mouth the Lord Jesus, and shalt believe in thine heart that God hath raised him from the dead, thou shalt be saved. For with the heart man believeth unto righteousness; and with the mouth confession is made unto salvation" (Romans 9:9–10, KJV)

The West have a misunderstanding of Christianity. The church was never to be the savior of the world. Many have suffered under the leadership of the church. The church is not growing as a whole. In fact, in some areas, church attendance is on the decline. The reason being is that the church elevated leaders above Christ. No church is perfect. No leader is perfect. Church is a hospital for the sin-sick to worship Jesus our savior. The reason we read of so many controversies with church leadership is because they are but human. We should never leave the church because there are imperfect people. The church is full of imperfect people that are repentant and want to be more like Jesus. Christianity is not about a church, pope or pastor, it's about Christ. Would Jesus be doing what we are doing? It's time we put on the mind of Christ and filter our actions through Him. Would He have the attitude we have? Would He treat our loved ones like we are treating them? Would He be doing what we are doing? Does it move us that much of what we do week in and week out looks very little like what Jesus did? Does it bother us that we want to imitate preachers and revivals of old more than Christ? Are we convicted that we get more joy out of every other thing than being with Christ? Christianity is about Christ. It's for Christ's sake that we are here.

If we sing about Him, and preach about Him, but don't have His life, fruit and character coming out of us is He even in us? Who are we radiating, who are we imitating? Do we get our inspiration from Christ and His words, or are we putting more money in Christian authors' pockets? We crave to read anything other than scripture. We crave to follow every movement and charismatic preacher, but what about following Christ? Don't be surprised when you hear of churches and leaders falling short. Every church and leader fall short. It's how we repent that matters. What makes us different than the world is our repentance. We never graduate from repentance while we are in this fragile, dying body. Whoever says that we are without sin is a liar. Anyone that says we don't need to repent after we get saved is blasphemous. It's time to get the attention on Jesus. We need Jesus.

Note

_____

_____

_____

_____

_____

_____

_____

_____

_____

229

*"Thy kingdom come, Thy will be done in earth,
as it is in heaven" (Matthew 6:10, KJV)*

The only way forward is His will. We have to trust that He is good. How can He not be good? The cross is the evidence. Even though we may not see His goodness now, we will in eternity! We want eternity more than temporality. There is so much trying to distract us or lure us out of His will. His will is the way we were originally designed for. The lie has been bitten into that our way is better than His by many in our generation. God knows our motives when we pray. He won't give according to our will because He knows the end of our will is destruction. When we hold onto our will, we will be eaten up with anxiety and bitterness. It's when we relinquish control that peace floods our soul. The "name it and claim it" movement are sending many to hell because they have set Jesus up like a genie in a bottle. They have made faith a whip for their god to do what they want him to. The purpose of the Gospel was to get us to repent, which means to state our total dependency on God. These lying messengers are charlatan business men living off the broken; their Jesus is their golden calf. There is nothing that God could give us that could satisfy our souls' thirst more than Christ. Run from these ministries that have turned Jesus into their cash cow. Flee the cheap talkers. We need demonstrators; if we want to see awakening, God wants a people that abandon their will and are set on fire for the glory of Christ. We are to be a people that burn for Jesus and His glory in sickness and in health, for richer or for poorer. "Jesus with everything I have, be glorified." We will contend for the truth; we will preach unashamed of what people think, so Christ will get the glory He deserves. How will they hear if no one preaches? We will preach and be accountable to the authority of scripture. We leave our rights at the cross and count all that we are as dung[39] in comparison to the glory of Jesus Christ. To you oh God we surrender our pride, sin, and will. On our watch, let the truth of the Gospel be preached. On our watch, use us to lift our Lord up above everyone and everything. Follow Jesus, make Him Lord. Live surrendered. It will be worth it in the end. We will have trouble; it won't be easy, but life is better with Jesus.

Note

---

[39]. *"Yea doubtless, and I count all things but loss for the excellency of the knowledge of Christ Jesus my Lord: for whom I have suffered the loss of all things, and do count them but dung, that I may win Christ." (Philippians 3:8, KJV)*

230

"But by the grace of God I am what I am: and his grace which was bestowed upon me was not in vain; but I laboured more abundantly than they all: yet not I, but the grace of God which was with me" (1 Corinthians 15:10, KJV)

We are loved. We are looking for acceptance and community. Your whole life you have felt rejected and an outcast. You just want attention and to know that you matter. You've been mocked and overlooked. I need to tell you something that I've found to be true for myself. Only Jesus loves you the way you are looking for. Battling with mental illness is really hard. No one fully understands you and we have all found it hard to connect to you. Now that we know your struggle, we want you to know that we love you. You don't have to live in denial or shame. We all have something wrong with us. We are all human. We understand that life is hard and you have not had it easy. Hear me when I say that you are loved. We are sorry that you have gone misunderstood for so long. We are sorry for judging you and blowing you off. We did not discern that your outbursts were cries for help. Just know, accepting your need for help is okay. Stop putting up walls, and isolating yourself even more. The biggest deception is that no one cares. We care. We can only help if you let us. Letting us help you, means that you need to get vulnerable with your illness. No one wants to hurt you. Believers in Christ want to do for you what He does for us. We want to see you accepted, whole and loved. We can only help those that want help. Jesus will only save those that want to be saved. Don't hurt yourself anymore by isolating from those that can help. Acknowledging that you're a finite human with an illness is your only hope for healing. Every person to be saved must acknowledge that they need to be saved. We will acknowledge this until the rapture or until we pass into eternity. We worship Jesus because we still need Jesus. We have not been saved to be God; we have been saved to need God. Church people should welcome all because God welcomes us all. We are called to show to others what was shown to us. I know you have been abused, hurt, and ridiculed by those that claim to be Christ's ambassadors, but you should know that they are human too. Read how He treats us in the scripture because He has not changed. He loves still today, just as He loved then. He knows you like no one else could.

Note

231

"And whatsoever ye do, do it heartily, as to the Lord, and not unto men" (Colossians 3:23, KJV)

Every believer is in full time ministry; it does not matter who pays us, what matters is that we are doing what we are doing unto the Lord? Ministry is not a career, it's a calling. A calling is not always our purpose but it's always His purpose. Very few that were called in scripture embraced it with joy. The call of God won't appease our flesh. In fact, no flesh would want to fulfill the call of God. If our flesh can fulfill the "call of God," we were probably not called by God. The call of God will always be impossible for us to do. If our call does not require faith to do it, then our call may not be from God. When the call of God became a career in the US, an influx of all types of ministers flooded Christianity. We hire based on resumes and education; Jesus did not call His followers like that. Religion really does everything it can, to hinder a relationship with God and limit Him to a resume. Let no one tell you what you can't do if God has called you to it. It's a fearful thing to stand in the way of God and His called. Peoples' negative opinions and hindrances on the "called" is fuel for God to show who is called and who is not. He uses blockages, hardships and opinions of people to refine faith in His called. Believe, no matter what people say. It's what God says that matters. Put Him first and obey God over everyone. Those closest to us will not always receive us or understand but they will when they see God do what only He could. God will silence the nay sayers by miracles and signs. Doors will open that could never have. Provision will come in ways no one could assume. I've seen this first hand. I want to tell you, "obey God." Step out of the comfort of the "boat" of the religious. Be what God has called you to be. Yes, it's impossible and ludicrous but that's how we know God is in it. Why would He ask us to do something that we would not need Him to do? When people stand in your way, don't take that they are from God. People always stand in the way; we stand in the way; get people out of the way and get out of the way so God will do what only He can. Don't cave into anyone or anything. Cave into God. Cave into his will. "God, have your way. Do what only you can. We are yours and yours alone Jesus."

Note

232

*"I am Alpha and Omega, the beginning and the ending,
saith the Lord, which is, and which was, and which is
to come, the Almighty" (Revelation 1:8, KJV)*

We are all replaceable. We are here today and gone tomorrow. What is mankind that God would even be mindful of us? We foolishly think God needs us. We have made ourselves more important than we really are. There is nothing that we could do that would impress God. We think that we are invincible until life happens. As important as you may be in the eyes of man, on our best day, we are sinners in the sight of God. No human should ever feel entitled to get something from God. The only wage we deserve is death. Much of the Western gospel feeds our entitlement generation. If some of our famous Western preachers were in the garden of Gethsemane, their doctrine would sound a lot like Satan's. "Your God would never will the Cross, and your God would never want you to be so stressed; God wants you blessed and wants you to live in abundance, don't pray, "God's will be done" name it and claim it." These false teachers don't need to be representing Christ anymore. It's time for the resistance to rise. There have been years of prayer and a lot of grace, but now we need to rise up and contend for the truth. If it were not for the grace of God, we would all be getting wages that we deserve. Stay humble, stay submitted to God's will, seek His will and not our own. God warns and gives time to repent before He judges. It's time to become biblically literate. Music, entertainment, emotionalism or no other distraction can disciple us like the teaching of the Word can.

Scripture is the greatest commentary on itself. Settle only for sound doctrine. We are not as important as we think. We need God. We need His Word. We are finite, but God is infinite. We are fallible, but He is infallible. We were created; Jesus is the uncreated One. Make Jesus Lord. Embrace His will, learn from Hezekiah.[40] We don't want our will. God's will is always best in the end. Our will sounds great and looks tempting but, in the end, only God's way leads to heaven. This is the way to contentment. The believer in Christ can tap into a realm of peace as we rest in His will like no other can. We need to repent from wanting our will over God's. Jesus is Lord; we are not. Even though God does not need us, He wants us. He is passionate about us. We see this in the cross.

Note

_____

_____

_____

_____

_____

_____

_____

_____

_____

_____

[40.] Kings chapter 20

233

*"Yea, so have I strived to preach the gospel, not where
Christ was named, lest I should build upon another
man's foundation" (Romans 15:20, KJV)*

What ever happened to "not building on another man's foundation"? Why are church planters planting where churches already exist?
Why can't they strengthen what already remains? Are our church
planters just church poachers? There are millions of unreached people; why are church planters just catering to the church goers when
we should be after those that are lost in the world? Why is business
determining the called of God? Businessmen must stay away from
influencing the leading of the Spirit. Judas never could understand
Jesus. He kept thinking to himself "budget could be better spent."
Success for a believer has nothing to do with crowds, budget or fame;
it has to do with obeying God. Church plants should be done where
God wants it and not where there is low hanging fruit. Planting a
church off of a split better be the leading from the Lord and not
just an opportunity. Church planters have become church splitters.
What was started in the flesh will end up in the flesh. Where are
the prayer meetings? Where are the evangelistic endeavors? Sunday
morning is not, nor was it ever intended to be an outreach. Pastors
lead churches, not evangelists. An evangelist as the lead of a church
will end up in works and strife. Pastors disciple and care for their
flock. The church is not your career. Get another career. The church
needs to be led by the called of God and not those that have nothing
better to be doing. If you are in ministry not because God has called

you, please do yourself a favor and get an honest job. The church is not for lazy script readers that don't pray, read their Bibles or care for their flock. It's easy to see who your god is, your belly. If you don't remove yourself, God will. There is going to be a shaking really soon. Ananias and Saphira have been running the show for a very long time but the grace of God will not always be taken in vain. The revival and growth we all want won't come by a business strategy, it will come when the fear of God is amongst the church again. God will be taken seriously. If you don't hear the alarm now, you will sleep in and miss out on all that God is about to do. If you don't want to be serving God, quit. God does not need you or me. We are replaceable.

Note

234

"But watch thou in all things, endure afflictions, do the work of an evangelist, make full proof of thy ministry" (2 Timothy 4:5, KJV)

The office of an evangelist is on the verge of extinction. There needs to be a clear description of an evangelist. An evangelist equips the church for the work of evangelism. He is not in the pulpit to lift himself up, so that the only way to evangelize has to sound like him, testify life him or look like him. To be an evangelist does not mean that you have to have a master's degree in theology, nor does it mean that you have to go out and make a testimony for yourself so you have something to say. An evangelist is not a mini-Christ that can save or persuade someone to be saved. Salvation is not of man, it's of God. God saves souls; the evangelist simply obeys the Great Commission. Evangelism is not benevolence; that's what the deacons are there for. An evangelist emphasizes the proclamation of the Gospel and is anointed to spark a fire in the church to preach the Gospel. No one should ever walk away from an evangelist and feel like they are inferior to him in any way. The evangelist is actually inferior to most in the church that have yet to evangelize because unlike them, he has been there and done that so He is not as reliant on God as a new Evangelist would be. An evangelist wants to elevate Jesus and the Gospel. The trivial strategies, people skills, and gimmicks come in second to being Spirit led. Jesus never evangelized anyone the same way. He tailored His message to His audience. The Spirit does this in us as we yield to Him. The more we realize that we can't evangelize, the better, because that's the truth. Only a Spirit dependent believer can evangelize. How our audience responds is not on us. We preach and God takes it from there. We can't force salvation or manufacture results. Why some respond and others don't is a mystery to us. We are wasting time trying to wrap our finite mind around how someone responds. We are simply called to preach the Gospel. As we obey, our level of success is not based on the outcome but on the obedience to the leading of the Spirit. Jesus told us to pray for laborers; we are mandated to pray for the evangelist. God is Lord of the Harvest but He calls us to pray for the sowers/laborers. Sowers sow; they can't grow the seed. Believers, in whatever office of ministry they have been put in, need to stay in their lane and obey God. Let's be about it.

Note

235

"How then shall they call on him in whom they have not believed? and how shall they believe in him of whom they have not heard? and how shall they hear without a preacher?" (Romans 10:14, KJV)

Who lied to you and said that you need a radical testimony or a doctorate in apologetics to be an effective witness? The more that evangelists build their ministries on their stories or personalities, the less effective they will be as evangelists. Evangelists equip the church for the work of evangelism. When an evangelist is using the congregation to only equip himself in his call, he no longer is functioning in his office as an evangelist. We are called to make disciples and not just be discipled. If we are not equipping the church, we will have no legacy our ministry will end with us. We should be known for how many we equipped to evangelize rather than how many we evangelized. That is the most successful minister. Every evangelist has his own strength but there is not one approach to evangelize. The greatest way to evangelize is to build on Christ and His Gospel. This levels the ground for the believer that wants to be discipled. We don't need radical testimonies; we need to know the Gospel that we claim to believe, so we can share Jesus with others. If a believer can't share the Gospel, do they even know the Gospel? Evangelism is easy when we know Jesus. As we walk in a relationship with Jesus, He will give us discernment needed to be effective witnesses for Christ. We need to know what we believe so well, that we can share it with others. Evangelists are not saviors. We must be cautious of a savior complex. Only Jesus saves. An evangelist is a sinner, showing other sinners where they find salvation. There is no believer that has grad-uated from a need for Christ. Once one is saved, they are ready to be an effective witness. When one is truly saved, they will want to share their life-change with everyone. It will be a passion and not a duty. Never evangelize out of duty. Evangelize because you have the desire to do it. That's what God does in us. The Holy Spirit will make us want to share Jesus with everyone. If we have no passion for the lost or the sinners around us, then do we even have the Holy Spirit? We really need to examine whether we are in the faith. Don't be "bewitched." You can do what God has called you to do when you are fully reliant on Christ and not your testimony or education. Our persuasion does not lead to conversion. Arguments don't save souls.

Note

236

"And the eye cannot say unto the hand, I have no need of thee: nor again the head to the feet, I have no need of you" (1 Corinthians 12:21, KJV)

A hand cannot say to a foot that it has no need of it. Just because it looks different and has a different purpose, does not mean that it's not important. God set the church up where we need Jesus for salvation but we need each other for discipleship. The church locally and universally is interdependent on each other. When one part is not functioning as it should, we need to do what we can to fix it. Many have turned a blind eye and have a "be and let be" attitude. The silence and passivity of the church has not helped. We can pray, but God has given scripture for doctrine, reproof, correction, and instruction. The inerrancy of scripture holds us all together. It is by preaching, that God grows the faith of His church. Faith comes by hearing the Word of God. Protestants bring their Bibles to church to hold the preacher accountable to scripture. Expository, contextual, passionate preaching of Scripture will usher in the awakening we all want to see. What happened in Acts 2 does not need to happen again because the spirit has not left the earth. Jesus never mandated for the church to wait again. The Holy Spirit came and has not left. The Holy Spirit would never take the attention from Jesus or elevate Pentecost over Calvary's cross. We test the spirits by scripture. The Holy Spirit will never contradict Himself. Jesus told us that He will lead to truth. Every manifestation must be limited to scripture. Every experience must be backed up with scripture. Every teaching must be verified contextually through scripture. This may be offensive, but only the truth sets us free not emotionalism. The Holy Spirit will give us self-control and a sound mind. Any spirit that does not is not of God. We need to be known for our biblical literacy. His word is all that sustains. What starts in the flesh, ends in the flesh. What starts in the Spirit will be maintained by scripture. When it's maintained by flesh or emotionalism, it will not last, but will end in the flesh. We are not to be passive anymore. Before we eat, we pray, but God never supernaturally transfers the food to our stomach. It's up to us to eat it. There are issues that we need to stop praying about and start preaching about. Salt stings the wound but in the end, it heals it. Coddling has not worked; it's time to follow our conviction.

Note

_____

_____

_____

_____

_____

_____

_____

_____

237

"And whatsoever ye do, do it heartily, as to the Lord, and not unto men; Knowing that of the Lord ye shall receive the reward of the inheritance: for ye serve the Lord Christ" (Colossians 3:23–24, KJV)

When we pray before we eat, God never transfers the food to our stomach, it's up to us to eat it. God does not answer prayers that He knows we can do. When prayer does not lead to action, then we must wonder who are we praying to? His people hear His voice. Hours of worship and prayer is wasted if we are not open to obeying His will. No one is called to prayer only or to warm the pew only. Our faith works unlike everyone else's. Faith in Christ saves but also ushers us into a relationship where God leads us to fulfill His purpose. His will always requires faith; if it does not, then it may not be His will. We live by faith. Faith is not a demand on God, it's a belief that God is with us. Every Bible study, every time of worship, every sermon, if it's of God, then it will lead us to fulfill the Great Commission. The church in the West is spiritually obese. It's time to work out. The only way to spiritually work out is to evangelize. It's time to obey the call of God. All we want is to talk about it, pray about it, and sing about it; but what about doing it? Leaders are not paid to be doing it only themselves, they are paid to get you to do it both in teaching and in example. Anyone can read from a script but discipleship needs to look more like Jesus did it. It's alarming that much of our discipleship looks very little like the way Jesus discipled. Apps, websites, YouTube, TV, and social media are not the way He did it. He did life with His disciples. They walked with Him through the streets.

They learned better than anyone could out of a text book or from a teacher. This is how an evangelist disciples. When an evangelist goes to a church, they take the church with them to the streets. They walk with the church and show them how it's done, then after a while they watch the church do it on their own. If Jesus discipled that way, then we want to do the same. As an evangelistic ministry, we must follow Christ as our example. He came to seek and save those who were lost. We are to seek but we can't save. Only Christ can save. Evangelism does not happen in a prayer meeting or in an outreach, it happens when the Gospel is preached. Just like when we eat, we pray for God's blessing and we go evangelize. This generation has overcomplicated it. We don't need a radical testimony or a doctorate in apologetics.

Note

_____

_____

_____

_____

_____

_____

_____

_____

238

"My little children, let us not love in word, neither in tongue; but in deed and in truth" (1 John 3:18, KJV)

Love is not an emotion. Grace is not a license. Mercy is not an excuse. No one ever walked away from Jesus the same. Salvation is not a mental ascent; it is an invitation to a relationship with God. Jesus bore our sin not so that we can sin but so that we can be saved from sin. We are saved when we first repent but then we are being saved until Jesus returns or until we pass into eternity. Don't settle in any area of our lives. Satan's strategy is to wrestle our faith until we can't fight for faith anymore. We are to fan the flame in us, we are to put on the mind of Christ, we are to take every thought captive, we are to draw near to God and He will draw near to us. Being saved does not mean that we lose responsibility but instead, we take responsibility for our sin and weakness. The more responsibility we take for our sins, the more Jesus can work a freedom in us to overcome our sin. The life of a believer in Christ is not a natural life, it is a supernatural life. We have not been left here as saved orphans but we are here as saved sons and daughters. In Christ, we have access to power that mortifies the deeds of our flesh. Never grow comfortable but continue to fight. Be cautious of those that emphasize a life of abundance, ease and comfort. Jesus told us that in this life, we will have trouble. In the West, we may not be persecuted externally, but internally we are. We have many people offering a form of godliness but deny the power of God to be what He has called us to be.[41] We can be disciplined, healthy, moral and obedient externally but God is interested in who is Lord internally. We can only serve one of two masters. Who is Lord of our lives? In the last major decision you made, did you consult with God? If not, then Jesus is not Lord. We are saved to be under His rulership. Satan deceives us by telling us that we can be our own lords but, in the end, we will get the same consequence as him. Heaven is not a republic or a democracy. It is a Kingdom. Jesus is the greatest King and He shall always do what is right. Jesus is love. Jesus is grace. Jesus is mercy. When we open the door to Him and let Him in, life gets better from His point of view. His eternal perspective changes our mind from prayer-*worriers* to prayer-*warriors*. Believe.

Note

---

41. *"Having a form of godliness, but denying the power thereof: from such turn away."* (2 Timothy 3:5, KJV)

239

"For what the law could not do, in that it was weak through the flesh, God sending his own Son in the likeness of sinful flesh, and for sin, condemned sin in the flesh: That the righteousness of the law might be fulfilled in us, who walk not after the flesh, but after the Spirit" (Romans 8:3–4, KJV)

What the Law could not do in changing us, Christ can do by making us born again. In Christ, we become new creatures. We are sanctified immediately in the sight of God but progressively we are being sanctified in our own sight. Every believer can testify that we are changing to become more and more like Jesus in character and righteousness. By our fruit, we will know how mature we are. Spiritual maturity is not defined by our knowledge but by the fruit of the Spirit coming out of us. Our fruit will be determined if our root is connected to Christ or not. If our root is not in Christ, we will not bear fruit. We can't manufacture fruit. Fruit grows when it's planted. As we abide in Christ, the radiance of Christ will be seen in us. The more we know Him, the more we will radiate Him. We don't stay the same in Christ, we change for the better. Helping people by giving anything other than Christ is hurting them. Christ gives a hand up and not only a hand out. All we do is enable poverty and addictions if we don't preach Christ. We can give free education, housing and money but without Christ it's going to people that love sin more than loving what is right. Only Jesus forgives sin and makes us desire what is right. Just look at the West. The reason we have so much success and favor is not because of race or hard work but it's because the West was influenced by the Bible. When Jesus and His Word is applied, everything gets better. Jesus did not come to teach laws and duties to get us right with God, He taught that Faith in Him gets us right with God. Faith in Him makes it possible for the Holy Spirit to dwell in us, who changes us more into the character of Christ. If we want to mature, we need to balance our time between reading theology and our relationship with Christ. We have a lot of Christians that know about God but will miss heaven because they don't know Him. As we walk by faith and in the light, then we will be in fellowship with Christ. As the scripture convicts us of areas of our life that is not radiating Christ, we need to repent and let God do what only God can do. We will never stop needing to repent while we are here. Repentance is the stem between the root and the fruit.

Note

240

"Though I might also have confidence in the flesh. If any other man thinketh that he hath whereof he might trust in the flesh, I more: Circumcised the eighth day, of the stock of Israel, of the tribe of Benjamin, an Hebrew of the Hebrews; as touching the law, a Pharisee; Concerning zeal, persecuting the church; touching the righteousness which is in the law, blameless. But what things were gain to me, those I counted loss for Christ. Yea doubtless, and I count all things but loss for the excellency of the knowledge of Christ Jesus my Lord: for whom I have suffered the loss of all things, and do count them but dung, that I may win Christ, And be found in him, not having mine own righteousness, which is of the law, but that which is through the faith of Christ, the righteousness which is of God by faith: That I may know him, and the power of his resurrection, and the fellowship of his sufferings, being made conformable unto his death; If by any means I might attain unto the resurrection of the dead. Not as though I had already attained, either were already perfect: but I follow after, if that I may apprehend that for which also I am apprehended of Christ Jesus. Brethren, I count not myself to have apprehended: but this one thing I do, forgetting those things which are behind, and reaching forth unto those things which are before, I press toward the mark for the prize of the high calling of God in Christ Jesus" (Philippians 3:4–14, KJV)

Preachers are just people. Who bewitched you to think that anyone is above another in Christ? God does not see pedigrees, education, ordination, race, or titles; He sees a soul that His Son purchased with His own blood. The only title that God calls us by is "sons and daughters." Our functions or positions do not define us in the sight of God. Jesus adopted us in as family. We are not servants, laborers, or employees only; we are primarily family. We must never value a title more than being in Christ. If we are chasing titles, promotions or positions more than a relationship with Jesus, we will never be satisfied. Ministry has become a rat race like any other career. Ministry was never meant to be a career; it was meant to be a calling. A career requires education, experience and a resume but the calling of God is based on the will of God. When God calls, nothing can hold that person back from fulfilling it if they believe. Normally God calls those that could never do what they are called to do so that they will need God. The called of God will need faith no matter what their education or experiences are. When they feel that they can do it without God, they will see how utterly useless they are without Him. Paul counted his resume as dung because he knew that knowing God is the only reason that He got as far as He did. Christ died so that we could know God. Knowing His leading for our lives, gives us peace when life takes a turn for the worst. Our belief in God is what gets us through the worst of times. God will turn it for good in the end. Don't look to a person more than looking to Christ, unless you want to be disappointed. Don't look to a sermon, more than Scripture, to speak to you or you will be deceived. The more we rely on God and His Word for ourselves, the stronger we will be in the faith. This will also be a safeguard to never be bewitched. We will be discerning and full of conviction. What we hear Sunday should never be "new revelation" but should be a confirmation to what God has already been speaking to you. We are to have church every day with Jesus. What we do on Sundays is more about fellowship and accountability than "hearing a word." The only word we need to be hearing is the word of God. Only the Bible is infallible.

241

"What is man, that thou art mindful of him? and the son of man, that thou visitest him? For thou hast made him a little lower than the angels, and hast crowned him with glory and honour. Thou madest him to have dominion over the works of thy hands; thou hast put all things under his feet" (Psalm 8:4–6, KJV)

We are all replaceable. There is nothing in this world that relies on us in order for it to continue. We are not as important as we would like to believe we are. In comparison with the largeness of our universe, our existence really does not matter. In a generation where atheism and "be and let be" mentalities are the majority; suicide is on the increase. Atheism is a cause for suicide. When we realize that we are nothing but dirt, we think to ourselves, "What is the point of facing life every day?" Satan wants us to believe that we would be better off dead. The church is not preaching on hell as much as Jesus did. Jesus was the one that introduced eternal punishment for unrepentant sinners. When hell is not preached, death is not feared. Sin has consequences, in this life and in the next. Jesus Christ forgives sin. That's why He went to the cross to take on Himself the penalty of all sin. He predestines for all to be saved, but only whosoever will believe shall be saved. God never created anyone to go to hell. Hell is the wage of sin and not the plan of God. He planned salvation before the foundation of the earth. He desires all to be saved and none to perish. Even though we don't matter in light of creation or the universe, we matter to God. Jesus shed His blood to show us how much we matter to God. God loves us and demonstrated His love in a very graphic way. God chose us. God desires us. We constantly turn away from Him and renounce Him but He still wants us. The love of God cannot be fathomed by our limited minds. His grace is accessible to those who will repent. God does not need us, yet He desires for us to know Him. There is no other foundation that a human can build upon that can compare to Christ. We need to preach hell because there is no repentance when we die. The time here on Earth is all we have to be saved. Once the time is up, the wrath of God will be poured out on Satan and sinners for eternity. The eternal weight of the Gospel is so serious yet we have preachers behaving like comedians or life coaches every Sunday. Preachers don't get their inspiration from Ted Talks or life coaches. They need to get an honest job if they do. Preachers, preach Scripture under the unction of God.

Note

242

"For what is a man profited, if he shall gain the whole world, and lose his own soul? or what shall a man give in exchange for his soul?" (Matthew 16:26, KJV)

Living for this life alone will only disappoint in the end. Billions have come and gone before us. A society that removes God and Scripture is an empty, pointless society. God set eternity in our hearts. It's what keeps us sane and puts a fight in us to live. Atheism must be educated because we are all born with a "God void" in our hearts. Everyone worships something. Even those that think they don't, actually do. When life happens and darkness of life floods our soul, that's when reality sets in: "There must be more than this." When we are at deaths door, and we don't know what to do, "call on the name of Jesus." Paul's born-again experience was not based on an argument or a logical persuasion; it was an encounter with Jesus. Throughout History, we read of testimonies like this. Jesus is alive. When He is called upon, He will save. His presence is real. I believe what I believe so strongly because I too have had an encounter with the resurrected Christ. I know He is true, not just because the Bible tells me, but because I have experienced Him more times than I can count in my life from the age of six. Believers are spiritual. This is more than doctrine and theology. This is a relationship with Jesus that is real, powerful and vanquishes doubt. In the dark of night, there is authority in the name of Jesus to destroy Satan and fill us with faith. We can have faith even when we lose our sight. This is not our home. Jesus is coming for us. Don't get too comfortable here.

A lot can happen in twenty-four hours. Prepare for the worst every day. Memorize the word, be disciplined in prayer, study scripture, remain in fellowship because Jesus said we will have trouble in this life. A foolish person let's their oil drain out. We need to keep oil in our lamp. Just as much as we are responsible for what we eat, we are also responsible for putting the word of God in our souls. The day has come. Disciples will be disciplined. We won't be perfect but the Holy Spirit will work in us the responsibility, self-control and the sound mind that is necessary to withstand all trouble. Any experience with Jesus and the Holy Spirit will always lead us to Scripture and be verified by Scripture. Jesus taught that "the Spirit will lead us into truth." Live for God.

Note

243

"And the Lord said, Behold, the people is one, and they have all one language; and this they begin to do: and now nothing will be restrained from them, which they have imagined to do. Go to, let us go down, and there confound their language, that they may not understand one another's speech" (Genesis 11:6–7, KJV)

It's amazing what we can accomplish without God; the infrastructure that we can build, the songs we can sing, the counterfeit presence we can muster up, the clever sermons we can preach. We can do a lot without God; look at the sheer discipline of our military and the grit of the religious. We can fool ourselves if we don't read the scripture. There is so much to pull us away from sound doctrine: books, sermons, seminaries. We have such a huge flow into us, with access to every resource from our devices, yet our streets have very little witness of Christ on them. We are a pampered generation; spiritually obese. We were never to be a reservoir for faith and the Spirit. Jesus said, "Out of your belly will flow rivers of living water." We are not lakes, we are rivers. Many of us have been spiritually damned up. Our society has sabotaged our obedience. We would rather please man, then please God. We would rather have people go to hell, then offend them by preaching the Gospel. We have many leading from pulpits but the pulpit is only 1 percent of discipleship. Jesus rarely used a pulpit like we do. His discipleship was His everyday life; living on mission. Every religion preaches to those that want to hear what their preacher has to say. Anyone can do that. It's preaching to those that don't want to hear what we have to say is where the Spirit of God is calling us to. We get discipled by doing what we believe and not by listening to what we be believe only. We have many that listened their whole Christian life but did very little with their faith. They never believed that they could do the will of God. They were fed that only the clergy could do that. We always want someone else to do the will of God. Only one out of twelve disciples in the boat stepped out toward Jesus. Not many ever say "I want to draw near to God because I can have as much of God as I want." Jesus is no respecter[42] of people. No matter what religion has told you or you have told yourself, the Bible is clear that if we draw near to God, He will draw near to us. Jesus makes priests of all believers. There is no believer in Christ with more favor than another in the sight of God. As we surrender, God will do what only He can through us. Surrender and see.

Note

---

[42] *"Then Peter opened his mouth, and said, Of a truth I perceive that God is no respecter of persons." (Acts 10:34, KJV)*

244

*"Pray ye therefore the Lord of the harvest, that he will send
forth labourers into his harvest" (Matthew 9:38, KJV)*

Jesus never said to pray for the harvest; He said: "pray for laborers."
God is the Lord of the harvest; we are not harvesters as evangelists.
We are seed-throwers. We obey, and God does the rest. Obedience
is a detested word amongst some in our generation. We know by the
law that none of us can obey God perfectly. Christ's obedience on
our behalf made it possible for us who believe, to be empowered to
obey God. If our Christianity only has us obeying our nature and its
lusts, then we don't truly believe. Belief is more than knowledge; it's
a relationship that desires the will of God more than our own. We
want the harvest without sowing seed. Jesus wants us to seek His
will and not seek the harvest. We want "revival," but we don't want
to make disciples. We are called to equip and not just be equipped.
Some leaders feel like the people exist for them to lord over; biblical
leaders exist to lead leaders, and are called to equip others. Believers
lead by obedience to what God calls us to. A successful believer has
nothing to do with what we accomplish, how big our budget is, or
how famous we are but it has to do with obedience. When we obey
God, it may lead to persecution or martyrdom. Today's definition
of blessing is attached to health and wealth, but the early church's
definition of blessing was surrender and obedience. Jesus obeyed
His Father to death, even the death of the cross. If Jesus obeyed His
Father, and He is our example, then we need to learn obedience too.
Evangelism is not a suggestion, but it's a commission. If the church is

discipling in everything but evangelism, then their discipleship must be questioned. Sugar does not heal wounds, salt does. Sugar causes wounds to be infected, but salt heals, even though it stings at first. Obedience to God is what blesses the believer. We don't come to God just for salvation; we come to God to do His will. We have many talking about miracles and healings, more than talking about the glory of God; they want God for what He can do for them but not for what He wants. It's time to disciple and raise up the next generation. The past generation did a great job equipping themselves, but we need to be known for how many we equipped and prayed for to replace us.

Note

245

"All scripture is given by inspiration of God, and is profitable for doctrine, for reproof, for correction, for instruction in righteousness: That the man of God may be perfect, thoroughly furnished unto all good works" (2 Timothy 3:16–17, KJV)

We have Scripture so that we may know doctrine, reproof, correction, and instruction. Scripture will teach us how different God is from us. It is the greatest mirror we can look into because it will show us our wretchedness in comparison to a Holy God. Our culture feeds entitlement, but the Scripture cultivates gratefulness. We all want to find out our purpose, calling and vision. We seek God for what we can get out of God. Scripture teaches us that God does not give according to our lust; He gives according to His glory. We try to fit God into our understanding. Scripture teaches us that we grow from faith to faith. Many people think that we grow from faith to works. We are saved by faith and kept by faith. Works do not keep us. Our purpose-driven works driven, dreams driven culture is not how we live. We live "faith in God" driven life. Anything other than faith in Christ for life will make us ungrateful and disappointed, and we will feel like God loves some more than us. The favor of God was given at the cross. There is nothing more that God could give us outside of His Son. When we live for the glory of Christ, no matter where we are, what our bank statements say, or what our doctors say, we will still bless the name of Jesus. Our praise of God is not based on what He is doing for us, but it's based on what He has already done for us. This is why Jesus wants us always to remember His death on the cross. Our joy is found in the cross, not in miracles, signs or wonders. If we go our whole life, never feeling or seeing but we have belief, then we will be rewarded greatly in heaven. Scripture needs to be enough. "Ted Talks" is not Scripture; our inspiration comes from the Word of God. Faith comes by hearing the Word of God and not by hearing the words of man. We live for the glory of God, which means all that is in front of us; we do for the glory of God with gratitude because of the cross. No believer is an entitled, judgmental brat. We are grateful that we are saved. We have been loved much, so we need to love much too. We have been forgiven much, so we need to forgive much too. Jesus is our example of success, favor, and character. It's His image alone that we should be conformed into and not the image of preachers. Our cry is, "Get glory from my life, Jesus."

Note

_____

_____

_____

_____

_____

_____

_____

_____

246

*"For all have sinned, and come short of the
glory of God" (Romans 3:23, KJV)*

On our best day, we can't be who only He can be. At our best, we still fall short of what God can do. It's why you have been disappointed by religion. It's why you felt weighed down about Christianity. There is no truth in Islam, Buddhism, or any other ism. Jesus Christ is the way, truth, and life. Look at our globe; no culture or community can compare with the power of Jesus's name. When He is lifted up in any amount, everything gets better. No one walked away from Jesus worse off. It was not always as they wanted it, but it was always better than it was. Life with Jesus is better. Look around you; every country that has been influenced by the Bible is better than any other country. Jesus is better than Allah; Jesus is better than Buddha; only Jesus rose from the dead. There is no question that Jesus was God. Only an "ignoramus" would doubt the resurrection of Christ. He lives. I know it to be true because He lives in me. Life happens to us all. With Jesus, life is better. We exist as a ministry until every Muslim, Buddhist, Catholic, Mormon, Jehovah witness, or sinner will convert to Jesus Christ. Only Jesus is Lord. There is no way to the Father but through Jesus Christ. Confession of sin, faith in Jesus, and repentance before God is our only hope of salvation. Don't look to people. Look to Him. Everyone on earth needs Him as much as you do. There is no one better than another without Christ. He leveled the ground. There is no Jew, Gentile, male, female, black, or white; we are one in Christ. God welcomes the "whosoever ever will."[43] You are reading this because He is speaking to you. You are loved. He loves you. We are all the chief of sinners, if we are honest. The only thing we love about ourselves is that Jesus lives in us. Jesus loves you. No matter what you have been through, call on Jesus, and He will save you to the uttermost. Our God is no respecter of people; "whosoever will," that's who our God saves. Call on Jesus and be saved. Every human has been chosen; it's up to us to believe. Everyone has been given the gift of faith. If only we will take that gift.

Note

[43.] *"For God so loved the world, that he gave his only begotten Son, that whosoever believeth in him should not perish, but have everlasting life." (John 3:16, KJV)*

247

"There is therefore now no condemnation to them which are in Christ Jesus, who walk not after the flesh, but after the Spirit. For the law of the Spirit of life in Christ Jesus hath made me free from the law of sin and death" (Romans 8:1–2, KJV)

No one can condemn another in the sight of God. The law condemns us all. The law was given to show us how condemned we really are. If we ever get a hint of self-righteousness, all we need to do is read the law. The law was given to condemn us so that we could see a need for salvation. The sacrificial system was set up because God knew of our sinfulness and that we needed forgiveness. God knows us. Just as no one can condemn, "neither does Christ condemn us." There is no condemnation for those in Christ. There is no one with a pulse that has gone far enough for God to condemn. We are not condemned. Christ took condemnation upon Himself at the cross. The church does not have the ministry of condemnation. We have the ministry of life. Christ came to give us salvation, life, and power to overcome what would have condemned us. The Jews have no sacrifice to this day. They have no way to atone for their sins. Jesus's words came true. He was the Christ and the sacrifice for all of our sins. We have access to life, forgiveness, and peace with God in Christ. Jesus does not condemn while we have a pulse. When we pass into eternity, Jesus will judge; but until then, Jesus is full of grace. This is our time of grace. That grace runs out once we pass away, so we need to avail of His grace now, while we have a choice. Choose this day to live free from condemnation. We can be free from all shame. We can be totally forgiven and cleansed. It's up to us to choose while we still have a choice. Believers in Christ are empowered not only to be free from condemnation but also to live free from what condemned us in the first place. Jesus makes us free. He gives us the spirit of liberty. His liberty is not to do what we want but to do what He wants. As we surrender to Him and communicate our need for Him, we can live above condemnation by not walking in the strength of the flesh but in the power of the spirit. It's our choice to live by the power of God or die by our own power. All we can do is sin and fail in our flesh. God set us up to need Him. We were not created to live without Him. We live for His glory and not our own. What the law could not do, Jesus does by saving us and empowering us.

Note

248

"Who did no sin, neither was guile found in his mouth" (1 Peter 2:22, KJV)

Jesus was Holy, yet His holiness drew sinners because they knew He had what they were looking for. Holiness is not a deterrent to reaching people; it's a draw. If what we have is not different than what people already have, why would they want what we have? Jesus was Holy, yet never compromised His holiness to reach people. The holiness Jesus had influenced everyone around Him. Believers in Christ are not being influenced but are influencers. What we have, the world wants; peace, joy, and the expectation of heaven. When we are in a relationship with Jesus, no matter what setting we are in, we are the influencers and not the influenced. The story of Joseph teaches us how strong a man can be with God. Thirteen years of rejection, pits, slave camps, and prison, but God kept Him in a position of favor the whole time. A believer should never let their circumstances define them; that's what makes us so different. Our faith is not based on what we see, so we can have joy in whatever situation we are in. The western culture teaches that Jesus shines brightest when we are prosperous, but scripture teaches us that Jesus shines brightest in the "furnaces" of life. Anyone without Christ would be responding in terror, but we are responding as conquerors. We have meaning when most would be hopeless. God redeems life's hardships for His glory. All things work together for good. If you're in the hardest time of your life, you have a reason to have hope. You are more blessed than you know. The fact that you need Jesus is a blessing. That's the greatest blessing because there are many on the highway to hell who think they are "blessed," but they don't see their need for a savior because they have health, wealth, and a great social life. The problem is, none of that saves the soul. Jesus is holy, and His holiness is attractive. No one wants to be around the self-righteous because their stench of pride keeps people away from them. Self-righteousness makes wretches look good on the outside, but anyone with street smarts can see past the front. We are all but flesh. The holiness of Jesus makes everyone want to be like Jesus and not like anyone else. His holiness is formed in us when we are about His glory and not our own. Hardship makes us about Jesus. Prosperity makes us about ourselves. Souls crave holiness, Jesus is holy.

Note

249

"Blessed are they which do hunger and thirst after righteousness: for they shall be filled" (Matthew 5:6, KJV)

Holiness is what our sin-ravaged souls are longing for. Holiness is the purest water to our soul that we could ever get. Many don't realize it, but humanity thirsts for righteousness. Many have tried to fill their parched need for righteousness with religion but have been let down. The truest holiness and the most real Righteousness that we could ever get is in Jesus Christ. Jesus is Holy. His holiness is placed in us when we are saved. Jesus quenches our souls' thirst for holiness. When we drink of His holiness, we will never thirst again. Our holiness and righteousness disappoint because we can't be holy in our flesh; we have sin at work in us from the Fall. We suffer from the original sin. We are totally depraved. Scripture gives us an explicit reflection of our wretchedness as we look into it. This is offensive in a generation that only wants to be told how good they are without God. Our goodness is never good enough to get to God's attention. This is why Christ died. He did not die for good people; He died for sinful people. "Good" people crucified Christ because their goodness was in themselves. Christ died for sinners. If you are a sinner, you are in good company with Jesus. Christ loves sinners but loves them enough to not leave them in sin. The only people that Christ drew were sinful. The religious and the self-righteous were the ones repulsed by Christ's message. How does it make you feel to hear that Jesus loves sinners? Do you love sinners? Do sinners run to you in time of need, or do they run away from you in their time of need?

As believers, we are being conformed to the image of Christ. His life that He lived here can be evidenced in us now. He said, "greater things than this shall ye do."[44] His life is accessible to those who believe. As believers, we have received a new life where our old ways pass away, and His ways become manifested in us. As we walk in relationship with Jesus, casting our sins, fears, and doubts on Him, He can make us more like Him to those around us. His holiness can be seen in us. The credit for the good that people see in us will be given to Jesus. We know in, and of ourselves, there is no good thing. The only treasure in our earthen vessels is Christ. He that is in us is greater than ourselves. We need the holiness of Christ.

Note

[44] "Verily, verily, I say unto you, He that believeth on me, the works that I do shall he do also; and greater works than these shall he do; because I go unto my Father." (John 14:12, KJV)

250

"And going on from thence, he saw other two brethren, James the son of Zebedee, and John his brother, in a ship with Zebedee their father, mending their nets; and he called them. And they immediately left the ship and their father, and followed him" (Matthew 4:21–22, KJV)

Jesus chose twelve young adults to be His disciples. Today, the youth are being shaped by culture. Their hunger for truth is increasing every day. They are tired of everything being watered down. Absolutes are deemed bigotry which has led to mass confusion in our generation; confusion about gender, confusion about sexual orientation, confusion about their purpose here. Sin is not a learned behavior. In the sight of God, we are sin. We are the enemies of God not because of what we do but because of who we are. Our nature from birth loves disobedience more than obedience. This is why we need a new nature. The Bible is full of absolutes. Jesus taught absolutes. He was clear about how one is saved, how one gets to the Father, how one will see the Kingdom of God. We are absolutely sinners. Jesus is absolutely the Savior. The Law proves that we are sinners; if you don't think so, Jesus made the Law even more impossible because He did not judge the action of sin but the thought of sin too. We absolutely need Jesus to be saved. Jesus prioritized young people as His closest followers because we are called to nurture the next generation. When we want to be served and catered to, after years of following Jesus, then there is a break down in our relationship with Jesus. If we love Jesus, we will feed His sheep. If we are passionate for Jesus, we will make disciples of those coming up behind us. This generation never had the Ravenhills, David Wilkerson's or Billy Graham's. They have a wash of political correctness but hear very little biblical correctness. The young generation does not need any more smooth-talkers, they need to hear from men who are passionate for the truth and preach the Gospel with unction. They are a discerning generation. They are not willing to be generous for generosity sake. They will be generous when they know that what they are giving will make a difference. Thank God for millennials. It's time to contend for the faith. Jesus left us here to preach His Word with no holding back. Read His Words to the seven churches in Revelation. Jesus is not what "Christianity" has forced fed us. Jesus is not the author of confusion. Jesus brings order, clarity, and holiness. Holiness is what we long for. Prioritize others.

Note

251

*"For we are his workmanship, created in Christ Jesus
unto good works, which God hath before ordained that
we should walk in them" (Ephesians 2:10, KJV)*

The way we pray before we eat is the best way to be praying. When we pray, we never ask God to "pick up the fork, stick it in the food, and put in our mouths." We thank God for the food and we eat it; then we eat it. He does not do the work for us, to get the food in our mouth. We do it. Prayer is not an excuse to do nothing. We are praying for revival and awakening but we are not evangelizing, we are not preaching the Gospel, we are not doing something about what we are praying about. If our prayers don't lead to action, then we need to check who we are praying to. The book of Acts is rightly named because it's the book of action. There is no "full-time" intercessor; there is no prayer and worship only office in scripture. If Jesus is not sharing His passion for souls with us, if Jesus is not telling us to go preach the Gospel, then we are not talking to the biblical Christ. Prayer gets us doing something when it's Jesus we are praying to. The Holy Spirit has not called us to be a reservoir; we are called to be rivers of living water. We need to stop waiting, sitting in indecision, and hoping that God will take over and do what He has called us to do. God will never do what we can do; we simply trust God and do what He told us to be doing. God will only work when He knows that we need Him to work so He alone gets all the glory. We will wait around our whole lives, starving to death, if we don't eat what is in front of us, hoping God will spoon-feed us. God won't feed us. It's up to us to eat. It's up to us to preach the Gospel. It's up to us to obey His conviction; when we can't, then He will take it from there. As long as we are asking God to do what He has told us to do and we know that we can do something but we are waiting for Him to do everything, nothing will get done. God called us to be His ambassadors. God called us to be His vehicle of expression. God gives us self-control and a sound mind. Decide today to pray for God's blessing and do what needs to be done. It may not be what you want it to be but it's what needs to be done. Jesus does not call us to do what we want to do; He calls us to do what needs to be done so that we don't rely on ourselves. We need to rely on Him. God rarely tells us to do what we want. He wants us to depend only on Him. Trust and obey.

Note

_____

_____

_____

_____

_____

_____

_____

_____

_____

252

"The steps of a good man are ordered by the Lord: and he delighteth in his way" (Psalm 37:23, KJV)

Not everyone is led by God the same way; Some were directed by talking donkeys, burning bushes and writing on walls. Not everyone was given clear signs as to what they needed to be doing. How do we make decisions when God seems to be silent? God is never silent and if He wants you to go in a different direction, He will send a "whale" to get you there. Stepping out of God's will is not easy. There is only one time that He spoke through a still small voice.[45] God does not hide His will from us. No good Dad wants to whisper their direction to their sons. Including God at the start of our decision-making process is a must. If God does not give clear direction, then we need to speak with godly counsel. If we still don't have clear direction, then we make the best decision we could make and commit to it. If it's not right, God is big enough to redirect. God sometimes won't steer us until we step in faith and start the momentum. Paul set out east but God redirected him to Macedonia. When Paul was arrested in Jerusalem, he used his Roman citizenship to get to Rome; as he knew God wanted him there. God steers us once we take steps of faith. God can use natural means to direct us, heal us and speak to us. We should never be chasing signs for guidance. God wants us to be real and not fake. Fake is not faith. Faith does not empty common sense

---

[45.] *"And after the earthquake a fire; but the Lord was not in the fire: and after the fire a still small voice." (1 Kings 19:12, KJV)*

from the brain. After we believe in Jesus, we still breathe on our own, eat on our own and move on our own. Faith is not the absence of a sound mind. Faith opens the way to the Holy Spirit to give us a sound mind and self-control. Faith in God may lead us to medicine, may lead us to college, may lead us to counsel. Any "faith person" that is against common sense or looks down on making practical decisions, need to prove their "faith" by driving into oncoming traffic and watch God work. Faith is not nonsense. If God audibly says it, then it will be verified by His Word. Scripture is our only source to discerning the voice of God. Without scripture, we are open to demons, lusts and emotions. Don't live indecisive. God is not the author of confusion. Believers should be the most decisive people on earth. We are to be confident that God will complete the work that He started in us, any way that He wants. Decide today.

Note

_____

_____

_____

_____

_____

_____

_____

_____

_____

253

*"Ye ask, and receive not, because ye ask amiss, that ye
may consume it upon your lusts" (James 4:3, KJV)*

Don't pray lust-driven prayers. Many are praying amiss because it's not for the glory of God but for their glory. Shouting passionately at God will not move His hand. The prayer meeting is supposed to be a shouting match or a time to shine. God does not want lip service. A "good" prayer is not a mini-sermon for all to "amen." Words don't move God; motives move God. God wants our thought life, God wants our motives, God wants our heart. We can't fool God with our knowledge, passion and charisma. We are only fooling ourselves. Scripture has been given for doctrine, correction and instruction. Where there is a lack of biblical understanding, strange spirits prevail. Scripture is the greatest commentary on itself. We don't need others opinions, passion or dominance; we need to study the scripture to show ourselves approved. If we want "revival" at the expense of biblical correctness, then we are invoking a demonic host. Jesus taught us that the Holy Spirit will not talk of himself; the Holy Spirit will lead us to rely on scripture. The Holy Spirit is the comforter. All miracles that distract us from Jesus are not the Holy Spirit. Flee from men who work outside of biblical boundaries. They are wolves in sheep's clothing. Their strange spirit is not holy, nor is it biblical. The lack of biblical understanding is leading to synchronization, which is ship-wrecking faith. Jesus will not be mixed with other philosophies, gods or religions. The lukewarm culture we are in has led to confusion and a lack of discernment. Synchronization has deceived our culture to think that discernment is judgment. Judgement is for Jesus but discernment is for the believer. Religion dumbs down discernment. Jesus gives us the gift of discernment. Our discernment as believers is stronger than the most discerning unbeliever because we have the Holy Spirit in us to give us a heavenly elevation of insight. Biblical truth strengthens discernment. If we want to discern, then we need to know the scripture. Don't read any book or author outside of scripture on discernment. Scripture will determine discernment; that's what the Holy Spirit will convict of. When we pray, get real. Uncover our soul and motives; glorify God and pray for His will to be done.

Note

_____

_____

_____

_____

_____

_____

_____

_____

_____

254

"And I knew him not: but he that sent me to baptize with water, the same said unto me, Upon whom thou shalt see the Spirit descending, and remaining on him, the same is he which baptizeth with the Holy Ghost" (John 1:33, KJV)

The title given to the Spirit of God is Holy. Holiness in our flesh can never be attained. We can have a form of godliness, which is religion, but it's just rules, dress codes and routines. There is none Holy but God. On our best day, we are still sinners in the sight of God. In our culture, the more rules you keep, the more righteous you are. This is not how salvation works, according to scripture. Many people feel like they are going to heaven because they are a good person. We might be good in the sight of our earthly justice, but God's justice is much different. God's justice is based on the Law of Moses, which is our tutor to show us how much we have fallen short of God. No matter which law you have broken in the sight of God, you broke them all. Sin is sin in the sight of God. The thought of sin gets the same consequence as the action, according to scripture. There is no amount of good that we can do, to outshine our sins in the sight of God. Our attempt of goodness will never be good enough for God. God knew this; that's why He gave the Jews the sacrificial system. He did not give the Law because we could keep it but so that we could see our need for Him to be our God. Jesus was the final sacrifice for sin. Seventy years after Christ, the Romans destroyed the temple in Jerusalem, proving Jesus to be true. Since that day, the Jews have had no way to sacrifice for forgiveness of their sins. Now, whosoever believes in Jesus is forgiven. To believe in Jesus, means that we confess our sins, renounce our goodness, and repent before God. Unlike the Jews, we confess our sin to Jesus and not to a priest. This is why we don't have priests as Christians. Jesus was our sacrifice and He is our priest. Coming before God with our goodness, may culturally seem right, but it's a total offense to God. Our righteousness is an offense to God. We are such an ignorant generation, even though we have scripture in our own language. If we go before our President in any way we want, we would get arrested. God won't let anyone before Him unless they go the way He wants them to go. Jesus is the only way to the Father. The Holy Spirit enters the believer to radiate the holiness of God through them. Let's walk in the Spirit and we won't fulfill the lusts of the flesh.

Note

255

"For now we see through a glass, darkly; but then face to face: now I know in part; but then shall I know even as also I am known" (1 Corinthians 13:12, KJV)

There will be a day where we will be face-to-face with our Beloved. He loves so deeply. He loves so purely. His presence is the only presence that we were first designed to be in. Alone with Him is the fullest experience that we could ever have. Humanity gets excited to be with dignitaries or famous people, but believers are privileged to sit with the creator of all. He takes time to draw near to whosoever will draw near to Him. Only He can draw near to as many as will draw near to Him and give undivided attention to each one. When we come before Him, it's like we are the only ones before Him. His value on us is unlike anyone else's. Everything stops when one sinner says, "Jesus, I need you"; in that moment, the attention of almighty God is given in its fullest measure. Joy fills His heart. A celebration is thrown. Anyone else would be saying "shame on you" but our beloved Father is saying "shame off you." His love is unlike any love that we could ever experience; yet His love is absolutely needed. We are famished for love. Love is not an emotion. Love cannot be fully experienced by another person. The love of God is the only love that satisfies our soul's thirst for love. Jesus celebrates over repentance. Jesus loves us. He is ready to save whosoever will call on His name. What religion can't do, Jesus does. What another person can't do, Jesus does. "Jesus, we want to sit across from you tangibly. Jesus, we want you to come back for us, but we know you are giving grace because you see millions of people that need to be saved before you return." Time with Jesus is unlike time with anyone else, yet time with Him always stirs us up for His will and passion. No believer walks with Jesus and does not weep over souls, as He does. His intercession to the Father is that none should perish. We are His mirror on earth. When the lost see us, they see His burning love for them. The lost know that we are as lost as they are but yet we have been found in the love of Jesus. We don't want them to see us. We want all to see Christ in us. We can't be what only Christ can be, to those that need to be found. We will disappoint, we will fail, we will fall, but Christ stays true to us and we want everyone to know that Christ is true.

Note

256

"For our God is a consuming fire" (Hebrews 12:29, KJV)

Our God is a consuming fire. Jesus baptizes not only in water but with fire. Fire is not passion. Fire is purification and mortification of the flesh. We need to throw out all of our doubt, sin, and carnality into the fire, to burn up all of our immorality. The fire of God has nothing to do with passion; it has to do with God sanctifying our ways. We need the fire of God to be consuming our ways, our desires, and our understanding so that we only rely on God. We will never be perfect in our flesh until we pass or until Jesus returns. This is not a license to walk in the flesh. We need to walk in the Spirit. That means we walk depending on God and not on our wisdom. If we burn for Jesus, then we will burn for holiness. It's good to every now and again write our sins on a piece of paper and throw it into a fire as a symbol of the Holy Spirit in us, working the holiness of God through us as we surrender to Him. Grace abounds toward those who have sinned the most. That grace is not a license but is the power to put sin away. Jesus does not want us sinning; He wants us to sin no more. If perfection could be attained in our flesh, then we would not need Jesus; but there is no graduation from a need for Jesus. We will always need Jesus. If Jesus called the churches to repent in Revelation, then we need to repent today too. Repentance is not a "salvation message only" it's an "unquenching of the fire of God message." Unrepentant sin quenches the fire of God in us to consume us. Embrace a lifestyle of repentance, so that there is no Luke warmness in our lives. To be hot for God means we burn for His life in us. We can't do this life on our own. Beware of charisma because emotionalism is a smoke-screen. No matter how bold the preacher is, he is as much human as anyone else. We all need to be spurred on in honoring Christ above everything. Any preacher or personality that elevates himself above Christ is on thin ice with God. Preachers need the message as much as their audience. There is no one above another in the sight of God. He wants us to fan/encourage each other into flame for Christ.[46] It's up to us to communicate our sins to God so that the Blood cleanses and the fire of the Spirit burns it out of our lives. This is why the Spirit has the title Holy. His title helps us discern what is of God.

Note

---

46. *"Wherefore I put thee in remembrance that thou stir up the gift of God, which is in thee by the putting on of my hands." (2 Timothy 1:6, KJV)*

257

"Neither give place to the devil" (Ephesians 4:27, KJV)

Guilt and shame will perpetuate the enemy's plan for our lives. These emotions will keep us bound. Condemnation never produces life. When we are constantly faced with our sin and wretchedness, we either invent a religion or run to a fix to get a temporary relief. Hobbies, business, sports, and careers are an escape; but they are all temporary. Vacations are temporary. The reality is, our biggest problems is ourselves. We can try to run from ourselves and numb ourselves, but the hangover will end. When we eventually come off of the high of religion, we face what we all have to face: "ourselves." The more depravity that we feel, the more sin that we have experienced, and the more of this world that we see, the more we will know that there is no thing that quenches the thirst of our soul. Jesus Christ alone will receive us as we are; but He will not leave us the way we were. A relationship with Him makes every day like a vacation; God makes the most horrible situation in our life, as if our favorite team just won the super bowl. A relationship with Jesus satisfies our soul more than any religion, church or preacher can. Jesus never lets us down. Jesus does not need the ten percent of your income. Jesus does not need your volunteer time. Jesus does not need anything. Jesus is self-existent. Jesus chooses to want us. He has no need of us and would be fine with or without us, but He wants us. Look at His nail-scarred hands. Even the hardest of men melt by the love that God has for us. Jesus knows that we are wretched, yet He still died for us. He took our sin on Himself; He does not leave us the way we were.

He will take us just as we are but He won't leave us in what hurts us. Jesus changes us. Beware of gnostic new covenant teachings. This "new covenant" is gnostic in its origin and its preachers are spiritually fat; preaching a message that keeps them in their suits and comfort. There is no repentance, there is no conviction of sin. They preach to the currency that makes their lifestyle perpetuated. It's time for the swamp to be drained. It's time like Paul did in 2 Timothy 4:20,[47] to call out the men that are utilizing the gospel for their own gain. At the end of Colossians, Paul had no issue with name-dropping those that had left the faith or taken advantage of the faith. We have all experienced them. Live shame and guilt free.

Note

_____

_____
_____
_____
_____
_____
_____
_____
_____

[47.] *"Erastus abode at Corinth: but Trophimus have I left at Miletum sick." (2 Timothy 4:20, KJV)*

258

"Jesus answered and said unto them, This is the work of God, that ye believe on him whom he hath sent" (John 6:29, KJV)

Up until Jesus, the teaching from the Law of Moses dealt with sin and righteousness. Jesus's teaching dealt with faith and unbelief. In the sight of Jesus, sin was sin. There were no levels of sin. The Jew that coveted and the prostitute that fornicated was loved equally by Jesus. He treated sinners equally, no matter what the fruit of sin was; He knew the root of it was where they were putting their faith for salvation. The law could not save. It was because of the law that we knew what sin was. If we didn't have the law, then we would do what was right in our own eyes and live as animals. Jesus fulfilled the law and taught righteousness came only by faith and not by works.[48] The whole Old Testament teaches us that we don't have what it takes to turn ourselves from our sin by ourselves. Repentance under the law was short lived. Faith under the law had no power to change the nature of a sinner that repented and believed in God. They had to continually sacrifice; they had to continually live fearing the law condemning them. Jesus taught that we are all condemned, no matter what level of sin we are at, in the sight of God. Jesus taught that the law condemned and we are condemned but the only way to live condemnation-free, according to Him, was to believe on Him. Jesus was not after behavior; He was after belief. Religion deals with behavior

---

[48.] *"Then said they unto him, What shall we do, that we might work the works of God?" (John 6:28, KJV)*

but Jesus dealt with belief. Jesus knew that the root of sinful behavior was unbelief. When a person believes in Jesus, we are empowered to live differently. The Gospel is not a gnostic teaching or a figment of imagination. The Gospel is the power of God unto salvation. When the Gospel is only demonstrated and not preached, someone is not reading their Bible. Jesus never said, "Show the Gospel." The Gospel is a message because the emphasis of it is not on the preacher or the believer but on the person of Jesus. The Gospel does for a person, what no political agenda could do. Ministries need to remember what sets us apart from government or humanitarian agencies. We have a message. The humanist "can lead a horse to water but they can't make it drink." The Gospel, when it's preached, "salts the oats so that when the horse eats, it gets thirsty." Ministries that are ashamed of the Gospel will be surprised by Jesus being ashamed of them.

Note

_____

_____

_____

_____

_____

_____

_____

_____

_____

259

"Moreover, brethren, I declare unto you the gospel which I preached unto you, which also ye have received, and wherein ye stand; By which also ye are saved, if ye keep in memory what I preached unto you, unless ye have believed in vain" (1 Corinthians 15:1–2, KJV)

The Gospel means good news. Anyone that says that they preach the gospel, but use words when necessary is biblically ignorant. The evangelical church no longer has prioritized evangelism. Sound doctrine is no longer sought after. Emotionalism and "ted talk" sermons have replaced the anointing and biblical sermons. Application is more important than conviction of sin. They feed the people how to live better lives but care less for their soul. There are no tears shed over souls going to hell. They are not bothered by His imminent return. They believe a false view that if God wants people saved, God will draw them to church. That's not the way God wants to reach people. He chose us. We are relying on lazy spirituality and not obeying the Great Commission. We are not saviors. The church is not salvation. Jesus saves. By not preaching the Gospel, we are setting our audience up for disappointment; we are not salvation, nor is the church or the services we provide. Your best life now could lead to your worst eternal life. hell Fire is fictional for most. The judgement seat of Christ does not fit today's belief system. All we want is to cherry-pick scripture to fit God into our understanding. Some of our evangelical leaders can't remember the last time that they shared the Gospel outside of a pulpit. They have no prayer life. Their advisors are all business men that are steering them to build the church without sound doctrine or biblical boundaries. The swamp will get drained if we really want awakening. We need salt even though it stings; it heals wounds. We need white blood cells, because they fight infections. We need to eat healthy, even though we crave dessert. It's time to wake up before it's too late. Hear the Spirit, let Him convict. Don't tune Him out; He won't always strive with your spiritual gluttony. If we are not taking our spiritual work-out seriously, we will be spiritually obese. The spiritual obesity is out of control in the West. We need salty sermons; we need white blood cell preaching. We need truth preachers who are not afraid of being invited back to the pulpit. We need men that are not preaching to the honorarium. We need men, whose consciences are captive to scripture and not their lusts.

Note

260

"But I trust in the Lord Jesus to send Timotheus shortly unto you, that I also may be of good comfort, when I know your state. For I have no man likeminded, who will naturally care for your state. For all seek their own, not the things which are Jesus Christ's. But ye know the proof of him, that, as a son with the father, he hath served with me in the gospel. Him therefore I hope to send presently, so soon as I shall see how it will go with me. But I trust in the Lord that I also myself shall come shortly" (Philippians 2:19–24, KJV)

Satanism is educating their following in the love of self. Self is god according to them, "love self, live for self." Self is the fuel of sin. There is no sin that is sinful enough to not be forgiven by Jesus. Jesus taught the denial of self. We want the self to be promoted, but it leads to destruction. When we reach the end of self and we get everything self wants, we find that at the end, there is nothing but death. Satan and Sin were made a public spectacle, as Jesus hung on the cross. The temptation of Satan and the power of sin was vanquished by the death of Christ. The Spirit that raised Christ from the dead is the same Spirit that lives in us; the Spirit that believes in Jesus to raise us from the temptations of Satan and the power of sin. We have unnatural power in Jesus's name. We have the kingdom of God within us. Jesus told the church in Smyrna to not fear the things they will suffer or the prisons they may get thrown into or the martyrdoms that are ahead because we should see death as a door to heaven. There is a crown of life for the faithful. We can't be faithful in righteousness but we can be faithful in Christ's righteousness that

He earned for us. Don't let the "name it and claim it" movement put fear that God does not hear because we face hardship. Embrace hardship, embrace demotion, embrace the decrease. Decreasing increases Christ. The less we rely on self, the more Christ will be lifted up. A person submitted to Christ will be used to slap Satan's smile right off his face. The day for his laughter is over. He will not rejoice anymore at the church. We have all fallen but we are rising in the power of Christ. We have sat in darkness but we are coming alive to the light of Christ. Reckon ourselves dead to self-strength. Die to self-strength daily. As we choose to not walk in self-strength, we will have Holy Spirit strengthen us to not fulfill the lust of self. Jesus Christ is Lord. His authority in heaven and on earth is in us, to put sin and Satan on the run in Jesus's name. Satanism is resisted in Jesus's name and the devil must flee when we submitted to God.[49] Sin has lost its dominion in Jesus's name. It's time for the militant believers to rise up from the valley where we have been slumbering and awaken to who we are in Christ. The gates of hell will not prevail.

---

[49] *"Draw nigh to God, and he will draw nigh to you. Cleanse your hands, ye sinners; and purify your hearts, ye double minded." (James 4:8, KJV)*

261

"And Jesus said unto them, Come ye after me, and I will make you to become fishers of men" (Mark 1:17, KJV)

We burn for souls because Jesus burns for souls. Souls can't be plucked from the clench of Satan's grip by anything other than the preaching of the Gospel. The proclamation of the Gospel is the only way to drive Satan out of a person's soul. Humanity can only serve one of two masters. Sinners are of their master the devil. This is why the Gospel leads to a decision of confession of sin and a declaration that Jesus is Lord. The Gospel demands a response if it's preached biblically. Jesus said to those that gave Him attention, to follow Him. At the end of the proclamation of the Gospel, everyone must make a decision to follow Jesus or follow Satan. Everyone is following someone but believers can't follow anyone other than Jesus because everything and everyone else will lead us astray. Only Jesus will lead us in life and peace. Every other way leads to a snare. This is why sinners repent, we state our need for a savior. "Jesus, we need you." Once we confess our sin and declare Him Lord, we follow His purpose for us, which to is preach the Gospel and make disciples. This is what disciples do. To be a disciple but not have an evangelistic desire, one must ask who are we a disciple of? Are we a disciple of Christ or are we a disciple of the church? A disciple of the church will only go as far as their church is willing to go. A disciple of Christ will go as far as Jesus wants them to go. We are called to follow Jesus. Following Him will always lead to a church but we won't be going where we want to go, we will be going where He wants us to go. We don't go to a church that caters to us; we go to a church that Jesus leads us to. We have many that have never included Jesus in their daily decision-making, yet have been hoodwinked into thinking that Jesus is their Lord. Who are we following? Follow Jesus, not trends, preachers or movements. Follow Jesus. When we follow Him, what moves Him will move us. We will become His ambassadors. He will use us as His hands and feet. This is how He chose to see souls saved, it's through the preaching of those that are following Him. Preaching may seem foolishness to our age, but it's God's vehicle to convict of sin and tear souls out of Satan's death grip, in Jesus's name.

Note

262

"And it shall come to pass in that day, that his burden shall be taken away from off thy shoulder, and his yoke from off thy neck, and the yoke shall be destroyed because of the anointing" (Isaiah 10:27, KJV)

Unction must be defined by passion, as it is by a lot of those in our pews today. Passion is not an anointing that breaks the chains of sin. Charisma can be faked. Our preaching strategy will wow the intellect but not transform a life. Some of the greatest preachers never had to raise their voice or use oratory methodology to convince their audience. Loudness does not make God listen and it does not earn the respect of the audience. A preacher that wants to be effective lays aside their foolish fleshly tactics and announces to their audience, from the beginning, that their absolute dependency is on God. The most important part of a sermon is the opening prayer. The opening prayer tells God and the audience that what is about to happen can only truly happen by God. We can't do what God can. We can try to imitate God, but it will always be counterfeit. If we want weight to our words, we must get transparent of our own total dependence on God for anyone to get anything good out of our exposition of scripture. Hermeneutics and homiletics are common sense; but when it comes to the preaching of the Gospel, we fully rely on God to do what we can't do. The Gospel is not a lecture. Preaching is not teaching. We are not evangelizing to educate only; we are preaching to see God save souls forever. The Gospel is an eternal message. It must be handled with care. Anyone that is dependent on God, can be effective at preaching the Gospel. As we look to Christ, who is in us, as we boast only in the treasure in these earthen vessels,[50] as we rely on God, the scripture will come alive, transforming our audience right before our eyes. We are overladen with teachers today. What we need are preachers. Preachers that are set on fire for the Gospel, so that their audience watches them burn and they hear the words of Christ drawing sinners to His grace and Lordship. Preaching is God's means to snap in two the chains of sin and Satan. We need unction. Unction comes from time spent with Jesus in prayer, repentance, and the study of His Word. Unction comes when the preacher is on His knees in total surrender before God in the quiet place. Unction is kindled in the private place and not the public place. Cultivate a relationship with Jesus that no one but you and Him know about.

Note

---

[50] *"But we have this treasure in earthen vessels, that the excellency of the power may be of God, and not of us." (2 Corinthians 4:7, KJV)*

263

"He that believeth on the Son hath everlasting life: and he that believeth not the Son shall not see life; but the wrath of God abideth on him" (John 3:36, KJV)

A Gospel that removes the responsibility and will of a person is only good news for those who believe it. The mystery of God's sovereignty will be a mystery for our finite minds to understand. Only Satan would offer a message that keeps us behind four walls and makes us be "like" God so that we can be seeker-hostile to those that we don't like. There is no one that can judge another person's eternity; we usurp God if we do. God loves the world and predestined the world to be saved. Jonah had to learn this the hard way. Whosoever believes in Jesus will be saved. When our theology does not burden us for souls or others, then we are in a religion and not in a relationship with Jesus. Religion loves the sound of their own voice more than the people. If we listen to sermons and read books more than share the Gospel with the lost, we have been lured away by the same serpent as Eve was. Satan has made religion into the apple for the West. "Religion will make us like god." We can give 10 percent, warm a pew, sing karaoke and hear a message that keeps us lord of our own lives, yet end up in hell. Religion is irrelevant to sinners. Religion loves their own and rivals the best social clubs. Religion will even pick and choose Bible verses but never read it in context. Religion emphasizes commentaries, theologians and opinions of preachers. Religion wants to make clones of themselves. They talk about Jesus but have more respect for their clergy and their clergies' image than

Jesus or conforming to the image of Jesus. Religion will quote every-one but Jesus. Religion does outreaches but has no passion for the Gospel. Religion wants it's converts to be relying on their services and not on a personal relationship with Jesus. Religion makes its buildings to be places of worship rather its followers being the place of worship. Jesus was put on the cross by religion. We are horrified by sinners because religion has crept its way into our culture. Jesus loves sinners; Jesus loves the world. If Jesus was here, He would be drawing sinners and be hated by the religious. Jesus came to begin an organism, not an organization. What thrills us more: scripture or our preacher? Follow Jesus, read the Bible, let God lead; discern or be deceived. Quit religion.

Note

264

"And he said unto them, Come ye yourselves apart into a desert place, and rest a while: for there were many coming and going, and they had no leisure so much as to eat" (Mark 6:31, KJV)

Millions sleep tonight, craving their next fix; they have nowhere to rest, no hope for tomorrow, and they are living from moment to moment. Government agencies, humanitarian charities and ministries have given handout after handout, shelter, on-ramps to employment, free education, apprenticeships; what is holding back these precious souls is not the lack of help but the lack of the Gospel. Sin destroys. There is no amount of education, resources or wealth that can drive sin out of a person's life. After talking with hundreds of precious souls, sending them to the best resources to make them better, getting them jobs, paying their way to get help will not get them what they need; unless sin is dealt with, there is very little that we can do. Most of the help they receive is enabling their lifestyle, hurting them even more in the process. We've worked the streets for years. Some of the greatest Gospel-preaching heroes of our past, would be horrified as to their legacy today. What began in the Spirit, preaching the Gospel in power has now led to the infiltration of every program, rehab, and discipleship tool we could invent to the point we are talking of a Jesus that saves us by faith but we need ministry resources to be kept saved. Today's gospel preaches salvation by faith but discipled by works. This limited born-again message is "right" on Jesus saves by faith but He also keeps us by faith. We are not kept saved by our works. Our discipleship is from faith to faith.

This is what has led to so much religion in Christianity. Discipleship was not to be Saul's armor that's only one size but it's supposed to fit everyone. David could not fit into Saul's armor. We do not fit into anything that is not the will of God for us. Jesus wants a relationship that relies on Him. Religion does not want anyone relying on Jesus; how would they pay their bills if that was the case? Silver and gold are what we are relying on but what Peter had, money could not buy. What the early Church had was not for sale. The anointing cannot be bought. We are either walking in a relationship with Jesus and relying on Him or we are not. The need on our streets will always be there until Christ returns. We are not motivated by need. As we need Jesus and know Jesus, the power that raised Him from the dead will be evident in us. The Gospel has power to not only give a handout but it also gives a hand up. Jesus put value on every soul when His blood was shed. As we rely on Him, He leads us, He cleanses sin and He makes us new.

Jesus never gave blueprints to what His buildings should look like. This is why we see Churches of all shapes, sizes, and locations. A better term for these places is assembly. Western culture has made a structure and organization out of His Church. Jesus allowed the church to grow organically to where it is today. We have so many different churches and that's God's will. The Church is a body, both locally and universally. Every church has its net and is tailored to draw what the Lord leads to their gatherings. Some churches reach old, some reach young, but the best is when the church is multigenerational, all valuing one another's part in the body. The church is the greatest gathering on this planet. There is no other community of love, acceptance, and commonality like it. The counterfeit churches out there have done a great job distracting the masses to the bars, sports games, gangs, hobbies and all other communities that were built on anything other than Christ. When a Church is built on Jesus and His Word, every cultural boundary is torn down. When a church is built on race, age or hobbies, the Church is not functioning as it should. Jesus showed no partiality toward Jews, Samaritans, or Gentiles. A Church that does not follow Jesus will be no different than any other religion. If we were to be conformed to the image of Jesus, then the fruit of Jesus would be seen in our lives. In order for a community to be a Church, they need to have the same love that Jesus had. The early church was a mess, yet most people dream of being like the early church today. When we read the epistles, there was mass chaos as to the organization of the early church. We have come a long way two thousand years later. Our Churches are defined, organized, and resourced; now all we need is to seek to be more like Jesus. We are the most blessed Church age ever with our rich history, amazing structures and the scripture being accessible anywhere we want it. We are set up for the biggest awakening that the earth has ever seen. It may be like the days of Noah in some parts of the earth, but it's not like that yet in the West. The earth has never been so civilized. We are truly in the greatest days of the Church. The more biblically literate and Sprit dependent we become, the greater Jesus will get glory out of our lives.

265

"But we all, with open face beholding as in a glass the glory of the Lord, are changed into the same image from glory to glory, even as by the Spirit of the Lord" (2 Corinthians 3:18, KJV)

When Christ comes into our lives, He works His nature through us. The way He loves will be seen in us. The way He forgives will be seen in us. Jesus restores years of division in an instant. The Prodigal had more hope than the elder brother. This does not license prodigals, but it warns us of religiosity and entitlement. Jesus wants all people to be restored. Restoration should make us celebrate and never cringe. How well we celebrate others' blessings is how much we have given over to the nature of Jesus. We can have as much of Jesus seen in us as we are willing to surrender. The more we let go of our culture, understanding, and wisdom, the more God works through us. Bitterness only hurts the person that's bitter. Religion hardens us, so that jealousy, anger, and resentment fester. Jesus makes us tender toward people but bold as a lion toward hell. Gates are defensive and not offensive; this is why the gates of hell will not prevail because we are called to storm the gates of hell. We are to take back what the enemy has stolen. When we are submitted to God, we can resist the devil. Believers are here to be offensive and not defensive. Believers are to be fearless. We are more than conquerors. We don't wait to be attacked; we attack. Evangelism is an attack on hell. Preaching the Gospel is like nails going down a chalkboard for Satan. It's time for ministry to become militant. Our passive and comfortable culture has made us spiritually obese. The only way we can work out

Salvation is by following Jesus in all that He wants us to be doing. When we follow Jesus, we will be evangelizing the way He did it. Jesus is the example of all of the offices of ministry, but especially the evangelist. It's no longer us that live as believers but Christ living His mission through us. Jesus sought and saved the lost. We are called to seek the lost, but only Jesus can save them. The quicker we get the attention on Jesus, the more effective we will be in evangelism. Don't deny the power by depending on yourself; deny yourself. Denial of self is not denying sin, but it's denying our strength to fight sin. We will lose every time. Sin is stronger than us. Satan is stronger than us. This is why we boast of He that is in us, for He is greater than us.

Note

266

*"And one of you say unto them, Depart in peace, be ye warmed
and filled; notwithstanding ye give them not those things which
are needful to the body; what doth it profit?" (James 2:16, KJV)*

Works don't lead to faith; faith leads to works. Preaching does not
follow miracles; miracles follow preaching. Discipleship does not lead
to salvation; salvation leads to discipleship. Discipling the unsaved is
like trying to produce oranges on an apple tree. We won't be able
to get the fruit we want to see in our Church, if they have not been
saved. Discipling the unsaved will only lead to a form of godliness.
Once a person is saved, they will want to be at Church, they will want
more of scripture, they will desire the fruit of the Spirit. Jesus makes
us new on the inside. He gives us the power to crave righteousness
and be mature in the faith. Faith in Jesus makes discipleship possible. Faith in Jesus puts the right behavior and a disciplined life in
reach. Faith does not excuse works but produces the desire to work
out our salvation; and if it does not, then our faith is dead. Faith in
Jesus empowers right living. Does this mean a believer is perfect? No,
we will never graduate from faith while we are here. We grow from
faith to faith. This means that maturity is not getting more and more
independent from God. True maturity is becoming more and more
dependent on God. As we grow in faith, we will learn that it is God
who works in us to do and to desire His will. Bible reading will be a
desire, righteousness will be a desire, praying will be a desire; everything changes when Jesus becomes Lord over our decision-making.
Working out Salvation is never for Salvation. Jesus saved us. Earning

Salvation is rejecting Christ's work on the cross. We can't get any more saved than we did when we first got saved. From the position of Salvation, we will want to be discipled and make disciples. To be a disciple, we must be discipled. This is why we have pastors. We need one another to stir each another on in the faith. Satan wants to knock the fight of faith out of us and his strategy is isolation. Like most predators, they pounce when their prey is isolated. Disciples only get discipled while they are discipling. We never graduate discipleship. No one can teach "teachability." Jesus makes us teachable. Most of us learn best the hard way and when we learn, we need to get back up believing that Jesus saved us. Follow Jesus to the end.

Note

267

"And Samuel said, Hath the Lord as great delight in burnt offerings and sacrifices, as in obeying the voice of the Lord? Behold, to obey is better than sacrifice, and to hearken than the fat of rams" (1 Samuel 15:22, KJV)

Obedience always leads to blessing, even when our flesh makes it out to be a sacrifice. What God has for us in eternity is nothing but prosperity, health, wealth, and every good thing that's beyond our imagination. Satan makes obedience to God feel like it's a sacrifice, when in reality, what we get in the end is eternal life. The correction God brings is only to promote health. The salt God puts in our wound is only to heal. Truth only offends that which is tempting us for our destruction, but all that gives life in the end. Those that want heaven now have sold out the journey of the cross for Satan's counterfeit temporal heaven. This earth will be destroyed. Don't get too comfortable here. There will be a new earth that we will live on. Don't sell out for our will over God's will. There are so many tempting us to turn the rocks into bread and to bow down to worship the devil just to get what we want in life. Don't sell out to their temptation. It's not true; they may offer temporal health and wealth but it will cost your soul. Don't sacrifice doctrine for unity. Don't sacrifice scripture for a spiritual experience. It's not worth it. Those that sell out doctrine for unity have sold out Jesus for their own agenda. Our agendas have no eternal gain. Scrap them. Seek God; do His will. His will may not be the most enticing but it's the most rewarding in the end. Obey His will; even if it's the cross He calls you to. Don't listen to smooth-talkers that make money from a limited gospel which says that life with Jesus is heaven now. This earth is not the believer's playground; this is the believer's battlefield. We need armor, we need spiritual weapons, there must never be a moment when we leave down our guard. The fight for faith will be daily if we are walking in His will. We may not be in His will if what we are doing does not require faith to do it. Obedience to God will always require faith. God does not ask of us what we can do; God asks of us what only He can do as we surrender to Him and allow Him to do it through us. Our obedience now will be worth it when we see Jesus. Hardship now is worth heaven forever. Don't sell out the will of God for the will of man. Don't pray out of His will, pray through His will. His will is eternal life.

Note

_____
_____
_____
_____
_____
_____
_____
_____
_____
_____

268

"For a day in thy courts is better than a thousand. I had rather be a doorkeeper in the house of my God, than to dwell in the tents of wickedness" (Psalm 84:10, KJV)

Better is one day with Jesus than thousands of days with anyone else. Jesus gives us a drink and we will never thirst again. We were created to walk with God; when we try to fill the void in our lives with anyone or anything else, we will be left dissatisfied. We were created with a need for God and a need for community. God first, because only He won't let us down; then others second. Church or community cannot come ahead of Jesus; if it does, we will get hurt. Many have gotten hurt at Church and they not only left Church but they have left Jesus. No one told them that the Church gatherings hurt people and as much as you need Jesus, they need Jesus as well. When Jesus is the focus, we bear with one another. When Jesus is first, we can commit to community; and rather than gossiping with others we gossip with Jesus. Secrets are safe with Jesus. Repentance is safe with Jesus. Confession is safe with Jesus. Don't deviate from Jesus. When we esteem anyone or anything above Jesus, we are prey to hurt. Be vulnerable with Jesus. Know Jesus. He has no stones to throw at you, He does not condemn you, He listens but also has the power to do for you what no one else could. Jesus saves, He also makes the burden light and the yoke easy. The church is our community, it's not our savior. Jesus is our founder and everyone else is a sinner just like you; we need Jesus as much as you do. When Jesus is first, He will lead you to church, He will lead you to community. Jesus knows that it's not good for us to be alone. As an evangelist, we need the Church. An evangelist without the pastor will be short lived. For years, the Pastor and the evangelist have competed; this is Satan's strategy. It's time for us to compliment, rather than compete. We need one another. It's how God set it up. There is no excuse for isolation or the lone ranger. We need the Church and we need community. It's how Jesus set up salvation; Salvation leads to a committed community of believers. When Jesus is the focus, that community will be healthy. When community is the focus, we are in trouble. The Church must build on the teaching of Jesus rather than gimmicks, music, entertainment or community. The world will outperform us but they can't compete with Jesus. Jesus is better.

Note

269

*"And I, if I be lifted up from the earth, will draw
all men unto me" (John 12:32, KJV)*

Let's get the emphasis off of what we can do and emphasize what He can do. We think we want our will. We think we know what is best for us. We think...that's the problem. Our thinking leads us in circles. What could have taken a few weeks of travel, took forty years for Israel to get to the promised land. A whole generation had to die to get to the next generation that were not willing to be led by their sight but led by what God said. Joshua and Caleb were the only two that were willing to believe that God could do what everyone else thought was not possible. Our thoughts will deceive us; that's why we believe in truth and not thought. Truth sets us free; thoughts keep us captive. Take thoughts captive and bring them to obedience in Christ. Repentance is a change of rulership from our thoughts to His truth. Repentance can only be seen in our behavior when our thoughts are submitted to the truth of scripture. When scripture is the lens we see through, our natural sight will no longer determine our faith. Our faith is determined by what we believe; it is not determined by our sight. Repentance is an acknowledgment of our need for Jesus to do what only He can through us. We can't behave as God would want us to in our own strength; Israel's history proves this. Christ died so that we would no longer live dependent on our thought-life but be dependent on His truth. The truth of scripture is not theology that entertains only our minds; it's power to live as God would want us to live. As we repent, which is stating our need for Christ and His truth, He puts to death our self-strength so that we can live by His Spirit-strength. Christ calls us to a life that needs Him. Satan calls us to a life that lives independent of Him. Beware of a gospel that appeals to our will, thoughts and behavior. The Gospel of Jesus calls us out of our life to have His life live through us. Don't be ashamed if you still need Jesus after being a believer for a long time, that's the will of God. We will need Jesus until He returns or until we pass into eternity. It's okay to need Jesus. It's okay to still repent. It's healthy to repent daily and die daily to our strength; this enables the Spirit to live the life of Christ through us. Christianity lifts Christ up above the apostles and the Church.

Note

270

"And he said to them all, If any man will come after me, let him deny himself, and take up his cross daily, and follow me" (Luke 9:23, KJV)

Denial of self is not denying desires of self or actions of self; it is denying self-strength to deny our desires and actions. When a believer surrenders, it's not the silver or gold that God wants from us it's us, He wants from us. God is not after what have, He is after who we are. Repentance is transparently saying to God "I need you for everything." God is our everything. He is not only our savior but He is everything that we have been looking for. When we repent, we are removing trust in ourselves and placing it on Christ, the solid rock. When repenting is about changing ourselves and cleaning ourselves by ourselves, we will live a similar life as Israel did in the Old Testament. Jesus did not only replace the sacrificial system; He replaced our hearts with His. Believers are supernatural beings. We are able to love the unlovable. We are able to forgive the unforgivable. None of this is possible because we are "trying" to be like Jesus; no, the believer does not try, the believer is empowered to do the will of God. We can't try what God is calling us to because what He calls us to, He does the work through us. That's why we repent for trying. We repent for trying to take matters into our own hands. If we miss this, then our whole Christian life will be no different than any other condemned religion. As we disengage our self-effort, the Spirit of God changes the "religious have-toos" into "want-toos." Never evangelize because you have to. People don't need to see the same old defeated life of "have toos." We evangelize because we want to; because we get to. What we have is different. We are unburned by the furnaces of life; we have joy in affliction and our faith gets fueled by hardships. The believer that is living the will of God is enflamed by the hardships belt; their fire is never outed. We crave to believe God. We are excited to repent. As we give God our root of self, He replaces it with the root of Christ; this leads to the fruit of the Spirit being seen in us. We don't pray "change me," we pray "have your way in me." Jesus said that we are clean by His Word; we are changed by His Spirit. Don't worship change, worship Jesus. Worship Jesus for what He did and not for what He can do. This is why He mandated us to remember Him. Repentance is not a remembrance of our sin but a remembrance of His sacrifice for our sin. Deny self, trust Jesus.

Note

_____

_____

_____

_____

_____

_____

_____

_____

_____

_____

271

"But without faith it is impossible to please him: for he that cometh to God must believe that he is, and that he is a rewarder of them that diligently seek him" (Hebrews 11:6, KJV)

Don't make our need for change a higher priority than our need for Jesus. Humanism in its extremity wants a prosperity god. The prosperity god that is worshipped today makes humanity its master and humans will only worship it if it gives them what they want. Its followers don't want boundaries, correction or doctrine. Their emotions are what they live by. When sound doctrine is pushed aside for a worship experience, they have been lured by the prosperity god. Satan came to Jesus in the wilderness with a prosperity message; Jesus used scripture to silence the temptation. Sound doctrine from scripture is what our society desperately need. When truth is replaced with emotionalism, we will be given over to lust and all forms of gluttony. A disciple of Jesus that has no discipline, no self-control, no sound-mindedness is not a disciple of Christ but a disciple of the flesh. The Holy Spirit leads us to truth, gives us the fruit of self-control, and brings a sound mind to us. The Holy Spirit ignites when we are submitted to God and live by His power. Change comes when Jesus is first. When our faith is not determined by our change or by what we see, but instead it is determined by what God says, then change happens in our lives. There is no one that believes in Christ and repents yet stays in sin. Jesus makes us Holy as He is Holy, not only by faith but breaks the lust of the flesh so we crave Him above anything else. No one could spend time with Jesus and not be affected by Him in lifestyle and countenance. Everyone can discern a man that's been with Jesus. We will be different; being with Jesus always makes us better. As we repent, which is stating our need for Jesus, nothing stays the same. When Jesus saves, there is nothing that can separate us from His love for us. We can be assured of eternal life. There is no believer that has to live by fear. We will always need to be changed because we will always need Jesus. Religion gives ordination and seminary degrees but it does not graduate us from our dependence on God. All God is looking for is a man that has repented, beating on his chest saying "God I need you." That's the person who gets the attention of God. God is not impressed by our education or titles; God is impressed by faith.

Note

_____

_____

_____

_____

_____

_____

_____

_____

272

"Not every one that saith unto me, Lord, Lord, shall enter into the kingdom of heaven; but he that doeth the will of my Father which is in heaven. Many will say to me in that day, Lord, Lord, have we not prophesied in thy name? and in thy name have cast out devils? and in thy name done many wonderful works? And then will I profess unto them, I never knew you: depart from me, ye that work iniquity" (Matthew 7:21–23, KJV)

Ministry is an outflow of our relationship with Jesus. Never evangelize because one has to. When we believe in Jesus, we will want to share Him. Anxiety and fear are not the emotions that lead us as believers. Anyone that invites Jesus into their lives does not stay the same. He calls us to His will. As we seek God, God leads us. Very few are taking time to pray anymore. We make the "best" decisions for ourselves. The Spirit-led life has been replaced with the religious-led life. As long as religion is happy with us, we must ask ourselves, "Are we doing the right thing? If everyone applauses and says amen, does that mean that we are right with God? As long as we stay in the boat are we really where God wants us to be? God does not lead us in comfort, He leads us in conviction. Jesus still speaks. His voice will be known by the believer. His yes and no will come from scripture. As we bring our decisions to Jesus, He may not give us a clear direction; if so, we need to make the best move we know, include Jesus in all our ways, and He will direct our steps. If we want to be Spirit-led, we will want to be praying. When we are Spirit-led, we won't be duty led. When we open ourselves to God, He will direct our lives in such a way, that faith will be required but we will be empowered to obey. The only thing that marveled Jesus was faith. When we set aside what we want for what He wants, God provides the way. When we follow God, He takes care of us and we will never beg for bread. Take time to pray; develop our relationship with Jesus because where He leads, He provides. If we have spent years of our life doing what seems to be right but have ended up in a mess, it's not too late to repent. God will restore those years in an instant. We don't have to live in shame. Get out of the boat and joyfully go into the belly of the fish. Our God gets us back on track. Repentance will be accepted until we pass. It's not too late. Religion may have written you off but Jesus wrote you in. Just repent. Repent of being lord of your own life and make Him Lord; this means that Jesus will be involved in our everyday life. Jesus wants all our mind, body, and soul, not just an hour on Sunday. Except the Lord lead us, what we are doing is in vain.[51] Follow Jesus, depend on the Spirit, and watch Him work daily.

[51.] *"Except the Lord build the house, they labour in vain that build it: except the Lord keep the city, the watchman waketh but in vain." (Psalm 127:1, KJV)*

273

"Trust in the Lord with all thine heart; and lean not unto thine own understanding. In all thy ways acknowledge him, and he shall direct thy paths" (Proverbs 3:5–6, KJV)

If our discipleship does not lead to dependence on God, then our discipleship will only condemn us. If our discipleship does not convict us to be more like Christ, then our education is irrelevant. Jesus never taught in a classroom, like we do today. The greatest form of learning is watching it being done and then attempting to do it. It's up to us to make the initial step of obedience; God will do the rest. God does not replace our responsibility when we follow Him. He enables our abilities to do what only He can do as we initiate to obey Him. It takes faith to initiate. If we draw near to God, He will draw near to us. The only time that Jesus marvels at us is when we believe. Belief is when we obey knowing that only God can complete the work we are about to initiate. Belief is not gnostic ascension in our mind; belief is obedience to the will of God even when we know that there is no way that we can do it. Those that came to Jesus were healed; those that called on Jesus were saved; those that followed Jesus were discipled. It takes faith for people to get the attention of God. Without faith, we cannot please God. Jesus rewards faith. Even if we have small faith as we initiate, God will make a way. Just like you can't steer a parked car, just like we don't drive into oncoming traffic, faith makes sense when we have God's point of view. Scripture steers our faith. Faith is built by hearing scripture preached. We don't exercise faith for our own gain, we exercise faith for the glory of God. Faith is more than positive thinking. The faith that God is looking for is honest faith that says, "I believe but help my unbelief." We don't need to be on "eggshells" with God. Faith is not words; it's initiated in our thought-life with Jesus. God welcomes honesty communication; He does not want lip service. This is the type of relationship that Christ died to give us. King David is an example of a man that was after God's heart because he was walking in a heart connected relationship with God. In Christ, we can come before God boldly, honestly and transparently. God does not work well with the religious. The religious make Him mad. Jesus was not willing to put up with the religious who turned God into a way to get gain. Jesus is passionate for an authentic relationship with us.

Note

_____

_____

_____

_____

_____

_____

_____

_____

_____

_____

274

"And that every tongue should confess that Jesus Christ is Lord,
to the glory of God the Father" (Philippians 2:11, KJV)

Tares and wheat, goats and sheep, leaven and unleavened, cold and hot; there are many comparisons given in scripture to help us discern our level of dependence on God and the dependence of others on God. When the Gospel is preached to an audience, there are both types listening. Not everyone that says Jesus is Lord means it from their heart. Jesus is not an eternal security while we remain lord of our own lives. Wheat is slouched over but tares are stuck up. Sheep need shepherds but goats are independent. Leaven puffs up, unleavened stays flat. Hot burns, cold freezes. Repeating a prayer is not what God is after, He wants to hear from us. When we genuinely come before God in repentance, the Holy Spirit will lead us to scripture, church and discipleship. The Gospel is power to make us like a wheat, dependent on God and not like a tare, stuck up before God. Humble ourselves before God or be humbled by life. Humility and dependence on God will be evidenced in every believer as they are discipled. Discipleship is not knowledge alone because knowledge puffs up. Bible studies, discipleship, church attendance can puff up if we are not humbling ourselves before God. Jesus did not come to teach theology only; Jesus came to teach us relationship. Theology and relationship must go hand in hand. One without the other will make us like one of the comparisons above. Let's discern where we are at today. Is Jesus Lord? Have we brought our major decisions before Him? Are we leaning on Him? A believer is not kept a believer by discipleship only but kept by the Spirit as we walk in relationship with God. Jesus reconciled us to the Father. If we miss relationship with the Father, we will miss heaven. Knowing God by communicating our need for Him and our need for His leading is what empowers us to live differently. When Christ is our shepherd, we will be content; nothing will thrill our hearts more than being with Jesus. We won't seek anything more than knowing Jesus. The world will try to get us purpose-driven but God wants us Christ-driven. We can either live for our purpose and dream but end up in hell or we can come under the Lordship of Christ and fulfill His purpose and end up in heaven. God's will is worth it.

Note

275

"Then shall the kingdom of heaven be likened unto ten virgins, which took their lamps, and went forth to meet the bridegroom. And five of them were wise, and five were foolish. They that were foolish took their lamps, and took no oil with them: But the wise took oil in their vessels with their lamps. While the bridegroom tarried, they all slumbered and slept. And at midnight there was a cry made, Behold, the bridegroom cometh; go ye out to meet him. Then all those virgins arose, and trimmed their lamps. And the foolish said unto the wise, Give us of your oil; for our lamps are gone out. But the wise answered, saying, Not so; lest there be not enough for us and you: but go ye rather to them that sell, and buy for yourselves. And while they went to buy, the bridegroom came; and they that were ready went in with him to the marriage: and the door was shut. Afterward came also the other virgins, saying, Lord, Lord, open to us. But he answered and said, Verily I say unto you, I know you not. Watch therefore, for ye know neither the day nor the hour wherein the Son of man cometh" (Matthew 25:1–13, KJV)

No one waits until the day of battle to sharpen their sword! Keep your sword sharp; you have no idea when the call for battle will be but when the battle happens, you will be ready. Every day we need to prepare like it's our last day or that a battle is imminent. Don't grow familiar with life or sin. Be on the offensive at all times because we never know when our enemy will attack. Don't shrink back. Ease and comfort will tempt us but a life surrendered to God will remind us that His mercy is new every morning. Be ready in season and especially out of season. God chooses the out of season a lot because He knows we can go a lot further depending on Him. Don't let anyone set your ceiling or limit your journey with God. You don't follow man. You follow Jesus. Where He leads, go. People love to cap others potential; God loves breaking caps into a million pieces. People strategize on how to make themselves look better than everyone else. No one enjoys being outperformed. Rather than success feeding inspiration, most get jealous and pick others successes apart. Flee communities like that. You don't want to be in a community that profiles you before you even say a word. You need to be in a community that believes anything is possible and celebrates what God is doing. We need to be in a community that spurs one another on and challenges one another to go further with God. If there is no challenge, then no one is discipling. Discipleship is like sharpening iron; it only sharpens when there is friction. Be around the believers that memorize more scripture than you; be around believers that get out of movie theaters when some offense against our God is said; be around believers that provoke you to do what is right. Our flesh wants friends that are worse off than us but they only bring us down and not inspire us to move forward. Ex-communicate those who laugh at spiritual disciplines, evangelism and holiness. They are no good. Believers are thorns in the flesh of the slothful and lazy. When we believe in Jesus, we receive an excellent Spirit. We do what we do unto the Lord and not unto the paycheck or employer. This means that we give our best at all times, in all situations, joyfully. Anyone that applies biblical truth will be light-years ahead of everyone else. Compare Christian influenced countries with all the others; none can compete.

276

"For our light affliction, which is but for a moment, worketh for us a far more exceeding and eternal weight of glory; While we look not at the things which are seen, but at the things which are not seen: for the things which are seen are temporal; but the things which are not seen are eternal" (2 Corinthians 4:17–18, KJV)

It won't be this way forever. The reason that we were not raptured after we were saved is because God has us here as His ambassadors. We are God's choice to represent Him. If every believer knew this, we would have a very different outlook on our everyday life. It's in our instinct to pay someone to do what we are called to do. The problem is that there are people who will receive Christ from you easier because of your influence. When we realize our importance in the Church, we will take our life seriously. The church is related to a body. The body can't function fully if all of the members are not healthy. In order for the church to be healthy, every part must believe its value. Our low self-esteem and insecurities get the best of our faith. Rather than boasting in our low self-esteem, we are ashamed of it. The lower our self-esteem, the higher our Christ-esteem. The more insecurities we have, the more we need Christ to be our security. Rather than standing on scripture as our confidence, the world's "truths" become our reality. This is why we are not preaching the Gospel because we don't believe it for ourselves. Eternity is a heartbeat away for all of us. We have prioritized poverty alleviation and discipleship as a church age because the Gospel is not believed. Our handouts and education won't save the soul. The only way the mind and body can be straightened out is when the soul is saved. The soul can only be saved when the Gospel is preached. Our government has so many resources for jobs, education and shelter, but because people love sin more than what's right, the government help is just enabling the sin. Jesus did not want to be known for miracles. He told most of the people that He healed, to keep the miracle to themselves. He wanted humanity to know what was more important, more than any miracle or dream, which is salvation. This life is like a vapor. He knew there was no profit in a healing, if our soul was not saved. The evangelist that emphasizes healing or miracles more than the glory of God is preaching a humanistic message. We need to learn from Jesus. He gives a hand up rather than a hand out. Christian-influenced countries, though not perfect are better than any other country. The Gospel is greatest for the whole person.

Note

277

"And the devil that deceived them was cast into the lake of fire and brimstone, where the beast and the false prophet are, and shall be tormented day and night for ever and ever" (Revelation 20:10, KJV)

Hell fire preaching is needed today more than ever. We have been so light on it, that we have many throwing their lives away, cheapening their soul to just dirt. Humans are eternal beings. Satan has successfully diminished the value of a person to just a mammal and our educational system teaches it. Imbeciles teach us that we evolved from apes. This teaching is from the pit of hell. The human race is the most valued of all of God's creation. God was willing to go to a cross to save us. The reason why there are still apes in the zoo is because we did not evolve from their species. We were made in the image of God. Death should be feared by the ungodly. The church must preach about hell again so that the conscience of our world will not cheapen them to throw their lives away. God saved us not just from bad manners or sin but from the lake of fire. We need to preach what it means to be saved. Salvation is emphasized as a behavior betterment message but that's the byproduct of being saved from hell. Sinners are going to hell. The religious are going to hell. The World is going to hell. Faith in Jesus alone is the way to the resurrection life. This is not bigotry; this is biblical truth. Humans can be saved from throwing their lives away if they would believe this message of salvation. Who's willing to preach the whole Gospel? If you're not, get an honest job and quit the ministry. If you believe this to be true, then pray that you get the right emotion when you talk about it.

This is not a lecture by some dead professor; this is passion from the heart of God, for sinners to be saved. If we can read this and not feel a burden for souls, then we are already veering toward a lukewarm faith. Faith in the whole council of the Gospel resists mediocrity, despises Luke warmness and produces a sold-out soul for the Gospel. This is the type of preaching that we need from our major platforms across our country. We don't wake up to lullabies; we wake up to alarms. We need to sound the alarm as preachers or we should look for a millstone for our necks. The Gospel was so tough to hear, it led to the crucifixion of Christ. Today's gospel has been turned into a money racket by men who preach what they think people want to hear. People need the Gospel!

Note

"It is of the Lord's mercies that we are not consumed, because his compassions fail not. They are new every morning: great is thy faithfulness" (Lamentations 2:22–23, KJV)

The believer's testimony does not end once we get saved, it begins. We are saved into a journey. Our salvation does not mean that we have heaven now or that we have perfection now. Some get saved and then their life gets worse. Many are saved and get persecuted or worse, martyred. Salvation is free but its journey involves a cost. Jesus paid the price for eternity but we have a life of sacrifice which is just our reasonable service. A gospel that tells us to enjoy sin, enjoy self, enjoy all our lusts, leads to hell and is so far from the Gospel of Jesus Christ. He calls His followers to eat His flesh and drink His blood. Jesus was a man of sorrows. This is why your life has been so tough. Satan won't leave you alone. What he did to the early church physically, he is doing spiritually in the western church. Suicide is at an all-time high amongst Christians. Our gluttonous gospel has led to such a spiritual obesity, that in the moment of onslaught, many depart from the faith. It's time to put metal in our faith. It's time to set our minds like flint. It's time to do spiritual drills, so that when the battle comes to us, we will be armed and ready. We are not in heaven now. We are in a battlefield, where the war began at the resurrection of Christ. Hell only has gates, it's time to storm the gates; Jesus said that they won't prevail. We are called to go and win souls for the kingdom before Christ returns; then it will be too late for the sinner to be saved. Jesus is coming. As much as we want Him to return, does it not grieve you that billions are going to burn in hell fire? Does hell make you feel uncomfortable? You can't believe in Jesus and reject His teaching on hell. Jesus is coming to battle in Armageddon. Blood will be spilt and Jesus Christ will be King of kings for the millennial reign. Narrow is the way to Him. Few want Jesus. They want Jesus for what He can do but not for who He is. Jesus wants all our mind, heart and soul but we only give Him an hour on Sunday. Jesus is only called on when we need Him. This is why we face sorrows and affliction as believers, to keep us needing Jesus. Woe to the rich, woe to the prosperous, woe to those that have a life of ease. Sell what makes you independent from God; lay aside the snare and follow Jesus.

Note

279

*"For I am jealous over you with godly jealousy: for
I have espoused you to one husband, that I may present you
as a chaste virgin to Christ" (2 Corinthians 11:2, KJV)*

The Church is Christ's bride. The Church is Christ's body. Jesus's seven letters to the seven churches in Revelation must be read by all believers. Jesus loves His church and loves the body of believers individually. The infrastructure of the church is not His passion; the people are His passion. The church hierarchy and separation of clergy and congregant is evolving into a more biblical perspective today. When Christ went to the cross, He made a priest of everyone who believes on Him. He made a way where we can all come before God. Jew and Gentile, male and female, we all have access to throne of God. The veil was torn from top to bottom so that the God of Abraham, Moses and the prophets are now accessible to whosoever will believe in Jesus. The temple is still in ruins in Jerusalem because the believer in Jesus replaced the temple. We have Christ in us. Every member of the body of Christ is important. The arm can't say to the head "I have no need of you." When Jesus is the focus and not the crowd or the tithe, we can really have unity. Our unity comes by the Gospel and not by Pentecost, Methodist or Baptist theology. Does the world know us for our love for one another or do they see the same competition, back biting and judgment they deal with every day? Jesus wants the Church to be known for their love for one another. When the Gospel is the same, then we have a reason to unite and love. There are pastors that have the same message and vision in the same city, yet they have never met; but we are family. The world knows our discord. If we want to reach them, they need to see our love for one another first. Church buildings look different but the Gospel is the same. We are a family. Loving the world but despising our brothers is exactly what the enemy wants us to be doing. The world won't be reached by that. We will have nothing different to appeal to them. Make the phone call. Let's be known for building the kingdom and not our own sandcastle Kingdoms that get blown away when we pass on. We can unite on the Gospel and it's okay to differ on discipleship. Discipleship does not save the soul nor does it keep the soul saved. Discipleship is overrated and it can be a distraction from a relationship with Jesus. Jesus saves and keeps us; flee religion.

Note

280

"And he saith unto them, Follow me, and I will make you fishers of men" (Matthew 4:19, KJV)

A preacher always preaches to a decision. What has been called an "altar call" is a time like when Jesus called His disciples to follow Him. Every day, we are faced with this decision, follow Christ or follow our flesh. Every day, we have a choice to walk in the Spirit and not fulfill our lusts or to walk in our flesh. Many are scared to surrender to Christ because "what if God's way is not our way?" What if God calls us to do something that we don't want to do? We have many people who are living their whole lives in the belly of a fish and they still won't repent. They have decorated their unrepentance. Jonah repented after three days but many have gone most of their lives unrepentant. Their disobedience to the will of God may have looked prosperous but inside they were tormented. No matter how much wealth one attains, if it's outside of the will of God, they will be ravaged by depression and demons. The most unhappiest people are those who heard the Gospel but rejected it. There is no choice for joy, follow Jesus and have joy or follow our flesh and be prey to the demonic host. A Jesus that makes us masters is not the Jesus of scripture. When we get saved, the evidence of that salvation is that we will want God's will more than our own. Many have a false sense of assurance that they are saved because they think that they want hell now and heaven when they die. We cannot serve two masters. Not every prodigal son makes it back to their Father. Many "don't come to themselves." The prodigal son story was not about Jesus teaching license to live the prodigal life but for those that are in it to be saved out of it. Jesus never condoned or licensed sin. He loved sinners but saved so we can sin no more. Following Jesus is a decision we all can make. Once our choice to follow Jesus is made, the power of God strengthens us to fulfill His will. Just because people claim to follow Jesus, does not mean that they will follow all the way. We can start out well but it's how we finish that matters. We need to surround ourselves with those who are older and more mature than us. Desire to be discipled by someone older in the faith than you if possible. They have not made it to where you're at. What do they know? Your life experience could teach them. Jesus chose teenagers to follow Him because He knew they would. Judas was chosen but never made it; will you?

Note

281

*"Then was Jesus led up of the Spirit into the wilderness
to be tempted of the devil" (Matthew 4:1, KJV)*

Not every wilderness is because of sin or Satan. The Spirit of God led Jesus into a wilderness to fast. Jesus was without sin, yet was tempted. Jesus relied on the context of scripture to not let Satan misuse scripture for his own gain. Beware of those that take scripture out of context. They will even use scripture out of context to tell you what you want to hear. They will tempt you in any way they can, just to get you to bail on the wilderness and the life of discipline that God has called you to. They will call devotional time, evangelism, and holiness—"legalism." They have even written books with themes of "three steps to getting out of the wilderness," "Your wilderness free life now." Satan has infiltrated the church and has counterfeits set up in it; they are wolves in sheep's clothes. They see the sheep as prey and not as people. They live behind curtains and behind bullet-proof doors; their room is called the green room. They have learned that Satan's message draws a lot more people than Christ's message. If you are in a wilderness, don't blame it on sin, Satan or punishment. Every man of God spent time in a wilderness; even Jesus did. Some were there for forty years or longer, like Moses; some were there for only forty days, like Christ. Don't sell out in the wilderness and give up. Don't turn the rocks into bread. Don't give up your birthright for soup. Stay committed and faithful to the best that you can and when you can't, call on the Spirit of God to strengthen you. God uses the wilderness for multiple purposes, but rather than having an explanation, just choose His will and believe that it is for the best. This life is short, and nothing is worth your soul, no matter what Satan tempts you with. He offers an abundant life here, and many have chosen it. His way will not work out in the end. It never does. Sin leads to death; holiness leads to true happiness. Read the scripture in context. Let scripture interpret itself. Scripture is the best commentary on itself. You are immature as a believer if you are quoting men more than scripture. The more mature we get, the more we will quote scripture: "it is written." Jesus taught us how to overcome temptation. You can overcome it with scripture. Listen to the conviction of the Spirit. Study scripture to be approved. Flee wolves, or you will become prey.

Note

282

"For such are false apostles, deceitful workers, transforming themselves into the apostles of Christ. And no marvel; for Satan himself is transformed into an angel of light. Therefore it is no great thing if his ministers also be transformed as the ministers of righteousness; whose end shall be according to their works" (2 Corinthians 11:13–15, KJV)

We have a lot of "testiphonies" being written and preached in our pulpits. Testimonies can be embellished, exaggerated, and lied about, but the Word of God is true and has the power to save the soul. The word of our testimony verifies the Gospel but it's not THE Gospel. When we want testimonies more than the Gospel, we are in trouble. Many have grown familiar with the Word of God so they feast on other men's words rather than God's Word. Don't depend on resources like this when you have the source of scripture. Be careful about raising any personality or manifestation above scripture. Don't go to church for any other person but Jesus. Even the best of our preachers is still human and needs Christ as much as their audience does. There is no other anointed Word than scripture. When a church is built on anything but scripture, it is setting its congregants up for a fall. Worship without the Word is sensual and emotional but the truth of scripture sets us free. Music has become entertainment, and personalities have taken over in our generation; it all has no power to save the soul. It's the preaching of Christ and Him crucified that may seem foolish to our generation but it's the only message a church should grow upon. The "Ted Talk" sermons coming from our pulpits are as weak as water. If you're a church, preach Christ and Him crucified. If ever the Gospel needs to be preached, it's today. Communism has failed every person and every country. Nobody can be God to a community, like Jesus can be. Jesus came to be our governance, to be our life and to be our dependency. He replaced kings, monarchs, priests, presidents and made away for all to have access to His throne of grace. Jesus does not discriminate but He made a way for whosoever to know God. We don't have to live under the limits of our family, race or pedigree. Time with Jesus makes us think like Him, and be like Him so when the world would deem us useless, He makes us useful, productive and Spirit-reliant. A believer has no cap limit but his own belief. Unbelief is our only limit. God can do anything through us if we believe. How much of the Gospel are we willing to believe? As we hear the Gospel, our faith gets fed and He gets formed in us so we could do what the world would have said impossible. Break the limits with belief in Scripture.

Note

_____

_____

_____

_____

_____

_____

_____

_____

283

"But whosoever drinketh of the water that I shall give him shall never thirst; but the water that I shall give him shall be in him a well of water springing up into everlasting life" (John 4:14, KJV)

Many live on empty emotionally, physically and spiritually. Jesus gives fullness and we will never be empty again, as long as we continue to believe. Jesus gives our soul water to quench our thirst. Anything we look to fulfill our soul with, other than Christ is idolatry. Believers need to be cautious of being led by goosebumps. That is not a determination of God's presence. God is omnipresent. Whether we feel it or not, we can believe it because His Word says. So many define the presence of God on their feelings, which tells of their immaturity in the faith. Immature believers walk by sight and their feelings but the more truth of scripture we anchor to, the more unmovable we become. Don't let the goosebumps determine the nearness of God to us. In fact, the less you feel, the more you believe. Faith purely in scripture which is not mixed with emotions or feelings is powerful faith in the sight of God. We are emotional beings and can easily be led by our senses more than by the Spirit. Our senses will deceive us but the Spirit will always lead us to scripture. We are not led by the Holy Spirit if we have no value for scripture. If ever we need to be aware of deception, it's today. So many are falling away because their lusts are lord more than Christ is Lord. Scripture is our weapon to fight our battles. Singing songs alone doesn't fight battles. Prayer meetings alone do not fight battles. Scripture conquers all battles. It reminds us that the battle was already won. A man that knows scripture is a powerful man. Let's be known for biblical foundation and not our spiritual confusion. Jesus said that the Spirit will lead us to truth which is the sixty-six books of the Bible. There is no other infallible word. Scripture is inerrant; our word is not. Forgiveness is found in Christ. Fulfillment is found in Christ. When we call on Him, He saves us and leads us to the church for fellowship as well as discipleship. His Word won't return void. Let's call people to salvation; after that, it's up to the Holy Spirit to do the rest. If they don't want truth, then their desire is not on us. We all are responsible for our own faith and on the day of judgment we will be held accountable for how we rejected the conviction of the Spirit.

Note

284

"But without faith it is impossible to please him: for he that cometh to God must believe that he is, and that he is a rewarder of them that diligently seek him" (Hebrews 11:6, KJV)

Our only hindrance is how much of the Gospel we are willing to believe. How much of His love are we willing to believe? When we know His passion for us is to the point where He is willing to give His only Son for us, why can't we totally surrender to Him? The reason that we don't lay down our lives as living sacrifices is because we don't believe that He loves us. God takes no pleasure in the affliction of His people. He knows what's best but Jesus weeps over our heartache. He is full of compassion over the broken. God knows what it takes to get us to our knees. We will not understand His every move but we will understand it in heaven. Everything will make sense in heaven. From our point of view, we can't see the good in a lot of what we face in life, but we will one day. We must not allow the definition of God's love to be shaped by our experience, life or feelings. The love of God is based on Jesus going through what He went through so we do not have to go to hell. This is why Jesus wanted us to remember His death as often as we can, so that we can take our attention off what we are going through and remember what He went through to save us. If we forget the cross, we will be eaten up with bitterness and anger. Life takes so many twists and turns, that the only thing that is consistent is God. Jesus is the same yesterday, today, and forever. We need consistency; our life does not offer that but Jesus does. He formed us in our mother's womb and has been with us through all of life so far. A relationship with Him is what we try to look for in everyone but only He can fill that need of relationship. No other relationship can do for our soul what Jesus can. God loves us the way we are but He does not leave us that way. He makes us more like Him in confidence and authority. Believers are the most confident, decisive and concrete people because Christ is in us. If a believer doubts or caps what God can do with them, they will be indecisive and bound to confusion. We are not to cast away our confidence by relying on our sight more than faith. Faith in Christ makes us want to surrender because what He has is better than what we could ever want in our flesh. The will of God is where we want to be, no matter what that looks like.

Note

_____

_____

_____

_____

_____

_____

_____

_____

285

"And some fell among thorns; and the thorns sprang up with it, and choked it" (Luke 8:7, KJV)

If we only preach Jesus when the mic is on, there is something wrong. If we only read our Bibles when we are preaching on Sunday, something is wrong. If we are only praying when times are tough, something is wrong. When ministry is done to pet our ego, something is wrong. So many ministries that have come and gone; the reason they had no legacy is because they started on the streets and ended up in the church. The temptation for any ministry is to leave the streets to do pulpit ministry. Once we take the emphasis off the streets and evangelism, we are on a downward spiral. We are in a generation of spineless believers. We need to be a generation that is on fire for truth, set ablaze by the Spirit to be bold for evangelism. When was the last time you evangelized unintentionally? Was it because the Spirit led you? We have preachers that will only preach in a pulpit because they like the sound of their voice. Cowards only preach in pulpits. If a believer wants to go to the next level of ministry, we need to be ready in season and out of season to give an account of what God has done in your life. This generation is willing to call out the hypocrites and wants truth more than religion. If we want weight to our ministry, we need to stop playing games with our relationship with God. We need to be memorizing the word, praying, fasting and spending time on our knees. Beware of false new covenant teachers that call spiritual disciplines legalism; their gluttonous spirituality will not stand the test of time. We need to be strong in the Lord and work out our salvation with fear and trembling. It's time to take God seriously. He will not be mocked. He knows everything. We can fool people with our charisma but we can't fool God. We may think we have gotten away with it, but we won't for long. Repent before it's too late. Come back to the heart of worship, come back to the Gospel, come back to evangelism. It's not too late while you read this. Years may have been wasted but repentance will get God to command the fish to spit you out where you need to be and do what God has called you to. Evangelize when God prompts. Follow His leading. Hear His voice. Listen for God. We have too many who are leaning on their own understanding.

Note

286

"Because it is written, Be ye holy; for I am holy" (1 Peter 1:16, KJV)

When the Spirit of God came upon the Old Testament characters, they were able to do the impossible. They had outbursts of strength, wisdom and power. The Spirit of God is Holy and cannot dwell in sinful flesh. Even though the law provided forgiveness of sin, it could only cover sin. Jesus was the lamb of God that took away the sin of the world. The law covered sin; Jesus cleansed the sin with His own blood. Even though our bodies sin still, we now have the Holy Spirit dwelling in us. We have power over condemnation and sin does not have dominion over us if we choose to walk in the strength of the Spirit and not the flesh. This wrestle in our flesh will be a fight until we pass or until Jesus returns. We have a will. We have a choice. Choose this day to walk in the power of the Spirit. As believers in Christ, the Holy Spirit makes us desire holiness more than sinfulness. Holiness won't be boring or forced; the Holy Spirit will make us hunger for righteousness. A sinner loves darkness more than light. A believer loves light more than darkness because He has the Spirit living through him. If we want to have the life of the Spirit, we need to get used to repentance. When we repent or walk in the light as He is in light, then we will have power over our sin. Shame keeps sin hidden. Grace exposes sin and gives power to overcome it. Gluttonous teachers that people have heaped up for their own itching ears, have taught to our generation that believers don't have sin anymore and we ignore sin in our lives; Jesus wants a real relationship with us, built on transparency. He knows all of us. While we were yet sinners,

He desires to walk in relationship with us. There is none sinless but Christ. We will sin less as believers but these bodies have sin at work in them; this is why we need to choose daily to reckon ourselves dead, so we can walk in the Spirit and not fulfill its lusts. This life is a spiritual life. Theological books won't get you through life. We are to walk in the Spirit. The Holy Spirit lets us know, by His title, what He produces in us: holiness. We can know that the Holy Spirit is at work in our midst, not by the lunatic manifestations or losing self-control but by the conviction of sin and hunger for righteousness.

Note

287

"For God so loved the world, that he gave his only begotten Son, that whosoever believeth in him should not perish, but have everlasting life" (John 3:16, KJV)

God does not condone sin, yet He loves sinners. When one sinner repents, God forgives and restores. The church is full of sinners. The only way to be a part of the church is to first acknowledge sin, then confess, repent and believe that Jesus takes us as we are. There are many in the church that can't remember the day they repented. They can't remember the day they were born again. They were raised in the church and never experience a prodigal life. The prodigal son story is not about Jesus excusing sin but letting those who are in the pig pen to know that they can come home. For us who have never went the prodigal direction, we must know that sin is sin in the sight of God. As much as blatant sin must be repented of, so must self-righteousness be repented of as well. It was not who religion defines as sinners who cried out for Jesus to be crucified, it was the self-righteous "sinners." Self-righteousness hardens the heart more than any sin ever could. Sin leads to brokenness and hopefully, repentance. Self-righteousness does not lead to repentance; it leads to the hardening of the heart. We don't read of the prodigal's elder brother ever coming home to his family. He grew so bitter, that his self-righteousness made him callous toward his sinful brother. When we grow callous toward sinners, we have lost the heart of Jesus. When all of our friends are self-righteous and we don't have one sinner as a friend, we might be serving a different Jesus. There is no sinner bad enough that when they repent, God would cast them away. There is power in the blood. For David, it was the blood sacrifice that was offered on behalf of him by the High Priest. For us, it's the blood of Jesus that cleanses us. Repentance of sin will be remorseful. God knows our repentance. We can't fool God. David was a man after God's heart because he genuinely repented every time he came under conviction. This is the same for the prodigal. The prodigal struggled with his Father's welcome to the point that he wanted to be a servant and not a son. The Father welcomed him back as a son. When we repent, we may think that He will put us through what any earthly dad would put us through; but Christ took our punishment for us. Christ redeemed us with His own blood. Our Heavenly Father welcomes us as we repent. Heed His conviction. Don't repent in vain; repentance gives power to be holy and live as He desires.

Note

288

"And when he is come, he will reprove the world of sin, and of righteousness, and of judgment" (John 16:8, KJV)

Lullabies put us to sleep; alarms wake us up. Salt heals the wound, sugar leads to bacteria. If we are not challenged, we will choose comfort every time. We need to realize our importance where we are at. We fall into temptation of focusing on what is next is but God wants us to value each moment and take no thought for tomorrow.[52] If we want to grow, we need to be prepared to be uncomfortable. Our flesh needs boundaries and disciplines. A body without a skeleton is just a sack of organs. If we are not provoked to grow, we won't grow. This is why we need sermons to challenge us, to make us better believers. A sermon should not be telling us what we want to hear; it should be conviction to give us structured faith. A sermon should provoke us to righteousness and repentance. Be around believers who know more than us. Be around believers that pray more than us. Be around believers that encourage us in godliness and evangelism. These believers are not legalists; they are inspirations to increase our spiritual hunger. If everyone around us are at the same place or worse in their faith compared to us, we will not grow. This is the type of preaching and community that will disciple. Satan has lured this generation into laziness, gluttony and lust. It is the foolishness of preaching that convicts us to believe fr another great awakening. Choose our com-

---

[52.] *"Take therefore no thought for the morrow: for the morrow shall take thought for the things of itself. Sufficient unto the day is the evil thereof." (Matthew 6:34, KJV)*

munity wisely. Be around those who lift us up. Our community can become backbiting chess pits if we are not hungry for truth. Don't be afraid to excommunicate. Love sinners, flee the religious, learn from those that love God more than we do. A disciple that graduates discipleship is no longer a disciple of Christ. They falsely think they have graduated their discipleship but that does not happen until we pass or until Jesus returns. Religion graduates its followers from discipleship and makes us gods but Jesus keeps us disciples who are dependent on Him. Disciples that remain dependent on Christ will make it to the end. It's when we can do ministry on our own, that we are in trouble. We need one another. We need a healthy community. Choose your community wisely so that you are provoked to grow and not stagnate in gossip. If we are not loving Jesus now, we won't be loving Him in hell. Salt heals and preserves, as does truth. This is why we need truth preachers today.

Note

289

"Peace I leave with you, my peace I give unto you: not as the world giveth, give I unto you. Let not your heart be troubled, neither let it be afraid" (John 14:27, KJV)

Numbing our way through hurt will help only temporarily. Prescription medication, alcohol, and illegal drugs are our idols for peace today. The side effects of these are not only physical but spiritual. What we thought would help with our depression has opened the door to strange spirits to decrease us even further down into the pit of despair. Our bodies are complex and our minds are complex but Jesus has power to lift us up from the miry clay of life. An idol is anything we go to first before we turn to Jesus for help. We are in a generation where Jesus is not our first choice for help. By the time we call on Jesus, we have been abused by every idol possible. Idols numb the pain and give a temporary fix but the long-term side effects are so destructive. Our idols need to be torn down in our lives. Jesus must be our first go-to and He will give wisdom from there for us to get the right help. Jesus has the power to heal depression. Jesus has the power to bring order to the mind. Jesus has the power to keep our soul decongested from bitterness, anger and disappointment; it's up to us to confess it to God. If we store it up, we will implode. Confess to God the idolatry of our heart and do not satisfy it. We are all human but we have a savior that has the power to pull us out of the pit, both physically and mentally. We have so much psychology, counseling and human wisdom today but at the end of the day, Jesus is the only one that has the power to heal the soul. It may seem like ignorance and foolishness to the world but whoever calls on the name of Jesus will be saved. Jesus works. I know it to be true in my life and millions of others throughout history could say the same. The church should be known for preaching Jesus because it's the message of the cross that saves souls and heals the mind. When the Gospel is lightly esteemed, then we set up idols for people to be ensnared by. A lot of our Christianity is idolatry. We are more excited about ministry than we are about Jesus. We are looking more to souls, revivals and fruit than we are Jesus. We are not content with being with Jesus; we are so busy that we have forsaken Jesus and are mastered by the church. The church is not Jesus. Ministry is not Jesus. Jesus alone saves the soul. Know Jesus, know life.

Note

290

"Jesus wept" (John 11:35, KJV)

Jesus wept. Jesus was filled with compassion. Our God is not heartless but has a heart full of love for us. He is still preparing a place for us in heaven. We have so much to look forward to as believers. While we are here, let's not grow weary because our time is so short. Don't settle for a mediocre life. We are only given one shot at life. One hundred years from now, everyone reading this will be long gone from here. Time is more valuable than any dollar that we could ever earn. Money can't buy time. Every second we get closer to Jesus. The only treasure we should be storing up is the treasure in heaven. Silver and gold here mean nothing after we pass or after Christ returns. Laying up treasure is done by our belief and obedience to Christ. The way to the Father is far narrower than we know. There are many who will not make it to heaven but they go their whole life with confidence that they're going to heaven. Saying to God "I was a good person" is an offense to God. Our goodness is not good enough. When we say that we are good enough for God, we are banging in the nails of Christ at the time of His crucifixion. Christ did not save good people; He saved sinners. Ignorance won't get anyone to heaven. We have the law and the prophets yet even though scripture is in our own language, people won't read their Bibles. If ever there was a more literate generation yet so lost its ours for sure, in the west. We have never been more civilized, educated, and wealthy yet ignorance of scripture is becoming more and more prevalent. We are too busy to read our Bibles for ourselves. We trust our preachers way too much. Crowds determine success more than the accuracy of the preacher. Scriptural literacy is seen as legalistic and confining so they would rather be led by strange spirits that give them emotional encounters than study scripture. Jesus loves us because our Bible tells us so. Don't base the love of God on anything other than scripture or you be deceived. The enemy has sent his counterfeits amongst us. Discernment is at an all-time low because the biblical literacy is at an all-time low. We need to educate our congregations in scripture. Our thirty- to forty-minute feel-good sermon is not discipling our people. Do we care for their convenience more than their growth?

Note

291

"And they were all filled with the Holy Ghost, and began to speak with other tongues, as the Spirit gave them utterance" (Acts 2:4, KJV)

"And when they had prayed, the place was shaken where they were assembled together; and they were all filled with the Holy Ghost, and they spake the word of God with boldness" (Acts 4:31, KJV)

It's going to take all of us to reach this generation. Hierarchy is what Jesus came to level out. God did not want mankind to get familiar with Him so He set up laws to come before Him. If God was approached in an unlawful, way they would die. We compare God to a republic or a democracy but He is God. When Christ came, God was going to permit His Son to die to save us from our sins so that we could become sons and daughters of God. Christ made a way for us to know God no matter our race, gender or pedigree. Jesus defrocked the priesthood so that everyone who believes in Him are priests before Him. We have no priest; we have no mediators; Jesus put an end to them at the cross. This is why God tore the veil, to make the way possible for the "whosoever"[53] to come before Him boldly, as family in Christ. This is a fundamental truth that even the protestant churches are not upholding. Ministers have set themselves up as mediators. Jesus chose average people to represent Him but

---

[53.] *John 3:16*

ministry today chooses seminary grads to represent Him. The reason that we have an organization run like a corporation today is because we have leaders who don't pray, read their Bibles, or fast; they are building the kingdom of God without God. They don't heed His word; they do what works. When we rely on strobe lights, concert style worship, and a hipster preacher to grow the church, we will see it explode like a ball of gas. It won't stand the test of time. A church grows off of sound doctrine, prayer, evangelism and the Holy Spirit. Everyone wants a thrill that caters to their emotions and identity for success but they are spiritual babes with no discernment. They crave goosebumps and happiness but are not open to the Word of God for correction or rebuke. They are accountable only to their lusts and flesh. As long as it feels good. Their "heroes" are laughing to the bank preying on the biblically illiterate. These cowards use widows' mites to buy suits, steaks, and sports cars. A ministry is not successful because of its silver or gold, nor by its crowds; a ministry is successful when their leadership glorifies Christ in Word and lifestyle. Everyone wants heaven but no one wants to live the life that Christ lived. They want His miracles but they don't want the people He loves.

292

"But even the very hairs of your head are all numbered. Fear not therefore: ye are of more value than many sparrows" (Luke 12:7, KJV)

No one but God knows what you've been through. Life weathers you in every way. We start out innocent, gullible, and full of faith but then we age. As we age, we see through the picture-perfect image into the depth of heartache. Don't be fooled by what you see. You will never know what someone has been through. It's decency to put the best foot forward; life is hard for everyone. We learn that being fake is safer around people than being real. We learn to be real with those who have earned with time a seat at our table. Trust gets shattered by those we look up to. Who we thought loved us, in fact abused us. Who we thought had our back, slashed it; and while we were down, backbit to deflect all responsibility from their own sin. The politics and bureaucracy put out the passion and replace it with a talking carcass. We age, we get bitter, we become what we swore we would never be. Years later, we ask ourselves "how did I get here?" Our world is dark and humans are of their father, the devil.[54] Jesus is the solution; Jesus is the solution to living burden-free. Don't grow weary from life. "Drink from the fountain that is filled with blood, drawn from Emmanuel's veins."[55] Jesus frees us from anger; Jesus causes our clenched fist to open in

---

[54.] *"Ye are of your father the devil, and the lusts of your father ye will do. He was a murderer from the beginning, and abode not in the truth, because there is no truth in him. When he speaketh a lie, he speaketh of his own: for he is a liar, and the father of it." (John 8:44, KJV)*

[55.] An old hymn

surrender. Vengeance is the Lord's. Let's let God fight our battles. The injustice will be judged. The backbiting will always come back on the backbiter. When we sow in gossip, manipulation, abuse, and shame, we will reap it back on us. Choose Jesus. Unload on Jesus. Go to the only one who has the power to redeem, Jesus. He has been with us from the beginning. He formed us in our mother's womb, our hair is counted, our steps are ordered. Jesus is the wonderful counselor because He hears and has the ability to do miracles. What we share with Jesus is safe with Jesus. We are dangerous men when we know Jesus relationally. Time with Jesus radiates Him through us to everyone around us. People looking on us are wondering how we made it this far; many lost bets because we are still thriving when they were ready to celebrate our demise. They did not realize that throwing us into the pit, selling us into slavery, and all of life's twists and turns were for God to get us to where we are so that they can have bread through us. Jesus uses broken people for His glory.

Note

_____
_____
_____
_____
_____
_____
_____
_____
_____

293

"And the man Micah had an house of gods, and made an ephod, and teraphim, and consecrated one of his sons, who became his priest. In those days there was no king in Israel, but every man did that which was right in his own eyes. And there was a young man out of Bethlehemjudah of the family of Judah, who was a Levite, and he sojourned there. And the man departed out of the city from Bethlehemjudah to sojourn where he could find a place: and he came to mount Ephraim to the house of Micah, as he journeyed. And Micah said unto him, Whence comest thou? And he said unto him, I am a Levite of Bethlehemjudah, and I go to sojourn where I may find a place. And Micah said unto him, Dwell with me, and be unto me a father and a priest, and I will give thee ten shekels of silver by the year, and a suit of apparel, and thy victuals. So the Levite went in. And the Levite was content to dwell with the man; and the young man was unto him as one of his sons" (Judges 17:5–11, KJV)

Our pulpits have been purchased by the biggest givers for a long time. "He who pays the piper calls the tune." Preachers need to find other ways to fund themselves if they don't want to sell out their anointing for "ten shekels and a suit." Only a small number of preachers are still not bought out by those who hold the cash. Preaching to the dollar means that we cherry pick through the scripture, to tickle the ears of those who have the fattest wallets. The more money you pay, the more attention you will get. Cash has replaced calling. Few are listening to the spirit; they are listening to where the cash is. We desperately need a ministry that is not moved by cash, business, or human wisdom but are follow the leading of the Spirit, no matter what. Repent of showing favoritism, repent of racial profiling, repent of discrimination; we need to be conformed to the image of Jesus and not successful celebrities who got to where they are at by elbowing their way forward. Be content where God has put you or allow your ungratefulness to elbow your way out of Gods will and into your own will, which leads to death. If Jesus is not enough and we are not content where He has put us, then we need to be concerned for our soul. Examine whether you're in the faith because of the way you are thinking, you might not be in the faith. Repent. Repentance is not an excuse for sin but an acknowledgment for God to intervene. We desperately need men who will preach the whole counsel of scripture. Our congregations are famished because of the spiritual diet that they have been on. When a personality is respected more than the person of Christ, something is wrong. The body of Christ has an overload of red blood cells and fat; it's time for the white blood cells to awaken and for preachers to get the body exercising their faith every day. If our preachers are not making us better believers, then we need to change who we are listening to. If they are not discipling their congregation but just soaking up all discipleship for themselves, then they need to take a break. The preacher should be preaching Scripture and glorifying Christ. If we are remembered after a sermon, it should be for how we magnified Christ.

294

"And my speech and my preaching was not with enticing words
of man's wisdom, but in demonstration of the Spirit and of
power: That your faith should not stand in the wisdom of men,
but in the power of God" (1 Corinthians 2:4–5, KJV)

The Gospel is power. Jesus does not need us to glamorize it any more than He already did. When Peter preached his first sermon, he lifted his voice and preached with such power that thousands were added to the church. The Gospel does not need a circus ring, entertainers or any Hollywood strategy for it to be effective. The rawness of the Gospel being preached is where the power is. It's so under-valued today that many don't want to have the Gospel preached at their outreaches. The ministry strategies today are based on heretics that teach "showing" the Gospel rather than preaching it. Showing the Gospel or using words when we feel is necessary, makes us out to be Christ or it makes the church out to be the Christ. This strategy puts the emphasis on our outreach and works more than what it's all about, Christ. The complacency and compromises made by this western church are becoming so humanistic that we can't even tell the difference between our outreaches and the humanistic charities. Churches have shied away from preaching outside of the pulpit for years now. It's like the time of Wesley, where sinners wouldn't step foot in the buildings, and no one was reaching them outside of the church. The Anglican Church defrocked Wesley because he was willing to preach where the people were at: in the downtowns and coal mines. Many pastors have settled for a salary and a pulpit today; Satan is holding the door open every Sunday for church, while hundreds of thousands wake up in sin, going to hell in our city streets, and for the most part are unreached. The church has become a country club where the pastor keeps the riffraff out by teaching dress codes, morals, and behaviors. The most dangerous place for a sinner to be at is the church. The safest place for a sinner, so they think is the bars and clubs. The religious spirit has lied to sinners that the church is only for upper echelons. This model of church is so far from the image and character of Christ that we need to question if it is even a church. A country club might be a better name. A 10 percent weekly fee to be a part of it is very expensive for a country club where there are poor services and staff. They get away with it because they teach to give to God and if we hold the church accountable, we are in rebellion. Con-artist is a better title for some of our pastors today.

Note

295

*"Let him that stole steal no more: but rather let him labour,
working with his hands the thing which is good, that he may
have to give to him that needeth" (Ephesians 4:28, KJV)*

How does it make you feel when you see someone succeed? Do you get jealous or do you get inspired? A culture, rooted in jealousy, back biting and gossip has given into Satan's strategy to divide. A community divided will not stand. The religious were so given over to jealousy and insecurity, that they could not see Jesus for who He was. When we are tearing everyone around us down who are doing better than us, we have fallen into the snare of the enemy. John the Baptist had the healthiest outlook on how to deal with others outperforming him. He knew he had to decrease so that Christ could increase. How we celebrate others, gauges how much we believe that God celebrates over us. The way of the cross is to put others ahead of us. Following Christ does not only change our direction in life but our emotions and purpose in life. Religion feeds jealousy, comparison, and discipleship. Discipleship is what religion cultivates. "Feed me, feed me, feed me" says the religious disciple. A disciple of Christ feeds, disciples, and puts others ahead of themselves. Its more blessed to give than it is to receive for a believer in Christ. We take more pleasure in giving complements than receiving them. We celebrate others success rather than being like the religious faultfinder. Jesus culture is full of life, joy and cheer. We motivate each other to sing in "prison cells"; we always have an outlook of faith at everything we go through. Christ gives the healthiest perspective of all things that we face in life. It is time to drive the religious spirit violently off of our attitude and culture. Look to Jesus; follow Jesus; be conformed to the image of Jesus. Don't settle for dead, nasty, gossip filled, cliquish religion. Religion is the number one enemy of Jesus. It's what put Jesus on the cross. Christ died to not start a new religion with rules, duties, and blueprints for buildings and discrimination. Christ died to bring us into a power-filled relationship with God that is real, life-giving, and vibrant. There is no community that can compare to a Jesus community when He is the center of that community. This type of community loves like no other, believes in one another, speaks the promises of God over each other, and it does not keep records of wrong.

Note

_____
_____
_____
_____
_____
_____
_____
_____
_____

296

"But fornication, and all uncleanness, or covetousness, let it not be once named among you, as becometh saints" (Ephesians 5:3, KJV)

Heartache is what millions are waking up to this morning. We numb ourselves to the grief but numbing never works out. Numbing the grief, stores it up until you hit the max capacity. Living at max capacity or on the edge is where the enemy strikes us. We are called to a relationship with God, where He can heal the grief and comfort us in time of need. Having an outlet to unload is key to making it through life. Who do we talk to that has power to heal? We can talk to many but we should not share our pearls with swine. Pearls are formed over the course of a long time and are fragile. Swine have no sense of class or respect. Our pearls were not made by ease but by time and hardship. We need to be slow to open ourselves up to people but when it comes to God, we can open all the way for Him. This is prayer. This is what prayer really looks like. Casting our cares on Jesus. No one has shown more love for you than Jesus. The only reason we can count the hardships of life joyful is because it keeps us waiting on God, to see what He is going to do to get us through this hardship. When we do evangelism, we open ourselves up to situations that the average person would never experience. God will use us to handle other's pearls with care, love and tenderness; just as God handled us. As we learn from Jesus, and how He is with us, we can be the same to others and they will see Him in us. When we are open with God, holding nothing back, He does not hold back from us too. He proved this with His Son. People will feel the love from us but they will know that it's not human love. As we speak, our words will be felt on our audiences' skin because God will anoint our words. Love covers a multitude of sin. Love is what every human needs to thrive. Human love is self-seeking and conditional but the love of God is pure. If sinners feel comfortable around us, it will gauge how much of the love of God we know. Jesus was safe for sinners to go to. Are we safe or would we be the last place a sinner would go to for help? Religion hates sinners but Jesus loves sinners. Religion loves their own but Jesus loves the unlovable. The more we read of Christ's life, then the more we need to unlearn what religion has taught us. The gospel requires a renewing of the mind.

Note

297

*"But I will forewarn you whom ye shall fear: Fear him,
which after he hath killed hath power to cast into hell;
yea, I say unto you, Fear him" (Luke 12:5, KJV)*

If we lived every day off of the opinions of other people, would we even get out of bed in the morning? Our community will be what makes us or breaks us. When we backbite or gossip, we can be sure that what we sow, we will reap. Once we are divided, we are ensnared in the enemy's trap. Physical battles are far easier for us to understand than mental battles. Our mind is a battlefield. Every day we take in the world's opinions of us and we entertain our own opinions. Most times, these are not good thoughts. If we are left to our own thoughts, we all would be bound in depression. This is why we need to know Scripture and choose the Church as our community. Our community will determine a lot of our decisions and potentially our future. Every Bible study and sermon should be combatting what the world says about us verses what God says about us. If we don't get molded by scripture, we will be molded by something else. We are all impressionable as humans. A community that is built on love, truth and belief is what the church is. As we spend more time with God, the more we will radiate His life. Whoever we are with the most will shape us the most. This is why spending time with Jesus and committing to fellowship with His church is essential. Face each day believing God's word or be prey to the lies of our enemy. What the world says about us may seem true but belief in scripture takes the world's "seemed" truth and proves it wrong. God can do anything

He wants through a believer. The world may deem you good for nothing but God makes everyone good for something. God has a plan for every person. Jealousy and covetousness despise God's plan for others. Many people think that the bar is the safest place for a sinner. It appears to be true. Unfortunately, the church has become a dangerous place for a sinner. Jesus is truly the safest place for a sinner. The Church should cause sinners to run to her but the religious spirit has come into her ranks and made the church detestable for the sinner to want to go to. Now we have wheat and tares growing side by side. Do we have a love for sinners? If we don't, we may not have Christ living in us. No one can separate Christianity from Christ. No apostle, pope, priest, or pastor has found what we believe. Jesus did. Christianity needs to come back to its founder, our Lord.

Note

298

"God is a Spirit: and they that worship him must worship him in spirit and in truth" (John 4:24, KJV)

If there was a global power cut on Sunday morning, would Christians know how to worship? Would they even go to church? We have relied so much on electricity that we have not needed the power of the Holy Spirit in a long time to grow His church or make disciples. We have so many crutches for the disciples of today that if they faced a power-cut, would they be able to worship without music or the right ambiance? This technological age has replaced God in so many ways. Few people study the Bible now; they Google instead. Electricity is a great convenience but must not be our reliance. We have everything so timed and scheduled, that our audience's comfort is more important than the will of God. We don't invite God to do what He wants; we ask Him to bless what we want. To be Spirit-led is not to be feelings led but it does mean that we are open to His conviction and leading. God will not be boxed into our buildings and told to bless what we want. He is God, and we are not. Are we open to allowing God to have His way in worship and in the preaching of His word? If all we are doing is read from a script because we plagiarize multiple authors to make ourselves sound profound, we are missing out on a much deeper well. There is a deeper well than music being worship and a "Ted Talk" for a sermon. We have scripture and the unction of the Holy Spirit. A church built on scripture and reliant on the Holy Spirit, does not need a synthesizer or a light show to encounter the glory of God. Our charisma does not change lives. Passion has defined anointing for too long. A "rightly"[56] divided word is what is anointed and not our clever speech. Music genres come and go; lights, cameras, and smoke change with the times but they never replace what we are all about. The truth of scripture is what matters more than strategies of men to get people into our services. God is not wowed by our services or events. The only record of heaven celebrating and God being filled with joy is when one sinner repents. Just because you have only led one sinner to repent, while others pack eighty thousand in a stadium to sing worship to Jesus, does not mean you don't have the attention of God. Our worship services and discipleship conferences do not move heaven like a sinners' repenting does.

Note

_____

_____

_____

_____

_____

_____

_____

_____

_____

_____

[56.] *"Study to shew thyself approved unto God, a workman that needeth not to be ashamed, rightly dividing the word of truth." (2 Timothy 2:15, KJV)*

299

*"He that loveth not knoweth not God; for
God is love" (1 John 4:8, KJV)*

Sinners were never in the hands of an angry God. From the beginning, God loved us; from the fall, God never gave up on us. Throughout history, God extended His hand to us of redemption and grace. God hates sin but loves people. Even though we are sinners, He still sent His Son to take upon Himself our sin. God works with repentance but He detests religion. This is evidenced with all the men and women He chose to represent Him in scripture. Many of them were neither religious or holy. Liars, murderers, prostitutes, adulterers, gentiles and the list could go on. These were who God chose to represent Him. Jesus got so fed up with religion, that He drove the religious money-changers in the temple out.[57] Jesus wants to drive the religious spirit out of us. Satan loves his religious ambassadors to paint an image of an angry god who hates sinners and loves judgment more than people. Satan uses these "Christ-like" preachers to condemn, beat up and rob the faith of a loving God. Religion raises personalities and preachers above Christ. The scripture must be read by every believer. For more than one thousand years, Satan successfully kept the Bible out of the hands of the average person. It's happening again. We have grown slack on bringing our Bibles to "Bible studies." Book studies, sermons and all other forms of disci-

---

[57.] *"And Jesus went into the temple of God, and cast out all them that sold and bought in the temple, and overthrew the tables of the moneychangers, and the seats of them that sold doves." (Matthew 21:12, KJV)*

pleship is inferior to reading the Bible with the illumination of the Holy Spirit. He makes the Bible come alive, better than any preacher. A lot of money would be lost by organized religion if they simply started teaching scripture, prayer, fasting and evangelism. We don't need fancy buildings, Jordans, and a rock band or rapper. The music needs to fade, the celebrity believers need to fade, the LED lights need to be stripped away. Let's come back to what it's all about. God loves people, not events. God wants one sinner to repent and not ninety-nine gathering and worshipping with goosebumps but they have no gospel preaching, no repentance, and no conviction of sin. We repent not because God is angry, we repent because the love of God compels us. It's with chords of love that God draws a sinner to repentance. It's His kindness that leads us to repentance. Hate, anger, condemnation or guilt is not the Gospel but a religious counterfeit of the Gospel. Sinners are in the hands of a loving God. Satan is angry; he hates us. His hatred is manifested in religion. God is love, for God so loved.

300

"For the wages of sin is death; but the gift of God is eternal life through Jesus Christ our Lord" (Romans 6:23, KJV)

It is appointed for all of us to die. Death comes to us all. We don't know the day or the hour. Like a thief in the night, our time here could be up at any moment. Death is a topic that hits home when we are faced with it ourselves. Some people go years without tragedy, and others live in tragedy. Don't get too comfortable, it won't be this way forever. No matter what miracle or healing God could do for you, if you miss out on Jesus, what does it matter that you were raised from the dead but die without Jesus? Healers want to keep us here as long as they can but they can't keep you here forever. When it's our time, it's our time. God is not the author of death; man brought it on himself but Christ died so we don't have to die; death for a believer is a door to eternal life. Do we believe this? Do we believe that death for the believer is not death but a door to eternal life? Death is a door for the believer. The wages for sin are death but there is an inheritance for a believer, which is eternal life. We don't want a wage as a believer, we want an inheritance. Employees get wages; family gets an inheritance. Jesus gives us what only He could have earned for us with his own blood. He died so that we don't have to. Jesus is the resurrection for all who believe. We will rise bodily from the dead at the second coming but once we are absent from the body, we are present with the Lord in the spirit form. These bodies that we are in will be called out of the earth again to meet our spirit and we will have glorified bodies. No more sickness, no more pain, no more old age. Eternally young, healthy and fit. Eye has not seen, nor ear has heard what God has prepared for those who believe. Jesus wants faith. Our faith makes us whole. Jesus is frustrated with little faith because of all that He has already done for us. It's time to lay aside the weight of doubt and believe what He has for us, by looking unto Him and all that He accomplished for us on the cross. We can't talk about death enough. It's not morbid to talk about death; it's exciting for those that believe. We experience a lot of death as we age but we have an assurance through it all that we, who believe, don't die but live forever. Just as Jesus rose, we too will rise. We not only follow Jesus in life but in death, we follow Him to where He is still preparing a place for us. Today, you can have confidence of the paradise with Jesus forever.

Note

301

"For God is not the author of confusion, but of peace, as in all churches of the saints" (1 Corinthians 14:33, KJV)

God does not author confusion. Truth is black and white. We live in a gray world that lures us into Luke warmness. Mixing God with our culture won't work because He does not come to add to our culture; He comes to replace our culture. Jesus broke all cultural boundaries because His culture is not ours, no matter what ours is. Jesus loves the sinner. He sees past clothing, sickness and employment. We would be so surprised at who Jesus would call His friends today. Would we be a friend of Jesus? I don't know if many Christians would have been a friend of Jesus. If you are a sinner, you are in company with Jesus. He is Holy, yet by His stripes we have been made whole; by His blood we have been cleansed. His word makes us clean; not our works or our efforts. The best work and effort we can do is hammer the nails into Jesus's hands and feet. Religion put Jesus on the cross. Sin is independence from God. Satan did not deceive Eve with immorality but with a temptation that she can be like God. The fruit what religion is today and millions bite into it every Sunday morning. They are not eating His flesh and drinking His blood, they are eating the fruit of independence from God. We don't want to need Jesus. We want to live without needing Jesus by eating the serpent's fruit. God knows that your religious blunt will not give you the peace with Him which only Christ can give. Eat and drink of Christ and experience the peace. Only Jesus can quench our spiritual thirst and appetite. God will not be ashamed of us if we trust Christ because He took our shame. Religion says "Shame on you"; Jesus says "Shame was taken on me, so it's off of you." The cross where Christ died is where our sin, shame and Satanic temptation was destroyed. Jesus carried our grief and sorrows. He knows what you have been through. Raise your hands as a symbol of our surrendered soul to Jesus. *Let Him wipe your tears from your eyes and speak love over you.* No human can love like Christ does. He wants nothing in return. There is nothing we have that He does not already have, yet He chooses us. He has no need of us, yet He wants us to know Him. Christ took our sin away; He is dependable. Christ brings clarity, soundness of mind, and decisiveness. Submit to God; decide now to resist confusion and the devil will flee.

Note

302

*"For we know that the whole creation groaneth and travaileth
in pain together until now" (Romans 8:22, KJV)*

Nature has been groaning from the fall. Our bodies have been dying since the fall. The fall of man ushered in the consequences that we see every day; from wars to tragic storms, our earth is aging and our bodies are dying. Jesus said that before He returns, there will be wars and catastrophes. We can't blame storms on God. Jesus was in a storm and the disciples feared for their lives; it was so bad. Not all storms are from God. The earth spins on its own, we sin on our own; we are living in an anarchist world, that because of the fall is heading toward an end. Once we are born, death is inevitable. We are only given one life and Satan has many distracted, bound by bitterness, blaming God for sin, storms, and violence. None of these were the will of God. We chose this. We can't blame Adam and Eve because we all would have done the same thing as they did in the garden of Eden. We are fragile created beings, that when given a choice, we will choose darkness over light. This is why God offered redemption all the way through the Old Testament. If we were the god of humanity, we would wipe these rebels out. We have very little patience; thank God no human has authority like that. Jesus came to redeem us once and for all. We will never find love which can compare to God's love. Redemption is in Jesus. The world will keep our record of wrongs and define us by our sins but Jesus wiped our records clean. Jesus cleared our history. He also gave a promise of a new heaven and a new earth where there will be no sickness, death or catastrophes. We have so much to look forward to. In this world, we will have trouble; the short pain here is worth the eternal gain. Many have sold out their eternal life for short term pleasure here on Earth. There is no car, vacation, job or fame that is worth our soul. Life has a funny way of stripping us of everything; economies crash, sicknesses strikes, wars come but Jesus stays our anchor through it all. If Jesus is not our rock, the storms of life will wash us away in depression and suicide. We need to prepare people for the worst when they get saved, so that they are not tempted to tuck their tail and run when the hardships in life happen. It rains on the believer and the unbeliever. There is no escaping life. We need to brace for it by putting on the armor of God every day. Prepare now to be ready; are you ready?

Note

303

"For it is God which worketh in you both to will and to do of his good pleasure. Do all things without murmurings and disputings" (Philippians 2:13–14, KJV)

It is God who works within us to do His will. We can pray and ask amiss if we want our will more than His. If we want our will more than His, then we need to ask who is Lord. It's common for us to make up a god that pleases us and only tells us what we want him to say. When we come to God in total surrender, laying aside our will, we think that we are sacrificing but we are really getting so much more in return. What seems like sacrifice here, when we get to heaven will be the biggest blessing there. The temporal pain that could be our reasonable service comes with eternal gain.[58] We are laying up treasure in heaven. The temptation to not sacrifice but have the enemy's abundance now is short lived with tons of strings attached. The Devil leaves out the small print of ramifications. His way never produces fruit. It's like living a diet of candy; it tastes great but destroys our health. Come to God for who He is and not for what we can get. He knows our needs but when we worship Him for who He is and not just for what He gives, God will bless us even more abundantly eternally. We need to get over ourselves and give God worship for

---

58. *"I beseech you therefore, brethren, by the mercies of God, that ye present your bodies a living sacrifice, holy, acceptable unto God, which is your reasonable service. And be not conformed to this world: but be ye transformed by the renewing of your mind, that ye may prove what is that good, and acceptable, and perfect, will of God." (Romans 12:1–2, KJV)*

what He gave in His Son. What more could He give? We emphasize healing and wealth but that's trivial in what He gave us in His Son. By His stripes, we have been healed in reconciliation. Anyone that got healed by Jesus is dead. We don't know where their soul is but many of them would be telling us today that health and wealth do not matter if Jesus is not Lord. Praise God in sickness, praise God in poverty, praise God in health and praise God in wealth. Our praise and worship of God is not because of what He does but for what He did on the cross. We are saved. When we glory in God with everything we have, we will never lack. God does not let us want. He is good. He clothes the lilies and feeds the birds. Worship God with everything and do everything unto Him; watch what He does. Only He will get glory. God won't abandon us. He will not forsake us. Be sure in the Lord that goodness will follow us all the days of our life. His way may seem the hardest but has the most rewarding end that we could ever dream of. Look unto Jesus, the author and finisher of our faith. He did not save us to forsake us.

Note

304

"Preach the word; be instant in season, out of season; reprove, rebuke, exhort with all long suffering and doctrine" (2 Timothy 4:2, KJV)

Be ready in season and out of season. Resist those who call spiritual disciplines—legalistic. A disciple without discipline is a disciple of their flesh. Those that don't check their lamp may run out of oil. If we are waiting to put on our armor on the day of battle, we will not be ready in time of warfare. An athlete trains, our military do drills, and believers "work out" seriously with fear and trembling.[59] We examine whether we are in the faith. Memorization of scripture does not magically happen, it takes work. Jesus did not save us from good works, He saved us from dead works unto good works. Dead works are any work done for salvation. Jesus did the work for salvation but it's up to us to do the work of a disciple from salvation. We are to make disciples. Most of the discipleship today is making cowards who will tuck their tail if hardship comes or depart from the faith if their life depends on it. Their Jesus eases their conscience on eternity but they remain lord of their lives. They have no reverence for the will of God. If they don't like His will, they whine to get their way and if He does not listen, they get bitter. The reason for this is the fast food that they are devouring is making them so unhealthy. What we put in our mouth affects our waste; what we put in our soul affects our faith. What we sow, we reap. We can't go wrong with spending

---

[59.] *"Wherefore, my beloved, as ye have always obeyed, not as in my presence only, but now much more in my absence, work out your own salvation with fear and trembling." (Philippians 2:12, KJV)*

time with God, reading His scripture and seeking His will. Give God quality time; study and take Him seriously now, while we can. A lot can happen in twenty-four hours. Be ready or be prey to the enemy. Don't be ignorant; don't grow weary in doing. Faith without work is dead faith. Our faith works. For it is God who works in us to do His will and not ours. As we surrender our inability, He is able to do exceedingly above what we could ever do. Talk to Him about your lack of discipline and set your alarm to give our first moment to Him each day. Write out our prayers, mark our Bibles, study to show ourselves approved.[60] Beware of those who take the grace of God in vain and mock repentance by confessing with their mouth but craving their flesh in their heart. God wants our heart. Until He reigns in us, we will only have a form of godliness but no power to follow Christ in discipline consistently. Be ready.

Note

_____

_____
_____
_____
_____
_____
_____
_____
_____
_____

---

[60]. *"That ye may be blameless and harmless, the sons of God, without rebuke, in the midst of a crooked and perverse nation, among whom ye shine as lights in the world."* (Philippians 2:15, KJV)

305

"Rejoice not against me, O mine enemy: when I fall, I shall arise; when I sit in darkness, the Lord shall be a light unto me" (Micah 7:8, KJV)

What keeps us on this planet when life gets dark? Our educational system is teaching that we are mere mammals. Animals die without funerals every second. "Why does anyone care if we die if we are mammals? After we die, we just become a memory and then with some time, life continues as if we never existed. What drives us to keep on fighting through every day, when the grass flutters in the wind? Would it not be an easier existence to nourish worms?" This is the most sinister strategy on mankind ever; suicide is an epidemic. God created us; we are made in His image. We are not mere mammals we have eternal souls. We live forever. The supernatural is real. Satan is using weak science, which requires more faith than believing in God. These satanically possessed scientists are blind to the responsibility of millions of suicides. Their unfounded theory is foiled because "nothing comes of nothing." Everything has a beginning, no matter how far back you go, and everything has a creator. The Bible is the infallible word of God. It gives us answers that scientists only have weak theories for. God fought for us when any other god would have given up on us in the beginning. We are foolishly trying to explain Him away, but not realizing the ramifications. Teaching us that we are mammals is cheapening the most precious of God's creation. Jesus did not lay His life down for any other creature. The human race, though sinful and rebellious is the apple of His eye. He made it possible for every human to know Him in Christ. God proved Himself inclusive which did not fit the Jews' expectation of an exclusive God to only Abraham's seed. We are all of Abraham's seed in Christ. Jesus showed humanity our worth; our redemption cost His blood. We are a significant creature to be given such a sacrifice. What manner of love is this? The Gospel is a love story. Why God so loves us, baffles the cleverest of minds. Our society may not believe Him but He believes in us so much; He paid the price of sin; sin was sending everyone to hell. The wages of sin is not only physical death but leads to the lake of fire. This is why we need Jesus to save our soul. The Bible is our instruction; it is our passport and legal assurance of salvation.

Note

306

"Jesus saith unto him, I am the way, the truth, and the life: no man cometh unto the Father, but by me" (John 14:6, KJV)

A first responder does and says whatever he can, to get someone out of harm's way. When we care, we will want to alarm of danger in any way possible. No one would sit by and watch someone about to hurt themselves, without saying something. When we love, we say what needs to be said. When we love, we do what needs to be done. Otherwise, our love is just an empty emotion. Love is more than an emotion. God did not just say that He loves the world; He backed up His love with His Son's crucifixion. Jesus's death was morbid and violent; it was God's way of showing mankind: "I love you." The crucifix is a symbol of the death penalty. It has been turned into an ornament or a piece of jewelry today. The "love heart" is an inferior symbol of love to the cross. There is no greater love that we could be shown outside of the crucifixion of Christ. The love that was shown to us, we are called to let it shine through us to everyone around us. God chose the foolishness of preaching, to be His means of communicating the Gospel to mankind. How it is communicated is so essential. Look at how serious God took our salvation. We need to be as serious about the Gospel. Jesus was passionate for us yet we shy away from the preaching of the Gospel at most of our outreaches. Sermons that have no urgency or passion attached, when it comes to the Gospel is dead religion. Do we believe that the Gospel must be preached urgently? Does it bother us that those without Christ are going to hell? The majority of evangelicals are not evangelizing. Why are we sleeping on the most populated generation earth has had? We need to awaken to our mission field as a church. Sports fanatics have more passion for their team than evangelicals have for their Jesus, who bled and died for them. What did your sport team ever do for you, other than take your money and disappoint you? Our idols and temples look so different in appearance than the Greeks and Romans, so many don't know that we are one of the most idolatrous generations ever. Very soon, our passive culture of believers will wake up and they will be shocked at the state of our cities because we have been too busy self-indulging. Church has turned into a Disney country club, where they go on tours and get their thrills. Their mission trips are excuses to go on paid vacations, where they might sing and maybe pray. Sound the alarm.

Note

307

"Herein is our love made perfect, that we may have boldness in the day of judgment: because as he is, so are we in this world" (1 John 4:17, KJV)

Self-image is important to any normal person. We care about our appearance. We want to be noticed as respectable in whatever culture we are in. We want our lives to count. These are instincts that should not be suppressed as a believer. When we believe, Jesus conforms us to His character and authority. He has all authority in heaven and earth; He lives in us. When the Holy Spirit filled the early church, they did not stay in a building to worship and pray. The Holy Spirit filled them so that they would leave their four walls to go win souls to Jesus. They were full of boldness and authority so much, that they sang in prisons, steered down lions, and praised God in furnaces. If you say that you have encountered God, but you can't preach Jesus where you are at, one must question what spirit you encountered; cowards only preach Jesus overseas. We have more authority spiritually than any president, king or emperor living in us. Christ is in us. Asking Him to hide us behind His cross is a waste of time because He chose us to be His ambassadors. As He is, so are we in this world. Christ does not lead a Christianity that is driven by fashion trends and fads. Who are you following? Why isn't Jesus enough? We don't have apostles today; the twelve apostles are long gone in heaven. We have been given something much more valuable than Paul, who wanted the early church to follow him; we have the Bible. Paul didn't even have what we have. We are the most blessed generation of all to be able to have a Bible and every resource necessary on our devices. Even with access to truth, people are foolish enough to give their first fruits to men who own million-dollar homes and drive fancy sports cars. Anointing has been cheapened to passion. Unction has been degraded to just an emotional experience. Worship has been cheapened to a rock band on stage. The pulpit has been devalued to just a "Ted Talk" like message. Many of these leaders would be told the same thing that Jesus told the rich young ruler. Some have even repented for preaching prosperity, but what would Zacchaeus ask them to do? What did Zacchaeus do? When he repented, it was demonstrated. It was not an emotion but an action. Don't give out of duty, give out of being led. Holding leaders accountable is not rebellion. Speaking the truth with the intent to restore is love. A first responder who cares aggressively does whatever he has to save those in danger.

Note

_____

_____

_____

_____

_____

_____

_____

_____

308

"But Peter said, Ananias, why hath Satan filled thine heart to lie to the Holy Ghost, and to keep back part of the price of the land? Whiles it remained, was it not thine own? and after it was sold, was it not in thine own power? why hast thou conceived this thing in thine heart? thou hast not lied unto men, but unto God" (Acts 5:3–4, KJV)

The Spirit of God has a title. His title should help us discern what is of Him and what is not. The Holy Spirit can be grieved, the Holy Spirit can be quenched, and the Holy Spirit can be blasphemed. He convicts of sin; He shows how different God is from us and He reminds us of the Judgment to come.[61] He is not to be lied to. Lying to the Holy Spirit is no light thing; read about Ananias and Saphira. The Holy Spirit is the third person of the trinity. He does not honor Himself above Christ or would ever allow anyone to take the glory away from Jesus. The Holy Spirit will always lead us to the truth of scripture. The Bible is that which is perfect.[62] It is not to be added to or anything should be taken away from it.[63] The sovereign Lord put

---

[61.] *"And when he is come, he will reprove the world of sin, and of righteousness, and of judgment." (John 16:8, KJV)*

[62.] *"But when that which is perfect is come, then that which is in part shall be done away." (1 Corinthians 13:10, KJV)*

[63.] *"For I testify unto every man that heareth the words of the prophecy of this book, If any man shall add unto these things, God shall add unto him the plagues that are written in this book: And if any man shall take away from the words of the book of this prophecy, God shall take away his part out of the book of life, and out of the holy city, and from the things which are written in this book." (Revelation 22:18–19, KJV)*

the sixty-six books of the Bible together. God is calling His church to fast from other people's books and have a diet only in scripture. Scripture is the greatest commentary on itself. The Holy Spirit wrote scripture through over forty authors in a span of more than two thousand years, all pointing to the glory of Jesus Christ. The Father and the Holy Spirit want to see us lift the name of Jesus up. When Jesus is lifted up, He will draw all men unto Him. We can try the Spirit by the fruit of self-control, sound mindedness, and a passion to glorify Jesus. A man that is dependent on the Holy Spirit will be biblically literate; he will crave holiness more than lust, pride, and fame. The Holy Spirit will always work through a repentant man. When we resist the conviction of the Holy Spirit and reject His leading, we will end up blaspheming. He will not always strive with us. It's a mystery but the Holy Spirit will give us grace upon grace, but when we take His grace in vain, we are on thin ice. Whatever needs to be repented of, repent. Turn from false teaching, recant false manifestations, heed scripture above any teacher. Humble yourself in the sight of God and He will lift you up out of the pit of despair, sin, and fear. Like David, repent, take responsibility, don't blame, own it, and feel the refreshing come over your soul as you repent.[64] Refreshing does not come in the dark, it comes in the light. When we walk in the light, which is openness before the Holy Spirit, not only are we forgiven but He conforms us to Christ's culture.

[64.] 2 Samuel 12:1–15

309

"Trust in the Lord with all thine heart; and lean not unto thine own understanding. In all thy ways acknowledge him, and he shall direct thy paths" (Proverbs 3:5–6, KJV)

Prayer gauges our dependence on God. The less we pray, the more reliant on our own understanding we become. Prayer is not a mantra; it's a relationship with God. Jesus gave us the example of prayer but never meant it to be tradition. We see in the beginning, that God wanted to walk with us. Don't get stuck in a rut of prayer. If we find it difficult to pray, do what David did: write your emotions to God. This is more than a journal or a diary; this is you getting all the dark out of your soul and putting it in writing. As we address God with our anxiety, sin, and burdens, we are learning to cast them on Him. It's like a release when we pray. Slowly, as we communicate to God, our clenched fist turns into an open hand of surrender. Open up your hands, receive the peace of God. The tighter our fist is, the more we are holding onto our fears and burdens. Jesus wants us to go to Him because His burden cannot be competed with and His burden is light.[65] The weight of the cross was so heavy, that Simon was called in to bear the cross for Christ.[66] The cross that we are facing is too

---

[65]. *"Come unto me, all ye that labour and are heavy laden, and I will give you rest. Take my yoke upon you, and learn of me; for I am meek and lowly in heart: and ye shall find rest unto your souls. For my yoke is easy, and my burden is light." (Matthew 11:28–30, KJV)*

[66]. *"And as they came out, they found a man of Cyrene, Simon by name: him they compelled to bear his cross." (Matthew 27:32, KJV).*

heavy for us; this is why we need to deny ourselves so that we can be empowered by the Spirit of God to enable us to carry the cross in our life. Following Christ and perfect obedience to His will is impossible in the flesh. This is what Jesus was trying to teach to the religious rich young ruler. The young man thought that he was able to follow Christ but left disappointed. Jesus does not invite us to follow Him because we can. If we follow Him without His strength, then we too will hear the rooster crow. It's not until we confess that we can't do what God wants and realize that it's only through Christ that we can follow Him. Then we are enabled. Denying ourselves by ourselves is religion. Denying our self-strength to deny ourselves is the only way to follow Christ. By denying ourselves, we are giving the burden over to the Holy Spirit to get us to where He wants us to go. This life of a believer is letting go of our ability so that we hold on to His ability, who is in us in Christ. If we lean on our own understanding, with no prayer or dependence on God, we are not believers in Christ. A believer in Christ knows that He is the way, truth, and life and there is no access to the Father but through Him. If life is too much for us, it was always supposed to be. Talk to Jesus, watch what He does.

310

"Go ye therefore, and teach all nations, baptizing them in
the name of the Father, and of the Son, and of the Holy
Ghost: Teaching them to observe all things whatsoever I have
commanded you: and, lo, I am with you always, even unto the
end of the world. Amen" (Matthew 28:19–20, KJV)

Successful parents' parent so that their kids will be self-sufficient as they grow up. Successful discipleship disciples to get their disciples Christ-dependent as they grow in their faith. A disciple that is still reliant on their "discipler" after years of discipleship is not being discipled. That's a cult. We are discipled to make disciples who make disciples. Until we pass or Christ returns, we remain a disciple but we are called to disciple as well. An adult that still needs his mother's milk is sick. Keeping people on milk because we want control over them is not discipling. Holding back lest a disciple outperforms you is sick. Discipleship is about working our way out of a job. The faster we can get a disciple onto the Scripture and the Holy Spirit, the more fruitful we will become. Jesus wants us making disciples; true disciples make disciples that make disciples. This is how the Gospel has advanced all over the world. A disciple is more than someone who stands in a crowd or warms a pew. Just because we pack auditoriums, does not mean that we are discipling. How did Jesus disciple? After three years, what was the best His disciples could do? They could not even pray for an hour. They fled off from Jesus. Our flesh can't be discipled. Our strategies can't make disciples. It's only when we depend on the Holy Spirit, that discipleship takes place. Christ knew when the rooster crowed what peter would do. The Holy Spirit leads us to truth which disciples better than any person could. Christ taught His disciples for three years on how much they we were going to need the Holy Spirit. Let's get our audience onto the scripture, so that they can quote it more than us. Don't push our literature more than scripture; quote scripture more than us, so that we can know that we have done our ministry. If you walk out of a sermon quoting the preacher more than the scripture, then the preacher failed. Preachers are failing their audience by sharing the glory with God. Our clever soundbites and opinions have nothing on the authority of scripture. Jesus did not fail in His discipleship; He set them up for three years to teach them their need for the Holy Spirit to come and live in them. They were not in-dwelt with the Holy Spirit, so they could not be discipled. Discipleship demands dependence on the Spirit.

Note

311

"For the Sadducees say that there is no resurrection, neither angel,
nor spirit: but the Pharisees confess both" (Acts 23:8, KJV)

Sadducees at the time of Jesus, were a sect that did not believe in the afterlife. Sadducees viewed the Old Testament as a moral code and it made model citizens but they missed the relationship God wants to have forever with us. It was good for humanity; that's all it was good for. It offered a better way of life than any other religion or philosophy. God just wants us to have "heaven" here and die was their mind-set. Not one Sadducee ever repented and followed Christ in scripture. The humanistic view of God's Word is only for their betterment but not for the glory of God. We have the Sadducee spirit in Christianity today. The "Christian culture" is a better way to live and it has great benefits but unfortunately this culture does not realize that it doesn't profit if we gain the whole world but lose our soul. The mind and the body are the emphasis of today's "gospel preaching" in some cases, but the soul is what Christ came to redeem. This is why Christ told many whom He healed, to not tell anyone. Only charlatans record their healings to puff themselves up above Christ. Flee anyone who preaches what we can get out of God more than how we can give glory to God. Jesus did not want to be known for His handouts, healings or feedings; He wanted the kingdom to be preached so that all would be saved. His kingdom is coming to earth soon. He will rule this earth for one thousand years and then for eternity, we will be with Him forever. The Pharisees were the most impacted by Jesus. They believed in the afterlife. Nicodemus and Saul were the most convicted Pharisees by Jesus's teachings. It was Jesus who introduced hell and its description of what is to come if we die without him. Christians can't cherry pick through scripture. The full Gospel must be preached. Donors, tithers, and givers should not slant the message. Preach whether it fills the room or empties the room. Fear God, who not only can take your life but who can throw you into hell. Jesus wants us to be free from the spirit of fear. Don't fear man. Don't fear what they think. It's God's word that matters more. The Gospel is more than a better way of living; it's salvation. Manners, dress codes, tax paying, and tithe paying is what religion focuses on. Jesus wanted the soul. When He has the soul and the mind, the body follows suit. Give Jesus your soul and His Spirit will indwell you, making you His temple forever.

Note

312

"If the world hate you, ye know that it hated me before it hated you" (John 15:18, KJV)

How do you respond when you are rejected? How did the early church respond when they were rejected? The Christianity we have today, does not prepare their followers for rejection. The evangelical church is shy to preach the Gospel at their outreaches. What has happened to our pulpit that it has confined its preachers to only preaching when the mic is on? Thank God that the early church never gave up in the face of rejection. When some evangelize today, after their second rejection, they squirm and quit. The tenacity and burden for souls has been outed by our experiences of rejection. When you preach the Gospel, it's not because of the acceptance of our audience but because of our obedience to Christ. We could get rejected for our whole ministry while working in our careers or in our communities but as long as we are preaching the Gospel, we are laying up treasure in heaven. We must not be results-driven. Profiling and discriminating is what we have been doing with our evangelism. CEOs need Jesus too. We preach to the poor, but Jesus preached to the "whosoever's."[67] Doctors need Jesus, attorneys need Jesus, your neighbor needs Jesus. Don't think that preaching the Gospel is only for the sinner on the street; be a light where you are at. If you are not a light in your career or school, you won't be a light overseas on your mission trip. Don't call it a mission trip, when it's really a paid-for

---

67. John 3:16

getaway or vacation. What a waste of time and money. Jesus wants a relationship now and wants to shine through you wherever you are at. If we don't wake up to this, we will have no weight to our ministry on Sunday's or overseas. Let Jesus shine through you every day. Don't fear rejection; fear God. If you are ashamed of Him, he will be ashamed of you on the day of judgment. The fear of man took over King Saul and drove him to fall on his sword. We live in a generation that cares more about what people think of them than what God thinks of them. We want to keep up with the appearances of our colleagues and family. To hell with what people think, follow God for Christ's sake. It's time to straighten up our back, lift our heads, and stand tall for our Jesus. A successful minister is not a full-time preacher to crowds, a successful minister hears from God and obeys. Obedience is greater than sacrifice. The believer's obedience is done by the power of God enabling us.

Note

313

*"It is the spirit that quickeneth; the flesh profiteth
nothing: the words that I speak unto you, they are
spirit, and they are life" (John 6:63, KJV)*

The Gospel is Power unto salvation. A person that has been argued
into the faith can be argued out of it. Gnostics have crept their way
into the church, to make the Gospel more about the accumulation
of knowledge more than power to Act. The Gospel does not pacify
the intellect; it gives us a new mind and heart. The conviction in our
minds when the Gospel is preached is more than our conscience; it's
the Holy Spirit revealing our need for Christ. Salvation is not just a
hand raised or a repetitious prayer; it's a transformative experience
which is rooted in biblical truth. Saul, on the road to Damascus is
a great example of what salvation produces. Jesus is alive. When we
call on Him, we will be saved. This does not emphasize emotionalism but it does remind the stoic that Jesus is alive and still changes
lives. We can encounter His presence. Not everyone has to have a
testimony like Paul but we can all encounter God. When we repent,
the Holy Spirit indwells in us and the old things pass away; behold
all things become new. Jesus makes us new. We don't have stay the
same. We don't have to get stuck in a rut. This is not a lukewarm
relationship with God; He sets His followers on fire. John the Baptist
said that Jesus will not only baptize in water but in fire too. The fire
of the Holy Spirit is not manifested in passion or charisma but in
holiness of life. We won't be perfect in our flesh but we won't stay
the same either. "He conforms our vile bodies like unto His glorious

body."[68] The Holy Spirit conforms us to the image of Christ. We are not Gnostics; the Holy Spirit gives revelation that manifests us in a Holy life. We can't do this in our flesh. If we walk after the flesh, we will feel condemned and fulfill the lust of our flesh while having a form of godliness. We have many who are denying the power of God. They figured out how to grow the church: with a rock band, LED lights, and a message that preaches everything but hell. Jesus preached on hell more than heaven. Until Jesus, hell was a mystery. The Sadducees did not even believe in an afterlife. No Sadducee ever repented or saved in scripture. They wanted religion. They saw the Torah as a moral code to live by, which made them "model citizens." The Gospel is power to save souls.

Note

_____
_____
_____
_____
_____
_____
_____
_____
_____

[68] *"Who shall change our vile body, that it may be fashioned like unto his glorious body, according to the working whereby he is able even to subdue all things unto himself." (Philippians 3:21, KJV)*

314

"But God hath chosen the foolish things of the world to confound the wise; and God hath chosen the weak things of the world to confound the things which are mighty" (1 Corinthians 1:27, KJV)

Whatever you think hinders you, in the sight of God, it actually qualifies you. The less we rely on our qualifications, the more we rely on Christ's qualifications that were earned for us by His blood. Resumes, pedigrees, zip codes, race, and genders are all barriers in our generation but Jesus turned all barriers into "easy-on ramps" for Him to pour His life through us. In Christ, we are no longer defined by our ethnicity, gender or education; we are welcomed as family before God. No matter what title we have or are aiming for, it profits nothing if we are not sons and daughters of God. Titles mean nothing to God; this is why Paul called his qualifications dung compared to knowing God. We have many people today, who are hiding behind titles and qualifications like Adam hid behind the bush. Come out from behind them. Jesus was shamed on the cross so that we could stand shameless before God. God knows that we ate of the tree; there is nothing that God does not know about us, yet loves us so passionately that His only beloved Son went to the cross to adopt whosoever will believe on Jesus. Harlots and tax collectors understood Jesus better than the religious. Jesus was inclusive of all people yet the religious only wanted a Jesus that was exclusive to them. Lay aside what we despise about ourselves, it does not define us. We are more of Abraham's seed than those who claim to be because we are in Christ. What gets the attention of God is not our pedigree or religion, what gets His attention is when one sinner repents. Come out from behind our religious smoke screen, come out from behind our titles, get real with God. He is the only one who knows everything about us yet loves us unconditionally. Jesus took the eternal judgment of our sin on the cross. He was the lamb of God who took away the sin of the world. Sin is not a hinderance; unbelief is. Jesus forgives sin but unbelief in His forgiveness reaps the consequence of our sin. To do the works of God, you must believe in Him who was sent.[69] Belief in Jesus for our qualifications is what invokes the Holy Spirit to work in us to do and to will of His good pleasure.[70] Lay aside the weight that easily besets you. Shame, guilt and unbelief are besetting thoughts that need to be taken captive to the obedience of Christ. Christ qualifies.

Note

_____

_____

_____

_____

_____

_____

_____

_____

_____

---

[69] *"Jesus answered and said unto them, This is the work of God, that ye believe on him whom he hath sent." (John 6:29, KJV)*
[70] *"For it is God which worketh in you both to will and to do of his good pleasure." (Philippians 2:13, KJV)*

315

"This know also, that in the last days perilous times shall come. For men shall be lovers of their own selves, covetous, boasters, proud, blasphemers, disobedient to parents, unthankful, unholy, Without natural affection, trucebreakers, false accusers, incontinent, fierce, despisers of those that are good, Traitors, heady, highminded, lovers of pleasures more than lovers of God; Having a form of godliness, but denying the power thereof: from such turn away. For of this sort are they which creep into houses, and lead captive silly women laden with sins, led away with divers lusts, Ever learning, and never able to come to the knowledge of the truth. Now as Jannes and Jambres withstood Moses, so do these also resist the truth: men of corrupt minds, reprobate concerning the faith. But they shall proceed no further: for their folly shall be manifest unto all men, as theirs also was. But thou hast fully known my doctrine, manner of life, purpose, faith, longsuffering, charity, patience, Persecutions, afflictions, which came unto me at Antioch, at Iconium, at Lystra; what persecutions I endured: but out of them all the Lord delivered me. Yea, and all that will live godly in Christ Jesus shall suffer persecution. But evil men and seducers shall wax worse and worse, deceiving, and being deceived" (2 Timothy 3:1–13, KJV)

Spiritual wickedness is exposing itself in our movie theaters, corporations, religions, and politics. The biblical literacy amongst the remnant is at an all-time low. Violence, decadence, and depravity will on day break out in every major city. There will be chaos. Darkness will cover the west. Those who have been abusing, taking advantage of their congregants, and preaching off the back of the cripple and widow will be brought low. Religion will no longer be attractive. The notion of God will be detested. The name of Jesus will be banned and anyone who preaches His name will be flogged openly. We will be sent into a darkness that is worse than the dark ages. Only the faithful will make it. Goats and sheep will be separated. It's not too late. It's time for the resistance to rise. Our candlestick may be dim but it's not removed. I am calling all intercessors to prayer. I am calling the remnant to know the Word of God. This is a call to repentance. Our statement of faith matters. Scripture must not be ignored. The time for preaching what people want to hear is over. It's time to take the Gospel to the streets. Let's reclaim our streets with the Gospel. It's not too late. Will anyone heed scripture? Evangelization is not only obedience, its storming the gates of hell which can't prevail to take back what Satan has held captive for generations. Our churches may be filled but we need to be open to who God calls. Gangs, hookers, pimps, criminals, drunks, drug addicts, and those forgotten are the dry bones in the valley which Ezekiel prophesized of. If we choose to speak about the Gospel to them, God will give them life. Redemption is in the Blood of Jesus. The resistance of spiritual wickedness is the preaching of the Gospel. We are at a fork in the road. Which way will we go? An awakening of resistance must rise in the body of Christ. We are the salt and light. Break the bushel of guilt, shame and unbelief in Jesus's name. Arise, God will give you life. Let's go together as one body, treading on spiritual wickedness in Jesus's name. Wickedness flees where we go; submitted to our Christ we are invisible. Arise and go. Go to prayer, then go to the streets. Go and go again. Don't relent; the Lamb's Blood was not spilt in vain.

316

*"For I would that ye knew what great conflict I have for you,
and for them at Laodicea, and for as many as have not seen my
face in the flesh; That their hearts might be comforted, being
knit together in love, and unto all riches of the full assurance
of understanding, to the acknowledgement of the mystery of
God, and of the Father, and of Christ; In whom are hid all the
treasures of wisdom and knowledge"* *(Colossians 2:1–3, KJV)*

There are mysteries about why some respond and others don't.
Trying to wrap our minds around faith is impossible. God knows
the state of the soul, whether it's open or closed. We can discern but
we can't see the state of the soul. Profiling who is open to be saved
is wrong. Everyone should get the same attention with the Gospel.
Jesus was willing to even meet Nicodemus in the night. We need to
remain open to God leading us to the "whosoever."[71] As Jesus would
set out to reach one family, along the way, He was ministering to
whosoever was in front of Him. Evangelism can't be just to one group
of people because Jesus loves the whosoever. As we walk in relationship with the Lord, a man can make His plans but the Lord orders
His steps. A relationship with the Lord takes us to where we could
never have gone if we were leading our own lives. Even though there
are mysteries and God wants faith, when the Spirit bears witness with
us, everything makes complete sense. God is God and we are not.
There are absolutes with no mystery attached and that is the love

---

[71.] John 3:16

of God. The crucifixion of Christ could not have revealed the love of God in a more graphic way. God did this so that all hindrances would be removed to know Him. No matter the extent of our sin, race, gender or lineage, Jesus loves us. Christ reconciled the world to the Father. Faith brings us into this relationship; unbelief takes us out. Sin can be repented of but unbelief sees no need for God or repentance. While we are here, we are to sow indiscriminately or we will learn the hard way like Jonah. Jonah believed that only his people were elect of God but God will do as He pleases. God will reach the whosoever. When we are willing and believing, we are poised to see God work through our faith. There are no limits on a man who is willing to believe God. Daily, we will face doubt, sin, and our flesh but as long as we stay willing, God will bring us through to the end. Life can make us congested with theology, doubt, and sin; the only way to decongest is by walking in relationship with Jesus. As we bring Him in on our internal struggles, He takes the burden of trying to figure it all out and gives peace. Jesus gives us peace unlike any peace we could get in the world. Confess to decongest the soul. God is listening. He made Himself available to us. Talk to Him in Jesus's name.

317

*"That if thou shalt confess with thy mouth the Lord Jesus,
and shalt believe in thine heart that God hath raised him
from the dead, thou shalt be saved. For with the heart man
believeth unto righteousness; and with the mouth confession
is made unto salvation" (Romans 10:9–10, KJV)*

Repentance is a faith change before it's a behavior change. Once we repent, which is removing faith from self and placing faith in Christ for salvation, power comes inside of us to desire what God wants for our lives. The Holy Spirit is convicting the world of sin. The Gospel is the means for that conviction to bring people to repentance. Why some respond and others don't is a mystery to us, it's the foolishness of preaching that the Holy Spirit uses to cause people to heed conviction and repent. Once we repent, we are empowered and refreshed. While we still have a pulse, it's not too late to repent. Repentance should be a part of the believer's discipline, along with evangelism and daily Bible reading. Wolves in sheep clothes have been teaching us that spiritual discipline is legalistic. A body without a skeleton is not a functioning body. We are the body of Christ, and we can be the most disciplined, righteous, and holy people because we are new creations in Christ. We have sin still at work in us as believers because these bodies have not been redeemed yet. Our soul and spirit are redeemed, but our bodies won't be until the resurrection. Our sin will haunt us and will get the best of us, so we must be quick to repent. Jesus taught us to agree with our adversary quickly. When the liar tells us that we sinned too much when he says we are too far gone, when he says it's over for us, agree and remind Him of the cross of Christ. We are clean by His Word over us.[72] We are saved by faith and not by behavior. This is why repentance is a discipline. It's healthy to examine whether we are in the faith. We need to check if our faith is in Christ, to live out His will or if our faith is in ourselves, to do it our way. Religion emphasizes what WE can do, but Christ emphasized what HE can do. Paul emphasized what we can do in Christ, who strengthens us. We are strengthened when we are worn-out, trying, and repenting. God expects us to draw near to Him. We need to call on Him. The Holy Spirit has been given to do what we can't do, but it's up to us to believe. This is why Jesus never got frustrated with sinners, but He did with unbelievers. Jesus works with sinners; He was frustrated with unbelievers who knew His Word but quenched the Spirit with doubt. Jesus, we need you.

Note

---

72. *"Now ye are clean through the word which I have spoken unto you." (John 15:3, KJV)*

318

---

*"By this shall all men know that ye are my disciples, if
ye have love one to another" (John 13:35, KJV)*

If someone does not know that you care for them, they won't receive
what you have to say. Love prepares the way to say an offensive yet
truthful statement, yet it is well received. They may not agree, but they
know that you have their interest at heart. What we must agree on, to
unite is the Gospel. Churches that known for Calvinism, Pentecost,
Methodologies, etc., have the Gospel but want to be known for non-
essential truth more than what is essential, which is obedience to the
Great Commission. They are more interested in reaching the reached
than the unreached. Church planters rarely plant churches where the
church is needed. A better title for some of them is "church poachers." Very few want to strengthen what remains. When we are known
for trends, fashion, and style but not known for reaching the sinner,
lost and broken, we are misrepresenting Christ. Paul's epistles give us
a lot of insight on how to tackle these issues. Religion needs draining
of the swamp. This is not harsh, but it's up to the five-fold ministry
to be activated again within the church. Pastors and teachers have
been holding the purse for a very long time. They have become like
pharaohs in their Egypt's, and we need evangelists to do what God
has called them to do so that we can hold the pastors and teachers
accountable to equip the congregation for evangelism. The evangelist has to ask the pastor, as Moses did Pharaoh, to let the people
"go" so that they can be all that God has called them to be rather
than just paying for the pharaoh/pastor to be all that he wants to be.

Rather than the five-fold equipping, they are making their audience dependent on them. This has caused more church hurt and abuse than anything else. Abuse has been covered up, misappropriation of funds has been covered up, they resemble the Roman Catholic cult in so many ways. Rather than one Vatican, now we have thousands of them with thousands of nondenominational popes at the top. Accountability is seen as rebellion. They are not open to be questioned. They separate parents from kids, they separate spouses, and their fruit is so spiritually manipulative, that they slide through every resistance. Their sins have not gone unnoticed. Using Jesus for gain, position and control is such cowardice that the Holy Spirit does not deal lightly with it. Hiding behind the Bible and colleagues may have worked for a while, but not for long.

Note

319

*"But there were false prophets also among the people, even as
there shall be false teachers among you, who privily shall bring in
damnable heresies, even denying the Lord that bought them, and
bring upon themselves swift destruction" (2 Peter 2:1, KJV)*

The dark ages lasted around one thousand years. The Remnant suffered severe persecution. The Bible was burned by the papacy and could only be read in Latin. This meant that the average person had no access to the Bible. The papacy replaced the authority of scripture. The papacy was more involved with commerce than theology. The pope replaced the roman emperor but kept the emperor's pomp and authority. No one can be saved by believing in the Roman Catholic doctrine. Every Roman Catholic that trusts the catechism for salvation is not saved. For the first time in years, we could see the fall of Roman influence over Christianity. This current pope would sit with Satan for unity if he could. He has tried to bring unity any way his can. Their center of worship, which is called the mass is blasphemy. Their priests and altars are the antichrist. The lines are so blurred today because the remnants are becoming more and more biblically illiterate. The statement of faith is not taught from the pulpits, so congregants are ignorant of what they believe. The Bible is a doctrinal absolute. Jesus came to bring a spiritual sword to the earth; the line has been drawn. Our generation believes in worship singing more than truth and obedience. We could be led into another dark age very soon. Most will be found unprepared. Our rock concerts and "light on doctrine" sermons are making our churches a mile wide but an inch deep. The church needs pastors to disciple them in sound doctrine. The pastor has to fulfill his function to earn the title "pastor." The five-fold listed in Ephesians are functions and not titles. Jesus taught doctrinal absolutes. The New Testament is full of warnings about false teachings and false teachers, but today the church only wants to preach what we are "for," and keep it encouraging. Scripture was given for doctrine, correction, rebuke, and instruction. Christ was crucified. The early church was persecuted not because they preached what everyone wanted to hear but because truth divides between bone and marrow. The Gospel divides sinners from believers. As it's being preached, it's falling on open souls and closed souls. What opens the soul to the Gospel is a mystery, but we are called to preach the Gospel. Roman Catholics must be evangelized to, and if they repent, they must renounce the papacy, mass, and all loyalties to the Vatican.

Note

320

"Come unto me, all ye that labour and are heavy laden, and I will give you rest. Take my yoke upon you, and learn of me; for I am meek and lowly in heart: and ye shall find rest unto your souls. For my yoke is easy, and my burden is light" (Matthew 11:28–30, KJV)

God wants us to run to Him and never from Him. Our natural instinct is to hide when we sin or lie about our disobedience, for fear of His reaction. There was no sin that man committed that made God utterly forsake him. His desire is toward us. The crucifixion of Christ is the extent of God's love for us. When we are rooted in the love of God, come hell or high water, we shall not be moved. God holds us through it all. His grace is sufficient for all circumstances. Many are not being taught how to face their cross in life; when they do face it, their faith is not deep enough in scripture that the storm washes their faith away. This is why discipleship is so important for the believer. How would we know if no one taught us? We need to be discipled in how to deal with hardship and affliction. Jesus prepared His disciples for trouble and look at how they responded to His death; they did not have the Holy Spirit and the full canon of scripture as we have. They were fishermen and tax collectors; they needed to experience the Holy Spirit who keeps us when times get tough. God wants us to know Him more than to know about Him. The calling on the twelve apostles was not Jesus's calling for every believer. Not every believer was told to leave all and follow Him. For some, Jesus told them to go back to their communities and testify of Him. The calling is not the same for every believer. As we walk in an honest relationship with Jesus, we don't have to fear God asking us to do something or go through something that His grace would not be sufficient for. As we walk in relationship with Him, we become everything that God wants us to be. God will be faithful to complete what He began in our lives. There is nothing that can separate His love from us. His love is a covenant, concreted by the cross of Christ. We have been forgiven since Christ died the death of the cross. Forgiveness must never be called into question; when we do question it, we are degrading the power of the blood of Jesus. We are forgiven. We are loved. The Bible tells us so. Sin does not determine the love of God; the cross does. Repent of sin and trust the love of God. Don't be shackled to doubt or unbelief. Scripture breaks the shackle of unbelief so that we can run to His throne boldly.

Note

321

"And he said unto me, My grace is sufficient for thee: for my strength is made perfect in weakness. Most gladly therefore will I rather glory in my infirmities, that the power of Christ may rest upon me" (2 Corinthians 12:9, KJV)

What God calls us to will have sufficient grace to get us through. Our God is jealous for the glory. He won't share His glory with us. When we shout grace to our mountains, they flatten by His might. Grace is the word that we all shout through life's peaks and valleys. It's by grace that we are saved; it's by grace that we are kept, and it's by grace that we will see His face. Grace is getting what we don't deserve. Grace is empowerment to do what He has called us to do. Grace is not a license; it's longing to glorify Jesus. We spend most of our Christian life praying for change; we pray "change me" every day. This may seem like a pious response, but we are what we are by the grace of God. We are so focused on changing that we are worshipping change more than Jesus. When we understand His grace and His passion for us, that we could never "outlove" God, then we find rest. When we rest, He works. When we know His grace, "praise Jesus" comes out of our mouth more than "change me." When Jesus is our focus, we can go through any buffeting of hell. We all have a thorn or multiple thorns in our flesh as believers. They are reminders that God won't share His glory. Jacob walked with a limp for the rest of His life after wrestling God. Not all sickness, thorns, and dislocations are of the devil; some are healthy reminders of who is God and who is not. Jesus uses our stubbornness, sin, and weakness for His glory.

We have nothing to be ashamed of; Jesus took our shame. The fruit of a believer is not health and wealth, but it's the fruit of the Spirit. This is why we can count it all joy when we are in the hardships of life because God is making us dependent on His Spirit, so His fruit is grown in our lives.[73] The fruit of the Holy Spirit grows in our lives as we learn to lean on the Spirit more than on our flesh. Hardship in our lives removes the option of walking in the flesh so that we only choose to walk in the Spirit. To walk in the Spirit is to be dependent on the Spirit. The less we have, the more we depend on Him. Thank God for affliction because it's more blessed to be poor and need Jesus than to be rich and live without Him. Don't let anyone sow unbelief about where you are with God, based on your circumstance. No one can be closer to God than when they first believed.

Note

---

[73] *"My brethren, count it all joy when ye fall into divers temptations." (James 1:2, KJV)*

322

"Behold, I stand at the door, and knock: if any man hear my voice, and open the door, I will come in to him, and will sup with him, and he with me" (Revelation 3:20, KJV)

God does not have a generic way of following Him. He leads everyone uniquely. For some, He speaks from scripture; for others, He uses burning bushes and circumstances, storms, and famines lead others. There is no "one size fits all" for direction for our lives. The life that Jesus called the apostles to was not His will for everyone. Some He told to go back to their communities. Not everyone had to forsake all to follow Him. Some had ravens provide for them, and others had to be a tent-maker to provide. Jesus told Peter to go fishing, and inside the fish was money to pay taxes. We are to follow Jesus and not just the way someone in scripture was led. We don't need to have a burning bush experience to follow God. Moses was not seeking a burning bush experience; he was making the best decisions he knew, and God intervened. If we don't have a clear direction, we need to go in the best direction for our family, with good counsel around us. Waiting for a Word from God or seeking an experience for direction, could become idolatry. Our purpose, while we are here, must not be more important than honoring Christ in all that we are doing. The way God leads each one of us is going to be different. Some get a clear directional word; some have to decide in faith and trust if it's wrong, that God will redirect. God will never contradict His character to lead us. Fear must be driven out of a believer's life. If we can say "Jesus is my Lord," then we can rest assured that if we got ourselves to where we are at, He could get us back on track as we repent. Jesus redeems and will turn all things for good; even bad decisions can be turned for good for those who are called. Every believer is called, but few are open to hearing. Some want Jesus for heaven but not for life. As we pray that His will be done on earth as it is in heaven, He will intervene. God has a purpose for us, but it may not always be clear. There are seasons in our lives where we won't know what God is doing until we get to heaven. In heaven, we will see our life here from God's point of view. God will fill in the blanks and the mysteries of life. If you don't know what to do, do the best option you know how to do until God says otherwise. As long as we remain open to God, we can't get it wrong. Indecision is not of God.

Note

323

"Beloved, believe not every spirit, but try the spirits
whether they are of God: because many false prophets
are gone out into the world" (1 John 4:1, KJV)

When the Spirit does not convict you to be a witness or to preach the Gospel, you might not have the Holy Spirit. If you have no friends who are sinners, and you judge those who sin differently than you do, you probably don't have Jesus living inside you. When you have nothing but sarcasm, negativity, and doubt flowing out of your mouth, you may not have the Holy Spirit living in you. When you love the lust of the flesh more than the holiness of God, you may not have the Holy Spirit in you. The word of God corrects, and reproves. We need truth more than ever. We need sermons that make us detest Luke warmness. We have many professional stone-throwers in our world today yet they don't realize the boulders of depression, gluttony, and gossip that they are under. If Jesus does not condemn, how dare we condemn another. Whoever condemns has the spirit of anti-christ at work in them. How dare anyone call unclean who God calls clean? When we read scripture, we should feel the grief of the Spirit in us, showing us how other God is of us.[74] We should feel convicted when we sin. The Holy Spirit is wrestling with our flesh every day. What we feed grows; what we starve dies. When we get fed religion, we get puffed up. When we feed on scripture, Christ gets puffed up

---

[74]. *"Endeavouring to keep the unity of the Spirit in the bond of peace." (Ephesians 4:3, KJV)*

in us. The only way to grow is to repent and never get comfortable. No one comforts like the Holy Spirit, when He comforts, it's not because of our sob story, it's because we are broken, repentant believers who know that without Jesus, we are empty. We need to welcome the Holy Spirit to have all of us. We are to fan the flame that is within us. As we yield to the Holy Spirit, we begin to change; our thoughts become His thoughts. We gain the mind of Christ. Christ won't get glory from the flesh; Christ will get the glory when our flesh is mortified, and we are dependent on the Holy Spirit. Don't quench the Holy Spirit in our lives. Passion and charisma are not the fruit of the Holy Spirit. The anointing that we need has nothing to do with goosebumps or weird manifestations; it's to do with sin being fought in lives, burdens for souls, lives transformed from walking in their flesh to walk in the Spirit. The Spirit of God's title should give us discernment; Holy, He is holy. Have your way in me, Holy Spirit.

Note

324

"Wherefore come out from among them, and be ye separate,
saith the Lord, and touch not the unclean thing; and
I will receive you" (2 Corinthians 6:17, KJV)

Come out from amongst them. Infiltrating from within won't always work. When we are bought, we are owned. When they pay you, they determine what is being said. Unbridle yourself from man, so that we are only bridled by God. No one has the right to silence the truth. The purse does not own the pulpit. We are entering a new era of pulpit preaching. Preachers are coming out of the wilderness that are not bought by their donors. They don't take tithes or love offerings; they are totally God-sufficient. Their message cannot be bought out. They are dangerous to religion because only scripture holds them accountable. Their loyalties are not to the wealthy but to Christ. Their conviction is shaped only by scripture. When they speak, they fear God and not man. Their conscience is captive to honoring God above man. A new breed of preachers is coming out of preparation. They have been broken by life, afflicted by sin, and they walk with a limp because they have been trained to lean only on Christ. They don't look like what we want them to. They are not attractive or appealing to the naked eye, but they carry the truth that scatters the demonic host. When they open their mouth, a light comes out, shining on our absolute sinfulness and God's absolute holiness. Christ alone gets glory out of their lives because they are nothing to look at. Their message will be followed with signs like no generation has seen—greater things than Christ they will do.[75] The fear of God will be all around them. God will be taken serious again. God is not mocked. The Gospel saves souls; it has the power to cleanse sinners, the power to heal but only Christ will get the glory. No one will dare touch the glory, and when someone does, they will feel the weight of it. God will be lifted up above all. A revival is coming, and the fire of God will consume all carnality. The Holy Spirit won't always strive with us for as long as He has with others. Too many souls are in need of salvation, so He will expedite judgment on His representatives, for the crowds to be led by Him and not flesh. No one should be elevated above God. God, come again in power. Our electricity has fed hype for too long. We are not entertained anymore. We need more than this. Come in your might, and show yourself. Show the demonic host who is Lord in our generation. The Lamb's blood was not spilled in vain. Come, Lord.

[75.] *"Verily, verily, I say unto you, He that believeth on me, the works that I do shall he do also; and greater works than these shall he do; because I go unto my Father."* *(John 14:12, KJV)*

325

"Then the Lord said unto Moses, Go in unto Pharaoh, and tell him, Thus saith the Lord God of the Hebrews, Let my people go, that they may serve me" (Exodus 9:1, KJV)

Religion must let their people go or face the plagues of God. They have been held captive for hundreds of years. If pharaoh does not let the broken go, they will very soon face the judgment. Let the people go to the uttermost parts of the earth. Let the people go out from the pew to preach in their pulpits of influence. Our designated pulpits must be lowered in view of the pulpit that the believer has been given in their everyday life. The believer's pulpit has more of an influence over their communities than the pulpit hiding behind the four walls. The pulpit is to push believers out of the pew to follow Christ every day, rather than following Christ only for the one-hour religious services. Let the people go. Don't keep them bound to only lifting pharaoh up but set them free to lift Christ up everywhere they go. Where the Spirit of the Lord is, there is liberty. We have been liberated from mediums and organization, to a life of intimacy with Christ, with an organism of the trinity residing in us. Arise from our slumber and let the light of Christ shine through us wherever we are. Revival will most likely happen next in our hospitals, places of employment, neighborhoods, schools and universities so that no church can glory. The "no-names" are coming out of the wilderness with a message for pharaoh. "Let my people go and preach the Gospel, making disciples everywhere they are at." The Lamb's blood was not spilt "for us four and no more." Calvinism must be renounced. John Calvin is not

Jesus Christ. Jesus Christ said that whosoever will believe in Him will be saved. Jesus Christ said, "All authority in heaven and earth has been given to Him, Go Ye Therefore."[76] Go and go again. Don't stop going. We have been endued with power to go and be a witness. We are not "result driven," we are obedience driven. Our conscience is captive to scripture. This is not rebellion. This is accountability. Roll up your sleeves, it's time to get to work; seven billion people need a savior. Let's present their only option to be saved. He gave us this responsibility, to be His ambassadors. We can't save but we can preach about who can save. Jesus saves. We know it because we have been saved. Pharaoh let the people go. Repent like Nineveh did. There is still time. God redeems.

Note

---

76. *"And Jesus came and spake unto them, saying, All power is given unto me in heaven and in earth. Go ye therefore, and teach all nations, baptizing them in the name of the Father, and of the Son, and of the Holy Ghost: Teaching them to observe all things whatsoever I have commanded you: and, lo, I am with you always, even unto the end of the world. Amen." (Matthew 28:18–20, KJV)*

326

"But our God is in the heavens: he hath done whatsoever
he hath pleased" (Psalm 115:3, KJV)

God is God, we are not. There will be mysteries for us that our futile minds will never comprehend. This is why it is the faith in scripture that reveals who God is. He will not be figured out. This universe is the size of a grain of sand, compared to our God. He is outside of our time zone. He is infinite, with no beginning or end. Christ Jesus made it possible for us to know Him. For us to believe that God would love us and not wipe us out, blows our minds. Why would God want us? Why would He love us? The power He placed in us is infinite power. He commands authority over time itself. If we were to believe who resides in us, we would never fear again. If we were to believe who is in us, we would stand in confidence, no matter what we are facing. The curse of fear is smashed. The heads of shame have been severed. The heritage of guilt has been cut off. Behold God has made all things new. We are no longer of this world; He is in us. Open ourselves to Him. Let Him in on all of us. Hold nothing back; let the Holy Spirit honor Jesus Christ through us in a way that no flesh could. We have been damned up for a long time but the damn is about to bust open and rivers of living water will flow out of the church like never before. We are about to see the greatest awakening that the earth has ever seen. If we will humble ourselves, repent of sin, we will see God heal our generation. If we resist repentance, we will experience sin's consequences seven times worse than any generation before us. No generation has been given as much resources as ours has yet slumbers as much as ours does. Awaken and God will give life. We are over entertainment. Karaoke is great, the motivational message by the guy that loves the sound of his own voice is sweet, but God almighty, we need you. Church without God is a brood of vipers. The most dangerous place for a sinner is the church without Jesus. Sinners should be flooding our churches but they see past the church people's fake smiles. They can discern gossip, judgment, and shame. Where sinners should be going to for help, which is the church, instead, they are going to the counterfeit church, the bar. Bar tenders could give today's pastors tips on how to love, counsel, and care for people. Satan has counterfeits for everything godly.

Note

327

"I have seen all the works that are done under the sun; and, behold, all is vanity and vexation of spirit" (Ecclesiastes 1:14, KJV)

Whoever says, "Do whatever makes you happy" has never lived. At the end of happiness, there is always regret. At the end of our dreams, there is disappointment. Happiness is an emotion that must not be trusted. Happiness without boundaries and conscience, can become demonic. Happiness must not be a principle to live by. No emotion should be followed more than Christ. "Do whatever God wants"; whether it makes you happy or squirm, God's way always works out in the end. As we do what God wants, day in and day out, we will learn a greater emotion than happiness, joy. Joy comes from the Holy Spirit as we yield daily to the will of God. Joy is not based on our circumstance or our location. We can be joyful when facing persecution, martyrdom, and affliction. It's time to dig deep and mature further in the faith. Keep our lamps full, lest He returns or we face hardship. Both are imminent. The West has experienced ease for a long time; we have grown comfortable. We need to prepare in these years of prosperity because when the famine comes, people will know where to go for bread. A major famine is imminent. It's time to fan the flame so it gets white hot. We need to be ready for when this famine hits. Memorize scripture as much as we can. We may go through a season where that's the only way that we will know the Word of God. No man knows the day nor the hour. We want Him to come now but He will come when He decides. While we are here, we will have trouble. Don't do what makes you happy, do what disciplines your flesh in scripture reading and prayer. Will you be ready? Don't say that no one warned you. God is trying to warn you now. Awaken from the spiritual slumber. It's time to fill the lamp. It's time to study to show ourselves approved. The day is coming where we will show ourselves approved. Hardship, affliction, and suffering come to us all. Be ready for it. Don't slack off, tighten up. We have a short time here. Nothing is worth our soul. No amount of temporal happiness is worth heaven. Put on the armor of God. Put on the mind of Christ. Don't be caught by surprise; it rains on the just and unjust. It's better to beat our thoughts into submission than to give into our thoughts and lose to the enemy. We are not ignorant of his strategies. With God, we will do valiantly. Trust God.

Note

_____

_____

_____

_____

_____

_____

_____

_____

_____

328

"Judge not, that ye be not judged. For with what judgment ye judge, ye shall be judged: and with what measure ye mete, it shall be measured to you again. And why beholdest thou the mote that is in thy brother's eye, but considerest not the beam that is in thine own eye?" (Matthew 7:1–3, KJV)

Religion that creates a culture of judgment will be judged. Suits don't deem a person righteous. Tax paying does not deem a person righteous. Our music style does not deem us righteous. A sinner can't judge another sinner's eternity. Only Jesus has the authority to judge. Our love for sinners and friendship of sinners[77] gauges our relationship with Jesus. He was known as a friend of sinners. Is the church known for this? Religions build country clubs but followers of Jesus build spiritual hospitals for the sin-sick. When sinners are scorned but the religious are welcomed, we are nothing like Jesus. Now is the time to repent and read about the life of Jesus. Jesus did not come to condemn but He came to save. Jesus was loved by sinners and hated by the religious. Our religious today would not welcome Jesus into their church if He turned up Sunday with His disciples. We need to wage spiritual war on religion. Sinners have a chance to be saved but the religious are securing their eternity with their judgement heaping more judgment on themselves. Don't follow any man if they live contrary to the culture of Christ in scripture. Jesus culture diminishes

---

[77.] *"The Son of man came eating and drinking, and they say, Behold a man gluttonous, and a winebibber, a friend of publicans and sinners. But wisdom is justified of her children." (Matthew 11:19, KJV)*

our culture if we want to be Christ followers. This is why He was so hated, because His culture of love and acceptance of sinners was offensive. Infrastructure was never to be the house of God. Buildings made with man's hands are not the house of God. Believers in Christ are the temples of the Holy Spirit. Jesus came to remove the prominence of the temple and buildings and put the emphasis on sinners that He loves to save, redeem, and make born-again. The fruit of the Holy Spirit is not white Americanism, republicanism, capitalism, suits, tithe paying members of a country club with church written on its signage.[78] The fruit of the Holy Spirit is the character of Christ. Some who say that they have the gifts of the spirit but don't have the fruit of the spirit are charlatans and are deviants from the truth. The gifts of the spirit don't puff up flesh but hide flesh so that only Christ gets glory. Filming the gifts of the spirit is so carnal. We are all broken flesh. We all need Jesus and we never graduate from our desperation for Christ to live through us. Religion graduates it's leaders like they are holier but with time the truth always comes out. Only honor Christ.

[78.] *"But the fruit of the Spirit is love, joy, peace, longsuffering, gentleness, goodness, faith, Meekness, temperance: against such there is no law." (Galatians 5:22–23, KJV)*

329

"Wherefore I say unto thee, Her sins, which are many, are forgiven; for she loved much: but to whom little is forgiven, the same loveth little" (Luke 7:47, KJV)

Those that are forgiven much, follow much. Those that don't understand how much they are forgiven, don't follow but lead themselves into destruction. As we look into the word of God, it's like a mirror; it shows us our unquestionable need for God. Other men's books and religion teaches us how we can attempt to serve God without God. Most of our best-selling book titles are basically saying "here is how to be a believer without God." There never needs to be reason of fasting books other than reading the Bible. It's time to go to the source than be fed from resources. Any parent that parents their kids to stay home and not prepares them to be self-sufficient has failed. Parents parent their kids to one day live without them. They should become adults and be self-sufficient. When an adult son still needs his moms' milk, there is something drastically wrong. We are weaned off of breast milk very quick in life. Discipleship should be about raising up disciple makers. A pastor that is not developing and eagerly desiring for his congregation to read their Bibles without him, hear from God without him, can serve God without him is a hireling and not a shepherd. When was the last time that a religious leader taught its followers how to do their job? How many have taught how to write sermons, seek God, and study the word? Religion lives to raise a man above another but Christ came to ruin that and level the ground. The call of God is available for everyone. In heaven, there will be twelve foundations, with only the twelve apostles of the lamb's names on them.[79] There are no other apostles outside of the original twelve. No one can claim the same authority as one of the twelve apostles today. There is no apostle in Rome. There were only twelve apostles. The apostolic church that gives out the title apostle and demands the same respect as the original twelve apostles should be ashamed of themselves. They are controlling hirelings, who love position and power more than people. Jesus kept teaching His apostles that the last will be first. Christ is our example of leadership not the suit wearing, high flying, cult leading, money grabbing, political maneuvering religious leaders of today. Their belly is their god. They use charity for their profit. They use the gospel to perpetuate their lavish lifestyle; shame on them. Repent now.

Note

_____

_____

_____

_____

_____

_____

_____

_____

_____

_____

[79.] *"And the wall of the city had twelve foundations, and in them the names of the twelve apostles of the Lamb." (Revelation 21:14, KJV)*

330

"And he gave some, apostles; and some, prophets; and some, evangelists; and some, pastors and teachers" (Ephesians 4:11, KJV)

Biblical leaders equip; carnal leaders want the people to equip them. People need leaders who live for their development and not use the people for their own development. We have so many leaders who foolishly think that the people exist for them, when God has them in leadership for the people's sake and not theirs. If our preachers don't preach to make us stronger in the faith, why are we listening to them? If we are not growing, we are dead. Everyone is growing in something. The day we stop growing is the day we died. There is no retirement on this side of eternity. We will need faith until the day we die. We will be a disciple to our last breath. Don't plateau in any way. Don't let someone keep you in one place but continue to journey ahead with God. Jesus led His disciples by staying on the move. Change, transitions, and new experiences are God's way of deepening our revelation of who He is. When we get comfortable for a long period of time, we slack off what is important; change comes to us all. Nothing stays the same on earth but God, our only consistent stability. God is the one relationship in our lives that does not change. We change but God stays the same. God is consistent when we and everything around us is inconsistent. Follow Jesus; even when He leads us through the valley and all we can see is Him, follow Him to the end. If we want to be good leaders, read how Jesus led. We need to tune out this world and tune into His Word. The more we apply His Word to our lives, as contrary to this world as it may be, it has eternal reward. Let's be known for how well we equipped and not just how well we were equipped. Let's be known for our spiritual generosity and not for our spiritual hoarding. Let's give all for the betterment of others, even if they use us as a doormat. Vengeance is the Lords. Those who took advantage of Jesus, faced the judgment and those who take advantage of you will also face the judgment. What type of leader are you? Who's our influence as a leader? It better be Christ because there is no one better than Him. It's amazing how Jesus, His ways, parables, and sermons are some of the least read from the majority of our pulpits today. Our suit-wearing, script-reading preachers need to come back to Christ. Do we reflect Christ more than our culture?

Note

_____
_____
_____
_____
_____
_____
_____
_____

331

*"Be not deceived; God is not mocked: for whatsoever a man soweth,
that shall he also reap. For he that soweth to his flesh shall of
the flesh reap corruption; but he that soweth to the Spirit shall
of the Spirit reap life everlasting" (Galatians 6:7–8, KJV)*

The earth has been groaning since the fall of man. Sin brought serious consequences. Man brought on himself the sin, sickness, shame, corruption, and all forms of pestilence. We all want to point a finger when catastrophe happens, but not all storms, famines, and diseases are from God. God can cause them and He has in the past but it always turns for the good and for His glory. God can intervene and stop the storms. Even the wind and the waves obey Him. God does not need to do anything for us. He does not have to listen to us. We are in a fallen world, with fallen bodies. Christ came to save the soul but the rain falls on the just and the unjust. Death comes to us all. It is appointed for all of us to die. We have Satan, sin, and the earth working against us. The cross is our assurance of God's love for us. When we face life, illness, and tragedy, we must aggressively fight to believe the love of God. Jesus wanted us to remember His death because He knew that everything in this world is after our faith in the goodness of God. We can't lose sight of the cross of Christ, no matter what we face. Even though it's a mystery, and we get confused as to why these hardships happen to Gods people, believe with all that we have, in the love of God; it's proved by the cross. The consequences of sin are all around us. We have no right to blame anyone because all have sinned. We would have all disobeyed just as Adam and Eve did in the garden. When we take responsibility, repent, and believe in Christ, we find life through the hardest of times here. Rather than whining or falling into the pit of despair, we are a voice of hope and assurance. God makes His believers shine brighter in the darkest of times because believers have confidence when everyone else is in the pits of fear. Mature believers should be prepared for hardship and trouble. We are not to be ignorant. Paul was shipwrecked but he turned the tragedy into an opportunity to honor Jesus. Believers who are mature are prepared for the worst so that they can shine the brightest. When we have a revelation of the love of God, there is nothing that Satan, sin, or the world could throw at us, that could persuade us out of the love of God. The cross compels us to worship Jesus, no matter what we face in life. We learn to boast in our afflictions and persecutions because Christ will get glory!

Note

332

"He that is faithful in that which is least is faithful also in much: and he that is unjust in the least is unjust also in much" (Luke 16:10, KJV)

If we can be trusted with little, then we can be trusted with much. Believers can be models in every way if we let God have His way in us. We can outperform anyone when we are following God in everything that He has called us to. We carry more favor on us than anyone else. Christians who do not return texts, phone calls, or handle their business in an efficient way should know that they are not to take the grace of God in vain. Church staff should be working unto the Lord which means that they should be early for meetings, prepared and take their position serious, as if their pay check depended on it. Volunteers work harder than most church staff do because for most staff, the paycheck robs the heart of the ministry. Some staff are not doing their work unto the Lord; they are doing it unto the paycheck. The world works way harder for a paycheck than some church staff do for the glory of God. A paycheck is of more value to the world than the glory of God is for the church staff; their work ethic proves it. Jesus sees our faithfulness in the secret place. Knowing Him and serving Him because of what He has done should be fuel to our fire. Slothfulness and laziness are not the fruit of the Holy Spirit. The early church was filled with ambition and worked tirelessly to advance the Gospel. It's time for laborers to rise. Jesus has been interceding for laborers whose faith will not be sifted like wheat. A new breed of believers is being raised up in this generation. We will be relentless for the glory of God. None will share His glory. We will be trusted with much because we have been proven with little. The hardships of this life prove the belief of believers. This faith is refined by fire. The refiners' fire has wrought a new breed of men and women of God. We are arising from the valley of the shadow of death, the wilderness of preparation, and the pit which stands for the "preacher in training." What we do is unto the Lord. We never clock out. Jesus does not want a couple of hours on a Sunday or forty hours a week; Jesus wants all of our heart, mind, and soul. Jesus is not just a PART of our life; He IS our life. Many will be surprised of who goes where on the day of Judgment. Be faithful to the secret place with Jesus. Follow Him. Do everything as unto Him.

Note

333

"Persecuted, but not forsaken; cast down, but not destroyed" (2 Corinthians 4:9, KJV)

Scars are reminders of how it could be; scars also show us that no matter the wound, there is healing. What we thought would ruin us, made us stronger. When we weather our first storm, we are reminded that there is nothing our God can't bring us through. What seems like loss has turned into the believer's gain. Come what may, still will we praise our God. The world and the enemy of our soul will try to sift our faith like wheat. Jesus prays that our faith won't fail. Faith can fail but rather than letting hardship attempt to fail our faith, let's let it fuel our faith. A person whose faith is not based on their five senses is a sensible person that has built their faith on a rock. While we still can, let's place our faith solely in the scripture so that we are not moved by the onslaught. Choose this day who we will serve: will we choose our five senses or our God, who always speaks a better word. It won't be this way forever. Things come and go; people come and go, but God is true from our beginning to our eternity. What the enemy meant for evil, God has already turned it for His glory. Bitterness only hurts ourselves. Hatred hurts the hater more than the hated. Stop trying to figure it out. Unclench your fist, open the fist to extend your palms to God, and surrender all. Surrendered believers are the happiest believers. This type of believer has had such an intense revelation of why Jesus died, that all that is coming out of their mouth is resurrecting words of life. Come forth, come out of your cave, come out of your grave clothes; God has given you life.

We don't need an abundance of stuff; we need an abundance of the Spirit of God. We have resurrection life in us. Christ is in us. As He is, so are we in this world. While He was here, He chose to be one of us but today He is not one of us, He is the almighty King, with all authority. This is who is enthroned within us. The kingdom of God is in us; few awaken to this higher reality, which is contradictory to our senses, the higher reality is called faith. The higher reality is that we are seated with Him in heavenly places. We have His attention when we come before His throne. There is no devil or demon that can snatch us from His hand. There is no sin that can remove us from the grace of God. Arise above our senses and believe. Believe and watch God restore.

Note

334

"As he spake these words, many believed on him" (John 8:30, KJV)

It's not over. It's just beginning. When all seems lost, we have the potential to be found. There is no one who can save our soul like Christ. Our soul can get congested with grief, rejection, bitterness, and hatred. When our soul goes unchecked for a long time, we all have potential to turn into the "Joker." When we suppress the lies spoken over us, it builds up hate on the inside which makes us do the craziest of things. We need to wake up to the R-rated things that we are capable of if we go unchecked. Jesus came to save the soul from the congestion of the world and sin. If your soul is not saved, you are prey to possession. Bitterness and hatred give the devil an open door to our soul. When we hold onto hurt, we are holding the door open to demons. We need to wake up from the bitterness and finger-pointing and realize that with time, differences can turn us into a monster. Religion and church hurt can turn someone into a worse sinner than any sinner on the street. We expect sinners to hurt us but sinners dressed in a suit, preaching Jesus is a stab in the back that hurts more than any other wound. Jesus conditioned His forgiveness of us on our forgiveness of others. The rage, bitterness, and hatred of our soul was taken out on Christ so that we can be saved. Those that don't turn their soul over to Jesus will be eaten up by the worm of bitterness. Forgive those who abused you, forgive those who despitefully used you, forgive those who stole from you; you are releasing yourself from bitterness more than giving them forgiveness. God will vindicate you. Leave the vengeance to the Lord and walk away free.

God's vengeance is way worse than ours or any earthly judges. Let rest enter our soul. The Holy Spirit comforts unlike anyone else. He liberates our soul and makes His life-giving fruit grow through us to everyone around us. Christ seen in us is the greatest compliment we could ever be given. Let's let His love and peace have His way in us. Come what may we are free people, yes free indeed.[80] We are free from hate, free from anger, free from judgment; Christ set us free so that He could be seen in us. Biblical maturity is to be conformed to the image of Christ so that His character would be evidenced in us, as we walk through the afflict.

Note

_____

_____

_____

_____

_____

_____

_____

_____

---

[80] *"If the Son therefore shall make you free, ye shall be free indeed." (John 8:36, KJV)*

335

"All things are lawful for me, but all things are not expedient: all things are lawful for me, but all things edify not" (1 Corinthians 10:23, KJV)

All things are permissible but not all things are beneficial. Christ fulfilled the law so that there is no work or effort that we could do to earn salvation. Where the Spirit of the Lord is, there is Liberty. Salvation was earned for us by Christ on the cross. If we come before God because of any good work that we have done for salvation, though it sounds right, it's the worst approach we could have. By doing this, we are stating to God that His Son's blood was spilt in vain. Jesus came to teach us that faith saves, and works condemn. Religion loves to make the Gospel be the bad news. Bad news sells, that's why we have hundreds of tabloids and news agencies. The Gospel, which means good news has been infiltrated by religion, where in order for someone to be saved, they have to dress and behave like that religion wants them to. If we read the New Testament without the understanding of the Gospel, we can have a works-driven religion or a license-to-sin-driven religion. When we are born again, we don't want to sin, and when we do sin, the Spirit in us will grieve us. Believers are not natural beings; we have Christ living in us. Faith in Jesus saves us but also gives us a longing to do what Christ would want us to do. There is a serious judgment for not preaching the Gospel; Paul said that if someone preaches another Gospel, let them be accursed.[81] The Gospel is good news for sinners and an offense to the religious. Jesus loved sinners, which fueled the religious' hatred of Him to the point that they wanted Him dead. Religion included all types of rules that only led to greater condemnation. The Gospel is not a powerless message that leaves us in our sin but it is the power to not only save us by faith but make us hunger for righteousness because Christ lives within us. It is God who works in us. We were born naturally but our second birth is spiritual. The religious buck this message because they lose their grip on their followers. Religion elevates its leaders and preachers above Christ. They live, look, and behave nothing like Christ. Religion sets up mini monarchies and places on their followers any burden they can to manipulate them in the name of god for their own gain. They take the New Testament scriptures and use them out of the context of the Gospel, to reintroduce the Old Testament with the New Testament verbiage.

---

[81] *"But though we, or an angel from heaven, preach any other gospel unto you than that which we have preached unto you, let him be accursed." (Galatians 1:8, KJV)*

336

"All scripture is given by inspiration of God, and is profitable for doctrine, for reproof, for correction, for instruction in righteousness: That the man of God may be perfect, thoroughly furnished unto all good works" (2 Timothy 3:16–17, KJV)

This is the purpose behind having the Bible. In a generation where absolute truths are resisted, conviction is deemed as condemnation, and discernment is seen as judgmental. We are all searching for encouragement, comfort, and unity but Jesus came to teach truth which works as salt to our sin. We are so light on the doctrine from our major pulpits, that anyone could sit through today's church and not feel any type of conviction. They want to feel good and leave motivated but that's not the primary purpose of the scripture. Our flesh needs boundaries and absolute truths; there can't be any gray area for our flesh because we are bent on darkness more than light. Our nature, without conscience or conviction is worse than the most depraved animal. Jesus must make us new before we can have the power to follow through on what God has called us to do. Scripture reminds us of the supremacy of Christ, it reproves us for not trusting Him, it corrects us when we are not depending on Him, and it instructs us in what genuine faith produces in a believer. Without scripture, we would not know God. The lack of scripture that is taught in our pulpits is raising a generation that does not have discernment. Discernment is not judgment, bigotry, or rebellion. Discernment offers healthy accountability when it is welcomed. Crowds and big budgets do not determine a blessed ministry.

Corporate America has defined blessing and success for the church but its measures contradict scripture. The emphasis on the community is unhealthy when it's just for the community's sake. Community must not be the focus, Jesus must be. When Jesus and His Word are the foundation of a believer's life, then community will happen. The glory of God is what separates the church from politics, capitalism, and communism. The glory of man is what our society wants and this is why we need scripture to renew our minds. Remembering the death of Christ is an ordinance that Jesus gave. He taught us that the Spirit will lead us to scripture. The Spirit of God will not contradict what He gave to us in the canon of scripture. We are mere sinful flesh that desperately need scripture for freedom.

Note

337

*"Humble yourselves therefore under the mighty hand of
God, that he may exalt you in due time: Casting all your care
upon him; for he careth for you" (1 Peter 5:6–7, KJV)*

We come into the world on our own, and we leave on our own.
The type of relationship that God wants to have with us is personal. A personal relationship with God can't be overstated. We read
through the Gospels of just how personal Jesus wants to be with us.
The Gospels have more stories of Jesus being one on one than Him
being one on a crowd. Cultivating a relationship with Jesus means
that we get alone with God, making sure that no one knows about
it, so it's genuinely about God and us. Religion boasts about corporate prayers, corporate evangelisms, corporate worship but Jesus
cultivates the anointing in the secret place. When we live to glorify
God, our relationship with Him will not be based on the opinions of
other people. The sooner we are held accountable by our relationship
with God more than others, the stronger believers we will be. No one
can understand us as good as God. No one loves us more than God.
When God becomes everything to us, we become unmoved by the
opinions of others. If we base our esteem on others, we will never be
good enough. We will never be enough for anyone but God. Christ
made it possible for God to be totally at peace with us. When we
trust Christ, we can know that we are in total peace with God. The
more confident we are with Him, the easier it will be to pass into
eternity. Don't hold on to anyone or anything more than God or be
prepared to be disappointed. People disappoint, but God never does.

Eternity will be worth every hardship and affliction we face for His glory. Don't grow weary in His will. Stay committed to His will even though naturally it's the hardest on our flesh and strength, it will be worth it in the end. Deny ourselves because we don't know what is best for us. We think we do, but in the end, only God's way works out. The tempter is doing all that he can to convince us otherwise, but that's why we read scripture. Scripture teaches us that history always repeats itself. The more we know it, the less agitated we will be through our difficulties. Whatever season you are in, study the Wore of God. To be forewarned is to be forearmed. Scripture is relevant to get us through the darkest of nights; God turns it all for good, look at history. God is with us. We are not alone.

Note

338

"And this is life eternal, that they might know thee the only true God, and Jesus Christ, whom thou hast sent" (John 17:3, KJV)

Have you ever wanted to fit in? Do you always feel like an outsider? Do you watch others in a community, wishing you had the same affection? Thanksgiving and Christmas for many is a reminder of how alone they really are. We live in a cold world. Most wake up every day with this weight on them. We assume that those who have a family or community don't think this way, but in reality, they do. This inner longing for recognition and love is found only in Jesus. Even the best of families, friendships and communities don't know you like He does. When we let Jesus in and build our confidence in His Word, everyone may come and go, but our souls are tied to Jesus. A relationship with Him is what carries us through all of life's changes as He stays the same. No matter how much of an outsider you are, you can be an insider with Jesus. He recognizes you as everyone else walks on past you. We are all searching for recognition; whether in our family, friendships, or jobs but no one compares to how Jesus celebrates when we repent before Him. He gives us all the recognition we are looking for. When we repent, we are lifting God and His word over people and their words. We were made to know God. He sees us. He knows us. Don't replace Him with church, family or friendships. If we are going to finish the race, this is an important truth. It's not how we start but how we finish, that matters. There are many misrepresenting Him; most of us will misrepresent Him because we are human. Our relationship with God can't be attached to a fickle person. We are called to know Him for ourselves. If we don't, we will get hurt deeply by those who even preach in His name. If we know Jesus and His Word for ourselves, there is no one that can convince us to depart from the faith. People fail each other but God is faithful to the end. It's time to know Jesus for ourselves. This is not rebellion; this is what Christ accomplished. There are no mediators between us and God. Overcoming the opinions of others is tough when it comes to knowing God. Our low self-esteem, loneliness, poverty, and pain all contribute to the lie that "we need a mediator because why would God want us to be an insider?" The cross silenced our foes and their lies. Jesus made the way for "whosoever will" to be children of God.

Note

339

"And it came to pass, when I heard these words, that I sat down and wept, and mourned certain days, and fasted, and prayed before the God of heaven" (Nehemiah 1:4, KJV)

Whose word do you believe the most? This world is broken. We see the evidence on the news every day. Rather than doing something to fix it, we watch it until the brokenness comes to our home. We are passive until the brokenness affects us. Those who could do something about it, sit around, living for themselves. Their selfish selves will be surprised one day, when they see how bad it gets on our streets. The church has pulled back behind the walls for years now. The youth are disengaged from worship and prayer. They are tired of the entertainment. Our generation is tuned out because they see past the preachers who talk well but live no different. We need an awakening before it's too late. Christians who are just waiting to get out of here, may be surprised by where they end up. Jesus is not only an eternal assurance but He affects our lives while we are here. Jesus would not be hiding out behind church walls. He would be with the ones that most church people would detest to sit next to on a Sunday. The lie that society has believed is that the brokenness is too big for us to impact. Rather than doing something about it, we are doing nothing because we have believed the lie as well. The Gospel ushers in a nationwide awakening. Billy Graham's generation could testify that the Gospel has power to change the course of history. How quickly we have forgotten. We need an awakening in this generation. The brokenness is not too much for God. If we would take the Gospel serious, we have no idea what it's potential could be. We need to remember what the Gospel has done and will do if we believe. Belief is not only a mental ascent but when our belief is in Christ, we will be empowered to obey. Belief leads to obedience. If it does not, then we don't believe. This is why evangelism is so essential. It's not a light thing to say that we believe yet have no passion for the lost on a daily basis. If we are not bothered that sinners around us are going to hell, how can we be confident that Christ lives in us? It's time to ask the real questions. It's time to examine whether we are in the faith. Don't be bewitched by those that just preach to your checkbook. If we begin in the Spirit, we are not kept by our flesh. We can't do this without God working in us.

Note

340

*"Who also hath made us able ministers of the new testament;
not of the letter, but of the spirit: for the letter killeth,
but the spirit giveth life" (2 Corinthians 3:6, KJV)*

The Gospel is not an intellectual argument that wins souls by clever speech. Arguing and debating does not lead to converts. The Holy Spirit uses the Gospel that's preached, to convict us of sin which leads to conversion as we repent. Teachers and apologists have flooded our church world. They are feeding the intellectual obesity of the church. Religion today is like a gym with no weights or treadmills but obese coaches that feed their congregants junk. If a gym operated as the church, no one would go. No one would pay for a gym membership and a coach and not lose weight or be challenged to break sweat. Our system has been infiltrated by carnal strategies that are only working to keep the sheep in the pen but are not raising them up to become shepherds in their homes, schools or places of employment. Who is willing to initiate a reformation in the church? Who is willing to get the church mobilized to do the work of an evangelist? Do we want to be challenged or comforted? God wants us to grow; stagnancy pollutes our spirituality. Grow in God and follow His leading. Never settle spiritually; there will always be someone that needs Jesus while we are here. Evangelism can never be graduated from while we are here on Earth. Every day, we are walking past hundreds of souls that are going to hell. When we put others ahead of ourselves, it gives us a better perspective on what we are going through. Help, love, and care for sinners because we receive the same grace every day. God gave so that we can give. If we have nothing to give or those around us don't need anything, then give them Jesus. We are God's ambassadors. The Gospel is power as we walk in obedience to His leading. We don't need to argue to persuade; God will draw sinners to Himself through us. Salvation is wrought by the conviction of the Spirit when the Gospel is shared by someone surrendered to Christ. Remember, the Gospel is power, supernatural power. Few people throughout history tapped into this revelation and walked in the full power of the Gospel. It's available for us all. God has no favorites but made it possible for anyone to walk in this power if we draw near to Him and follow Him. Let's believe, against all odds. We don't need a PHD to evangelize. We all have a testimony. Go!

Note

341

"Wherefore, my beloved brethren, let every man be swift to hear, slow to speak, slow to wrath" (James 1:19, KJV)

Listen more than talk. Evangelism makes us better listeners. Jesus never preached without knowing His audience. Jesus took time to hear the needs of those that He knew He was to minister to. Sharing the Gospel like a robot, won't work. We are people who are called to reach other people. How would you want to be reached? Reach people with the same dignity, without compromising the message. People won't care what we have to say until they know that we care about them. Don't talk about church, talk about Jesus. We are not trying to fill the church with people; we are trying to fill people with Jesus. All we can do is try; God must do the rest. The problem is that few are willing to try. The great thing about evangelism is that the results are not up to us. As we do the best that we can, to share Jesus, the Holy Spirit will do the rest. Many give up because they see no results. Believers are not result driven; we are Christ driven. No one can separate faith from obedience. Faith leads to obedience if the faith is in Christ. Spiritual results and spiritual performances are up to the Holy Spirit, as long as we are doing what we are called to unto the Lord. Sinners work harder for a paycheck than some believers do unto the Lord because people love money more than Christ. That's why we need to surrender our flesh to Christ. This life that we are called to live, can't be done by our flesh. Our flesh does not want to honor Christ or to preach Christ. We know that we are obeying Jesus when our flesh is uncomfortable. Obedience is not supposed to be easy; it's supposed to be impossible so that we only glorify in Christ, as we obey. The church has tried to replace Christ but all that the church can do is set up LED lights, a rock band, cheap entertainment, and backbiting community groups. This is why we need to preach Jesus to the lost and not the church. The worst community that we could ever invite people to is a church community without Jesus. The church was never supposed to be a building; believers who obey Christ are truly the church. Very little of Christianity wants to address obedience. The great commission has become a shameful act in our upper echelon of Christianity. They have even invented a doctrine that keeps them from evangelizing, so that they sit comfortably in their elected clubs.

Note

_____

_____

_____

_____

_____

_____

_____

_____

_____

342

"And I, if I be lifted up from the earth, will draw
all men unto me" (John 12:32, KJV)

Evangelism honors Jesus above the church. Inviting people to church is not evangelism. Giving out invite cards for a church is not the great commission. Sinners are not drawn to church because in the West, most of them discern the church as a cult that wants control, money, and service. Most sinners would choose a bartender over a pastor to talk to; a bar over a church service to go to. Inviting people to church only works for those who don't like the church they're at, so they might try out another one. Jesus builds the church better than any church growth strategy. Church growth consultants should be ashamed of themselves if they are talking about anything other than the great commission to grow a church. The evangelist is the church growth consultant and not the skinny jean millennial that could not quote John 3:16 to you if you asked. We need to equip the church to invite people to Jesus. When someone comes to Christ, the Holy Spirit will make them committed to church fellowship. They won't be going because of the music or its compromised message, they will be going to assemble joyfully because Christ is in them and gave them the desire to be there. They are not consumers. They are givers. They are not choosing church based off of the music, kids' ministry, or youth group; they are following Jesus to church to worship Jesus. We need to be lifting Jesus up and not the church. Any church that is lifting themselves up above Jesus has already been bewitched and is tinkering with being a cult. Cults make their congregations appreciate their leaders more than Christ. They love to appreciate themselves more than appreciate their congregations. When is church appreciation day on the calendar? No one should demand a title, yet call Jesus by His first name. Church is not about the fallen man behind the pulpit. Preachers need Jesus just as much as their audience. Don't be surprised when you see the humanity of preachers. Jesus won't share His glory with another. Invite people to Jesus. Only someone who believes in Jesus will make it in the church. If they don't, they will be hurt. Church hurt is worse than any other. Many have fallen prey to it and rather than them just leaving the cult, they left Jesus too. Cult leaders, choose your millstone.

Note

343

*"Whose voice then shook the earth: but now he hath promised,
saying, Yet once more I shake not the earth only, but also heaven.
And this word, Yet once more, signifieth the removing of those
things that are shaken, as of things that are made, that those things
which cannot be shaken may remain" (Hebrews 12:26–27, KJV)*

When everything gets shaken that can be shaken, we are left with what remains. Christ is all that we have as a firm foundation. All other foundations are sinking sand. What are we building our joy on? The things of this world can be so distracting from what matters most. When things get stripped away from us, what we thought was a curse is really a blessing. "Things" change people for the worst when "things" are trusted in more than Christ. A soul, captive to Christ is the greatest freedom that any human could have. Freedom, defined by the world is a life without boundaries and perimeters but that's not biblical freedom, that's chaos. Jesus came to set us free from the rulership of Satan, and to be under the rulership of Jesus. We can only serve one of two masters. Satan's freedom looks free to our flesh but has serious consequences here and in the afterlife. Build joy on Jesus. When Jesus is our foundation, the shakings of life won't shake our faith but solidify our faith even more. We can count hardships as blessings because they make us rely on what remains. In this season, we need to draw near to God, we need to draw near to His Word. Don't be slothful but be disciplined because it won't be this way forever. In this world, we will have trouble. If we are not prudent, we won't have oil in our lamp when we need it most. A disciple of

Christ must be open to God 24-7. Once we let our guard down, once we make peace with the world, once sin is welcomed, then we can believe that the enemy of our soul sees us as prey. Put on the armor of God, don't make peace with the world, fight sin, and never give place to the enemy. We need to get militant in our disciplines of reading scripture, prayer, and evangelism. Don't relent but rise up and fight. This life is a fight to believe to the end. We will be shaken but we can stand firm through it all, on Jesus our rock. We shall not be moved if we are grounded in the infallible Word of God; the inerrant sixty-six books of the Bible are what we feed on, to grow our faith. What we feed, grows, and what we starve, dies. Healthy habits are formed by initial discipline and routine which turns into our everyday practice. What is initially uncomfortable, turns to a harvest; faith produces a strong foundation.

Note

344

"In this the children of God are manifest, and the children of the devil: whosoever doeth not righteousness is not of God, neither he that loveth not his brother" (1 John 3:10, KJV)

Rejected, hated, misunderstood, criticized, mocked, back-bitten, maligned, accused, cast down; these are some of the emotions we receive as kids, teenagers and adults. Some get more than others because of their image, impoverishment, race, or gender. We live in a base generation that if it had no accountability, we would be worse than the animal kingdom. Sin knows no limits. If the church was removed from the earth, we would see mankind at our finest. It's the grace of God that keeps it in some measure of order. Satan is pining to bring destruction to mankind; many people welcome him into their homes this time of year. When we let these emotions build up in our souls, it opens the door to possession. We either get in-dwelt by the Holy Spirit or possessed by a demon. It's up to us to let in who we want. When life takes its toll on a person, their rage turns them into vile sinners. They begin to act on their unchecked thoughts. This is why the believer is responsible for taking their thoughts captive. We must not let these real emotions fester, no matter how much we deserve to feel them. Vengeance is the Lord's. We are called to surrender all to Christ. We are called to unclench our fists, raising our open hands to God in worship. Examine whether you are in the faith. How much of our soul are we giving over to God? Jesus wants all of it, in order for Him to have His way in us. Don't leave any of it vacant, for the enemy to get a foothold. Slam the door in his face, in

Jesus's name. We can rise above these emotions by casting them on Christ, who replaces them with His peace, joy, and confidence. We won't get this revelation until we let it all go, which is the evidence of trust in God. Every day of our lives, until we pass or Jesus returns, we must decide to trust God over our emotions. Bitterness eats at our soul; it wrinkles our face and takes years away from us. Give it over to God. Don't worry about the opinions of others, worry about not walking transparently before God. The worst that a human can do is take our lives but God not only can do that but also has authority to throw us into hell.[82] Jesus must be taken seriously. He experienced every emotion that we have. We are reconciled to walk in a real relationship with God. Let Jesus know you.

Note

---

[82] *"But I will forewarn you whom ye shall fear: Fear him, which after he hath killed hath power to cast into hell; yea, I say unto you, Fear him." (Luke 12:5, KJV)*

345

"How God anointed Jesus of Nazareth with the Holy Ghost and with power: who went about doing good, and healing all that were oppressed of the devil; for God was with him" (Acts 10:38, KJV)

W hat do you do when you don't know what to do? Do the right thing. How do we know it's the right thing? Check scripture, and if it's not contradictory to the righteousness of God, then go ahead with it. God gives us options in life; as long as we want His will, we can't make the wrong choice. Few get very clear directional words for their lives. We must keep making the right decision, and watch God steer as we initiate the momentum. If you say for days on end that Jesus is Lord, you can be confident that you are where God wants you to be. If you are not, as you remain under the Lordship of Jesus for our decision making, He will get us back on track whether by using a fish, storm, or famine; He is big enough to get us on track. God is not the author of indecision or confusion. Religion is full of confusion, politics, and manipulation. If an earthly father would want to make his will clear to his kids, to keep them out of trouble, how much more does our holy God want to be like that for you? There was only one time in scripture that He spoke through a still small voice,[83] but for the most part, He made His will crystal clear. God wants us to walk in the light before Him. With God, there is no gray. He is all in with us. He did His best to walk with us. The believer is the clearest-minded,

---

[83.] *"And after the earthquake a fire; but the Lord was not in the fire: and after the fire a still small voice." (1 Kings 19:12, KJV)*

concrete-minded, and confident-minded that a human can be. The believer has the answer to our origin, purpose, and destiny. No one else has what we have in Christ. If we don't, we must detox from the religious spirit. Where religion is, there is confusion, but where Christ is, there is clarity. Many believers who have grown up in Christendom need to renew their minds with scripture. When we are quoting scripture more than our preacher, we are prepared to take on the religious spirit. Let God lead by making the right decisions after opening ourselves to His will. As we remain open to His will, we can be confident that we are in His will. Be strong and courageous; again, He says, *"Be strong and courageous.*[84]*"* Strength and courage are the emotions of a believer as we open ourselves to the glory of Christ. Fear won't rule us. Faith in Christ rules our emotions. Ejecting out of His will is rebellion; resisting His conviction will make us blaspheme the Holy Spirit. Do the right thing.

Note

---

[84] Deuteronomy 31:6, Joshua 1:9

346

"And thine ears shall hear a word behind thee, saying, This is the way, walk ye in it, when ye turn to the right hand, and when ye turn to the left" (Isaiah 30:21, KJV)

This is the way, walk in it. Jesus came to make the way for us. He is the way. We are prone to be more fulfilled by serving Him than spending time with Him. We are not servants of Him more than we are sons of Him.[85] There is no title that can compare with being His son. Insecure men want titles for their self-esteem, cheapening the esteem of Christ placed on all of us at the Cross. Christ esteems us higher than any self-esteem we could work up on our own. God put a ghastly price tag on our soul that He was willing to pay for. God set the price. Jesus's sacrifice was sufficient to take our sin away and redeem our soul. We all want to know our purpose but it won't be revealed when we are purpose driven. Our purpose is to glorify God. How can we glorify God in this life? What decision could we make that would glorify God more than anything else? What drives us to be healthier or better than anything else is Christ. Honor Christ, in all things glory in Christ. Living for the glory of God is truly an abundant life. There is no life that compares to a man who has totally given over to glorify God. If we are driven by any other motive or purpose, we will be disappointed. The world disappoints, religion disappoints, health disappoints, wealth disappoints; glorifying God will never dis-

---

85. *"Wherefore thou art no more a servant, but a son; and if a son, then an heir of God through Christ." (Galatians 4:7, KJV)*

appoint. A believer that says "Come what may, still will I glory in my Christ" is a major threat to evil. What can the hoard of hell throw at us, when we are abandoned fully to the will and glory of God. Worship God not for the results, worship God for no other reason than He sent His Begotten Son to pay our debt of sin. We have been redeemed eternally. This life will be hard; there will be persecution and possible martyrdom but the Lamb's Blood was not spilt in vain. Disciple with the potential of the believer to be martyred. Discipling a believer to be successful and a billionaire while they are here is not how Jesus discipled. Teach what Jesus taught. Prepare the believer for life here and not heaven. We won't have heaven here until Christ comes back; prepare the church for battle. A spiritual battle is about to come on the earth and even the elect will depart because of the deception. Scripture is our source for discernment. Come out from amongst the epicurean philosophies that have fed into our culture!

Note

347

*"Wherefore God also gave them up to uncleanness through
the lusts of their own hearts, to dishonour their own
bodies between themselves" (Romans 1:24, KJV)*

God will turn us over to our lust with time. "Don't give us what
we want!" We don't want what we want. What we want will always
fall way short of what God wants for our lives. It never worked out
for anyone who took matters into their own hands. We will regret
our will more than His will, no matter how glamorous our will may
be versus His will. The will of God may not look glamorous to the
naked eye. Our will may turn the rocks into bread but if it's not His
will, then we will miss out on the bread of life. We settle for bread
here, but we need the bread of heaven. His presence must be sought
after more than the presents of our pleasure. We were created for His
pleasure. Our pleasure never pleases like living for the pleasure and
glory of God. Pleasing Him, more than pleasing ourselves will always
leave us more pleased than anything that we think could please us.
Break away from self so that we can live for the glory of Christ more
than the glory of self. Joy and peace are found in Him. Whether we
are in the belly of a fish, slave camp, furnace, or prison, there is no
circumstance that adds to our peace more than being where God has
us. It won't be this way forever. Forever is not worth the temporary
counterfeit peace. His presence will fill anyone whose heart is open
continually to glorify God. May God be praised in all circumstances.
Don't be disappointed; tell your emotions to praise God in faith.
Praise God in the rain of life and watch Him wash the shackles off

your mind away. Don't be led by the naked eye; let the eye of your soul be on Jesus. He stabilizes our outlook; He puts joy in reach in all our circumstances. Let the well spring of Christ in us flow out of us, which will affect our world. This type of believer will be a testimony wherever life takes them. God is raising up biblical believers who are not influenced by the culture but are built on scripture. The teachings of Jesus will sustain us as we are yielded to the Holy Spirit. The Apostles did not have the indwelling, so when Christ was taken away, they could not withstand the hardship. We can stand strong in hardship because we have the Holy Spirit. After the Pentecost in Acts 2, the Apostles became empowered men. They were bold, strong, decisive, and confident. This way of living is available to this very day. Believers today have the same spirit as the apostles had in the early church.

Note

348

"Now all these things happened unto them for examples: and
they are written for our admonition, upon whom the ends
of the world are come" (1 Corinthians 10:11, KJV)

We learn best the hard way, more than we do by history. History always repeats itself. Ignorance of history makes us fall into the same trappings as those that have gone before us. The scripture sheds light on the pitfalls of those in the past. Scripture is unashamed of teaching us the sins and failures of the men whom God used because we are all broken in our own way. Scripture does not enable sin but teaches us how to respond when we do. There is no one who loves God yet wants to sin. There is no one who truly loves Jesus yet takes pleasure in sin. The Holy Spirit leads us by scripture and also convicts us when we fail. Asking the Holy Spirit to never take the grief of sin from us will keep us to the end. It's when we sin without grief or conviction, that we end up like Ananias and Saphira. The gnostic teachings of today are breeding "Ananias and Saphira's." What they call Calvinism and New Covenant teaching is really a strand of Gnosticism. It allows them to live without conviction or a sense of grief over sin. They lie, cheat, malign, and gossip without any conviction. This gluttonous Gnosticism teaches mental ascent; it's a form of godliness but has no power. They love their pulpits more than the people that they preach to. They want to conform to the image of "crowd following preachers" more than the image of Christ. They quote men more than scripture. Their financial books and receipts would shock most congregants. Their followers are told that accountability is rebellion, and discernment is judgmental. "Ananias and Saphira" are the "apostles of today." We don't have a major voice to clean out these "apostates." Their Gnostic teaching never teaches on repentance, hell, or disciplines. They cherry-pick scripture but hardly ever preach the teachings of Jesus. They live so much different than the way Jesus lived. They think that they are protestant but they mirror in leadership the papal apostates in Rome. Like the Galatian Church, some began in the Spirit but ended up in the flesh.[86] Their gnostic teaching is not new; it's why we have the Pauline and general epistles to deal with them. A great deception is imminent. The biblical literacy rate amongst believers is so low, that some are bewitched by every passionate, money grabbing speaker they hear.

Note

[86.] Galatians 3

349

*"Simon Peter saith unto them, I go a fishing. They say unto him,
We also go with thee. They went forth, and entered into a ship
immediately; and that night they caught nothing" (John 21:3, KJV)*

What did the disciples accomplish after three years of discipleship by Christ? After three years of discipleship, they could not even pray an hour! Our discipleship must not make disciples who are dependent on discipleship. Organizations can make great disciples but as soon as their disciples graduate or are on their own, most go back to their old ways, and some even seven times worse than before. Discipleship today has become a Christian version of the Mosaic law yet even more condemning because it's not about actions but attitudes. The heart of flesh can't do what the heart of Christ can do. Christ was getting His disciples ready for Pentecost. He knew that without Him, they could do nothing. He went to the cross to make repentant sinners clean, so that the Holy Spirit could indwell us to do what we could not do via structure, organization or religion. The church is not an organization, it's an organism. Christ in us, working through us is the life of a believer. The longer we are dependent on anything to keep us more than the Holy Spirit, we have been bewitched. No organization can keep us to the end but the organism of the Holy Spirit keeps us to the end. We can have the knowledge but without knowing Jesus, we won't make it. A life that is dependent on the Holy Spirit makes us do what we never could on our own. It's amazing what religion can do without God. Discipleship is not just to scratch our intellectual itch, it's to get us to depend on Christ for life. Any work that is done without God will be judged as iniquity. Sin is independence of God. Religion breeds this type of sin. For three years, Jesus was teaching His disciples this but they did not get it until they received the Holy Spirit. We have many who have the baptism of John but have yet to know the baptism of Jesus, which is not of water only but fire too. Many Christians will hear the rooster crow at some point of their lives. They will realize that they were bewitched and are bewitching others. They attempted to organize the organism but that cannot be done. A seed won't grow in a machine. It grows in soil. God does not need our bricks and mortar. Except the lord build the house the laborers labor in vain.[87] As the temples of the Holy Spirit, we can't glorify Christ by our own might or strength.

Note

---

[87] *"Except the Lord build the house, they labour in vain that build it: except the Lord keep the city, the watchman waketh but in vain." (Psalm 127:1, KJV)*

350

"And for this cause God shall send them strong delusion, that they should believe a lie: That they all might be damned who believed not the truth, but had pleasure in unrighteousness. But we are bound to give thanks alway to God for you, brethren beloved of the Lord, because God hath from the beginning chosen you to salvation through sanctification of the Spirit and belief of the truth: Whereunto he called you by our gospel, to the obtaining of the glory of our Lord Jesus Christ. Therefore, brethren, stand fast, and hold the traditions which ye have been taught, whether by word, or our epistle. Now our Lord Jesus Christ himself, and God, even our Father, which hath loved us, and hath given us everlasting consolation and good hope through grace, Comfort your hearts, and stablish you in every good word and work" (2 Thessalonians 2:11–17, KJV)

Discipleship is not a means to scratch the intellectual itch. Discipleship that is educational only is not how Christ discipled. Does it matter to us that scripture is not as much read as sermons are heard today? Does it bother us that the great deception is on the brink of happening? It's up to us to contend for the truth not to be "judgmental" but to be discerning. Our society believes that unity happens when we remove moral absolutes but what really happens is chaos. Believers feel the same way about unity. Some want to remove all doctrinal absolutes for the sake of unity. That unity is perversion. The Jesus that they worship is not the biblical Christ. We can't know Christ without scripture. The Bible is our manual for salvation. Without scripture, we have no instruction. Our generation is destroyed for the lack of knowledge. There is no unity without doctrinal absolutes. Christ without doctrine is not Christ. The Holy Spirit without scripture is not the Spirit. Jesus told us that the Spirit will lead us to truth, which is the sixty-six books of the Bible. The sovereign hand of God gave us the complete Word of God, which is inerrant in every way. A church that does not teach scripture is like a restaurant that does not serve food. The purpose of our fellowship is to build one another up in the faith; faith comes by hearing the Word of God. A church which is built on any other foundation is built on a shallow foundation. Our worship of Christ can't be done by spirit only but it needs to be done by truth too. Worshiping in Spirit only will give way to emotionalism, which ends in perversion. Worshipping in truth only leads to religion, which has a form of godliness but no power. We must be known to have sound doctrine. Our sound must be tuned like we would a stringed instrument. If the tension on the strings is too tight or too loose, it won't sound right. We need the right tension to have the right sound. God tunes us with scripture and the Spirit so that we have sound doctrine. Our interpretation will never be infallible compared to scripture; we are called to study, to show ourselves approved. When we are open to scripture and the Spirit, we will be tuned to preach the sound doctrine rightly dividing scripture.[88] We have many people who are either too loose or too tight. Pray to have the right tension.

[88.] *"Study to shew thyself approved unto God, a workman that needeth not to be ashamed, rightly dividing the word of truth." (2 Timothy 2:15, KJV)*

351

"Holding fast the faithful word as he hath been taught,
that he may be able by sound doctrine both to exhort
and to convince the gainsayers" (Titus 1:9, KJV)

If a stringed instrument does not have the right tension on the strings, it won't sound right. We need the right sound in our doctrine when our doctrine is too tight or too loose means that we won't have the right tension on our message, for it to have sound doctrine. We have churches and denominations that are either too tight or too loose. We need to pray for the right tension so that when we preach, it's sound doctrine. Relationship with Jesus tunes our scriptural and spiritual sound to be just the right tone. It won't be infallible because we are still mere flesh. God won't let anyone preach inerrant truth; all we preach is the interpretation, the scripture is the final authoritative Word of God. There is no one that has a Word outside of the written Word. No matter how passionate, articulate, or clever a preacher is, there is no other inspired Word outside of the sixty-six books of the Bible. Even the best sermon has got nothing on scripture. The most anointed sermon will have the audience quoting the scripture more than the preacher. The best sermon is the one that elevates scripture more than their commentary. We need to get people onto scripture as quickly as possible because His Word is all that won't return void. Unfortunately, our generation has elevated authors, commentaries, sermons, and teachers above scripture. This is why we have so much deception accepted today. We have no excuse for deception because everyone has access to scripture, yet even with the ease of access it's neglected. If only we knew what it took to get the scripture into our language and into our hands. How can anyone still claim to be Roman Catholic after all that we know from scripture and history? This shows how ignorant we have become. Western Believers have been bewitched to think that Roman Catholics are saved based on their doctrine. No one can be saved based on the Roman Catholic doctrine. The statements of faith are posted on our websites, but when are they taught? Soon, churches won't even have a statement of faith. This deception will replace the scripture with music that they call worship and with teachings that are not based on scripture but instead are based on psychology and "Ted Talk" style sermons. There is no generation that will be held as accountable for having the Bible and not read reading it, as ours.

Note

352

"For the life of the flesh is in the blood: and I have given it to you upon the altar to make an atonement for your souls: for it is the blood that maketh an atonement for the soul" (Leviticus 17:11, KJV)

The Law of Moses provided atonement for sin by blood sacrifice. Once a year, the High Priest of Israel would enter through the veil, to the holy of holy's with blood from a lamb. The blood signified that the wage of Israel's sin was death but the lamb took the punishment, so Israel was atoned. What was the difference between the blood of a lamb and the blood of the Lamb? Christ's blood was shed once and for all. We don't sacrifice Jesus at communion; we remember what He accomplished by His death. The primary difference is that believers in the Lamb of God are born-again after they believe in Christ. This means that we get a new heart, the indwelling of the Holy Spirit, and all things become new.[89] This is what Jesus accomplished on the cross. The temple in Israel is in ruins to this day because believers in Christ have replaced the temple. The veil was torn so the Holy Spirit could live in us; not because we are holy, but because Christ makes whosoever believes, Holy. We are holy as He is holy because of the Lamb of God that was sacrificed on the altar of the cross. Our bodies are the altars, where every day we can choose to lay our lives down as living sacrifices so the Holy Spirit has His way in us. We have a choice as believers, to walk in the flesh or to walk in the Spirit. Walk

---

[89] *"A new heart also will I give you, and a new spirit will I put within you: and I will take away the stony heart out of your flesh, and I will give you an heart of flesh."* (Ezekiel 36:26, KJV)

according to our own understanding or lean not on our own understanding and lean on the Holy Spirit instead. If we remove the Holy Spirit from the church and from believers, then we are left with a book and a religion. The letter without the Spirit is dead. Rejecting the Holy Spirit and quenching the Holy Spirit[90] leads to the blasphemy of the Holy Spirit, which Christ said was unforgivable.[91] We can discern the spirits by the title of the Spirit of God. He is Holy. We can trust that we are walking in the Spirit when we hunger and thirst for righteousness. When we sin without conviction or grief, we need to examine whether we are in the faith. When scripture is not our source for truth, we need to examine who is leading our lives. The Spirit of God will always lead us to the truth. We need to fan into flame, the gift that is within us, and allow Him to have His way because He does a much better job at glorifying Christ than we ever could.

---

90. *"Quench not the Spirit." (1 Thessalonians 5:19, KJV)*
91. *"Verily I say unto you, All sins shall be forgiven unto the sons of men, and blasphemies wherewith soever they shall blaspheme: But he that shall blaspheme against the Holy Ghost hath never forgiveness, but is in danger of eternal damnation. Because they said, He hath an unclean spirit." Mark 3:28–30, KJV)*

353

*"For my thoughts are not your thoughts, neither are your
ways my ways, saith the Lord. For as the heavens are higher
than the earth, so are my ways higher than your ways, and
my thoughts than your thoughts" (Isaiah 55:8–9, KJV)*

As we study scripture, we realize how other God is of us. God is Holy and we are not. Our conscience must not be the gauge for our righteousness. It will deceive us. The law sheds light on right and wrong. If we were to remove the law, then there would be chaos. Removing moral absolutes does not create unity. We have many people who are confused because we want a lawless lifestyle. We want to live in the gray. While the Western church has been passive, lukewarm, and enjoying the "abundant life," Satan has been aggressively destroying our communities with drugs and influencing the government to take our freedom away as believers. We have freedom of speech, yet we live confined more than the persecuted church, warming the pews and getting on with life. We may as well be a state church. Jesus does not produce a mediocre life. We are either all in or all out. We should either be ice cold or white hot. In a society now, where sin is accepted, wrong is right and there are no moral absolutes; we are unaware of how seriously dark it really is. The only way to shine is to follow His conviction and repent. We have all sinned but no one who believes in Jesus, can sin without grief. We need scripture to convict us and reinforce our conscience. Even though God is Holy and we are not, this does not give us the license to live any way that we want. We are to repent before Him when we sin and allow conviction to have its way in us. The difference between condemnation and conviction is that condemnation gives no opportunity to repent; conviction not only gives us the opportunity to repent but it also gives us the power to turn away from what we are being convicted of. Until we pass or until Christ returns, we should pray to feel the conviction of the Spirit when we sin. Knowing that we are going to sin as believers is not an excuse to sin but it reminds us that there is no condemnation in Christ. Jesus, in revelation, told the church in Ephesus to repent. His Words ring true today as well. We are to let His Word convict us, which always provokes us to depend on Christ. We will not graduate from a dependent state before Christ. This is why we need scripture daily to remind us how desperately dependent we are on Him. When we quote sermons and preachers more than His Word, we are open prey to deception. Study scripture.

Note

_____

_____

_____

_____

_____

_____

_____

_____

_____

354

"That they should seek the Lord, if haply they might feel after him, and find him, though he be not far from every one of us" (Acts 17:27, KJV)

Do you see what I see? None of us see the exact same. We all have our own take on what we see. This is why the four gospels are the way they are. All three apostles wrote what they saw and John Mark wrote what Peter told him. Even though it's the inspired word of God, we see their personalities coming out of the text. There is no denying our personalities as believers. We are not called to be robots or clones. We are set free to be who we are. We are what we are, by the grace of God. Our unique DNA and personality must never be quashed. Religion makes clones; Jesus made us be who we originally were. We were made in His image, with a voice and a will. Jesus gives us life and assures us that it's eternal. There will be no serpent in heaven to deceive us. Once we are in heaven, we will always be in heaven. Salvation does not take work because Christ did the work for us, but a relationship with God does take work. We have not been saved from good works but in fact, we have been saved unto good works. We have been saved unto the obedience to Christ. Christianity without obedience is Gnosticism and is a deviation from the truth. We have so many deviating spirits today, trying to get us preaching on anything but what matters most: Christ and Him crucified. Unessential truths for salvation have been given way too much importance. The body of Christ is divided mostly by unessential truths for salvation. Satan has severed the body of Christ successfully by getting believers bitter over the music style, color schemes, instruments, dress codes, etc. Salvation is not based on any of these trivial preferences. Our community knows our division and rarely sees us together under the banner of Christ. They don't know us by our love for one another, they see that we are full of strife just as they are, what do we have that's different than them? They don't see our love for one another. They see our signs competing on the highway, they hear the gossip about one another in the work place, yet we all worship the same Jesus and have the same statement of faith up on our website. The body of Christ could fulfill the great commission by coming together to lift Jesus up above the church. We do outreaches, to grow our church but not glorify Christ. Look to Christ.

Note

355

*"For the time will come when they will not endure sound
doctrine; but after their own lusts shall they heap to themselves
teachers, having itching ears" (2 Timothy 4:3, KJV)*

The statement of faith cannot be over taught. We are living in an age where the statement of faith is under scrutiny daily. Most could not quote their statement of faith. Many have their own set of beliefs on essential Christian truths that err from scripture. Why it's not taught more should baffle the churchgoer. We have series for life skills and purpose but what about the doctrines that make them possible? The lack of doctrine being taught from our pulpits reaches "everyone" but saves no one. Doctrine produces a healthy division between tares and wheat. Doctrine defines Jesus. Many who worship a Jesus without doctrine or call on the spirit without scripture are open prey to deception. Scripture alone defines worship; scripture alone defines the church and scripture alone defines doctrine. Without the Bible, we are worshiping our emotions. It's the Bible that keeps our emotions in a boundary, which is essential. Roads without boundaries would lead to chaos. We are not to check our brains at the door of the church. Church and doctrine make us more sensible than anyone without it. We don't lose "sense" as believers; we gain sound-mindedness and self-control. Naturally, we can't, but supernaturally, we can. We have all seen the fruit of our flesh and emotions. This is why we need the fruit of the Spirit. To grow the fruit of the spirit in us, we need to go to the root. What is nourishing our root? Where is our root planted? Sound doctrine is what nourishes faith, which makes us more dependent on the Holy Spirit. We are called to root ourselves in the truth of scripture. Whatever we feed, grows, and whatever we starve, dies. Whatever we sow, we will reap. False teachers today call spiritual disciplines legalistic. They resist boundaries and want liberty that does not convict of holiness. This is a gluttonous spirit and not the Holy Spirit. We all sin, we all will sin until we get the glorified bodies, we have sin at work in us. This is why we need scripture to convict us of sin. The Holy Spirit uses scripture to guide us and keep us within His boundary of liberty. This sounds like a paradox to have liberty and boundary coexisting. The liberty of the Spirit is not lawless but liberates us to follow Christ.

Note

356

"Likewise reckon ye also yourselves to be dead indeed unto sin, but alive unto God through Jesus Christ our Lord" (Romans 6:11, KJV)

Give up and depend on God. Giving up is the art of maturing as believers. The sooner we give up and let God give in, the faster we get to where He wants us. We hold on so tightly; what we could have learned ten years ago, we could learn today if we let go. A believer must give up on letting the opinions of others or themselves define them; we are to give into scripture. What God says matters more than what others say. Where He leads, He provides. When we let go of our strife and give in to the Spirit, then we tap into the supernatural life. On our best day, we are riddled with anxiety because we try to figure life out, but we won't be able to do that without God. We are born with eternity in our hearts, but our generation has tried to educate eternity out of our society. Everyone in the moments before death wonder, "what if I'm wrong?" We can be so stubborn over very destructive issues in our lives. We can be like dogs that return to our vomit over and over when we have a perfect fillet ready to be eaten. Surrendering to God is only sacrifice for our flesh, but it's prosperity to our soul. Jesus never asks us to "give up" to give us something worse in return. God's way always works out in the end for the better. Heaven for eternity is better than any measly counterfeit heaven here. Satan offers us counterfeit heaven here. He can turn the rocks to bread, he can give us fame and fortune, but it costs us our soul. Be wary of those who offer heaven here at the cost of following Christ. Following Christ is not always prosperity and it's not always poverty, but it is always leading to a dependency on Him. Not everyone in history had to give up everything to follow Christ. Jesus did not tell everyone to do such a thing. The calling of God for the apostles was a life of financial faith. Others prospered as they followed Christ and as they did, they supported the early church leaders to do the will of God. Paul was not always a tentmaker; he did that to show the early church that he had no financial motive when he preached. Preachers who live way above the average believer should consider having all things in common with their congregations, so they flee the appearance of evil.[92] Swindlers use the Gospel to live in luxury.

Note

[92.] *"And the very God of peace sanctify you wholly; and I pray God your whole spirit and soul and body be preserved blameless unto the coming of our Lord Jesus Christ." (1 Thessalonians 5:22, KJV)*

357

*"Whosoever believeth that Jesus is the Christ is born of God: and
every one that loveth him that begat loveth him also that is begotten
of him. By this we know that we love the children of God, when
we love God, and keep his commandments. For this is the love of
God, that we keep his commandments: and his commandments
are not grievous. For whatsoever is born of God overcometh
the world: and this is the victory that overcometh the world,
even our faith. Who is he that overcometh the world, but he that
believeth that Jesus is the Son of God?" (1 John 5:1–5, KJV)*

The Gospel is not a poverty message, nor is it a prosperity message; it's a "surrender to the will of God" message. Religion makes
following their god a clone of their followers. A rich man gave Jesus a
tomb to be buried in. Barnabas gave all his wealth for the Gospel to
be spread. Jesus was not bought out by the rich but showed no partiality between rich or poor. He acknowledged that it was harder for
the rich to be saved. This did not mean that only the poor would be
saved; His call was to the poor in spirit to be saved. Jesus knew that
poverty will always be a challenge here because the root of poverty is
sin. Whether it's because of the greed of the rich or the slothfulness
of the poor, it won't be solved on this side of eternity. The Gospel is
for everyone who chooses to believe. One can be rich yet be poor in
spirit. One can be poor yet want the lotto more than Christ. No one
who gets saved should stay in poverty in the West. God blesses us
with a life that gives us a hand up out of poverty and not what religion gives, which is a handout. If they do, then they are not applying

biblical convictions for work ethic and business. The Gospel does not promise prosperity here, but it does not mean that we will be in poverty either. Being in poverty does not make us spiritual; it might mean that we are lazy and unwilling to follow God's conviction. The Gospel is about His will being done, more than our will being done. The Gospel is good news for our soul, but it's not always good news for our flesh. Jesus said that we will face hardship in this life. We will get the common cold, and it is appointed for us to die lest Christ returns.[93] We can't prolong it. Believers can eat right, work hard, and live a healthier life than any other religion or lifestyle in this world. This is why Christian-influenced nations are better than all others in every way. The Bible prospers everywhere it influences compared to the fallacies of all other religions and political "isms." The Gospel produces testimonies from addicts to model citizens. The Gospel produces the best kind of husbands and workers. The Gospel does not only influence the mind, but it changes the life too. The born-again experience is a holistic message. It transforms the whole person. Only Jesus makes a person born again. No one else can change the inside desire of a person like Christ can. We are born with a nature that loves darkness more than light. Christ regenerates like no other. Behold, all things become new!

---

[93] *"And as it is appointed unto men once to die, but after this the judgment." (Hebrews 9:27, KJV)*

358

"And there came unto me one of the seven angels which had the seven vials full of the seven last plagues, and talked with me, saying, Come hither, I will shew thee the bride, the Lamb's wife. And he carried me away in the spirit to a great and high mountain, and shewed me that great city, the holy Jerusalem, descending out of heaven from God" (Revelation 21:9–10, KJV)

Heaven is as prosperous as we will ever be. For all eternity, we will be healthy, wealthy, and socially secure. The Gospel promises prosperity for eternity. Prosperity in this life is not promised, but neither is poverty. Satan offers prosperity here and tempts us to settle for our best life now at the price of our soul. This does not mean that God won't prosper us. If it were not for wealth, we could not advance the Gospel as we have. God uses silver and gold to do His will, just as He uses the power of the Spirit to do His work on the earth. Throughout history, God prospered His people like Abraham, Joseph, David, and Daniel. When wealth became god, it was taken away, but when God was God, financial favor came their way. Jesus won't be coming back riding on a donkey. Poverty is not the fruit of a believer; it's the fruit of sin. The prodigal son did not end up in poverty because of God but because of sin. Sin is the root of poverty whether it's because of the greed of the rich or sometimes the laziness of the poor. God does not want us to be poor. We are to be no man's debtor. We give to Caesar what is Caesar's. We give to God what's His. When wealth is accumulated with the intention to advance the Gospel, then we have the right attitude on prosperity. Most start out with good intentions to gain wealth, but money changes the heart of a person. Money leads to materialism, greed, and selfishness. Few believers can manage billions as God would want them to. Billions come with spirits that make the best of us greedy, unsatisfied, and selfish. We need to be careful what we pray for. If it's not His will, yet we pine for it more than we glorify God, then He will turn us over to it. Mammon is a destructive spirit. Even the best of believers, who want prosperity more than the will of God, get turned over to their lusts. This is why Jesus talked to the rich young ruler as He did. He could see that the young man's identity was based on his wealth. Whatever defines us more than Christ, we must hold very loosely. God has a higher calling than prosperity, and that is to do His will. To obey His leading, whether that is to be rich or persecuted, we are more prosperous in His will, no matter what that looks like. There is no wealth here that is worth our soul.

Note

_____

_____

_____

_____

_____

_____

_____

_____

_____

359

"For I know that in me (that is, in my flesh,) dwelleth no good thing: for to will is present with me; but how to perform that which is good I find not" (Romans 7:18, KJV)

In sinners, there is no light, just darkness. We either walk in the light or walk in darkness. Religion defines walking in the light as righteousness. Their righteousness white-washes the tomb. Jesus came to turn our tombs into temples of the Holy Spirit. Walking in the light is not a behavior; it's transparency. When we walk in transparency with God, then we can have fellowship. The blood of Jesus cleanses us of sin. The Holy Spirit works with those who bring their darkness into the light. Faith does not mean being fake. Faith is honesty before God, "I can't, but I believe You can." Every one of us is brought to the same place where we need God and others. We enter the world needing help, and we never get to a helpless state; we need community. As successful and self-sufficient as we may be, we still need community. The higher we get on the ladder in whatever career or ministry we are in, the lonelier it gets. It's like being on a tight rope with no net below. One wrong step and we fall to our death. When we gain the world, we are still not satisfied. Contentment is a discipline and not an emotion. Many don't know that it's a discipline, so they turn to narcotics for counterfeit contentment. The peace and contentment that Christ can give cannot be rivaled; this only comes by transparency in our relationship with God. If you are not content, talk to Him. If you are not at peace, talk to Him. This world appeals to anxiety, but Christ gives peace. Anxiety does not bear good fruit.

This is why casting our cares on God is so important. It can't be said enough: "Take every thought captive to the obedience of Christ." If we are bound to anxiety, sin, or doubt, talk to Jesus about it. Satan does not want us to walk in the light, so he makes God out to be "Zeus-like," who wants to pour wrath on us all, but God is love, everyone is redeemable, no matter what state they are in. This is the power of the shed blood of Jesus. We must not trample on His blood by taking His grace in vain, but as we walk in the light, Jesus tells us, "Go and sin no more." He gives us the power to overcome sin. There is no unredeemable sin. Jesus had more of an impact on sinners than He did on the religious. He did not enable sin but gave power over it.

Note

360

"Who was before a blasphemer, and a persecutor,
and injurious: but I obtained mercy, because I did it
ignorantly in unbelief" (1 Timothy 1:13, KJV)

Y ou are redeemable. When we believe the lie that we have gone too far, it enables us to continue on the path of destruction. The Gospel gives hope to everyone, especially those who feel like they have gone too far. It's not over until our pulse stops; it's not too late to get right with God. The church is not always a reflection on Him because the church needs Him as much as you do. The church is not Jesus. Jesus is in the church, but the church depends on Him as much as you need to. Religion casts stones while those that are casting them are under boulders themselves. We can't judge another person's eternity because if we are all to be honest, we deserve the same judgment. We can discern, and we are called to discern but judge not, lest we be judged.[94] Discerning between right and wrong is what we are called to do, but judging someone to heaven or hell is not our place. Compared to some, we may not be as bad as others, but compared to Christ, we are vile wretches in our flesh. Arrogance, pride, haughtiness, and judgment, when sown, reaps a blight and disease. To have a contrite heart does not mean that we are cowards; it means that we are aware of our desperate state for grace. Discernment is not judgment; it's a warning

---

[94]. *"Judge not, that ye be not judged. For with what judgment ye judge, ye shall be judged: and with what measure ye mete, it shall be measured to you again. And why beholdest thou the mote that is in thy brother's eye, but considerest not the beam that is in thine own eye?" (Matthew 7:1–3, KJV)*

to repent. We can ask for the gift of discernment. We are to desire the spiritual gifts eagerly. We have not because we ask not. There is so much that we could have if we only asked. Many don't know to ask and may have been brought up where asking is rude. We don't ask as entitled brats; we don't ask for our lust; instead, we ask for the glory of God. It's not too late to ask. If you are reading this, it's not too late to be redeemed or to see your situation redeemed. As hopeless as it may be, we can have hope in Christ if we ask. For some, it's time to ask. That's what prayer is; prayer is asking. Worship is honoring and praising, but prayer is mostly asking. A healthy balance of prayer and worship will give us a healthy perspective on what we are going through. There is a time to ask and a time to thank Him for what He already did in giving us Christ. Jesus loves you; He takes care of His own. His hand is outstretched to anyone who would believe His word over the lie of Satan. When we have doubts about His love for us, remember His death!

Note

361

"Saying, Father, if thou be willing, remove this cup from me: nevertheless not my will, but thine, be done" (Luke 22:42, KJV)

Every believer will have their own Gethsemane. It's lonely, it's internal, we know the right decision, but it's a wrestle to make it. For some, this is their everyday life with God; for others, it's once or twice in their lifetime. It's a good thing that the prosperity gospel preachers were not with Jesus in the garden of Gethsemane. We need to be careful who we listen to. Some today preach against the Gethsemane experience as if the early church martyrs died in vain or did not have a revelation of the love of God because they suffered. Their view of the Father is like a dad who spoils his kids, never disciplines, and never prepares his kids for real life because he "loves" them so much. If we never have a Gethsemane experience, we may never have been saved. This life as believers in Christ is about obeying the will of God. Naming and claiming, declaring, and decreeing, treats God like a genie in a bottle and not like He is Lord. We are not Lord or God; we don't know what's best for us. Jesus knew what the crucifixion was going to be like. Three years before the crucifixion, Satan offered him the earth if only he bowed down and worshipped him. That's what prosperity preachers preach. "Have heaven now, don't trust a God who would make you face a 'cross.'" They call the cross "child abuse." "What Father would take pleasure in watching His Son suffer in such a way?" Our humanity will never understand the magnitude of who our God is. We can't try to relate it to our experiences and culture. Our God is a mystery; we behold Him dimly right now. Our logic will talk us out of faith, but our logic is left with unanswered questions as to our origin, purpose, and destiny. This is why we can't walk by logic but by faith alone. The Spirit bears witness with us when we believe God's word for what it says. It's in the Gethsemane, that logic can override faith. Not everyone makes the right decision as Jesus did. Jesus went to the cross to show us that we can make it through anything. There is nothing that He can't bring us through. He saved us, but He also empowered us with the Holy Spirit to do, through us, what our flesh could never do. Choose today whom you will serve. As believers, we are faced with this choice daily. Our testimony is ongoing, our wrestle is daily, and our fight for faith is urgent!

Note

362

"Wherefore, as by one man sin entered into the world,
and death by sin; and so death passed upon all men,
for that all have sinned" (Romans 5:12, KJV)

We all wanted a hero growing up but as we get closer to who we thought were heroes, really they were villains that just made heroic decisions. In the sight of God, we are all villains; even the best of us. There is only one hero who will not let us down, take advantage of us, or abuse us; He is Jesus. We look to those afar off as heroes but the closer we get, the more disappointed we will become. It's in our nature to want a hero. There is no person on this planet that is a hero; it looks like there is, based on heroic decisions made, but once you get to know them long enough, you will be reminded that they are human. This is not to disappoint anyone but it's to remind us that Jesus is the hero. We can all decide to follow Him and make the greatest heroic decision we could make but that does not make us the hero. In all of us, there is a villain nature. Whatever we feed, grows; whatever we starve, dies. If we store up bitterness and hate, we feed our villain nature; it will get the best of us at some point. Jesus is the only one who can heal our soul. He does this divinely as we open our soul up to Him. This won't make us perfect in our flesh but He will make us want to be perfect as He is. We will want to be like Jesus. We will give off the appearance that we are heroes but let's always remind ourselves and everyone around us that Jesus is the only hero worth trusting. Our sin reminds us that we still need a savior, long after we are saved. Our sickness reminds us that we still need Jesus. Let's live a life of dependence on Jesus. It's not hard. Life throws so many obstacles at us; who else can we turn to, get us through? Let Jesus be your focus to prevent you from any further disappointment. He carries us through life, like no other. We are held more than we know. Make the most heroic decision by trusting Christ with your life. Trusting Him, means that when all seems lost in the sight of the world, we are still held, found in the grace of God. Trust is not trust until everyone wonders: "how did he make it that far?" God and God alone will be our testimony. What we learned from man is what not to do; what we learned from the Bible is what to do. When we decide to follow God more than man, we are set up for success in life. Christ made this possible at the cross.

Note

363

"And we know that all things work together for good to them
that love God, to them who are the called according to his
purpose. For whom he did foreknow, he also did predestinate
to be conformed to the image of his Son, that he might be the
firstborn among many brethren" (Romans 8:28–29, KJV)

Purpose, destiny, strength test, identity, personality test…these are the hot topics of today but they are not what the Gospel is all about. The Gospel should not lead us in a self-focused life but should lead us to a Christ-focused life. We need to stop thinking about all of our benefits all the time and get our minds on the glory of God. When our attention is on the glory of God, more than ourselves, we will have a better perspective. This means that we ask ourselves: "how will God get glory in this situation?" We all face hardship; rain falls on the righteous and the unrighteous. How we respond, shows where our faith was all along. Hardships should not weaken our faith but fuel our faith. Any gospel that cheapens hardship, or slanders diffi-culty, or does not prepare their audience for obstacles in life is not the Gospel of Christ. God qualifies the unqualified. God redeems the sinner. God shows His glory through the furnaces in life. This does not mean that we seek affliction, no not at all; we seek God's will for our lives but if affliction comes, we should be prepared. Our eternal prosperity and health are coming but, in this world, we will have hardship. Prepare in whatever season you are in. It's not too late to memorize the Word; go to prayer and follow Jesus in whatever He has in front of you, in sickness or in health. God is not the author of disease, famine, or tragedy; these are all the ramifications of the fall. God is not playing games with humanity; He values our souls so much. Look at what Christ did for us at the cross. God has a purpose for all of our seasons but some seasons will be a mystery to us until we see Jesus. We see dimly now, but when that which is perfect comes, we won't be in confusion about some of life's tragedies. We must trust that if God could bring good out of the cross, He can bring good out of all of our hardships. Believe in God when it all looks lost and watch Him turn it for good. God always brings beauty out of ashes. Faith always has great results, but those results may be a mystery until we get to heaven. Love Him in the hardship, praise Him in the prison, and glorify Him in affliction. Our adversary does not know what to do with a believer who sees affliction as an advantage to depend on Christ!

Note

_____

_____

_____

_____

_____

_____

_____

_____

364

There is so much to feed unbelief in our every day. If we don't study scripture, we will be overrun by the spirit of this age. The world is dark, and the people are negative; the best way to make it forward in our society is to talk about what's wrong with us because when they hear what is right with us, they get jealous and make us a target. Some people only want to hear what's wrong with you, in order to have a friendship. We have a small few that we can celebrate with and trust that they won't get jealous. Some talk about other's failures and fragility more than about accomplishments because they are so insecure about themselves, that they find a need to feed off of the negative comparison. As long as they compare with someone who is worse off than them, they will encourage, but anyone that they compare with, that is better off then them, they are covetous and tear them down. This is how most of our corporate and employment culture is. We need to resist this mind-set in the church. John the Baptist set the example to us of how to deal with others' success. Does others' success inspire you or does it muster jealousy? Jealousy will make a "joker" out of us. Self-pity, covetousness, jealousy, and bitterness will make a "joker" out of us if it goes unchecked. Let's be known for how we encourage others, even when we correct; is our correction for the betterment of others and the glory of God? Narcissistic men are a danger to themselves. People are bent on narcissism. Narcissism is the love of self to the extent that we will step on anyone, just to get us where we want to. Jesus taught is that we can't love our neighbor until we love ourselves; this means that He wants us to believe that we are loved uniquely, personally, and eternally. Satan teaches the love of self by telling us that we are god or by teaching us the hate of self, by making us out to be mere mammals. Jesus made us in His image and went through a lot to have a personal relationship with us. The opposite of narcissism is not the hate of self. Insecurity makes us narcissistic. We can be secure in Christ. Our significance is not in ourselves; John the Baptist taught us how to overcome narcissism by celebrating others more than ourselves. Narcissists discourage. What do we do more: encourage or criticize? Narcissism makes us cynics! Be secure in Christ and encourage.

Note

365

*"All scripture is given by inspiration of God, and is profitable
for doctrine, for reproof, for correction, for instruction in
righteousness: That the man of God may be perfect, thoroughly
furnished unto all good works" (2 Timothy 3:16–17, KJV)*

Who sets out to parent to not see their kids become self-sufficient adults? Who pastors to not see their congregations know Jesus and read scripture for themselves? Who disciples to not see their disciples make disciples? Narcissists are jealous of their kids; they keep their congregations dependent on "their word" and make disciples that can never disciple. A biblical leader will have a legacy; every other type of leader will have their accomplishments die with them. The spirit of Joseph's family and king Saul is what narcissism produces, which leads to death. This spirit wants no one outperforming each other; it discourages, it's critical, and it makes us worship self. This spirit pulls people down, holds people back, and emphasizes what people can't do. Satan fell like lightning because of covetousness. Jealousy that goes untamed will turn family on itself, churches on each other, and society against itself. Division is a strategy of evil against us. When we are insecure, it will cause us to make the most damning decisions. Discrimination, sectarianism, and racism are all fruit of narcissism. When we don't live for the development, discipleship, and growth of others, we are not a reflection of Jesus but are actually a reflection of Satan; there are leaders who make themselves "kings," call accountability rebellion, and use people rather love people. Every investment decision and show of love is for their own elevation. Beware of kindness and love from a narcissist because for some reason, they see you as an economic value or servanthood value; once they get what they want, it's as if you never existed. Once the prodigal son was out of money, he was out of narcissistic friends. He had to learn the hard way. The narcissistic religious is the most demonic. They use Jesus and His word for their own fame and gain. This is the darkest of all narcissism. This is what makes the church unsafe for sinners today because it is not built on the image and character of Christ, but the image of Satan, pretending to be an angel of light. There is no light when you talk to their accountants. Their donations are never disclosed; if someone asks, they are demoted and called rebellious. We desperately need a reformation in leadership, biblical literacy, and evangelization today!

Note

366

"Who also hath made us able ministers of the new testament;
not of the letter, but of the spirit: for the letter killeth,
but the spirit giveth life" (2 Corinthians 3:6, KJV)

The Bible brings death but the Spirit gives life. The reason why few people read their Bible is because discipleship has been so watered down, that we give every resource to the new believer, but what really matters, the source. If the Bible is not enough, then we don't have the conviction of the Holy Spirit. He will lead us to scripture to build our faith and He will make it understandable. When we realize that the Bible is a spiritual book, we will not read it like another book. The Holy Spirit gives us revelation from scripture. We need to stop depending on other resources and go to the source directly. There has never been a generation with such ease of access to scripture yet it's so ignored by our generation. If we read the New Testament without the Holy Spirit, we will form a worse religion than what put Jesus on the cross, look at Rome and what their apostate church has produced. When that which is perfect is come,[95] we won't need all the resources that we have today because we will see our Lord face-to-face. We need the Holy Spirit for empowerment to live as believers; we need the Holy Spirit so that all will know the treasure in us is of Him and not of us. The Holy Spirit will do a better job lifting Christ up than we can in our flesh. The Holy Spirit would never elevate Himself

---

[95.] *"But when that which is perfect is come, then that which is in part shall be done away." (1 Corinthians 13:10, KJV)*

above Christ, nor contradict the sixty-six books of Scripture that He inspired. He is our comforter because we can't be what Christ has called us to be without Him. Denying the Holy Spirit, quenching the Holy Spirit, or rejecting His conviction is a very dangerous state of mind. When the church organization replaces the Holy Spirit, it forms a religion with no power. The life source of the church has been electricity, music, and clever orators but that's a counterfeit life-source if relied upon. Few people pray or even acknowledge the Holy Spirit when they do ministry; we think we have it figured out. We have many that have mimicked the Holy Spirit by using strategy, passion, and talent as their reliance to do ministry. There is nothing wrong with these but where they become sinful is when they are relied upon. If there was a power cut, would Christians in the West even know how to do ministry? You can't expect a seed to grow in a machine. As organized as we become, the temptation is to rely on the organization more than the organism. "Don't end in the flesh."

Note

367

*"Faithful is he that calleth you, who also will
do it" (1 Thessalonians 5:24, KJV)*

W hen we hear a call from God, it will be questioned but it's always
proved in the end because He never fails. We have the Bible to testify that no matter how impossible it is for us, with God, all things
are possible. God rarely asks us to do what we can, He won't share
the glory. He asks us to do the impossible so that only He gets the
glory. There are few that had audacious faith which we read about
in scripture. It does not take much faith for someone to obey God
when they have the strength, resources, and wealth to obey. Faith is
not faith unless only God can get us through it. Serving God is not
for those who can do it but for those who serve through Christ who
strengthens them. The famous here may not be as well known in
heaven. God rewards faithfulness to Him when all hell comes against
us to take us out. Our faithfulness won't be our boast; if we are honest, it's because of His faithfulness that we are faithful. He will keep
us, He will not forsake us, stand still and watch the salvation of the
Lord. It's when we take matters into our own hands, that we begin to
realize that we should not be walking on the waves and the gale force
wind should be blowing us away; that's when we sink as peter did.[96]
Our soul's eyes must be disciplined to see only Jesus, no matter what

---

[96.] *"And straightway Jesus constrained his disciples to get into a ship, and to go before
him unto the other side, while he sent the multitudes away. And when he had sent
the multitudes away, he went up into a mountain apart to pray: and when the eve-
ning was come, he was there alone." (Matthew 14:22–23, KJV)*

our naked eye sees. Jesus will pull us up out of the pits of anxiety and fear as we bring it all to Him. We tried to figure it out, we tried to budget, we tried but, in the end, only God can bring the increase. We will continue to walk on the waves and the winds will blow around us; we will not be shaken. God speaks peace to our soul and peace to our situation when we release it all over to Him. God, have your way. We will step toward you, so we can walk in your strength and not in the flesh. If could, we would rather walk in our flesh but we have no choice than to walk in faith. To where would we go, to whom else could we serve?[97] As we surrender to God alone, we can trust that just as He took care of the faithful in scripture, He will take care of us. No matter what, our soul will be taken care of. In the hardships, He will be our comfort. There is nothing that could disappoint the believer, we see the nail scarred hands, God get glory from our lives no matter what we face. We will be known for how trusted Christ through it all.

---

[97] *"Then Simon Peter answered him, Lord, to whom shall we go? thou hast the words of eternal life." (John 6:68, KJV)*

368

*"When Jesus heard it, he marvelled, and said to them
that followed, Verily I say unto you, I have not found so
great faith, no, not in Israel" (Matthew 8:10, KJV)*

Our education, our wealth, our pedigree, our social status; none
of these marvel God like faith in action does. The only time that
Jesus marveled at anyone, was when he saw the faith of the Roman
centurion who expressed more faith than all of Israel; an ungodly
gentile believed in Jesus and believed in the authority of Jesus. We
don't marvel God by anything other than faith. There is a "hall of
faith," where it lists the men and women, who by faith, accomplished
great exploits. It says "by faith," not by God. Faith is a mystery but
it gets God's attention. Who do we want to marvel more: man, or
God? What do we fear more: what people think or what God thinks?
When a man breaks free from the opinions of people and follows the
voice of God, he has found life. Life is found when we are dead to the
opinions of ourselves and others; life is found in the Word of God.
God qualifies us to be more than conquerors, no matter what He
calls us to. Our faith will fail if we look at our failures and our "cant's"
more than God; this is why Jesus prayed that Peter's faith would not
fail. Like Peter, we all will hear the rooster crow. Years later, he heard
it again when Paul had to challenge Peter for bringing discrimination
into the church. Paul was not as easily influenced because he was
more grounded in scripture than Peter. The more of the Bible that we
can quote, the stronger our faith will be. It won't give us an excuse to
sin but in the heat of temptation, we will know how to respond using

"it is written."[98] Faith is a mystery; we see Jesus getting interrupted by men and women that had faith. In the New Testament, such as the woman who was sick and touched the hem of Christ's garment and was healed.[99] Even when it was not His time to do miracles, faith moved Jesus to turn the water into wine. When we run out, when we don't know what to do, when we don't know where to go, have faith in God. Faith is faith when we have no other option but God's intervention. We will all be brought to this place in our lifetime. We either get crushed by our feelings or get held by our faith. Faith in God keeps our feelings in check. Any belief, thought, or person that has more sway on us than scripture, must be cast out of our minds in Jesus's name. As we follow Jesus, faith won't always get us what we want but it will get us through to the end. Science and wealth can't do for the soul what faith in God can.

---

98. *"But he answered and said, It is written, Man shall not live by bread alone, but by every word that proceedeth out of the mouth of God." (Matthew 4:4, KJV)*

99. *"And a certain woman, which had an issue of blood twelve years, And had suffered many things of many physicians, and had spent all that she had, and was nothing bettered, but rather grew worse, When she had heard of Jesus, came in the press behind, and touched his garment." (Mark 5:25–27, KJV)*

369

"But when that which is perfect is come, then that which is in part shall be done away. When I was a child, I spake as a child, I understood as a child, I thought as a child: but when I became a man, I put away childish things. For now we see through a glass, darkly; but then face to face: now I know in part; but then shall I know even as also I am known" (1 Corinthians 13:10–12, KJV)

When that, which is perfect has come, we will see Him face-to-face. Right now, we see dimly; right now, we have spiritual mysteries; right now, we need faith. While we are here, we have scripture, the church, and the Holy Spirit to keep us to the end. When Christ comes, who is the perfect one, we will be caught up with Him. The Holy Spirit came on Pentecost and has not left the church since. What took place in the upper room and the sign to Peter, that the gentiles were included in the Gospel has not ceased but continues to this day. The Gospel is not an argument; it is power unto salvation. The Holy Spirit is the power that we receive in Christ. He is the third person of the trinity. It is the Spirit that quickens our flesh and abilities profit nothing compared to what He can do through us.[100] He is in us and He is greater than us, so we can do what we could never do on our own as His will permits. The Holy Spirit does not elevate Himself above Christ, nor does He elevate a person above Christ. As we walk in the strength of the Spirit, we will not fulfill the lust of the

---

[100.] *"It is the spirit that quickeneth; the flesh profiteth nothing: the words that I speak unto you, they are spirit, and they are life." (John 6:63, KJV)*

flesh. The Holy Spirit gives us self-control and a sound mind. The Spirit of God has been given a title, which opens our eyes to what He produces in us and that is holiness. He is holy, which means that if He is in us, we will be grieved by sin. We will not take pleasure in sin but we will genuinely repent of it and detest it because He is in us. He is our life source, He is our teacher for scripture, He makes us a witness of Christ. If we speak in the tongue of an angel but have no burden to preach the Gospel to the lost around us every week, then what spirit do we have? If we have miracles and signs happening through our life but we don't hunger for biblical accuracy, what spirit do we have? If we have all the fruit of the spirit but we are ashamed of Christ in our everyday life, what spirit do we have? The liberty that the Spirit gives us is not a liberty to sin but a liberty to overcome temptation. Repent and continue to do so as the Spirit convicts us throughout our journey with Christ. When we rely on our flesh, to produce the life of Christ, we will fail; when we rely on the Spirit of Christ, the fruit will grow. Renounce your strength and yield to the Spirit of God; then you will experience regeneration.

370

"Withdraw thy foot from thy neighbour's house; lest he be weary of thee, and so hate thee" (Proverbs 25:17, KJV)

When we get familiar with anything or anyone, it breeds contempt. Familiarity has crippled faith in our generation. We have grown familiar with scripture, church, and Jesus. Many are unmoved by the crucifixion of Christ. The love of many is growing cold.[101] When people are out of sight, they are out of mind because we are a selfish generation. We do what we feel like doing, we follow what we want to follow, and no one will tell us differently. This lifestyle comes with serious ramifications. Even though we think we are free in the west, if everyone could be famous and rich, we would realize how empty this world is. Religion teaches us "to do more" but Jesus taught us "it's done." The reason that we have grown familiar is because although we began in the Spirit, we have ended up in flesh. This can be our testimony too if we stray from Jesus into the works of religion. Religion curses with lethargy and liturgy. Religion is all about our works but a relationship with Jesus is about His work. A relationship with Jesus means that we talk to Him. He is closer than a brother. He is our Lord but He made the way so that we can be His family. We can leave our first love as believers. When we leave our first love, we end up with religion. Religion makes us focus on unessential doctrines, practices, rituals, and traditions for salvation,

---

[101.] *"And because iniquity shall abound, the love of many shall wax cold." (Matthew 24:12, KJV)*

which the enemy of the church uses to divide us. A house divided will not stand the test of time. When Christ is the foundation and the focus, we will burn for truth and live impassioned for His glory until we pass or until He returns. We can experience a personal awakening every day as we walk in relationship with Him. We don't have to wait to be awakened; we can walk awakened every day as we open ourselves to Christ. If we need an experience outside of scripture and our relationship with Jesus to be awakened, then we need to grow out of the milk and get on to the meat of the Word. In this season, we need to prepare for hardship, or if we are in the midst of hardship, it's not too late to be awakened to who is with you in your midst. God will see us through. Let's fight familiarity or it will get the best of our faith. We are all susceptible to this. This is why we need each other to spur one another on. When the light is shone on our sin, run to Jesus and never away from Him. Awaken.

Note

_____

_____
_____
_____
_____
_____
_____
_____
_____
_____

371

"The heart is deceitful above all things, and desperately wicked: who can know it? I the Lord search the heart, I try the reins, even to give every man according to his ways, and according to the fruit of his doings" (Jeremiah 17:9–10, KJV)

Would anyone love you if everyone knew you? If our thoughts could be read by each other, would we like each other? If our internet history was published, what would the world read about us? Are we as good as we want to portray? Scripture sheds light on our heart and thoughts; it explicitly says that our hearts are wicked and we love darkness more than light. Scripture is clear; we have all sinned. The more we read the Bible, the viler we realize we are and holier God really is.[102] If it were not for Christ, none of us could be holy enough. The holiness of God is so out of reach, that it would be like telling humanity to jump and touch the moon in order to be holy. God is Holy, we are not. Even on our best day, we are not holy enough to earn access to Him. This is why Christ died; He put holiness in reach to whosoever believes. Belief in Christ makes us holy instantaneously before God. Belief also affects our behavior but while we are in these bodies, we will always need Jesus. This does not excuse sin but makes us contrite before Him and others. We should need Jesus more and more if we are being biblically discipled. Discipleship that graduates us from Christ to our efforts will only condemn us. We don't have what it takes and we won't have what it takes but Jesus does. Until we

---

[102.] Jeremiah 17:9

get our glorified bodies, we are in a wrestle between faith vs unbelief, flesh vs spirit, and sin vs righteousness. Until we get to eternity, fight for faith in Christ, no matter how great the opposition gets. Belief in Christ produces right behavior; right behavior does not produce faith in Christ but it produces faith in self, which is the basis of religion. Let's not deviate from the supremacy of Christ for salvation and sanctification. What's up to us is the choice of whom we will serve. We can either serve self or surrender to Christ. Serving God without surrender to Christ, only regurgitates the law of Moses, which produces the ministry of condemnation. This is every believer's statement: "I stand condemned in myself. What you see is a wretch. My need for Christ is more evident today than it was when I first made Him Lord. I still need Jesus and I'm grateful for that. God, keep me dependent on you, continue to remind me as you have until now about how much I still need you; may all know Christ and not me!"

Note

_____

_____

_____

_____

_____

_____

_____

_____

_____

372

*"Speaking lies in hypocrisy; having their conscience
seared with a hot iron" (1 Timothy 4:2, KJV)*

What would happen if the church pulled back behind the four
walls? What would happen if the human race would stop having
kids? For nearly a thousand years, Christianity hid out in monasteries
because of the sin and persecution during the dark ages. They did not
know any better. They hid out in the country, while the cities were
dying in sin. That's a long time for God to allow His church not to be
the light that He has called it to be. We live in an unusual age since
the birth of the church. The church never had the influence it has
over the world as we have it today because of technology. The church
is the most resourced it has ever been with Bible apps, thousands of
discipleship tools, and infrastructure; we are poised for the greatest
awakening we have ever seen. Jesus called His church to be His light
on the earth. Our enemy is real, but many make light of him in the
West. We live every day allowing our society to believe that they're
mere mammals, and the enemy of their soul is a fun figment of their
imagination. The day that Christianity left the dark ages has become
the darkest day of the year. Martin Luther began the reformation on
October 31 when he hung the 95 Theses on the Wittenberg Roman
Catholic Church. We have forgotten our history as Bible-believing
Christians. Our generation is the most resourced yet the most ignorant ever. Rather than praying and trusting for another reformation,
we are dressing up in costumes, being entertained by the dark pow-
ers that are worshipped on that day. Evangelists are under onslaught

daily in their physical health, family, and finances; many have left the office of an evangelist to be a pastor. Denominations that once had active evangelists in their fellowship have made church growth their priority without the evangelist at the helm. They are growing the church with every method possible but not getting the church to evangelize. The church's education on evangelism is "invite people to church," rather than inviting people to Jesus. The church is the light, but it's not the savior. The pulpit preaches Jesus, but those in the pew have more influence over their community than the pulpit. Envision everyone in the pew preaching from their pulpit every day. We all have a pulpit to preach behind every day.

Note

373

"And he gave some, apostles; and some, prophets; and some, evangelists; and some, pastors and teachers" (Ephesians 4:11, KJV)

The people in the pew have more of an influence over the lost than the pulpit in the church. The church is our seminary and our everyday life is our mission. If the pulpit is not equipping those in the pew for ministry to their families, neighborhoods, and work place, then they are not fulfilling their mandate. The pew does not exist to make a disciple of the guy behind the pulpit but the guy behind the pulpit is to make a disciple of the people in the pew. The marketplace is full of unreached people; our public schools are full of unreached people; our city streets are full of unreached people. The devil has his evangelists working outside, night and day, through to the Mormons, Jehovah Witnesses, and Hollywood. While the church is complaining about the worship styles and dreaming of the good old days, millions all around them are going to hell. Cults look more evangelical than we do. We have relied on TV, Social Media, and the "evangelist" to reach people. What this generation needs are not a pamphlet or a video, nor do they need a superstar evangelist; they need you. You are the only Bible that someone may ever read. You are the hope that someone will ever listen to. Your career is sacred, do it unto the Lord. Don't look to the "full time" ministries as an example, at least you have an honest job and have influence over the lost every day for the glory of God. Some "full time" guys are more about raising themselves up than raising up anyone else up. After years of ministry, all they want is to hear the sound of their voice or the voice of anyone who will blindly follow them. Very few actually want to equip biblically. So, it's up to you to reach out where God has put you. Don't rely on prayer because God has chosen you. Prayer can be an excuse for us to do nothing. Prayer was never designed for that. The prayer before we eat is the best kind of prayer. We pray, then we eat. When it comes to evangelism, we pray, then we evangelize. God won't do what He has called us to do. Everyone has a purpose; everyone has a place. Believe that God can do anything He wants through you. Surrender to His will and follow His leading. Don't listen to the opinions of others who tell you all that you can't do. *Philippians 4:13.*

Note

374

"For from within, out of the heart of men, proceed
evil thoughts, adulteries, fornications, murders, Thefts,
covetousness, wickedness, deceit, lasciviousness, an evil eye,
blasphemy, pride, foolishness" (Mark 7:21–22, KJV)

How do we feel when we are outperformed? How do we think about the person that outshines us? Christianity today defines worldliness by behavior but worldliness can also be defined by culture. Our corporate culture of ministry has led to greed, selfishness, and jealousy. Unless one is the "son of" or born into wealth, then one will have to rely fully on God; there is no "hand up" except from God. The world only gives a "hand out." God won't be interested in what we know when we pass away, He will be interested in who we know. Knowing Jesus, matters more than what we know about Jesus. Our culture of who we know is more than about our education or skill set. Accountability is not rebellion. Discernment is not judgment. Gods leading is not arrogance. Joseph's family responded to Joseph like much of our culture does when we follow the leading of God. When success does not inspire but makes us jealous, we have entertained the spirit of the world. Worldliness and sin are best defined by living independent of God. Envy, greed and comparison are so destructive. We need to repent quickly when these emotions rise up. We are to examine whether we are in the faith. If we are going to disciple, we need to be ready to deal with these emotions. God works best with the person who surrenders fully to Him and says, "Have your way." When we accept that we are nobody without God, when realize that we can do nothing without Jesus, then we are a major threat to the enemy. Our culture sees this mind-set as a doormat but vengeance is the Lord's. The Lord raises up and He shields His sons, who have nothing without Him. When we grow confident in our flesh, we must be open to Him bringing us low. This is His grace because nothing good comes out of our flesh. Good only comes out of God; let's lay our pride down so that He has His way in us. We can rejoice when someone is being discipled, we can be inspired when someone is successful, we can celebrate others when others are celebrated. The is the culture of Jesus that comes into us. No one encourages like a believer in Jesus. We never have a reason to lose heart. Christ made us more than conquerors, so we don't have to achieve it; He won it for us. Christ made whosoever believes more than conquerors. Rejoice and rejoice over each other.

Note

375

"For there shall arise false Christs, and false prophets, and shall shew great signs and wonders; insomuch that, if it were possible, they shall deceive the very elect" (Matthew 24:24, KJV)

Saul and Judas have a lot in common. They both were chosen, both were called, both walked with God in very unique roles; Saul as a king and Judas as an apostle. God knew the end from the beginning for their lives. They served their purpose. They were chosen by God yet both have failed. God did not will their death but they both took matters into their own hands and faced the consequences. One fell on a sword and the other hung himself. Elijah and Paul both despaired of life also, yet they never gave up. Peter is an example of how to respond when you fail; he spoke out of turn, sank in the waves, denied Jesus to a maid, welcomed discrimination into the church but he never stopped repenting. Saul never behaved like David did, Judas did not fail as much as Peter did, but they both would not repent and instead, their sin drove them to suicide. Whatever the reason for their unrepentance, let their testimonies be a warning to all of us. Don't conceal your thoughts, emotions, or doubts from God; this way of living leads to self-harm. Jesus made the way so unlike Judas, when we sink, instead of reaching for a rope, we are reaching for the hand of God. When we sin, instead of blaming everyone as Saul did, we take responsibility as David did. Don't fear men or their opinions, take God seriously. Saul showed signs of taking God seriously, so did Judas; how we finish, matters more than how we are right now. Many people change drastically with the wind. One day they are one way, and the next day, they are another. We can't rely on people because they change; we change but Jesus remains constant. Knowing that Jesus receives us, knowing there is no hope outside of His mercy, knowing that no matter how convicted we get, no man can condemn and neither does He condemn. Jesus did not come to condemn but to seek and save the lost. He is seeking the lost but most people pretend that they're found when inside, they're so lost. We may look found but truth is, we are all deeply lost until we are found in Christ. Christ does not condemn, neither do I, neither should we. One will experience conviction when the Spirit is at work; if you don't grieve over sin, you may not have the Spirit in you. Repent, believe in Christ, and receive the indwelling of the Spirit. Examine whether you are in the faith until we see Jesus.

Note

376

"So shall my word be that goeth forth out of my mouth: it shall not
return unto me void, but it shall accomplish that which I please, and
it shall prosper in the thing whereto I sent it" (Isaiah 55:11, KJV)

Awakening happens not because of the sound of a preacher but to the truth of scripture. A preacher without scripture won't have any power. It's the Word of God that won't return void. It's a lack of the knowledge of scripture that is holding back our generation. We are called to study to show ourselves approved. The scripture must be rightly divided. When reading the Bible, we must not read it like a lucky charm. We need to understand the context of what we are reading. Reading one verse at random is not smart. We are to read scripture from the beginning of the book or chapter to the end, so that we can understand the context of each verse. Many cults have begun because they built a doctrine off of a verse without using intelligence and reading the context. If we hear a preacher not giving context, then he is just a "con" using the text for his own gain. Anyone can make a verse say what they want it to say but without context, we won't have correct interpretation. Scripture interprets itself and is the best commentary on itself. Scripture is our constitution as believers. It's our go-to. We are all held accountable to scripture. The more we know, the more discerning we will be. It's time for believers to know their constitution and not rely on the agendas of our preachers to influence them more than scripture. May we all be men and women of the Word. Context is important in our personal lives too. If we don't have context to our lives, then we won't know our origin, purpose, or destiny. The Bible gives us context and perspective. We may feel like another small insignificant piece of creation but scripture tells us how important we really are. Christ died for us. Preachers should talk less about themselves and more about Christ. As impactful as our stories are, it has nothing on History. History is His story. He is writing history right before our eyes each day. Don't cave into the lie that you are not significant. You are significant, you have a voice, purpose, and pulpit wherever you are. Ministry happens when we are engaged in our everyday life; that's our mission. Church is the pep talk for when real worship takes place as we honor God in our everyday life. Let's not confuse worship with karaoke. Worship is obedience and not songs. Awakening is coming.

Note

377

"Who comforteth us in all our tribulation, that we may be able to comfort them which are in any trouble, by the comfort wherewith we ourselves are comforted of God" (2 Corinthians 1:4, KJV)

Praying before we eat is the best example of prayer. We pray, then we eat. Prayer has become an excuse to not do anything. We often pray for God to do what He has asked us to do. If we pray without it leading to action, then we must question who we are praying to. There is no book of prayer in the New Testament but there is a book of actions. The book of Acts teaches us that our faith works; the Spirit calls us to action. Real prayer makes us doers. We pray, then we eat. We pray, then we work. We pray, then we do. Religion makes prayer an excuse to do nothing. Jesus said, "My sheep hear my voice." We are His ambassadors. Dreams, visions, miracles, and signs are not His ambassadors, we are. He has chosen to use us. Religion and Darwin have a lot in common; they cheapen the soul any way they can. Jesus determined the value of a soul with His own blood. Don't let anyone cheapen your soul; you matter. God left us here to be a light. Each of us are a light in our own sphere of influence. Society determines value by wealth, family, title, and education but God determines value by belief. When we believe our value before God, we are open to what He leads us to. When He leads us, faith in Him will be our only security. He does this so that no one can explain His miracle. The reason that we are facing an impossible situation or that God waited for it to get to this point of impossibility is for Him to show humanity who is God. We have story after story in scripture where God waits until there is no other deliverer but Him. He knows how quick we are to point to coincidence or science to take away from the glory of God. This is why we don't lose faith when we pray and nothing happens as if He does not care; He is, but He knows what's best. Trusting Him even when He does not work on our time schedule is real trust. God rarely does what we want Him to do because we don't always get it right. Our will rarely lines up with His will, so it's best to surrender to His will. Sara laughed at the will of God. Abraham would not follow God's leading, so he took matters into his own hands. We are still dealing with his sin to this day. Islam boasts of Ishmael. He was an illegitimate son and Islam is an illegitimate religion. Let's learn from history.

Note

_____

_____

_____

_____

_____

_____

_____

_____

378

*"For if we sin wilfully after that we have received
the knowledge of the truth, there remaineth no more
sacrifice for sins" (Hebrews 10:26, KJV)*

*"No man can serve two masters: for either he will hate the one,
and love the other; or else he will hold to the one, and despise the
other. Ye cannot serve God and mammon" (Matthew 6:24, KJV)*

A ship was not built to stay in the port. Believers were not saved to
stay in a structure which we call the church. Jesus never gave blueprints to the structure that we call church. The church is believers
that follow Christ in their everyday life. We were not saved to just sit
and wait until we get to heaven. If we warm a pew our whole lives
and never engage in our community, family, or place of work, then
we have not stepped into the fullness. Going to church conferences
and worship nights, if they're biblical should make us excited to follow Jesus in our everyday life more than those gatherings. A ship in
port is not fulfilling its purpose but gets maintenance and cargo so it
can continue to fulfill its purpose. Christianity that makes us excited
more about the "port" than the "voyage," will lead us in a life of disappointment. It trains us to be Christians only at "church" or around
other "Christians" but that's the reverse of what discipleship should
be producing. Discipleship should be getting us "self" sufficient in
our relationship with Christ, so we are shining forth His glory in the
middle of our workplace and everyday community. Religion teaches
that "bad company corrupts good morals" but Christ came to reverse

that proverb by giving us the power to influence bad company more than them influencing us. One person with Christ is the majority wherever we go in this world. We don't cave into peer pressure; we stand against the current so that all will see the glory of God. We were designed to befriend sinners without being influenced; He that is in us, influences them. The monastic temptation is exactly what the devil wants us to do. He wants us to pull back from sinners and shy away from the world but Jesus ran toward it without being influenced. We have the Holy Spirit in us; as we follow Jesus, He will keep us no matter where He leads. Our "high" as believers is to evangelize in the darkness to be a light for Christ; it's not only about singing songs and hearing a motivating message. The best type of worship leads to obedience to Christ; the best type of preaching makes us intentionally share Jesus with everyone around us. Get out from the port and fulfill your mission. This does not mean that we need to go overseas; it means to go across the street.

Note

379

*"And let us not be weary in well doing: for in due season
we shall reap, if we faint not"* (Galatians 6:9, KJV)

W hat are you waiting for? Why are you making rash decisions?
We will never please everyone, one way or another. There comes a
time when we will be accountable for our own decisions whether
people are happy with them or not; we need to make the right decision before God. The opinions of people rarely have our interest at
heart. People's opinions are filtered through their interests and jealousy. We all go astray and can lead people astray. The voice of the
world and the voice of Satan can drown out the voice of God if we
are not intentional on knowing His voice. God has separated us unto
Himself. Mute the world, be ablaze for the voice of God. Counsel
is good but our conscience matters more than counsel. Don't make
strategic decisions first; wait on God first, then make the decision.
Give margin for God to work. If we don't wait, then we will work
as lord of our lives; ask anyone in scripture how that fared for them.
The war was waged at the crucifixion of Christ. Hell rejoiced; the
world rejoiced but God too rejoiced, for it was the joy of salvation
that Christ died.[103] Christ's death will go down for all eternity as the
greatest sacrifice ever. God in the flesh, being sacrificed by us who
rebelled against Him, to save us from our sin. Why are we heeding
the voice of others more than the voice of God? Did they rise from

---

[103.] *"Looking unto Jesus the author and finisher of our faith; who for the joy that was set
before him endured the cross, despising the shame, and is set down at the right hand
of the throne of God." (Hebrews 12:2, KJV)*

the dead? Read scripture; listen to God. Make decisions after consulting with the only one who matters first; when there is silence, make the right decision for His glory and watch Him steer as we initiate in faith. Initiate after surrendering to Jesus so that He can steer the momentum of our decision. People won't always celebrate with us but we are serving the only one who matters. When we are at peace with God, to hell with the opinions of the world. Feed on faith; His scripture nourishes the soul. We are bolder, stronger, ambitious, aggressive, and abrasive in Jesus, more than all the force of the world. The spiritual military are arising on fire to honor Jesus. We will tread on darkness in Jesus's name so that the light of the Gospel will advance through us. As we step in the power of Jesus, we are treading on the dark lies that hate us. Everything in this world wants to steel, kill, and destroy our soul. Our soul is bought with the Lamb's Blood. Arise.

Note

380

"And of the angels he saith, Who maketh his angels spirits, and his ministers a flame of fire" (Hebrews 1:7, KJV)

Arise and blaze for the glory of God. The flame is being kindled in the quiet place. The heat of His presence is increasing. We will live possessed only by the Holy Spirit. We have opened our soul for Jesus to take over. We will rise in the power of His might. Spiritual wickedness will be threatened by this force because this is not the force of the flesh, it is the person of the Holy Spirit having His way in us. We are tired of fads and trends; we want Him to have all of us for the glory of our Christ. We know our sin, we know our wretchedness, we don't want anyone to look to us and if they do, may they see our flesh so they will only glory in Christ. We can't hide behind our baggage; we can't use false humility as our escape to not follow God. Follow God, eagerly desire spiritual gifts, and glorify in Christ, passionately. Let's decide to be fervent and ambitious to glorify our God. Don't justify fear or false humility, cast it out and be set ablaze to glorify our God with everything we got. Religion controls, holds back, and focuses on what we can't do; break free from religion. Jesus set us free from the sin of religion. Religion is the worst kind of sin because it masks the inner torment with false doctrine. Jesus takes us as we are, uses us as we are, and loves the world through us. Reject Calvin, reject reformed theology; its heresy is only good news to those who believe it. The Gospel is good news for all. Rise in the might of the Spirit with a plea for the masses to repent so that all will know our Christ. Religion makes disciples who act like Jonah when God calls them to do His will. Follow no man more than God. Be open to His leading. Come out from behind the bush, come out from behind the baggage, come out from behind fear and sin; God takes us as we are. He loves us enough to not leave us in what hurts us but calls us to lift His name up above every other. Speak freely, preach the truth whether it fills the room or empties the room. We will be held responsible; teach the Word in its fullness. We will only understand His word by faith, our futile minds won't know all the mysteries of truth until we see Him face-to-face. The Gospel is not based on a cast system, preach the Gospel more than any other weak teaching.

Note

381

"For we walk by faith, not by sight" *(2 Corinthians 5:7, KJV)*

Reject sight as a determination of faith. Our faith is not determined by anything but scripture. Faith must be fought for while we are in these bodies of flesh. We are prone to depression; our minds without faith will spiral into despair. Faith stops our thoughts from free-falling and sets them into the hands of God. Scripture binds our thoughts that are contrary to faith, and God casts them out. The less of His word we know, the more our thoughts will plummet. Don't let the enemy get the best of us; confess and depend on His Word. When we quote anyone more than scripture, we are on thin ice. The enemy does not submit to the flesh or the wisdom of man, but by the name of Jesus, he is vanquished. We are called to live valiantly in Christ.[104] The Spirit of God makes us a weapon while we are here, for the glory of God. Religion deviates us from our call as evangelists. It gets us sidetracked by all forms of religious charades and doctrines. Music and motivational messages have taken over the house of God. We summon the Spirit when we gather so that our time together is not just accumulating knowledge, but we are baptized in the fire for the glory of our Christ.[105] We gather to hail our King; we gather to remind ourselves that we have no rights of our own, we gather to lift Jesus overall. A successful minister makes His congregation quote

---

[104.] *"Through God we shall do valiantly: for he it is that shall tread down our enemies." (Psalm 108:13, KJV)*

[105.] *"Thy God hath commanded thy strength: strengthen, O God, that which thou hast wrought for us." (Psalm 68:28, KJV)*

the Word more than him. The artistry of a preacher leaves the people thinking about Christ when he is done preaching. The pulpit is not for testimonies or egos; it's for the Word to be rightly divided. No one needs to hear about us; they need to hear about Christ. Share testimonies one on one but when you stand behind the pulpit, preach Christ and Him crucified. Paul had one of the most incredible testimonies, but he chose to preach Christ more than his own story. Jesus saves, our testimonies verify that He still saves, but our testimonies are not the Gospel. A pulpit built on testimonies will be filled with "testiphonies." The pulpit is for the scripture to be taught in such a way that the bondages of sin are broken off the audience, and they walk away not only with a changed mind but with a changed life. The Gospel is a power unto salvation. The Gospel does not need discipleship when preached. The Gospel makes us want discipleship and not detest it!

Note

382

"I can do all things through Christ which strengtheneth me" (Philippians 4:13, KJV)

There is nothing you can't do if God calls you to it. When God calls us to do something, it requires faith in Him. If no faith is needed, then we must question if God really called us. We can believe that if we are facing hardship, tears, and anguish of the soul, that it won't be this way forever. If we are not reading scripture, we will be ignorant of the "called" who have gone before us, who made it through way worse times. Scripture is the best lens to look through on life. The Bible teaches us how He brings beauty from ashes. When people say it's impossible, when they say "you can't," trust God that He will prove them wrong. God can do anything; He teaches the opinionated gossips that their words are empty. We should be spurring one another on to follow God. We can know if it's of God, if it's for His glory. No flesh wants to glorify God, unless the Spirit of God is in him. A culture that spurs one another to follow God is so contrary to the religious culture. Religious culture is disingenuous. They will give a handshake and sum you up within seconds. Community can't be built if people are not vulnerable with one another. Religion does not breed community, it breeds clicks. Have you ever sat during a religious service and wished that you could connect like others do? After a while, you realize that everyone is friends with each other based on how they benefit one another. It's a networking opportunity for everyone's own interests to be met. Jesus came to look out for others interests more than His own. Jesus sought the outcast and called him a friend. Jesus sat with the newcomer. Jesus led by washing feet and serving. Religious leaders want their feet washed. They would not dare do such a thing. Who do we want to be like more: our leaders today or our Jesus? Many leaders today don't behave like Jesus at all in their mannerism, love, and friendliness. If our gatherings kept challenging us to let Christ's life live through us, we would be dependent on the Holy Spirit. We can't be like Christ in our flesh. Our flesh is self-seeking but Christ seeks the lost. Find community in Christ. Don't let anyone limit you, judge you, or look down upon you. Christ is better than any human that we could look up to or be inspired by. Don't let anyone influence you more than Jesus! Follow Him!

Note

383

"But we have this treasure in earthen vessels, that the excellency of the power may be of God, and not of us" (2 Corinthians 4:7, KJV)

Finishing strong matters more than starting strong. How we finish life, determines our eternity. We can start in the spirit but so easily end in the flesh. We can start like a flash in the pan, here today but gone tomorrow. Our testimonies should not only go back in years but should go back to this morning. Yesterday's relationship with God is not enough to get us through today. He is with us at all times. There is no break from Him, there is no hiding from Him. God wants us. We all desire to be wanted but end up just being needed as someone else's resource. To be loved unconditionally, to be wanted for nothing in return is an experience that only God can give. He is closer to us than any other. We can easily drift and coast but in the end, it does not end well. Be intentional to obey God, be intentional to acknowledge God in all your ways. There is more to life here on this planet than nourishing our pleasures. There is no fulfillment for our flesh, its lusts are bottomless. Our flesh will never hit the bottom and be satisfied in this world. Giving ourselves over to our wants all the time will lead us to death. Living for the glory of God, now this is life. There is so much in this life that would tempt us to live for but nothing compares to the glory of God. Oh, that God would get glory out of our lives. Laying ourselves down, laying our wants down, telling our flesh "no" is the greatest experience we can get here. Jesus gives an abundance of life but this abundance has nothing to do with our lusts or wants; it all has to do with giving God glory.

Loving as He loved, giving as He gave, caring as He cares, this is when we flow in the Spirit. We are spiritual beings and we can either open ourselves to the possession of the Spirit or to the possession of demons. We all serve one of two masters. Jesus is the only choice that produces eternal life. We can trust our soul and life into His hands. This life will be filled with hardship and death because sin is at work all around us. There will be a day when Jesus returns and the battles of sickness and sin will be done away with forever. While we are here, it should be expected. None of it determines the favor of God. His favor was defined by the crucifixion of Christ. God loves us! Believe it no matter what!

Note

384

"Among the gods there is none like unto thee, O Lord; neither are there any works like unto thy works. All nations whom thou hast made shall come and worship before thee, O Lord; and shall glorify thy name" (Psalm 86:8–9, KJV)

When we look up to anyone more than Christ, we are prey for disappointment. This does not mean that we dishonor those who inspire us. They inspire not because of who they are but because of the decisions of faith they made. The book of Hebrews honors the decisions of faith more so than the people of faith. Each one listed had short comings but what was honored was their decisions of faith. Their faith was a decision to obey God, it was not their perfect life. There is no perfect person outside of Christ; there are perfect decisions that imperfect people can make by faith. "By faith," not "by God" or "by the will of God" but "by faith." Don't be inspired only by preachers or teachers, be inspired by doers. Anyone can talk but not everyone decides by faith to obey God. God does not reward orators, He rewards decisions that require faith in Him, to glorify Him. We live in a generation that honor talkers more than doers. Times are changing. The day for "do as I say but not as I do" is over. Millennials won't follow or support that foolishness. For years, charlatans have been getting away with that as preachers; this is one reason why millennials don't go to church. When we look up to a person, more than Christ, we are prey for cults. No person or group of people deserves that much honor. Jesus and His word speak for itself. The power is not in the preaching alone, it's in the actions of faith. Anyone can talk but only a dependent believer on the Holy Spirit can live this life every day. Most ministers would not even go to church if they were not paid to be there. When we raise a preacher higher than Jesus, we are setting him up for a fall. God won't share His glory. We are all fallen and the quicker we can get the attention on Christ, the more anointed we will be in our ministry. This is an important lesson for a disciple. Christians get it wrong; they fail and fall. There is no person that has graduated from a need for Christ on this planet. Once we get this truth, we will be unmoved from our faith in Christ when others we looked to more that Him disappoint. Many have walked away from Christ, based on Church leaders. Jesus gave the church leaders a serious mandate. He recommended them to choose a millstone if they lead their following astray. Church leaders must be notified of their responsibility.[106]

[106.] *"It were better for him that a millstone were hanged about his neck, and he cast into the sea, than that he should offend one of these little ones." (Luke 17:2, KJV).*

"But whoso shall offend one of these little ones which believe in me, it were better for him that a millstone were hanged about his neck, and that he were drowned in the depth of the sea." (Matthew 18:6, KJV)

385

"Be ye not unequally yoked together with unbelievers: for what fellowship hath righteousness with unrighteousness? and what communion hath light with darkness?" (2 Corinthians 6:14, KJV)

If we want to be good at what we do, then we need to put around us the people who are better than us; so that we can be challenged rather than comforted where we are at. Comfort may seem like what we want but what we need is challenge. Challenge keeps us white hot but comfort makes us lukewarm or worse, cold. We need one another for accountability. We need one another to be challenged, corrected and inspired. Scripture was not given primarily to comfort or encourage but to instruct and correct. Our flesh uncorrected, leads to death. If our flesh is given a blank check and all we want in life, we will self-destruct because we can't handle a life without Jesus being our Lord. A life without absolutes or boundaries leads to chaos and addictions. We think we want what we want but what we really need is what God wants for our lives. It's hard to hear this, but God knows best. Taking matters into our hands, makes us bitter, angry and gives us over to hatred. These emotions without conviction put us in a dangerous place. When these emotions get the best of us, we will be surprised at what we are capable of. We are all one decision away from being where those we judge are at. Examining whether we are in the faith should be practiced more often. It's amazing how quick we can go from being in the faith, to being in the flesh. The deeper our faith is in scripture, the longer it will take to get us in the flesh. There is such a lack of biblical literacy in this generation that many go from faith to flesh within seconds as they leave the church. What gives a preacher weight to their sermon is the life that they live. Anyone can talk but only God's power makes a person do. This power comes by depending on God and spending time with Him. We can talk, but in order to get doing we need be believing who is in us. Christ in us gets us doing. Being in a church community that seeks God and depends on God is essential. Believers get built up in faith as we are around people with more faith than us. This is why we are not to forsake the assembly. We need one another. The church can't be the church without people. We need to challenge and inspire one another more than comfort. Our lives should speak a thousand words. When they elevate us, we can't say that this is our life; this is His life. What you see is God at work. God, have your way in me. May He alone receive glory.

Note

386

"For what saith the scripture? Abraham believed God, and it was counted unto him for righteousness" (Romans 4:3, KJV)

Reject sight as a determination of faith. Our faith is not determined by anything but scripture. Faith must be fought for while we are in these bodies of flesh. We are prone depression; our minds without faith will spiral into despair. Faith stops our thoughts from free falling and sets them into the hands of God. Scripture binds our thoughts that are contrary to faith, and God casts them out. The less of His word that we know, the more our thoughts will plummet. Don't let the enemy get the best of us; confess and depend on His Word. When we quote anyone more than scripture, we are on thin ice. The enemy does not submit to flesh or to the wisdom of man but by the name of Jesus, he is vanquished. We are called to live valiantly in Christ. The Spirit of God makes us a weapon while we are here for the glory of God. Religion deviates us from our call as evangelists. It gets us sidetracked by all forms of religious charades and doctrines. Music and motivational messages have taken over the house of God. We summon the Spirit when we gather, so our time together is not just accumulating knowledge. We are baptized in fire for the glory of our Christ. We gather to hail our king, we gather to remind ourselves that we have no rights of our own, we gather to lift Jesus overall. A successful minister makes His congregation quote the Word more than him. The artistry of a preacher leaves the people thinking on Christ when he is done preaching. The pulpit is not for testimonies or egos, it's for the Word to be rightly divided. No one needs to hear about us; they need to hear about Christ. Share testimonies one on one. When you stand behind the pulpit, preach Christ and Him crucified. Paul had one of the most amazing testimonies but he chose to preach Christ more than his story. Jesus saves; our testimonies prove that He saves but our testimonies are not the Gospel. A pulpit built on testimonies will be filled with "testiphonies." The pulpit is for the scripture to be taught in such a way, that bondages of sin are broken off the audience and they walk away not only with a changed mind but with a changed life. The Gospel is power unto salvation. The Gospel does not need discipleship when preached. The Gospel makes us want discipleship and not detest it!

Note

387

"But God hath chosen the foolish things of the world to confound the wise; and God hath chosen the weak things of the world to confound the things which are mighty" (1 Corinthians 1:27. KJV)

When we conclude or make a judgment, God tends to use it as fuel for Him to remind us of who has the final say. We can say "It's dead" but Jesus said, "It's just asleep." We like to write off what God writes in. We are warned by Scripture to not assume because our five senses tell us so.[107] We are challenged to believe the statement "She's not dead but she's asleep." The church is not dead in the West, she is asleep. No one who believes in Christ is dead but is asleep if they are not spiritually alive. The only people that need to be revived are those that are dead in sin and trespasses. Since Adam's fall in Eden, we have all been dead. The wages of sin are death. This is why Christ died a brutal death to take on Himself what we deserved. We have millions of Christians who are asleep. A great awakening is coming. This church age won't awaken to the sound of a lullaby but to the sound of an alarm. Awakening happens when preachers call out the sleepers. When the Gospel is preached, it will call forth who we thought were dead; the light of Christ has given them life. An awakening is coming but it will be through the unexpected in the most unexpected of places. So many "no name" preachers will be used so that the only name that is honored is Jesus. These men won't want

---

[107] *"There is a way which seemeth right unto a man, but the end thereof are the ways of death." (Proverbs 14:12, KJV)*

glory for themselves; they resent to be talked about more than Christ. They burn for Jesus's name to be lifted up. They have been prepared by seasons of grief, hardship, and rejection to not touch the glory of God. God will do as He pleases. He anoints whom He chooses. When the awakening happens, it won't be known for the experience but for the power to change lives. Life transformation will be the evidence. Those who thought that they were dead will be made alive. Spiritual tombs will be emptied. A generation will come forth and say "we were dead in sin but God gave us life in Christ." The church is asleep. She is not dead. Christ will have a bride that is ready before He returns. Let's put our five senses aside and trust scripture as our hope for today. Believe and watch the church awaken to all that He wants her to be. Don't be a scorner or a naysayer; the millennials have hope as you did when you were first saved. Remember where you came from and begin to believe for others. By faith, we will see God do what only He can do.

Note

388

"I can do all things through Christ which strengtheneth me" (Philippians 4:13, KJV)

God never gave us eyes on the back of our head for a reason. We were designed to not look back. The only time that Jesus told us to look back, was to remember what He accomplished. We have many people who are looking back on their last decisions, thinking that those decisions defined them. In Christ, we always have hope for redemption, as long as we have a pulse. Looking only in the rear-view mirror will lead us into a crash. Some need to forget those things that are behind them, which haunt them and steel their faith. Our faith must not be in what we did but in what Christ did. Our opposers want to remind us of the last season to shame us but we need to tell them that "yesterday" does not define who we are today. His mercy was new this morning. Let's choose to look ahead to today. Many have aged looking back, turning them into pillars of salt because they would not heed the conviction of scripture to not look back. This is the day that the Lord has made, rejoice and be glad in it. Every day, we are given a new start in Christ. When we succumb to our enemies, we start every day defined by who we were in our "yesterday." Shake off the past; look to Christ. Our past will let bitterness and resentment get the best of us; this is why we need to look to Christ's past. What He accomplished is for us today. His blood will never lose its power. Christ is relevant today and it's never too late to trust Him for a new start. Who you were without Christ is not who you are in Christ. No matter what the outcome, our faith is unshakable. We already won because He won, no matter our seemed defeat. We have a reason to keep going. Our reason to continue is for His glory and not our pleasure. With the same excellence that He showed us, we can show others in all that we do, that we do it unto Him. Let's give our all for His glory by not letting our past define us; His past is our definition of worth and value. Don't look back; forget those things in the past. Remember only what Jesus accomplished and keep pressing ahead to glorify His name. This mind-set frees us from bitterness, breaks our limitations, and launches us into life. The taunts of our opposers may sound true but in the end, we know what really matters. Decide today to believe, no matter what yesterday reminds us of. Finish strong!

Note

389

"Repent ye therefore, and be converted, that your sins may be blotted out, when the times of refreshing shall come from the presence of the Lord" (Acts 3:19, KJV)

Repentance leads to refreshing. There is no refreshing in gratifying our flesh. Living in sin is far from refreshing. There is no good fruit from sin. Sin may seem pleasurable but, in the end, it leads to death. We all have sinned. This is why repentance is an urgent message. God does not need a man-made lie-detector to use on us, which we can manipulate. God cannot be fooled by anyone. We are prone to pretending but we can't do that with God. In order for repentance to be refreshing, it has to come from the heart before God. It's refreshing because His grace never runs out. No matter how we squandered life, or how long we worked in the pig pen, God is waiting with arms wide open, to receive us. Christ took our punishment on Himself. God won't allow His Son's blood to be taken in vain. This is why we can't use Christ as a license to do what He bled and died for. We must be warned of trampling the blood of Christ under our feet by choosing to use Him as an excuse to sin. When repentance is from the heart, we will hate sin and feel the grief of the Holy Spirit. If we sin without grief or without conviction, we may quench the Holy Spirit. Repent, it's not too late. Repentance is not a negative word; it's the most encouraging word that we could ever hear. Repentance is a part of the Gospel and without it, we don't have good news. We want to be encouraged the way we are and comforted in our sin, but that does not lead to refreshing. There are only two books where

Jesus Himself speaks outside of the Gospels, 2 Corinthians 12:9 and Revelation 1:4. Both times should be noted. His grace is sufficient and His corrective words to the Church are what we read. These are the least preached sermons in the West. We want health and wealth but Jesus told Paul that His grace would be sufficient. We want to be encouraged but Jesus tells the church to repent or He will remove His candlestick from them.[108] The most encouraging sermon for a believer is what makes us see our need for Christ, whether in repentance or in Worship of His glory. The glory of God teaches us that we are "wretched, pitiful, poor, blind, and naked." This is our state without Christ. The good in us is Christ at work in us. In our flesh without Christ, there is no good thing. Be refreshed, repent!

Note

[108.] *"Remember therefore from whence thou art fallen, and repent, and do the first works; or else I will come unto thee quickly, and will remove thy candlestick out of his place, except thou repent." (Revelation 2:5, KJV)*

390

"For God sent not his Son into the world to condemn the world; but that the world through him might be saved" (John 3:17, KJV)

God did not send Jesus to condemn us but to save us. The warnings of God and the convictions of God are always for our benefit and His glory. His passion is to love us. Even the hardest of words that God speaks are motivated from His abundance of love. Kids don't always understand the discipline of their parents but when the parents follow Christ, they must train their kids in the way they must go. God is our parent. He is our Father. We may not know all that is going on right now but He does. If an earthly dad knows to do good for his kids how much more does our Father in heaven. The Gospel is a message of prosperity and abundance but not in the way that we want it to be. Judas wanted prosperity and was willing to sell out eternity for temporal pleasure. The Western prosperity gospel only disciples Judas': people who are in their relationship with Jesus for the wrong reason. Satan preached the Western prosperity gospel to Jesus while He was in the wilderness for forty days. His lie will not tempt the remnant. Today's prosperity gospel makes people despise their cross and hardship but those who follow Christ, boast in their cross and hardship. God is not shunning you or is too busy for you. God is with us through whatever it is that we are facing. Don't let the storms of life uproot the anchor of faith. Rejoice in the hardship. Dance and sing when everyone would expect you to be down in depression. Affliction is a blessing. The conviction of God is a blessing. Thank Him that we see a need for Him. What does it profit if we are spoiled rotten here and get everything we want, when we want it but end up in hell for eternity? Don't despise what causes you to need God. Resist the heresy. Contend for the faith. When Jesus said that one will betray Him, it was not obvious who would be. False teachers are not obvious. Wolves have the best of costumes. Try all that we hear with scripture. Remember, scripture interprets itself. Remember, scripture is the best commentary on itself. Remember, His body and blood. His death is our way to resurrection. The resurrection power is found when we reckon ourselves dead. It's in our death that we pass into eternity. Know that our Father is always good, no matter what is going on.

Note

391

"We then, as workers together with him, beseech you also that ye receive not the grace of God in vain" (2 Corinthians 6:1, KJV)

Preachers have been bought for too long. Their salary and health insurance are keeping them in blind submission. Accountability will lead to their termination so that they choose provision over truth. They have families to feed. The widow's mite has been spent on outlandish clothing, houses, and vehicles for too long. To use single mom's generosity so that ministers can live a life of luxury is embarrassing. No one is saying that a preacher should live in poverty but they need to exercise modesty. When the pastor is the wealthiest congregant, then there is something wrong. Living off of the widow, elderly, and vulnerable is the height of cowardice. God will warn before He will judge. God wants all to repent before He exercises judgment. We must be warned that there is a time when the grace of God is taken in vain. The deaths of Ananias and Saphira are a lesson to us. Zacchaeus has a testimony that we need to see our celebrity pastors have. Who will be the first to repent? We need repentance from our leaders before we will see repentance from those on the streets. We will never graduate from a need to repent while we are in these bodies. Humble ourselves. May all see our humanity so that all they will look up to is Christ. Preachers must get free from depending on the tithe so that they are only dependent on the Spirit of truth. Preachers who are dependent on the tithe more than the Spirit are in a dangerous position. Don't sell out the call of God for temporary provision. What is more important, your birthright or the satisfaction of your hunger? Scripture was given so that we don't need to be ignorant. We can have clarity about our call and purpose but it's all about our faith in Christ. Will we trust truth more than trusting our need for provision? God is raising the standard against His enemy. There will be a voice of truth in our generation, we won't be purchased or bound to politics. We are free agents who preach the Word and are accountable to scripture. We will not compromise for anyone. We will preach truth whether it fills the room or empties the room. We are not in it for ourselves but for the glory of God. Be excited because the greatest awakening is about to happen. We must believe all the way to His return.

Note

392

"There is no fear in love; but perfect love casteth out fear: because fear hath torment. He that feareth is not made perfect in love" (1 John 4:18, KJV)

We need fear cast out of our church age. The love of God casts out fear. Fear must not be welcomed. Fear must not be entertained. Every headline feeds fear, everywhere we go is a breeding ground for fear. Fear must be feared and that's all that must be feared. No anti-Christ, no calamity, and no tragedy must dictate our faith or grip us in fear. God doesn't want to tell fear to just leave; throw fear out of our soul, in Jesus's name. We are not as audacious or as bold as we can be in Christ. We are unrestrained to believe what the end of our existence tells us. We know how life is going to end. Christ won; we have won, no matter what we face, we have grace that's more than sufficient. Eschatology taught in the right way fills us with faith and not with fear. The Holy Spirit fills us with faith when our flesh wants to be filled with fear. Don't make peace with fear. Violently, brutally, and viciously remove fear in Jesus's name. Beat fear into submission to faith and watch it be cast out by the perfect love of God. Jesus wants to drive fear out of our lives. Jesus's death was to crucify doubt in the love of God, so that none could ever question the love of God toward us. His love is toward us. Not only does His crucifixion show us His love but it also shows us His hatred of sin and fear. Don't hide in fear like Adam and Eve. Come out from behind fear and feel the warmth of Jesus. He will throw His arms around us because He loves us to death. The same Spirit that rose Him from death is in us.

Relinquish fear to the Spirit and He will mortify the deeds of the flesh. Surrender fear, let the Spirit and the Word wash our souls, so that we can live bold, fearless and on fire. The fire of God will consume as much of us as we are willing to surrender before Him. He wants to start a spiritual fire through us that makes us hate sin, cast out fear and preach Christ with such power that no one can resist His grace. Hold onto nothing that keeps you from faith. Let go of fear, embrace the love of God. Take God seriously. Take fear seriously. Fight the fight of faith like never before. Don't let the devil wear our faith out. Have audacious faith where only the grace of God is what keeps us moving forward, so all will know who is Lord.

Note

393

"But the fearful, and unbelieving, and the abominable, and murderers, and whoremongers, and sorcerers, and idolaters, and all liars, shall have their part in the lake which burneth with fire and brimstone: which is the second death" (Revelation 21:8, KJV)

F earing man more than fearing God affects our salvation. Who is Lord of our life, God or man? The fear of man is more of a dangerous way of living than any immoral sin. Many think that they have never violated the moral law, but the fear of man gets the same eternal wage as any other sin does. The spirit of fear is so prevalent yet goes unchallenged. How can we fear to preach the Gospel? How can we fear to preach what needs to be said? How can we fear if we say we believe all that Christ did for us? When God speaks, we are responsible to obey. The spirit of fear keeps us from obedience. It tempts us to value the approval of man more than the approval of God. There is too many souls going to hell to be wrapped up in the politics of what people will think about us after we preach the Gospel. Let's live unashamed of the Gospel. May truth always prevail. May we remain open to the Holy Spirit so He can call out what needs to be called out. We need to break free from the spirit of fear in Jesus's name. Only the fear of God produces good results. Fearing God means taking Him seriously. When God is not magnified and worshipped, we will grow familiar with Him and no one should want to get loose or frivolous in our relationship with Him. God is not one of us. He is the uncreated One. Magnify God or we will live oppressed by the spirit of fear. God is with us and loves us, so we have no reason to fear. There is never an excuse to fear when we believe in the love of God. Christ vanquished fear. We can only have a sound mind when the fear of man does not rule us. When we believe that God is bigger than whatever we are facing in life, we will make it to the end. Don't be afraid of not getting people's approval. It's God who we need to honor above mankind. When we honor God above all, we will walk in order and favor. Seeking approval and the recognition of people is such a waste of time. It will never happen. People will never be pleased. There will always be something that you won't be able to do for them. The void in the soul can only be filled by Christ. We will only disappoint each other when we look to each other more than Christ. The church will disappoint, preachers will disappoint; none of us are the Christ. Fear only God, take God seriously.

Note

394

"Pure religion and undefiled before God and the Father is this,
To visit the fatherless and widows in their affliction, and to
keep himself unspotted from the world" (James 1:27, KJV)

No one can help an adult if they are not willing to help themselves. The widow and the orphan are who we are commanded to help but not those who can help themselves. Jesus helped those who needed Him and challenged those who did not. God won't get us out of bed; God won't use our utensils to feed us; God won't take the wheel of our car; God gives us self-control. The Holy Spirit gives us self-control so that we are not controlled by sin but by our will. Our will matters to God so much, that He put a tree in the Garden of Eden, the tree of the knowledge of good and evil. Believers in Christ have a sound mind. This may surprise the world because Christians rarely are a good example of having a sound mind. The foolishness that comes out of ministries today, one would wonder if they ever read the Bible. We have the Bible in nearly every language and it has been paraphrased so that anyone could read it but it's not being followed. With all the knowledge that we have, with all the access to Scripture that we have, yet there is such an ignorance in our society. No generation will be held more accountable than ours. The biblical illiteracy is a disgrace. What preachers are getting away with is a shame on the congregation more than the preachers. So many people bash the preachers but it's the donors that will be held responsible. The congregation can try to deflect the responsibility onto their preacher but they are the ones paying his salary. These preachers are such hirelings, that they will say what their donor wants them to say. The way to speak to our preachers of today is with our money. Many preach to the pocket book. "Just tell me what I want to hear and I'll pay my tithe." A massive number of pastors preach to the largest donors in the church. "What do you want to hear so I can keep you giving?" It's sad because so many are silenced by these pastors for fear that they will lose their job or their severance pay. Washington is not the only place where the swamp needs to be drained. Politics, nepotism and fraud is going on in our churches. It's like the church has Nanci Pelosi as their apostle. The foreign budget of most churches looks more like the liberals of today than the will of God. We need to make where God has put us great again.

Note

395

"Now as touching things offered unto idols, we know
that we all have knowledge. Knowledge puffeth up,
but charity edifieth" (1 Corinthians 8:1, KJV)

A new wave of clergy is coming to our nation. They won't look like we expect, they won't talk like we thought they would, but they will stand in an anointing like no other generation. Their ordination won't come by their knowledge, which is received from books. Their anointing will be on their testimony of what Christ did in their lives. Knowledge puffs up and for the most part and that is what we are dealing with in our puffed-up church age. We have many leaders who learned to preach, know the Bible but have never experienced the power of God. Our Church today has a great form of godliness but has little to no power. There are many centers today that are breeding grounds for the next wave of pastors to be standing behind our pulpits. They will have the knowledge of Scripture but also a testimony that cannot be refuted. These men and women won't only show in the Scripture that Jesus lives but they will show you by their life that Jesus lives. Those who doubt the power of Christ need to stop serving in the church and start serving these centers where ministry is needed the most. These centers do more for the community than most churches. If Jesus were here today, where would He be on a Sunday morning? Read the Gospels and follow the life of Christ. The men who Jesus chose as apostles, were not seminary grads. We have emphasized education and knowledge so much in our church age, that ministry has become a career choice and not a call of God.

Run from ministry if it's a career choice. The Devil does not relent. The battle is too great. We need men and women who have heard the call of God. We need to be cautious when the church becomes so focused on image and knowledge that they neglect the vulnerable and those who need Christ the most. A man of God is simply a man who needs God. Let's pour into the ministries' prayers, resources, and finances. Church, it's time to mirror Jesus and not celebrity pastors. Church, it's time to look to Jesus and not the trends coming out of our mega ministries.

Note

_____

_____

_____

_____

_____

_____

_____

_____

396

"I tell you, Nay: but, except ye repent, ye shall
all likewise perish" (Luke 13:3, KJV)

Love keeps no record of wrong as long as the wrongs have been repented of, otherwise that love leads to abuse with power and manipulation. Minors must not feel shame to speak out about abuse. When wrong is done, holding the one who sinned accountable is not rebellion. We have all sinned but sin that's done to you as a minor must be taken seriously. The church has overlooked multiple cases of abuse for the sake of the "Gospel." We have all sinned. The Gospel does not elevate our perfection but our sinfulness. Why would we think that sin hinders the Gospel? Unless we acknowledge sin, we cannot be saved. Believers still sin but the difference is they don't enjoy the sin. The Spirit of God won't let us. Minors are not "defective" if they have been abused. Jesus can heal. No human is a true reflection of Christ. Don't let the accuser lie and tell you that God turned a blind eye on who abused you. We all get haunted by our past about what happened to us while we were unaware fully of what was going on. We were young and impressionable. There is no shame that Jesus can't cleanse from our soul. There is no sin done to us that Jesus will let go unpunished. Just know that Jesus would not have used you like that, just know that Jesus won't take advantage of your gullibility, just know that Jesus does not steal of your time, talent or treasure for His own gain. There is nothing that Jesus needs of us to fellowship with Him. He loves us. We are safe from all abuse in His presence. The church is made up of sinners, that if we go unchecked are no different than any other sinner on the street. Elevating a man too high is setting him up for a fall. The most respected man has a past, the most respected man has a nature like you. Fools teach that believers don't have a sinful nature. Fools don't warn against sin. Fools lie when they say that Jesus keeps no record of wrong when the wrongs have not been repented of. Bring Jesus in on our own sin but also bring Him in on the sins that were done to you. We need healing from the abuse committed to us. The record of wrong is held because there was no repentance and the offenders are still getting away with their sin. There is a time to let God to fight our battles but He also does lead us to authorities to stop the abuser from continuing.

Note

397

"And he saith unto them, Follow me, and I will make
you fishers of men" (Matthew 4:19, KJV)

The majority profession of the apostles prior to meeting Jesus were fishermen. Their trade had equipped them to be what God called them to be. Fishing is not catching fish; it's fishing for fish. No one catches a fish without going to where the fish are at, with the right bait and using the right tool to catch the fish. No one has ever caught a fish by prayer alone. No one has a caught a fish by holding up a welcome sign in a boat with a trendy music group and a clever orator preaching the fish into the boat. To be a fisher of men, takes obedience to God. The growth strategy for churches coming out of our major ministries are mostly carnal. They offer strategies that do not come from scripture but from charlatans who found a way to turn Jesus into a cash cow. They teach how to build God's church without God. Where is the prayer meeting? Where is the evangelistic training? Where is the evangelistic service outside of our Sunday gatherings in the community that we are called to be ministering in? Sunday was supposed to be the Lords day and the day to Worship Jesus. Western churches have turned Sunday into the people's day. The day is designed to fill the services with people but has little to no room for God to be in attendance. The worship tracks, video announcements, sermon notes on a projector, give little to no room for God to lead. God won't come if we close the door to Him and tell Him that we can do a better job than Him. Many Churches have no room for Christ. Many churches keep Jesus on the outside; the elders are too mature, the board is smarter, the pastor can do it better than God. How can we discern this? It's very easy: is prayer important there? Is there a prayer meeting? Has prayer become as trivial as our prayer before we eat? If we believed the scripture, would we be so lukewarm in our Gospel presentation. There is more passion over politics, sports and hobbies than there is for the Gospel. It's time for repentance to be preached, it's time to get honest with the diagnosis! Turning a blind eye to this will reap serious ramifications on our generation and fearfully on us. God won't bless ignorance. Does it not move your emotions when we read of Jesus's reaction to a lukewarm believer[109]?

Note

[109.] Revelation chapter 3

398

"The fear of the Lord is the beginning of wisdom: and the knowledge of the holy is understanding" (Proverbs 9:10, KJV)

The fear of man is a snare. Our fear reveals to us who is more of a Lord in our life. The only fear worth having is the fear of God. The fear of God does not mean to be afraid of Him but it does mean to take Him seriously. He is coming back with a military force. He is not weak but strong and mighty. Many people think of Jesus for who He was prior to the cross, as a lamb. When He comes back, He will be coming as a Lion. Do we take God seriously? Our human nature is bent to become familiar with what is important. Familiarity with God and His Word is very dangerous and it will lead to a spirit of entitlement and lukewarmness. Familiarity will fill us with contempt for what is important. It is so self-destructive. Take God seriously. Take our call seriously. Don't let our faith be determined by fear. So many in the West are fearful of evangelism, but why? What are they afraid of? Are they ashamed of their Savior? Jesus was rejected unto death, why are we fearful when our rejection will only hurt our feelings? It's time to grow up spiritually. We have many adults that have childish faith. Jesus wants us to have childlike faith that simply says yes to His call without knowing how all the details will come together. A childish faith is different. How can you have gone a whole year without sharing the Gospel with someone around you in your community? Do you even have friends who are sinners like Jesus had? Is Jesus your example of what it looks like to be a believer or is it today's celebrity pastors your examples? God is repulsed by most Western Christianity that worships self-image, materialism, and entertainment more than obeying His commission. We think that we know what is best for mankind but God told us what is best and that is "every soul must hear the Gospel." The Gospel will always be a message as offensive as that may be of "St" Augustine, the heretic, who did not write scripture when he said, "Preach the gospel and use words when necessary." Jesus never said that. Jesus said, "Go, preach the Gospel to everyone." When our works become the Gospel more than His work on the cross, we are blaspheming the work of Christ. It's time to fear only God and preach what is on His heart. Don't please people, don't fear man, take God and His Word seriously.

Note

399

*"And Jesus being full of the Holy Ghost returned from Jordan,
and was led by the Spirit into the wilderness" (Luke 4:1, KJV)*

*"And Jesus returned in the power of the Spirit into
Galilee: and there went out a fame of him through
all the region round about" (Luke 4:14, KJV)*

Anointing oil is made one way only and that's by crushing olives. The anointing is not just charisma, passion, fluency, oratory or exuberance. No one can get an anointing without embracing the afflictions that come with life. Everyone wants the anointing; few want the process to have it. To walk in the power of God, means to walk less in our power and more in His. Suffering, affliction and hardship summon an anointing that no seminary or conference could ever give you. Knowing God in the valley deepens our anointing more than knowing Him on the mountain top. On the mountain top, there is no vegetation; it's in the valley that we see the greatest variety of life. Take advantage of this pressing, boast in this crushing, preach from this pain, let all see what determines our faith. Scripture alone determines our faith. Stand on His promises. Don't cave into any other way of thinking. His Word is sufficient to not only bring us through but He will bring us through on dry ground. God does not abandon us. Even in death, we can die the death of the righteous. In our last breath, we can see His hand taking our soul to be with Him in paradise. We are all allotted time while we are here. Don't let anyone replace God in your life. Don't let anything replace God in your life. We live off of His Word. His Word is manna to our famished soul. We could not be more anointed when everyone looks on in disbelief that we are still pressing ahead in the call of God. Satan will use anyone and everyone that is open to him, to rob the call of God from our lives. Jesus wants us to say, "It is written" and "the Bible says." His Word is our weapon to cut down the lies of hell. Worship Jesus when our flesh does not want to. Worship Jesus when all would wonder why. The revelation of the cross will keep us to the end. Considering Christ will keep us to the end. God, we surrender to you. It's in surrender that anointing pours down our heads; it's in our surrender that the anointed words we preach do not fall to the ground. Still will we praise Him. In life we will praise Him, in sickness we will praise Him, and in death we will praise Him. There is nothing that could move us because we are not planted in our strength or might.

Note

_____
_____
_____
_____
_____
_____
_____
_____
_____

400

"But ye shall receive power, after that the Holy Ghost is come upon you: and ye shall be witnesses unto me both in Jerusalem, and in all Judaea, and in Samaria, and unto the uttermost part of the earth" (Acts 1:8, KJV)

How long will our city streets be void of the Gospel? How long will pastors hoard the tithe for themselves and their own endeavors? How long will the congregation financially give to keep the Gospel of the pulpit in their church? How long will we turn a blind eye to our cities? How long will the human condition dominate the condition of the soul? How long will the evangelical church be okay with not evangelizing in their local community? How long will our outreaches be ashamed of Gospel preaching? How long will the office of an evangelist lay in ruin? How long will we allow the evangelist to do all the work, when he should be equipping the church for the work of evangelism? How long will we have pastors coddling pastors at pastors' conferences? How long will the pulpits be closed off to evangelist's? How long will Gospel preaching be an embarrassment to the local church? How long will the Gospel be the least preached message in our evangelical church age? How long will hell be omitted from the content of the Gospel? How long will repentance be seen as an offensive word and dated word? How long will feeding programs, building projects, well digging and sustainable ministry be emphasized more than the souls of men? Where is the passion for souls? Is it more important for someone to gain the American dream than have their soul saved from hell? When was the last time we were moved to tears when we read of hell fire and the torment that awaits? Does it not bother us? Have we grown so cold? Is our church culture more backslidden and on the verge of reprobate as we even know? Will you get behind a ministry that preaches unashamedly about the Gospel of Jesus Christ? Will you support an evangelistic mission that wants to be in every city of this nation, holding crusades and gospel preaching in the open air?

Note

401

*"But without faith it is impossible to please him: for he that
cometh to God must believe that he is, and that he is a rewarder
of them that diligently seek him" (Hebrews 11:6, KJV)*

What if we believed that awakening can happen? What if we
believed miracles can happen? What if we believed the best days of
the church age is right before us? What if we believed that it won't
be the way it is right now for the rest of our lives? Satan does not
want anyone to believe any of this. The scheme of hell has been
keeping many in unbelief, worn out, hiding behind our walls, and
not looking up for the return of the Lord; few believe that "greater
things than our Lord, we will do." If we are going to be extreme one
way or another, let's choose to be extreme in faith. Our faith must
not be shaped by our past disappointments. Our faith must not be
determined by logic or what we see. Faith is only determined by
scripture and scripture alone. We live by faith in God's Word and by
His promises alone. We are commanded to fight the fight of faith.
If ever there was a generation where our fight needs to get spiritually
violent, if ever there was a generation that needed undignified faith,
it's ours. We can become earth-shaking, demon-slaying fire brands
for the Kingdom of Christ if we believe. Will we believe in the promises of God? Many have had their faith shipwrecked because they
trusted in their faith for too long to no avail. Don't trust in faith,
trust in Christ. Believe more audaciously when we have no reason
to believe, other than Gods Word commanding us to believe. Don't
let your senses dictate your faith, let God's word dictate faith. The

only F-word Satan hates is Faith. This is a call for believers to stir up their faith. Let's remind ourselves of what God did in scripture, what He has done in the history of the church. Let's believe that we can see, the greatest outpouring of the Spirit that the earth has ever seen. Let's believe for the glory of Christ. Let's believe all the way to glory. His word is all that nourishes faith. Stand on the promises of God, declare Jesus Christ is Lord and surrender before Him our whole selves. Satan will try every means possible to knock the fight out of us but He who saved us will keep us to the end. We will not be forsaken. Our Lord will have the last Word. Scoffers, maligners, and doubters will be brought to shame. Those of faith will not be brought to shame in the end.

Note

402

"Being confident of this very thing, that he which hath
begun a good work in you will perform it until the
day of Jesus Christ" (Philippians 1:6, KJV)

When we are lost for words and we don't know what's next, go to your knees. It's in the posture of repentance and humility that we feel God is with us. Hardening our heart does no one any good. Rendering our hearts before God in surrender is all that we can do through the darkest times of our lives. The only place that we will find comfort and relief from all that the enemy throws at us is before our God in worship. When we mature as believers, we will not only learn how great our sin is but how even greater the price that He paid for our sin truly was. The more life experiences we get, the more we realize that we need Him as much today as we did when we first were saved. The attacks of our enemy and the storms of life will bring us to our knees before God, telling our Lord Jesus that if He does not intervene, there is no way that we are going to make it. Many live in the lion's den but they can't harm our faith. Our faith will not shipwreck, our faith will not fail because our faith is not in our faith, Jesus will keep us to the end. He will not leave us nor forsake us. A bruised reed He will not break. We may be battered and bruised but God will keep us to the end. When our faith is in anything other than Christ, we will not make it to the end. When Christ is all we have left, we are in the best place we could be. Everything around us may be falling apart but He is our rock. Christ is interceding that our faith will not fail. We all will hear the rooster crow; even later on in our journey, we will be reminded of our continuing need for Christ. There won't be a day where we will be able to live without God. There is no graduation from a need for God. If we need Him right now, rejoice because we even see a need for Him. There are many that turn to other means, idols, and distractions but we are turning to the only one that has power to keep us going. Christ in us is our assurance of life and eternal life. When He returns, every knee will bow willingly or unwillingly. Christ will never go to a cross again. His return will be for vengeance and to conquer forever. Let's make Him Lord in a culture where no wants to be accountable or told what to do. We will stand out when we make Christ Lord. It's so counter for our culture to bow. Take a knee.

Note

403

"It is good for me that I have been afflicted; that I might learn thy statutes" (Psalm 119:71, KJV)

Following Christ is an adventure. Saying yes to Him is the greatest decision anyone could make. His grace is sufficient. Many on the outside of our journey would wonder how we have made it this far. Transitions, afflictions, demonic attacks, rejections, betrayals, malice, gossip, financial hardships, the list could go on but through it all, the grace of God is sufficient. Trust less in ourselves, trust less in people and put our full trust in God. Jesus never disappoints. When we consider Him through all of life's peaks and valleys, He remains constant. Don't look to anyone or anything more than Christ. Satan attempts to get our focus off Christ and onto the distractions of this life. Don't fall for the temptation, God will deliver us from temptation if we bring Christ in on all of life's battles. When we run from His presence or over time backslide away from our time with Him, we will notice that our fight against bitterness, anger and self-pity will weaken. When God has our focus, we will be emboldened and become ready to fight like never before. The spiritual military is awakening. Life has trained us for the Spiritual warfare that we need to engage in every day. This is a call to spiritual arms. Memorize His Word, curse the enemy in the name of Jesus, evangelize to everyone and live unashamed of our Lord. When Satan attempts to put out our fire what he is actually doing is pouring gas on our flame. The gospel spreads through the affliction of the saint more than through the prosperity of the saints. Mature believers boast in their affliction, "it is good that I've been afflicted." The more dependent on Christ we get through our journey as believers, the greater our threat to spiritual wickedness we are. The flame of the Spirit in us cannot and will not be extinguished. We resist the devil and he flees because he is no match for who is in us. Who is in us is greater than any authority on this earth. None can stop in His way, none can hinder the called of God, none can quench the anointed of God. Don't be bitter at the agents of hell, pity their souls. They are tormented night and day. Their abuse, manipulation and shame did not work as they thought. They schemed for our demise but God vindicated.

Note

404

"These things I have spoken to you, that in Me you may have peace. In the world you will have tribulation; but be of good cheer, I have overcome the world" (John 16:33, NKJV)

When God calls, we typically don't know who we should or should not tell it too. Abraham, Joseph and David had their families ridicule them for the call of God on their lives. There were times when they second guessed the call. While they were on the journey in the wilderness, going through the process, there were times of deep doubt. The temptation to take matters into their own hands and make the call of God happen in their flesh became so strong but it never worked out. Much of today's Christianity does not prepare their followers for hardship. Many get saved because they want to go to heaven but they don't know of the cross that they will bear to get there. The believer faces a cross every day. We face a decision every day to follow God or to follow our flesh. Choose our will or choose His will. Foolish preachers preach that the will of God for today is wealth, health and abundance. These foolish preachers are not preparing for their congregation to have faith when the feelings run out, instead the congregation becomes more led by their five senses than faith in Scripture. Any preacher that teaches "in this world, we won't have trouble" is a liar. Any preacher that talks about heaven without a cross is leading their people to disappointment. While we are in these bodies, we will fight sin and face the appointed time to die lest Christ should return. Many that were healed by Jesus and saw His miracles were nowhere to be found on the day of His trial with Pilate;

if they were there, they were shouting for the crucifixion of Christ. Judas wanted abundance and fame so desperately, that He was willing to sell out Jesus. Look what that got him. We don't need health or wealth just like we don't need poverty and sickness; we need the will of God. We need to start praying that His will be done. Thank God these foolish preachers were not preaching to Jesus in the garden of Gethsemane, they would have tried to talk Jesus out of going to the cross. That's what most Western preachers are doing, they are trying to talk their congregation out of the cross. Unfortunately, the congregation gives financially to their message because it's what they want to hear. Who wants to hear about the cross? Even the apostles were offended at the cross.

Note

405

*"Nor height, nor depth, nor any other creature, shall
be able to separate us from the love of God, which is
in Christ Jesus our Lord" (Romans 8:39, KJV)*

There is nothing we could ever do to stop God from loving us. From the beginning, God loved us. He loved us to death. When we base the love of God on anything other than scripture, Satan will get a foothold. The love we need can only be found in God. This is why God must be first because if we replace Him with anyone or anything else, our souls will never be fulfilled. We come into alignment when He is first in our lives. Obedience to Him is what will give us joy. Obedience to Him may not make sense to those around us. We have story after story in scripture where God intervenes in a man or woman's life and directs them in His way. The call of God will not always be accepted by those we thought would celebrate it after we naively shared it with them. God uses others rejection, jealously, mockery and spite to affirm the call on our lives. The process of the wilderness molds our character and reminds us of our total reliance on God. Don't take their reaction personally because God has allowed it so that we would find comfort and celebration in Him alone. Sometimes only you and God will ever know what is going on, other times only God knows what is going on. When the call of God has no opposition, we need to examine if we heard it from God. If Christ and every follower that followed Him went the way of suffering and martyrdom, we are not exempt. The opposition in the West is mostly spiritual, more than physical like those in the East. Our afflictions and persecution are spiritual wickedness that taunt our minds. Physical persecution is easier to discern but spiritual attacks are the worst kind because we can't discern it as easily. Many in the West have taken their lives, fell into addictions or are distracted by things that don't matter. This is why we need to walk in the Spirit. Daily we need Him for discernment, daily we need Him to fend off the darkness. Don't get lazy because you are in ease. Hear from God, obey, say yes with joy. No matter what it is, consider Christ; nothing can compare to what Christ went through for us. His chords of love will pull us through even when we are left without strength. God is with you even when no one seems to be. Rest in Him. Let His Word enter you into the rest. God is love.

Note

406

"And he said unto them, Unto what then were ye baptized? And they said, Unto John's baptism" (Acts 19:3, KJV)

There are many today that have only experienced the baptism of John. John's baptism was of repentance. The baptism of John was only water baptism. The baptism of Jesus is more than just water. His baptism takes place as soon as a sinner repents and trusts Christ for salvation. He made us a Holy place by taking upon Himself our sin so that we can be a dwelling place for the Spirit of God. Without His Spirit, we are cadavers. Without His Spirit, we are sinful defeated humans. Jesus's baptism is of the Holy Spirit and fire. Jesus did not give His life so that He can have a lifeless church. He gave His life so that His church can have His life living through us. When we surrender to His Spirit, we will have a river of living water flow out of our mouths. He will make us relevant to sinners; we will be understood by sinners and will be compelled by His Spirit to preach the Gospel to sinners. Any Spirit that does not make convict of sin or make us on fire to preach the Gospel is not the Spirt of Christ. Jesus wants us to do greater things than He did. As we yield to Him, what He can do through us is limitless. Will we open ourselves up to the Holy Spirit or will we quench Him? We are bent on quenching Him, we are prone to think that we can do a better job than the Holy Spirit. The Church without the Holy Spirit will be no different than those under the law of Moses. The Bible without the Holy Spirit will not be understood. Discipleship without surrendering to the Holy Spirit is no different than the armor Saul offered David to defeat Goliath.

Evangelism without the Holy Spirit is just a debate and an argument. The church is spiritual, the worship of God is spiritual. Truth without the Spirit will not produce life. Any Spirit that does not lead us to the truth of the sixty-six books of the Bible is not the Spirit of Christ. The Spirit of Christ will not elevate Himself above Christ or add to what He has already given to us in the sixty-six books of the Bible. Don't lie to the Holy Spirit, don't quench the Holy Spirit, don't blaspheme the Holy Spirit. When the Holy Spirit is ignored, we will only reap what our flesh can produce, death. Take the Holy Spirit seriously, take His conviction seriously, He will not always strive with us.

Note

407

"And the second is like, namely this, Thou shalt love thy neighbour as thyself. There is none other commandment greater than these" (Mark 12:31, KJV)

The world teaches the love of self but religion teaches the hate of self. Religion looks down on those who love themselves and the world thinks there is something wrong with those who deny themselves. What did Jesus teach about self? He certainly paid a huge price for our "selves." God not only demonstrated His love for us but He also demonstrated His disdain for sin by dying the death of the cross. Jesus taught us not only to love God but also to love our neighbor as we love ourselves. We are not mammals or mere evolved creatures. We are advanced because we were made in the image of God. God treasures humanity, He deemed our value to be worth the blood of His only Son. We are not mere sinners predestined to burn in hell. We are fallen beings; we once walked in the tangible presence of God in the cool of the day. He listened as we named the animals. He desired a personal friendship with humanity. For thousands of years, we suffered the consequence of sin and disobedience. What Jesus accomplished is more than humanity had in Eden. We have more understanding because of scripture and the indwelling of the Holy Spirit. We need to unlearn the world's definition of the love of self and unlearn the religious definition of self. Christ's demonstration of love is clear in His crucifixion. It not only shows the love that He has for us but it also shows His hatred of sin too. We still see the consequences of sin all around us to this very day. Jesus's salvation was spiritual and eternal but until He returns, we will all pass bodily, we still have sin at work in us. Sin wants us to love ourselves more than Christ but religion wants us to deny our value that Christ purchased for us. We must love ourselves or we will lower ourselves to just mammals. When a society removes eternal life, the moral compass and stability of that society crashes. Suicide is on the increase because our educational system is godless. Religion also is seeing a rise in suicide amongst their leaders and congregation. Eternity has been pushed out of our society. Everyone wants to go to heaven but nobody wants to die. Nobody wants to go to hell but few look into how to be saved. Ignorance is not bliss. We have so much access to knowledge, yet so many choose ignorance.

Note

408

"John answered, saying unto them all, I indeed baptize you with water; but one mightier than I cometh, the latchet of whose shoes I am not worthy to unloose: he shall baptize you with the Holy Ghost and with fire" (Luke 3:16, KJV)

Biblical unity and biblical love are not compromising or immoral. The unity of the world teaches us that we should compromise and remove all moral absolutes. This is not unity or love. Love does not look away from accountability to truth. Love does not set us free. Love is just an emotion to the world. To God, love is more than an emotion or a feeling, it is a demonstration. Christ demonstrated the love of God. Everyone wants the blessing but looks away from the means of the blessing. Love came at a price, Christ died. The love that humanity needs is not the love that keeps us in our sin, which only hurts us, but love that pulls us up out of our sin, which sets us free. Christ's love does not condone sin but condemned sin in His own body on the cross. He bore our sin and our transgressions so that we can be free to know God. The Spirit of God is Holy. When we say "we feel God, sense God, or God is moving" yet there is no conviction of sin in our lives, we don't have the Spirit of God at work in our midst. The Spirit of God convicts us of sin and causes us to desire holiness more than sinfulness. The love of God does not leave us in what hurts us but leads us into what gives us life. We need biblical unity. We need to stop fighting about the non-essentials for Salvation. Many churches in the same city preach the same Gospel yet won't show the lost that they are different by loving one another.

The world will know us by our pastors' love for one another in the city. If we have the same Gospel, why can't we work together to reach our city? Let's not worry about how full our churches are but worry about how much we are obeying Christ. Do we even feel convicted to obey Christ's command to love one another? There will be a commanded blessing when we love one another. There will be a commanded blessing when we unify together. As long as we are divided, hiding behind our walls, we will not see the awakening that God wants to do. God is patient and will wait until the next generation if we would rather live in fear than walk in the promises of God. Those that have faith are a minority, the remnant is a minority but few is many when God is in it. An awakening is coming; we will see even greater things than our predecessors.

Note

409

"For God hath not given us the spirit of fear; but of power, and of love, and of a sound mind" (2 Timothy 1:7, KJV)

When was the last time you shared the Gospel as the Spirit led you to? Not at an outreach, not at a church but in your everyday life? Has the Lord led you to share the gospel? When we follow the leading of the Spirit in evangelism, we will experience the best results. A machine can't give birth, only an organism gives birth. The church is not only an organization, she is an organism. She is called to multiply. Each one of us believers in Christ make up the bride of Christ. Christ's bride does not need a mini skirt and scandalous makeup. The church could not get any more perfect in the sight of Jesus than when she simply depends only on Him. His blood cleansed us, He put a robe of righteousness on us and His Spirit is in us. We can stand in the power of His might and do what He has called us to do. The spirit of fear has dominated Western Christians. We are afraid of getting our feelings hurt by being rejected. We are afraid of offending people by telling them the truth. If we truly believed in the eternal consequence of sin, would we carelessly breeze past sinners every day. We would rescue anyone if we could see physically that they need to be rescued but what about the soul needing rescue? Does not the soul matter to you? For many Christians, the church is a culture or a tradition but they have never given Christ their soul. Does this not alarm you? Have we become so spiritually dull that we are not moved by the many we know who are going to hell? Satan has activated angels of light and wolves in sheep's clothing as the shepherds of our Christendom. They are more about politics, power and wealth than they are about the truth of the Gospel. They want to entertain crowds than stand in the conviction of scripture. When we fear man more than God, the same spirit that tormented Saul will torment us. Don't be fooled they are being tormented. Until we surrender, God won't let us rest in compromise. They may seem blessed but inside they are dead because they are not alive to the Gospel. They would rather call people to pray than call people to preach the Gospel. We need less praying and more preaching. The book of Acts is rightly titled; it's not the book of prayer. Follow the leading of the Spirit.

Note

410

*"For they that are such serve not our Lord Jesus Christ,
but their own belly; and by good words and fair speeches
deceive the hearts of the simple" (Romans 16:18, KJV)*

Just say what needs to be said. Tell it like it is. Most in this generation are tired of politics, people-pleasers and phonies. They can discern fake from faith really fast. They know when someone means what they say or when someone is acting. Studying the art of public speaking can be such a snare. We can be the best communicators but preachers need more than clever techniques. Preaching is different than teaching and lecturing. Preaching should be full of conviction, passion and anointing. It's more than a persuasive speech because the content came out of their intimacy with Christ and His Word. It won't only be apologetics, it will be the Gospel preached in such power the congregation will be left with two options, walk away in rebellion or kneel in submission to the Lord Jesus Christ. Many evangelicals have forgotten what it means to kneel before their God. The nondenominational church is told to scrap kneeling by their trendy church growth strategists. God will be taken seriously, even if the preacher in the pulpit does not. This generation does not need comedians, script readers, plagiarists, or charismaniacs, they need preachers of the Word who know Jesus intimately and fear only God. When God is not taken seriously, when the pulpit is not taken seriously, when our purpose in evangelism is not taken seriously, we are right where the devil would want us to be. Any church growth strategy that does not include preaching the gospel and evangelism is anathema. The church does not need her legs waxed and make up, that is blasphemy. The church does not need anything more than the message we have been given in the Gospel. The Gospel does not need our help. Preach the Gospel under the anointing and leave the rest to God. We need preachers in our generation. We have too many gluttonous men and women in the pulpits. They are in ministry for what they can get, not for what they can give. Rend your hearts before God. He is tired of the act and the show. Get with Jesus when you are all alone and the mic is off. Knowing Jesus will make a preacher out of you. God has chosen the foolish, so stop trying to make yourself wise in your own flesh. True wisdom is found when we take God seriously. No compromise.

Note

411

"And because iniquity shall abound, the love of many shall wax cold" (Matthew 24:12, KJV)

Coldness is sweeping across the earth. Many are becoming indifferent toward one another. Everyone has their own mountains to climb and it's tough to see others around us struggling. "You do you"— that's the general statement of the western culture. When we show interest in one another, motives are called into question. When help is offered it comes at a cost. Love is earned and conditional. Inside our society, there is a cry for value, love and care but many are so focused on themselves that they can't see anyone else around them. Many feel invisible. If they never got up, would anyone notice? If they passed, would they be missed? What is the solution to this coldness? The Bible is clear—in the end, the love of many will grow cold. There may not be a solution until Christ returns. The Bible has been accurate on how the end is playing out before our eyes. Knowledge has increased, Israel has its country back, we are nearing economic globalization. We are all faced with a decision to live indifferently or decide to make a difference. We can feel like the problem is too big and wonder what can we really do? Jesus taught us that heaven values the one lost sheep over the ninety-nine safe sheep. He does not celebrate over the crowds as we do, He celebrates when each one of us takes care of the broken right in front of us. Don't let this world make you cold. Let His love for us pour through us to everyone around us. We love best when we know we are loved. We can only give what we have received. God gave His love to us in His Son, Jesus. Jesus demonstrated the love God. His love warms the hardest of hearts. How can we say that we believe in Jesus yet not love others as He loved us? We can't affirm another person's salvation when there is no character of Christ in their lives! Let's examine ourselves before we cast a judgment on another. We will notice very quickly what hypocrites we are, when we cast judgment on anyone else. When we start looking at our inconsistencies and our weaknesses, it makes us realize that we are all in the same state of need for Jesus as anyone else. The only way to deal with our own coldness of heart is by repenting before God and staying true in our relationship before Him. This leads to obedience of His will.

Note

412

"Hell and destruction are never full; so the eyes of
man are never satisfied" (Proverbs 27:20, KJV)

Are you still not entertained are you still not satisfied, how long will you search for an experience to fill the void of your soul? What will it take for us to realize that our relationship with Jesus is enough for our soul? We have been so deceived that Jesus is not enough that we have added music, lights and smoke, yet the Gospel does not need our help. If His nail-scarred hands are not enough to bring peace to our soul, nothing will. Many believers live in constant turmoil for revival, miracles and experiences but never enter into the rest. In the stillness, when all is stripped away, alone in the quietness, that's where we will know Him the best. We seek an experience on earth to fill our soul but get disappointed every time. Only Jesus can be enough for our soul. This is why He wanted us to remember His bloodshed and His death because our flesh needs a constant reminder. How quickly we forget His accomplishment. We make the cross of no effect when we seek revival, miracles and healing more than Him. Be anxious for nothing. Jesus is the remedy for anxiety but religion fuels anxiety. Religion makes us chase experiences, religion makes Jesus never enough, religion leads us from hype to hype but the lows are so low, that we fall into the devils snare every time. Jesus is enough to make us consistent; Jesus is enough to make us disciplined; Jesus is enough to keep us when life takes a sudden turn for the worst. Don't be enamored by the glamour of today's religion, it's just smoke and lights. Don't be enamored by the preacher, he is just flesh and blood.

Be enamored by the cross of Christ. There is nothing and no one that deserves our worship more than Jesus. Everything changes but He remains the same. Seasons come and go, awakening comes and goes, feelings come and go, but His Word anchors our soul through it all. This generation is crying out for consistency, but music, entertainment and heroes will fade away; there is only One who remains faithful to the end. Follow Him, Follow His Word and you will make it to the end. We are in a race. What matters more about a race, how we start or how we finish? God can make us finish strong if we lay our pride down before Him and humble ourselves into His mighty hand.

Note

413

"But rejoice, inasmuch as ye are partakers of Christ's sufferings; that, when his glory shall be revealed, ye may be glad also with exceeding joy. If ye be reproached for the name of Christ, happy are ye; for the spirit of glory and of God resteth upon you: on their part he is evil spoken of, but on your part he is glorified" (1 Peter 4:13–14, KJV)

No one can really prepare us for the twists and turns of life. We can know the theory of change but the emotions we experience through the change, only a daily relationship with Jesus can carry us through. Throughout life, Jesus becomes closer than anyone could ever get to our hearts. His Word becomes our assurance that these changes will work together for good. Change is not always a choice. Life, circumstances, other people's choices are also the cause of change. Change that we cannot control, causes some to end up blaming the only One that can bring them through. Satan loves to tease us with blame. When we fall into the pit of blame, self-pity and bitterness, the changes through life become mountains that are impossible to get over. When we surrender to Jesus and blame sin, we are empowered by almighty God to flatten the mountains. Don't separate from the only one that can get us through. Don't stitch a veil, don't build a wall. Jesus went through so much so that nothing could separate us from Him. Pour out our fears on Him. Let Him take all our pain and rest, knowing He turns everything good in the end. The temptation is to turn to other means to get us through when change happens. Nothing can compare to Jesus. Go deeper in His Word, tell everyone you know about Him, sing worship to Him and let the world wonder. The light of Christ shines brightest when all that the world sees is darkness around us but it does not put out His light. The darker it is all around us, remember you could not be shining brighter in the sight of the world. God won't let us go even in death. The believer sees death as a door. When our time comes, we will stair through the door of death to see the face of our Lord welcoming us home. Let Jesus be who our soul relies on for healing and peace. Let His Word and promises be our comfort and assurance. There will be change. Growth, aging, ups and downs will come, but Jesus remains constant. He knows us like no one else could. Many search for love in this world but never find what their soul is longing for because only Jesus can fill our need to be loved. We were made for Him first. When He is first, everything around us comes into alignment. We get out of alignment when He is not first! Make Him first!

Note

414

"But he that shall endure unto the end, the same shall be saved" (Matthew 24:13, KJV)

God wants all or nothing. He gave His all, how can we give anything less than our all after reading of the crucifixion of Christ? What does it mean to give our all? God does not need our talent, treasure or time, that's what people want but God wants us. He wants you. He wants me. If we only give our stuff but we don't give our hearts, then we have missed why He came. His blood was not shed for our stuff, His blood was shed for us. We must not neglect our relationship with Him. We can get caught up with everything in life and miss out on what is most important. Church can talk about everything and anything yet miss out on talking about what matters most. Our personal relationship with God matters so much, that God went to great lengths to make it possible. God wants all of us and when we surrender, giving of our time, talent and treasure will be an outflow of our relationship with Jesus. When we yield to God, our soul, strength and lives, He takes us on a journey that we won't regret in heaven. There will be times when we will feel regret and disappointment here because we gave our all yet we only seemed to face hardship after hardship, but we must not make this life longer than what it really is. This life is a vapor. For most of us, we can still remember getting ready for school. Years ago, feels like yesterday. The temptation gets strong in the hardships of life to sell out giving our all to God for a temporal fix. Selling out for a temporary fix is not worth eternity, stick out the hardship to the end and watch the blessing of God be poured out. If we have sold out, it's not difficult to return to your first love. Repent, surrender, yield to the power of the Spirit and immediately He will get you back on track. What would take years for the world to fix, God can in the blink of an eye. Getting right with God takes simple faith in what Christ accomplished at the cross. God will always take us as we are, if we are willing to believe that He will. One of the assurances of the Gospel is that not only will He take us as we are but He won't leave us in what is hurting us. When we give God our all, He will do everything necessary to make old things pass away and make all things become new. Give God our all and watch Him work.

Note

415

"Beloved, when I gave all diligence to write unto you of the common salvation, it was needful for me to write unto you, and exhort you that ye should earnestly contend for the faith which was once delivered unto the saints. For there are certain men crept in unawares, who were before of old ordained to this condemnation, ungodly men, turning the grace of our God into lasciviousness, and denying the only Lord God, and our Lord Jesus Christ" (Jude 1:3–4, KJV)

Loyalty can be a great trait to have but it also has a weakness. Believers must be loyal to scripture over any church leader or relationship. When our loyalty is to scripture alone, then we can hold everyone around us accountable and they can hold us accountable. When any person or organization has our loyalty more than scripture, then we become prey to a cult. Holding ourselves and others accountable is what true fellowship is built on. When accountability is labeled rebellion or the one that is holding their leaders accountable is called a maverick, then we need to exit that fellowship as quick as we can. When we don't want accountability and isolate ourselves from those who would tell us the truth, we are on thin ice. Many leaders put around them people who only say what they want to hear. This is not biblical leadership. The scripture teaches us what real leadership looks like. Elevating one man and his teaching above scripture is very dangerous. Most non-denominational churches have no eldership or board and if they do, it's their family members or easily influenced individuals. This is toxic. No one is above scripture. No one's opinion is above scripture. Scripture is the best commentary on itself. When people follow a man more than their Bible, they're prey to the enemy to devour them. There is no hierarchy in the sight of God. He sees us all for who we are. Churches that elevate a person as if he is a priest are going directly against scripture. Jesus put an end to the priesthood at the cross. There are no mediators between man and God besides Jesus Christ. No one should claim that type of control over another. We can seek counsel but we don't need to seek an inspired word from another person, God will speak to us from the Bible for ourselves. We are foolish to depend on another person's interpretation; the Holy Spirit was given to lead us into the truth. Preachers should be confirming what God is already speaking to you in your quiet place. No one has a "new word" or a "new revelation"—they are cult leaders if they do. The Bible speaks for itself. It's a fearful thing to add to the word of God or take away from the Word of God. Tie your loyalty to scripture over everyone and anything.

Note

416

"Now the Spirit speaketh expressly, that in the latter times some shall depart from the faith, giving heed to seducing spirits, and doctrines of devils; Speaking lies in hypocrisy; having their conscience seared with a hot iron" (1 Timothy 4:1–2, KJV)

Every believer's loyalty must be to scripture alone. What is right, matters more than who is right. When we are loyal to a church or a preacher more than scripture, we will end up in a cult. The reason Protestants bring their Bibles to church is to remind the fellowship what our foundation is. Our church culture is rapidly ridding themselves of scripture and embracing music, entertainment and other books. There is no other infallible Word of God but the sixty-six books of the Bible. The less a congregation knows scripture, the more manipulated they can be. The nondenominational churches that have built their crowds on music, video and personalities are very dangerous. Any church that has a congregation coming for any reason other than for scripture to be taught are prey for deception. Churches are being selected for the services they provide more than the soundness of the pulpit. We need to sound the alarm. Paul said any other gospel that is not derived from scripture is accursed. The wolves in sheep's clothing are in the highest ranks of our churches today. They elevate their personality above the person of Christ. Rather than them serving the people, the people are expected to serve them. They feel that the congregation is there to equip them rather than what the Bible mandates all leaders to do, which is to equip their congregation. We are all held accountable to scripture and no one is above scripture. Jesus is our example in character, ministry and passion, not the celebrity pastors today. Why do congregations financially support these leaders? Like Israel, we want a man more than we want Christ. Like Israel, we want a king more than we want God. We need Samuels that will preach to "Eli and his two sons" before it's too late. Using the church to live a lavish lifestyle, comes with very serious consequences. If we want revival and awakening, we need to take God seriously. Who we are when the mic is off, matters more to God than what we do in front of people. Repent, wholeheartedly repent, it's not too late. We have all sinned but there is hope until God says enough. The candlestick will not always be lighting. There is a time when the candlestick is removed. Does this move you? Repent!

Note

417

"And the Lord God said, It is not good that the man should be alone;
I will make him an help meet for him" (Genesis 2:18, KJV)

It's not good for us to be alone. If we don't talk out what we are harboring in our hearts, it has the potential to take over us. Talking it out with God but also talking it out with another trusted person, keeps us living free. We need one another to keep each other accountable; there is wisdom in multiple counselors. Holding on to bitterness and unforgiveness only leads to further isolation which leads to defeat. There are many just reasons to be bitter at what life has thrown at us but the only person that un-forgiveness hurts is the person that's bitter. How can we say that we love God but hate who God loves? How can we worship and read the Word yet not forgive others like we have been forgiven? If we were forgiven, we too need to forgive. We want to get revenge but that never works out well. Leave revenge to God. Taking matters into our own hands only makes a mess of things. We need to forgive and let God serve justice. Having accountability is so freeing. We should not be accountable with just anyone. We should not seek counsel with just anyone. We need to be discerning but as the Lord leads, we will have the counsel, friendships and accountability that we need. Don't seal off any areas of our lives. Stay transparent before God. Confess any guile and surrender before God in worship. This is how we experience freedom in our lives. This is how we make it to the end. May we all stay open to the conviction of the Holy Spirit. When we live without the conviction of the Holy Spirit, we need to ask ourselves, do we have the Holy Spirit? Not a day should go by where we don't feel the conviction of God, convicting us of wrong motives, sin or calling us into His mission. Every believer received the indwelling of the Holy Spirit when they repented and trusted in Christ as savior. He will cause us to desire holiness. He will cause us want be more like Christ in character. Be alone with Christ but don't stay alone. Our posture before God is submission to His Word and His will. Western Christianity has lost the discipline of kneeling before God. If it's been a while, try kneeling when you pray, to remind your flesh and self who is God. Our culture encourages everyone to "have it your way," "do whatever makes you happy." This could be further from the truth. We are called to surrender to Christ and obey what He calls us to. What He calls us to, He empowers us to follow through.

Note

418

"For as many as are led by the Spirit of God, they
are the sons of God" (Romans 8:14, KJV)

Yield to the Spirit, say yes to God no matter what it looks like. Don't follow logic, follow the leading of the Lord. Everyone and our own selves will be a deterrent to following God when it comes to some of life's choices but we must choose to follow God. Follow God when He calls, even if it looks like you've made a mistake and everyone says you misheard God, don't stop believing. God's way may seem the hardest but it always has the best results in the end. We can read story after story in scripture of men and women who followed God; it's when they took matters into their own hands, that their stories were tougher than it should have been. Wait on God. Even if it's the eleventh hour, God won't abandon you. At some point, God will ween you off of depending on people to hear from Him so you can hear from Him for yourself. The sooner the better. Jesus made this possible so we can rely on Him alone to get through life. Tune into His voice. Mute the voices all around you and lean into hearing from Him. Fast, pray and get away from the bustle of life, God still speaks directionally for our lives. God will never contradict the Bible but He does still lead our lives. Even when we are at the eleventh hour, even when we feel trapped, even when we see no way out, God will see us through either miraculously or we will pass to be with Him forever. There is no loss for the believer. We can rejoice in life and in death, we can rejoice in sickness and in health, our joy is not built on what we see but on the authority of scripture. The Bible fills in the blanks for our need to know our origin, purpose and destiny. When we are where God wants us to be and we believe that His sovereign hand, no matter what the scoffers say, we can have total peace. Build the Ark, go to the land you do not know, cross the Red Sea, dance in the midst of the scorn, sing in the prison cell, our joy is in the hardship set before us because God will get all the glory the harder it gets for us. The believer's testimony will include "only God could have brought me this far." Surrendering to God brings peace, doing our will brings turmoil. If we want to get rid of anxiety, surrender to the will of God. There is no peace outside of His will. Yield!

Note

419

*"Be ye therefore ready also: for the Son of man cometh
at an hour when ye think not" (Luke 12:40, KJV)*

Are we ready for His return or when we receive our call to heaven? Our military spend most of their careers doing drills so that they are ready. It may seem monotonous but it's essential so they are ready for when their call comes to be active duty. It's very unfortunate that most only seek God when they are going to be "ministering" but in the "off season" they have no time for God. Seminary does not graduate us from a need for God. The disciplines we learn at Bible School are to be maintained whether we are in "ministry" or not. Ministry must never replace our relationship with God. When ministry replaces our relationship with God, we will be ineffective and could potentially miss heaven. Jesus was clear that our number one ministry is first to Him, otherwise we will preach in His name but it will be counted as a work of iniquity.[110] Are you bored in your relationship with Jesus? Would revival, awakening, healings, signs, and wonders be enough to fulfill our soul? Don't allow emotions, dreams or desires to excite our soul more than knowing Jesus. This is controversial because we live in a culture that emphasizes "know your purpose" and "know your identity" but what we need to know is Jesus. The more we look past ourselves, the more we reckon ourselves dead, the more we deny ourselves, the more we get ourselves out of the way then the more we will see Jesus at work in our lives. Be ready in sea-

---

[110.] Matthew chapter 7

son and out of season, examine whether you are in the faith. Are you full of yourself or are you full of the Holy Spirit? We need to warn in this generation because many sadly believe that they are saved by confession alone but they also must believe in their hearts that Jesus is Lord. To be saved is to be empowered to do His will. If we don't desire His will, His way and His truth, then questions must be asked. Believers receive power in the Holy Spirit to do what He has called us to. The Gospel is not a cheap faith just to live the way we want to and go to heaven when we pass. Jesus called His disciples to follow Him. Some followed Him to martyrdom, some followed Him to the courts of Rome, some followed Him to the ends of the earth but only those who followed Him made it in the end. Follow Jesus daily.

Note

420

"Let your conversation be without covetousness; and be content with such things as ye have: for he hath said, I will never leave thee, nor forsake thee" (Hebrews 13:5, KJV)

Nothing in this world will satisfy the soul like Jesus. Materialism is the god of this age in the West. Stuff matters more to this generation than the Truth of God's Word. Carnality offers no solution to the state of the soul. There will be many spiritual leaders held responsible on the day of judgment. We will be surprised at who actually makes it to heaven. "Making it" here on earth does not affirm that we will make it to heaven. Carnality is a deterrent to millennials when it comes to ministry. We are tired of the politics, we are tired of the political correctness, we are tired of the manipulation. It's the truth of the Gospel that sets us free. We need to resist lukewarmness, resist mediocrity and compromise. It's spreading into the western culture rapidly. Without surrender to Christ, we won't make it. Secularism and worldliness are infiltrating our Christianity like never before, our churches are starting to look no different than a night club. Entertainment has consumed our interest more than the truth that sets us free. When the music fades and the hype is gone, that's when we will be the closest to God. It's who we are in private that matters more to God than who we are in public. Never neglect the truth, no matter how compromised a society gets. Don't follow the crowd or the leader that values crowds more than the Word of God. Jesus always had an uncompromising and challenging Word. He still does to this day. His Word to the seven churches in Revelation is still relevant to this day. He is listening even when you don't get a text back or a call back from those you thought you needed the most; who we need the most is Jesus. This why we are facing such hardship, so God can get us to seek His face more than anyone else's. We like noise but if you are not hearing God, turn down all the noise and hear Him in the silence. Don't get lost in the crowd. You are as valuable as anyone else. Don't neglect sound doctrine; don't neglect the truth or your feelings will deceive you. If we miss this truth, we potentially could miss heaven. This is why we need to be reminded of the truth of the Gospel over and over because it can get out of sight very quickly. Don't be bewitched.

Note

421

"Choosing rather to suffer affliction with the people of God, than to enjoy the pleasures of sin for a season; Esteeming the reproach of Christ greater riches than the treasures in Egypt: for he had respect unto the recompence of the reward" *(Hebrews 11:25–26, KJV)*

Moaning, complaining, and disappointment are the results of today's false gospel. The emphasis of today's false gospel is all about an abundant life here and now. It's deceptive because some get an abundant life here and now but the majority don't. Does God love those who get an abundant life here on earth more than those who get a life of persecution, illness and affliction? Absolutely not. It is better to be afflicted and know our need for Jesus than to be rich and see no need for Jesus at all. It is better to live a life of need for God than to live a life without a need for God and end up in hell-fire for eternity. Hell does not get preached today as much as Jesus taught on it. Most of today's Christianity does not follow Christ's teachings, and one should wonder why they claim to be Christian yet live nothing like their founder in character, truth, and love. It's false to think that someone who is physically healthy is blessed. It is false to think that someone who is financially rich is blessed. Their health and wealth could be a curse and not a blessing yet we define them as blessed. We are blessed not because of any other reason but that we believe in Jesus. Come what may, we are blessed no matter what comes our way. This is the mind-set of the overcomer. When we have a revelation of what it could be like for eternity in hell, we will never murmur again. Our culture has created entitled, selfish, spoiled brats. They don't know discipline and they turn a blind eye to the wages of sin. The ramifications are being exposed by our news outlets every day. When we remove the Bible, people lose their compass both morally and spiritually to the point that common sense is not common anymore. The end result is destruction, judgment and hell for eternity. The Church is mandated to speak up and preach the Gospel. The church has been silent on their city streets and communities for years now! Now their youth and college students are feeling the effects. The world has more sense than "church people." No one on the street would give 10 percent of their income to someone who spends it on themselves and their lifestyle. Sound the alarm. A reformation is about to begin. It will have nothing to do with Calvinism or Arminianism it will be about obedience to God.

Note

422

*"For the time will come when they will not endure sound
doctrine; but after their own lusts shall they heap to themselves
teachers, having itching ears" (2 Timothy 4:3, KJV)*

The fear of man will beat us into silence. Fearing what people think is so dangerous to our faith in Jesus. We can't have faith in Jesus and fear what man thinks of us too. The fear of man will make a coward out of us. Revelation 21:8[111] is clear what the consequence of cowardice will be on the day of Judgment. Our culture has silenced our preachers when it's offensive to tell it like it is. It has led to a lukewarmness with no moral boundaries or doctrinal absolutes. We are an age of music and motivational sermons. Christianity is mile-wide but an inch deep in the West. Truth alone sets us free, not music or motivational messages. We desperately need a reformation in the church or we will continue to turn a blind eye on the millions of souls that are going to hell all around us. Does it bother us that our loved ones without Christ are going to hell? The love of many has grown cold. Love is waxing cold because love without truth is immoral love. We need to care less about what people think and be more concerned with what God says. We need to follow God over following anyone else. The veil was rent to do away with mediums. You and I can know God as much as anyone else. There is no human

---

[111.] *"But the fearful, and unbelieving, and the abominable, and murderers, and whore-mongers, and sorcerers, and idolaters, and all liars, shall have their part in the lake which burneth with fire and brimstone: which is the second death." (Revelation 21:8, KJV)*

that has more access to God than another, no matter what foolish title they claim. In Christ, we all have equal access to God. When we look to another person more than God, when we fear another person more than God, when we quote another person more than His Word, we will be a part of the great deception which we are on the cusp of. Even the elect will depart from the faith when it begins. Many have deviated from scripture and the Gospel that they first heard because they love this world more than their God. It's time to call the church to an examination of their faith. Many gave into the enticing spirit of music, entertainment and a motivational message because they would rather have the presence of a large crowd than the presence of God. The congregation will be just as responsible because they pay for this type of ministry to continue each week. They heaped up for themselves lazy teachers and dare any of them challenge the congregation lest they be out of a job. "Itching ears" is a good description of those in our pews.

Note

423

"For the which cause I also suffer these things: nevertheless I am not ashamed: for I know whom I have believed, and am persuaded that he is able to keep that which I have committed unto him against that day" (2 Timothy 1:12, KJV)

Positive thinking, being fearful of the diagnosis, being cautious of saying it like it is, is so ridiculous. Realists must not be suppressed in our generation. Hiding the reality behind superstition or religiosity is such a waste of time. If you are sick, you are sick. Don't let anyone tell you to not say what the Doctors report says. It is what it is. The "faith" movement tries to get God to work on behalf of them when they fake what they're going through and then claim that to be faith. That is not faith. Faith is not fake and fake is not faith. God does not want our strategies or foolish manipulations. God simply wants relationship; a real relationship built on honesty and not fear. God does not punish those who are going through affliction, God does not shame people who are sick, Paul was unashamed of his suffering. Anyone who looks down on the sick will have God looking down on them. Don't rush to lay hands on someone. Get the mind of God and His will. The pompous religious want to be god and do whatever they want. That's not what it means to declare Jesus is Lord. This "faith" movement make themselves Lord of Jesus, telling Him they know better than He does when it comes to the church and His people. God knows best. Doing what seems to be right, leaning on your own understanding, relying on a certain methodology is such a waste of time. Know God. Yield in relationship with Him. Tell Him like it is. Allow the pain, tears, disappointment and doubt to flow out of you because He cares. Don't damn it up or hide behind religiosity. Be real even if that means we need to be like Thomas. It would be better to be real like Thomas than be fake like Judas. God is not interested in how many scriptures we quote or how many of His promises we know, God is interested in us. Satan deceptively is destroying relationships, especially our relationship with God because He knows that when we are isolated, we are prey to his onslaught. Be real before God. You can't always be real before people because they need God as much as you do. They will sometimes judge, ridicule and shame you but Jesus comforts like no other. With God, we can find love, comfort, and acceptance. No relationship can compare to knowing Jesus!

Note

424

"O Timothy, keep that which is committed to thy trust, avoiding profane and vain babblings, and oppositions of science falsely so called: Which some professing have erred concerning the faith. Grace be with thee. Amen" (1 Timothy 6:20–21, KJV)

A gnostic teaching is spreading across the West. Discipleship has become all about teaching and education more than action. It gives way to spiritual laziness and blunts discernment. It elevates personalities above the person of Christ. It elevates sermons above Scripture. It preaches "church" more than Jesus, as if the church can save a soul. Evangelism for this gnostic teaching is basically inviting people to Church. The gnostic teachers applaud crowds and aesthetics more than truth and the presence of God. The early church had to battle Gnosticism and we are still dealing with it to this day. The teachers of this gnostic Gospel have a form of godliness but their lifestyle and love of materialism exposes what they are really all about, they deny the power of the Holy Spirit. They only want to teach in a pulpit but as soon as they step off the pulpit, they run from the people they are supposed to pastor. They are in it for the lifestyle more than the people. They preach a message to the people that keeps them in the pew but "dare any of them walk in their call of God lest they be rebellion." It is not rebellion to obey God more than man. We are each called to obey God, even if that means it goes against the grain of our culture. God does not always lead us as our church leaders would like. They are not gods. God made it possible so that He can have a personal relationship with us. Their leadership is supposed to lead us to Christ and not control us for their own gain. No one mediates on behalf of God. Jesus removed all our mediators. The Gospel teaches us to know God for ourselves. What the reformation tore down, nondenominational churches have tried to set back up. Pastors are not priests. The evangelist is not a savior. We must not look to man more than Christ. We must quote scripture more that sermons. If we don't, we are not as mature as we thought we were. We have the source, why waste our time on man's resources. It's a dangerous church when accountability is taught as rebellion. We see this today. The leadership silences anyone that holds them accountable and shuns them as rebels. It destroys lives, families and friendships. To whom much is given, much is required.

Note

425

"And all things are of God, who hath reconciled us to himself by Jesus Christ, and hath given to us the ministry of reconciliation" (2 Corinthians 5:18, KJV)

The born-again message that Jesus taught is an essential result of the Gospel. If the Gospel is just a message, then it won't impact our lives. We have focused so much on theology but we must not neglect Pentecost. The sign to the Jewish believers that the gentiles could be saved was the infilling of the Holy Spirit. The Holy Spirit is who makes the church come alive, the Holy Spirit is who makes the Bible come alive, the Holy Spirit is who makes us come alive. When we remove the Holy Spirit from Christianity, we are left with a social club that sing karaoke and try to figure out God. The Tower of Babel warns us what man can do without God. We have millions of "Towers of Babel" today called churches; they are all built without the Holy Spirit. They were built by good intentions; these buildings were made to confine God to a location, times of week and restrict Him to their service schedule. Jesus never gave blueprints for buildings. He prophesied of the destruction of the temple. Thank God that it's still in ruins to this day as a reminder to all of us that God desires the church to be His people. Believers in Christ are the Temple of the Holy Spirit. We are not "Towers of Babel" built by our hands, led by our own ideas and followed by our good intentions. We are spiritual beings led by the Spirit within the boundaries of the Bible which the Spirit of God wrote through men for our understanding. The Holy Spirit has been overlooked, silenced and quenched for a long time and it looks like we have done a good job because of the crowds. Will it really last because we look so trendy? Ignoring the Holy Spirit is a dangerous place to find ourselves. Jesus honored the Holy Spirit and Peter honored the Holy Spirit. Are we lying to Him? We can put on a great front to the crowds and the people can be fooled but the Holy Spirit sees all our motives. This should send a chill down our spine if we are true. If it does not, one might need to examine whether they are in the faith. We have many today who have a false security of salvation. Some preachers today are more interested in filling their buildings than preaching the truth of the Gospel. They may tell you that you're saved because you give of time, talent and treasure but are you born again?

Note

426

"And all things are of God, who hath reconciled us to himself by Jesus Christ, and hath given to us the ministry of reconciliation" (Luke 19:10, KJV)

What is more important to us, that we are changed or that we are saved? What took more effort, for Jesus to forgive sin or to tell a lame man to rise and walk? Jesus did not go to the cross to heal our physical bodies or to make us rich while we are here. Jesus went to the cross to reconcile us into a relationship with God. Jesus taught us that in this world we will have trouble. What is more important, for us to know God or for us to be used by God? We cheapen the work of Christ when we find our identity in anything other than sons and daughters before God. If we seek revival, church growth, or any other spiritual thing more than God, we can quickly fall into a religious mind-set which led the Jews to Crucify Christ. When Jesus is not our focus, we will be bitter, angry and live empty. When we preach the Gospel and people show interest in responding, asking why they want to be saved is very important. Why do we want to be saved? Is it just so we don't go to hell? Is it so we can be fulfilled? Is it for our own self-gratification? God sees our why, He knows our motives so let's be unashamed before God and walk in relationship with Him. There is nothing that we could confess to God that He would be surprised by. There is power in confession before God which not only saves us but leads to change in our lives. The less we focus on ourselves, the more Christ will do through us. We can be our own worst enemies by overthinking, hiding our motives or letting our senses dictate our level of faith. Not only do we have spiritual wickedness working against us but we have our flesh at work against us too, this is why we need to be confident that God is for us. If God is for us, who can be against us. He that is in us is greater than anyone or anything on the earth. As we look unto Jesus, we can be assured that He will guard us from the enemy and empower us against our fleshly desires. Jesus Saves. He saves to the uttermost. Our challenge is to look unto Him and know that we are saved. So much things fight for our attention every day to distract us as to why we have been left here after we were saved. Many are slaves to bills, selfishness or self-gratification. Jesus came to set us free. He will provide for us; He will take care of us.

Note

427

"Woe unto you, scribes and Pharisees, hypocrites! for ye are like unto whited sepulchres, which indeed appear beautiful outward, but are within full of dead men's bones, and of all uncleanness. Even so ye also outwardly appear righteous unto men, but within ye are full of hypocrisy and iniquity" (Matthew 23:27–28, KJV)

The work of the Gospel does not change from the outside in but from the inside out. Religion changes from the outside but unless we have power, we will never truly change. No matter what we do to try to change, without the power of Christ we can't change. This is why we must be born again. Our first birth came with a nature that loves what is wrong more than what is right. When we are born-again by repentance and faith in Christ, we are given a new nature. Our old nature still wars against our new nature but as we feed our faith and rely on Christ, we can suppress our old nature. If we feed our old nature, we must not be surprised when our old nature gets the best of us. This is why we need to examine ourselves today; are we feeding our faith or are we feeding our flesh? We feed our faith by reading scripture, hearing scripture and fellowship with other believers. Our relationship with Christ will always lead us to feed our faith. As we surrender to Christ and worship Christ, we will see the power of the Gospel at work in our lives. We never have to be separated from God. Christ died a bloody death to show us that there is nothing we could do to separate us from God. No matter where we find ourselves, God will take us as we are if we confess our sin and believe on Christ, but He will never leave us in what will hurt us. Christ makes us new. He causes the old nature to pass away and makes all things new. Our old nature will permanently die with our bodies and at the resurrection of the dead in Christ, we will receive glorified bodies. There will be a day where we won't have sickness or sin in these bodies. Until that day, we are to fight the fight of faith. Let's decide to feed our faith. Don't let the devil or our flesh knock the fight of faith out of us. Christ will train our hands to war and our fingers to battle as we walk in relationship with Him. We must not be ignorant of our enemy or our sinful nature. It's up to our will to keep our lamps full of oil. Are we full of the Holy Spirit or are we full of the flesh? In Acts, we read of the early church continually getting filled with the Holy Spirit. We all get filled by something each day but nothing fulfills like the Holy Spirit, everything else disappoints.

Note

428

"For they that are after the flesh do mind the things of the flesh; but they that are after the Spirit the things of the Spirit. For to be carnally minded is death; but to be spiritually minded is life and peace" (Romans 8:5–6, KJV)

We are prone to fear. We are prone to wander. Our humanity can't cope when life changes for the worst. Our minds can't see past the darkness of this life. When we live this life without faith, when we live this life without the power of God's Spirit, we will not overcome. The enemy of our soul has a strategy against us and that is to get us to run from our fear by distracting us with prescription pills, alcohol, entertainment and anything else that we would be tempted by. Running from our fears will work for a short amount of time but it will catch up with us. We don't get younger. The older we get, the more fragile we become and the more of this dark world we experience. Many make it through life without faith, warning us of the hardness of the human heart. Resisting the conviction of the Holy Spirit and rejecting the Gospel of Jesus Christ is so tragic; countless have passed into eternity with that coldness of heart. Believers in Christ must give no place to fear in our lives. It is contradictory to say we have faith in Christ yet be overcome by fear. The Holy Spirit in us gives us power, love and a sound mind. The spirit of this age cripples us with fear, bitterness and no self-control over our sinful desires. If ever we need to preach the Born-Again message, it's today. Many Christians have never been Born-Again. To be Born-Again is to born of the Spirit and receive the Holy Spirit's power to do what we never could. The Spirit gives us the power to love and resist our sinful desires. Believers in Christ who repent, receive the power of the Holy Spirit to do what we could never do in our humanity. To have life and to have confidence, we need to choose to go to Christ first before we are given over to the temptations of our enemy who wants us to turn to anything other than Christ first. We are to have no other God, we are to have no other Lord but Jesus, we are to open ourselves to no other spirit other than the Holy Spirit. If we do, we will reap the consequences. We are all given this choice every day. Whatever we sow, we will reap. Let's sow into scripture, let's sow into the Holy Spirit, let's surrender our fears to our Lord and watch Him do the miracles only He can do. We will not be forsaken.

Note

429

*"There is therefore now no condemnation to them which
are in Christ Jesus, who do not walk according to the flesh,
but according to the Spirit" (Romans 8:1, KJV)*

We will never graduate from a need for Jesus. The longer we are believers in Christ, we will learn to depend on Him more and more. Discipleship that teaches us how to be Christians without Christ, only leaves us empty in the end. If we don't need Him more today than we did yesterday, there might be something off with our relationship. It's okay to feel wretched sometimes. It's normal to feel broken. There are seasons where life teaches us that there is only One who can give us meaning. Jesus alone gives meaning. His love cannot be compared with any other type of love on earth. Paul writes Romans chapter 7 late in his ministry, with a personal declaration of his continued need for Jesus Christ. The first seven chapters of Romans deals with our origin and the expectation of God on humanity to be Holy. Romans chapter 8 shifts from our wretchedness to what Christ accomplished by His death and resurrection. In Christ, we have the power of the Holy Spirit, the same power that raised Christ from the dead, lives in us. While we are in these bodies, we will be reminded daily of our need for Christ and His power to work in us. After three years of discipleship from Jesus, His apostles needed Him more than ever at His crucifixion. We must not be surprised as we mature in the faith when we experience Romans 7 as we did when we first were saved. Many that hit Romans chapter 7 late in their walk with God are bombarded with doubt and condemnation; some choose the path of Judas but prayerfully we will choose the path of Peter. We see years after Pentecost that Peter still was reminded of his humanity when Paul addressed him for bringing discrimination into the church between Jewish Christians and Gentile Christians. Don't let anyone judge you when you hit the bottom. Christ is near to the broken hearted. Trust and believe Jesus is for you, no matter how you feel about yourself or how others feel about you. Our Father loves us the way we are. We don't need to put up a front with Him. He loves us the way we are but as we walk in relationship and dependency on Him, He will give us the power to not leave us in what hurts us. We can overcome as we choose to walk leaning on Him, which is a daily decision. "Keep me needing Jesus all my days."

Note

430

*"Ye are the light of the world. A city that is set on
an hill cannot be hid" (Matthew 5:14, KJV)*

Discipleship is more than education. Prayer is more than us doing all of the talking. Church is more than community for fellowship. We have been left here to let the light of Christ shine where we are at. We are all fallen, we are all broken, as true as these statements may be, they are not an excuse to continue to be fallen and broken as believers. Believers in Christ have the power to get back up when life hits us down, believers have the power to obey the great commission, believers have access to hear from God and be led through this life; it's when we are walking with God, holding nothing back, that we find out why we are here. We are not here to wait out life to get to heaven. We are here to be His ambassadors so that we can bring as many people to Jesus as we can. We all are a part of the body of Christ. The evangelist is not who we need to be relying on to reach our nation. When we rely on anyone more than Jesus, get ready to be disappointed because you will see their humanity the closer you get to them. Honor Christ above any man. Fear God if you're going to fear anyone. The fear of God does not mean to be scared of Him; it simply means to take God seriously. Preachers are not comedians, entertainers, motivational speakers; they are convicted sinners that found a real savior and want everyone to know Him. Every preacher needs Jesus as much today as they did when they first got saved. We are all one decision away from being where those we preach to are at. Friends, don't miss out on the "more" of this walk with Jesus. Don't ever "arrive" and get comfortable until we get to heaven. Keep your lamps filled with oil because we don't know the day or the hour that will be our last here on earth. Let's be ready in season and out of season. Don't stay down, get up in the grace of God; don't stop getting up, no matter how many hits you take. God will complete the work He started. If Jesus prayed for Peters faith to not fail, He is also interceding at the right hand of our Father for our faith to not fail. Let's believe through it all. Jesus won't forsake us no matter what. The cross is the evidence of His deep love for us. Let's step out of comfort and lukewarmness as He is convicting and leading.

Note

431

*"Therefore leaving the principles of the doctrine of Christ, let us go
on unto perfection; not laying again the foundation of repentance
from dead works, and of faith toward God" (Hebrews 6:1, KJV)*

*"How much more shall the blood of Christ, who through the eternal
Spirit offered himself without spot to God, purge your conscience
from dead works to serve the living God?" (Hebrews 9:14, KJV)*

The works that Jesus honors are the works done by faith from
the place of acceptance in the sight of God. A gnostic strand has
infiltrated the western culture. Discipleship has become educational
only for the most part. Somehow our generation has divided discipleship from evangelism. There are discipleship ministries and there
are evangelistic ministries. There is no biblical way of separating the
two. Jesus's way of discipleship is the way we need to come back to.
The youth that sits and listens only but never goes out and does
evangelism are the ones prey to departing when they hit college.
Entertainment and music have replaced the passion to obey Jesus but
it does not sustain the young people past High School. The reason
they are not engaged and are full of apathy is because they are not
persuaded by those who are teaching them even believe what they are
teaching. They will know we believe what we are saying when they
see our lives sold out to Christ when the church service ends. How
can we entertain, joke and sing songs when the message we have is
a matter of heaven and hell? Jesus calls us to a fundamental life with
Him. He does not permit a halfhearted approach to His Word or to

Him. Our church today encourages mediocrity and anyone who is fundamental or "all in" is labeled a legalist. It is not legalistic to pray, it is not legalistic to read the Bible, it is not legalistic to evangelize when these works are done from our salvation, they are good works. The problem is when these works are done for Gods acceptance, they become dead works. God is more interested in *why* we do what we do more than *what* we do. Jesus finished the work of salvation for those who believe. Discipleship without evangelism is not biblical discipleship. Jesus does not want you to be filled with His Word for your own sake. In the free countries of the west, we live as if we are under the state church in China. We have the right to evangelize but we only do it in the church or in its parking lot. We won't have the freedoms we have very soon. The Bible is clear about who is coming. We must not rely on media or technology. Believers will have a better impact on reaching their community than YouTube.

Note

_____

_____

_____

_____

_____

_____

_____

_____

_____

432

"For of him, and through him, and to him, are all things: to whom be glory for ever. Amen" (Romans 11:36, KJV)

The Gospel in the West has become more about our identity, our purpose and our life. Knowing who we are has more interest today than knowing who He is. As much as we want to make God all about us, before we were, He was. As much as we want a God that loves us, thinks of us, showers grace on us, He still is God. God is self-existent. What He did with His Son will never happen again. Jesus finished the work it took to save us from our sins. God is gracious, loving, and tender hearted but don't let that feed our entitled nature. The elder brother of the prodigal son had an entitled nature but it did not end well for him after he saw the love of his father for his younger rebellious brother. The elder brother knew his identity and purpose, followed his father's direction to the best he knew but still, he was as much a prodigal in his heart as his brother. Jesus confronted the entitled religious, who scorned His love for sinners, by revealing to them they were the elder brother in the story of "The Prodigal Son." The elder brother should be a warning to our generation who live a life of entitlement. "Blessed are the poor in spirit," Jesus never said, "Blessed are those that name it and claim it." If discipleship equips us to tell God how He should do something, then our discipleship will lead to disappointment. Our discipleship should lead us to a surrender and worship of almighty God. Our discipleship should cause us to follow His Word rather than follow our impulses. There is a way that seems right to a man but in the end is destruction. What matters more to us, our will being done or His will be done? When we want our will more than His, we will be anxious and disappointed. Rest in His will. Let His sufficient grace wash over our anxiety and replace it with His peace. Shouting God down does not always work. Claiming our will, no matter what His will is, only ends in disappointment. The religious allowed their disappointment with Jesus and His teaching of the cross to make them bitter until they pleaded for his death before Pilate. Jesus was not born how they wanted, did not look like what they wanted, nor did what they wanted and then He taught about dying on a cross. They did not get what they wanted but they did get what they needed.

Note

433

"But the people that do know their God shall be strong, and do exploits" (Daniel 11:32, KJV)

"And this is life eternal, that they might know thee the only true God, and Jesus Christ, whom thou hast sent" (John 17:3, KJV)

It is clear in scripture that God desires a personal relationship with us. There is key men and women in the Old Testament who believed God, and their belief was credited to them as righteousness. Their belief was not a mental ascent but an act of obedience to God. He called "whosoever" would believe in Him. It was humanity that wanted a mediator or a king. God gave them what they wanted over and over but they would not learn from the consequences of getting what they wanted. Christ removed the middle person when He went to the cross. Now we all have unhindered access to God. Our faith in Christ is credited to us as righteousness. Christ makes us righteous by faith in what He accomplished at the cross. The temptation for all of us is to replace our direct access to God with a church or mediator. It has been the age-old temptation to rely on another to know God. This is the root of religion. Jesus made the attention of God available to those who would believe. We can know God for ourselves. The best teachers and preachers get their audience to rely on God as quickly as they can. No one should rely on another to get to God, Christ must be our only reliance. Christ is the way maker. When we put another ahead of Christ, we will be eaten up with guilt, fear and shame. Adam was designed to walk directly with God, there was no angel or mediator who visited Adam or Eve on behalf of God. Jesus restored the direct relationship that was broken in Eden because of Sin. They did not have foreknowledge; scripture enlightens us of the plots of hell against us. Scripture reveals the temptation of Satan and teaches what happens to those that give into it. Jesus resisted Satan's temptation because He knew nothing good comes out of his will. Satan appeals to our sight but conceals the unseen consequences of following him. This is why at the source of every religion; there are popes, priests, and religious men and women who "only" have the full revelation. The only full revelation is the Bible. As much as we need pastors and teachers, their mission is to get us to depend on Christ for ourselves. We must be reminded that God wants to know us personally. We easily revert to routines, traditions and mediators more than simply trusting God. Remember Christ's death.

Note

434

"And we have known and believed the love that God hath to us. God is love; and he that dwelleth in love dwelleth in God, and God in him" (1 John 4:16, KJV)

Have you faced death at one time in your life? Have you come to the end of yourself, have you lost hope? We have all failed, all have sinned, we have disappointed our loved ones; even though we believe in the grace of God for others, we struggle to believe it for ourselves. We know the Gospel and would believe the good news for everyone but why do so many people struggle to believe it for themselves? This type of personality gives an abundance of grace and love but when it comes to themselves, they hate what they see. They would never shame anyone yet live under a cloud of shame. They love the unlovable but hate themselves. One of the most difficult truths to believe is that the Gospel is as much good news to the believer as it is to the sinner. If we are not willing to believe the love of God for ourselves, how are we going to convince anyone else that God loves them. Can you say with no hesitation "God loves me!"? Many people love and serve but they use it to hide behind their hatred of themselves. If we want power in our lives, we must first believe the love of God for ourselves before we can believe it for others. A lot of our evangelism is done by people who love others more than themselves. Jesus was clear that we can't love our neighbor until we first love ourselves. Who is willing to believe that the grace, love and mercy of God are accessible to all in Christ? God extends His love to us all, it's up to us to believe it for ourselves. For years, many people lived steeped in a hatred of themselves. We mask it with our care and love for others but when it comes to our own personal walk with God, we detest ourselves. God loves the world but does that include "me"? Yes, it does. God cares for us equally and uniquely at the same time. People may make you feel invisible, as if you don't exist. Just because few would miss you if you passed (died), does not mean that you do not matter. God loves you. God cares about each one of us not only equally but uniquely. Many believers need to start believing for themselves as much as they do for everyone else. When we believe the love of God for ourselves, we won't be swayed by people's love. We can be secure in who we are when we ground ourselves in Christ. Make Jesus your foundation.

Note

435

We are to give honor to whom honor is due. The US military have put their lives on the line to keep order all across the globe. Their sacrifice is felt by every country. We are safe and protected because of the US military. As believers in Christ, we are to honor our government and pray for our leaders. Jesus was tolerant of everyone. He taught freedom for all to choose. He never formed a military or used weapons to advance His message. Tolerance and freedom must be defended. Other religions force their followers with military force. Jesus used love to win over His followers. When Peter reached for a sword, Jesus rebuked Him. Jesus does not need military power like the weak false gods of Islam and other false religions. The USA is the land of the free. Our military fights to protect the freedom of religion and speech. We must pray for the US Military as they defend our Lord's will for freedom of choice. No one should be forced to be a part of any religion. No one should be persecuted to follow any God. On this side of eternity, every human should be born with the right to encounter God for themselves. Jesus never baptized children or brainwashed anyone to follow Him. Jesus never asked for time, talent or treasure in exchange for heaven or Salvation. The USA Constitution is the greatest constitution that humanity could have. It protects the right of every human to make their own decision and follow what they want to follow. Believers in Christ made a choice to follow Him. In order to be saved, we choose to repent, confess and believe in our heart that Jesus is Lord. The USA is a free country. Jesus did not come to set up a nation here or have a kingdom here. When Jesus returns, He will conquer the earth but until He returns, every human has the right to choose Him or follow the Devil. Anyone that used the name of Jesus to be violent or wage a war is not a follower of the biblical Christ. Jesus Christ is the founder of our faith, not a pope or an apostle. There is no one we follow more than Jesus Christ and His Word. God bless our US military.

Note

436

"Wherefore I say unto thee, Her sins, which are many, are forgiven; for she loved much: but to whom little is forgiven, the same loveth little" (Luke 7:47, KJV)

Let the broken come and find healing. In this cold world, many go about their every day like robots. We go through the routine but when life gets rudely interrupted, we are knocked off course. Life has a way of doing that to all of us. When these times strike, that's when we need a net to fall into. There is no community better than the church on earth. It is the safest and most resourceful community we could have. The church is full of people who have been redeemed at one time or another so they're prepared to be gracious and loving. They don't judge; the church loves as they have been loved. They want to see you thrive and unlike other communities, they celebrate when you do well rather than get jealous like all other communities do. The church is a community that truly desires to decrease so others can increase in Christ. They look out for each other and discern when we are going down a path that will hurt us. This is why we are not to forsake the assembly. Jesus chose twelve apostles and had three even closer. We need to be in a community of at least twelve and have three that are even closer. We can't choose our family but we can choose our community. Jesus modeled community. Rarely was He alone. It's when we isolate ourselves from community for an extended time, that we are outside of the will of God. God's will always lead us to community and will be accomplished by community. We have so many great resources to stay in community, like social media. We should take advantage of all types of community. Staying in community is easier than ever. We can talk to someone dear to us within seconds. It just takes intentionality. Staying in community requires work, intentionality and effort. If we wait around for others to initiate community, it may not happen. If everyone waits for someone to initiate community, we all will live in isolation. Be known as the one that always initiates. Humble yourself and engage in community. Pride keeps us from entering community because we don't want accountability. Don't wait, reach out. We are stronger together. Jesus left the church here so that we can have community to get through this life together. The church is as much our family as our biological family, in fact even more if the biological family is not.

Note

437

"For by grace are ye saved through faith; and that not of yourselves: it is the gift of God" (Ephesians 2:8, KJV)

Grace is our only means to God. There is grace for all of us. Grace is getting unmerited favor. The prodigal son in our day would have been given the cold shoulder or worse. Jesus taught a different parenting style then the way we are taught. Rather than discipline, the prodigal's dad threw a celebration for the return of his son. This was not to make light of sin; Jesus didn't make light of sin because we read of the price that He paid so that our Father can throw a celebration over every one of us sinners who repent. There is grace. If we don't preach grace and with grace, we will spiritually die under the ministry of condemnation. The law will only condemn all of us. Jesus did not come to condemn. Condemnation was not Christ's method to get people to respond to Him. He showed grace. Sinners were not put off by Him, they were drawn to Him because He was full of grace. Grace without truth is grease and is powerless. Jesus was full of grace and truth. "Grace to the sinner and truth to the religious." There is more grace than we could ever need from God. Jesus's sacrifice was brutal but it was not in vain. The extent of His sacrifice shows the extent of God's grace on us. Grace and peace can only be experienced in Christ. We won't get that from another person or church. Few people show what they have been given, making one wonder if they even know what has been given to them in Christ. Their judgment, condemnation and arrogance mean all that they see is the sin but have no compassion on the person. Jesus was moved with compassion for sinners. Sarcasm, coldness and putting sinners down should have no place in us if we are in Christ. Compassion is what fills our soul when Christ is Lord. He will never cast you away no matter what state you are in. When those around you distance from you and gossip about you, they are no reflection of Christ. When those who you thought would be there for you abandon you, they are no reflection of Christ. When all forsake you for whatever reason, they are no reflection of Christ. Religion runs from others' brokenness; Jesus comes to all our brokenness and offers healing at the cost of His own blood. Dignity and pride make us give off that we are not broken and have it all together. Truth is, we are all in pieces without Christ.

Note

438

"He must increase, but I must decrease" (John 3:30, KJV)

"Be more than I could ever be. Go further than I went. Learn from my mistakes. Improve what you can. Believe with no limits, break all restraints, don't give up. No matter what, I'm proud of you. You don't bless me for what you can do but because you're my son." If an earthly dad knows to bless his kids, how much more does our Heavenly Father. If all you have known is conditional love, you have not experienced real love. Human love can't compare to the love of God. God is our Father. Jesus taught an inclusive God of both Jew and Gentile. The Jews wanted an exclusive God and this is one of the reasons they pleaded for Christ's crucifixion. They thought that God only predestined their blood line. They felt that God would only elect them because of their heritage. Jesus sat with sinners, spoke with the Samaritan women, allowed a prostitute to wash His feet, had dinner with a tax collecting thief to show humanity that God was never exclusive to a race or a lifestyle. God loves humanity equally, passionately and cares for each one of us unconditionally. He elects all to be saved but the election is conditional to belief. His atonement is unlimited. His grace is resistible. Jesus is the most famous person in all history yet billions resist His message, conviction and call. We are totally depraved by sin yet have the ability to choose to believe His love as we hear the Gospel preached. As long as we believe, we will be preserved; but if we give place to the enemy, we can depart from the faith and enter a state the Bible calls apostate or reprobate. Jesus marveled at faith and was frustrated by unbelief. The Jews thought their messiah would have honored their righteousness and would have detested sinners. We see through scripture that sin is not what separates us from God but unrepentant sin feeds what really separates us, which is unbelief. Jesus knew we were sinners but the religious used their works to distract everyone from their sin. Jesus's name—called the religious, He called them hypocrites, white washed tombs, blind guides, He said they make their disciples twice as much a child of hell as they are, they clean the outside of the cup but inside they are full of greed and self-indulgence. Jesus loves you, don't hide behind religion. Believe in His love for you.

Note

439

"In every thing give thanks: for this is the will of God in Christ Jesus concerning you" (1 Thessalonians 5:18, KJV)

Many look on and wish that they had what you have. We can be so ungrateful for the blessings we have. We never have an excuse for ungratefulness as believers. There is always someone wishing for what you have. Whether it's your health, roof over your head, or clean water, the believer has more than all of that in Christ. If Christ is not your source for thankfulness, we will never experience true gratefulness. Our culture breeds entitlement. Western Christianity raises entitled believers. They treat God like Christ was enough. They try to ignore the suffering and bloodshed of Christ even though He specifically told us to remember His death. All that our culture wants is to remember their identity, their benefits, their blessings but not remember what Christ told us to be remembering. He never told us to remember who we are in Christ. He wants us to remember Him. The more we decrease and He increases, the more grateful we will become. Magnify Christ and forget about what we get, just give Him praise for who He is in sickness or in health. Life is found in Christ. As long as we trust God only for what we can get, we are still on the milk of the word. The sooner we learn to look to Him in all thing and be content where He has put us, then we have real gratefulness. Moaning won't produce fruit. It's time to grow up and drive out the sulking spirit. It could be way worse, no matter how bad it is. The flames of hell await unbelievers. Believers don't complain, believers are not ungrateful, believers are not spoiled entitled brats. Believers are grateful that they are saved. Hell and the damnation of the soul is not preached enough. Most think salvation is living well-mannered, paying taxes and going to church. They ignorantly think that we have been saved from a bad life. No, we have been plucked out of a destiny of hellfire. Jesus did not come to better our life here and improve our experience as a human. Jesus was clear what salvation was. He preached more on hell than He did on being born-again or heaven. He never used the words identity, purpose, or destiny. These three buzz words have been the focus of many preachers. We have been focusing on ourselves and on our benefits way too much. Forget self, reckon yourself dead, magnify the Lord, and glorify Christ.

Note

440

"And then will I profess unto them, I never knew you: depart from me, ye that work iniquity" (Matthew 7:23, KJV)

Our definition of iniquity is breaking the law of Moses. Christ's definition of iniquity is doing ministry without knowing Him. There is a difference between a calling and a career. Ministry is not a career. Following God is a calling. Jesus called His followers; some even heard their name spoken to follow Him. Throughout scripture, we read of men and women who were called by God. It was never a good idea, or logical for them to follow God. Following God will require faith. It will cost us our comfort, reasoning and our lives. We are promised that He will never leave us but we are not promised that it will always be easy. We can hear the call of God when our prayer time is more about listening than praying. We hear the call of God when we seek God more in secret than only in the sight of the public. The religious only do their religion in the sight of people yet in the quiet place, they are no different than the world. The called of God care more for their relationship with Jesus than the opinions of people. Caring more for what people think than what God says, means we have fallen for religion. Religiosity is so deceiving but needs to be taken seriously. Religion may make model citizens but it won't save the soul. Truth itself does not save. Christ did not come to only tell us the truth but embodied the truth that we need Him for freedom. Truth is more than a written word, it's Jesus. He is the truth. When we know Jesus, then we will know freedom. Freedom is not doing what we want, but doing what He wants. Religion is a worse hindrance to our relationship with Jesus than sin is. Sin shows us our need for Jesus, religion hides sin and disciples white-washed tombs. Jesus does not give license to sin, but knows that we will sin as long as we are in these earthly bodies. Religion makes us turn to rituals, creeds, and traditions more than Jesus. God desires reconciliation with us more than our religious works. Jesus knows us. Don't hide motives, sin or agendas from Him. Open wide our soul, let Him come into our tombs of bones and call us forth into an empowered life. The called of God stand in the power of the Holy Spirit, declaring Christ is supreme; Jesus is Lord of all. From this relationship with Jesus, we will do what He calls us to do!

Note

441

"And rend your heart, and not your garments, and turn unto the
Lord your God: for he is gracious and merciful, slow to anger, and
of great kindness, and repenteth him of the evil" (Joel 2:13, KJV)

We will have no weight in our missions if our missions are not flowing out of our life. When missions are a time or place or people group, we are ignorant to what missions are. We have many missionaries ignorantly trying to save their people group by digging wells and giving them education only to conform them to their own image. Western missions want third-world countries to be like the West more than like Christ. Humanism puts the needs of humanity ahead of the glory of God. Every believer is a missionary. A believer who hears from God and follows through is a successful missionary. We applaud those who go overseas but God applauds those who obey His will for their lives. We must never discriminate between those who go overseas to do missions and those who do missions where they are at. As long as they are following God, then they are a success. Humanism puts the mind and body ahead of the soul. Many ministries that started out preaching the Gospel now look no different than any humanitarian charity. Like Chick-fil-a, they have brought in businessmen to increase their prosperity by compromising their message. The founders want sustainability more that following scripture. Like the Galatian church, they began in the Spirit and ended up in the flesh. It's an age-old cycle. It's the same for our own lives. We are tempted to leave our first love every day. Today's discipleship has been the cause of many leaving their first love. Today's discipleship is about knowledge more than knowing and obeying God. Today's Missions is something we do once a year rather a lifestyle we live. This is why they have no spiritual weight on their ministries. They are so spiritually weak, that the only good they can do on their mission trips is "build a church," pass out free stuff and sightsee. Sinners don't need stuff, they need Jesus. The church needs to give the same dignity that was given to them. Rather than giving handouts, let's give them a hand up. Jesus got us to where we are at, not silver or gold. Why would we give anyone anything other than Jesus? Without realizing it, we are enabling sinners and poverty by just giving handouts rather the hand up, which is Jesus. We have so much silver and gold that we have set ourselves up to be the Christ.

Note

442

"Let no man despise thy youth; but be thou an example
of the believers, in word, in conversation, in charity, in
spirit, in faith, in purity" (1 Timothy 4:12, KJV)

A new type of clergy is arising. Some of the most unreached people today are in our public schools, businesses, athletics, and the medical field. This clergy will be self-funded. There have been too many "ministers" living high off the widow's mite. They have pimped out Jesus by putting makeup and a mini skirt on Him. They found a way to take 10 percent of their followings' income and get away with just talking behind a mic for an hour a week. We applaud missionaries who go overseas but what we need to be applauding is believers who do the will of God. Every believer who follows God in whatever it looks like has the applause of God. There are many that have given their lives to overseas missions but came back bitter and enraged that they gave their lives to sinners who love their sin more than Christ. Pity is not a good motive to minister. We minister for the glory of God. God takes care of the rest. We can't save souls. Only God can save the soul. We need to live for the glory of God and follow what He tells us to do. All we can do is give a hand out. Jesus gives a hand up. If ministries are shying away from the proclamation of the Gospel, then they are on the verge of Ichabod. When the mind, body and soul become more of a focus than the glory of God, we are on a downward spiral. Overseas missions or local missions are not our primary calling. If we foolishly think it is, we could end up getting the same judgment as those we are trying to "save." Our primary calling is to know God and glorify Him. The poor, we will always have, and sinners will always love their sin; the world is heading for destruction. We can't do anything about it in our flesh. We would be surprised at what God can do through us if we stopped living for the souls of men and just glorified God by doing what He tell us to do. He can save the soul. Glorify Jesus Christ, obey His call. It's time to raise up a new generation of believers who are more passionate about honoring Jesus than reaching people. Don't put people or pity ahead of God. None are equal to Him. When we put God first, we are more of a resource to those around us. They don't need our stuff; they need our savior. We are nobody's savior. Preach Christ, get the attention for Him, He will do what we can't.

Note

_____

_____

_____

_____

_____

_____

_____

_____

443

"There is no fear in love; but perfect love casteth out fear: because fear hath torment. He that feareth is not made perfect in love" (1 John 4:18, KJV)

The open air is where Jesus spent most of His ministry preaching and teaching. He discipled by teaching and demonstrating. Anyone can teach a script, but not everyone can live what they teach when it matters most. Talk is cheap if there is no power to cause what we say to be what we do. We have enough teachings and teachers; we need some doers. Ranting and raving from a pulpit is not where the Gospel is needed the most. Local churches are not community centers or social clubs but they are equipping centers to see the church raised to be the church in their everyday life. The gathering of the church was not supposed to be evangelistic, it was supposed to be a time of refreshing and equipping to cause believers to be all that they can be as evangelists in their sphere of influence. When the church gathering becomes the evangelistic service, then the congregation will be equipped to be laborers who will lift up the name of a church more than Jesus. Rather than the congregation raised up to invite people to Jesus, they are equipped on how to invite people to Church. This can work and has worked but we need to be about making disciples of Christ and not a brand of Church. Church won't save anyone, no matter how trendy it is. When someone is invited to church, they are taught attendants, tithe and volunteerism to keep them saved rather than faith in Christ alone. If we want committed believers, let's get them off reliance on a church and onto a reliance on Christ as quickly as we can. Churches that desire to lift Jesus above their brand, style and image will not compete with other churches in their community. The world can see the division between churches that have the same statement of faith. This division is working against our church growth. Having a God-driven passion to glorify Him will grow the church of Jesus Christ. Allowing corporate America to make us purpose-driven has made us step on each other to get to where we want to go. Planting churches next to seasoned churches is cowardly. The Bible is our manual for the church's origin, purpose, and destiny. We depend on celebrity preachers who are doing what God has called them to do. Rather than copying, we have the same source they have, scripture and Jesus; what more do we need?

Note

444

*"And now why tarriest thou? arise, and be baptized, and wash away
thy sins, calling on the name of the Lord" (Acts 2:1–2, KJV)*

The more we work together, the stronger we are. Our unity can be used for our glory or the glory of Christ. When humanity was in one accord, we built the Tower of Babel but it was for our glory; in the New Testament, when we united for Christ's glory, we were empowered to be the church. Unity for the glory of man may make sense, but unity for the glory of God won't always. God requires faith to be saved, faith to follow Him and faith to make it to the end. By faith, the men and women of old got the attention of God. By faith they did great exploits. A life of faith is best defined by our dependence on God. When we do what He says, it will always require faith. Without faith, it is impossible to please God. It's only when we set out to follow God and there is no explainable way to how we are going to make it, that God will see us through, now that's faith. Jesus was only upset with unbelief, doubt, and faithlessness; Jesus only marveled at the faith of a person. If we need God right now and there is no way forward unless God shows up, we are in the most blessed place we could be. Anyone can preach when they have everything going for them. Religion elevates men who can do the things of God without God. This is why there are very few prayer meetings anymore. This is why the prayer meeting is the first service millennials axe when they want their services more appealing. What Jesus defined as a place of worship is the least practiced in our places of worship, prayer. We sing and we preach, but when do we have corporate prayer? The early church had corporate prayers constantly. The church began and was built on the prayer meeting. When prayer is replaced by marketing, lights and a rock band are we building the kingdom of God or the Tower of Babel? We sound so intelligent with our sound bites, trendy styles and skilled band but what pleases God more than anything is when we pray, believe and do as He says. Following trends, styles and preachers more than following Christ leads to lukewarmness. The way we lift up men today is exactly what Israel did with Saul. Where are the Samuels? Men who lift their teachings above scripture are not fulfilling their calling. Don't look to any man more than Christ. Don't quote any book more than the Bible.

Note

445

"But continue thou in the things which thou hast learned and hast been assured of, knowing of whom thou hast learned them" (2 Timothy 3:14, KJV)

This world is so broken. People's souls are so lost. Sin and Satan have had our streets for too long. When we do what God has called us to do, which is the Great Commission, our hearts get broken by the suffering that people are going through every day. A prayer meeting is not the only place where we can get the call of God, putting feet to our faith can lead us to hear the call of God for people. "God, give us your heart for people. Let people feel your love through us." When we let people's pain affect us, we can't help but weep for their souls. "God, give us souls for the glory of Christ. May people not only pray a prayer but truly be born again." No discipleship in the world can keep someone saved like the Spirit of God. As we have been kept by the grace of God, may those we pray with be kept by the grace of God. We can't carry the weight of the world but we can do what God has called us to do. God chose His church to be His hands and feet. Outside of the church the world has no hope of hearing the Gospel. Prayer meetings, worship nights, benevolence, outreaches, and block parties are all ineffective to save the soul. The only way for a soul to be saved is to hear the Gospel, repent and believe in the heart that Jesus is Lord. We must not be ashamed of the Gospel by emphasizing "showing the Gospel." Showing without preaching is lifting our works up above the work of Christ. Only Jesus saves the soul. Humanism is very deceiving. We don't do what we do for humans' sake; we do what we do for the glory of God. As we continue to glorify God in evangelism, we will see the power of God do for the people what we never could. Only God can make someone born again. No amount of clever speech, cultural relevance, or strategies can compare to what the power of God can do. Christianity is not an argument, the Gospel is not a philosophy, this is a supernatural encounter with the resurrected Christ. The Bible is more than a history book; the words of scripture are powerful enough to change us from the inside out. We can't separate the power of God or the Holy Spirit from Christianity; if we do, we are left with a dead religion. The book of Acts was just the beginning. The power then is the same power that we have now. Will we choose to walk in the Spirit?

Note

446

"Confirming the souls of the disciples, and exhorting them to continue in the faith, and that we must through much tribulation enter into the kingdom of God" (Acts 14:22, KJV)

Do we see what God sees? Life throws at us every situation unimaginable. Few could've foreseen where they are today when they were younger. When all we hear is health, wealth and prosperity, we can get so disappointed following God if He does not produce that lifestyle. Following God, promises that lifestyle in heaven but while we are here, we will face trouble. Our gratefulness as believers is a decision no matter what we are going through. Rich or poor, health or sickness, we have a reason to rejoice in Christ. This is why we are to remember His death as believers. He emphasized remembering His death because He knew what was ahead for His followers. When He comes, He will wipe every tear. There will be no sickness in heaven, there will be no sorrow in heaven. Until He comes, we are to remember His death. There is nothing we could face in life that should rob our gratefulness. Our thanksgiving is based on Christ and nothing else. We know that life changes, seasons come and go; hold onto nothing here too tightly. Jesus is all that stays the same, He is our rock and consistency. When we see as He sees, we will not be moved by our sight but in all things have joy because God will get glory out of all circumstances. Let's be about His purpose for our lives. We can love God yet not be about His purpose and never enter into the peace that all things will work together for the good. Many love God but by not doing as He says, shows what we really love. By not living for His purpose or mission, our words of love for Him are hollow. When we decide to obey even though it's against our will, against our flesh and against our wants, then we can see as God sees. God gives us His vision for our lives. Seeing as God sees, makes us notice what we would never notice in our flesh. As we live surrendered to God, then the power of God leads our lives. Let's decide to be grateful, let's decide to obey God; when we take the initial step toward His will, God will use our momentum to steer us in His direction. Don't wait to move. How we pray before we eat is the type of prayer that works for everything in life. Pray God's blessing and then do something about it. Staying in a state of prayer will only make you starve. Pray then eat. Be a doer.

Note

447

"For where two or three are gathered together in my name, there am I in the midst of them" (Matthew 18:20, KJV)

It takes a community to do the will of God. Not only does He call us but He uses community to accomplish His will. We can't be discipled in isolation. We can't be the church isolated. We are called to hold each other accountable and sharpen each other. Iron does not get sharpened without friction. We can't choose our family but we can choose our friends. Who we put around us, determines our spiritual distance. Choose those who spur us on, choose those who challenge us spiritually and not sinfully. Golfers don't hire a soccer coach, the obese don't hire a sumo wrestler to be their gymnast. Who is coaching you? Who is pastoring you? The temptation is to only go as far as our coach is, but a real coach will want you to grow way beyond him. Jesus wants you to never get lukewarm in your relationship with Him. He will use all that life throws at us to keep our faith challenged so we make it to the end. Jesus is praying that our faith won't fail because He knows our faith can fail. Fight to believe through it all. Put those around you who encourage you daily in truth so we don't get hardened by "sins deceitfulness," which leads to a "departure from the faith." We are all one decision away from being where those we judge are at. Pride always goes before a fall. Spiritual pride is defined as living for God without depending on God. Examine whether you are in the faith by how much accountability you have in your life. When we get hurt by those who were supposed to be there for us, we are tempted to close off. There are genuine believers who won't throw stones at you because they're aware of the boulders on them, they will be there for you to walk you through it, loving on you the whole way as family should. We will be effective in evangelism as we love on one another. It's easier to love a stranger than it is those closest to us but loving those closest to us is key for the world to see our love for them. Love everyone without compromising the truth. Our motive behind every rebuke, criticism, and discipline is restoration and growth. The reason we preach so straight and with fire is because there is a higher calling for all of us and the devil has made many settle when we have been created to be white hot. Give Christ your all.

Note

448

"But he giveth more grace. Wherefore he saith, God resisteth the proud, but giveth grace unto the humble" (James 4:6, KJV)

Gratefulness is what Christ produces in every believer. Entitlement is what religion produces in every adherent. He that is forgiven much will love much. The law, hell, and the judgment of God are three rarely taught topics in the church. Without these topics that Jesus taught, the spirit of entitlement can overrun us. Entitlement breeds unhealthy competitiveness, comparison and jealousies. Rather than celebrating with someone who does well, we pick it apart. We become fault finders not to be productive but just to distract us from our own faults. We all have faults. As we walk in the light before God, He conforms our thoughts to His thoughts. We need His mind so we can have His perspective. He produces gratefulness as we realize what we have been saved from. The law is our schoolmaster to teach us our dire need for Christ. Hell is our reminder of why Christ was bloodied and died such a violent death. Judgment reminds us of what is to come when every person will stand before almighty God, giving account for every action and motive. If it were not for Christ, we would all be damned to hell. There is not one human born predestined to hell. God has made a way where "whosoever will" believer in Christ can be saved. Those that believe that some humans have been elected to hell just don't want the responsibility of the Great Commission. We all know what we are entitled to, if we are honest. Hinduism has a caste system that is demonic at its core but this spirit has taken over much of the evangelistic philosophy of the church. As if God shows favoritism to some by saving some and damning others. God wants all to be saved. It will always be a mystery to us on why some resist yet others respond but we must believe that every person we meet can be saved. Let's love much, let the gratefulness we express be seen by how we evangelize. May we be filled with thanksgiving as we evangelize so all will look to the sacrifice of Christ and be saved. Are we being formed into the image of the Pharisees or Christ as we read scripture? The Bible can be used for what we manipulate it to say if we deny its whole counsel. The truth is God loves us, Jesus took our penalty of sin; repent, believe and be saved.

Note

449

"But watch thou in all things, endure afflictions, do the work of an evangelist, make full proof of thy ministry" *(2 Timothy 4:5, KJV)*

So many evangelists start on the streets but over time, they settle for the easier option, the church. An evangelist that only pulpit preaches to church people, may need to relook at his title. An evangelist that does not equip the church for evangelism needs to relook at his title. History tells of ministries that were evangelistic but the enemy lured them from being a threat to darkness to reaching the reached. Every day an evangelist will share the Gospel, in season or out of season. An evangelist that basis his message on his testimony rather than the Gospel needs to relook at his title. Our testimony does not save anyone and if we are not careful, our testimony can be a hindrance making the church feel like if they don't have a story like the evangelist does, then they can't evangelize. You don't need to be relevant or relate to be an evangelist. Jesus did not have to sin to reach sinners. The message that evangelists champion is the Gospel. Anyone can preach the Gospel. Not everyone has a dramatic testimony but everyone has a dramatic Gospel. Evangelists that don't equip the indigenous or the local church but raise themselves up are not fulfilling the office of an evangelist. An evangelist is not a savior. In fact, the evangelist needs Jesus as much as His audience. A successful evangelist gets his audience onto scripture, the Gospel and Jesus as quickly as he can. There is nothing in us that can persuade a sinner to convert. If we lift Christ up, He will do the rest. It's a mystery why people some resist but others receive. It's okay to not understand it, but don't let it be an obstacle to obeying what Christ told us to do, which is preach the Gospel. When was the last time you preached the gospel outside of your routine or pulpit? It's shocking how we mute the leading of God outside of church. The evangelist lives the most exciting life that anyone could live and that fire should be contagious. There will be no need for an evangelist in heaven. These few years we are here is our only opportunity to preach the Gospel. Follow Jesus as He leads you. We live in a very ignorant and selfish day where many turn a blind eye to sinners and even came up with a doctrine to keep them from the Great Commission.

Note

450

"For even hereunto were ye called: because Christ also suffered for us, leaving us an example, that ye should follow his steps" (1 Peter 2:21, KJV)

A ship was not built to stay in port. Believers were not saved to stay in a structure which we call church. Jesus never gave blueprints to the structure that we call church. The church is believers that follow Christ in their everyday life. We were not saved to wait out until we get to heaven. If we warm a pew our whole lives and never engage in our community, family or place of work, then we have not stepped into the fullness. Going to church, conferences, worship nights if they're biblical should make us excited to follow Jesus in our everyday life more than those gatherings. A ship in port is not fulfilling its purpose but gets maintenance and cargo so it can continue to fulfill its purpose. Christianity that makes us excited more about the "port" than the "voyage," will lead us to a life of disappointment. It trains us to be Christians only antichurch around other "Christians" but that's the reverse of what discipleship should be producing. Discipleship should be getting us so "self" sufficient in our relationship with Christ, that we are shining forth His glory in the middle of our work place and everyday community. Religion teaches that "bad company corrupts good morals" but Christ came to reverse that proverb by giving us the power to influence bad company more than them influencing us. One with Christ is the majority wherever we go. We don't cave into peer pressure we stand against the current so all will see the glory of God. We were designed to befriend sinners without being influenced, He that is in us influences them. The monastic temptation is exactly what the devil wants us to do. He wants us to pull back from sinners and shy away from the world but Jesus ran toward it without being influenced. We have the Holy Spirit in us, as we follow Jesus; He will keep us no matter where He leads. Our "high" as believers is to evangelize in the darkness to be a light for Christ; it's not only singing songs and hearing a motivating message. The best type of worship leads to obedience to Christ, the best type of preaching makes us intentionally share Jesus with everyone around us. Get out from the port and fulfill your mission. This does not mean that we have to go overseas; it means to go across the street.

Note

451

"Wherefore he saith, Awake thou that sleepest, and arise from the dead, and Christ shall give thee light" (Ephesians 5:14, KJV)

"She is not dead; she is just asleep." Only sinners are dead in sin and trespasses. The sleepers are awakening. The nominal church is awakening to who she has been called to be. We have been lured to sleep by smooth talkers and worship that's more like lullabies. The awakened preach with fire and passion. The mellow lukewarm Christianity that only leads to nominalism has neutralized the church for far too long. Their teaching numbs the brain from activating the believer to do what they hear. Slowly but surely, the awakened are gaining more ground. The sleepers are seeking to be awakened. The more irritated we get as sleepers, the more we will want awakening. Awakening comes when truth impacts our state of being. It is not educational only but also empowers us in our lifestyle. Jesus does not only change our minds but our lives too. Many would deem the church dead but the fact we can discern, tells we are not dead but awakening. There are only a few people awake right now, standing in our pulpits. The awakened don't preach sound bites or a "self-focused" messages but rightly divide scripture with passion. When scripture is preached with genuine fire and power, then awakening comes. The attention will not be on the preacher but on Christ. The congregation won't be in awe by the preacher's clever speech but by the Words of scripture. God will share His glory with no one. Anyone that attempts to share the glory with God will disappoint everyone who looks to them more than God. The church is not dead, she is just asleep. God, send an awakening to our generation. There must be more than this. So many have lost heart in the church. The church does not need a revival because she is not dead in sin or trespass. The lost are dead in sin and have needed to be revived since the fall. All the church needs is an awakening. If we would just awaken to who God called us to be; if we would seek God for a revelation of His Word. We need to draw near to God and press past our lukewarm state. Let's fan into flame the gift that is within us. Scripture opens the eyes of our understanding. Awaken, rise from the dead, Christ will shine to reflect the world around us. Christ calls us to fulfill His will while we are here. Christ alone is the light.

Note

452

"For our gospel came not unto you in word only, but also in power, and in the Holy Ghost, and in much assurance; as ye know what manner of men we were among you for your sake. And ye became followers of us, and of the Lord, having received the word in much affliction, with joy of the Holy Ghost" (1 Thessalonians, 1:5–6 KJV)

The Gospel is the power of God unto Salvation. We have two thousand years of history to prove that the Bible brings prosperity, hygiene, society, order, freedom and family. There is no other book that can come close to the benefits of scripture. How can anyone argue that Jesus Christ is not God? Look what His death on a cross accomplished globally. Look what His disappointed followers accomplished after they encountered the resurrected Christ. He lives. Millions around the globe can testify that He lives. We don't need to look to any other book to understand our origin, purpose or destiny. We have the clearest answers to the mysteries of humanity. When we yield to the power of God and preach the Gospel, not as an argument, for the glory of God, it's the conviction of the Spirit that converts. Conversion does not happen off of a clever speech or an argument, conversion happens when the soul is opened to Jesus Christ to save. The Gospel opens the door of the soul for Jesus to enter. His kingdom is within the believer. This is why we live from within. Our life source is Christ in us. Without Him leading our lives or empowering us, there is no way that we could honor Him. The Holy Spirit does a much better work in us than we ever could. It is God who works in us as we surrender to Him. We must never forget the most important benefit of salvation, which is reconciliation. We have been brought back into relationship with God. He made us His temple. We don't need to go anywhere to meet with God, He is in us. God never leaves us, nor forsakes us. The more we realize that He is with us at all times, the more we will know Him. We are never alone. We can call on almighty God. Our generation has billions of souls without Christ; God gave the church the responsibility to be His ambassador on earth. This does not mean that we are only His ambassadors when we are on missions or on Sundays but in all times, He is shining through us. He is as near to us on Monday as He was on Sunday. We need to stop letting goosebumps determine the nearness of our God. He is near to us because His Word tells us He is. If we draw near to Him, He is always ready to draw near to us. We can know as much of God as we want. If we believe the Gospel, we will proclaim the Gospel.

Note

453

"There is a way that seemeth right unto a man, but the end thereof are the ways of death" (Proverbs 16:25, KJV)

Let's not do what seems to be right, let's do what the Word tells us. The biblical literacy of Christians today is lower than any other generation, we have no excuse because we have never had such ease of access to the Bible. How can we put up with ignorance when we have scripture to "study to show ourselves approved"? Every major decision needs be balanced with scripture and conviction. We need to press through our emotions and filter our thoughts through scripture. Our thoughts will deceive us, our emotions will lie to us, we are to follow Christ by using scripture as our guide. Scripture was not given to tell us what we want to hear but what we need to hear. If we only give our ears and bodies what they want, we will end up addicted, broken and wrecked. This is why we need to rise in the power of the Word and quote scripture to our flesh, to our wants and to the temptation of Satan. Jesus used scripture to overcome the temptation of the enemy. A believer's arsenal is not his passion, charisma, loudness or eloquence but His ability to recite scripture. In the heat of battle, that's when the believer uses the Word to cut down the lies of Satan. Truth is what gets us through life. Without it, we are shackled to our emotions. Lift your attention to Jesus. No matter what we are facing, our sight is not what determines our faith. Faith alone in scripture determines our faith. As we are discipled in the Word, we can have hope through all of life's battles. No matter how tempting it is to do what seems to be right, we must acknowledge God first, give Him an opportunity to speak, then we can be assured that He will direct our ways. This is what it means to have Jesus be Lord of our lives. Jesus gives more than eternal security; He gives us His will for our lives, which requires a relationship with Him. Our reconciliation to God is not only to worship Him but seek His will in all situations. We are not the Lord of Jesus. He is our Lord. Christianity that disciples their followers to "name it and claim it" or look to God as a "genie in a bottle" will only disappoint their followers. God does not always heed our prayers or give us what we want; this may make Him seem like He is unloving but He is actually protecting us, God knows best!

Note

454

"Look not every man on his own things, but every man also on the things of others" (Philippians 2:4, KJV)

Are you alone? Does anyone reach out to check you? Loneliness is taking out so many in our technological age. We have acquaintances but who do we go deep with? The art of friendship is slowly deteriorating. We live in a transient age that few do life with each other for an extended time. Life is busy. We are like ships that pass each other in the night. This disconnection and lack in families gives arsenal for our enemy to take us out. We were designed for community. God saw Adam and gave him a companion because He knew He could not be to man what another person could be. We need each other. It's more than multiplication. It's a need for community. Community today has been twisted where our society treats each other as commodities more than family. It's all about what we can do for each other. We answer our phones by saying, "What do you want?" We are bread to only make calls when we need somebody. We make friendships to use people to better ourselves. It's a "tit for tat, quid pro quitches for that" generation. Jesus redirected the foundation of our community when He went to the Cross, which was totally unconditional. The cross was God's way of showing humanity a different type of love. His love was not based on our response. God loves you. We should also love people. Anyone I'm with, no matter how many years incarcerated or how bad they were, I always love people. I know now that it's because Christ loves me. If He loves me, He can love anyone. Sometimes while going about my day, I'm so moved by the cross that

I just weep; "how can someone love me that much?" If it were not for the love of God, love would be dead in our world. The love of people has grown cold. People use each other and when they get what they want, they throw you out of their lives. There is no community that loves like Jesus does. Even the church, like Eve will disappoint. As much as we may try to fill the need for community with humans, at the end of the day, only Jesus can fulfill that need. Why don't you text someone, "How are you?" Those who know you, probably will be surprised by the question. I know I would be. We are so used to texting to get something, but what about texting to give something? God loves us so that we can love others.

Note

455

"Remember therefore from whence thou art fallen, and repent, and do the first works; or else I will come unto thee quickly, and will remove thy candlestick out of his place, except thou repent" (Revelation 2:5, KJV)

The difference between believers in Christ and believers in religion is the conviction of hidden sin. The prayer of a genuine believer is "don't let me take pleasure in sin." Conviction of sin must be heeded to. Religion either condemns or excuses sin but the Holy Spirit convicts us and grieves us of sin. There is not a single human that will attain sinlessness while we are in these bodies. The wages of sin is death and that's why these bodies age. Death was never the will of God. We brought death on ourselves. Believers in Jesus live forever; unless the rapture comes, we all will die. The Joker movie is about a man that allowed hidden sin to build up in his soul to the point that the sin took over his soul. Unconfessed sin to God will make us what we never thought we could be. If we don't deal with bitterness, insecurity and insignificance, it will give place to the enemy. We are to give no place to the enemy. We are to allow no emotion have our souls more than Jesus. When we clench onto anything but the hand of Christ, we will fall into despair. There is no assurance of life or eternal life outside of Jesus. This is why we need a relationship with Him because not a day goes by that the world does not want to influence us. Satan wants our soul. Distracting us or shaming us from a relationship with Jesus is the devil's strategy. Whether it's religion that binds us or sin that binds us, they both lead to the same end, death.

It's only when we have an open relationship with Jesus that we can go deep with Him. Confess sin to God, repent as often as you sin, not for salvation sake only but for a strong relationship with Jesus. God knows we are flesh; God knows everything about us but calls us into relationship with Him no matter our daily struggles. When He has His way in us and we feel His conviction, then we can walk in the life that He has called us to. Christ did not die so that we can sin but so that we can hate sin and have power over sin in our lives. God wants us to go and sin no more. As we allow the conviction of the Holy Spirit to have its way in us, we will repent and be empowered to be Holy as He is Holy. Don't let any gentile philistine dwell amongst us. The Holy Spirit mortifies the deeds of our flesh.

Note

_____

_____

_____

_____

_____

_____

_____

_____

456

"Where is the wise? where is the scribe? where is the disputer of this world? hath not God made foolish the wisdom of this world?" (1 Corinthians 1:20, KJV)

When the world sums you up, we must make a decision to either cave into the opinions of people or rise above the people to what God calls us to. Many who are born today, hit their ceiling from birth. Christ came to remove ceilings, limitations and restrictions. This is what the cross accomplished for all who would believe. When we believe on Christ, we stand out. Our joy is contagious. Our faith is insane. When the world says "No way," we say "Bring it on." We thrive in challenge, we dream to do the impossible, we believe against all odds. Believers in Jesus make a difference. We seem like the most foolish, the underdog; we have even been told that nothing good will come of our lives, and they were right!! The only "good" that we want to come out of our lives is the glory of Christ. That's the only good we live for, "God, get all the glory from my life." Rather than let criticizing opinions incapacitate us, let's let their negativity be fuel for our faith. "How will God confound them this time?" God won't forsake us; we can be confident that He will bring us through, even in death. Christ advances His kingdom through opposition, persecution and affliction. Rather than praying for prosperity, let's pray "God, in all seasons, get glory out of my life." We have been so distracted by materialism, things and self. Living for the glory of Christ alone is where life is found. Believers must only be moved by God. If we allow people, emotions or society to define us, we will live under a weight. When we find our significance in Christ alone, we will tap into another realm of living. The believer in Christ is a spiritual person, we are not natural. We were born of the Spirit. Without the power of God, we can't have life. Our flesh only produces death. This is why the believer reckons Himself dead and alive only to Christ. When we live without God, we have a counterfeit life. It's only when we realize that we no longer live but Christ lives in us and we walk in the spirit, that's when we see the transformation. If we walk in the spirit, we won't fulfill the lust of the flesh. God will enable us to do what we could not do on our own. He produces life. In Christ, there is life. The world may have "summed" you up but God did too when Christ went to the cross. Believe to the end.

Note

457

*"There is no fear in love; but perfect love casteth out
fear: because fear hath torment. He that feareth is
not made perfect in love" (1 John 4:18, KJV)*

Many feel every day like they are walking a tight rope with no net below if they fall. This mind-set leads to crippling anxiety. When we entertain the enemies lies, we fall into the clench of fear. The spirit of fear isolates us and turns everyone against us in our minds. Fear is more than a feeling, it's a spirit. The root of fear is a depletion of faith. If ever we need to be intentionally building faith, it's now. Faith in God's promises, which tells us that He will catch us if we fall and He will not forsake us, these have been fulfilled in Christ. It's the love of God, demonstrated by the cross of Christ, that drives the spirit of fear out of our minds. As we are read of the love of God toward us, this truth casts out fear. We can gauge our revelation of the love of God by how much the spirit of fear can oppress us. We can know in our mind that God loves us but, in our heart, we are full of doubt. By doing this, we lightly esteem the cross and make mountains out of grains of sand. Diminishing the cross and basing the love of God on how full our bank account is or how much family we have around us or how many friends are here to help us is dangerous. These things are important but they can fluctuate over time. What stays the same is what was already accomplished at the cross. It won't be this way forever. Believers have a net to fall into, the grace of God. We are not alone on this journey. Remember Christ when all you can see is the height you are walking at on this tight rope called life. Life is not easy.

It's full of cycles, seasons and change. Time waits for no one. When we fall, the spirit of fear will try to keep us free falling for the rest of our lives. That is no way to live. God so loves us. Not only does He catch us, He puts us back on our feet so that we can tread on fear, in Jesus's name. Pray to be perfected in the love of God. The Holy Spirit does not manifest fear in us but reveals the love of Christ for us. When we take the Spirit of God seriously, we will have power, love and a sound mind. He is residing in us. He reveals Christ and His scripture to us. We can't drive out the spirit of fear in our flesh. We need the comforter. Yield to the Holy Spirit of God, "Build up your most holy faith, praying in the Holy Spirit."

Note

458

"Be not deceived; God is not mocked: for whatsoever a man soweth, that shall he also reap" (Galatians 6:7, KJV)

Salt stings but it always helps with the healing process of a wound. Truth offends but always has the best outcome. We want a diet of candy but sweets alone won't make us healthy. We want to be fit but enjoy to sit more. Whatever we sow, we will reap. A disciple of Christ, without spiritual discipline is really a disciple of their flesh. Work out your salvation. Put on the armor of God. Study to show yourself approved. Fight the fight of faith. Decide to believe and let faith in Christ give you the power to be who you never could be on your own. The Holy Spirit is not in us to excuse work and keep us in a prayer meeting. It's not time to pray. It's time to act. Talk is cheap, roll up the sleeves and get to work. The best type of prayer is exemplified by how we pray before we eat. We pray, then we eat. God does not pick up the fork for us. God does not chew for us. It's time, wake up and take responsibility. Blaming, sitting, and waiting is exactly what the devil wants you doing. Our faith works. The book of Acts is rightly named. The Holy Spirit was put in us to work and do. Human beings need to start doing. We were not created just to be, we were created for purpose. God gives us a sound mind and self-control to do the will of God. Every day, decide to pray and do. Each one of us has a purpose and a calling. We are not here to consume oxygen alone. Rise to what we are called to do. Don't let anyone get in the way of what God has told you to do. You will be surprised at who will try to stand in the way of God's call on your life. Don't worry, God always proves them wrong. Their scorning, gossip, naysaying attitude will only be heaped on them so that they repent and rise too in their call. God will never abandon a doer of the Word. Walk that talk; quit talking about the streets when you do nothing about it yourself. The reason few are doing it is because all they hear is what we should be doing, but who is going to quit the talk and start doing? If you're so grieved and burdened but you are not doing anything about it, you're no different. If you want it different, be the difference. If you want to lead millennials, do what you say. Your lifestyle makes your words hollow. If Christ is not lived through you, what do you really have to give? Go and preach the Gospel!

Note

459

"Now his elder son was in the field: and as he came and drew nigh to the house, he heard music and dancing. And he called one of the servants, and asked what these things meant. And he said unto him, Thy brother is come; and thy father hath killed the fatted calf, because he hath received him safe and sound. And he was angry, and would not go in: therefore came his father out, and entreated him" (Luke 15:25–28, KJV)

When the "elder brother" replaces the Father, there is no celebration over the prodigal. Prodigals will not return because they know their elder brother will just rebuke, judge and condemn, so they die in the pig pen. Jesus never tells us the end of the elder brother. We don't know if he repented or allowed bitterness to ruin his life. The Dad in this parable teaches us the heart of God. While the religious scorn the sinner and the fallen, Jesus is filled with compassion to restore. The elder brother had a religious spirit which ended him in a worse situation than all the sins of the prodigal. At least the prodigal came to the end of himself but the religious rarely come to the end of themselves because their religion has blinded them. It was the religious that cried out to crucify Christ. Religion makes sinners the toughest to reach. Their traditions and rules harden their hearts. It's better for a human to be a prodigal and learn to repent than be religious and strive to be god, based on self-righteousness. The parable about the "prodigal son" is more a rebuke to the religious than it is to the prodigal. It was hope for the prodigal and hell for the elder brother. Jesus does not judge as we do. The reading of scripture is so essential to understand our God. We must not be left to our imagination. Without education or instruction, we would conjure up our own image of god. We have the scripture to give us understanding. Without scripture, we would have no moral compass; right and wrong would be left to individuals' discretion. What a chaotic world it would be, if each one of us had our own definition of right and wrong. The Bible gives us clarity on life and eternity. Without it, we would be left with weak theories. Our society either follows faith in God or theories of man which change with the wind. God's Word has stood the test of time. No one can question the success of Christ. Who would not want to live in a "Christ" influenced society? All we have to do is compare it with all the other false gods, religions and theories of the world. It's a simple choice, Jesus and the Bible are better than every other religion, to the point where there is no competition. Jesus Christ was the Messiah and the Bible is the only Holy book.

Note

460

"I know thy works, that thou art neither cold nor hot: I would thou wert cold or hot. So then because thou art lukewarm, and neither cold nor hot, I will spue thee out of my mouth" (Revelation 3:15–16, KJV)

Read the words of Jesus. He name-called, He discerned, He held frauds accountable, He exposed the secrets of religion; we have this weak view of Christ today. He is not weak. He is to be feared, for He has the authority to cast us into hell. He is not humanity's door mat. He is not your dog, that comforts you when you need Him. Jesus Christ is Lord. He does as He pleases. He will never be tried by man again. No matter the opinions of man, no matter creed or tongue, every knee will bow to the Lord Jesus Christ. He will throw every sinner into hell, He will spit out every lukewarm Christian into the eternal fire of hell, He will judge. Jesus Christ will have the last Word. Read your Bible. Don't let your "goodness" or "kindheartednesses" deceive you of the truth of scripture. God is God. We can try to figure Him out or attempt to wrap our minds around Him, but we never will be able to. Our finite minds will never understand. The truth is, He is God; we are not. Sinners don't put themselves in hell, God judges them there. He will punish unrepentant sinners. This is why Christ died. If we don't choose Christ, then we will reap the consequence of sin. Fools preach that God predestines sinners to hell. Preach the whole council of Scripture. Cherry picking through scripture is dangerous. Every human has the opportunity to be redeemed. Christianity is not another "cast" religion. The Gospel is good news to "whosoever will" believe. Election is unlimited, atonement is unlimited, everyone can decide who we will serve. Choose Jesus. Get out of the valley of decision and choose Christ. Once you are saved, stay in relationship or you won't always be saved. Jesus is not a ticket to heaven; He is your Lord. Many have been saved but like Judas, they chose their will more than His in their everyday life. Choose Jesus every day or be prey to deception. There is a falling away happening right before our eyes. The departure from church has begun. Thank God finally, that religion is no longer a "go to." Now people won't hide behind their white washed tombs of religion. Religion is a tomb for the dead to assure its adherents of hell forever. Flee religion, trust in Christ. God replaced rituals with a relationship. Christ reconciled us into this relationship.

Note

461

"But when Peter was come to Antioch, I withstood him to the face, because he was to be blamed. For before that certain came from James, he did eat with the Gentiles: but when they were come, he withdrew and separated himself, fearing them which were of the circumcision" (Galatians 2:11–12, KJV)

What coward flees from his wounded brother and says, "Serves him right?" What hypocrite uses the tithe of a widow to jet all over the world, to have fine dining, enjoying the delicacies of the bullet proof enclosed green room? The empire of that coward will die with him. Where they spend eternity will shock them. Scorners will be scorned forever by their own scorning. Rather than accountability, they set up a monarchy. Those that tithe have no voice, they set themselves up a king who passes his empire to his son. He thinks he can hide behind scripture but anyone with common sense can see the truth. Only those who have had discernment beat out of them by abusive handling of scripture will sit under this oppression. Scorning, judging, maligning, and shaming to maintain leadership is so satanic. Anyone can preach and teach, it's who we are that makes us be us. We can hide behind clothing, preaching and religion but at the core of all of us is wretchedness. There is only one who we should be lifting up, there is only one who we should be imitating, there is only one who is worth talking about and that is Jesus. Call no man teacher or father, nor elevate anyone above Jesus. When you elevate a coward like me or them above Christ, you will be disappointed. I am a repentant sinner; Jesus alone is the savior. Don't build up our inheritance or who we are in Christ higher than Christ. Don't focus on anything or anyone more than Jesus. Everyone will disappoint, there is only one to be trusted with our soul. He does not require your tithe, He does not require flattery, He does not want your time, God has no need of us but chooses to want us. God loves us. We are only fulfilled when God is lifted above everything and everyone. Worship Him. Even the angels had enough sense to not share any of the glory with God. Satan tried to but he will get what is coming to him along with all unrepentant clergy. Satan has not only infiltrated our gutters; he is also in the board room of churches. The only way to drive him out is to "drain the swamp of religion." The church needs to be taken back by the congregation. The greatest form of government is a republic on earth, yet the church is run like a monarchy. No believer has a king outside of Jesus, monarchy is an offense to God.

Note

462

"But if ye forgive not men their trespasses, neither will your
Father forgive your trespasses" (Matthew 6:15, KJV)

Bitterness only hurts the person that is bitter. It is unavoidable on this journey. Everyone is susceptible to the trapping of bitterness. Jesus took forgiveness so seriously that He said, "If we don't forgive, He will not forgive us." This is not an easy command because most bitterness is "just." We were treated wrong, taken advantage of, used, despitefully used, abused…the list could go on. We live in a world full of sinners. Sinners, sin. Forgiveness of the offender does not mean that they will get away with their injustice but it does mean we release vengeance over to God and correct authorities. When we clench onto our past hurts, they will clench onto our soul as a dead weight. Bitterness will make us lose sanity. It leads to all forms of mental, physical and relational sickness. Jesus was clear that it also leads to hell. Christ offers forgiveness to us so in response; we are called to offer forgiveness to others. We all have to take personal responsibility for our own sin. We have all sinned. Not all sin was done to us, we have all sinned. Comparing sins is what the world does but in the sight of God, sin is sin. It all gets the same judgment. You can miss heaven by a mile or miss it by eighteen inches; we all get the same results no matter how far we miss it. Salvation is not knowledge but it is power when it goes down into our soul. Many confess salvation with their mouth but their soul is full of bitterness. What is the state of your soul? Is it full of bitterness, resentment, rage and anger? You can't say that you love God but hate your brother. Jesus wants our soul. Search within, examine whether your faith is from your heart or just in your mind. To get our faith from our mind to our heart, this can only be accomplished through a genuine relationship with Christ and a real church community around us. Many have fallen into the pitfall of bitterness because no one told them that it's sending more people to hell than the blatant sins religion rails about from the pulpit. Cast bitterness on Christ, write out the offenses before God, don't carry it to hell. This is urgent. Bitterness is not a light issue. None are exempt. Forgiving our offenders does not mean we trust them or that they should escape prosecution. Vengeance is the Lords. Forgive!

Note

463

"But, beloved, remember ye the words which were spoken before of the apostles of our Lord Jesus Christ; How that they told you there should be mockers in the last time, who should walk after their own ungodly lusts. These be they who separate themselves, sensual, having not the Spirit" Jude 1:17–19, KJV)

"Rejoice not when thine enemy falleth, and let not thine heart be glad when he stumbleth" (Proverbs 24:17, KJV)

When we rejoice at other's downfall, or find humor in our brothers' stumbling, we do not have the spirit of Christ. When the human body turns on itself, it does not function. Religion loves sarcasm, coldness and judgment. It gloats when others fall. It feeds off of comparison. The religious feel good when those who they compare with are worse off than them. They see sinners and thank God that they are nothing like them. Religion is "revived" by gossip, rumors and other men's failures. All they want to read is what is wrong with someone. Religion has no passion for restoration or reconciliation, it is cold and cuts off anyone that shows weakness. Its culture tries to outdo one another. Religion is a greater curse than any blatant sin that the religious detest. The love of many is growing cold. If we are gratified reading about others failures, we do not have the spirit of Christ. When one part of our human body suffers, the other parts don't rejoice, our entire body suffers. Believers have become fans more than family. We celebrate Jesus but have no connection with one another outside of our biological family. This makes us no different than anyone else. What makes the church unique is that its members are bonded as family in Christ. Some churches treat their congregants as donors and not as a body. They have time for the biggest giver. All their prepping and events are to maintain their biggest donors. Those that have wealth must realize that they are accountable to who they give to. Wealth should not be used to influence the pulpit for an agenda. Their wealth should be used to protect the pulpit so that the preacher rightly divides scripture and not just tickles their ears. Wealth that is blindly given is foolish. No one should give blindly. We give to vision that is dictated by scripture. The congregation speaks with their wealth. When there is misappropriation of funds, religious judgment and no biblical accountability, the enemy is welcomed in. God is raising up the "whosoever will" to outshine the status quo of religion. God's choice of representation is not what we would choose. We look at character, religiosity and education but God looks to the heart. Religion manufactures a form of godliness but has no power. Christ, be seen through us.

Note

464

"But this shall be the covenant that I will make with the house of Israel; After those days, saith the Lord, I will put my law in their inward parts, and write it in their hearts; and will be their God, and they shall be my people. And they shall teach no more every man his neighbor, and every man his brother, saying, Know the Lord: for they shall all know me, from the least of them unto the greatest of them, saith the Lord: for I will forgive their iniquity, and I will remember their sin no more." Jeremiah 31:33-34 KJV

Who you know is more important than what you know. What you know is not what gets us to heaven, it's who we know. Many will stand before God and quote scripture; they will boast of their service to God but they will get the same response as the vile sinner that they would have shunned during their ministry. No one told them that their works of righteousness, miracles, and preaching were iniquity because they never knew God. Knowing about God won't get us to heaven; knowing Him will. Heaven and hell hangs in the balance of this truth. Our discipleship emphasizes knowing about God but that's not what matters most. Do we know Him? Do we have a relationship with the resurrected Christ? Who is Lord, you or God? What is more important to us, our will or His? The more we read scripture, the more we realize how surrendered to Him we should want to be. Do we know Christ? Are we talking to Him? Is He one of our counselors for life and decision making? Most Christians in the West have knowledge of Jesus, but do they know Jesus? By their fruit, one will know it and not by their works. Works can be deceptive; that's why the fruit of the Spirit should be sought after more than the gifts of the Spirit. The gifts of the Spirit without the fruit of the Spirit can be counterfeit power. It takes discernment in the West to know who is who. We have great forms of godliness but for the most part, our generation has denied the power. If we want our will more than His, then we need to question who is Lord of our lives. One of the ways that we can discern this is by the manifestation of the fruit of the Spirit in others' lives. What is more important than the discernment of others is the discernment of ourselves. Are we in relationship with Jesus? The most fearful words a Christian could hear on the day of Judgment is "I never knew you, depart." Religion teaches about God; Jesus taught us to know Him. God is relational. This is why reconciliation matters so much to God. When we seek life, contentment, and fulfillment by anything spiritual or natural outside of our relationship with Christ, we will be left disappointed. No one can be a savior to our souls more than Jesus, no place can bring more joy to our soul than being in the presence God. Know God, Christ made it possible.

Note

465

"Saying, Father, if thou be willing, remove this cup from me: nevertheless not my will, but thine, be done" (Luke 22:42, KJV)

Jesus offers a decision, His will or our will. Adam and Eve chose their will in Eden but Jesus chose His Fathers will in Gethsemane. Every sinner has the same freedom as Adam and Eve but we are spoiled by a sin nature. The believer lives in Gethsemane every day. Until we see Jesus, we are to decide daily, "His will be done on earth as it is in heaven." We need to be delivered from temptation to not go our own way. Every day, we are faced with the temptation to follow our flesh or follow faith in Christ. Jesus chose the way of the cross yet look what the cross accomplished. The will of God may be the hardest decision for us to make but it always has the most fruit. Choose His will over every other person or temptation and reap the eternal fruit. Learn from the decision made in Eden, our will is not what we want, as good as it may look. Satan was able to infiltrate the garden of Eden but Christ beat the power of darkness at the cross. The believer in Christ has the power to choose God's will and resist the devil. We are called to a life of submission to the will of God. We can't resist our flesh on our own. We need Christ. Our first birth leads to death but He offers a new birth. To be born again means we have a new nature that is empowered to follow Christ rather than our cravings. Submit to God and step in His direction; He will be faithful to complete the work that He started. We would be fools to think that we don't need to decide to follow God; following our cravings leads to death. We follow one of two Lords in this world. Say no to the tempter and lift our hands to Christ in surrender. God won't call us to something to forsake us. Jesus was not forsaken; we won't be either. He proved our Fathers' faithfulness. He cleared the way so that we can follow Him with His protection. We don't want to get ahead of Christ. We were created not for God to follow us but for us to follow Him. As He leads, He gives us the grace to follow. We are not on our own. Choose what Christ chose in the garden of Gethsemane over what Adam chose in the garden of Eden. Learn from Christ the "second Adam," who reconciled us all back to God because of the "first Adam's" sin. God's Will will lead us to eternal life; choose His will!

Note

466

"Repent ye therefore, and be converted, that your sins may be blotted out, when the times of refreshing shall come from the presence of the Lord" (Acts 3:19, KJV)

Repentance leads to refreshing. There is no refreshing in gratifying our flesh. Living in sin is far from refreshing. There is no good fruit from sin. Sin may seem pleasurable but, in the end, it leads to death. We all have sinned. This is why repentance is an urgent message. God does not need a man-made lie detector to use on us, which we can manipulate. God cannot be fooled by anyone. We are prone to pretending but we can't do that with God. In order for repentance to be refreshing, it has to come from the heart before God. It's refreshing because His grace never runs out. No matter how we squandered life or how long we worked in the pig pen, God is waiting with arms wide open to receive us. Christ took our just punishment on Himself. God won't allow His Son's blood to be taken in vain. This is why we can't use Christ as a license to do what He bled and died for. We must be warned of trampling the blood of Christ under our feet by choosing to use Him as an excuse to sin. When repentance is from the heart, we will hate sin and feel the grief of the Holy Spirit. If we sin without grief or without conviction, we may quench the Holy Spirit. Repent, it's not too late. Repentance is not a negative word, it's the most encouraging word we could ever hear. Repentance is a part of the Gospel and without it, we don't have good news. We want to be encouraged the way we are and comforted in our sin but that does not lead to refreshing. There are only two books where Jesus speaks outside of the Gospels, 2 Corinthians and Revelation. Both times should be noted. His grace is sufficient and His corrective words to the Church is what we read. These are the least preached sermons in the West. We want health and wealth but Jesus told Paul that His grace would be sufficient. We want to be encouraged but Jesus talks about repentance or He will remove His candlestick. The most encouraging sermon for a believer is what makes us see our need for Christ, whether in repentance or in Worship of His glory. The glory of God teaches us that we are "wretched, pitiful, poor, blind and naked." This is our state without Christ. The good in us is Christ at work in us. In our flesh, without Christ, there is no good thing. Be refreshed, repent.

Note

467

"Then said Jesus to them again, Peace be unto you: as my Father hath sent me, even so send I you" (John 20:21, KJV)

What will the next great awakening hook like in this technological age that we live in today? Technology must never replace face-to-face ministry. We have relied on the internet and TV; it has its place but must never replace believers being who they were called to be. For years, we have been giving tracts, fliers, food, gifts, and whatever we can, to open a conversation with someone we don't know. The believer will have more of an impact on those they do know. It's easier to reach strangers than it is reaching those we work with or do life with. We might be the only tract or biblical truth they will ever read. Our lives impact those around us more than any piece of literature or YouTube video. Living our lives online won't have the same impact as we do on those who we do life with every day. We think that people will see Jesus when we put our best foot forward but that attitude won't make us relatable to those we are reaching. It's when people see our vulnerability and how we respond, that's when they see the light of Christ the most. Those that do life around us will testify of our imperfections; but they should also testify of our willingness to repent. Those around us should be able to say that we trust Jesus no matter what we go through. We can win the world online but what about being a light to those that are right in front of us. Religion can get away with anything online. We are so prone on giving off the appearance that we are great but truly we are in as much need of Jesus as anyone else. We are not called to be Christ; we are called to point to Christ. If we elevate ourselves above Christ, we will disappoint everyone around us. Believers will need Jesus to the day we die. This does not give us an excuse to take His grace in vain. His grace will make us quick to repent. Our tears won't be self-pity but personal responsibility for our choices. Tears during repentance must be discerned whether they are tears of self-pity or genuine personal responsibility for sin. Those around us can discern us the best. The internet makes it impossible for anyone to discern, unless God gives insight. There is no comparison between face-to-face discipleship vs technology. Jesus wants us to disciple as He did, face-to-face.

Note

"Draw nigh to God, and he will draw nigh to you. Cleanse your hands,
ye sinners; and purify your hearts, ye double minded" (James 4:8, KJV)

W e can't change someone that does not want change. If someone does not want help, there is very little that we can do but pray. This is the problem with our socialist generation. We can only help those that want help. How to get people to want help is the miracle. The help is there but getting a person to want the help is what is needed in the West. The preaching of the Gospel changes from the inside out. Religion, education, and hand outs, change only the outside but Jesus gives a hand up. The Gospel message is power unto salvation. When Jesus is made Lord of our life, then our desires follow Him and not our flesh. He knew the earth will always have poverty but what they really need is their soul saved. The preaching of the Gospel alone has the power to say "take up your mat and walk." Today's Christianity has so much silver and gold, that we have used wealth to replace the power of the Holy Spirit. Rather than proclaiming the Gospel and praying for people, we are giving stuff away in our outreaches. Humanists have moved into the leadership of our major ministries who mock the Gospel and slander its power. These shrewd business men are about their business and not the Fathers. They write the script for their preachers. Their goal is to make major ministries even more dependent on mammon. We need to steward the Gospel being preached more than our nest eggs. We want awakening but it won't happen until we value the Gospel so much so, that we preach it on the streets of our cities. If we believe the message to be true, we would be sharing it daily. When we go months without a desire to reach sinners, whose kingdom are we building? If we only preach to those that will grow our church, do we really have the heart of God? We will be anointed when we preach to honor Jesus more than get people in a pew. The church will grow when Jesus is lifted up above her needs. When we choose to preach the Gospel and lift Christ up, the promise is, He will draw all people unto Himself. Let's use the silver and gold He has given to us to evangelize, preach the Gospel and honor the name of Jesus. Judas would much rather do many other humanitarian things with it but Jesus was clear "what does it profit the soul if we gain the world but lose our soul?"

Note

469

"And when he had removed him, he raised up unto them David
to be their king; to whom also he gave testimony, and said,
I have found David the son of Jesse, a man after mine own
heart, which shall fulfil all my will" (Acts 13:22, KJV)

If we don't take a stand, someone else will. We are all replaceable. God will use anyone who is willing. Our society relies on talent, birthright, education and a resume but God looks for willingness. When we say "yes" to God, we have no idea where that yes will take us. Following Christ is unlike anything else. It's exciting and so fulfilling. When we obey God, then we are living. If what we are doing is disobeying God no matter how good it is, we will be unfulfilled, anxious and bound to fear. When we are following after His leading, we will be bold, courageous and do what everyone would've said was impossible. The more people say to you "you can't," "you'll never," "nothing will come of your life," don't heed it because God will have the final say. God loves to confound the wise. The wisdom of the world will always limit, cap and criticize but faith in Christ removes the ceilings of the world so heaven becomes our ceiling. With God, anything can be done if He calls us to it. We know that we are the called of God if we know we can't do it. Ministry is a life of faith and not a career built on what we can do, but on faith in what we can't do. Be encouraged if what you are facing looks impossible, be faithful to His will because He will never forsake us. As we continue in what He has called us to, He will come through for His glory. Don't lose heart in doing His will. It is impossible, so rely on what He can only make possible. We are most blessed when we rely on Him the most. There is nothing like relying on Him and following His leading. God will accomplish His will with us or without us. When we say "no" to His will, He will continue with someone else that says "yes." The called of God don't sign up for a career but sign up to follow His calling. A calling makes ministry pour out of us. A career makes our ministry nine-to-five. God does not need our time, treasure or talent, God wants our heart. He is self-existent. He does as He pleases. He is almighty. Have you heard the call of God but went the other way? Jonah's testimony teaches us that it's never too late. Repent in the mess life got you into and watch Him put you back on track where you fell off. He restores the years that we wasted on ourselves. Give Jesus your "yes," it's not too late.

Note

470

"For this ye know, that no whoremonger, nor unclean person, nor covetous man, who is an idolater, hath any inheritance in the kingdom of Christ and of God. Let no man deceive you with vain words: for because of these things cometh the wrath of God upon the children of disobedience" (Ephesians 5:5–6, KJV)

Everyone turns to something or someone to get them through life. Our hearts are idol factories. Whatever we turn to first, can become idolatry to us if it's not God. God is our source for peace, God is our counselor, He is almighty God. The people and things we turn to before Him can't compare to what He can do for us. God must be first in order for us to experience life. Everything else gives temporal and counterfeit life. God gives life. His presence and His Word are our source of eternal life. Without God, we will try to fill our void with "nothing" that will ever satisfy. Even the "good" won't fit the God hole in our life. This is why many who are saved and are even in ministry are empty. When our satisfaction and purpose is found outside of our relationship with God, we won't be content. Knowing Jesus is all that completes us. No one, nor anything else will ever do for our soul what Jesus can. Our earthly dreams, our spiritual ambitions, our eagerness for revival won't ever give us fulfillment outside of knowing Jesus. We know Jesus by talking to Him about our lives, talking to Him about our decisions, turning to Him first in all we go through in life. We were created to walk with God. Christ made it possible for us to be reconciled back into this relationship that was broken. For generations, we were separated from God. We are at enmity with Him outside of faith in Christ. Jesus's death bridged the separation between us and God. We can know God. Unconfessed sin leads to hardening of our hearts toward Him. Believers know God by confessing our sin and giving our lives over to Him for His glory. When we let God be who He is in us, we enter a state of euphoria that nothing in this world could give. Many turn to drugs, alcohol or their pleasures to get the devils counterfeit peace. Jesus gives peace that costs us nothing. He paid the price for this peace. Give Jesus Christ your soul. Relinquish your mind to Him. Come under His rulership and watch the fruit grow in your life. Humans blossom in Christ. Sins shackles are torn off. Our minds become healthy. Our bodies denounce its cravings to only do what He wants us to. We won't be perfect but we will crave perfection. We will want as much of God as He gives for His glory only.

Note

471

"That there should be no schism in the body; but that the members should have the same care one for another. And whether one member suffer, all the members suffer with it; or one member be honoured, all the members rejoice with it" (1 Corinthians 12:25–26, KJV)

When our body works together, we are at our best. Division or competition in our body leads to disease and even death. Comparison in an unhealthy way, leads to jealousy, and jealousy unchecked leads to death. We don't realize how dishonoring it is to God when we lower our value because of where we are in the body of Christ. We honor the seen members of the body but it's the unseen members that are just as important. If the hidden members compare and get jealous, they don't realize the toll that will have on the seen members. The body of Christ can't do what she is called to if we are not united. Individually, we are sons and daughters; that's where we should find our value. That's of greater value than whatever part we are in the collective body of Christ. Seen or unseen by man, we are all seen by God. God sees us even when we feel invisible and alone to people. Our value, assurance, and our life source are found in God's sight. He sees us. Whatever part of the body we are collectively, let that not define our importance. Our importance is evidenced by the shed blood of Christ, not by our titles or positions given by man. We are altogether lovely. There is not one spot in the body of Christ. More than Solomon loved the Shulamite woman, Christ loves His bride, the Church. You are important. Evolution will tell you that you are a mammal, religion tells you that you are nothing, Jesus told us that our God so loves us. God, Our Father, did not tell us that He loved us alone. He proved it with the blood of His only begotten Son. Comparison, competition, and jealousy must be addressed in the body of Christ. Covetousness is rampant; we judge those "worse off than us" yet we are facing the same judgment. When we unite, there is no telling what we can do. We must honor the seen and the unseen parts of the body. We need one another. God set humanity up to be interdependent on one another. God saw that He was not enough for Adam. His provision of Eve teaches us that we need the church as our community. We can't function with God alone; we need one another. Jesus and His church come hand in hand. When we encounter Christ, He will lead us into community at a local church. We need one another.

Note

472

"Who also hath made us able ministers of the new testament;
not of the letter, but of the spirit: for the letter killeth,
but the spirit giveth life" (2 Corinthians 3:6, KJV)

The spirit realm is real. Our age of science and evolution try to explain away the fact of spirituality. Spirituality is more real than any theory they try to condor up. Christ is not a figment of our imagination. Scripture is not a theory on how we got here, it is truth. Without scripture, we have no idea of our origin, purpose or destiny. It's more than a history book. It feeds our faith. The Spirit of God makes the Words of scripture alive like no other book. Our soul is cleansed, our minds are sharpened, transformations happen by the authority of scripture. No preacher, no interpretation, no commentary is equal to Scripture. It speaks for itself. Scripture is the best commentary on itself. Once the enemy gets God's people distracted from their daily scripture reading by using music, preaching, outreach, or entertainment, we have opened the door to him. Satan has infiltrated. We can't discern because he is posing as an angel of light. He says enough truth to deceive even the elect. Slowly he is pulling Western Christianity away from scripture and into his deviating spirituality with a false gospel. We have more access to scripture than any other generation but we are reading everyone's literature rather than what feeds our faith. We have time to sing, we have time to be encouraged, we have time to be told what we want to hear but we have little time for biblical truth. Worship is not music; it's obedience to God's word. Satan has elevated music in Christianity above the pulpit. Our generation wants music more than the Word. They will pay for a concert to get tickled more than an evangelistic crusade to our generation. They foolishly believe the lie that obedience is legalistic. The deception that evangelism, Bible reading, and prayer meetings are legalistic from the pit of hell. Spiritual wickedness is nearer to the West than we can discern. We pray for the persecuted church but the persecution on the Western church is far more sinister. Overseas, we can see the persecution. Here in the West, only those that have eyes to see spiritually will know just how dark it really is. To truly see spiritually is to know scripture. The Spirit uses scripture to increase discernment. Pray for discernment or be prey.

Note

473

"That ye put off concerning the former conversation the old man, which is corrupt according to the deceitful lusts; And be renewed in the spirit of your mind; And that ye put on the new man, which after God is created in righteousness and true holiness" (Ephesians 4:22–24, KJV)

When we are first born, we are born with a nature that craves wrong more than right. Christ's salvation is not only an assurance of heaven but we are also born again. Christ makes the sinner righteous so that the Holy Spirit can reside in us. The Old Covenant had the law and blood sacrifice for atonement but it lacked in the power that we have in Christ. When the Spirit came upon those under the Old Covenant, it was to make them do what they never could in their flesh temporarily. The Holy Spirit resides in the believer to do what we could never do. Old things pass away and all things become new. Until we get our glorified bodies, there will be a wrestle within us between our flesh and the Holy Spirit. This is a mystery to us. Our righteousness for God's acceptance of us will only ever be in Christ. We never move on from a need for Jesus as our savior and Lord. Many Christians feel so condemned but quote Romans 8:1 *"There is therefore now no condemnation to them which are in Christ Jesus, who walk not after the flesh, but after the Spirit"* (KJV) like it's real yet their life is bound to condemnation. To live condemnation-free is conditional, walk after the flesh and be bound or walk after the Spirit and be free. To be born again is to be born of the Spirit. He enables us to walk in such a way that we never could on our own. For those that have been raised in Christianity, it's harder to see drastic change when they were born again, but the truth is, we are born again because sin grieves the Spirit in us. We must be born again to get to heaven. Knowledge of Christ won't save us, knowing Christ will. If we grieve over sin and desire to repent, then we can be sure He is in us. Our nature only wants to gratify itself. It's not natural for our nature to worship Jesus or want to be Holy. What is natural for us is to sin and crave darkness. To say, "Jesus is my Lord" without any hesitation is the evidence that the Holy Spirit is in us. No flesh can say that unless the Spirit is in us. The born-again message teaches us that this life is spiritual and not carnal. Our discipleship must be spiritual and not carnal only. What this means is that the Gospel is more than an argument, it's more than knowledge, it's power unto salvation. We can't live this life on our own. The fruit of the Old Covenant is condemnation. Christ came to make us do what we never could on our own.

Note

_____
_____
_____
_____
_____
_____
_____
_____
_____
_____

About the Author

Adam Field is a native of Ireland and has known Jesus as his Savior since the age of six. After graduating from Summit International School of Ministry, Adam served in pastoral roles in Ireland until God called him to the United States as an evangelist. He served as an evangelist in West Florida District Assembly of God. Moving to Colorado, he worked in the evangelistic department of World Challenge, a ministry founded by David Wilkerson. Inspired by the story of David Wilkerson and Nicky Cruz, Adam founded Comission, to ignite a passion for evangelism in local churches across the United States. Currently, Adam lives in Florida with his wife, Ashley and two children Anabella and Ashton, where he spends most of his time studying the Word of God and heading up Comission. These writings came out seasons of sickness, transitions, and hardships. Adam has been writing for over fifteen years in his daily journal. What you are about to read has come out of experience and revelation that only comes by the way of the cross.